Willow and Strix

A spiritual journey

A spiritual novel

Including the appendices

"Practical Steps" and "Spirit Animals"

A. Wakan

Published by
A. Wakan
c/o Block Services
Stuttgarter Str. 106
70736 Fellbach
Germany

Mail: info-awakan@gmx.net
Visit the author's website at: https://awakansspiritanimals.wordpress.com/

Cover design by Nayeli A. Wakan

First edition
Printed and bound by KDP or IngramSpark

The German National Library lists this publication in the Deutsche Nationalbibliothek; detailed bibliographic data are available on the internet at dnb.dnb.de

ISBN paperback: 978-3-949149-00-9
ISBN eBook: 978-3-949149-01-6

Disclaimer

The fictional parts of the book are just that – fictional. They are the product of the author's imagination and any resemblances to persons, places, names, events and incidents are entirely coincidental.

The factual parts of the book are based on research and the current level of knowledge of the author. Although A. Wakan has made every effort to ensure that the information in this book is correct at press time, the author cannot be held personally, legally, or financially liable to any party for any loss, damage or disruption caused by errors, inaccuracies, omissions or any other inconsistencies herein, whether such errors or omissions result from negligence, accident or any other cause.

All information obtained in this book is to be taken as solely advisory in nature and any use or misuse of information is at the reader's discretion and risk. The author also makes no guarantees concerning the level of success you may experience by following the advice within this book. The reader accepts that results will differ for each individual.

A. Wakan is not a psychologist or medical professional and the content of this book is for informational purposes only and is not intended to diagnose, prescribe, treat, cure, or prevent any condition or disease. Always consult a licensed medical practitioner for professional medical advice and treatment.

Anyone using the information in this book acknowledges that they have read and understood the details of this disclaimer.

For my mother, whom I chose;

For my dog, who chose me;

And for the one I named brother, who gave me no choice but to awaken.

TABLE OF CONTENTS

World map – Strix's journey

1. Sloth, Costa Rica ° 2. Badger, Ireland ° 3. Wolf, Germany ° 4. Eagle, Italy ° 5. Chameleon, Egypt ° 6. Warthog, South Sudan ° 7. Giraffe, Kenya ° 8. Wild Ass, Somalia ° 9. Octopus, Indian Ocean, African Coast ° 10. Clownfish, Indian Ocean, Australian Coast ° 11. Swan, Ethiopia to Saudi Arabia ° 12. Crocodile, Cuba ° 13. Dolphin, Arabian Sea ° 14. Squirrel, England ° 15. Red Panda, China ° 16. Bumblebee, USA ° 17. Tortoise, Indonesia ° 18. Snake, Australia (North) ° 19. Platypus, Australia (East) ° 20. Kangaroo, Australia (South) ° 21. Penguin, Antarctica ° 22. Snowy Owl, Southern Ocean

Part 1 - A spiritual journey

Willow's introduction

I'm Willow, an old and weathered weeping willow tree.

I'm used to the fact that people don't notice me when they walk past. But I do wish that more humans would sit underneath my branches and listen to everything I have to say. Because I've heard and seen and felt and experienced so much over the centuries.

Plus, I have lots of stories about my good friend Strix, a short-eared owl, who travelled the world and let me be part of his journey. The more I hear about his adventures and all the wonders he saw, the more I want to share these tales with everyone else.

But alas, so many humans have become deaf to the sound of nature, and no one ever stops to listen to me.

Until one fateful day, that is, when a young woman stumbled into the meadow that I call my home. Meeting Nayeli was a gift – not just because she's become one of my closest friends, but also because she came up with the idea to put everything I have to say into a book for humans to read. Nayeli did all the work on that, as neither my roots nor Strix's claws are suitable for holding a pen. But she did ask us for our opinion along the way and integrated our ideas into her writing.

The most important thing for me was to include as many different topics as possible. I think many humans who read this book might be beginners in spiritual practices. Therefore, I wanted to give you a good overview of all the subjects that could be important for your life. This means, of course, that not all chapters will resonate with everyone. Maybe you're interested in the Law of Attraction but don't care about developing your clair-senses. Or maybe you want to know more about chakras and how to heal them, but the topic about oneness holds no relevance for you right now. That's okay. Trust your intuition when reading these stories. Whatever you feel drawn to will be what you need to hear most right now.

Saying this, I'm glad that you want to join Nayeli, Strix and me on this journey: a journey that doesn't only span the continents of the world but one that'll also help you to travel deep within yourself, to remember what you once knew but have forgotten.

Prologue – The Other Side and the Dual Reality

The sun looked like a centrepiece in a painting, hanging seemingly weightless in the sky and casting the meadow in a warm golden glow. Flowers in every colour of the rainbow were scattered over the gently rolling hills and bees and butterflies competed for the best pollen.

In the middle of the meadow was a small hill with a lone weeping willow standing on top of it. To the left, a babbling brook wound through the landscape before it disappeared between a line of trees on the horizon. And on the other side, a group of rabbits was playing in a field of clover.

Normally, Nayeli would have felt at peace here: in the midst of nature, surrounded by wildlife. But today the songs of the robins and sparrows did not reach her heart. And instead of feeling comforted by the warm rays of the sun, today she felt vulnerable.

Running through the tall grass, tears were dripping down her cheeks, making her sight blurry and unfocused. As Nayeli reached the hill with the willow, she ducked underneath the low-hanging branches that almost touched the earth and which created a shadowy cave away from the midday heat. Feeling physically tired after having run so far on this hot summer's day, in addition to being emotionally drained, she sunk down to the soft grass and allowed exhaustion to consume her.

It was only when Nayeli sat underneath the tree that she realised she had chosen a weeping willow, of all things, as her hiding spot. She smiled at the irony of it as she had done little else but weep for the last couple of days – ever since she had got that fateful phone call, which had ripped her out of her comfortable life.

More tears spilled from her eyes as she remembered the moment she had been told of her beloved grandmother's death. She wiped them away, berating herself for dealing so badly with the situation. She had known that her grandma was sick; it had come as no actual surprise that a goodbye was imminent.

Just then, her jumbled thoughts were interrupted by a gentle voice that addressed her out of nowhere.

"Why are you crying, my dear child?"

The voice sounded as if it was coming from all directions at once.

Startled, Nayeli let her eyes dart around. Who could have followed her from the funeral service? The voice hadn't sounded like anyone she'd ever known. Besides, there was no one here. She was alone in the meadow.

"No, you are not," the soft voice answered her. "I'm right here."

A cold shiver ran down her spine. Nayeli stood up and looked behind the tree's trunk, then let her gaze drift up into its branches to see if anyone was hiding there. But nothing. And even if there had been someone, Nayeli thought, how could they possibly have answered her when she hadn't spoken aloud?

Or had she?

Maybe the funeral had taken more out of her than she had believed.

But no, she was sure that she had said nothing in the last few hours – not since she had bolted from her grandmother's house, needing to get away from all the people in black, gathered to tell funny and heartfelt stories.

Laughing hysterically, Nayeli realised that the voice she had heard must have come from inside her mind. "I'm only thirty-three and already going crazy," she muttered, disbelief colouring her voice.

"Don't worry, Nayeli. You are not crazy. And neither are you imagining this. I'm as real as you, I promise."

"What the heck?" Nayeli's hands balled into fists as her grief and agitation turned into anger. She looked around for a hidden microphone or speaker, beyond furious that someone would dare to play such a trick on her. Especially today.

"Who are you? And how do you know my name?"

"Sshh," the voice said. "There's no need to freak out."

"NO NEED TO FREAK OUT? Nayeli shouted. "How dare you tell me there's no need to freak out? Do you think this is funny? When I find out where you're hiding, you'll regret ever thinking of this!"

"My dear," the voice said, even more gently than before, "I'm sorry that you're in pain. But I'm not playing a trick on you. Let me show you that I'm real – as real as the brook running through the meadow and as real as the sun above my leaves."

"Above your leaves?" Dumbfounded, Nayeli couldn't do anything but stare at the willow tree.

She had no idea what was happening and briefly entertained the possibility that she had really gone crazy. That the shock and grief had been too much for her to process. But then the truth hit her like a speeding truck. She was dreaming! And, if she was lucky, the dream had already started with the phone call a few days back, telling her that her grandma had passed over. Yes, she thought giddily, that must be the answer. She would wake up before long. And her mum would phone and ask how work had been, and then she'd chat with her grandmother and make plans to meet her.

Feeling as if a heavy weight had been lifted off her, Nayeli sat on the ground and faced the tree, gazing challengingly up into the crown.

"You want to make me believe that you, a tree, are talking to me? Prove it, then. If you can ..."

As soon as Nayeli spoke, the weeping willow came alive. Its branches began to sway and its leaves rustled against each other.

Looking through the gaps between the tree's foliage, Nayeli noticed that the other trees she could see in the distance weren't moving at all. Likewise, the tall grass and flowers stood calmly on this hot summer day.

Only the willow tree was becoming more active by the second, swinging its branches around and tapping the longer ones onto the ground below.

Nayeli was fascinated by the spectacle taking place. But then she shook her head at her naivety. Of course, in a dream anything was possible, even a tree uprooting itself and starting to walk. Which this one obviously wasn't about to do. Slowly, it calmed down again, standing as still as it had before.

"Impressive," Nayeli said. "Anything else that you've got to offer, old Willow?"

"It's Willow, not old Willow," the tree responded. "My bark might be gnarled, but I don't feel *that* ancient yet."

"Willow then." Nayeli nodded. She wasn't actually concerned about how to address this figment of her imagination and more interested when she would wake up.

As if it had read her thoughts, the tree responded. "You really do think that all this is just a dream, don't you? Well, if you'd rather think so, I'm happy to go along with that. Whatever you need to accept this situation, my dear child."

"I'm not a child," Nayeli responded hotly, being mildly curious that this was the part of the tree's statement she was most bothered about.

"You are to me, though. I've been here twice as long as you," the tree retorted. "If not longer than that ..."

Since Nayeli wasn't interested in idle chit-chat, she shrugged dismissively. A more interesting topic occupied her brain: "At least dreaming of being able to speak to a tree is better than going mad, isn't it?"

"I'm aware that you humans are a bit strange," the tree said carefully. "But I don't think you go mad for no reason at all – or do you?"

"But what if I had a reason?" Nayeli asked, not sure why she was continuing with this line of questions since she had already evaluated that nothing she had experienced in the last days was real.

"Because your grandma died?" Willow asked in a caring tone.

"Because my grandma died in my dream," Nayeli corrected the tree, pushing down the lump in her throat. "From which I'm going to wake up any moment now."

"I can feel your pain," the tree said, unfazed by her response. "And I'm sorry that you have to go through it. But please know that your grandma is all right. She's crossed over safely to the other side. Which is where you'll see her when your time comes."

Nayeli decided not to correct the tree again that her grandma had passed nowhere. It would be futile, since it obviously wanted to stick with its opinion. Instead, she humoured it.

"By all means, speak then, wise tree. Share your knowledge with a mere mortal. Where do we go when we die?"

The tree didn't answer immediately, and silence spread over the meadow between them. Nayeli thought the weeping willow couldn't back up its claims after all and had just wanted to assume an air of importance. But then it spoke again, sounding confused.

"What are you talking about, my dear? Isn't the answer obvious?"

"What answer?" Nayeli asked. "That everything is over in the blink of an eye when we leave this world?"

"But that's not the case," Willow responded.

Nayeli interrupted the tree hotly. "Why am I even talking to you about this? You're only a tree – you have no idea what death means."

The tree made a sound that resembled a deep sigh. "I'm sorry, but I think it's the other way around. I think it is you who has forgotten everything about who you are, where you came from and where you go once your incarnation here has come to an end."

Nayeli snorted. "I know exactly what happens when we die, Willow. Sometimes I wished I didn't, but I do. Death is a big black hole of nothingness. It's the one certainty in life that no one can escape. And when you're dead, nothing is left of you but memories for those who mourn you. And as to your statement that I don't know who I am – I do. I'm Nayeli, a human. Nothing more and nothing less."

"I accept that this is your current level of truth. Now, would you like to hear my take on death and the other side?"

Nayeli shrugged carelessly. "Since I obviously won't wake up anytime soon, why not? Currently, I have nothing better to do."

"Fine, fine," Willow mumbled, more to itself than anyone else.

Then the tree fell silent for such a long time that Nayeli believed it must have fallen asleep. If trees slept, that is.

When she couldn't take the silence any longer, Nayeli cleared her throat loudly. "I thought you wanted to tell me something?"

The weeping willow stirred, as if waking from a trance. "Yes, yes, coming right up. I was just thinking about a good place to start. It's an important subject, after all, and one we could talk about endlessly. You know, I had downright forgotten that most of you humans don't remember your true nature, like the rest of us do."

"Who's *us*?" Nayeli asked, bewildered.

"All the trees and plants and animals, from the biggest blue whale to the tiniest flower. *We* all remember where we come from and where we'll go when we leave this world. Because death is not the end. When you *die*, you are going back home."

"Home? What are you alluding to?"

"I'm saying that you're not human, my dear Nayeli. You are an eternal soul, which is having a human experience. And as soon as you've completed this journey that you call life, you cross over to what I call the other side. That's where we look back on the life we've had and the lessons we learned. It's where we reconnect with our soul-family. And it's where we plan out our next life when we decide to incarnate again."

"So, reincarnation is real?" Nayeli asked, feeling herself being drawn in by the tree's words, despite her earlier indifference.

"It is," Willow answered. "Our souls incarnate countless times."

"Tell me more about this *other side*."

"Gladly. The term 'other side' is nothing else but a name to help us visualise something that exists beyond the human consciousness. You humans think in terms of space and time and endings. But the other side is an infinite source of energy that does not have a beginning or an end. And it doesn't have a shape or form or any other kind of limitation, either. You could call this source of energy 'God' or 'Allah' or 'the universe' or simply 'source', or whatever else fits your beliefs. It is all there ever was, all there is and all there'll ever be. Nothing exists outside of it. And we're all part of it – you, me, and that white billowy cloud drifting by overhead. Being fully integrated inside this source is truly beautiful. It's a feeling of total peace. It feels like you are sinking into an ocean of pure white light that purifies your very being and fills you with tranquillity."

Willow painted the picture so vividly that Nayeli felt an echo of that peace resonate within her. As if her soul faintly remembered that state of being. And as Willow continued to talk, the feeling only intensified.

"It's unlike any feeling here on Earth because the vibration is so much higher on the other side. You see, every thought or emotion causes your energy to vibrate at a particular frequency. Love, for instance, is a high-frequency emotion, while fear and powerlessness are some of the lowest ones. Humans experience a mix of frequencies and are constantly switching between higher and lower emotions. The minute you cross over, all lower frequencies cease to exist, though, and solely the higher ones remain. It's like being reawakened. You feel much more alive there than you ever do when you have a physical body. Which is why you humans have it backwards when you say you die. It is when you are born into the density of life that you experience something akin to a small death. It's as though you sleepwalk through your incarnation here without ever being aware of your true self and your potential. This is why remembering your eternal self is called an awakening. This awakening can happen during any incarnation as soon as you are ready for it. Or, if you aren't, you will be reconnected with your eternal soul once you cross back over."

"That all sounds beautiful," Nayeli said. "But tell me, Willow. If this other side is so perfect, why do we leave it to come here?"

"To learn. To grow. And to become conscious. We want to experience different lives, learn different lessons and see everything from different perspectives. This helps us to ascend."

"But why? Couldn't we just stay on the other side and learn the lessons there?" Nayeli dug deeper.

"Technically, we could," Willow answered leisurely. "But then again, any lesson is more intense when you live through an experience as opposed to only hearing about it, no? And that's why souls choose to incarnate into a body."

The tree's leaves whispered in a wind that didn't exist. "Anyway, that's the basic truth about the other side. On the other hand, here on Earth, while we are incarnated, we are faced with an entirely different reality: the 3D or dual reality. In this reality, everything is made up of two opposing sides. When there's night, there's day. Summer has winter as its opposite. And health does not exist without illness."

"Wait, you're telling me there are no opposites on the other side? But how can that be? When you say it's made up out of light, then shadows must also exist there, no? And if not literally, then at least figuratively?"

"No, there aren't any shadows," Willow countered. "You only think that because you base everything on your human perception. Living inside this dual reality makes you automatically assume a source of darkness must exist when you hear about a source of light. But this is wrong for two reasons. First, because the source of light is everything there is and nothing can exist outside it. Don't make the mistake of visualising this source as something physical, like a sun, which casts a shadow. In truth, the light is all around you: it is in front of you and behind you, it is above and below you, it comes from all sides and it's even within you. It permeates everything, and there's simply no place for anything other than light to exist."

"And what about the second reason?" Nayeli asked when the tree stopped talking.

"The second reason is that darkness does not exist at all. Not even here on these lower planes where duality exists."

"Then what would you call the opposite of light?"

"The opposite of light is the absence of light."

"But isn't that the same thing as darkness?" Nayeli questioned.

"No, there's a huge difference. And what better thing to use to explain this than this sunny summer day? Look at your legs, my dear. They are momentarily cast into shadow because my leaves block the sun. But what if I shifted some of them?"

A gap appeared in front of Nayeli, getting wider as Willow moved its branches apart and let in the sunlight. It spilled onto the grass and Nayeli's legs.

"As soon as there's light, all darkness ceases to exist, disappearing into the unknown, does it not? If the darkness you saw were real, it would need to go somewhere – because something that exists can't stop existing. That's a fundamental physical law of this reality. Water that flows in a stream does not disappear into thin air just because a large rock is blocking its path. It finds another way – either flowing around or over the rock or seeping into the surrounding earth. Or it can change form, becoming ice or evaporating. But what water can't do is to disappear into nothingness. Which is what darkness does. It stops existing when light touches it. Therefore, it's not real. And this proves the fact that the opposite of light is, in fact, the absence of it."

"All right, Willow. Say that I believe you – what does that mean for us? That we come here into this dual reality to experience pain?" Nayeli asked disbelievingly. "To be miserable and feel things like grief and loss because we don't get to experience these emotions on the other side? Cause if that's the case, our souls must be crazy!"

The tree moved its branches back. As the gap closed and Nayeli's legs were freed from the burning rays of the sun, the air underneath the tree immediately felt a bit cooler again.

"Not that crazy ... It's true that this dual reality and all its negative aspects – like abandonment, rejection and loss – have a huge influence on us wanting to incarnate here as we want to experience the entire range of emotions. But only for as long as strictly necessary."

"Where are you going with this?" Nayeli asked.

"No one *wants* to be in pain. But our souls sometimes choose to experience it to gain something from the experience. Because how can you otherwise know what you're missing? How can you know what love feels like when you've never felt lonely before? Or how do you realise what happiness means when you were never sad?

"Imagine that everyone was wholly healthy from the moment they are born. No headaches, no colds, not even a scratch. You would have no concept of what health means because you would not know what being sick feels like ... You do not know a coin until you've looked at both sides of it. And that's what we do when we incarnate. We pick lessons that show us the negative side of the scale in order to move towards the positive end."

"But then why do some people have a hard life and never catch a break, while others have an easy life with no big problems? Are they not invested in making the most out of this experience?"

Willow's branches lifted from the ground, as if the tree was shrugging. "First off, every single human has problems and difficult times. There is no exception to that rule. Everyone who is incarnated here knows to some extent what pain and loss and loneliness feel like. But beyond that, a soul is free to choose whatever life and lessons it wants. Anyone can choose an easier life or a more difficult one, depending on the events they want to add to their wealth of experience."

Nayeli frowned. "I guess what I'm trying to figure out is whether I got a good deal, y'know? Or whether I was ripped off and could have done better ..."

"That's understandable," Willow replied.

After that, silence reigned between them. A silence that Nayeli didn't know how to break. When it got too oppressive, she mustered all her courage. "And? Aren't you going to explain this whole matter of us coming here further?"

"I am. But give an old tree a little time to think about how to best illustrate this subject, my child."

A few more seconds of silence followed before the tree continued to speak. "You could think of life as being like a boarding school. Your home is the other side. But to learn, you come here and take certain courses that you choose in advance. You can concentrate on one subject or pick several. You can choose to take a short course or a longer one. And while you're in this boarding school, you'll meet other pupils and teachers. You might fall in love or teach a course yourself. But whatever you choose, one universal truth remains. Once your course or studies are finished, you go back home. There you can look back on everything you've learned, enjoy your summer holiday, so to speak, and choose what further lessons you want to take the next time you incarnate."

Emphasising these words by whipping its branches up and down, the tree concluded: "But I'm aware how difficult it is for your species to remember this truth."

Tilting her head, Nayeli looked up into Willow's canopy. "You've said that before. That humans are the exception to the rule. That we are the only ones who cannot remember our soul-state. Why is that? What makes all other species remember this when we can't?"

"Your ego, my dear – your ego is the difference. Adult humans are the only beings who have a fully developed ego, which you could see as the opposing counterpart to your soul. This colours your whole perspective while you are incarnated here."

"You are saying our ego is bad?" Nayeli asked.

"No," Willow said earnestly. "Your ego isn't bad at all. Why would you think that?"

Nayeli raised her eyebrows, beyond confused by the tree's reaction. "When you say that our soul-state is something good and that the ego is the opposite, what am I supposed to think? Besides, you've just said that it's our ego that makes us forget both who we are and that life doesn't end when we die. And I don't like to be taken for a fool and to be in more pain than necessary."

"Maybe I didn't express myself adequately," Willow admitted. "Let me put it like this. The ego is a useful tool, and you need it for your experience here. Its main job is to allow you to perceive yourself as separate from everyone else by constantly making comparisons. By recognising that you are taller than this person or more fluent in English than that person, you automatically know that they are not you and you are not them. Likewise, when your mind concludes that your friend left the room while you are still standing inside it, you know that you exist separately from them. These comparisons are an automatism playing out in the back of your mind all day, without you even being aware of it. But it's what allows you to experience life through your unique perception.

"Imagine that ten people experience anxiety. You might think that everyone feels fear alike, but that couldn't be further from the truth. One person may feel the anxiety in their belly as a growing ball of stress, while another person's hands shake or sweat. One person might be scared about something that hasn't even happened yet, while the next person is reliving the fear of an earlier experience. The physical symptoms and their magnitude – as well as the reasons for it – will be different for everyone."

Nayeli watched as Willow's leaves danced in front of the sun, making them sparkle.

"Think of the source as being like an infinite pool of different colours. Your individual life experience is adding a new shade to it with everything you feel and think and do. And no one else could recreate that exact shade of colour because anything in your life is unique. Your wants, your needs, your beliefs, your wishes – anything. Your ego is what makes you you and differentiates you from all else."

Nayeli smiled. "I have to agree that it doesn't sound so bad in that case. It would be pointless for us all to come here if we all had the identical experiences."

"Yes," the tree agreed. "That's the best news about the ego."

"Are you implying that there is some bad news about it, too?" Nayeli queried.

"I don't know if I would call it bad news, but there's a shadow side to everything inside a dual reality. And one of the shadow sides of the ego is that it wants to survive at any cost."

"So? What's the problem with that?" Nayeli asked, taken aback. "I like being alive."

Willow chuckled. "That you do. But you asked me why you humans are the only ones who don't remember your true soul-state. And this is why. Your ego goes overboard when it feels threatened. And it feels especially threatened when you reconnect with its opposite, your soul. Because of that, it makes you forget all about it and the other side when you grow up. Which it does rather effectively in most cases, I might add. Meanwhile, animals, plants and even human children do not have a fully grown ego, so they can remember all or at least some of it."

"But why would our ego feel threatened?" Nayeli asked. "I thought you said we don't die when we cross over? That we are eternal beings?"

"Your soul is," the tree corrected her. "It is your soul that lives forever. But your body and your ego will die eventually. Thus, they do everything they can to keep you alive for as long as possible."

"That sounds rather egoistical of the ego," Nayeli said.

"It's called an ego for a reason." Willow laughed. "Because it *is* egoistical. When all is said and done, though, a healthy ego can be a real blessing. And you humans can call yourself fortunate to have them because they make you learn everything so much faster."

"But doesn't a baby or a dog perceive itself as separate, too? The same as an adult human would?" Nayeli asked bewildered. "I mean, I don't remember what I thought when I was little, but it can't have been that different, can it?"

"Oh, it is. In the first years, a child is still emotionally connected to its primary caregivers, especially its mother. It feels the emotions the mother feels and can't separate those from its own. That's also why a small child doesn't understand that pulling a cat's tail hurts the cat. They don't feel any pain themselves by doing so, and they haven't learned that the cat has separate feelings. This awareness grows alongside the ego until it is fully developed. And as for animals – they have what I'd call a mini-ego. It helps them to see themselves as separate and to distinguish between other members of their species, their prey and the predators that prey on them. But it's not as developed as the human ego."

Willow's leaves rubbed together, creating a soothing tone. "You know what, my dear? I have a proposition for you. Let me take you on a journey. A journey during which you will gain the answers to many hidden truths that are just waiting to be discovered."

Nayeli thought about this offer. "I suppose it can't hurt to listen to you. I don't have to take everything at face value, after all, and can always disagree."

"That you can," Willow said. "Then make yourself comfortable. Because I've got a lot of lessons to teach you. Lessons on how you can access the infinite wisdom hidden inside you and how to reawaken it. Lessons on how to access all the abilities you've forgotten over time. And lessons on how to trust that inner knowledge deep within you. And I'm gonna begin by telling you a story about a close friend of mine, a friend who has travelled the world."

Nayeli laid down on her back. "Fine with me. But tell me, who's this friend? Another tree?"

"No!" Willow laughed brightly. "Have you ever seen a tree travelling the world? My friend is a short-eared owl, called Strix. He has been a bundle of energy since the day he hatched, looking for adventure wherever he flew. But then, one day, he outdid himself. He decided to cross the big ocean to see the Old World – which was farther than he had ever been before."

"Where did he fly to?" Nayeli asked curiously.

"To Europe and Africa and Asia and Australia. But before he set out on this trip, his very first stop was Costa Rica, where he wanted to meet up with an uncle of his who had moved there. Years ago, this uncle had already safely flown to the Old World and back, and Strix hoped for some tips regarding his own journey. Only that he got lost on the way and met someone else ..."

1. Olive, the Sloth

Strix let his eyes roam over the endless ocean of green treetops beneath him and turned his head every which way. But currently, his excellent vision that he prided himself upon was no use to him. The jungle beneath him stretched in all directions, and he could make out no sign of the Pacific coastline he was searching for, nor any other landmarks that could help him find it.

Normally, he would've had no problem navigating using the Earth's magnetic field. But today, his inner compass was off, and the sun wasn't cooperating either. Instead of telling him where west was, it hid behind heavy grey clouds that were emptying torrents of water onto him, drenching his plumage – something that didn't help his mood at all.

Strix's internal voice kept berating him for having lost his way in the first place. But he had been so occupied thinking about his surprise visit to his uncle and all the questions he wanted to ask him that he hadn't noticed he was lost until it was too late.

Finally giving up the attempt to find the way by himself, he gazed around for someone that appeared trustworthy enough to ask for directions. At first glance, every living being seemed to have fled the downpour of rain, but then he spotted a brown-green blotch in one of the higher trees that blended almost perfectly into the surrounding foliage. *Almost* wasn't good enough to fool him, however.

Strix soared lower to take a closer look.

The animal in question wasn't moving. And strangely, it was hanging upside down from a sturdy branch. Caught off guard at the sight, Strix forgot to beat his wings and only brought them back under control when he was close to colliding with the tree.

Landing skilfully on the same branch as the animal, Strix turned his head to study it. He concluded that it was truly the weirdest species he had ever come across. It had long brown fur that was covered by a greenish layer of algae, and it hung from the tree by long and razor-sharp claws.

Upon noticing those, Strix took an involuntary step back; for all he knew, this stranger could be aggressive and lunge at him at any second. Curiously, so far, the animal hadn't even raised its head or taken notice of him, though.

Dead, Strix thought clinically. But before he could hop over to inspect it further, the creature refuted his suspicion by blinking its eyes open, looking blearily up at him and then yawning widely.

"What's the flurry about, owl? Is there a reason you are disrupting my nap?"

Strix was startled at the fact that the animal, who was clearly female if the high voice was of any indication, had come alive after all. Then he reined in his surprise.

"There is," he said urgently. "I've lost my way. Can you tell me the quickest route to the west coast, please?"

"Naturally, I can help you. But why the quickest?" the female said while a relaxed smile spread across her face. "Tell me, why is everyone always searching for the quickest way to do things? The quickest road, the quickest hunting technique, the quickest mating ritual. Okay, I can relate to that last item on that list. But what I'm trying to say is that you need to slow down a bit if you want to stay healthy. Take a few breaths, relax and be present, why don't you? I promise you'll feel much better for it ..."

The animal spoke at a snail's pace, pausing between every word, and Strix feared that she would fall back asleep before she could make her point. Even he felt tiredness overcome him, thanks to the creature's monotonous voice. Shaking his head to rid himself of the fogginess, he wondered if this was her tried-and-tested hunting method: first, lull your prey to sleep and then slash it open with those outrageously long claws.

Taking his eyes off them, Strix let his gaze drift back up to her face. "Much better, Lady?" he asked, feeling miserable in this humid heat and on edge because he'd lost his way. "Thank you for your concern, but I'm fine. And the only thing that could improve my mood even further is for you to give me the right directions."

"I beg to differ." The animal grinned widely. "You seem quite agitated and stressed. I would even venture a guess that you seem angry. And from my own experience, I know that taking a little time to centre yourself helps wonders with that. Let go of your problems and meditate, why don't you? And if you don't know how, just look at me. I'm the perfect role model: I'm one with the universe. The trick is to be so present that you feel the flow of life energy."

Strix wasn't fazed by this stranger's opinion of his lifestyle, but he sure didn't like his patience being tested. "Listen, my weird friend," he said but was immediately interrupted by the female waving one of her long arms about. Taken aback at the fact that she could move this fast, Strix fell silent and took another step backwards to be on the safe side.

But instead of lunging at him, she grasped a few leaves hanging overhead and brought them to her mouth in slow motion.

"It's Olive. My name's Olive. And I'm a sloth," the female said while munching sedately on the greens. "I think we have enough time for some pleasantries, don't you think?"

Grumbling under his breath at the nerve of this animal – sloth, whatever – Strix breathed deeply a couple of times and tried to get his anger at being unnecessarily delayed under control.

"Fine, Olive. My name's Strix, and as I was trying to say, I would —"

"It's nice to meet you, Strix," Olive said and yawned heartily, presenting the half-eaten leaves in her mouth. "It isn't all that often that I get visitors."

Strix huffed. "Well, maybe your disgusting table manners keep others away. Or perhaps it's the fact that you bore people to death and don't get to the point. Would you *please* just tell me the way to the coast? And tell me right now? That way, I can fly on and leave you to your peace and quiet. It's a win-win for everyone."

Strix had expected Olive to oblige his request or at least to answer him. But, instead, she simply closed her eyes, as if she intended to go back to sleep.

Staring at her with wide eyes, Strix was torn between nudging the sloth to wake her up or flying away to search for someone else to ask for directions. But before he could decide between these two options, Olive opened her eyes again.

"Hmm," she said, drawing the syllable out to its maximum. "The coast ... yes, yes, I remember overhearing some birds speak about it. They said it's pretty, but I also learned that it's a long way from here. It will take you a few weeks to get there. Why don't you take a nap in advance of setting out on that arduous journey?"

"A FEW WEEKS?" Strix shouted, aghast. "Why are you talking such nonsense? I haven't gone *that* far off course. It can't take me more than a few hours, tops. If I find the direct route, that is."

Then he became aware of his mistake. Of course, Olive wouldn't know the way to the coast! Considering how slowly the sloth moved, Strix wondered if she had ever travelled any farther than the next tree. Feeling anger bubbling up inside him because he had wasted his precious time here, Strix spread his wings and took off into the air. He flew a circle over Olive.

"Since you don't know the answer to my question, I'll find someone else who does. But you could have said so from the start instead of making false promises that you can't keep."

He looked daggers at the sloth, but Olive was completely unfazed by his rage. She just ripped off another handful of leaves and calmly brought them to her mouth.

Turning around in the air, Strix swiftly left the tree behind him. His ire had grown into a fiery ball that sat in the middle of his stomach, making him feel as if he was burning up from the inside. It made Strix want to scream and curse and to lash out at someone. Which was unlike him, as he rarely got angry or upset. And this made him feel even worse.

Ultimately deciding that the best thing was to forget about this incident, he pushed the anger down and concentrated on his real problem: finding his way to his uncle. After staying clear of other sloths he saw hanging around in trees and a crocodile that he deemed too dangerous to go near, Strix noticed a quetzal that could finally help him out.

Following the bird's directions, he arrived at his destination after three additional hours and a long detour, right when the sun appeared from behind the grey clouds and began its descent towards the horizon. It illuminated the clearing below that his uncle had described to him. But Strix couldn't reconcile the image in his mind's eye with the reality lying before him.

His uncle had used words like 'peaceful' and 'green paradise' when going into detail. What Strix beheld, however, was a battle-ground. There were ripped out feathers strewn everywhere and spots of blood on the forest floor. Strix had to swallow a few times to keep himself from retching.

"Uncle?" he called out. "Are you here? Uncle? Answer me!"

Hoping against hope that his uncle had escaped the massacre that must have taken place, Strix flew higher to get a better view of the clearing. But he could see no signs of life. Even the insects had ceased buzzing for the time being, leaving a deadly quiet in their wake. Then, right when Strix was giving up hope, an owl emerged from behind a bush.

"Uncle!" Strix called out as he flew over to him, having never been this happy to see the old coot.

"Strix?" his uncle asked, confused. "What are you doing here, boy? My, how you've grown in the couple of months since I last visited my sister. I almost didn't recognise you."

"Uncle, what happened here?" Strix asked, staring at the feathers that littered the ground.

"A jungle ghost," his uncle muttered darkly. "He came out of nowhere and killed four of my friends before anyone could even call out.

"A ghost?" Strix asked, perplexed. "This doesn't look like something a ghost could manage. It looks more like something a big cat would do ..."

His uncle lowered his voice until it was nothing more than a whisper. "It was a black jaguar. But sssh, don't call them that. When you say their name, it brings them back. And this specimen seemed famished. You can count yourself lucky that you weren't here a few minutes ago, boy. It was a terrible sight to behold. And the ghost has only just left."

"I can imagine," Strix said sympathetically. "How did you escape that massacre unharmed?"

"The sole reason I wasn't ripped apart by the cat's claws was that it didn't see me. I was sitting in that bush over there to meditate when it appeared."

"Wait, uncle. You too?" Strix felt flummoxed because he had never known his uncle to be into this esoteric stuff. "Why is the whole world suddenly so interested in this nonsense? Don't you have anything better to do with your time?"

"Better than avoid being eaten?" his uncle laughed, his sarcastic nature coming through again now that the shock was wearing off. "But let's not talk about my latest hobby. Tell me about yourself and your mum and what everyone else is doing back home."

Strix and his uncle filled each other in on everything that had happened since they had last seen each other. With every hour that passed, his uncle, who had always been an adventurer and bon vivant at heart, became more relaxed as the stress from earlier fell off like leaves in the fall. And as the jungle around them once again filled with the sounds of birds and insects, their laughter mingled with those background noises.

"So, you want to imitate me and travel the world? That's a mighty big goal you've set yourself there, boy. What did your mother say to that? I bet she wasn't exactly happy, was she? I mean, she told me I was crazy when I migrated, and *I'm* not her son ..."

Shifting his weight onto his other foot, Strix looked uncomfortable. "Er, I didn't tell her. Or anyone else, for that matter. I just kinda up and left."

"You did, did you?" His uncle laughed heartily. "My, I wish I'd seen her face when she realised you were gone."

Shrugging, Strix scraped the ground with one of his claws. "It's not like she can say anything about it. I'm grown-up now, and I make my own decisions. Granted, owls aren't usually known to migrate that far, but I don't see why I should let that stop me."

"You're right," his uncle agreed. "Never let anything get in the way of you following your dreams, simply because those aren't 'the norm'."

"Why don't you accompany me?" Strix asked, the idea just having come to him. He grinned winningly up at the older owl. "It would be great fun to travel together."

"It would be," his uncle agreed. "But I'm too old for such a long and taxing journey. No, boy, my adventuring days are over. I've built myself a nice home here with lots of friends. I feel content for once, and this is where I'll stay."

Although Strix was sad to hear this, he could understand his uncle's point of view. After all, the prospect of crossing the ocean and entering an entirely unknown world was beyond scary. And he was still young and fit.

"But even if I'm not travelling with you," his uncle interrupted his thoughts, "I can tell you a few valuable facts that'll keep you safe. I can speak of the friends I've met who'll help you when you are in need and the customs of some species that are foreign to us here ..."

They spent the next couple hours huddled together, planning Strix's route, discussing where it was best to cross the sea and where to turn to first. And it was only when the sun rose that Strix looked up again.

He blinked in the bright light, surprised by how quickly the night had passed. Stretching after sitting for so long and abuzz with all the interesting tales his uncle had told about his own journey, Strix felt a wanderlust spreading within him.

Noticing the gleam in his eyes, his uncle grinned knowingly. "Off with you then, kiddo. Don't let an old bird keep you from your adventures. But come back and tell me all about them if you are ever in the region, agreed?"

"Agreed," Strix grinned, saying goodbye to his uncle and taking off into the sky, which shone in hues of orange and pink. He flew north-east, where he had come from, as discussed in length. While he was soaring on the thermals and the wind ruffled the tips of his feathers, Strix admired the colours of the sky and the way the rays of the sun painted a magic picture on the carpet of trees beneath him. It was a breath-taking sight and Strix felt utterly calm. He could practically feel how the sweet smell of the morning air stripped him bare of all negative thoughts. And how the sound of the many birds striking up a song made him fall into a dreamlike trance, which resulted in an incredible feeling of peace permeating him.

Laughing in pure delight, Strix didn't know how long he flew like this. But when he gazed downwards, after what felt like aeons passing by, the trance-like state gave way to a feeling of astonishment. For there, directly below him, was a familiar tree. And a very familiar sloth hanging from one of its branches. Olive!

Strix felt disbelief that fate would have him cross her path twice in two days. But being in such a good mood, he wanted to use this opportunity to apologise for his rude behaviour yesterday. He soared downward and landed on the branch beside the female.

Today, Olive was already awake and munching away on the leaves surrounding her. Strix noticed that even this mundane act resembled a tranquil experience when done by her as she gave her full attention to her food.

"That looks unappetising," Strix said to start the conversation.

To his dismay, Olive seemed to still be mad at him, though. Because, instead of responding, she continued to chew her leaves in slow-motion while fixing him with a gaze.

Strix spread out his wings in an apology. "I'm sorry, okay? You were right. I wasn't feeling great. I was angry and upset, and I took that out on you. Which I shouldn't have. Especially since you were not the reason for it ..."

"No need to apologise," Olive answered after swallowing her mouthful. Smiling at him, with no accusation in her eyes, the sloth stretched out a long arm to grab another twig.

"You aren't mad at me?" Strix probed. "Then why didn't you say anything?"

Moving in slow motion, the sloth grinned. "Not long ago, some bird told me that my table manners weren't the best. And I had to agree. It's not nice to speak with your mouth full. But to answer you now ... these leaves are delicious. Do you want one?"

"Nope, thanks," Strix said. "They're all yours."

"All the better," Olive replied and let a few more leaves disappear inside her mouth. After swallowing them, she then winked at Strix. "If you don't mind me asking, how was your day? Did you find what you were looking for?"

"It was good," Strix answered, puzzled by the question. "And I did reach my destination. Why do you ask?"

"Merely because you appear more relaxed and happier. As if a weight has lifted from your shoulders."

Shrugging, Strix gazed up at the azure sky. It was a welcome change to the endless curtain of rain that seemed to be normal for this region.

"I was just flying around and enjoying the morning air. Nothing special. And, sorry to say this, but the reason for my improved mood has nothing to do with the new-age stuff you were trying to sell me. All this stuff about meditating is too airy-fairy for me. Besides, if I were as relaxed as you are, it would spell big trouble for me. The attentive owl catches the mouse. My mum told me that when I was little. And she's right. If we were to sit around and meditate about life all day, I'd starve! Not everyone has the luck – or should I say misfortune – to eat awful green stuff that doesn't run away."

Olive remained unperturbed by his opinion and plucked yet another leaf from the branch above her.

Watching her, Strix was torn between his desire to find the answer to an issue that had plagued him since yesterday and his desire to not upset Olive. He turned his head in indecision, first one way and then the other.

"Go on and ask before you get a crick in your neck," Olive said mildly, making Strix wonder how she had read his thoughts. But he was not one to reject a free earthworm when offered.

"I was wondering how you sloths can survive for longer than a day. I don't want to offend you or anything, but you're moving so damn slow that it would be the easiest thing for any predator to kill you."

"No offence taken," Olive said after swallowing her leaf. "To answer your question, we are pretty good at camouflaging ourselves. Look at me. The algae in my fur make me practically melt into the trees surrounding me. It's the best survival strategy if you ask me."

Laughing, Olive winked at him. "Especially since it gives me the time to relax all day long."

"And isn't that dull?" Strix asked curiously. "If I was forced to hang around all day, I would probably die of sheer boredom. I need action. And fun. I need to soar and tumble in the sky; I want to be carried by the warm draughts or speed through the cooler night air. When I fly, it's as if time stops. It's about the only thing that can make me feel absolutely free and relaxed at once."

A grin was tugging at the edges of Olive's mouth.

"What?" Strix asked. "Why are you smirking like that? As though you know something I don't?"

"It's nothing," Olive said dismissively. "I just realised that you should ignore everything I said about my way of handling life and the advice I gave you. It appears as If you've found a much better way of being mindful and present."

Strix stared suspiciously at the sloth, not yet fully trusting her. "That's the first reasonable thing you've said, Olive."

The sloth laughed loudly, but then her face scrunched up in a grimace as her laughter turned into a jaw-splitting yawn.

"Sorry," she said sheepishly. "I think it's way past time for me to take another short nap. All this eating and chatting has tired me out."

"You do that." Strix agreed as he prepared to fly away. Once he was up in the air, he looked back down at Olive.

The sloth had fallen asleep – quicker than Strix would have expected – and was hanging limply from her branch. Shaking his head at the absurdity of nature at creating a species that was the epitome of laziness, Strix flew up to continue his journey east and to new shores.

Countless dangers might await him in the unknown, in a world thoroughly different from the one he was used to. But if those were part of the deal, then so be it. He wouldn't allow his doubts or fears to tie him down to a life that was too small for him anymore. And he definitely wouldn't sit inside a tree until the end of his days to stay safe. Because it was quality of life he was after and not sheer survival.

Meditation and Mindfulness

Nayeli was so caught up in the story that it took her a little while to notice Willow had stopped talking. When she did, the tree let its branches sweep over the grassy ground.

"I'm interested in what you learned from the story, my sweet child."

"That I need to learn how to fly?" Nayeli asked jokingly.

The willow tree apparently didn't get her humour and stood silent.

"It's just that I'm totally on your friend Strix's side. I'd rather spend my time flying than sit around for hours doing nothing. It might work for Olive, but I'm not into all that airy-fairy stuff either. I've tried to meditate once, back in school, when our sports teacher thought it would be a good idea to do something else for a change. But he soon gave up on the idea because we couldn't stop giggling long enough to count our breaths. It's honestly the most boring thing I've ever done."

"I think that you have a false idea regarding what meditation means, my dear," Willow answered. "Because it is anything but boring. It is a beautiful and peaceful state of being. And it's one of the best ways to access all the wisdom and abilities you have forgotten."

Snorting disbelievingly, Nayeli rejected the tree's claim. "I don't know about that."

"But I do," Willow replied steadfastly, "and I bet I can convince you of it. If you give me a chance."

Nayeli laughed. "Ha, I doubt you can. But go on – I'm curious."

"What if I tell you that you have been in a meditative state more than once in your life? Without even knowing it?"

"Then you would be wrong."

"You think so?" Willow asked, a grin being visible in the tree's voice. "You've never watched a sunrise or sunset and been in awe of the beautiful spectrum of colours in the sky? You've never done anything creative in your life where you lose yourself in the flow? You've never lain on the grass and gazed at the clouds, seeing animals or other shapes in them? You've never done a jigsaw and concentrated so much on where to put the next piece that all other thoughts fled? And you've never stared into the flames of a bonfire or a candle?"

"Sure I have," Nayeli said, perplexed at this change of topic. "But what does any of this have to do with meditation?"

"All of these things are forms of meditation."

"Come again?" Nayeli said, surprised.

"Meditation means nothing else but to be completely in the present moment. It's a state of peaceful mindfulness. Yes, there's your typical meditation where you sit cross-legged and consciously empty your mind to reach that state of being. But there are also countless other moments where you reach the same state without even intending to do it."

Nayeli opened her eyes wide in surprise. "And what's the one technique or form that is the most useful?"

"No technique is better than the next," the tree chided softly. "It depends on what works best for you. And that answer will be different for everyone. In the end, all moments in which you are present are important. Because the present isn't called present for no reason – it is a gift to everyone. It is the only state of being where we can truly live. When your mind is stuck in the past or in the future, you'll never be able to create your life and manifest all that you wish for.

"Change is merely happening when you recognise the truth of your reality. Truth is requiring awareness. And awareness comes as a result of being mindful. Thus, being present is the foundation of all healing taking place. That's not to say, however, that you should ban all times you spend in the past and future. There's nothing wrong with reliving memories or daydreaming. But if you're never in the present, your life is gonna be over before you've started to live it ..."

Nayeli blinked. "You think that humans live too often in the past or future?"

The tree shrugged by first raising and then lowering its branches. "I haven't talked to a whole lot of humans in the last years. But based on the ones I met, I noticed some similarities. About half of all humans are too stuck in the past. They have trouble letting go, and they escape from their present life by reminiscing or by wallowing in regrets based on decisions they made previously. And the other 50 per cent are doing the opposite: they're constantly thinking about the future. They're daydreaming or worrying about what might happen next."

"And it's either one or the other?" Nayeli asked.

"Actually, everyone alternates between the two. If you're driving a car, for example, you are mostly in the future because you're planning what turn to make next, which detour to take or where you can find the best parking space. But you can also be stuck in the past – when you're cursing about a near miss or think about your bad luck to have got a speeding ticket. On the other hand, humans are mostly inside the past when they're using social media. They're looking at pictures and texts that others have posted prior, telling them about things they've already done and seen and experienced."

"Or I can be inside the future when I see an update about a movie release I'm excited for ..." Nayeli extended the list.

"Correct," the tree agreed. "As I said, everyone switches between the past and the future all the time, while being predisposed towards one. The only thing you have trouble with is to stay in the present."

Nayeli accepted that Willow was doubtlessly right since the tree seemed to know more about this topic than the average human. "Fine, I get all that. But what can I do to change this status quo?"

"First off," Willow said, "it's important for you to be able to de-stress as many humans have lost that ability based on the fast-paced lives you live."

"But doesn't that depend on the human?" Nayeli interjected. "Sure, there are people who are stressed out by life and all their responsibilities, but there must be a lot of others who are perfectly okay?"

Feeling some discomfort because one of Willow's roots was pressing into her backside, Nayeli shifted around and settled in a lotus position that reminded her of meditating monks.

"There are indeed differences from individual to individual," the tree pulled her back to the present. "Some people can deal with more stress than others. You can even thrive on positive stress in your life. And how you handle it is unique and depends on the stressor. But I've yet to meet a human who is dealing well with constant stress without using some sort of technique to counter it – which can be sports or naps or meditation.

"Just look at how unhealthy your lifestyle has become. You are always in competition with each other, wanting to be accepted, wanting to be successful, wanting to reach new goals. Not to mention that you bombarded with information from the TV, newspapers and the internet all day long. You are connected with others 24/7 through social media. Your mobile phone accompanies you everywhere, making you available round the clock. And I'm talking about your free time alongside your career."

The tree paused. "Tell me, my dear Nayeli, what job do you have?"

Surprised at the question, Nayeli took a few seconds to gather her wits. "Nothing special. I'm an office administrator. Why?"

"A desk job then, sitting in front of a computer for hours on end. How is that going? How much time do you have each day without being interrupted by the phone ringing or emails coming in?"

"Not a whole lot," Nayeli conceded. "Sometimes I have a calm day, but usually the piles of papers on my desk get ever higher because each time I finish one task, two new enquiries have arrived. Yes, I begin to see what your point is."

"And I could keep this going forever. You humans are not living at a natural pace anymore, and it must be incredibly tiring to try to keep up. Unless you've got so used to this level of activity to notice how tired you really are. In that case, your exhaustion only becomes visible when you take a break and your high stress level lowers. These are the times you will get sick or when you'll feel bored and get cabin fever because you aren't used to this state of relaxation any longer."

Embarrassed by how closely Willow's description matched her own life, Nayeli blushed. She admitted to herself that she would have likely looked at her mobile – scrolling through any new messages – two or three times by now if she hadn't left it at her grandmother's house.

Luckily for her, Willow wasn't saying these things to put her on the spot, though. Instead, the tree continued its teaching.

"You humans don't give 100 per cent each day but 130 per cent. And it's time to slow down. That's not to say that you have to spend your entire day sitting around and never logging into your beloved computer anymore. Just taking half an hour every day to be present with yourself can already make an immense difference in your life."

"That sounds logical," Nayeli said thoughtfully. "But I still don't see the need for meditation. Why do we need to sit down and empty our minds?"

"Empty your mind?" The tree chortled. "No, we're not talking about that here."

"But isn't that the whole point of meditation? To get rid of all thoughts?" Nayeli asked, flummoxed.

"I'm not saying that you can't do it," the tree said, "but it's only the second step and not what we are concerned with for now. To break it down, there are two main forms of conscious meditation. The one you're thinking about is the one where no thoughts are present and where you experience the sound of the source, as I would call it. You may be able to master this when you have spent months or years training yourself in the art of meditation. Meanwhile, the other form is available to everyone right here and now. Its goal is not to empty your mind but to meditate despite and with your thoughts. Cause you have to know one important fact: When you try to push your thoughts away when meditating, they get stronger. And thoughts will come, especially in the beginning. But this is perfectly okay. When we watch our thoughts, we can actually use them to improve our meditation practice."

"How's that?" Nayeli questioned.

"Whenever you become aware of a thought, you will know that you are doing everything right. Because by looking at that thought and letting it pass by, you are already practising awareness. Look at it like this: when you watch a thought from an outsider's point of view, you are not stuck inside it. And thus you are not stuck in the past or the future, which the thought represents. Or, to say it otherwise, as soon as you notice that you are thinking about a memory or a future problem, you are in the present because you know that the thought itself is not."

"Hmm," Nayeli said slowly. "This reminds me that I often catch myself ruminating about a problem after I've already spent a few minutes pondering it. It's a weird sensation to realise there was something on my mind all along, but I wasn't conscious of it."

"Yes, that's because most of your thoughts run on autopilot," Willow explained. "You are only aware of a small number of them throughout your day. Which makes it even more important to become aware of them as much as possible. Because when you are, you can steer them in the direction that you want."

"But what if there are too many when I'm meditating and they keep flooding my brain?"

"When your thoughts pull you in when meditating, imagine them to be clouds in a blue sky that drift by. Accept that the thought is there, look at it without passing judgement and then let it go."

"That will be hard," Nayeli stated. "To not judge my thoughts when they come, despite you saying that they're allowed to be there ..."

"But why?" Willow asked. "It's natural that they are with you. They are a part of you – and an important one at that. Besides, sometimes when you are meditating you might get the best ideas from watching your thoughts. Creative breakthroughs, solutions to problems or insights into an issue that has been troubling you. So, why not see thoughts as the blessing they are?"

The tree stirred and created moving specks of shadow and sunlight on the grass in front of Nayeli.

She followed them with her eyes, feeling her earlier resistance crumble, and squared her shoulders. "Okay, how do I do it then? How do I meditate?"

"That sounds as if I've already convinced you to try it?" Willow asked cheekily.

Nayeli shrugged nonchalantly. "It doesn't sound as bad as I initially thought. I guess there's no harm in giving it a shot. And what better time is there than the present to try it out, right?"

Willow's twigs swished in agreement. "Right. The trick to enjoy and master meditation is to find a technique that works for you. One of the most popular ones is a simple breathing meditation where you concentrate on your inhales and exhales. This has the added bonus that you can do it anywhere because your breath is always with you. But you can also use any other form of meditation, like focusing on your senses and what you perceive through them. Or you can do an active meditation like yoga. Keep in mind, though, that meditation is not about *getting better*. It's about choosing to take time out of your day to be present and mindful."

Nayeli nodded in understanding and straightened her spine. She breathed in deeply a few times and noticed how the air travelled through her body and into her belly. At first, she was only aware how her chest and stomach rose and fell. But then she let her awareness move outside her body and towards the meadow around her. To the blue sky that shone through the gaps in Willow's foliage, to the deep green hue of the grass and the ladybird that was climbing a flower beside her left leg. Nayeli listened to the water gurgling in the brook and to the faint sound of an eagle calling. A feeling of peace spread within her, as if nothing outside this meadow existed or mattered.

Nayeli did not know how long she sat like this. But the next thing she became aware of was that the sky had darkened, plunging the meadow into twilight. At first, she was confused by how quickly dusk had approached, but then she remembered that she was still sleeping and that the passage of time didn't necessarily have to follow a linear order inside a dream.

Just then, a thought came to Nayeli. Maybe this was all she had to do to end it? Stand up and go away?

Nayeli was about to test that theory when a question from Willow made her stop.

"Will you come back tomorrow? As I said, there's a whole lot more I could teach you if you'd like to hear about it."

Nayeli was cautious when she answered, as she didn't want to hurt the tree's feelings, despite it being only a figment of her imagination. "I've never been good at managing my dreams and I don't know if I can. But I'll do my best to dream of you again tonight."

She stood up and laid her hand on Willow's rough bark, wondering if it would be the last time she talked to the tree. "Goodbye, Willow," she said. "And thank you!"

Not waiting for a reply, Nayeli ran back the way she'd come earlier, after the funeral service. The funeral service, she reminded herself steadfastly, which had also been part of this weird dream.

Nayeli crossed the meadow, which was being consumed by the

looming darkness of the night and walked through the streets towards her grandma's house. It stood at the far edge of the village and by the time she reached it, the path was only illuminated by some light posts and the headlights of a lone car driving past.

The cooler evening air made her shiver in her short black dress, and Nayeli quickly walked up the front steps to the house. Standing in front of the wooden door, she paused, not daring to move for a minute or two. She told herself that it was to recover her breath, not because she was steeling herself mentally for what might happen next. But she couldn't deny the fact that her heart beating loudly behind her ribs.

Finally plucking up her courage, she fished her keyring from her handbag. But before she could insert the key into the lock, the door was flung open, as if the person behind it had been waiting for her arrival.

"Nayeli, where have you been the whole afternoon?" her mum asked in her most anxious voice. "You can't run away like that. The memorial service ..." Breaking off mid-sentence, Nayeli's mother wiped her eyes.

Seeing that they were red from crying, Nayeli felt her grief come back full force, with a sense of guilt settling atop on it. Once again, she reminded herself that she simply needed to find a way to wake up. Only that this conviction resembled more of a leaky bucket now. And with every second she saw her mum's anguish, new holes were added to it.

Pushing past her mother into the living room, Nayeli had no idea what to say. She ultimately settled on the apology she would have given if this day had been real. "I'm sorry, Mum. I know I should have stayed, but I couldn't take it anymore. I needed to be alone."

"Nayeli, I'm aware that all this isn't easy for you," her mother said. "It isn't for me either – my mother died, for God's sake. But you can't run off without a word. I was worried about you. I was just about ready to go out there and search for you myself. I was afraid that something had happened to you ..."

"I'm fine," Nayeli croaked. "I just need some time alone."

Dodging her mum's arm, Nayeli walked to the guest bedroom at the end of the hall where she was sleeping. Shutting the door and lying down on the mattress, she closed her eyes, hoping that this would end the spell. She didn't notice when exhaustion made her slip into a fitful sleep.

***

When Nayeli woke the next morning, she didn't feel rested but groggy and a little dehydrated. But the sunlight shining in through her window and the smell of fresh coffee quickly roused her. Jumping out of bed, she was about to pull on a shirt and joggers, when she registered she was still wearing the black dress from yesterday.

Nayeli sank down onto the bed in shock as her thoughts and feelings tumbled all over each other, vying for her attention. She blocked out all of them except one. The one that told her to accept the inevitable truth. It hadn't been a dream; her grandmother *had* died.

The grief that struck her felt all-consuming, like a black hole that was sucking her in, leaving nothing but a shell behind. As fresh tears spilled from her eyes, making them red and puffy, Nayeli pummelled the pillow lying beside her. But then she reined her feelings in – she had to be strong for her mother now.

Springing into action, Nayeli took off her dress and left it lying crumpled on the floor while she put on some fresh clothes. Then she left her room and entered the kitchen.

Her uncle, who was her mother's older brother, was sitting at the wooden table, eating breakfast, while Nayeli's mother stood at the counter.

"Hey," Nayeli said awkwardly, not knowing how to react. But luckily neither of the two seemed upset anymore. Her uncle pulled out a chair for her to sit, and her mum raised the can of coffee in invitation.

"It's freshly brewed," she said and poured a mug for Nayeli.

"Thank you," Nayeli said and then asked the question that had been at the forefront of her mind since she'd left her room. "Is my sister ...?"

"She left early." Her mother cut her inquiry short. Her forced smile transformed into a stony mask that showed no emotion.

Being aware that she was treading on dangerous ground, Nayeli cast her uncle a glance before facing her mother again. "I'm really, really sorry for rushing off yesterday."

"I know," her mother answered. Her eyes were red-rimmed, as if she had cried all night. "I know how much she meant to you. You were always eager to visit her, even as a small child ..." Her voice broke.

As Nayeli's uncle turned away to hide the tears welling up in his own eyes, Nayeli had to swallow hard to not break down.

"Anyway, what will we do today?" Nayeli asked, both to break the silence that had taken over the table and to distract herself from her thoughts.

"Your mum and I will begin to organise things," her uncle answered. "It will take a while to sell the house."

"I can help you with that," Nayeli said confidently, but her mum declined the offer.

"Nayeli, we can manage ourselves. You should do something else that distracts you a bit, hm? I'm sure my mother would have wanted you to enjoy the rest of your holiday, even under these circumstances."

She knew that her mother hadn't said those words to hurt her, but the word 'enjoy' reverberated inside Nayeli's mind, as if mocking her. Angrily, she jumped up from the table. "Grandma died a couple of days ago and you are telling me that I should ENJOY myself? Are you serious?"

Enraged, she wanted nothing more than to throw her cup of coffee against the wall but managed to hold back. "You know what? You're right. Do your stupid paperwork alone. It doesn't matter, anyway. Grandma is dead and I'm not interested in splitting up her possessions, dividing everything that once mattered to her."

"Nayeli!" her mother called out. But Nayeli didn't stop. She ran out of the front door and slammed it shut behind her.

At first, her anger resembled a storm clouding her judgement, but the farther she ran through the streets, the faster it released its hold on her, leaving her feeling tired and drained. And guilty that she'd abandoned her mother the second day in a row, despite knowing how hard things were for her.

It was difficult for all of them. Their feelings were currently so close to the surface that it only took one wrong word to ignite an impulsive outbreak of anger. And Nayeli felt like a firecracker, ready to explode as soon as a spark came too close.

Coming to a stop in a side street she didn't recognise, she decided to call her mum and apologise. But when she fished around in her pockets for her mobile, Nayeli came up empty-handed. She swore loudly. Realising that she had left it behind again, Nayeli considered going back to the house: she could pick it up and apologise to her mother in person. But she disregarded that idea almost immediately. It might be better to let everyone cool down first, or they'd go straight from one dispute to the next.

Wondering what she should do with the next couple of hours, now that she had this much free time on her hands, Nayeli dug out everything she found in her pocket. An old sweet and some coins. Not enough to buy a bus ticket to the next town. But enough to purchase a bottle of water and a croissant in the town's bakery. Although she wasn't hungry yet, Nayeli knew from experience that when the appetite came, she'd get cranky if she didn't have anything to appease it.

It was only after she walked out of the bakery, a paper bag clutched in her hand, that she pondered where to go. The air was already warm, and the day promised to get even hotter. But the village didn't give her a whole lot of options to escape the burning sun. Apart from a church and a children's playground, there was only a small grocery store and a bar that would open later.

Before long, the picture of a willow tree popped into her mind, unasked. But Nayeli quickly discarded the mental image and concentrated instead on the older man walking his dog, who was coming towards her. And after he had disappeared around the corner, she focused on three children running towards the swings. Remembering how she had needled her grandma to bring her to this playground whenever she had visited her as a kid, and how she had pleaded to push her ever higher on the swings, Nayeli felt the sadness return in huge waves, crashing over her head. Tears ran down her cheeks and Nayeli wiped them off, wondering if they would ever stop coming.

Walking on blindly, she didn't even care where she was going anymore and let her feet lead her wherever they wanted to. It wasn't until she was standing at the edge of the forest that she became aware of where they had brought her. Seeing the hill in the distance with the solitary weeping willow on top, Nayeli was about to turn back around when her stubbornness stopped her.

Straightening her shoulders, Nayeli marched through the tall grass, not being able to avert her gaze from the tree. The willow stood so innocently in front of her. It appeared to be a regular tree, exactly like the thousands of others she had passed in her life. And it was just as silent as them; the wind murmuring through the leaves being the only sound she could hear.

It was as if yesterday had never happened.

But Nayeli knew that it had.

What she didn't know, however, was what it all meant. Maybe, she thought, she had disassociated from reality due to the trauma of her grandma's death and had taken refuge in a fantasy she'd dreamed up? A fantasy in which reality couldn't hurt her anymore? Yes, this was a logical conclusion. But there was something else she needed to ensure. Namely, that it had been a one-off event.

Gathering her courage, Nayeli ducked underneath the low-hanging branches and touched the rough bark of the tree. To her relief, nothing happened, and Nayeli felt the tension drain out of her body.

She had already turned around to walk back the way she'd come, when a tender voice halted her in her steps.

"Hello, my dear Nayeli. How did you sleep?"

It was a voice that Nayeli remembered only too well.

Gasping in surprise, she took a step back. Her eyes went wide with fright as she looked into the tree's crown.

Nayeli had calculated every possible emotion that could be sparked by the willow tree remaining silent. That she'd feel regret that all they'd talked about had been nothing but a fantasy. That she'd feel fear because she'd hallucinated something so vividly. That she'd feel the crushing weight of despair because it would lead to the verdict that all she'd heard about the other side and eternal souls was nothing more than her mind desperately searching for answers. But what she hadn't expected was for the tree to actually address her anew.

Her legs suddenly felt like rubber. Nayeli hastily knelt before they could give out beneath her.

"You are talking to me again ..." she said disbelievingly.

As the weeping willow answered, its voice felt like a caress. "I know that you secretly wished that the last days were nothing but a dream. And I'm sorry that it isn't so."

"It's ... a tree ... I ... you ... talking ..." was all that Nayeli could get out, laughing shrilly. "This is by far the weirdest thing that has ever happened to me in my entire life."

"I for one have seen much weirder things in mine," Willow answered cheerfully. "You won't believe half of them ..."

But Nayeli wouldn't be side-tracked. Hugging her knees and rocking back and forwards to calm herself down, she felt as if she would break apart at any moment. She didn't want to go crazy, and she certainly didn't want to have these hallucinations anymore. Leaning her forehead against the willow tree's bark and breathing deeply in and out, Nayeli tried to get some semblance of control back.

The weeping willow was silent during those minutes, obviously sensing that any further words would be too much to handle.

But then Nayeli became aware of a faint vibration inside the trunk, as if energy was flowing through it and into her forehead. And from there into the rest of her body. She meant to pull away from the strange sensation but couldn't bring herself to do so. It felt soothing.

"Are you feeling a little better now?" Willow asked, sounding similar to her mother when she was concerned.

Nayeli nodded, wanting nothing more than to quiet her thoughts, which were running in an infinite loop. "Willow, can you please tell me another story?"

Surprised by her own request – since she hadn't planned to address the tree, let alone ask it to recount another tale – Nayeli pursed her lips. But it was too late to take back the words. And when the weeping willow began to talk she was glad of this. Because, she realised with sudden clarity, this was exactly what she needed. A story to focus on. Something to distract her from her worries and fears.

2. Brownie, the Badger

The weather was turning.

It was only midday, but the sky was nearly as dark as if it were the middle of the night because a storm was brewing behind Strix, chasing him east. So far, he'd been able to escape the worst of it, but the closer he got to the rocky Irish coast, the faster the wind picked up. Black clouds pursued him and gained ground more rapidly than he'd have thought possible.

When the first raindrops hit, he'd barely made it to the cliffs in front of him, which were being cast into a murky grey twilight. Looking around for a hiding place to wait for the storm to pass, he saw nothing that would shelter him from the heavy rain. What made matters worse was that now he could also hear the distant echo of thunder joining the whistling wind.

Turning his head back in mid-flight, Strix was blinded as a lightning bolt broke open the sky. For a moment, he saw nothing else but colourful lights that danced before his eyes, and the seconds it took for him to focus his gaze made him scared to fly straight into an obstacle in his path. But even when the spots faded into the darkness surrounding him, did his vision remain bad. Because the rain was now coming down in sheets and did not let him see more than a few distant shapes in the distance that could belong to a mountain range or a wooded area or anything in between.

He felt like swimming inside an ocean rather than flying through the air.

Cursing his bad luck at having to brave this weather in a landscape that was totally alien to him, Strix tried to shake the water from his plumage as it was beginning to weigh him down. But he realised that he was fighting a losing battle because every rain droplet was immediately replaced by three more. Abandoning his attempt to keep dry, he instead focused all his energy on staying alive.

Lightning brightened up the sky in fast succession now, accompanied by the constant echo of thunder. It enabled Strix to see some thin trees that stood far apart from each other. But none of them provided the safe place he was looking for as they were bending underneath the onslaught of rain and increasing wind, looking as if they would snap in half at any second. And neither could he spot any caves or thick bushes or rocks that would act as a barrier against the storm.

The situation was dire.

Strix flew lower as a loud thunderclap deafened him. A moment later, a gust of wind hit him from the side and he lost his balance. Tumbling downwards, he stopped himself from crashing into the earth beak-first just in time.

"Come inside, quick!" he heard a voice say. Turning towards it, Strix tried to see its owner, but rain poured in his eyes. All he could make out was a black hole in the earth, which was even darker than its surroundings. And inside it, someone was moving.

Not being in any situation to be picky, though, Strix didn't think for long but hopped towards the hole in the ground, The entrance appeared big enough for him to fit in, and so he jumped inside – and not a moment too soon. Because, a split second later, a thunderbolt hit a tree that was standing a few meters away, accompanied by a clap of thunder that shook the earth itself.

Jerking around, Strix gazed back, terrified of what he would find. But the faint flickering of flames licking over the trunk and branches was already hidden by a veil of thundering raindrops.

"That was close," the male voice said.

Swallowing hard, Strix turned back around in the tunnel and waited until his eyes had adjusted to the darkness. He smiled in relief when he recognised that his saviour was a badger: a badger that admittedly looked a bit different to the American species he knew from home but who was clearly related to them.

His uncle had told him about the European ones and that they were a lot more friendly and social than their counterparts in the new world, sometimes even sharing their setts with other species. Knowing this, Strix felt it was safe to take another step into the tunnel and towards his host.

"Mr Badger," he said. "Thank you for sharing your den with me in this storm. How can I repay you?"

The badger grumbled. "My name's Brownie and you're welcome. I saw you struggling out there when I was coming home, and I couldn't leave you unprotected in this storm. What were you doing anyway, flying around in that weather? Why didn't you search for cover when the storm was coming in?"

"I was over the open sea when I saw the first signs and couldn't get to safety in time. As soon as I had reached the coast, it was already over me."

"Ah yes." Brownie smiled warmly. "This region is notorious for that. You aren't from around here, are you?"

"No. I'm just passing through, travelling the old world and looking for adventures."

"In that case, it's a stroke of luck that the wind pushed you right in front of our lovely home, isn't it?"

"Our?" Strix asked, trying to gaze past Brownie into the passage. But the badger was so stocky that he almost completely filled the space. "Who else is living here? Your family?"

Brownie's grunt confused Strix at first. But then he successfully interpreted it as a laugh. "Among others. I'm living here with my beloved and our cubs, which are lively little things. And then there're a couple of rabbits and a fox family that moved in shortly ago."

Brownie turned around and walked deeper into the passageway. "But now enough small talk. Come in, come in. I'll introduce you to them. Besides, we'll get soaked if we continue to stand in the entrance."

Brownie's comment reminded Strix that he was already wet to the skin. He shook himself, letting the water clinging to his feathers fly in all directions.

"Hey," Brownie grunted from deeper inside the passage as a few of the droplets hit him. "Leave the rain outside."

"Sorry," Strix answered cheekily.

His merriment was quickly replaced by a sense of foreboding, however, as he followed the badger deeper underneath the earth. Halting briefly, he tried to figure out the reason behind it and if it was at fault for the tight knot in the pit of his stomach. But when there was another crack of thunder behind him, Strix decided to ignore it in favour of being in safety. Stumbling forward after his host, he reasoned with himself that he didn't have another choice in any case; the thunderstorm was not going to be over anytime soon. And, beyond that, he had always been curious about how badgers lived. So he'd be stupid to refuse this once-in-a-lifetime chance to examine a sett with his own eyes.

Brownie was walking fast, navigating easily in the dank, dark passageways of his underground realm.

Half walking and half hopping after him, Strix was glad of his keen eyesight, which enabled him to see any obstacles, like tree roots growing into the tunnel or small rocks that were sticking out of the walls. But despite his ability to see well in these passages, he had trouble keeping up because he concentrated on keeping his wings folded so that he wouldn't brush the walls on either side. On top of that, with every step he followed the badger, the strange feeling in Strix's stomach intensified – like a stone that was getting heavier.

They had walked around three bends by now and past four side passages, and the thunder sounded muted, which told Strix how thick the earth between him and the outside must be. Chasing away the mental image of the sett collapsing on top of him, burying him alive underneath layers of dirt, Strix told himself that he was safe and that being here was by far preferable to being outside in the storm.

Just then, Brownie stopped and directed him into a chamber that opened in front of them.

"My sleeping chamber," the badger said, stepping aside and motioning for Strix to enter it first. "You are welcome to stay here tonight until the storm settles down."

"Thank you," Strix said as he walked tentatively over the threshold. The roundish chamber itself was a dead end and padded with grass and leaves for bedding. If it hadn't been so cramped, it could have felt quite homely. But as it was, Strix felt dizzy as he looked around.

"Cosy, isn't it?" Brownie said proudly, not noticing Strix's discomfort. "I dug it out myself, as an extension to the existing sett. It was ..."

But his words were cut off mid-sentence when a small furball slammed into him from behind.

"Sorry, Dad," the badger cub called out, already turning around again and racing after his brother, who had bowled him over. "Just you wait. You'll get that back!" he called while disappearing around a bend.

Grinning proudly, Brownie looked at Strix. "My two youngest sons. Some real troublemakers in the making. We have our work cut out for us."

"Ah," Strix responded. But before he could think of something more intelligent to say, the two cubs had come back, making a racket as they raced each other down the passageway. One skidded right past his dad and into the wall behind Strix.

Clumps of dirt rained down upon them.

Alarmed, Strix froze and waited for the ceiling to fall, burying them all alive. Nothing of the sort happened, but that didn't alleviate his fear.

"Sorry," the cub said with a lopsided grin as he noticed Strix for the first time. "Didn't know we had a guest tonight."

It was the last thing Strix heard. Brownie's answer was drowned out by a loud buzzing in his ears. The sound increased until it resembled a tidal wave rushing over him. Horrific images flicked through his mind, and when Strix tried to draw in air, his inhale turned into a gasp of desperation. Smelling nothing but earth, he felt as if he was drowning in it. And the walls closing in on him restricted his breath even further. Flailing around, Strix tried to hoot, to talk, but no words came out.

It was only when a paw touched him that he came back to the present. Staring fearfully into Brownie's concerned eyes, he grounded himself in the calmness he saw shining out of them.

"Come," the badger said, at the same time friendly and assertive. "I'll take you outside. We'll use the quickest route."

Unable to make sense of the words, Strix's mind repeated the only one his brain had registered on an infinite loop: *outside, outside, outside*. Getting his trembling legs back under control, Strix walked after Brownie as fast as he was able to, being super-mindful not to touch any of the walls so as not to set off a landslide.

Instead of taking the way they had come, Brownie turned into another tunnel and pointed towards the end of the passage, which sloped upwards.

Although his gaze was blurred and black dots danced in front of his eyes, Strix could see that the darkness at the end of the tunnel had a different quality to the surrounding darkness. And when lightning brightened the sky behind it, he knew why.

Strix hopped towards the opening at a surprising speed, only stopping when he felt the wind on his plumage. Drawing fresh, clean air into his lungs, he tilted his head upwards to let the rain drip down his face and beak. Already, he was feeling much calmer, and his heartbeat and pulse were returning to normal.

"Feeling better?" Brownie asked in a concerned voice as he appeared behind him. "That was quite the panic attack you had there. I have to say I was a bit worried."

"Panic attack?" Strix asked shakily. "That was a panic attack?"

"It sure looked like one," Brownie muttered. "I don't know what triggered it. But something must have ..."

Strix chose his words cautiously, as he didn't want to hurt Brownie's feelings after the badger had been this accommodating to him. "Your home is a little on the scary side, don't you think?"

"Scary?" Brownie asked, guffawing. "No, not at all. The chamber I showed you was one of my cosiest."

"Ha, yeah, I dare say you could call it cosy. But I'd be more inclined to use the words 'constricted' and 'stifling'."

By now Strix was dripping wet and he was shaking in the cold wind. He walked a few steps backward until he stood in the entrance to the sett – far enough in to not get rained on, but not so far that he couldn't see the sky or smell the rain.

"What are you talking about?" Brownie asked, baffled. "I couldn't imagine a better home than the one I have. Moreover, inside it, we are protected by her."

"Her?" Strix asked. This time it was his turn to be confused.

"Mother Earth," the badger explained. "I'm talking of Mother Earth, of course. That's her name because she is like a mother to us. Nourishing, loving. She provides us with all we need. Just look around you – at all the earthworms and bugs that live inside her. And all the plants that grow from her. In the end, everything we eat and drink comes from her. And she keeps us safe, not only from storms and rain but also from predators that are too big to enter our sett. Additionally, Mother Nature's presence is healing and grounding. Nothing else comes close to the warm, secure feeling we get from being inside and connected to her."

Pensively, Strix tilted his head. "I know the feeling you are speaking of," he said. "But I don't need to be inside the earth to feel her presence, because she's in everything around us. She's in the trees, in the rain and wind and the clouds drifting by. She's in the very air that we breathe. I feel closest to her when I'm flying. Not stuck inside some grave."

Strix gazed up into the sky and at the wall of dark clouds that were pelting the ground with rain. "I hope you don't mind if I wait out the storm in this entrance? I think I must be allergic to the smell of earth."

Brownie snorted. "By all means, be my guest. If you prefer a muddy entrance, where the wind is howling and the rain is sweeping in, over my comfortable chamber, who am I to deny your wish? I reckon it would be too much to ask for a bird to appreciate the lovely home I have built for myself and all the amenities it comes with." But Brownie's voice was good-natured and the twinkle in his eyes was kind.

"It's true." Strix grinned in answer. "But I'm positive that you wouldn't be able to cherish the dizzying heights and the infinity of the sky either, if I were to take you on a ride – or would you?"

"You? Me?" The badger guffawed. "Please, you would collapse underneath my weight if you tried to lift me."

"Hey!" Strix called out in mock outrage. "I'm stronger than I look." Then he joined in Brownie's laughter, and the last traces of the heavy weight disappeared from Strix's chest.

They both spent the next hour sitting comfortably inside the entrance to the sett, talking about their lives while the storm whistled past. Then Brownie stood up, saying it was high time to check up on his cubs.

Strix looked after the retreating form of the badger until he went around a bend, the tip of his tail the last to be seen, before turning his head back towards the sky, which was the colour of charcoal. It did not take long for the sound of the rain to lull him into a relaxed sleep. And when Strix woke up some time later, he knew that he must have rested a few hours at least, for the night had fallen and the rain had stopped. Only the leaves on the trees continued to drip water.

Immensely refreshed after his nap – just as nature was refreshed after the cleansing rain – Strix spread his wings and catapulted himself into the sky. The freedom he felt when flying filled every pore of him and he soared around the clearing before he landed on the sturdy branch of an oak, which had survived the storm without any damage. As he landed on the wood, he felt the Earth's energy run through the tree and into him. Right then, he felt that everything around him was connected – to each other and to him – a feeling that was rarely this clear but that was always there in the background, giving him a sense of peace and belonging.

Savouring the moment, Strix smiled before flying high into the sky where the first stars were blinking into existence between the clouds.

Grounding and Mother Gaia

"I wish I could feel that way too," Nayeli said forlornly.

When Willow answered, the soft sound of the tree's leaves crinkling against each other highlighted the calmness of its voice. "Pull off your shoes, my dear child."

"What?" Nayeli asked, puzzled by the request.

"You are wearing shoes, aren't you?" the tree pressed.

Nayeli looked down at her blue trainers, which she had snatched before rushing out of her grandma's house. "Sure. But what does that have to do with anything?"

"Just trust me for a moment."

The kindness in the tree's voice convinced Nayeli to follow its lead. Bending forward, she took off her trainers and set them to one side. "And now?"

"And now you place your feet on the earth and imagine being a tree."

Snorting, Nayeli stared up. "Willow, I know you mean well and want to help me, but I'm a human. Why should I pretend to be anything else?"

"Just trust me," the tree repeated. "Place your feet on the grass and imagine roots growing out of them and into the earth beneath you. Imagine them growing ever longer until they reach through all the layers – through the rocks and granite and through the lava deep down. Imagine your roots extending into the inner core, which is filled with light. Now take some deep breaths. With every exhale you let go of dense energy, negative thoughts and feelings and everything else you don't need. See this as a dark cloud that flows out of you and through your roots into the core, where it's transformed into pure light. And with every intake of breath, you inhale this clean energy: it travels up your roots and fills your entire being. Do this until the light fills you from head to toe."

Letting the last of its words fade away, the tree fell silent.

Nayeli did as Willow had told her. She breathed deeply into her belly while visualising all her negative emotions flowing out of her, to be replaced by a lighter, calmer energy.

"I feel better," she said after a few minutes, surprised to realise that it was the truth. "There's still a lot of grief inside me, but all those sharp edges are gone."

It was also the first time Nayeli was able to let go of her worries about her current hallucinations. So what if all this wasn't real and she was losing her mind? At least, her visions were the nicest she could imagine and made her feel better after everything that had happened. Speaking to Willow was, in fact, the only thing that made her feel calm right now. And because of this, she would damn well continue to do so, no matter what it said about the health of her mind.

Looking up at the tree, Nayeli inclined her head in thanks. "That was exactly what I needed. How did you know this would work?"

"Because," the weeping willow said in its most soothing voice, "when we connect to Mother Gaia and accept her healing energy, she always helps us. Mother Earth – or nature, as she's often called – is able to calm, energise, heal and ground you. When you have lots of anxiety or are lost inside a stream of worries, grounding yourself can relieve you of those feelings and thoughts. And when you are feeling depressed or confused, grounding yourself can give you renewed strength or a new sense of clarity and direction. Grounding has many positive effects and using these techniques will not only improve your health but help in all other areas of your life, too."

"And how do you know that?"

"My dear Nayeli, if there's any topic I'm an expert on, it's this one. As a tree, my roots are constantly connected to Gaia."

Willow swept its branches in a broad gesture, encompassing the whole meadow. "But tell me, have you never noticed that being in nature revives or calms you?"

"I have. As a matter of fact, being in the woods near where I live or close to a source of water brings me a sense of peace and tranquillity. It quiets my anxiety. And when I jog in nature, it's a foolproof method to clear my head of any baggage. Sometimes I even get my best ideas this way. But why is that?"

The tree shook out its crown. "Now, you're mixing up what it means to be connected to Gaia versus being connected to source," Willow said gently. "But that's only natural since these are the two sides of the same coin."

"What are you talking about?" Nayeli asked, confused.

"When you jog inside nature, you have the benefit of Mother Gaia healing and grounding you, simply because you are surrounded by her. But then there's also your breath to consider. You automatically inhale more oxygen when doing sports. And your breath is your number-one connection to the source. Think of it as being a bridge between the two planes. You use it to receive energy or to download knowledge when you breathe in and to send out energy to manifest your reality when you breathe out."

Nayeli massaged her temples. "Now you're confusing me. Do I need to ground myself or meditate? They sound identical. And why use two different techniques to practise being present?"

Willow grunted. "You can use both meditation and grounding to bring you back to the present moment, that much is true. But, apart from this, they are unlike each other.

Meditating helps to reconnect you with your eternal self; it presents you with intuition, ideas and messages from your soul and the source. Meanwhile, grounding enables you to connect to the physical level of existence and your body; it enhances your health and well-being here."

"But isn't that contradictory?" Nayeli interjected. "If I use one technique to connect to the higher planes and the other to bring me back down, I'll stay stuck in the middle and move nowhere, won't I?"

"No," Willow said calmly. "Grounding and meditation techniques actually enhance each other because spirituality doesn't mean to transcend the physical, but to integrate the higher and lower levels. What will you do with all the intuitive knowledge you receive if you have no way to translate it into your life and don't know how to apply it practically? Grounding can help you with that. And, what is more, it can stop you from making a common mistake – to become addicted to spirituality."

"I beg your pardon?" Nayeli laughed disbelievingly, unsure if she had heard right. "Are you saying that something like a 'spiritual high' exists?"

To her amazement, the tree answered in the affirmative. "Indeed. I assume you know that you can become addicted to anything, not only drugs or alcohol or cigarettes?"

"Should I?"

"Why, yes. You could, for example, become addicted to watching TV or to eating junk food or to shopping or to cleaning your house every day. Or you could become addicted to feeling good. Which is where the spiritual high comes into play. Meditation can help you feel peaceful. And the more you experience the stress and fear lessening, the more often you want to feel it again."

"But why is that bad? I'm not hurting anyone if I want to feel peace or happiness. I'm not even hurting myself."

"And that's where you're wrong, my dear. You're hurting yourself in a roundabout way if you constantly deny the parts of you that don't feel good, if you can't sit with your negative emotions, if – instead of practising healing and integration – you're pushing parts away and if you're using meditation as an escape from reality, *then* you are harming yourself."

Nayeli tilted her head to the side. "If I understand you correctly, any technique – be it meditation or grounding – can be valuable when I use it to improve my life, but it can also be detrimental if I use it to ignore my problems?"

"Undoubtedly. It's best to face any negatively perceived emotions or situations and deal with them directly because rejecting, denying and suppressing your feelings isn't possible in the long run. When you resist something that you see as negative, you might be able to push the feeling down temporarily, but it will come back – and stronger than before. What you resist persists. Always! That's a universal law, and one that cannot be bypassed."

Nayeli was intrigued by this topic and wanted to hear more. "And how do I ground myself? Is there any other way apart from the one you showed me?"

"There are many options. Being in nature, as I already mentioned, is one. Especially when you walk barefoot on natural surfaces. The reason this works so well is that you continuously exchange energy with Gaia as you humans are a part of her – just like any other living being. Your bodies came from Mother Earth, they depend on nature for their survival, and they go back to being part of Gaia once you cross back over to the other side."

"I know we couldn't survive without the air we breathe or the food we grow, but aren't you overstating that a tad?"

"Overstating?" Willow laughed. "Oh, I've heard that humans have done their utmost to remove themselves from Mother Earth. You've unplugged yourself from her by living in concrete cities and towns where nature has been banished to the outskirts. You live in houses whose walls and roofs act as a barrier to the sky. You do not get up with the sun any longer or go to bed when it sets but use artificial lights instead. You don't live in tune with the phases of the moon anymore. And, beyond that, most of you have lost your initial knowledge of all the other creatures with whom you share this planet. So much so that – rather than living in harmony with wildlife – you are at war with other species, forcing them to give up their habitats and resources.

"But no matter how much you deny your connection to Mother Earth, nature is still an integral part of you and you cannot exist without it. Mother Gaia can continue without you, no problem. She doesn't need any species to survive – and certainly not one that's spreading like an uncontrolled virus. She was doing fine in the thousands of years when nothing else but plants and animals populated her and even before that. But what will you do when you've succeeded in poisoning the water and air? What will you do when all living beings die, one by one, because you've changed the environment to such extremes they can no longer survive? The wounds you deal out to Mother Earth will come back like a boomerang and hurt not only you but also all other living beings, including me and my brothers and sisters. Solely Mother Gaia herself will recover when we are all gone."

"I suppose so," Nayeli admitted haltingly. It wasn't the first time she had thought about how dependent humans were on a healthy planet. But it was the first time she'd felt personally responsible for the unhealthy conditions humans had created – for themselves and for all other species.

Nayeli cast her eyes downward. Willow was right. Throughout industrialisation, nature had taken a back seat in many human lives. And if she was honest with herself, the same was true for her. How often had she voluntarily confined herself to her own four walls? Unlike all her ancestors who had known what plants they could eat and where they needed to go based on the constellations of the stars without having to consult the internet first.

It was sad, now that she thought about it, because she loved nature and animals. But she had never taken the time to truly connect to them. Before her regret could turn into full-blown shame, though, the tree interrupted her reflections with a question.

"And speaking of you humans being disconnected from Mother Gaia – have you ever bothered to think about the food you eat and how it affects you?"

"My food?" Nayeli asked, perplexed. "I'm a vegetarian, if that's what you mean. But aside from this, no, I've no idea what you're getting at."

"I'm getting at the fact that everything in the universe has its own energy, including everything you consume. Potatoes, carrots and other vegetables that grow inside the earth, for example, are grounding foods, in contrast to fruits that grow on trees. Meanwhile, meat and fish have the lowest frequency of all foods. That's because animals have a higher awareness than plants, and when they die they pour out a lot more stress hormones. These hormones do not disappear when an animal dies; they stay stuck inside the meat, which you humans then eat."

"Oh," Nayeli said tonelessly. "Are you implying that people are correct in saying that we should all become vegetarians or vegans then?"

"No, my dear," the tree replied, its voice both firm and gentle. "If it's in alignment with your life, it's a great thing to become a vegetarian or vegan. But I'm not a fan of forcing people into a lifestyle that they don't want. It never works in the long run. People will always choose what they think is best for them, and the only way they'll stick to a path is if they pick it themselves. They must decide that the benefits will outweigh all the disadvantages that might come along with any decision. But everyone can play their part in saving the environment. Whether you do so by becoming a vegan, by reducing the amount of meat you eat or by eating local products is up to you. You could change something completely different as well – like taking public transport instead of driving a car or by reducing your plastic usage. The answer lies in people doing what they can and choosing any improvement that's in alignment with their path. That's what leads to lasting change.

"But to come back to the topic of food – you have to consider what types your body needs most – which can depend on your lifestyle, your job or hobbies, any food allergies you have and so on. For example, an advertising designer who spends a lot of their time in front of a monitor, creating, can have entirely different needs than a construction worker who's doing hard labour outside."

"So, what's the verdict? Is it a good thing to eat meat and fish now?"

As she waited for the tree to reply, Nayeli felt a gnawing sensation in the pit of her stomach. All this talk about food had made her hungry for the first time in a few days. Pulling the croissant out of her paper bag, Nayeli bit into it and rolled her eyes in bliss as the buttery taste hit her tongue.

"No," Willow answered, bringing her back to the topic at hand. "Obviously, the overpopulation of your species has negative effects. If you all carry on as always, leaving a giant ecological footprint behind, humankind will erase life itself. But saying this, eating meat isn't the core problem. Humans are omnivores by nature, and your ancestors have hunted just like predators in the animal world do. This means your species can survive on a plant-based diet alone or you can eat a bit of everything. The crux of the matter isn't that you eat meat. It is how and in what quantities it is produced. Your factory farming causes animals to suffer *and* harms the environment. Beyond that, the meat you eat is laced with hormones and antibiotics, which are bad for your health. And the fish that land on your plates contain micro-plastic particles because the oceans are littered with it. To say it plainly – you are slowly poisoning yourselves on top of this planet."

"But we are also poisoning ourselves by eating other things," Nayeli argued. "We are poisoning ourselves by eating plants that contain insecticides and pesticides. And we are poisoning ourselves by pouring chemical cleaners into our toilets, particles of which then end up in our drinking water."

"That's true, too," Willow agreed and sighed. "Look, there are no easy answers to be found here. Everyone needs to decide for themselves what to do. But whatever food you do decide to eat, you should all do one thing – be thankful for it. Realise that getting food from Mother Earth or her inhabitants is part of the natural circle of giving and receiving that's integral to living here. Step back into this cycle instead of exploiting your host – before it's too late. For no hunter can survive long without prey ..."

The willow tree let some time elapse and then raised its voice so that it rang loud and clear over the meadow. "I'm only asking you to not become so digital and pixelated that you can't see the wonders anymore that are part of your existence here. Did you know, for example, that trees communicate with and help each other? That there are estimated to be more than 400,000 species of plants, at least half of which are edible to humans, but that you only use about 200 of them? That leaf sheep exist, which are small sea slugs that can do photosynthesis? Are you aware that all your cells are regenerating every second of every day, no matter whether you're dancing or sleeping or laughing? Are you consciously aware that you are living on a planet consisting in large parts of water that circles a burning ball of fire – a fiery ball that lets the moon shine at night, which in turn makes your oceans move in tides? That this is a planet on which cocoa plants grow, providing you with chocolate? A planet on which animals sometimes foster orphaned young ones of another species? We live on a planet full of wonders, some of which are still undiscovered by humankind. And every blade of grass, every raindrop, every song a bird strikes up and every sunray that reaches the Earth is a miracle in itself."

Nayeli closed her eyes and felt after the feelings these words had triggered within her. "I know that you speak the truth. But being aware of all this is a far cry from being able to do anything to help save Mother Gaia. Cause, Willow, I can't even help myself. My own life resembles a construction site, and I could spend hours naming all the things that are wrong with it. Which leaves me lost where the heck I should start ..."

"This is a difficult question to answer, my dear child. Because every soul coming here is unique, with different needs and wants and dreams and goals, which are written down in their soul-plan. This means that no two people asking this question would receive the same answer."

"That makes things easier. Not!" Nayeli groused. "And what is a soul-plan?"

"Ah, to explain that, let me first tell you another story ..."

3. Hazel, the Wolf

"I understand you want to work with us." The alpha wolf spoke matter-of-factly, circling Strix and letting his eyes rake up and down his body.

Strix felt slightly uncomfortable underneath this thorough scrutiny, and he swallowed nervously when the wolf sat down in front of him and signalled to the other members of the pack that they could come closer.

"There's nothing we can say against it. We normally only cooperate with ravens, but a bird is a bird when it comes down to it."

"I don't just want to work with you, though," Strix croaked. "I want to join your pack as a real member!"

"Yes," the alpha wolf said, gazing back towards another wolf standing directly behind him. "Hazel mentioned something along those lines, but I thought she was joking. I think I'll have to disappoint you on that end, little Strix. You are not a wolf and you'll never be one. And why would you even want that? Isn't being a bird enough for you anymore? This whole idea is foolish at best."

"I ..." Strix began, not knowing how to say what was in his heart.

He had met Hazel in the woods yesterday, and she'd been so kind to him that, for the first time since setting out on his adventure, Strix had felt his desire to travel and see the world shrivel up. Instead, he had wondered what it would be like to stay here. To settle down in this new place, alongside the female wolf and her pack mates.

Looking at her now, Strix found some inner strength when Hazel winked at him encouragingly. Sitting up a bit taller, he made his voice sound steady and firm while facing the alpha wolf. "I want to begin a new life here. I've left my home in Massachusetts and I flew across the big ocean. I've done all this to experience something new, to broaden my horizon. But now I think what I've been searching for was something entirely different, and that it was a stroke of fate when I met Hazel. And that's why I'm asking you one more time to please assign me a spot in your pack. I know that I won't disappoint you. I can be a great asset to your group."

The alpha wolf remained quiet, his vision turned inward. When Strix had already given up all hope that he would be accepted as a member, the big wolf raised his head and fixed him with an intense stare. "Very well then, we'll try it out for a few days. But if by then I'm not convinced ..."

"... that won't happen," Strix interjected, bowing his head in silent thanks.

"We'll see," the alpha wolf said firmly. "But first, let me introduce you to the others. You've met my mate Hazel, who gave birth to our four little pups some weeks ago. One of her main jobs is to take care of them. And, besides that, she's one of the most successful hunters I ever met. She knows exactly which animal to single out and go after.

"The female wolf with the scar on her face is our best scout. When we go hunting, she runs in front of us, looking out for prey. Aside from this, she warns us of any danger she sees, calls for reinforcement or gives the all-clear signal.

"The wolf on my left with the white markings helps me to keep harmony in the pack. He's the calmest and most sensitive. It's easy for him to perceive when anyone is being treated unfairly. And he's the voice of reason on our hunting trips when we get a bit too excited. I can't count how often we would have dashed forward and lost our prey if it hadn't been for his great observation skills.

"And the wolf beside him with the scruffy coat helps Hazel to look after the young ones. Additionally, he watches our backs when we are moving, by running as the last in line and noticing any danger that could sneak up on us from behind.

"As for me ... I keep everything under control. I mediate when there are fights. I find a middle ground between the pack members who are highly energetic and want to press forward at all times and the ones who are more laid-back. And I have the final word when it comes to decisions – although, needless to say, I take everyone's wants and desires into account for that. Listening to everyone's opinion is one of the most important parts of my job. Because a pack is only as successful as each of its members, and I would be lost without my family. They mean the world to me!"

The alpha wolf stared down at Strix, who puffed out a breath. "That's a lot of new faces to remember."

"Don't worry about it," Hazel laughed, speaking up for the first time. "You'll soon feel as if you've always been part of our family, especially now that we have pups. They make time fly fast."

"And what are their tasks inside the pack?" Strix asked in curiosity.

Hazel looked down at her offspring. "At present, their job is to keep us on our paws, which they do with commitment and passion. Whenever you lay down to get some sleep, they will nibble on your ear or hunt your tail. Little nuisances!" But the last part was said with so much love and fondness in her voice that Strix knew she wouldn't swap her life for anything else.

Watching the pups tumble over each other in the grass between the wolves' paws, Strix had to admit, reluctantly, that he had already got a liking to them, too. But before they could win his heart over entirely, his attention was redirected to the alpha wolf once again, who rose to his full height. "But now, enough of the chatting. I'm starving and wouldn't mind filling my stomach. LET'S GO HUNTING!"

He shouted the last words and raised his snout heavenward, howling long and deep.

The rest of the pack joined in, their voices intermingling, sounding resonant and piercing.

Strix tried to copy them, but what came out of his beak was more of a throaty hoot than anything else. To his relief, none of the other pack members laughed at him, though.

Lowering their heads almost synchronously, they rose and took up position, the tenseness of their muscles proof of their excitement to get going – all except Hazel, who was propelling her pups back to the den at the other side of the clearing.

Wondering what he should do since no one had given him a task till now, Strix harrumphed loudly. This caught the pack's attention.

"Right," the wolf with the white markings said. "We need to figure out what job he'll get. I think he should stay here with Hazel and watch the youngsters."

"Nah," the scruffy wolf answered. "Let him scout the area for foes. He has wings and can see farther than any of us."

The suggestions went back and forth until the alpha wolf straightened up. The other wolves fell silent as he turned to face Strix. "Strix, what task would *you* like to have?"

Strix was about to give an answer when he realised, horrified, that he didn't have one. "Em ... I ... I ..." he stuttered. "I don't know." He had not thought further than having wanted to stay here.

Noticing his trouble, the big alpha wolf inclined his head. "It's okay not to be aware of the answer yet. We all have to discover who we are in life and where our soul-path leads us, and sometimes it takes time. Why don't you try out a different task each day and we'll see what suits you and what doesn't? For today, you could stay here with Hazel and watch over the pups. You think you can do that?"

"No problem!" Strix said confidently, puffing his chest out. Babysitting wasn't anything new to him, as he had previous experiences in looking after his little cousin back home. And that owlet had been a real troublemaker. One time his cousin had made them both crash into a riverbed after tumbling into him on his first flying lesson. And another time he had set a skunk on Strix, making him smell so atrociously that all his friends had fled for a whole week whenever he had come near them. At least whelps couldn't get stuck in the top of a tree. Which made Strix reasonably sure that this task would prove to be child's play.

But when the other pack members disappeared between the trees and the small wolves woke from their naps, he was quickly disabused of that notion. And only an hour later, Strix knew that tending to four curious and highly energetic pups was a full-time job. They were constantly roughhousing, chasing each other across the meadow or playing hide and seek behind the bushes. And every time one of them lay down to rest, another one would take over and think up even more mischief.

Strix felt bone-tired as he tried to keep his eyes everywhere at once. The trouble was, he wasn't much larger than the young wolves, and his plumage didn't offer the same protection from their needle-sharp teeth as thick wolf fur did. So, all he could do when he saw one of the pups sneaking away or playing too roughly was to call Hazel's attention to it.

"I don't know how you do this every day," he finally said, exhausted, after once again jumping to safety as two of the pups almost knocked him over in their play.

Laughing, Hazel swatted playfully at her smallest daughter as the pup climbed up on her shoulder and bit into her right ear. Howling in mock pain and wiggling her paws, as if under serious attack, her hazel eyes gleamed with pride and happiness.

"It's rewarding," she said when the pup tumbled down. "What could be more fulfilling than playing with the little ones and watching them grow?"

"If you think so," Strix muttered, not wanting to hurt his friend's feelings.

The affection he had felt earlier for the youngster had stolen away and made room for the certainty that he would never have kids of his own, since they were too much work. But before he could tell Hazel about this resolution, she was up and gone, mock growling at her oldest son, who had attacked her tail and chasing him to the other side of the meadow.

It was at this moment that Strix noticed the youngest pup – which was the biggest ruffian of the bunch – creeping up on one of his sisters. Only this time, it didn't appear to be harmless play. A low but dangerous-sounding growl emanated from him, and his teeth were bared threateningly.

Startled by this recent development and unsure what to do, Strix looked over towards Hazel, who was disappearing beneath the shadows of the trees. Realising that he was on his own for now, Strix gulped uncertainly.

Then the pup snarled and attacked his unsuspecting sister from behind.

Strix abandoned all thoughts in favour of taking action. Fluttering over, he dived between the two pups, who were rolling across the grass, doing their best to gain the upper paw by biting each other. His instincts told him to separate them as fast as possible. But then a paw hit him in the chest and he was thrown backward.

Strix landed hard on the hard-packed earth, his breath driven out of his lungs.

The next second, Hazel stood over him, a concerned expression on her face. "Strix! Are you all right? Are you hurt?"

Peering past Hazel's shoulder, Strix's eyes went wide in alarm when he saw that the two pups were still going at each other. And that the female one went straight for her brother's throat. "Why are you still standing here? Go and separate them or one of them will die!"

Following his gaze to her fighting children, Hazel tilted her head questioningly, staying totally relaxed in the face of the imminent danger.

"What are you talking about, Strix? They are measuring their strength against each other. That's important to find their role in the pack, you know? It won't take long now until one of the two will relent and the other will assert their dominance. We'd best let them finish this naturally and not intervene."

Strix was taken aback by Hazel's words. The skirmish looked way too rough to be harmless. But the fact that the female wolf was this calm eventually convinced him that it must indeed be as she said. And then, exactly as Hazel had predicted, the female pup gained the upper hand in the fight and pressed her brother to the ground momentarily before releasing him. To Strix's surprise, the pup who had lost accepted this calmly and after they had both shaken themselves, they chased their tails, as if nothing out of the ordinary had happened.

"I can't believe it," Strix said, stunned. "You wolves do have some strange customs. And there isn't even a drop of blood on them."

The thought of injuries reminded Strix of his own impact with the earth. He took the time to scan his body for any pains and aches and noticed that, luckily, no lasting damage had been caused.

"Are you really all right?" Hazel inquired as she saw him test his wings.

"Yeah, yeah, I am." Strix was embarrassed at having miscalculated the scene this thoroughly.

Apparently Hazel wasn't buying his answer, though. She kept staring at him with an inquisitive gaze. "I don't think you're fine." She poked him tenderly with her wet nose. "Come on, tell me what's wrong. We are friends, aren't we?"

Sighing, Strix scratched at the ground in embarrassment.

"The way I see it, it's my first day in your pack and I'm already misjudging situations. If your mate knew about this, he'd certainly rethink his offer and toss me out." Strix let his eyes dart up to Hazel. "On second thought, maybe that would be a good idea. Maybe I *should* leave. I don't wanna be a burden to you all."

"Now, now," Hazel said affectionately. "Don't be so hard on yourself. As you mentioned, it's only your first day, and no one is perfect. We all make mistakes, especially when we set out on a new leg on our journey. Do you have any idea how many I made, especially when I was young and inexperienced? Besides, your lifestyle, habits, customs and practices differ from ours. It takes time to tune in to our way of doing things."

"You don't think I'm a lost cause?" Strix asked hopefully.

Her warm hazel eyes landed on him. "Would I have invited you to join us if I did? Come, let's forget this incident. I'm sure you'll have mastered everything in record time. And in a few days, you'll laugh when you look back at your beginner's mistakes."

Strix forced a small smile onto his face. It didn't quite reach his eyes but seemed to please Hazel nonetheless. "If you say so."

"I do!" Hazel's answer was confident and strong, which made Strix feel a bit better. But some doubts remained. Was he doing the right thing? Were his talents useful enough for him to become an integral part of the pack? Or was there something wrong with him?

***

Strix's second day as an honorary wolf started roughly and painfully when one of his tail feathers was pulled so violently that it almost ripped out. Spinning around, he saw one of the wolf pups jump forward and sink his sharp baby teeth into his plumage a second time.

"Ow," he called out in pain and flew into the air as soon as the teeth released their hold. "Watch it. That hurts!"

"My family always let me bite their tails ... they say play-fighting is a good way to hone my hunting skills and instincts," the young smarty-pants answered. "And they say you're part of the family now."

"Do they?" Strix asked, peeved. "And have you considered that their fur is thicker than my feathers? No? Then let me tell you something now. Stop ripping them out. I do need them to fly."

As a short-eared owl, Strix was used to sleeping on the ground amid grasses as opposed to in a tree, like some of his distant relatives did. But he wondered if he should keep up this habit, now that he was living with these little beasts, who evidently didn't know that respecting their elders was crucial. And the brawler who had tried to massacre him in his sleep was the worst of the bunch, continuously goading the other pups to carry out all kinds of shenanigans.

But before he could reprimand the pup further, Hazel was picking up her struggling son by the scruff of his neck and mumbled an apology in Strix's direction.

Landing on the ground, Strix inspected the damage to his tail feathers and was happy to note that they were all still attached. He hoped that him getting off lightly was a good omen. Especially since this day's task was even more challenging. He'd been asked to scout out big prey, maybe a deer or stag.

Taking to the air again, Strix flew over to the other members of the pack, who were waiting beside some beech trees that circled the meadow. Everyone, that is, apart from Hazel and the scruffy wolf, who were herding the four pups together. Then Hazel said her goodbyes to them and trotted over.

The big alpha wolf rose when she approached. His gleaming eyes held reproach that she'd let the entire pack wait for her. But Hazel wasn't fazed by that and grinned at him innocently. "What's the rush?"

Growling half-heartedly in answer, the alpha wolf muttered something under his breath, which sounded like 'Females, always taking forever to get ready' that raised a laugh from the other male wolf with the white markings.

Strix sniggered himself and had to evade Hazel's paw swipe.

"Hey," he called out, mock offended. "Careful with those. Tiny owl in close range – you could hit me."

"That was intended," Hazel said before she joined in with the pack's laughter. Once they had calmed down, the alpha wolf gave the signal to get moving, and the wolves left the clearing in their accustomed order, the alpha male in the middle and Hazel in front of him.

Strix rose higher and higher in the air until the tops of the firs and birches were beneath him and he had a clear, unobstructed view over the forest that stretched towards the horizon. He watched the wolves weave in and out beneath the trees that stood tall and proud. Then, when he had memorised the wolves' direction and speed and was sure that he would easily find them again, he approached the task given to him by flying ahead and scouting the area.

Strix normally hunted over meadows and plains and wasn't used to this many trees blocking his view, which presented quite a challenge. But his name wouldn't have been Strix if he hadn't accepted it wholeheartedly. He was intent on proving his worth to the group. And he *had* been one of the most successful hunters back home – a fact he had always prided himself on.

To show that he had not lost his edge, Strix got himself into the right mindset, concentrating fully on his senses to scan the woods below him and chasing out all other thoughts. While his sharp eyes noticed any irregularity in colour and texture, his ears picked up the sounds of the forest, from the faint drumming of a woodpecker to the almost inaudible steps of the wolves, who trotted with softly padded paws over the solid earth.

The sound of a dry twig snapping redirected Strix's attention. It had come from not too far in front of him. Automatically, he gauged the distance and glided lower, plunging into the woodland. Strix manoeuvred between the trees, which stood wider apart in this area, giving him room to speed up.

When he reached the spot where the sound had originated from, he was quick to spot its source. Five moving specks of brown, walking between the conifers. Deer!

He turned his head back to listen for the wolf pack, then ascertained their position regarding his own and the prey he had found. They were behind him, and the path they were taking was leading them away from the deer, as the wind wasn't in their favour and they wouldn't be able to pick up their scent.

Feeling excited that he could at long last establish his usefulness to the pack, Strix assessed his options. If he flew back to the others and told them about his discovery, the deer could get a safe distance away. And if he let them out of his sight, there was no telling whether he could find them again. Not wanting to look stupid by losing the prey, which was practically already theirs, he rejected that idea. This left him with one option. Hooting shrilly to get the attention of the pack, he called out loudly, "Come here, hurry!"

What he hadn't considered, though, was that the deer would hear his shout as well.

Jerking their heads up, they stared at him. Then, as if they had silently agreed with each other, they reared back as one and took flight in the opposite direction, their hooves flying over the shrubs and plants standing in their way.

Cursing loudly, Strix sped up to follow the fleeing deer and made a snap decision to attack the smallest one himself. Maybe, he thought, he could detain it until the pack could bring it down.

Diving and extending his sharp claws to grasp the deer by its fur, he missed his target by a hair's breadth as it jumped forward, panicked. Moments later, and before Strix could attempt a second attack, the deer reached the edge of the forest and the open plains behind it. Startling a few hares, who had been sitting in the shadows, they broke out between the last trees and leapt away through a wheat field, accompanied by a clamour of birds.

Just then, the wolf pack reached the edge of the woods. But to Strix's surprise, they made no move to chase the fleeing prey. Instead, the alpha wolf sat down, his back ramrod-straight while his eyes glittered angrily.

"What are you doing?" Strix called out, confused. He let his eyes dart from one wolf to the next and then towards the deer, which were running away as fast as their legs would carry them. "Why aren't you chasing them?"

"Strix," the alpha wolf scolded, somehow managing to make the syllable sound foreboding despite being totally calm. "Come here and sit down."

Following the order, Strix gulped with trepidation, feeling the wolf's gleaming eyes bore into him.

"Strix, not only did you chase away good prey, but you destroyed our chances of finding a decent meal in this part of the woods with all the ruckus you created. We told you that your task was to scout out the area and then to communicate with us about anything you found. Not to scare it away. What do you have to say?"

Feeling uncomfortable and not enjoying being reprimanded, Strix pulled his shoulders up. "I'm sorry," he said ruefully. "I guess, I didn't think things through. I didn't intend to make them bolt." Not wanting to take all the blame for himself, he looked up defiantly. "But it isn't *all* my fault. You didn't follow them ..."

The alpha wolf stared sternly at him until Strix averted his eyes.

"Going after any large prey can be dangerous, as we could be injured by a well-placed kick or sharp antlers. That's why we need to assess carefully which individual to go after. Not to mention that we need to factor in the terrain and other variables, which can make the difference between a full and an empty stomach. We could, of course, trail this group of deers for some time but that would lead us a good bit away. And since we have pups right now that's not an option." His tone grew softer. "I know you meant no harm, Strix. And for that reason, I won't punish you any further. But please remember this lesson: if the prey is alerted too soon, it isn't worth pursuing it."

"I'm so sorry," Strix apologised, chagrined. He realised that the worst thing wasn't the wolf's reprimand but his own guilt at having messed up such a simple task. Thinking about how he could make amends for his mistake, Strix had an idea. He perked up as he addressed the group of wolves.

"I know that it isn't much of a substitute for a big deer that would have been enough to feed you all, but I'm a skilful mouse-hunter. And I've noticed a lot of signs of them all around here. How about I catch you a few?"

"That won't be necessary," the alpha wolf answered, his stern voice replaced by a kinder one. "We can hunt our own mice to tide us over." He fixed each of the other wolves with a look. "Let's head back, pack. There's nothing for us here anymore."

They had run for some minutes when the female wolf with the scar, who was the first in line, halted the group abruptly. Her neck fur was standing straight up as a warning sign.

Immediately all the other wolves were at attention, their muscles tense, ready to flee or fight for their lives.

"What is it?" the alpha wolf called to his pack mate, who had slunk over to some thick shrubs and was peering through a small hole while sniffing the air.

"I'm not sure," she said. "There's nothing to see, but I'm sure there's danger near."

Strix was just about to ask the alpha wolf for permission to fly ahead and scout out the scene from above when the female wolf suddenly reared back.

"Humans – it's humans!" she shouted, panic layering her voice.

The alpha wolf lost no time to take action, shouting out instructions to his pack mates. "Run back and hide near the clearing until the danger has passed. Be fast, but stay calm and silent."

No one needed to be told twice. All the wolves instantaneously obeyed his orders.

Strix flew high into the sky and was about to follow suit when he gazed back and saw two humans emerge from between the trees, carrying long metallic sticks that glinted in the sunlight. The sight froze Strix heart as he had seen the likes of them once before in his life. He had been a young owlet back then, but the sight of his friends and neighbours falling from the sky, mid-flight, had ingrained itself into his brain forever. The last time he had seen those magic tubes, they had been accompanied by loud bangs. This time, they were eerily silent, but Strix still recognised the deadly danger they promised.

Without losing any time, he called out a warning to his friends. "Look out! They have something that can kill you from a distance!"

The warning was just in time. Because, at that moment, one of the humans came into range of the fleeing wolf pack. Surprise written on his face, he hastily composed himself and pulled the long tube forward, aiming it at Hazel. And then, similar to Strix's memory, a loud bang came from it while clumps of earth sprayed up, raining down on the female wolf.

Hazel made a panic-stricken U-turn and raced off in a zigzag line between the trees. As if that had been a signal to the others, order gave way to panic, and when there were two more bangs, the wolves scattered and ran off into different directions between the trees.

It wasn't only the wolves who were panicking, however. Rabbits and squirrels ran blindly in every direction while the air was abuzz with birds fleeing the scene.

Strix flew as high as possible to avoid any collisions with the other birds and to get out of range of the deadly bangs. Aside from that, he hoped that by flying this high up, he could keep track of the pack. But he soon had to accept that it was a lost cause.

Almost immediately, they had disappeared into the thick undergrowth, leaving Strix behind. His heart pounding viciously inside his chest, he thought it would break free of his ribcage, all the more so as a small blue bird not far from him screeched brokenly and plummeted to the earth, one of its wings hanging limply while the other flapped desperately in an attempt to stay airborne.

The scene brought back all the horrors from his youth and, from one minute to the next, all sense and reason fled from Strix's mind. He sped away, not knowing or caring where he ended up. There was just one thought left in his mind: to get out of this nightmare alive.

It was only when he had found a densely planted part of the woods, where the humans would have trouble following, that Strix slowed down. Strix landed on the branch of a sturdy tree and concentrated on his breathing, feeling the fear and stress course through his body in dizzying waves.

For a couple of minutes, his panic demanded his sole attention, but then the feelings ebbed away and the anxiety was replaced by worry for his pack mates' safety – especially Hazel's since she had been far too close to that first bang.

Taking his time to look around at this foreign part of the woods, Strix tried to get his bearings. He knew that he had flown south and that he could therefore easily locate the clearing where they had left the pups. Thinking of them gave rise to a whole new onset of panic. Strix hoped with all his heart that the humans hadn't stumbled upon them, as they were way too young to run away in time.

Shaking himself to get rid of these dark thoughts, which wouldn't help anybody, Strix concentrated instead on what his next steps should be. But before he could decide on any appropriate action, he noticed movement between the trees beneath him.

Instantly, Strix worried that the humans had found him. But then a familiar figure emerged, and a breath of relief rushed out of him.

"Hazel!" Strix called out and soared down to her. "I'm so glad to see you. Is everything all right?"

"No," Hazel answered, her eyes huge and fearful. "My pups – I need to get back to them. What if the humans found them?"

Withholding the fact that the same thought had crossed his own mind, Strix was determined to be the rock Hazel could lean on for help. And having her calm down was taking precedence over anything else at this moment. "Shh, I'm sure everything will be fine. Let's go back and you'll see for yourself. Agreed?"

"I can't," Hazel answered, motioning to her front paw, which she held off the ground.

Strix didn't see any blood or broken bones, but it was obvious that it pained Hazel to put any weight on it.

"Did one of the humans get you?" he asked, concerned.

"No," Hazel answered. "But the ground exploded right in front of me when I fled, and it spooked me so much that I jumped into a thorny bush. At first, I didn't notice that one of the thorns had pierced the skin between my pads because I was in a panic, and I just kept on running. But that drove it in deeper. And now, I can't grasp it with my teeth to pull it out."

Craning his neck and inspecting her left paw more closely, Strix saw that she was indeed speaking the truth. There was a large spike embedded in it. "Shall I try to get it out?" he asked tentatively.

"Please," Hazel answered and held out her leg. Strix opened his beak and grasped the short end of the thorn with it.

A soft hiss escaped his friend as he pulled it out and spat it onto the ground.

Hazel licked her paw where a bead of blood had welled up, and used her saliva to disinfect the wound. "Thanks," she said and limped forward eagerly. "Let's get back as fast as possible. I need to see with my own two eyes that the others are all safe."

No further words were needed.

Strix flew ahead to warn her of any danger from the humans and to look out for the other members of the pack, while Hazel trotted slowly after him, hindered by the fresh wound on her paw.

By the time they were near the clearing, Strix had neither seen nor heard any signs that indicated the presence of the humans nor of the other wolves. But when he flew over the last treetops, he saw, to his intense relief, that the rest of the pack was already assembled, standing near the burrow and watching the woods vigilantly.

Since everyone appeared to be unharmed, Strix circled back to

Hazel, who was lagging behind.

Hearing the good news and being eager to be back with her family, she increased her pace. And no longer than two minutes later, she hobbled into the clearing.

Immediately, Hazel was bombarded by a bundle of wolves, big and small, who all tried to get to her and lick her face to reassure themselves that the last member of their pack had come home. Even the alpha wolf, who was normally guarded when it came to showing emotions, ran up to her and buried his muzzle in her fur, sniffing her unique smell.

"Thank heavens you are back in one piece," he said and let his eyes dart up to Strix. "Both of you."

Smiling at his words, Strix felt a warm feeling spread through him, especially when the sentiment was mirrored by the others. Once everyone had taken their turn to greet them and examined Hazel's paw, licking the wound for good measure, the alpha wolf gathered the pack around him and looked seriously at each member before letting his eyes sweep over to the next one in line.

"This situation could have ended badly. We can count ourselves lucky that the universe was well disposed towards us today and that we haven't suffered more than one small wound. This was because of our scout who first noticed the humans, and Strix who warned us in time of the danger lurking in the objects they carry." Turning around, the alpha wolf inclined his head. "If you hadn't called out that warning who knows what else might have happened. Strix, my friend, you kept a cool head and assessed the situation correctly – which is what makes up a true leader."

Strix shrugged off the compliment, feeling awkward at being in the spotlight. "I wasn't thinking about any of it, I was merely reacting. It's what I do best, being the lone hunter I normally am. I don't have a pack to count on, so having quick reflexes and acting on them in a timely manner has kept me alive in the past more times than I can remember. Aside from this, I have wings and had a clear overview from above."

"Exactly," Hazel cut in. "And that's what I – what we all ignored – these last two days. You are an owl, not a wolf. And you should never aim to be anything else. I'm sorry that I didn't see that earlier, and that we only looked at our skills and capabilities and how you should adapt to fit in. Neither of us took the time to recognise that you have just as many good qualities yourself. Wolves and owls are obviously unlike each other: we have different ways of living, but one is not better or worse than the other. Strix, you are who you are, and you are perfect like that. Don't deny your nature to fit into a group that's not yours."

"Are you casting me out?" Strix asked, shocked. "But I can still fit in with you if I try a bit harder ..."

"No!" Hazel responded. "You misunderstood me. I'm not abandoning you as a friend. Strix, I would count myself lucky if you decided to stay here and live with us. But not as an honorary wolf or some such nonsense. You would not be happy in the long run if you betrayed your true nature."

"Eloquently spoken," the alpha wolf agreed. "And to make this official ... You are always welcome here. As a dear owl friend! "

Upon hearing these words, Strix first felt a tinge of bitterness that his momentary dream of being a real member of the wolf family was over. But underneath this emotion was a warm and fuzzy feeling that he had made such great friends in the last few days. Friends who would continue to accompany him while he found his way back to his own soul-path, and whom he would support while they travelled theirs.

Soul-Plans and Individuality

"So, what's this soul-plan you mentioned, Willow?" Nayeli asked, taking a swig from the water bottle sitting beside her.

"The soul-plan is the plan your soul makes prior to you incarnating here. It establishes what you want to learn and how you want to learn it. It includes the sex you choose, what culture and family you will be born into and what traumas you are likely to experience in childhood – based on the life situation and characters of your caregivers that are build by the past traumas they lived through and the beliefs they carry. It includes when and how you'll meet other important soulmates in your life and what lessons they'll teach you. It includes the profession you want to pursue. And it also includes when and how you are gonna exit this life. In short, your soul determines everything that will be important to you in this incarnation."

"Ha, I knew it. There *is* something akin to fate."

"Indeed. Your soul does plan out plenty of things in advance, and going along with that blueprint of your life is not the worst decision you could make."

"But why? Why should I follow a plan that was made before I was even incarnated? What if I don't like it now that I'm faced with the reality? What if life isn't how I imagined it would be?"

"Look at it the other way around, though," the tree said, evading a direct answer to Nayeli's question. "What if you said you wanted to adhere to the plans you'd made? Then you'd have everything you needed to live a happy, successful life. Your soul has endowed you with all the attributes, abilities and talents you need for that specific soul-path, making you perfectly suited for it.

"But let's look at a specific example. Let's say that your soul wanted to be a member of an Irish pop group. In this case, it would not only have you living in, or moving to, Ireland but would have also endowed you with a great voice and an ear for music. Wouldn't it be sad not to use these talents? To be a footballer or an accountant instead? Sure, you can be successful in another profession. You can study any subject you want. But it might be more of a struggle, because your soul-given ability to connect to a crowd on an emotional level, your ability to write deep and meaningful lyrics and the unique timbre of your voice won't help you if you choose a path that does not lead to you being a singer. If you decide to be an accountant, you'll actually be at a disadvantage compared to anyone who wrote the profession of an accountant into their soul-plan as they have what it takes to excel in it."

"Ah, is that why happiness and success keep evading me? Because I'm not on the right path and lost access to my soul-plan? That would explain why I feel like I'm walking into a hurricane that's pushing me backwards a step, each time I take two forward."

"If you feel that way, my dear, then yes, you have most likely lost your path. When it takes a lot of energy for you to get somewhere, it's a direct message from your soul that you're not following the course it intended for you. But the good news is that you don't need to do anything else but turn around and go in the other direction, letting the wind push you forward."

As if to underline the tree's words, a refreshing wind blew by them at this moment, cooling the sweat on Nayeli's skin.

"And what if I don't want to move in that direction, either?"

Willow laughed fondly. "But that's the issue. The wind always pushes you towards what brings you happiness. The fulfilment of your soul desires comes easily – as soon as you stop resisting them."

Nayeli huffed. "But this would imply that the choices our souls made restrict us regarding what we can and can't do in this life. And that's not fair!"

"It's correct that all attributes have restrictions. If you chose to be small in stature, it's pretty unlikely that you'll become a top basketball player. But any attributes also have values. And your soul chose your deepest desires first, followed by the traits and features you will need to turn these dreams into your reality."

Nayeli turned her head back to look at the tree. "And what if I don't have any positive abilities? What if I'm utterly untalented and can't find anything I'm good at? What if my soul chose to find out what it feels like to be a failure?"

"Oh no, my dear, oh no!" Willow cried. "There's no such thing as having no talents. If someone believes that, it's only because those parts are stuck within their subconscious. Sometimes these inner truths can be buried so deep that it takes some effort to unearth them. But one thing is for sure. Everyone has got several desires along with all abilities they need to fulfil them. You humans just need to rediscover what is that you have forgotten."

Nayeli mulled this over. "So, how did we lose our way in the first place? What does our ego do to make us go astray? Why are so many humans lost? How can we get back on our path? And can we even do that, or is it too late once we've moved away from it?"

"Slowly, slowly!" Willow fended off her questions, laughing. "One thing at a time. Let me start by answering your last question first. You can definitely align your life with your soul-plan again. It's never too late to do that. And as for how you became lost ... most people stray from their soul-path by losing their passions when they're very young. When you are a child, you are socialised by your parents and primary caregivers. Additionally, you are indirectly influenced by the society you live in and the values you are raised with. All these conditions not only shape you; they also drown out your inner voice and its inherent knowledge of who you are and what you had intended to do here. Let's take the example of the singer once more. This child might have been raised in a family where logic and analytical thinking are rated highest. A family in which all members work in scientific fields. The parents might have disapproved of the child's wish to become a singer based on the belief they'd never make it. Maybe the parents dismissed it as a stupid dream. In this family, the child would likely have adopted the belief that singing was not a suitable profession. They might have even stopped singing altogether at one point."

"And will someone who is meant to be a singer stay unhappy unless they sing professionally?" Nayeli asked.

"Not necessarily," the tree replied. "This person could fulfil their desire to sing by doing it as a hobby while working in a different profession. There are lots of ways to work with the plan, your soul put into motion. You don't have to follow it to the letter to make it work. But unless this person uses their soul-given musical talent in one way or another, they will remain unhappy to some extent, yes. Desires and needs never leave you until they are fulfilled. They're a constant reminder of what you hoped for but don't yet have."

Nayeli let her right hand sweep over the blades of grass beside her as she thought of the one thing she had ever been passionate about doing. From the time she had learned to read until her late teenage years, she had loved the art of writing. Even now, she felt a sense of accomplishment when she remembered the drafts in her drawers she had completed. But what good would it do to take that hobby up again? Now that she had a full-time job, she had few spare hours and not enough energy to pour it into a creative outlet that would yield no results. No, the answer to finding more happiness must lie somewhere else. Maybe the solution was to find another profession than her current one – a profession that was more meaningful than her office job and, at the same time, more likely to bring an income than writing. Nayeli looked back at Willow, knowing what she needed to ask and determined to get the answers.

"Then what should the many people do who are unhappy with their lives because they chose a job to earn money and not because they care about it?"

"You sound as if you are talking from personal experience, my dear?"

Nayeli snorted, in equal shares amused and peeved. "You could be on to something there."

"I take it, having an office job is not to your liking then?"

"God, no!" Nayeli cried. "I hate it – I despise it. I wish I didn't have to go there each morning. It doesn't fulfil me. But I need the money, so I ignore all those feelings. And besides, I don't have the first clue what I'd want to do instead. I just know that I feel fed up to be stuck in this company for eight hours each day and slave away for someone else."

"That's a common feeling if you've left your soul-path," Willow affirmed. "Fatigue and resentment. That's when most people start to search for some additional meaning in their lives."

As the tree paused, the sound of the water gurgling over the pebbles in the stream came to the fore. But when Willow continued to speak, the brook reverted to a faint background noise again.

"You humans might not initially notice when you stray from your soul-path, but you definitely notice it once you are feeling unfulfilled."

"Right, but how does that apply to my life?" Nayeli cut in. "That I need to leave my job and apply for medical school instead?"

"That depends," the tree said, its branches swinging softly in the wind. "Do you want to become a doctor or nurse?"

"No," Nayeli said firmly. "Not any more than I want to stay in my current job. But you said to find something that makes me feel fulfilled. And helping people is something worthwhile, isn't it?"

"Don't forget about the part to choose something that makes you happy," Willow replied. "It's equally important."

"And how am I supposed to find something that brings me both joy and fulfilment?"

"To find the answer where your passions lie, look back at your childhood. What were your dreams when you were growing up? As a child, your ego wasn't fully grown yet and you were thus much more connected to your inner knowledge of your soul-plan than you are today."

"Are you alluding to the fact that every soul who incarnates as a human has planned to be a firefighter, a vet, a police officer, a rock star or a princess?" Nayeli joked. "Cause those must rank as some of the kid's top wishes."

"You can't take it all literal." Willow chuckled. "When a child dreams of being a teacher, it doesn't necessarily translate to them having written the profession of a teacher into their soul-plan. More interesting than the profession itself is the reason behind their desire. One child might want to be a teacher because they're interested in a certain subject and want to become an expert in it. Another child might enjoy school so much that they don't want to leave it. And a third child might want the long summer holidays every year. Don't only look for obvious reasons. Look at all the layers beneath. Ask yourself why you wanted something, and go as deep as possible until you reach the core desire."

"All right, let's say I do that and find out that my core desire is to sit on the sofa my whole life, watching TV – what then?"

Willow raised its branches, imitating a shrug. "If that were truly your soul's passion, then that's exactly what you should do. Because whenever you feel fulfilled and happy, you feed those feelings into the collective consciousness, which is the combined consciousness of all souls and influences everyone."

Nayeli interrupted the tree. "You mean the more people who follow their soul-plan and the happier they are because of it, the higher the frequency of the collective consciousness, and the stronger the pull for everyone else to fulfil their dreams as well?"

"Precisely. It's a snowball effect. But saying this, I bet that relaxing all day, every day, is not anyone's core desire."

"Ha!" Nayeli exclaimed. "You'd lose that bet. Plenty of people would love nothing more than to play computer games or binge-watch TV series weeks upon weeks. To wind down without any responsibilities."

"I do know that this is the case. But it's due to people having lost their soul-path, and not because it's a core desire of anyone. When you're struggling with a reality that's not in alignment with your soul-given abilities, you need a great deal of strength and energy to deal with everyday life. It's natural, in that case, that you want to do nothing else but sit somewhere and rest. But once your basic need for relaxation has been met, boredom will set in and you'll start to notice you have other needs: a need to create something, for example, or to go on an adventure and experience something thrilling and new."

"Hmm," Nayeli made, reckoning that the tree was on to something. "But what if I can't remember any desires I had as a child? You can't expect everyone to know what they dreamed about?"

"No," Willow responded. "Sometimes the desires were buried too early or never had the chance to see the light of day. In general, a person who doesn't have a clue what wishes they have, left their soul-path at such a young age that they have no memory of it – nor of the traumas that discouraged them from following the plan their soul made. In that case, do what children do to find out what they're good at. Try out all kinds of different things and see what makes you happy."

The tree ended on a challenging note.

Knowing what was coming before Willow had given voice to its next question, Nayeli averted her eyes from the trunk, intently studying a yellow butterfly that had landed on a flower beside her. But Willow was not deterred by her sudden silence.

"Anyway, my dear, I get the distinct impression that you remember something. What did you want to be when you were little?"

Nayeli hesitated. Would Willow laugh at her desire?

But the tree immediately quietened her fears, as if it had heard her doubts. "You can tell me anything. I won't judge you."

For a minute, Nayeli's emotions were still caught between her fear of being vulnerable and her hope that the tree would support her dreams. But, in the end, her trust in Willow's sincerity won. "I've wanted to be a writer for as long as I can remember. I recently found a stack of stories I wrote when I was a teenager, which I had totally forgotten about. And it made me realise how fun it was. Developing characters, creating plots, thinking up settings and bringing it all together to take readers into another world. I love the process and the creativity of it. And if others would read and enjoy my stories, or if I could help people in some way through my writing, that would be beyond amazing!"

Noticing how her voice had taken on a dreamy tone, laced with a hint of passion, Nayeli quickly came back down to earth. "But that would never work. Few people make a living from writing books, and I'd need a whole lot of luck to be one of them. To be blunt, I'm not sure if I'm good enough to do it professionally."

"Luck has nothing to do with it," Willow answered. "Putting in the hours to practise and learn your craft is what's important. And that you are this passionate about it, is a sign that you're meant to do this. Whether you will be successful is another question altogether. Maybe your soul intended for you to write as a hobby and to have another profession to earn money. But write you should. See where it leads you."

"Really?" Nayeli asked, her uncertainty making her voice waver.

"My dear Nayeli," Willow chided, "the whole point of your dreams and desires is to make them your reality! Because by following them, you are not merely making yourself happier, but you are also helping all others. Look at it like this ... Everyone's come here because they have to give something to this world. And by fulfilling your desires, you're carrying out the purpose you accepted as your role in the grand scheme of things. A task that no one can accomplish quite like you."

"What are you saying?"

"I'm saying that everyone could write a book. It's nothing more than arranging words into sentences. Some people have more talent at it than others, but everyone has the potential to do it. Only that no one else can create the books that *you* are meant to write. Nobody else has had the same experiences as you, no one else feels the exact same emotions or thinks the same thoughts as you, and no one else sees everything the same way as you do. Even if you and someone else wrote a book on the same exact topic, your stories would be entirely different. On top of that, no one else but you could teach readers in the same way. There might be someone out there who's – without realising it – waiting for the book that you haven't written yet. And although there are countless other ones with a similar theme, it will be your unique way of writing that touches and inspires them."

"I guess ... if you put it like that ... I do feel that I should start writing again," Nayeli admitted, a small smile playing around the edges of her mouth. But a second later, it was gone. "It's just ..."

"It's just what?" Willow asked, laughing good-naturedly. "Do I need to put in more effort to convince you?"

Nayeli crossed her arms in front of her chest. "It's just that ... why do I even want to write? Some people's desires will help the world. Like the desire to clean the oceans of plastic or to discover a cure for cancer or something along those lines. But wanting to be an author – that has no real use, does it? I mean, the arts and sports aren't needed to keep society going."

"No? Then think about your life and what it would look like if there were no movies or music or books or games. Imagine a world like that! A world without beauty and joy. A world that's solely focused on productivity and things that are *necessary*. A world where emotions are not considered important. Don't you agree that a world like this would be terrible to live in?"

"I do," Nayeli said instantly. "But still ... although writing fulfils me on an individual level and brings joy to people, there are other professions that are more valuable, no? I mean, a surgeon is more important than a pilot because we humans will survive just fine without flying anywhere."

"Tell that to someone who's completely healthy until old age and never needs a surgeon but who spends their life building wells in countries where people die because they don't have enough clean water," Willow tossed in before listing a couple more examples. "A bus or tram driver won't be important for those who own a car, but for the people who need to commute each day without having a driving license, they are essential. And a baker is needed by many as they sell a staple food, except for those who always bake their own bread and pastries.

"Desires, my dear, can't be divided into categories of 'better' and 'worse' or 'acceptable' and 'unacceptable'. Because every wish you or anyone else has is valuable and useful, no matter what it is. It's simply a matter of matching the people who need something with the people who have to give that product or service. That's the beautiful thing about individuality. Every soul has chosen a different path and has something unique to give to this world. Which is necessary ...

"Just imagine that every person would have the exact same life that you have. With the same beliefs, ideas and experiences. The same wants and needs as you. And the same desires. Ultimately, they would *be* you – there's no other way. Besides, if everyone was good at the same thing, it would create chaos. Think of it in terms of the wolf pack. If every wolf wanted to be the alpha wolf, what would happen? They'd constantly fight, while no one would deal with the other tasks that are equally important for their survival. And this can be transferred into human society as well. What if everyone wanted to be a police officer but no one a farmer? You'd all die of hunger. Diversity is what makes you thrive and what can fulfil all your needs."

"Isn't that unfair, though?" Nayeli interjected. "That some of us plan an interesting life prior to coming here, while others have to choose a dull job like, say, a mathematician or a cleaner, so that all occupations are covered?"

"And who decides what is interesting?" the tree asked gravely. "Everyone has an opinion about those things, but they're all subjective. Don't make the mistake of projecting your feelings onto another person. For one person, being an author would be perfect, but for someone else it would be terrible, and they'd think it was more boring than juggling numbers or washing dishes. In the end, all jobs and talents are not only useful but interesting - for the right people."

"Even the profession of a cleaner?" Nayeli pressed. Having always hated doing housework herself with a passion, she couldn't get behind the possibility that someone else might enjoy it.

"I take it you haven't heard the story of the famous street sweeper then? It's a real-life story about a man who refused offers to model and act in movies and make loads of money. When he was asked why he'd turned down those offers, he said that nothing could make him as happy as sweeping the streets. Will everyone agree with him? No! But not everyone will agree with your opinions, either."

Nayeli adjusted her collar. "Yes, okay, you know what? You did it. You convinced me that it would indeed be a good thing if we all followed our soul-path ..."

"But?" Willow asked, as usual reading Nayeli's energy.

"But, on the other hand, it makes me want to rebel."

"Why?"

Nayeli shrugged her shoulders. "Isn't it obvious? That we have no freedom once we're here because we have to follow a plan that our soul created – it feels constricting."

"But you can live your life as you want it," Willow argued. "I'm sorry if I didn't make that clear until now, but one of the greatest gifts you humans have been given is free will. You're free to decide what to do in life – and whether you want to follow your soul-plan or not ..."

4. Azure, the Eagle

The view was breathtaking.

The sun was setting, colouring the sky in shades of pink, violet and orange, accentuated by hues of blue and red. Before this backdrop, the silhouettes of the mountaintops were outlined, and the beginning twilight cast shadows into the rocky valleys below.

Breathing the fresh air deep into his lungs, Strix let himself be carried by a thermal, enjoying the freedom to fly wherever the wind took him.

After having stayed with the wolf pack for a little longer, he had felt the first stirrings of unrest within him and knew it was time to hit the air again. At first, Hazel had begged him to stay but, when she'd seen how important it was for him to move on, she'd wished him well – after making Strix promise that he'd visit them whenever he was near.

Starting on another leg of his journey, Strix wasn't sure what awaited him. Maybe he would find somewhere else to settle down, or maybe he'd tire of wandering and come back to Hazel to live with her pack. But he wasn't anxious about what the outcome would be. For now, the air was his home and the wind his companion.

Strix had made good progress flying south. It had been mild and sunny during the days while the nights were clear, with millions of stars showing him the way. It wasn't until he'd neared the first mountains that the air had become chillier, but it was still agreeable – especially since Strix was rewarded by the view of the setting sunlight gleaming off the rough cliff faces and sparkling in a small stream that wound its way down into a valley.

Strix was so distracted by the beauty of the landscape that he almost missed a dark shadow plunging down from a ledge above him.

Avoiding a collision in the last possible second by flying towards a crevice in the rocky wall, Strix watched the shadow plummet straight down towards the valley – so close to the cliff face that Strix thought the animal would graze it.

At first, he was afraid that the bird of prey – for it could be nothing else, considering its size – was after his blood. Back at home, he'd had his fair share of run-ins with over-eager eagles, who wouldn't have said no to catching a curious young owl. But the bird didn't change its course.

Figuring that it must have a broken wing – especially since the bird made no attempt to save itself as it neared the ground – Strix quickly closed his eyes because he didn't want to watch it crash into the rock-strewn earth. He waited for the impact, but no sound came. Confused, Strix blinked his eyes open again and saw an eagle spiral up in front of him. He then looked into the abyss to see if there was another body lying shattered on the rocks, but there was neither a dead bird nor any blood to be seen.

The mystery was solved only moments later, when the big eagle rushed down past him a second time, letting out a whooping laugh along the way.

This time, Strix kept his eyes open. He observed how the eagle spiralled down and how it waited until the last instant to spread its wings. It had been so close to the ground that its claws almost touched the sparse clumps of grass between the stones. Then, catching a rising thermal, the bird of prey used it to soar up.

The eagle, who on closer inspection turned out to be a male, was bigger than Strix. But the look of joy that was plastered on his face, let his hooked beak and long talons appear somehow less dangerous.

Thus, gathering his courage, Strix dared to fly after him.

"Hey!" Strix addressed the eagle when he had caught up with the bird of prey. "Were you the one who nearly barrelled into me?"

"Did I?" The eagle, who introduced himself as Azure, laughed, his eyes sparkling as brightly as the sun. "I'm sorry. With the speed I was going, I didn't even see you."

"Why were you falling down the cliff?" Strix asked the bigger bird, "And twice in a row? Is there something wrong with your wings? You were so close to the mountain, I thought you'd get speared by a sharp rock sticking out from it, not to mention that you almost smashed right into the ground."

"Nope," Azure said. "My wings work fine. This is just a fun pastime to undertake. Have you never done it?"

Strix grimaced. "Done what? Commit suicide? No, I am adventurous, but I do happen to like being alive."

"Ah, but it's not dangerous," Azure refuted, settling down on the cliff's edge. "At least, not when you know how the winds work in the mountains and have two functioning wings. And I've heard that you owls are pretty good fliers, all things considered?"

Strix knew that Azure was intending to goad him into doing the stunt, but he was having none of it. Instead, he settled on a rock near the eagle and looked at him. "I don't see what you get out of it."

"You mean apart from joy?" Azure grinned. "It's the most amazing feeling in the world. You feel so elated when you fall off the cliff. It's the purest form of freedom you could experience – nothing else comes close to it. The speed at which you fall, the wind blowing by you. It's this huge rush of energy beyond your wildest dreams. And then there's the moment when you spread your wings – you feel totally weightless for a second. To say nothing of the feeling of power as you take back control over your body and the element air. But if you don't want to do it, that's okay. I figure it's not for everyone."

Feeling his resolve to stand firm in his decision to not do a cliff fall crumble, Strix looked down the mountain's face. "You think I can't do it?" he asked.

"I only think that not everyone has the guts to try it out. Despite the fact that anything in life can be unsafe. Heck, you could fall out of the smallest tree and break one of your wings, which would result in a wretched death from starvation. Or you could be hit by one of these stupid human birds."

"Are you talking about aeroplanes?" Strix asked, remembering that his family had mentioned those when he'd been a fledgling and how dangerous they were.

"Yeah, I think that's what they're called. I always say that humans have no business flying. The air is our world. But be that as it may, nothing is 100 per cent safe. And this is a fairly minimal risk I'm taking. We're birds, Strix. Flying is in our nature. Tumbling, diving, being carried by the wind – we can practically do all that in our sleep."

"And do you do this often? Diving from the cliff?" Strix asked, feeling excitement arise within him as he contemplated doing the fall.

"Every day," Azure answered. "And before you ask, no, I've never had an accident. Anyway, are you gonna join me now, or not?"

Being asked this directly, Strix's common sense was pushing his curiosity into the shadows once more. He stepped back as Azure spread his giant wings. "No thanks, I think I'll pass. It's still too dangerous for my taste."

Shrugging, Azure leaned forward slightly. As his feet left the cliff, he screamed at Strix while plunging towards the ground. "HAVE IT YOUR WAY!"

Strix gazed after the quickly receding bird. Thanks to his great eyesight, he could watch the fall and see how Azure pulled up moments before he would have hit the ground. Hearing the eagle's raucous laughter from his perch, Strix hooted uneasily. Then Azure appeared in front of him again.

"That's was soooo much fun," he beamed.

Strix couldn't help but mirror the eagle's smile, but then it turned into a frown. Had he made the right decision to not try the stunt? It did look like fun ... Making a split decision, Strix spontaneously turned towards the Azure. "Okay, tell me what to do!"

After listening to every eventuality that could make the difference between a safe or deadly plunge and repeating all the steps three times, Strix felt as ready as he'd ever be. Gathering his courage, he walked towards the edge where he stood motionless, following the rocky walls with his eyes and picking out the safest route to go down. Azure had assured him that when a gust of wind would come out of nowhere or the ground would rush up too fast, instinct would take over. But Strix wanted to make sure to avoid any unnecessary dangers.

Then, not giving himself any time to change his mind, he leaned forward and let himself fall.

At once, Strix felt a cold wind blow past him, filling his ears with a roaring sound as he gained speed. The ground rushed towards him faster and faster, and the rocky walls around him were nothing but a grey blur.

But instead of being scared, he felt pure joy – and total freedom. "I'M THE KING OF THE WORLD!!" Strix called loudly and burst out into whopping laughter.

When he was still a good bit away from the ground, he spread his wings and caught a warmer draught, flapping back to the cliff ledge. There, he sat down next to Azure, who had watched him the whole time. Strix beamed so widely that he feared his beak might fall off.

"That was fantastic!" Strix laughed, high on adrenaline. "I wanna do it again!"

"Told you it's addictive," Azure grinned back and pointed downwards with one of his claws. "C'mon, I'll race you there. Bet you won't catch me."

And with that they were rushing towards the ground, side by side, their laughter and screams mixed in with the wind.

They jumped four more times, and Strix was out of breath as they ascended after the last fall. Instead of flying to the starting point as before, he landed on a rocky outcrop halfway up to catch his breath.

"What's wrong?" Azure asked, soaring before him.

"I need a break," Strix breathed out heavily and declined Azure's invitation to jump another time. "Maybe later."

Shrugging, Azure flew up to the edge of the cliff alone and catapulted himself from it, giving the impression that he could continue this all night.

"Ah, how long has it been since my last jumps? It was such fun," a voice from behind Strix said.

Surprised, he spun around and saw that there was a cavern in the rocky wall. And in its entrance, an aged male eagle sat, holding a faraway look in his eyes. Bowing his head in respect, Strix turned around to face his elder. "I didn't see you there," he said. "If this is your home and you want peace, I can go."

"Nah." The eagle laughed. "I'll have peace soon enough when I exit this life. In the meantime, I'm more than happy to enjoy watching the exuberance of youth. Anyway, how was it? I take it, these were your first cliff falls? I've not seen you around before."

Strix couldn't contain his excitement as his eyes tracked Azure, who was spiralling upwards yet again. "Yes. And it was the best feeling ever. The best in the whole world! Claws down."

Looking deep into his eyes, the old eagle inclined his head. "It might be the best feeling you have experienced *until now*. But don't be too hasty and say there is no better to come. There's a lot you haven't tried in life, and many things can make you feel as elated and alive as jumping from a cliff."

Strix followed the eagle's gaze and noticed a nest that had been built into the rocky wall opposite them. It was occupied by a pair of young eagles, who were grooming each other lovingly.

When the old eagle spoke anew, his words came slowly, as if they were carried from far away, but the conviction behind them was strong. "Love and a faithful partner who understands and accepts you are the real treasures in life. And nothing makes you feel as alive as having young ones around."

"Um, I don't know ..." Strix didn't want to offend the old eagle. But the mention of offspring had reminded him of the wolf pups he had left behind and how much trouble they had been. "Little ones are loads of work. And love? A relationship isn't exactly the epitome of freedom, but more like an invisible cage, where you have to give up a good chunk of your wishes and make compromises."

The old eagle chuckled and pointed with a claw at the pair. "Do they appear caged to you?"

Strix watched the couple closely. They seemed happy. More than that, they seemed to glow from within. But Strix shrugged that phenomenon off as being caused by the reflection of the full moon, which had steadily climbed into the sky over the course of the last hour.

He looked back at the old eagle. "They appear to be happy enough. But being in love and happy doesn't necessarily mean you feel free, or does it?"

The old eagle smiled absentmindedly. "Oh, but they do feel a sense of freedom. Which you'll understand when you're older and have gained some further life experiences. Until then, trust an old bird and don't pass up the chance of love when it comes into your life. You would miss out on much."

Turning his head, first one way and then the other, as he tended to do when he wasn't sure about something, Strix shrugged uncomfortably. "If you say so."

"I do," the eagle responded. "Take it from a bird who has been in love for almost three decades and still is to this day. It all began when I was a mischievous eaglet who liked to play tricks. I was ready for any adventure or thrill. Jumping off the cliff was one of my favourite pastimes. That, and soaring as high in the sky as I could or plunging into cold mountain lakes to catch fish. I thought that I'd found all the happiness that life could offer. But then I saw her ... From that day on, I had someone at my side with whom I could share all my adventures, and it made those all the better. It's difficult to explain if you haven't been there yet. But true love doesn't equal losing anything. You gain from it."

Feeling a faint stirring deep inside him at the eagle's words, Strix shook his head to ward off a memory and concentrated on the present moment instead.

"And where is she now? The love of your life, I mean?"

"On the other side, waiting for me," the old eagle answered.

Strix averted his eyes. "I'm sorry to hear that."

"Don't be, don't be," the eagle replied. "I will not be here for much longer. My old wings are tired of carrying my weight, my bones are weary and my soul is yearning to cross over – not only so I can be back at her side but so that I can finally be free of the restrictions of this body and all its aches and pains. I'm truly ready to take on this last great adventure of life and to feel the infinite freedom that awaits me on the higher planes."

"I don't know if I can see death that positively," Strix admitted, shifting restlessly from one foot to the other. "To be honest, I'm a bit scared of it. Or maybe that's my survival instinct talking?"

"I think it's more than that." The eagle smiled knowingly. "You are young, little owl, and you have a lot left to do in this life that your soul looks forward to. You still have a purpose and a reason to be here. But I've finished my lessons. I am ready for the next journey that awaits me."

Gazing up at the night sky and the stars twinkling above them, the old eagle sighed. "But before I go, let me give you some last words of advice. You can find countless things in this world, which will make you feel free. Travelling around the globe, jumping off cliffs or falling in love are just some options you have. So chose wisely by using your free will, which ones you want to experience."

Strix nodded. "I just hope that I'll not regret my decisions when I'm old and look back." Contemplating the path lying ahead of him and all that could go wrong, Strix shook off the worries trying to take hold of him.

"At any rate," he said, allowing his carefree attitude to chase away the profoundness of the moment, "I know what I want right now. My free will is screaming at me to jump off that cliff once more."

"Then don't let me keep you." The old eagle shooed him off gruffly.

Strix bowed his head to the old bird in farewell a last time and took to the air, being all too aware that, when he left these mountains behind, he wouldn't see the eagle again in this world. If he ever came back here, the old bird would be gone, having travelled to a dimension that would be out of Strix's reach for some time to come.

Shaking off the sadness that clung to him at that thought, Strix flew back up to Azure, who was sitting on a rocky outcrop, taking a much-needed rest.

"I see you met our grandpa," Azure greeted him as Strix landed on a nearby rock.

"Your grandpa? I didn't realise you were related."

"We aren't. That's what we all call him, simply because he's been around these mountains for such a long time." Azure grinned devilishly. "Anyway, want to beat me in another fall? You've yet got to be faster than me."

Strix wanted to complain that this comparison was unjust since Azure had years of training on him, but the eagle had already tipped himself forward and was disappearing over the edge of the cliff.

"Hey," Strix called out after him, "that's an unfair head-start. Come back here."

But Azure only laughed, and Strix had no choice but to fold his own wings and dive after him, hot on the eagle's claws.

Free Will and Exit Points

"Is it really that great on the other side?" Nayeli asked, swallowing past a lump in her throat.

"Yes. But I've covered that topic earlier, haven't I?"

"You did." Nayeli bit her lip to stop herself from crying. But, despite her best efforts, a single tear slid down her cheek. She wiped it away resolutely. Unfortunately, she wasn't as successful at wiping away the tenseness in her voice, though.

Willow picked up on it in an instant. "What is wrong, my dear?"

"This is just the first time I've truly got it, y'know?" Nayeli choked out.

"Got what?" Willow asked gently.

"That my grandma is all right on the other side, and that we haven't seen each other for the last time. That all what you've been telling me is true. It's not that I didn't believe you before. But this story, the old eagle ... something about the way he spoke ... maybe it's because he was close to death's door himself and he wasn't scared at all. It touched something within me. Now, I don't merely understand what you've been saying on an intellectual level; I know it's the truth because I feel it deep within me."

"I'm glad the old eagle could help you," Willow said sincerely.

Nayeli laughed amidst the tears that had begun to drip out of her eyes. She still hated the fact that her grandma wasn't here anymore and that she could never hug her again in this life. But now she was able to see some light. Nayeli knew she would be happy again, as her grandma would have wished her to be.

"It's like the eagle told Strix," Nayeli pondered. "I might not have been able to fully comprehend this truth till now because I'm young and haven't completed my life's journey yet. Maybe it's natural that the thought of crossing over scares me. But I assume that when you're ready to leave, you're ready. And my grandma *was* old. I think she had made her peace with leaving?!"

Her last question had been rhetorical, and Willow seemed to be aware of that as the tree remained silent.

Settling back, Nayeli looked into the distance, dwelling on her own memories for a while. It was only when she saw an eagle soar high in the blue sky that she remembered the story as well as Willow's earlier comment – about humans having free will – that had sparked it.

As If the willow tree had been woken by Nayeli's thoughts, it stirred behind her. "Anyway," Willow said slowly, dragging the word out, "we were going to talk about free will, weren't we?"

"What I can't wrap my head around is how both can be possible at the same time," Nayeli tossed in. "How can we have a soul-plan on one hand and free will on the other? If I have the freedom to ignore my soul-path, why bother creating it at all?"

"But your soul-plan and free will fit together quite nicely, my dear," the tree answered. "When this dual reality was created, there was a choice. To give the souls incarnating here a free will – or not. And I don't think the decision was hard to make. What sense would it make to plan out your entire life, with every little detail and all eventualities, prior to incarnating here? If you knew everything that would happen in advance, it would be pointless coming here and living through it, wouldn't it? If there were no surprises, there'd be no learning experiences and no growth."

"Are you now saying that it's a *good* thing if we stray from our soul-path?" Nayeli asked, perplexed by this shift of opinion. "That's not what you told me before."

"What I'm saying is that from the perspective of the universe, every experience is valuable, no matter if it's based on your soul-plan or on your free will. Therefore, it's up to you to decide, which path you want to follow. You can follow your soul-plan to the letter or parts of it. You can follow it immediately or later. You can run down the road or go along the path slowly. You can find alternative routes to it that are similar or take a detour that will eventually lead you back to the main path. Or you can throw the soul-plan away and decide on an entirely different course of action."

Willow moved, making its leaves quiver in the otherwise still air. "To better understand this, imagine life being like a play. Your soul-plan is the script and your soul is the writer, additional to being the director and producer and stage designer and every other person behind the scenes who is needed in order to create the story in the first place."

"And as the incarnated human being, I'm the actor?" Nayeli asked before answering her own question. "Clearly I am. But then I'd just read the script that was given to me, wouldn't I? Where's the free will in that?"

"This script only contains the key aspects of the story. It tells you the general direction where the play goes, more akin to an improvisational theatre piece than anything else. Aside from this, when you're on the stage, you're free to ignore the script altogether and to move the story where you want it to go instead."

"And there'd be no repercussions for that? The director wouldn't be angry?"

"No – your soul would be fascinated to watch how everything would play out with this alternative storyline. The one thing that could happen is that you don't like the story you create as much as the script you held in your hands. That it won't make you feel as happy and fulfilled as the other story would have done. It can be trickier to create a happy life when you're not following your soul-path. But you can achieve it if you find other ways to meet your existing needs and desires."

Willow lifted some of its lighter twigs. "And, by the way, it's not that your soul or source *won't* interfere with your free will. It's that they *can't*. Your free will is a fundamental law of this reality, and it cannot be bypassed. The universe and your soul can only provide help when you ask for it. Which, by the way, also applies to all relationships here on Earth – a truth that can be painful at times."

"How so?" Nayeli asked, frowning.

"Since we all have free will, we have to respect other people's decisions, too. You can't help anyone until they allow you to help them. And you can't prevent anyone from taking a wrong turn if they're not ready to listen to you. Imagine that a family member has a serious illness but doesn't want to go to the doctor or accept any treatment. Maybe you fear losing them. Maybe you even know about the spiritual reasons why this illness manifested and how it could be healed. But if they don't want to hear about it, there's nothing you can do about it."

"I'd have to watch them die, in the worst-case scenario?" Nayeli asked, aghast. "Then what about me forcing my help on them? I could blackmail them into going to a doctor. Or trick them somehow."

Willow grunted. "You can decide, based on your free will, to do all of that. But likewise, it's up to the other person how they react to you. They can give in to your blackmail – or not. They can let themselves be persuaded by your arguments – or not. And they can let themselves be swayed by your pleading – or not. In the end, it's their free will that determines what road they take. Free will is absolute, my dear, and can never cease to exist. Even if you decide to let someone else choose something for you, you use your free will to hand the choice over to them."

"But that's terrible. If I knew more about something than another person and couldn't make them believe me, there must be some other way to help. If it would save them?"

"Do you know more than anyone else, though?" Willow asked. "It can be true that you have more medicinal knowledge, for example, and maybe you know more about the healing arts. But since you've never walked in the other person's shoes, you definitely do not know more about their unique life path. Maybe they need this experience of being ill. Maybe their soul chose it for a reason. Maybe the situation will turn out to be a blessing in disguise. And maybe their reality is different from your perception. I'm aware that this might be a hard pill to swallow, but free will is something good and we've all got to respect it. No one knows as well what they need as the person itself."

"In other words, there's no way at all to help someone else?"

"Of course there is," Willow said. "You can offer help to others. When they accept it, you're free to help them in any way they allow. On top of that, you can help others by example. When people see that you're leading a happier, healthier life after making some changes, they're more inclined to follow you than when you use empty phrases to convince them."

Nayeli nodded. This she could get behind. But something else the tree had said was still bothering her. At first, she couldn't put her finger on what it was; the thought kept lingering on the edges of her awareness, receding into the shadows of her mind as soon as Nayeli tried to take a closer look at it. But then the reason behind that feeling revealed itself to her, and Nayeli's breath caught in her throat as she beheld the implications. "Willow, you said we all have free will and that even our souls can't force us to do anything we don't want to do, correct?"

"Yes, that's correct."

"Then my grandma actively chose to cross back over? It was her free will to die?"

Willow's tone was loving as the tree answered. "Death is the only exception to free will. Or to say it better, death and where and how and when you're born. But since these decisions are made before you come here, and thus before you have free will, they don't really count."

"But why is death an exception?" Nayeli asked, confused.

"In short, anything that affects your soul directly can be decided or overruled by it. And that includes the decision when and how you leave this incarnation."

"So, I can't die if my soul doesn't think it's the right time for me to cross back over? And I can't stop myself from dying when it's the right time? Is that it?"

"That's indeed what I'm saying."

Nayeli sighed in relief – relief that her grandma hadn't consciously chosen to leave her and her family behind.

Then that relief was replaced by fear.

"In other words, we're at the mercy of our own soul when it comes to our death?"

The tree's voice spread out over the meadow, as if it was carried by the breeze. "Don't worry, my dear child. Your soul doesn't discount your wishes, as you're part of it. If it hurts you, it would automatically hurt itself. But let me explain what I mean by first defining exit points and how they work. Then it might make more sense to you ... Every soul has several exit points spaced out over their life. These exit points can range from illnesses and accidents to dying of old age. They're written in your soul-plan prior to you incarnating here. But your soul can choose to adjust them over the course of your life, just like the script you hold on stage is constantly being rewritten with every decision you make."

"And how do our souls choose, which exit point to take and when – and how – we should cross back over?"

"By assessing whether staying in this life continues to be in alignment with your path or not."

"Are you implying that death can ever be in alignment with someone's path? That's outrageous!"

Willow's leaves rustled in the summer breeze. "I understand why you think this because you are looking at this matter from your human perception. It is completely normal to want to hang on to life and to see death as the enemy, as it takes loved ones from us. But when you change to the perspective of the source, you can see that it's the multitude of experiences that enable its growth."

Nayeli huffed. "Fine, maybe our souls can get something useful out of death because it enables us to switch into other incarnations. But that still doesn't explain why death can be in alignment with my path specifically."

"Sometimes you humans get stuck in a dead end in life that feels like hell. For example, when you're facing big health problems on top of being homeless and jobless. In this and more cases, your soul can consider changing this incarnation for another life, one that will be better. Saying this, you're not close to an exit point every time you face a problem. Difficulties and troubling times are part of this dual reality, like the air you breathe. I'm simply saying that, after weighing up all options and considering your wishes, death can be the answer your soul chooses. And, additionally to that, your soul might choose to take an exit point when you've fulfilled your soul-path and have no desires left. If you have nothing more to gain, why not choose a new incarnation with new goals?"

Nayeli leaned forward expectantly. "And why do we have several exit points? We can only die once, after all."

"Yes, but our souls seem to like having a few options to end our stay here," Willow joked before becoming serious again. "It's not a problem, though, because you'll pass the exit points you don't use without ever noticing they were there."

"Pass them by unnoticed? How?"

"Let's say one of these exit points was to have a car accident. Your soul would rewrite the situation leading up to it. It could send you a warning and you'd feel uneasy about walking down a dark alley, choosing to take a different route home instead. Or it could line you up to meet a childhood friend, and you'd chat to them for a while; and by the time you reached the street where the accident would have occurred, the car is long gone. Or maybe the car never arrived, because the driver called in sick and stayed at home that day. There are endless ways you can avoid an exit point and not notice it ..."

Nayeli blew out the breath she had been holding. She was still miffed that her soul could decide when she had to leave this life. But then her mind made a U-turn as she remembered the fight with her mother this morning. "You know what, Willow? I might have initially balked at the idea of being at the mercy of my soul, but the longer I think about it, the more relieved I feel that we aren't responsible for choosing the time of our own death. Because, honestly, this free will is wasted on us humans. Or at least it's wasted on me. Even my small day-to-day decisions suck."

"Why do you say that?" Willow asked, picking up on her changed mood.

Nayeli scratched the nape of her neck absentmindedly. "I said some things to my mum today, which I now regret. Ever since the funeral, our emotions have been running high, and we've hurled accusations at each other. I don't like it. I love my mum. And I don't want to add to her burdens and bring her more pain. But I don't seem to be able to stop myself, either."

Willow hummed lightly. "You're both in an exceptional situation, my dear child. You've lost your grandma, and your mother lost her mum. You are both grieving. It's understandable that you're not dealing particularly well under these circumstances. But this position you find yourself in provides you with a unique learning experience."

"What kind of learning experience?" Nayeli asked dubiously. "That we can't use our free will after all, since it's overruled by our emotions, over which we have no control?"

"No, nothing like that." Willow laughed loud and brightly. "I thought more along the lines of learning how to reconcile with your mum and connect to her on an even deeper level. But since you have the wrong idea about emotions, I will have to postpone this talk and address the basics first."

"Which are?" Nayeli asked, grumpy at being called out. She had never liked being told she was wrong. Or being laughed at. Least of all by a tree who, when all was said and done, was a figment of her hallucinations.

"Emotions, they are ..." Willow began, then paused. "Did I say anything wrong just now? You seem to be in a bad mood all of a sudden."

"I'm not in a bad mood," Nayeli said tersely, squaring her shoulders and glowering at the tree's trunk.

Willow was clearly unconvinced but shrugged the matter off. "If you say so. Anyway, what I was trying to say is that, while the mind is the tool of the ego, emotions are the language of the soul. As such, emotions are an important part of any relationship. The relationships you have with others, but also the relationship you have with yourself. And if you like, I can tell you a story I heard from Strix that might help shine some light on this?!"

Sitting in frosty silence beneath the tree's crown, Nayeli refused to answer the tree. She had half a mind to stand up and walk away without another word, never to return.

But the weeping willow must have taken her silence as an invitation to start its tale. And, as always, Willow's talent at storytelling didn't leave Nayeli unaffected. Before she could decide otherwise, her curiosity had won over her upset, and she decided to stay to hear this one last story out before leaving.

5. Bronze, the Chameleon

When Strix met Bronze, it happened by accident.

Having flown all night, Strix felt tired and his wings were starting to ache. Deciding to take a break to recharge his batteries, he found a suitable tree and was about to land on a branch when something right in front of him moved and made the leaves rustle in the otherwise still air. Startled, Strix jumped back into the sky, only avoiding the animal that was camouflaged in the tree's foliage by millimetres.

Circling above the spot, Strix partially blamed his tiredness for his mistake. But there was also the fact that the animal in question was a deep vibrant green that matched its surroundings perfectly. Or rather, it had been green. Because now, the stranger's skin was an alarming yellowy-orange. Strix took this as a warning sign and landed a good bit away from the foreign creature.

"Wow!" Strix said, impressed. "How the heck did you do that?"

But the animal evidently wasn't willing to answer him. It just sat, unmoving, while the one eye that was turned his way fixated Strix.

"Can't you talk?" Strix asked after some time. Then a realisation hit him. "Wait, you think I wanna eat you? Nah, you can relax. I'm full. Found a tasty mouse half an hour ago. And to be honest, I've never much cared for reptile meat. You are a reptile, aren't you?"

"Yes, yes, I am," the male said, coming to life. "I'm a reptile for sure. A chameleon, to be exact, and we taste absolutely disgusting. My name's Bronze."

"Nice to meet you, Bronze!" Strix said, relieved at these turns of events. Because if the reptile had feared him, Strix was confident that he was in no danger of being eaten himself. Introducing himself, he came back to his earlier question. "Anyhow, I'm genuinely interested in how you can change your colour to match your environment. You're practically invisible if you want to be, which is why I almost sat on you ..."

"I'm not changing my skin tone to match my environment," Bronze corrected Strix. "We chameleons change colour to adjust to the heat and humidity, as a mating ritual and to communicate. Different colours translate to different emotions, you know? And if we sometimes happen to blend into our surroundings – that's nothing else but an added benefit, meaning predators like you don't spot us."

"Oh?" Strix asked, interested. He studied Bronze more closely, noticing that his skin had a green tinge again. "And what colours can you turn? Can you be bright red, for example? I'd love to see that."

Hissing in anger, Bronze let his long tongue whip out of his mouth, his skin changing to an orange-brown tone. "Never tell me what colours I should wear! Do you hear me?"

"Whoa, whoa," Strix said, taking a step back and spreading his wings in case he needed to escape the angry reptile. "Calm down, okay? What's got your scales in such a twist?"

But Bronze ignored his question, turned his back to him and walked away, his pace slow and his motions jerky.

"Hey, hang on," Strix called out. "What did I say wrong?" Sighing when he didn't receive an answer, he lifted his tired body and hopped over, landing between Bronze and the tree's trunk.

"Look," he said earnestly, "I'm sorry if I said the wrong thing, but I have no idea why you reacted this strongly to my request. I've never met a chameleon before, and I was simply impressed by your ability to change colour so easily. It's cool! I might even be a tad envious. Just know that whatever upset you, I didn't intend any harm with my words."

Strix didn't expect much of a response but, to his surprise, Bronze relaxed and the tension drained from his body. Which was highlighted by his skin turning a yellowish-green again.

"I guess I reacted too strongly," Bronze admitted sheepishly. "But I've had some bad experiences in the past, and your question triggered those memories. I don't like to revisit them very often."

Spellbound, Strix watched Bronze's skin showing off alternating patterns, unable to take his eyes off the strange lizard.

"You're green when you're calm and relaxed, right?" he asked curiously. "And orange-brown when you're upset?"

"Am I?" Bronze said, flummoxed.

Then he burst into raucous laughter, his tongue extending and retracting a few times. "I'm kidding. You should have seen your face. We chameleons aren't blind, bro. We do know how our feelings influence our skin colour. And if we didn't, we could just take a good look at ourselves as our eyes are pretty damn flexible."

As if to demonstrate how far his eyes could swivel, he stared back over his shoulder with his left eye while gazing up at the sky with his right one. "See?"

Strix gaped at Bronze before closing his beak with a snap. "Wow!!" he said breathlessly.

At once, Strix felt real envy creep up on him. Changing skin tones didn't even compare to two eyes that could move separately from each other. The things he could have done with those, if only owls had been given that gift!

Feeling challenged by the chameleon's ability, Strix didn't want to come across as inferior. And so he bethought, which of his talents he could show off, finally settling on the most exceptional one. Sitting up proudly to tower over Bronze, he deliberately used his most arrogant tone. "Nice one. But can you do this?" Turning his head to gaze behind himself, he spun it first to the left and then to the right.

"Cool!" Bronze declared, his eyes bulging out more than usual. "How do you do that? It looks painful."

"It isn't," Strix responded, demonstrating again how easy it was. He smiled in satisfaction that the chameleon was suitably impressed by his talent, but his grin was wiped off his face at Bronze's next words.

"I prefer my eyes to your neck, though. We might both have the ability to see what's behind us, but I can look into two different directions at the same time."

"Pff, who cares?" Strix said, offended. "I can fly. Soundless. While hearing the softest rustle under tons of earth and snow. Not to mention that I can see everything, even in the pitch black of the night. That beats all else!"

"Yeah," Bronze said sarcastically. "I noticed *that* talent up close when you almost skinned me with your claws. Y'know, if you're that good at flying, the next step should be to learn how to land without killing someone."

"For the record, I didn't kill you," Strix threw back. "And how is it my fault when you blend into your surroundings? Watch out yourself, will ya? So much for your great eyes."

"I saw you perfectly well - my eyes weren't the problem," Bronze retorted. But his tone wasn't that aggrieved anymore, and at the end, the chameleon chuckled. "Look at us. Fighting like two adolescents."

Strix joined in the laughter.

Soon after, he noted that the relaxed atmosphere settling between them led to Bronze showing off the same deep green he'd been prior to their almost collision. It made him ask the question that was burning on his tongue.

"Are you sure you don't want to tell me what caused your upset? I know it's not my business, but you were literally seething when I asked if you would show off your different skin tones. I think it might do you good to talk about it. I'm a great listener. And discreet …"

"And noisy," Bronze rounded off the list. He sighed. "But maybe you're right and it would do me good to let it all out. It's just … it's a very personal story. And not one of the highlights in my life."

The chameleon looked pensively into the distance. He remained silent for so long, Strix thought he wouldn't say any more. But then Bronze turned his right eye back to him. "Ach, what the heck, why not? You might learn something from my stupidity."

"I doubt you've been as stupid as you make yourself sound," Strix said, shaking his head. "You seem smart."

The reptile laughed sarcastically. "Wait till you hear my story. I was naive in my younger years and made a lot of questionable decisions … It all started in my first mating season. I was walking around the border of my territory in search of a female chameleon. After a few days of having no luck, I reckoned I'd have to wait another season to find a partner. But then I saw the most beautiful female sitting on the branch of a tree. She was breath-taking. Sleek, graceful and bug-eyed. But there was a second male chameleon who had set his sights on her as well. He was bigger and stronger than me, and I had no chance to win against someone that fit. Naturally, the female only had eyes for him, despite me trying everything I could to woo her. Until one fateful moment, that is, which I'll never forget. I can remember it as if it happened yesterday ... An eagle was circling in the sky above us. He didn't see the beautiful female or the bigger male, who was climbing her tree. But I was sitting on the ground and had nowhere to hide. In short, I was easy to spot and therefore easy prey.

"The eagle saw me and dived. As his shadow grew bigger and bigger, I knew my end had come. I felt the draught of air from his massive wings as he extended his claws to grab me and was paralysed by shock. Normally I would have hissed at him and tried to appear as big as possible to fend him off, but I could merely roll up into a ball and shake in terror. I closed my eyes and mentally prepared to cross over early. But then something amazing, and totally unpredictable, happened. A second eagle I hadn't noticed had selected me as his snack, too. Diving, the two birds of prey got into a fight and hacked at each other with their sharp beaks. Since they weren't paying any attention to me, I scuttled off to a shrub, where I hid. From there, I watched them fight each other before they flew off in different directions.

"I had never been this close to dying in this life. And, along with that, I had never felt this panicked. My skin colour, which matched those feelings, had turned a brown that was bordering on metallic. It was a shade I had never seen on me – or any other chameleon, for that matter. And neither had the female who had observed the whole scene from the safety of her branch. For the first time, her eyes sparkled with interest as she looked at me. And I was allowed to approach her. So, I did. I risked the open ground between us and raced out of the shrub as fast as I could, running to her tree, which I began to climb. Being completely focused on that task, I lost a lot of my terror. The bad news was, however, that when I stopped panicking, I also lost my bronze colouring. And by the time I reached the branch she was sitting on, my skin was a boring brownish-orange again, with specks of green in it. As quickly as her interest had been piqued, it vanished when she saw me like this.

"I was confused and sad when she rejected me. And when the other chameleon chased me away from the tree, I felt like even more of a failure. Which is why I developed a plan to prove myself to my beloved. The next days, I put myself under as much stress as I could. I refused to eat anything despite my stomach growling in hunger. I ran around in the burning sun until I could barely breathe. I didn't sleep or rest. But nothing I tried yielded the results I wanted. My skin was brown, as it usually is when I feel stressed, but not the sparkling bronze tone it had been. Needless to say that the beautiful female continued to ignore my advances.

"Which is why I decided that more drastic measures were needed. And an opportunity soon presented itself. I saw a snake slithering over the ground beneath the low branch I was sitting on. In hindsight, I know how stupid it was, but I let myself fall from the tree, right into its path. Before I hit the ground, my skin had already turned bronze, and my heart beat so fast that I thought it would burst inside my chest. I would've had no chance of survival if the snake had attacked me, but, to my incredible luck, it had eaten shortly ago and showed no interest in me. Other than the female chameleon who instantly flirted with me again, telling me that my skin was exceptional and beautiful and I should wear this colour all the time because she would never tire of looking at it. Well, what can I say, I took her words to heart. I searched out more and more dangerous situations to get back my bronze colouring, and I practised staying in a panicked state for longer periods of time. I did everything to reach that goal – and was so damn reckless that it's a wonder I'm still alive today. But at the time, it all seemed worth it because the female encouraged my advances.

"The only sad thing was that I couldn't enjoy her company. Because whenever I did, my stress levels reduced and my skin would change back to a boring brown, yellow or green. Then she would withdraw from me, saying she could have lots of green mates who were all stronger and fitter than me. Before long, I was miserable 24/7, either because I was terrified of the dangerous situations I created for myself, or because I was doing my best to keep my stress levels up when I was with her. Soon I had forgotten what it was like to feel relaxed or happy. Until yet another fateful evening when, once again, my world turned on its axis.

"I was on the ground, a good bit away from a fig tree. Not being the fastest species on Earth, it isn't particularly safe for us to leave cover. But I was even more of a target than usual because I was stressed out and my bronze skin sparkled in the sun. I heard a noise above me and curled up, waiting to go over to the other side – as I did so often in these days. But it wasn't an eagle or hawk flying above me. Once I dared to look up, I saw another female chameleon sitting on an extended branch of the tree, half concealed between the leaves. She called out to me a second time.

"The interest in her eyes reminded me of my beloved, but it quickly became clear that she wasn't intrigued by my colours but my strange behaviour. She asked if I was all right and invited me to join her. At first, I wasn't sure if I should, being embarrassed that she'd seen me cover in fear for no reason. But then I took heart and climbed the trunk to sit beside her.

"Something about this female chameleon – maybe it was her calm aura or the gentle look in her eyes – made me feel safe enough to relax a little bit, for the first time in forever. Initially, that actually didn't feel good, because it brought forth all my suppressed emotions, the strongest one being rage. Suddenly, I felt burning anger towards the other female rise within me – anger that she'd ignored my advances unless I was feeling so bad that I sparkled bronze in the sunlight and anger that she had never really cared for me. But more than that, I felt angry at myself for having given up my health and safety for nothing else but a passing infatuation. It took a long time for the rage to bleed out of me, which was followed by regret that I had wasted this much time on someone who didn't deserve a second of my day and a belated feeling of dizzying faintness at having gambled with my life this carelessly. Meanwhile, my skin colour was changing rapidly, depending on the emotion that was flowing through me, until it finally settled on a neutral yellowish-green.

"Afterwards, I became aware that the female was staring at me intently with one eye while the other darted around to look for any potential danger. She asked if I felt better. I nodded, and before I could even consciously decide to tell her what had happened, the entire story spilled out of me. I'll never forget the expression on her face as I revealed what trying to impress this other female had done to me. And I sure won't forget what her next words were ..."

"What did she say?" Strix asked in curiosity when Bronze stopped speaking.

"She said," Bronze smiled, "that she thought all my colours were beautiful and that I should appreciate every single one of them. She said that true beauty lies in my ability to show my emotions in hundreds of different tones and patterns."

"That's sweet." Strix smiled. "And what happened to her? Where is she now?"

Bronze swivelled one of his eyes to the right. Strix craned his neck around to follow the chameleon's gaze to a second tree that stood nearby and saw that one of the green specks he had taken for a leaf was moving differently from the others. True enough, a few yellow spots that hadn't been there before began to show on the female chameleon's skin.

"Hello!" Strix called over to her. "If I'd known you were there, I wouldn't have been so rude as to ignore you this whole time."

"No worries. I like to be ignored," the female called back jokingly. "And especially by birds of prey who enjoy us as a snack."

Strix called back. "I promise I'm not going to eat you."

The female reptile looked him straight in the eye with one of her own. "Yeah, that became apparent when I listened in on the conversation you had with Bronze. But by then I didn't want to interrupt."

Strix turned his head back to the chameleon beside him and noticed that the eye he could see from his position shone with love and care for his female companion.

"We're normally not that sociable and rarely share our territory," Bronze answered Strix's earlier question. "But we two are such a great team that we chose to stick together."

"That's nice," Strix said.

He felt genuine joy that Bronze had found his match and a connection that was so full of love and understanding. But he couldn't ignore the fact that beneath this feeling was also a spark of jealousy. Shaking himself to get rid of it, Strix smiled as Bronze continued to explain their living arrangements.

"But you know how it is – forever an exception to the rule. Or do you want to tell me that you've never met an owl that didn't like to fly?"

"Actually," Strix grinned, "I have a cousin who's never longer in the air than absolutely necessary to hunt for meals. He hates flying with a passion. I always wondered why he chose to become an owl, but I reckon he must have had *some* good reason for it ..."

"That sounds like an interesting story," Bronze said and grinned at him. "And since I've just told you a long tale, I think it's only fair that I get to hear one of yours, don't you think?"

Strix couldn't help laughing at Bronze's challenging tone. "Okay, okay," he said, waving his wings about. "I can't refuse a polite request like that." And with that, he plunged right into the story of his cousin: the owl who was deathly afraid of heights.

"Why wouldn't Bronze's partner say that his green colours are the most beautiful, though, and he should wear those more often?" Nayeli asked, having completely forgotten that she hadn't intended to talk to the tree anymore. "When you care about someone, you want them to be relaxed at all times, don't you?"

"But that's neither possible nor healthy while living in a dual reality," Willow argued. "There are always highs and lows. And, as I've said before, living a spiritual life does not mean to be always happy. Instead, it means accepting all parts within you, including the ones that make you feel negative."

"It's the dual reality that's at fault again? I'm beginning to hate it ..."

The tree shook its crown. "There's no need for that. We've already established how useful it is, didn't we? Besides, whether or not we care for it – it *is* the status quo."

The weeping willow sighed audibly before continuing to speak. "My dear, I know that you humans perceive some emotions as being 'better' than others. But every emotion is important. Every single feeling is valid and necessary."

Snorting derisively, Nayeli turned her eyes heavenwards. "For real? Tell me only one good reason why I have to feel fear or anger."

"The specific reason can differ from person to person and from situation to situation. But, generally speaking, the emotions that you rate negative keep you safe."

Nayeli thought she knew what the tree's point was. "You are saying that, without fear, we wouldn't have survived as a species, right? That our fear triggered our fight-or-flight response whenever we came near a predator? And we still have these instinctive reactions that help us survive when we feel threatened?"

"Yes, that's part of it," Willow agreed. "Your brains are wired for survival – even now that you live in concrete cities where you're in no danger of being eaten by a tiger or lion. Because of this genetic predisposition, you automatically concentrate on any dangerous or negative situation over any positive ones because they're a potential threat to you, which you need to avoid in the future. If a friend forgets your birthday one time, it can affect you as much as fifty positive experiences you have with them.

"And, contrary to popular belief, fear isn't the only negative emotion that keeps you safe. Other feelings, such as anger or shame, keep you alive and functioning as well. Anger, for example, helps you to reinforce weak boundaries when someone oversteps them. And shame is your safety alarm: it rings when you feel threatened in a social situation, protecting you from the thing humans fear most – disconnection."

Nayeli tilted her head. "Can you explain what you mean by that?"

"I mean," the tree said, "that connection is a basic human need. When someone rejects or abandons you, you feel threatened. And to avoid that, we install a subconscious pattern of shaming ourselves, which takes effect the second you think someone might disapprove of you. We hope that, if we beat ourselves up early enough, we'll prevent others from doing the same, and from leaving us."

Nayeli felt amazed at this new revelation. "How exactly was this pattern installed? And can we change it when we become aware of it?"

"Those, my dear, are questions I'll gladly come back to later."

"Why not now?" Nayeli asked, petulantly. "I want to hear more about this."

"Because we haven't finished talking about emotions in general yet and need to address these lessons one after the other, as each topic I tell you about is important."

"Fine." Nayeli huffed, resigned. She had sat underneath the tree's crown long enough by now to know it was futile trying to change Willow's mind when it was made up. And if she argued further, it would only result in her having to wait longer for the answers she desired. Thus, she bowed to the inevitable and waited for the tree to decide what it was it wanted to talk about while letting her own thoughts wander. As they did, a new question crept into her mind, skirting around the edges of her consciousness before it became louder and demanded an answer.

"All right," Nayeli finally voiced what was bothering her. "Maybe we do need to feel negative emotions inside a dual reality. But why do we need to be subjected to them for such long periods of time? Why can't they come, say hello and then leave us alone? Why do they have to stay for hours or days or even weeks on end, making us feel bad?"

"And this is precisely what's wrong with a lot of humans' perceptions," the tree declared.

"What? That we feel negatively?"

"No, that you don't *want* to feel negative emotions and try to avoid them at all costs. This is why they stay for longer than necessary. Remember the spiritual law 'what you resist persists'? It's not one of the most used spiritual quotes for nothing. And it's especially true when it comes to the emotional body. Any negative emotion you have is there for a reason: to be seen and heard and felt and be understood by you. And it's only after you've done this that it can run its course and leave, making room for another emotion to take its place."

Willow let one of its longer twigs tap the ground beside Nayeli's foot. "This is a mistake that some spiritual teachers make, too. They'll tell you to move away from emotions with lower vibrations, like fear or anger, and to concentrate exclusively on emotions with higher vibrations, like happiness. But there's a problem concerning this. When you ignore, suppress, deny, reject, disvalue or disown a negative emotion – if you run from it or fight with it, if you push it down or shove it away, if you ridicule or trivialise it or if you distract yourself from it – you're resisting that emotion and what it embodies. And resistance makes the thing you are resisting stronger because you are placing your whole subconscious focus and energy on the thing you don't want to face.

"Imagine you've made plans to meet a friend, but she stands you up. Later, she apologises for not coming, telling you that she met this nice guy and forgot the time. You might feel angry at being cast aside. But since another part of you understands your friend and is happy that she's met her dream guy, you tell her it's all right. You suppress the anger and distract yourself from it. This works. For a time. But the anger is still stored within you, and each time this friend does something to make you feel angry, more energy is added to it. Until you reach the straw that breaks the camel's back. And this holds true for any emotion. Sadness can be stored inside your body, just like fear or powerlessness. For as long as those emotions aren't healed and released."

"And how do I heal a negative emotion?" Nayeli asked.

"There are several ways. Sometimes it's enough to sit with the emotion and feel it consciously. To accept and value it and to look at the reasons that caused it. And sometimes you need to heal the underlying trauma, which is another topic that I will explain in greater detail later on. In both cases, one thing is for sure, though: running from a negative emotion only helps in the short term. If that. Because, sooner or later, it will rise to the surface again."

"Like with thoughts in meditation? You said when I push them away, they get even more persistent."

"Exactly like that," Willow agreed. "Negative emotions are not intended to prolong your suffering or for you to wallow in them. They act as an alarm bell, ringing to alert you to the fact that something within you needs attention. Once this alarm bell has gone off, the emotion itself has played its part. At this point, your job begins. Namely, to make the emotion your friend, no matter if you consider it 'good' or 'bad'. Rather than judge the feeling, spend time with it. Get to know it – and the reason it arose."

Nayeli frowned. "I get that we have to endure negative emotions sometimes. And I can even see that they have their uses in certain circumstances. But isn't welcoming them a bit much to ask?"

The tree chuckled. "But what else would you do with an old friend who knocks on your door? You invite them in instead of putting up a barricade against them."

"And by doing that I can control the situation?"

"It's not about controlling your emotions, but about actively releasing them from your emotional body," Willow corrected Nayeli.

"That's the second time you've mentioned the emotional body," Nayeli interjected. "But what is that exactly?"

"Surely you're aware that you have more bodies than your physical one, don't you?"

Nayeli arched her eyebrows. "Nope, I actually wasn't."

"Then let me enlighten you. You also have an emotional, mental and spiritual body. You can divide them even further, but these are the layers that are the most important to know about in the beginning."

"Ah, of course," Nayeli interrupted the tree, irony lacing her voice. "Then why haven't I seen any of them in all these years I've been alive?"

"Because, my dear child, your physical body is the only one that's corporeal. The other bodies are ethereal. You can't see them with your physical eyes. Think of them as invisible globes of light that fill out and surround your physical body. The emotional body has the smallest circumference. Your mental body is a little larger than your emotional body. And the spiritual body is the largest of them all."

"All right, let's say I have all these invisible bodies I'm not aware of. What purpose do they have?"

"Each subtle body has its own important tasks to fulfil. For example, one of the main jobs of your emotional body is to ensure the flow of emotions."

"And when I think something, I do it with my mental body?" Nayeli inquired.

"You are spot on."

Nayeli laughed out loud as a comical thought entered her mind.

"What?" Willow asked, confused. "What's so funny about that?"

Giggling, Nayeli pulled her legs to her chest and wrapped her arms around them. "I just imagined being on a date or at a job interview and my emotions and thoughts appearing in a bright red colour or something, for everyone to see what's going on inside me. Ugh, what an awful idea! You know, Willow, considering this, I'm glad that we don't wear our emotions on our skin for the world to see, like chameleons do ..."

"But the subtle bodies can be seen," Willow said seriously.

Wondering if the tree was having her on, Nayeli squinted over her shoulder at its trunk. Obviously, this didn't help her discover the answer, though, because, unlike chameleons, trees didn't show their true colours for everyone to see either.

"Are you joking?" she asked to get clarity.

"Not at all," Willow said lightly. "I'm talking about auras. Every body, from your physical body to your spiritual bodies, has its own auric field, or aura."

Hearing Willow mention this, Nayeli was reminded of watching a documentary once about Kirlian photography, which could record something that looked like colourful fog surrounding a person.

"Oh wait, I think I've actually seen that on TV a few years ago. Auras can be lots of different colours, right?"

"Yes. The colours can give information about a person – for example, how healthy they are. And some people have the ability to see or feel or even hear those auric fields. Actually, everyone has these natural abilities since they're a soul-given talent, but some people have learned to consciously use it."

"Woah, wait," Nayeli said, dumbfounded. "You can *hear* auras?"

"Yes, it's possible," the tree answered. "Since sounds and colours are simply different expressions of the same frequencies of energy, it can be done. It's more common to see and feel an aura, however."

By now, Nayeli was keen on hearing more about this topic. "Are these subtle bodies created by my body when I incarnate?"

"No," Willow said firmly. "It's the other way around. Your subtle bodies are the blueprint for your physical body. Everything exists on the energetic plane before it manifests into the physical reality. Accordingly, your body exists as an energetic imprint first, from which it becomes physical. And, knowing this, it's obvious that not only humans have an aura. Everything does – animals, plants, even objects. The physical form is always a result of the energetic blueprint and everything moves from the higher planes into the lower ones."

The willow tree mumbled to itself for a minute, so softly that Nayeli couldn't discern any words. But then Willow raised its voice again. "Ah yes, I know just the example to use to better explain this. If you have a traumatic experience early in your life, such as your parents divorcing, it originally arises in your spiritual body as a potential threat to your survival. From there it moves into the next vibrational layer, which is the mental body. In this subtle body, it manifests as negative thoughts, for example 'I'm powerless to do anything about this'. The thoughts then move into the layer beneath it, your emotional body, where they will transform into emotions – for example, fear, anger or hopelessness. And from there, the emotions move into your physical body, where they are perceived as sensations, such as your chest seeming tight or your throat feeling closed up."

"And this happens every time?" Nayeli asked, surprised. "Our thoughts prompt our emotions and these become sensations?"

"Every single time," Willow confirmed. "Which is yet another reason your emotions – both positive and negative – are important. They enable everything to move from the higher energetic form into the denser level of your physical body. And without them, you'd feel stranded because many of your thoughts run on autopilot and you aren't aware of them."

"Right," Nayeli said astonished. "Wow, I knew we were complicated beings, but I had no idea *how* complicated!"

Willow sounded amused. "It's not that complicated once you've learned a bit about it. You can simply see your subtle bodies as translators. They translate messages until they're in a form you can understand. And, additionally, the auric fields act as a great communication tool between you and others."

"I communicate with others through my aura? Without even knowing it exists?" Nayeli asked in surprise.

"For sure. Have you never wondered why you feel tired after you've spent a day shopping in the city? That's not only due to you being on your feet for hours. Every time you're near someone or something else, your auras mingle, and the subtle bodies exchange energy with each other. On the downside, this means that when you are in a higher vibrational state and your aura touches the subtle bodies of others who are in a lower vibrational energy, your energy reduces. When this happens and you're exposed to this for too long, you feel drained."

"Is there no way to protect my aura and to prevent that from happening?"

"There are several ways you can do that. There are techniques to heal and replenish your auric fields and others to protect and shield them. One simple technique is to imagine standing inside a crystal sphere of light. It surrounds all your subtle bodies and fills you up completely. This bubble of pure light will allow nothing else but energy of the same vibration or higher than your own to flow to you, while it will repel any lower energies from your field."

Nayeli's mind was running at a mile a minute, and with every piece of information she learned, it went faster.

"Do you see now that emotions are nothing to fear, my dear?" Willow interrupted her train of thoughts. "And that even emotions you perceive as negative are useful when you learn how to handle them, instead of seeking to escape the feelings?"

"Yeah, I see it," Nayeli said. But at the same time, she noticed that her voice still held a note of resistance. Squaring her shoulder, she gazed up into the tree's crown. "Look, I *do* get that negative emotions have their purpose on a purely logical level. But I can't help it that I don't like to feel them."

Looking at the colourful flowers that scattered the surrounding meadow, Nayeli sighed. "You know, Willow, it's not always easy to see the value in everything. Sometimes the positive aspects and hidden blessings are buried so deep that they're hard to discover. Not everything is as visibly beautiful as these wild flowers."

"That's true. But if you shift your focus, you'll see it all. The beauty that exists everywhere around you – and inside yourself."

Nayeli wrinkled her nose. "You don't, by any chance, have a story from your friend Strix where he finds out about that, do you?"

"Hmmm." Willow drew out the sound before laughing loudly. "Now that you mention it ... I remember one that fits quite nicely. Do you want to hear it?"

Nayeli peered up at the sun, which had almost completed its journey into the west, and decided that one more story couldn't hurt. It would, at any rate, prolong the moment when she had to go home and face her mother again.

"Hit me with it," Nayeli said teasingly, lying back on the grass and letting her gaze become unfocused as Willow's voice carried her away from the meadow, into another land.

6. Plum, the Warthog

The first time Strix saw Plum, the warthog sat in front of his burrow and stared unseeing into the distance, looking like the most depressed animal in the world.

Initially, Strix had planned to make good use of the cooler morning hours and to make up ground before finding a suitable resting place for the day. But when he saw the sad warthog, he couldn't fly by without at least trying to cheer him up.

Landing in front of the boar, Strix regarded him closely. His grey skin was practically naked, with the only hair being a mane-like stripe on his back as well as a tuft at the end of his tail. But the most prominent feature were the wart-like bumps on his face, which were accentuated by curved tusks sticking out from his snout. All in all, Strix thought to himself, Plum was the ugliest animal he had ever laid eyes on. But since he had learned early to not judge a book by its cover and to hear the story first, Strix tilted his head enquiringly. "Is everything all right? Can I help you in some way?"

"No," the warthog answered sorrowfully. "No one can help me."

"Are you sure?" Strix asked. "Because I think that every problem has a solution. And I've become an expert at finding those."

"Pff. Unless you can find me a new body, the only thing you can do is to leave me alone."

"A new body?" Strix asked curiously. "Do you have any problems with yours? A rash, maybe? I heard a mud bath can help with that."

"I don't need a mud bath. I need a sleek, strong lion's body with a bushy mane. Or a powerful crocodile's body with smooth dark-green scales. Or the body of a proud bird with a colourful plumage." Ending his list with a deep sigh, the warthog looked tiredly at Strix and let his head hang down.

"Okaaayy," Strix said, half amused at the melodramatic way Plum talked and half worried for the poor animal, who was clearly in a lot of emotional pain.

He knew how bad that felt and that it could be worse than any physical illness, so Strix decided then and there to help Plum feel better. Naturally, the first step would be to find out what was weighing on the warthog's heart. Which could prove difficult, as Plum didn't appear to be very forthcoming in sharing his worries. Unless, Strix thought, he was tricked into revealing them.

Fluttering up, Strix let his eyes dart around the savannah that stretched out before him. The sun had ascended a good bit by now, and its bright light flooded the plains, which were dominated by grasses and interspersed with some shrubs here and there. These were growing randomly, some grouped together, while others stood alone, which gave off the impression as though they had been thrown from the sky and left where they had landed.

Almost immediately, Strix saw something glitter in the sunlight. He flew over to inspect it and smiled in satisfaction when he saw his assumption confirmed. An idea was taking form in his mind.

Hooting in excitement to get the warthog's attention, Strix circled in the air above him.

Slowly, and as if every movement was done against his better judgement, Plum raised his head. "Yes?" he muttered wearily.

"I might not be able to swap your body for someone else's, but what do you think about enhancing it with a shiny snakeskin? I mean, all that glitters is not gold, but this one comes pretty close. Cause when the sun sparkles off it, it looks like diamonds ..."

"It does?" Plum asked. Instantly, there was a glint in his previously dead eyes. "Where is it?"

"Right over there, behind that shrub."

Strix had to somersault out of the way of the warthog. None of the sluggishness that he had associated with Plum remained as the animal leapt up and dashed towards the bush, as if he was scared the snake would come back to repossess its skin.

"Fabulous, this is perfect," Plum gushed excitedly. "Quick. Help me slip it on."

But, suddenly, the elation left his body, and the warthog hunched his shoulders in abject misery. "You know what? Forget it. I'll never fit into this skin. Look how plump I am compared to a snake."

Strix landed on the rock beside the boar and let his gaze glide first over the warthog and then towards the snakeskin, wondering how to voice his thoughts without hurting Plum's feelings. Weighing his options, Strix eventually decided that honesty was the best course of action. "You won't fit fully into it. But you could put it over your tail. The way it sticks up in the air when you run – it's basically made to be carrying this skin."

"You think so?" Plum asked uncertainly, before his eyes lit up. "Yes, you're right; we'll do it like that. C'mon, don't just sit there. Help me."

Strix sighed at being ordered around and wondered if he shouldn't have flown past this crazy warthog, after all, But now that he was in for a penny, he was in for a pound. So, Strix soared down and grasped the snakeskin.

At once, Plum reprimanded him again. "Be careful with your claws. Don't break it. It needs to be whole."

"Yes, yes," Strix said tonelessly as he flew over Plum's back. He tried to let the skin slide over the warthog's tail, but it was a lot more difficult than he had thought, especially since the boar was so excited that he couldn't manage to stand still. But then, Strix finally managed to put it over the tassel at the top from where it slid down. Contemplating his creation for a moment, Strix felt pleased with himself. "There you go. It fits perfectly, as if it was made for you. Now, care to tell me what all this is about?"

"There's no time for idle talk," Plum answered hastily as he jumped around in an attempt to see his backside. "This is too perfect to pass up. I gotta go."

Without hesitating, Plum turned east and dashed over the grassy plains, his tail held proudly erect, as if he wanted the whole world to admire his treasure.

Looking after the retreating warthog, Strix blinked once, surprised at how quickly Plum had left. Then he jumped into action and caught an updraft to trail the boar and find out what his plan was. To Strix's dismay, his curiosity soon gave way to frustration, though, when the first mile or two, nothing happened.

Plum simply trotted on at a steady pace through the long grass, which was growing everywhere.

But when Strix began to fear that the warthog would continue to walk all day, the boar finally halted behind a bush and panted.

Not being sure if Plum did so because he was out of breath or if he had another reason, Strix wanted to ask him what was going on. But before he could follow through with that thought, Plum grunted a last time, ran around the shrub and into the open plains beyond, where he came to a stop and stood tall.

At first glance, Strix didn't notice anything out of the ordinary that would explain such odd behaviour. But then he saw four holes in the ground and, in one of those, the unmistakable snout of another warthog – a snout that was layered with even more wart-like bumps than Plum's, making Strix change his mind about him being the ugliest animal he had ever come across.

Plum, meanwhile, seemed to disagree with his opinion, as his eyes took on a dreamy expression the moment he saw his female counterpart.

In an instant, Strix knew what all the wallowing had been about: Plum was lovesick and wanted to impress his chosen one. His assumption was immediately confirmed as the boar ran over to the burrow and turned around to show off his embellished tail.

Strix was curious how this makeover would be received by the female warthog, and so he observed her every reaction carefully. He noticed the joy on her face as she saw Plum, and he also noticed how her eyes widened as she fixated Plum's tail, a hint of panic becoming visible in them.

Plum meanwhile seemed to be oblivious to her change in mood. He simply laughed in delight that she had noticed his accessory and shook his behind so that the sun reflected off the skin.

Strix could foresee the catastrophe before it happened – but not swiftly enough to warn Plum about it, as the female warthog had already lowered her head and raced forward, out of her burrow, to ram her tusks into Plum's backside.

Shrieking loudly in pain and shock, Plum leapt to the side and stared at the sow, aghast. "What the heck did you do that for? That hurt!"

Instead of answering, the female squared off and lowered her head for a second attack.

Suddenly, understanding gleamed in Plum's eyes and he quickly turned his tail away from her. "It's not a living snake, I promise!" Drawing himself up to his full height, the warthog's next words were laced with pride. "But doesn't it look pretty?"

Panting angrily at him, Plum's love interest apparently had another idea. She pawed the hard-packed earth with her left front hoof, whirling up dust. Flashing her eyes at Plum, she jerked her head backwards, motioning to the holes in the ground, where the heads of three younger warthogs had emerged. They were watching the scene unfold as intently as Strix was.

"Do you find this funny, you stupid ass? To scare a lady and her offspring? Is this your idea of a sick joke?"

"No," Plum said, taken aback and obviously not realising what he had done wrong. "I wanted ..." he began but was interrupted by the angry female who was advancing towards him.

"I don't care what you wanted. Get lost, you stupid fool, and take your damn dead snake with you. Go!"

To underline that she was serious, she lowered her head once more.

Plum didn't need to think long in the face of this much rage. He turned tail and ran.

Looking after the misunderstood warthog, who was galloping as fast as he could into the direction they'd come from, Strix followed in his wake. It wasn't hard to do, even if he wouldn't have remembered the exact route. He just had to track the path of crushed grass, which must be an accurate symbol of the poor animal's heart.

The whole way back, Strix pondered about how to help Plum patch up the damage that had been done. But by the time he had reached the warthog's burrow, he was none the wiser.

The boar was rolling around on his back to scrub off the remains of the snakeskin. "Stupid," he muttered to himself. "I'm so stupid. Why didn't I remember that her eyesight isn't the best? Of course, she'd get scared by a snakeskin on my tail."

Strix flew closer carefully, unsure what welcome to expect since the whole fiasco wouldn't have happened if it hadn't been for his idea. He needn't have worried, though. The warthog's anger had subsided and left nothing but misery behind.

Shuffling inside his burrow, backside first, Plum laid his head on the ground wearily. "Don't bother," he said bitterly. "I'm aware that I embarrassed myself beyond measure. So go and let me suffer in peace."

Strix's first instinct was to object to that and to console the warthog. But he restrained himself at the last second and instead complied with the boar's wish. Knowing from personal experience that the best thing he could do for Plum was to give him some time to come to terms with the rejection he had received, Strix opened his wings and let himself be carried away by a warm updraught.

Flying to a small group of trees he had passed before, Strix chose one that would provide an acceptable resting place and landed on a branch.

As soon as his claws wrapped around the wood, tiredness overcame him and he slipped off into a dreamless sleep.

***

When Strix woke up hours later, the sun was descending beyond the horizon and his mind immediately went back to the lovesick warthog. Wanting to see for himself how Plum was holding up, Strix didn't lose any time and flew back the by now familiar route.

Even from afar, Strix could make out the boar, who was lying half inside his burrow, exactly as he had left him earlier. Wondering whether the warthog had moved at all during the day, he flew closer and registered one difference, after all. A colourful feather had fallen onto Plum's head and was lodged between two of his wart-like bumps.

Harrumphing to make his presence known, Strix landed on a patch of bare earth before the burrow.

Sluggishly opening his eyes, Plum looked up and reared back. The end of the feather, which he apparently hadn't noticed until now, was hanging in front of his left eye and blocking his view. "What the hell?" Plum asked, shaking his head to dislodge it. But then he stopped dead in his tracks and turned to Strix, an excited gleam in the one eye that was visible. "How do I look?"

"Tired," Strix said straightforwardly. "You didn't sleep very well, did you?"

"No," Plum said impatiently. "The feather. How do I look with the feather?"

"Eh, I don't know," Strix said, unsure what the warthog wanted to hear from him. "It looks like you're wearing a feather? Nothing special about that, I've got hundreds of them."

"Yeah, but yours are brown and not as colourful as this one." Plum laughed as he shoved past a baffled Strix and trotted away.

Confused, Strix stared after the warthog until the meaning behind Plum's words reached Strix's brain. He groaned and muttered underneath his breath. "No, please not again ..."

Taking off and flying after the boar, Strix called out. "Plum, wait!"

"Why?" Plum exclaimed excitedly, not slowing his steps. "This is perfect."

"The same words I heard you say hours ago," Strix reminded him. "And we both know how that turned out."

"But back then I was wearing the skin of a venomous animal. Now, I'm wearing the feather of a harmless bird. She has no reason to be scared of this. Besides, it's much more beautiful than a stupid old skin."

Strix was speechless at Plum's one-track mind, but for only a second. "Don't you warthogs have any other mating rituals? Like using your tusks to fight one another? Or digging up some food for your lovely lady?"

"Normally we do," Plum admitted. "But look at me. I'm a lost cause. I have fewer bumps than most warthogs, and the ones I have are tiny. Not to mention my tusks, which are short compared to those of my brothers and sisters. Thus, even if I were to showcase my strength and skills, my ugliness is the deciding factor. No female as beautiful as her would ever consider me if I don't change my appearance."

Plum had fallen into a trot while talking. The feather stuck between his bumps was whipping up and down with every step, as if agreeing with the warthog. "I mean, have you looked at her? She must be the prettiest creature you have ever laid eyes on, right?"

"Er," Strix said noncommittally, wondering how bad Plum's eyesight was if he called his beloved 'beautiful'. He might have merely seen her once for a few short minutes, but his visual memory was usually spot-on. And what he recalled was that she hadn't looked very different to the boar, being disfigured with the same wart-like bumps as Plum – only that hers were bigger and more numerous. It wasn't exactly the image that came into his mind when the word 'pretty' was mentioned.

Realising that he had been silent for the better part of a minute and still hadn't answered the warthog's question, Strix was about to fish for the right words when he became aware that they had reached their destination.

From one moment to the next, Plum appeared to have forgotten all about Strix's presence, as he was entirely focused on the dark burrow in front of him and the head sticking out from it.

Strix shook his head in resignation. The boar was too damn stubborn to listen to his wisdom either way. And so he fell back to watch the drama unfold – preparing to pick up the pieces afterwards.

To Strix's surprise, Plum's chosen one wasn't attacking the warthog, though. Instead, her guttural laughter floated over the grassland. Hearing this unexpected cheerfulness gave Strix hope that the situation wouldn't end as badly as he had feared. Until the sow voiced her first thoughts, which quickly disabused him of that notion.

"Oh my, this is hilarious. You look as if you collided with a bird. What, did one mistake your head for a nest?" She laughed, not noticing that Plum's head was drooping.

"You look ridiculous," she put more wood on the fire. "A fool if there ever was one."

It was too much for Plum. He turned around dejectedly.

As the sow continued to joke about how silly he looked, the warthog trudged back the way he'd come, giving off the impression of having been run over by a rhinoceros.

"Did you have to do that?" Strix called out angrily once Plum was out of earshot. He flew up to the female warthog and circled over her head, staring down furiously at her. "Why the hell did you laugh at him?"

"Why not?" she asked, giggling. "If he wants to make an ass out of himself by adorning himself with borrowed plumes, he should realise that others will call him out on his arrogance."

Strix hooted angrily. "I really don't know why he fancies you. Gosh, you're so blind. Don't you get that he's courting you? He wants to impress you!"

The female warthog's laughter stopped abruptly, and she gazed up at Strix. "He ... he is? He does?"

"Yes," Strix said hotly, but then decided that an explanation would be wasted on someone this dense. Preferring to make better use of his time by finding Plum and helping the warthog see that someone as insensitive as her didn't deserve his love, Strix flew high into the air. Flapping his wings, Strix made haste to catch up with the boar, who had disappeared from view. The only thing that was left were his tracks on the ground, which soon told Strix that the warthog had swerved from his original path and had trotted further south into the vastness of the savannah. Strix followed him.

Once Strix found Plum, the warthog was running as if on autopilot, not seeming to care where he went – or taking any notice of the feather, which was still sticking to his snout, being held in place by one of his tusks.

"Shall I remove that?" Strix asked tentatively.

"Please," Plum said sadly. He halted so abruptly that dust billowed up from the ground and stood still just long enough for Strix to take it off. Then he trotted on through the tall grass, as listlessly as before.

Not knowing how to cheer Plum up, Strix flew above him for some time, silently offering his company. They covered some ground like that, the landscape never changing until the shadowy outline of a lone tree appeared in the moonlight. And, along with that, the shapes of six lionesses and one male lion, who wore an impressive mane.

"Hey, Plum, stop. Halt!" Strix called out when his sharp eyes made out the danger ahead of them.

But the warthog kept his head down and trotted on, as if he hadn't heard his warning.

Strix took this to mean that he needed to take more drastic measures and flew right in front of the warthog's face.

Plum put on the brakes and looked up at him. "What is it? I'm not gonna go back there."

"I never said you should," Strix answered. "But if you follow this path, you'll walk straight into a pride of lions."

"Great," the warthog said uninterestedly, walking around Strix and trudging on, not altering his course in the slightest. "Whatever awaits me there can't be any worse than what I already survived, can it? And hey, maybe a fight with a lion is exactly what I need right now to feel better."

Strix was about to respond when Plum stopped dead in his tracks once more. "A fight with a lion," he said to himself. "She was laughing at me. But if I can win against a real lion, she won't be able to do that anymore. She'll see how strong and brave I am. So strong and brave that even my ugliness won't matter. And as a sign for my bravery, I'll pull out the lion's mane and lay it around my neck."

Strix felt disbelief at Plum's lunatic idea rise within him, and he swiftly blocked the warthog's path again.

"You stop that rubbish right now," he said urgently. "Throwing yourself to the lions because you are unhappy in love? If that isn't the stupidest thing I've ever heard, I don't know what is."

"I agree," a female voice affirmed.

Surprised, Strix peered over Plum's head while the warthog spun around, shock written in his eyes when he came face to face with his beloved, who, undetected by both of them, must have followed in their wake.

Looking chagrined, she stepped closer to Plum. "I'm sorry I laughed at you earlier. It was just such a funny sight how the feather stuck on your head, and I didn't comprehend why you did all that. If I had known that you tried to impress me, I wouldn't have reacted in the way I did."

Plum fixated the ground. "And I'm sorry for scaring you with that stupid snakeskin," he said, his voice almost inaudible.

"I simply don't understand why you think you need all these accessories to court me," the female continued. "I think you're a lot more dashing without them ..."

"For real?" Plum asked, taken aback.

She rolled her eyes. "Yes, you dimwit! And now let's go back. I don't need you to pick a fight with a lion. You've already done the bravest thing in the world."

"I ... did?" Plum stuttered.

The sow's eyes shone with kindness. "You allowed me to see the real you. That's worth more than a hundred wart-like bumps on the face."

Plum's face lighted up at hearing those words, and a silly smile formed on his face.

Feeling a bit queasy at all this mushy talk, Strix intended to steal away unnoticed since Plum had got his happy end and he obviously wasn't needed anymore. But just as he was about to leave, the female warthog looked up at him and smiled brightly.

"Thank you for the wake-up call, owl. It was much needed. I'm glad that Plum has found such a good friend in you."

Smiling shyly at her words of approval and the way Plum nodded along to the statement, Strix fended off her thanks and quickly wished them both well. Then, catapulting himself high up, Strix flew further south.

When he was passing the lone tree, the male lion lying beneath it opened his giant mouth in a yaw-splitting yawn and showed off his impressive canines that sparkled in the moonlight. Meanwhile, one of the females was stretching, presenting her razor-sharp claws, which left incisions in the earth.

Realising what a close call it had been for the boar to make acquaintances with both, Strix was beyond glad that Plum had been deterred from challenging the pride of lions because it would have meant to fight a losing battle.

Beauty and Soul Ages

Nayeli wiped a few tears from the corner of her eyes. Her laughter rang bright and clear over the meadow. "You know your sayings, Willow, don't you? All that glitters is not gold? Adorning himself with borrowed plumes? Throwing himself to the lions?"

"Excuse the poetic licence I took here – but it fitted perfectly with the story."

Giggling, Nayeli held her hurting ribs. "It did indeed. Thank you, Willow. I needed this. It felt good to laugh again and to forget all my worries, if only for a little while."

"I'm glad I could help," the tree mumbled and bowed its branches down. "At your service, madam." Then Willow stood up tall, making a creaking sound. "Anyway, what else did you take from this story?"

Nayeli let it play out in front of her eyes one more time. "That beauty is in the eye of the beholder? That although a warthog isn't overly pretty in our eyes or an owl's, they're beautiful to each other? And that this can be translated to the human world, too? Because tastes differ?"

"Not bad at all. You've touched on something important there. Even if you don't see someone or something as pretty, someone else will disagree with you. Beauty is subjective – and who are we to tell anyone else what it should look like for them? This in turn means, of course, that we're all beautiful to someone. If you don't fit the beauty standards of the society you live in, you might not be at the top of everyone's list. But you can be sure you're at the top of *someone's* list. Someone who's a match to seeing the unique beauty that is you and which cannot be replicated by anyone else."

Something occurred to Nayeli at that moment. "Beauty – be you. I never realised how similar these words sound. But that's what you are saying, right, Willow? That we're most beautiful when we're ourselves?"

"Absolutely," the tree agreed. "As the infinite soul you are, you are always beautiful. And for you to become beautiful as a human being, you don't need to do anything else but to let your true self shine through. It's, in any case, more important than to solely concern yourself with your outer appearance because superficial beauty is not only fleeting but also a meagre substitute for the real thing."

"Hmm, I guess you're right," Nayeli said hesitantly.

"You guess?" the tree chuckled.

Nayeli nodded, then shook her head. "No, I actually know that this is the truth because I've experienced it myself in the past when I was in love with someone ... I don't think I've ever had a type. But if I'd had one, they definitely wouldn't have been it. They were nothing like the person I expected to fall for, and the first time we met, I wasn't attracted to them in the slightest. Only, the closer we became the more attractive they were in my eyes – not just their character but their physical appearance as well. Until they were the most beautiful person in the whole world. I guess, the longer I spend with them, the more I saw their soul ..."

"That's what I was getting at," Willow confirmed.

"And you said it all beautifully," Nayeli replied. "But no matter what prose you use or how right you are, it still doesn't help us humans in this reality when our outer appearance is seen as ugly by most people. How am I supposed to find love, if no one ever finds me attractive?"

"Wait, my dear," Willow said, surprised. "You think *you* are ugly?"

Nayeli waved the question away like an annoying fly. "I'm definitely nothing to look at. I'm too short, my nose is too big and my —"

She broke off just in time. Clamping a hand over her mouth, Nayeli felt frozen in shock at having been so close to revealing her worst feature to the one friend in her life who would never judge her for it.

"And your what?" Willow asked.

Sitting in silent trepidation underneath the tree's crown, Nayeli felt sweat beading on her forehead as she tried to answer in as neutral a tone as possible. "Nothing. I was meaning nothing."

Waiting anxiously if the tree would comment on her obvious lie, Nayeli breathed out a sigh of immense relief when Willow ignored it and steered the conversation in another, safer direction.

"Superficial beauty can make life a lot easier, that's true. But then again, it can make things harder, too. Because people can be blinded by it and won't bother to look beneath that outer layer."

"I still find it unfair, though," Nayeli declared. "That some people match the beauty standard, while others, like me, differ so much from it. And how can it even be that something like a beauty standard exists? How can people in a society agree that a six-pack or a flat stomach is more beautiful than the opposite? You've said yourself that anyone finds something else pretty. So how does this fit in with your teachings?"

"The answer to that is normalcy, my dear."

"Normalcy?" Nayeli asked, taken aback. "But our beauty standards are model-like figures, not the *normal* people we see on the street each day."

"Your consciousness might have some blind spots, but that doesn't mean your subconsciousness is in the same boat," Willow said cryptically. "But let me explain ... You only need to walk by one newspaper kiosk or go on a social media channel, and you'll see countless photoshopped models or influencers smiling at you. Likewise, movies, TV shows, and adverts are full of people who've spent hours in the mask before daring to face a camera. You see hundreds of those people daily compared to a few dozen *normal* people like your colleagues or your neighbours. Thus, the celebrities become the norm everyone else has to compete with."

"Are you sure about this? That normalcy is the deciding factor?"

"Just ask yourself the following," Willow countered her question. "How many women in your friendship circle shave their legs?"

"All of them," Nayeli said. Then she slapped her forehead in realisation. "I get it now. It looks initially *strange* when a woman doesn't do it, because we are so used to seeing them have smooth legs."

"Precisely, my dear. It's been a beauty standard in many countries for decades. But the same would hold true the other way around. If all women stopped shaving their legs, you'd soon find the sight of hairless legs odd. Or, if all men decided to wear skirts and dresses from this day on, in a very short time you'd not find that remarkable at all."

"I don't know about *that*, Willow," Nayeli said doubtfully. "Cause some humans can be mean bullies when they feel threatened in their own masculinity. I've certainly encountered my fair share of those in my life."

"I'm sure you have," the tree affirmed. "But if something is done by the majority of people and established as the new norm, it will automatically be accepted by society. And our perspective and view of what is beautiful would shift along with it. Similar occurrences have already happened. Or didn't you know that high-heeled shoes were originally invented for men? Or that red and pink were considered to be men's colours for a long time because they were the most expensive to produce, while women wore the cheaper blues, greys and greens? This only changed more recently when baby girls were made to wear pink and boys blue. And when women started to wear high heels."

"Honestly, Willow," Nayeli muttered, "is there ever a question you don't have an answer for?"

"Actually, there is one that seals that deal," the tree responded lightly. "Tell me, how can it be that you agree with me that beauty is subjective and that anyone can become beautiful in the eyes of someone else – based on the fact that you've experienced that phenomenon yourself in the past – but that you think there's a difference when it comes to you?"

"I don't know." Nayeli shrugged. "Maybe the difference is that my self-esteem is on the floor?"

Although she'd tried to pass the words off as a joke, Nayeli knew it was the truth. She didn't, couldn't, fully believe that others would see her as valuable, let alone beautiful. Nayeli had always blamed her childhood for that, in which she had been told continuously she wasn't smart or interesting or brave or pretty enough – not that the reason mattered now. What had been done couldn't be undone ...

So, Nayeli just grinned lopsidedly and shrugged her shoulders a second time. "No matter how many times you tell me that I need to see myself as beautiful, I can't do it."

"I'm not going to ask that of you," Willow argued against her. "Your feelings and thoughts are always valid and there's a good reason why they exist, based on the trauma you experienced. It would be a recipe for disaster to not accept them. What I would like you to do, however, is to accept something else alongside these negative thoughts and emotions - namely the fact that they aren't representing an objective truth. They are rather based on subjective beliefs. And other people won't necessarily feel the same way about you."

Nayeli snorted. "How the heck can it be valid that I think of myself as ugly whenever I look in a mirror? There's no point in that. All it does is lower my already low self-worth and make me think that I'll never find love."

"On the contrary. There can be a multitude of good reasons. These beliefs can, for example, be a protective measure that you've installed."

"A protective measure?" Nayeli asked disbelievingly. "Willow, that's nonsense. If anything, when we perceive ourselves as ugly, it makes us feel more unsafe, because of bullies who make it their hobby to demean us."

"Look at it from another angle, though," the tree tossed in. "If you're afraid of connection and intimacy and you avoid going on dates because you think of yourself as ugly, you're keeping yourself safe from being abandoned later on, aren't you? In the end, my dear, your soul chose this body with all its perceived imperfections for a reason. Maybe their task is to teach you to love yourself. After all, it's easy to love your body if most people consider it beautiful, but it's harder to do when it differs from the norm. Or maybe any blemishes you have will help you set healthier boundaries because of being exposed to disparaging remarks as a teenager. Or maybe you installed those imperfections as secret weapons to weed out the wrong people in your life as opposed to those who are worth keeping around ..."

"How so?"

"Let me ask you a counter-question," Willow said, its voice sounding simultaneously soft and firm. "Why would you want to waste time on a partner who is more interested in your outer appearance than your personality?"

"You are right that I wouldn't want someone like that in my life," Nayeli confirmed. "But then again, some people don't seem to mind being a trophy to others. I know a woman who's undergone countless plastic surgeries to be more attractive for her partner. Not that I judge her for it. She can do what she wants and for whatever reasons – I simply don't get why she changes herself to be liked by someone else instead of finding a person who will love her for who she is ..."

"Well, aside from the fact that she probably lacks self-love, which is something I'll elaborate on at a future date, this can easily be explained by the different soul ages."

"Soul ages?" Nayeli asked. "Our souls are not all the same age?"

"No, they're not," Willow responded. "Just as a human grows in life, so does a soul. They start as infant souls then grow into young souls. After that, they become mature and then old souls, based on how many experiences they've lived through."

"And why do some souls have more of those at present than others?"

"For one, there are only a limited amount of bodies to incarnate into, which entails that not all souls can come here at once. Besides, some souls like to remain on the other side for longer periods of time, while others prefer to jump straight into another bodily experience. Eventually, though, all souls become old souls."

"Right, but what has the soul age got to do with beauty?" Nayeli probed.

"Depending on how old your soul is, you will have different desires. Similar to a teenager being interested in walking the wild side of life and going on adventures, younger souls are more likely to choose a life that matches these wishes. Meanwhile, old souls will more often choose to experience lessons that relate to gaining more knowledge and wisdom."

"But not always?" Nayeli questioned.

"No, not always. An adult soul can choose a life of adventure and a young soul can go on a life quest that's based on finding inner truth. But those are the exceptions rather than the rule. In general, the first clue you have regarding the age of a soul is to look at the desires that were picked for this life. Or, at least, by looking at your unique desires, which are at the forefront."

"Wait, is there more than those?"

"Of course. When you dig deep enough, my dear, you'll see that everyone – no matter how old their soul – has one desire at their core. And that is to be connected and loved, as this is the natural state for all souls. We all gravitate back towards the feeling of oneness. But above this one ever-present desire, there are the other, unique wishes, which align specifically with our soul-paths. Not everyone wants a spouse and a dozen children. The dream of someone to live the life of a rock star would be a nightmare for someone else. And while someone might have the desire to reach a *perfect* beauty standard they set for themselves, someone else will dream of moving into the wilderness and saving animals."

"I understand." Nayeli felt like she had gained new insight into a topic she had never thought much about before.

But her complementation was cut short by the tree.

"It's getting late," Willow stated. "You should go home, or your mum will be worried."

Gazing through the willow tree's branches and seeing the stars light up in the darkening sky, Nayeli had to agree with that assessment. She stood up and collected her bottle and empty paper bag. "You'll be here tomorrow though, won't you? There's a lot more I still need to ask you."

"I don't plan on walking anywhere, considering I have no legs to do so," Willow joked.

"Ha ha," Nayeli responded dryly and rolled her eyes heavenward at the tree's questionable sense of humour.

Walking across the meadow and through the streets towards her grandma's house, she wondered what welcome to expect there. The question was answered as soon as Nayeli set foot on the front steps and the door was flung open.

Her mother stood on the threshold, glowering. "Where have you been all day, Nayeli?" she asked loudly. "First yesterday and now today? What's wrong with you? You can't run off whenever you feel like it!"

Nayeli's sense of serenity she had gained in the last hours evaporated in the face of her mother's anger, and she could feel her body tense up at the accusations being flung at her. Clearly, her mum had no intention of apologising for her words this morning.

"You don't get to tell me what to do," Nayeli therefore retorted, pushing past her mother. "I'm an adult and I can bloody well do what I want. You're just picking a fight with me to distract yourself from the fact that your other daughter didn't stay."

Nayeli regretted the words immediately after spitting them out but knew it was too late to take them back.

Her mother's eyes narrowed into slits. "You will *not* talk to me like that, Nayeli!"

Ashamed at having lost her cool, Nayeli shouldered past her mother and ran to her room, not wanting to hear what else her mum had to say as she feared it would escalate into another full-blown fight. Slamming the door behind her and leaning back against it, she tried to block out the sound of her mother continuing to rant at her.

Breathing deep into her belly, Nayeli hoped that some of the calmness she'd felt earlier in the day would return. But it didn't.

***

The next morning, the mood was still frosty, but Nayeli had expected nothing less. Her mother could be resentful for ages, and Nayeli had never been very good at apologising. But this time, she wanted to do better.

Squaring her shoulders, she dared to take the first step.

"There's nothing to forgive," her mother responded, to Nayeli's surprise. "Neither of us is at our best right now. And I hope you accept my apology, too."

Smiling relieved, Nayeli pulled her mother into a hug, glad that – at least for now – everything between them was well again. Nayeli pulled away and looked at her mum, who gently tucked a stray strand of hair behind Nayeli's ear.

"I also thought about what you said. You weren't wrong. It's not fair to exclude you from dealing with the legal papers about the house and everything else. And if you want to help us – there's a lot left to be done."

Nayeli didn't know how to react. On one hand, she didn't want to let her mother down by refusing to do what she had wanted to be part of so desperately only yesterday. But on the other hand, she wanted nothing more than to go out to Willow and hear more about what the tree had to teach her. Wavering between both options, Nayeli finally made her decision. "I'm sorry, but if it's all right with you, I'd rather go out. I've agreed to meet someone."

Seeing her mum's shoulders sag, Nayeli added quickly, "But if you need me, I can cancel my plans. No problem!"

"No, no," her mother replied. "I'm glad you haven't been alone these last two days. I wasn't aware you had friends left here. Who is it? Do I know them?"

"It's none of the kids I used to play with. They've all moved away by now. It's ..."

The words *'a tree'* had been on the tip of her tongue but Nayeli swallowed them down, suppressing a giggle at the thought of her mother's reaction at being introduced to Willow.

"Ah, I get it," her mum said, excitement in her voice. "It's a guy, isn't it? When do I meet him?"

"Mum!" Nayeli groaned pitifully, wondering if her mother would ever lay the topic of a romantic relationship to rest. At the same time, she doubted it. Her mother was famous for her persistence, alongside her talent to hold grudges.

"Fine, fine," her mother said seamlessly. "You keep your lover secret for now. But promise me you'll introduce him to me as soon as it gets serious."

"Mum!" Nayeli called again, embarrassed by her mother's antics but even more bothered that she was keeping the truth from her. Only, how could she tell her mother that she was hallucinating about talking to a tree without being carted off to an asylum? There was simply no good reason to worry her, especially since Nayeli didn't know how long this phenomenon would continue to occur. Maybe today, when she arrived at the meadow, the tree would have already gone back to being a regular tree and wouldn't answer her any longer.

Feeling sadness creep up within her at that thought, Nayeli shook her head to dislodge these bleak images.

"Don't shake your head at me," her mum said. "As your mother, I'm entitled to meet my future son-in-law. Oh, and take something to eat with you. You're getting way too thin for my liking. I've some fruit and sandwiches. Let me pack up something."

Nayeli accepted this as the peace offering it was and waited patiently until her mother had filled a bag with everything edible she could find in the kitchen.

Half an hour later, Nayeli reached Willow. She swept one of the tree's low-hanging branches aside to walk into the green cavern they formed and dropped to the ground dramatically.

"Didn't you sleep well, my dear?" Willow inquired.

"No!" Nayeli said mournfully. "I had another row with my mum last night, and I never sleep well after an argument."

"I'm sorry to hear that," Willow answered. "Is there anything I can do to help? Maybe you could bring your mother with you tomorrow and I'll tell her all that I've told you in the last two days?!"

"No, that definitely wouldn't help," Nayeli said adamantly. "My mum is very different to me. She has no interest in all the things we've been talking about. She always says topics like these make her nervous."

"She could be a younger soul then," Willow considered. "They are usually not as interested in spirituality as older souls."

"Yeah, could be," Nayeli said. "Either way, she doesn't like to talk about her feelings or dive too deeply into the reasons behind her thoughts and beliefs."

"In that case, I agree that bringing her here won't be of any help. But is there anything else I can do for you?"

Nayeli stuttered helplessly. "No – yes – I don't know. Willow, what am I gonna do? A lot of the pain my mum feels isn't even due to her mother's death. I mean, she's grieving, the same as I am. But my grandma has been ill these past few months, and we knew she would pass on sooner rather than later. My mum was prepared to say goodbye – as prepared as one can be."

"But if that isn't what's causing most of her pain, then what is?"

"That my sister didn't stay after the burial to help," Nayeli admitted. "She and my mum aren't on good terms. Haven't been for a while. And it's driving my mother crazy. No matter how often she tries to call or goes by my sister's house, she rarely gets the chance to speak to her. My sister is blocking every attempt."

"And you?" Willow asked. "Are you on speaking terms with your sister?"

"No, but I don't mind it as much. Sure, it would be nice to have a sibling I can depend on. But because she's seven years older than me, we've never been close, not even when we were children. Her calling me 'boring' is probably the nicest thing she's ever said about me. So, it's not like I've lost something. But it's different for my mum."

"I can imagine," Willow said earnestly. "That would be tough for any mother."

"And I'm making it worse by not being there for her now," Nayeli said, suddenly regretting not helping with the estate.

"If you want to go and be with her, I understand. We can talk later. There's no rush."

"But there is, kind of. I'm only here for two weeks. After that, I need to go back to work. I won't be able to see you anymore. And I've got this gut feeling that I need to learn about all this stuff for some reason. That it's important. Or will be ..."

Feeling jittery, Nayeli sat up and crossed her legs underneath her. "Y'know what, Willow? Don't listen to me. I don't think I'm making any sense today. Lack of sleep and all that."

"Don't sell yourself short, my dear child," the tree responded. "If you have a gut feeling, you would be wise to listen to it."

"Why?"

"Because your intuition is a direct link to your higher self."

"My higher self?" Nayeli asked. "What's that?"

"It is essentially your soul-perspective, which stayed on the other side while you have this human experience here on Earth."

"Now you're speaking in riddles," Nayeli replied, drawing her brows up into her hairline. "You said that I'm a soul who incarnated here and now you say the total opposite. But how can I be both here and on the other side?"

"Sorry." The tree sniggered, not sounding sorry at all. "I believe I missed the chance to make one fact clear to you: namely that you hold two points of perspective from the moment you incarnate. An error I'll remedy immediately ..."

7. Mauve, the Giraffe

As Strix was flying over the African savannah, he knew it wouldn't be long until the gruelling heat of the day returned. Already, the unforgiving sun was peeking over the horizon from where it would climb steadily into the sky, frying everyone who wasn't careful enough. And so, he kept a lookout for a shady spot to rest.

Not being used to this climate, Strix had noticed over the past several days that he felt more exhausted than ever before in his life. It made him question whether it had been a clever idea to travel this far south. But his uncle had told him of so many wonders from his own journey that Strix had wanted to see those for himself: The animals with the long necks who were taller than a tree, and the grey giants with the huge ears and the noses that were so long they dragged on the ground.

Up till now, he hadn't met any of these creatures. But Strix hadn't given up hope yet on finding some. For now, he would be satisfied to find a sleeping place, though.

Just as Strix thought this, he spotted a few acacia trees. Veering from his course and heading for them, he tried out different branches before settling on one near the top, which he deemed high enough to keep him safe from any predators.

Sighing in content, Strix closed his eyes and slipped into a weird dream in which a giant mouse sprouted wings to hunt him. Seeing it swoop down on him, he tried to avoid it with some daring manoeuvres. But whatever he did, the mouse was too fast. And then it was upon him and touched his head with a dripping wet cloud, which it held in its paws.

Jerking awake at the strange sensation, Strix opened his eyes –

and almost fell off the branch in fright. For right in front of him was a huge brown eye, framed with long eyelashes, which belonged to a face that was twice as big as he was. Being frozen to the spot, Strix hoped that the creature wouldn't notice him if he didn't move a muscle. But his hope was shattered when the giant addressed him directly.

"Don't mind me," the large mouth said. "Didn't want to slobber all over you. But there were some tasty leaves beside you, and I had to have them."

Strix's emotions tumbled all over each other, and he wasn't sure which one would gain the upper claw in the end. There was immediate relief that the female animal who could have swallowed him with ease was obviously a herbivore and more interested in her vegan diet than trying out owl meat. Then there was disgust at being covered in the creature's spit. And finally incredulous wonder: how could her head be at his level when he was sitting at the top of a tall tree? Letting his gaze wander down, Strix saw the head merge into a neck, and then even more neck, before it transitioned into a torso and long, lean legs.

Closing his eyes and opening them a few times to ascertain it wasn't a dream or a mirage that was brought on by the African heat, Strix eventually realised what the image meant.

"Oh my gosh, you're a real giraffe! My uncle wasn't exaggerating! Animals with long necks as tall as trees, he said. And he was right. This is incredible!"

Looking around, Strix registered other giraffes standing around them, who were plucking leaves from the surrounding trees with their bluish tongues. It was at this point that he had a second insight: the female standing in front of him wasn't even one of the taller ones. She was a teenager.

"Yep, I'm real," the young giraffe replied, snorting. "And you have a lot to learn if you don't even know the most basic things."

"The most basic things?" Strix asked, undecided whether to be amused by the adolescent's energetic way of talking or annoyed at her over-confident tone.

"Of course," the juvenile said haughtily. "Like the fact that we giraffes are the best animal species in the world. Everyone worships us for our superior eyesight. The herd of zebras that joined us this week, for example, and the ostriches that ran with us prior to that. You, out of all animals, should know what I mean. You might be nothing more than a tiny bird, but you can fly and see the world from the same higher perspective as we can. Don't you think that's better than being a zebra or a wildebeest, who always eat dust when we gallop on?"

"And don't forget our conceit and arrogance," an older giraffe to their left chimed in. "Darling, how many times do I have to tell you that we are not *better* than anyone else, just different?"

"But Mum," the young giraffe responded petulantly, "we can see a lot farther, thanks to our long necks. And we can reach the highest, freshest leaves in the crowns of the trees, which no one else can snatch away."

"And we should be grateful for the abilities we have been given," her mother agreed. "But pride comes before a fall. And don't forget, we also have disadvantages that others do not have. Having a long neck and long legs makes it a real hassle to lie or bend down to get some rest or drink." The older giraffe sighed deeply. "And how often have I told you that no sense – sight, hearing or smell – can rival the one sense every animal calls their own? Intuition is the most important of them all. Because no matter how far you can see, your higher self has a clearer view. And trusting it over your physical senses is an important lesson you need to internalise if you want to reach my age."

"Yes, Mum," the adolescent responded glumly, not sounding pleased about the impromptu lecture.

Strix, meanwhile, was captivated by the interaction of the two giraffes, because he was gleaning so much new information. Cocking his head to the side, he was curious to hear what else he would learn. But to his disappointment, the young one's mind was already somewhere else.

Her bad mood after her mum's reprimand was being fast replaced by mischief as two other giraffes – who looked about the same age as her – galloped by. The juvenile swung around and joined them in their game of tag,

"I'm sorry."

Strix turned to the older giraffe to ask what she meant by those words. But before he could open his beak, she already explained herself. "My daughter gets ahead of herself sometimes. But she'll learn. As we all do. My name's Mauve, by the way."

"I'm sure she will," Strix agreed, introducing himself to this female giant who would have appeared threatening if it weren't for her gentle brown eyes, filled with wisdom and kindness.

Tearing his gaze away from her, he watched the three youthful giraffes chase each other around, running among their older relatives and some black-and-white-striped animals that looked similar to horses and which were cropping the dry grass.

"Are those the zebras your daughter mentioned?" he asked Mauve, pointing with one of his claws at the animals in question.

"Yes, they are zebras. And you really aren't from around here, are you?" The female giraffe laughed.

"No, not exactly," Strix replied. "I'm from the other side of the big ocean. But I'm not the first of my family to come here. My uncle visited these lands a couple of years ago. Did you meet him by chance?"

Strix described his uncle and watched for any signs of recognition, being slightly disappointed by her response. "No, I'm sorry. I can't remember meeting anyone like you. But there's an old elephant cow who lives around these parts with her herd. She knows everything and everyone and you could ask her ..."

Strix inclined his head in thanks. "I'll do that. But tell me more about yourself and your kind in the meantime. I'm always interested to learn about other species and how they live." Strix tilted his head questioningly. "These zebras, for example – do you do this regularly? Join up with others?"

Mauve nodded. "Africa is a dangerous place, especially for us herbivores. There are a lot of predators here. Needless to say, many of those can't kill a grown-up giraffe. But our calves are small enough to fall prey to them if we aren't careful. And we've learned that, sometimes, the survival of the fittest means to create symbiotic relationships with others."

"But what can others bring to the group that you don't have?" Strix wondered.

"Most predators, like lions, aren't easy to see in the long grass and their smell is strongest near the ground. Zebras have an excellent sense of smell, and if the wind is blowing the right way, they could spot them long before we do. In the end, every individual has some advantages they can play out, and we combine all our abilities to survive."

Mauve ripped off a few green leaves and chewed them slowly. "But what about you? What's your life like where you come from? Do you not join up with others?"

Happy to comply with the giraffe's request to swap stories, Strix told Mauve about his home and how vastly different the landscape was. Mauve listened intently, plucking a few more leaves from the branches around him and chewing them with relish.

"That sounds fascinating," the giraffe said as Strix ended his narrative. "And you're sure that you don't have deserts and savannahs there?"

"Not where I lived," Strix said. "But I haven't been to every corner of my country or the ones behind it. Which brings me to something else I wanted to ask... All this heat here might be almost bearable if there were enough shadowy places and more sources of water. But you aren't blessed with those, are you? Does it ever rain here?"

"We do have a rainy season," the giraffe explained. "And when the rain falls, it's usually heavy and lasts for some time. But otherwise? No. You need to know where to look for water."

"How do you bear that? If the birds I met on my way hadn't told me where to find some, I would have died of thirst a couple of days ago."

"We giraffes are actually able to live a long time without drinking. We take most of the liquid we need from the plants we eat. Otherwise, life here would be unbearable for sure. But even for us, it's getting harder. The weather has become unpredictable and it's getting hotter and dryer every other year. This year is especially bad as the last rainy season was the shortest since I was born ..."

"Great, which means I picked the wrong time to come here, right?"

Mauve was about to respond, but before she got the chance, another tall female in the group signalled that it was time to move on. The other giraffes fell in line behind her, intermingling with the zebras, who didn't seem to be bothered to trot beside these towering giants, which could probably kill them with one well-aimed kick.

Peering at Strix questioningly, Mauve lingered for a second longer. "Do you want to come with us? We could swap more stories about our lives."

On one claw, Strix wanted to take her up on the offer, but on the other claw, he knew he'd have to face the burning midday sun if he decided to join the giraffes. The idea scared him.

"We're heading for a river that carries water," Mauve continued, as though guessing his thoughts. "It's not far from here and you can freshen up there."

The prospect of bathing in cool water and drinking his fill of it was tipping the balance. Strix agreed.

Leaving the shade of the trees behind, he flew above Mauve and her daughter.

The first few minutes weren't as bad as he'd feared, and he talked amicably with the older giraffe. But the longer he flew, the more he noticed weariness settling in. The constant heat had taken quite a toll on his body, making Strix dizzy and weak. But he managed to hide the fact that he wasn't feeling good and concentrated on keeping his balance while following the herd through the savannah, which seemed to stretch on endlessly.

Finally, when Strix felt that he couldn't flap his wings one more time without falling from the sky, he saw a silvery blue line in the distance. The sight gave Strix enough hope that he mobilised the last reserves of strength he had.

As the blue salvation got closer, he was mesmerised by the burning sun glistening on the water's surface, making it look as if it consisted of millions of gems – only that water was much more valuable than any diamonds in the world.

To Strix's astonishment, the herd didn't immediately run towards the river, though. Instead, they halted and watched their surroundings carefully while the zebras smelled the air.

One of them in the front of the group gazed up at the tall giraffes interrogatively. "What do you say? Can we go on? We zebras can neither smell nor see any danger."

"We see nothing either," the female giraffe answered. "Not even trees or bushes where any predators could hide. It should be safe to proceed."

Despite their mutual consent, they all stood rooted to the spot. No one dared to make the first step.

Mauve put their reluctance into words. "It feels off, somehow. As if there's danger awaiting us. I think we shouldn't go further."

Strix would have groaned at that statement if it hadn't been for his parched throat. He could already visualise diving into the cool water, which was so close and yet so far away. But it wasn't only that he wanted to refresh himself. Strix knew that he had no other choice left. If he didn't get some water inside him soon, he wouldn't last another hour.

Desperate to convince the others of that fact, Strix cleared his throat. "That's all rubbish – there's no predator for miles around. One of us would have seen or heard them if there were any. Let's go. I'm sure everything will be fine. Aside from that, no one in their right mind would dare to attack a group as large as ours."

As though roused by his words, the whole herd talked across each other, their voices intermingling and reaching a crescendo.

"Can't you feel the threat?"

"I don't know why. I just KNOW there's something wrong."

"Look at the water – it's like there's an invisible shadow lying over it."

"I smell danger the closer we go."

"I'm gonna listen to my intuition. It's not safe there."

"Maybe we should move a few miles south."

Then, surprisingly, Mauve's daughter broke out of the group and headed towards the water. Dashing forward, she called back over her shoulder to the others. "I think the bird is right. There's no danger here."

"No!" Mauve called, meaning to run forward to block her daughter's path. But before she could do so, she was cut off by one of the zebras who broke out of the group and was galloping for the water. "I've had enough of all your worries," the black-and-white-striped animal called back. "You giraffes might be able to last a long time without water, but we can't."

A few others nodded and chased after their friend, creating a landslide of movement until all the zebras were running towards the river, keeping Mauve's daughter amid their bodies.

Although Strix had wanted to fly to the stream himself, he felt as if he was rooted to the spot – much like Mauve who gasped in fright, standing stock still as her daughter moved further away from her.

Then, a surge of adrenaline shot through her, setting her into action. Her hooves trampling the dry earth, she raced after the group to intercept her child.

Watching the proceedings warily, Strix was unsure what to do. But when another dizzy spell seized hold of him, he knew that the time for thought was over and the time for action had come. Flying as fast as he could towards the sparkling water, he just hoped that he would reach it before he lost consciousness.

Rallying all his strength, he overtook most of the zebras – apart from the first one who had reached the river bank.

At that moment, the quiet and peace of the scene showed itself to be the illusion it had been all along. The second the zebra lowered its head and its mouth touched the water, a green-scaled body shot out of it, its jaws clamping around the black-and-white-striped animal's neck and dragging it deeper in.

Hooting in terror, Strix catapulted himself away from the crocodile, which had forced the thrashing zebra below the surface, leaving the water churning, as if there was a fight taking place underneath it. But only for a short while, after which the river calmed as though nothing at all had happened.

His heart in his mouth, Strix gulped in air as he stared at the spot where the zebra had disappeared. That could have been him, he realised in shock. The second jolt of adrenalin set in when it dawned on Strix that there could be other crocodiles hiding in the water, which could snatch him out of the air at any moment. Squawking in fear, Strix flew higher and turned back the way he had come, flapping his wings as fast as he could to get away from the river and the danger it held. He was only marginally aware that the giraffes and zebras were emulating his actions. The whole herd, including Mauve and her daughter, were fleeing from the gruesome scene they'd witnessed and had soon overtaken him.

Strix tried to keep up with the group, but realised quickly that it was futile. His body was too weak from the scorching heat, and instead of gaining speed, he felt himself getting slower and slower.

Before long, the last members of the group had disappeared out of sight on the horizon, leaving nothing else but a dusty cloud behind.

Just then, another fit of dizziness overpowered Strix, this time even stronger, and he tumbled to the ground, half-unconscious. Seeing a small bush nearby that would provide at least a little shade, Strix staggered over to it and collapsed on the ground. But the shadow didn't help to ease the delirium that overtook his body and mind.

Strix felt as if he was burning up from the inside. Yet, at the same time, his body trembled, as if he was freezing. The world was coming in and out of focus, flickering as blackness closed in on him from all sides. The last functioning part of his brain told him he was having a heatstroke and that, if he survived it by some miracle, he'd surely die of thirst because he didn't have the strength to move anymore, let alone fly, to reach a source of water.

Strix hooted feebly for help and cursed his own decision to have come here. The African savannah was simply no place for an owl. But this knowledge, not to mention his regrets, came too late.

Strix lost consciousness and everything went dark around him.

Higher Self and Clair-Senses

"Oh no!" Nayeli cried when Willow stopped talking. "You can't end your story there. What happened to Strix? He's alive, right?"

"Patience, patience, my dear." Willow laughed. "That's something you'll find out soon enough. But one thing that I can guarantee you is that Strix is okay – whether or not he survived."

"I know he is," Nayeli conceded, thinking that it was those who remained behind in this 3D reality who suffered, not the ones who passed on. "But I still hope that Strix made it."

"Maybe he did," Willow said mysteriously, a small smile evident in the tree's voice.

"You are terrible," Nayeli complained. "Why is it so difficult to get a straight answer out of you?"

The willow tree only chuckled, and Nayeli shook her head good-naturally. "Fine, keep your secrets for now. But at least tell me this – what did you mean about the two points of perspectives you mentioned before? I thought that when we incarnate, our soul comes here into this body and that's it?"

"That couldn't be further from the truth," the tree replied earnestly. "And I'm sorry if I gave you that impression. No, your soul always stays on the other side and never comes here. Instead, it sends out an energetic stream of consciousness, which incarnates into a body. You! And just like that, you are two points of perspective at the same time. On one hand, you have your human perspective, including your ego, which is also called your lower self or temporal perspective. It is created when you are born and ceases to exist when you cross back over. And the second perspective is your higher perspective or higher self, which is also called your eternal or soul perspective. This is your immortal soul."

"So, my soul isn't here? I'm an extension of it while it remains behind?" Nayeli mulled this over.

"Correct. You were right when you said that we'd be crazy if we left a state of unconditional love and oneness behind for this dual reality where we perceive ourselves as separate. And since our souls aren't insane, they do stay there. Only, your ego perspective isn't aware of this happening, as most of you humans forget all about your soul and the other side. You see this temporal aspect of yourself and this reality you live in as everything that exists."

Nayeli watched a butterfly dance between the flowers. "I take it that my soul has the benefit of being aware of both perspectives, though? My higher self and my lower self? How can I imagine this? Is my soul sitting in front of something akin to a TV screen and watching my life while being aware of its own separate existence?"

"No." Willow sniggered. "Since your soul is energy and has neither eyes nor ears, it can't *watch* you. Instead, it feels the energy that you send out."

Nayeli leaned her head back against the tree's trunk. "So, what's the deal with this higher self? Is it better than my ego-self? Does it have more wisdom because it isn't exposed to this 3D reality, or what?"

"No. Both points of your perspective are valuable. Naturally, your eternal perspective has a higher awareness when it comes to your soul-path. It knows what goals you planned prior to incarnating here and what lessons are to come. Its knowledge and wisdom are based on a whole lot of factors that your ego-perspective can't see. But it's not all-knowing. And it's not here like your temporal self, which is experiencing everything first-hand. In the end, they are both deeply invested in your well-being and are acting in your best interest. Since your ego perspective is a part of your human self and since you are an extension of your own higher self, them hurting you would automatically entail hurting themselves."

"And that means what?"

"That both aspects continuously give you advice. Your ego does this most often via an internal voice you hear inside your head, while your higher self uses your intuition, which comes in many forms. Through a strong gut feeling or as yet another internal voice, for example."

"But when they both talk to me inside my head, how do I know, which one is speaking?" Nayeli asked, feeling lost.

"By listening to what they say. Your ego's overriding need is survival. It emphasises everything that's negative and could be a threat to you. It says things like 'don't do this as you aren't smart enough' or 'don't get your hopes up because no one will ever love you'. Meanwhile, your higher self comes from a place of love. Its voice sounds positive and uplifting, saying things like 'you got this' or 'trust in yourself'."

"And when I've made the distinction, then what?"

"Once you've tuned in to both voices, your job is to decide, based on your free will, whose advice you want to follow."

Nayeli frowned. "There's a problem in that case. Because I can hear my ego chattering away inside my mind all the time, telling me what to worry about or narrating things I've done wrong. But the positive voice is a faint whisper at best. Sometimes I can't hear it at all. Honestly, Willow, if my soul wants me to know stuff this badly, why can't it find a way to say it more clearly? Why must it let everything be translated through my subtle bodies until it's nothing more than an obscure belly rumble, which could mean anything, or a whisper in my mind that's drowned out by my ego? That's not helpful! I'm bad at solving mysteries, and trying to figure out what my thoughts and the sensations in my body could possibly stand for, is one of the hardest ones to date."

Willow inclined its crown knowingly. "That's because, over the years, you humans have forgotten how to listen to your intuition."

Nayeli squinted at the tree. "Another thing we have forgotten? How many more are there?"

The willow tree ignored her question in favour of explaining things further. "Think back to how you humans grow up. Your parents and the other people in your life teach you to rely on your physical senses to ascertain whether or not something is accurate. The invisible friend you had as a small child doesn't belong in that category. But the green, rolling hills covering the land do, alongside the songs of the birds, the salty sea air, the sweetness of a fruit and the soft texture of a blossom. Over the years, you are being taught that only what you can perceive is real, that only what you can prove scientifically is true. And just like that, you don't trust seeing auras or hearing spirits anymore because no adult around you can, until you too have forgotten all about it. By learning your human language, you are unlearning the universal language and become blind and deaf to everything that's outside your limited physical awareness.

"Losing access to your intuition and the channels it comes through is just one step in that process. The inner voice of your higher self becomes fainter and fainter with every year and gets overshadowed by other voices telling you what's right and wrong: the voices of your parents and family, the voices of your teachers, friends and neighbours, the voices from strangers in the media and the voice of your own ego ... until it's nothing else but a faint whisper that you can ignore. Or that you can't hear at all anymore. It's the same as when you'd chose to not use your legs for a decade. If you tried to walk after such a long time, you wouldn't even be able to make it across the room without help. You'd need to strengthen your muscles first. Likewise, your intuition needs to be strengthened by practise to have access to it again."

Nayeli stretched out on her back, letting the warm summer sun fall on her face through a gap in Willow's foliage, and folded her arms underneath her head. "What do you mean by the channels my intuition comes through?"

"Your clair-senses, of course," the tree said, as if those words alone were enough to answer her question.

Nayeli wrinkled her forehead in thought. "Clair-senses? I've never heard of those. What are they?"

"Then let me extend on them. There are several clair-senses, some of which are similar to your human senses. But, instead of perceiving the physical world, you use your clair-senses to perceive the higher dimensions beyond this reality. The four main clair-senses are clairvoyance, which can be translated as clear seeing, clairaudience, which is clear hearing, clairsentience, which is clear feeling and claircognizance, which is clear knowing. Each of these senses uses a different method to receive the information we need. With clairvoyance, for example, you can see a message as a picture or as a moving image or as letters in your mind's eye. If you use your clairaudience ability, you could hear an internal voice, music or other sounds. If you use clairsentience, you feel the answer as an emotion or a sensation in your body. And if you use claircognizance, you *know* what the message is, without being able to figure out how it came to you. There are a few more clair-senses as well, like clair-salience, which means clear smelling, and clairtangency, which is clear touching. But those aren't used as often."

"And which clair-sense should I concentrate on first when I want to relearn how to use them?"

"There is no superior clair-sense, my dear. Maybe some people pride themselves on having developed a specific one but that's nonsense, if you ask me. Every spiritual sense is as good as the next, and the best one for each of us is the one that comes most naturally. So, the answer will be different for everyone."

"But some of these senses work better for us than others?"

"Yes, at least in the beginning. Based on your life path and the abilities that go hand in hand with it, most humans have one or two dominant clair-senses, which will be the easiest to access – usually the ones that correspond to your best developed 3D sense. In other words, if you have great eyesight, you might have a talent for clear-seeing, musicians might have a dominant clear hearing sense and empaths might have an advantage with the clear feeling sense. Your higher self, meanwhile, doesn't care, which sense you use. It will use any form of communication you can understand, as it is able to send messages via all of these channels."

"But we can learn to use all of our clair-senses in time? Not merely our dominant ones?" Nayeli continued to pelt Willow with questions.

"Sure. With a little practise, you can use them all. These are your natural, soul-given communication tools, after all. But I'd advise you to first focus on those that you are predisposed towards. Because when you've mastered one, learning to use the others will come that much faster. Imagine the senses as a fountain with four levels. Your most dominant clair-sense is the top level, which is the smallest basin, and your least dominant clair-sense is the bottom level, which is the largest basin. Now, to use a clair-sense, you need to fill the corresponding level with water. If you started at the bottom, you'd need a long time to fill that large basin, and once you'd managed this, you still wouldn't have access to any of your other clair-senses, as their basins would remain empty. But if you start at the top with the smallest basin, it would be full in a short amount of time, and the water would spill over into the basin beneath it, making it a lot easier to learn them all."

"That makes sense," Nayeli said. "But how do I find out what my most dominant clair-sense is? I neither have spectacular eyesight nor hearing. And, as far as I can remember, I've never seen an aura, nor would I know the first thing about talking to a spirit."

Only moments after she'd said this, Nayeli became aware of a faint gurgling sound she couldn't place. It wasn't coming from the stream rushing over the pebbles or from the bumblebee flying past her head.

Sitting up curiously, Nayeli laid a hand on the tree's trunk to support herself while ascertaining the noise's direction. The moment it touched the rough bark, she felt the vibrations underneath her skin. Startled, she tore her hand away from the tree and gaped at Willow.

"Are you laughing at me?" Nayeli asked incredulously.

"I would never do that," Willow defended itself, still rumbling with suppressed laughter. "I'm simply finding this situation funny. You wouldn't deny an old tree a bit of joy, would you?"

Nayeli felt defensive as she looked at the weeping willow.

"What's so funny about what I said?" she asked testily.

The tree continued to chortle. "I think, my dear, that there's been some miscommunication between us. And that's my fault, not yours. I'm sorry."

"What miscommunication? Willow, I've no idea what you are talking about."

"I know, which is why it's high time I told you a story about my old friend Oak ..."

"Who's Oak?" Nayeli interrogated the tree. "I don't see an oak here. You're the only tree on this meadow. Or is Oak another bird-friend of yours?"

"No, certainly not – who in their right mind would name a bird Oak?" Willow giggled. "No, no, it was a tree. I might be the only one standing here now, but this was not always the case. Do you see that green bush at the bottom of the hill behind me? If you go over there, you can see its remains."

Standing up, Nayeli followed Willow's directions and, sure enough, found the tree stump as Willow had stated, hidden behind the bush that now grew there. The wood of it was black, as if scorched.

Nayeli walked back into the cavern of Willow's low-hanging branches. "What happened to your friend? Why is there nothing else but a stump left?"

"A couple of years ago, lightning struck the oak tree and it went on fire."

"I'm so sorry for your loss," Nayeli said.

"Loss? What are you talking about? Oak's pestering me from the other side continuously."

Not knowing if Willow was making a joke, Nayeli wasn't sure

how to react to these words and chose to stay silent.

"It's true," the tree added brightly, obviously sensing her discomfort. "I can communicate with Oak as easily now as I could before. For you humans, it might take a bit of an acclimatisation process to talk with anyone in the spirit world since you're accustomed to looking each other into the eyes and being able to touch. Having that taken away can be a huge adjustment. But for me, as a tree, it's not something I needed to get used to – Oak and I stood so far apart that our branches didn't touch each other, not even when the wind bent us."

"Wait, Willow," Nayeli said, surprised. "We can all talk to those who passed before us? Not just people born with a psychic gift, but everyone? Are you saying I have a chance to talk to my grandma while I'm still alive? Cause I'd love to do that!"

"Naturally you can," the tree replied, making it sound like the most obvious thing in the world. "There are techniques anyone can use to connect to those on the spirit planes."

Nayeli poked the tree impatiently. "Well, what are they? How do I use them? What do I need to know? Is this about using the clair-senses? Or is there more to it? Don't keep me waiting here."

Willow wagged its branches. "If you stopped asking a hundred and one questions, I could have already started with the story, which might explain some of them."

Grinning at being called out, Nayeli pretended to zip her mouth closed. "You can start. I'll be quiet. Promise!"

True to her word, she settled back down onto the grass while Willow's voice echoed over the meadow, carrying her into the tree's past.

Interlude A: Willow

My story begins when I was a little shoot. My first conscious memory is of a strong wind bending me so far that my budding leaves touched the ground. It was scary to be exposed to such a storm. But I distinctly remember that, when it died down and the grey clouds passed, everything around me felt fresh and lively.

The brook had swollen with all the rain and rushed by me, full of energy. And the birds all came out of their cover and sang to the sun.

This was also the first time I noticed Oak. The tree was groaning as it shook off the rain clinging to its leaves. It was a gnarled, grumpy-looking tree, but behind its surliness, it had a big heart and a kind, funny personality to match it.

The oak tree soon became one of my best friends and confidants. Not astonishing, considering we were the only trees living in this meadow. The deer who venture out of the woods to graze are merely visitors who disappear once they're sated, the mice scurry into their holes in the ground and the bees fly back to their hives. But Oak stayed here, like me.

I talked to the old tree every day and got to know it better with each season. I learned about its dreams and beliefs and its opinions and aspirations while sharing my own feelings and thoughts.

In the meantime, life around us was ever-changing. The rabbits were raising one litter after another, and the caterpillars were transforming into beautiful, colourful butterflies.

Naturally, Oak and I changed too, in accordance with the seasons. In the autumn we would lose our leaves and grow new ones in spring. But since it was always the same, year after year after year, it eventually lost its appeal, and I was fast becoming envious of all the animals around me: the squirrels that could hop from branch to branch and the birds that could fly wherever they wanted, whenever they felt like it.

At first, this feeling was nothing else but a faint whisper, but as the years went by, it grew louder and louder, making me increasingly aware of my roots, which bind me to the earth.

Then, one spring day, the migratory birds came back from their winter quarters, and a few ducks rested near the brook, directly beside my hill. They talked to each other about everything they had seen and experienced. They talked about the thick jungle they had overflown, where the light filtering through the treetops casts a green sheen on all life below. They talked about the mountains in the distance, with their snow caps that reached up so high into the sky that they appeared to touch the white clouds. And they talked about all the strange species that occupied these regions. They talked with such passion about it all that I could imagine it in my mind's eye.

Compared to them, my life seemed empty and hollow. I felt a huge desire to do all that they did and more. I wanted to fly, raise a family and swim in the cool waters. I wanted to travel the world. I wanted to know what the ocean looked and smelled like, and I wanted to see the endless fields of flowers from a bird's eye perspective. But I couldn't. My roots were my prison.

In the coming weeks, I became depressed. I asked myself why I was here since my life was boring and pointless. I knew, logically, that this wasn't the case. I had learned from Oak that it was important for trees to exist – especially for humans and animals. Without us trees and other plants that provide oxygen through photosynthesis, none of you could survive for long on this planet. But that wasn't a satisfactory enough reason for me. Not anymore.

The depression sank so deep under my bark that I felt the life force running through me lessen. It felt like my energy was stagnating. But the worst of it all was that Oak wasn't talking to me any longer. I didn't know why and questioned the tree's silence. Had I upset it with my desire to be something different? Was it offended that I didn't value us trees? Had it got fed up with my negative moods?

No matter the cause, Oak's silence hurt. And the more I tried to speak with the older tree and didn't receive any answer, the more depressed I became. After some time, I felt so drained that I didn't have the energy to draw water up through my roots any longer. Which, slowly but surely, showed. My bark began to look dry, my twigs hung down more than they usually do, and my leaves began to turn brown. Later, Oak told me that everything indicated I would dry out from within and that I wouldn't make it.

But then, one day, something inside me rebelled. Part of me wasn't ready to move on to the other side, and it put up a good fight. I suddenly knew that I had chosen this life to fulfil a specific purpose. I didn't yet know *what* it was, but the knowledge that I *did* have a reason to come here made all the difference to me. I took my remaining strength and drank deeply through my roots.

It was only the first step, but it was the most important one. Over the next few weeks, I got better. And then, one day, I could hear Oak again. The tree had never stopped talking to me; I just hadn't been able to hear it because my energetic frequency had been very low. From that day on, Oak was there for me. The old tree was a constant source of help and comfort whenever the effort to continue living seemed to be too much. Step by step, I recovered, and over time I felt a sense of happiness returning.

Speaking to Oak again, I hoped the other tree could help me figure out the reason behind my existence. But when I voiced my idea that maybe my soul had intended for me to be felled and for my wood to be processed into something useful, like paper for books – books that could help transform people's lives and guide them on their healing journey – Oak just shook its crown uncomprehendingly at me, saying this was unlikely as the wood from willows is generally used for other things, like furniture. Still, it remained the sole reason for coming here I could think of.

That is, until years later Strix stumbled into my life. He was a fledgling at the time, who had only learned to fly days ago. We connected instantly, despite us being so different. And when I learned that he had the same desire that I'd had as a small tree, namely to someday travel the world, it gave rise to an idea. The idea to collect his stories and experiences and to pass on all his knowledge to others while adding my own wisdom to it.

In hindsight, I'm grateful that this was the purpose I chose for this incarnation. And I'm beyond glad I persevered long enough to experience these days with you, my dear Nayeli.

"Me too," Nayeli said forcefully. Scrambling up from the ground and wrapping her arms around the tree's trunk as far as they reached, she rested her cheek against the rough bark. "I'm glad because otherwise we would have never met and I don't know how I would have handled this situation without your help. I've learned a whole lot from you already, and I don't think I'd be as centred without your guidance."

"Thank you, my dear," Willow said, sounding choked up. "It means a lot to hear that I've been able to make a positive difference in your life."

A thought came to Nayeli at these words, and a worry line appeared on her forehead. "Willow?" she asked carefully.

"Hmm-hmm?" the tree replied.

"I stand by everything I just said. But have you really made your peace with being a tree? Or are you still envious of other species sometimes? I don't want to open any old wounds by coming and going as I wish, while you have to stay here. Damn, I shouldn't have reminded you of that. I'm sorry. Let's talk about something else, shall we?"

Fidgeting nervously, Nayeli looked up into the tree's crown.

"Don't you worry. I don't do regrets anymore. I was wrong to compare myself with others, who have chosen an entirely different path, and to recognise only their blessings, not my own. Plus, I finally did get to travel myself – if not with my body, then at least in my mind. And seeing everything through Strix's eyes is amazing. It might even be better than journeying alone. For what could be more fulfilling than to share your life experiences with a close friend?

Strix and I complete each other perfectly. He carries me away to faraway lands, while I'm the grounding presence in his life when his head is too far in the clouds."

Willow extended its branches. "Maybe in another incarnation I will travel for myself. But for now, this is exactly what I want and need."

"Good." Nayeli breathed out, relieved to notice the sincerity in the tree's voice. And as a wide grin broke out on her face she added cheekily: "I guess I'm allowed to come back then?"

"What?" the willow tree asked, mock offended. "You want to leave already? I can feel the sun burning brightly on my leaves. It can't be later than midday ..."

Nayeli sat back down demonstratively. "I didn't say I would leave right now. I have nowhere else to be today – and I definitely won't go before you answer my question."

"Which one?"

"Why did you laugh at me earlier? I still don't get it."

"I didn't laugh at you, but with you," the tree corrected her.

"Whatever you want to call it to make yourself feel better," Nayeli joked. "Anyway, you said we had a miscommunication. But nothing in this story explains this. And there was no mention of any technique for talking to someone on the other side, either. That's not like you. Usually, your tales include the things you want to teach me. But in this one? Nada, niente, nothing."

Willow snorted loudly. "But it did clarify that I'm a tree, did it not?"

"Yes?" Nayeli said.

"Nayeli, you said that you can't use any of your clair-senses. Which raises the question – how do hear what I say?"

"Um," Nayeli said, blinking in surprise. "Normally? Like I hear everyone else in my life? I mean, your voice is kinda strange. Not strange in a bad way, mind you, just different. It's, I don't know, as if it's not my ears that pick up your words but my brain. If that makes sense?"

"It makes perfect sense," the tree said. "Because we're talking telepathically to each other. We are talking in the same way in which I talk to Oak or Strix."

"We are … what?" Nayeli asked, confused by that revelation. "But I don't know how to do that. As I said, I'm talking normally to you."

"I take it you're speaking out loud then?" Willow asked in a strained voice, as if trying to keep from laughing further.

Nayeli nodded, feeling insecurity settle into her being because the tree was making such a big deal out of this.

Willow made a sound that resembled a cough, which Nayeli suspected was the tree's way to disguise its mirth. "My sweet Nayeli. In that case, you should be glad that I'm standing remote and that there are barely any passersby. Because let me tell you, they would think you highly weird for talking to yourself."

"What?" Nayeli asked, perplexed, her mind resembling a maze in which the information went missing as soon as it arrived.

Despite continuing to chuckle, Willow explained the matter patiently. "I'm a tree. I have no ears to hear with and no mouth to speak to you. Which is why we are speaking energetically to each other – telepathically, from mind to mind."

"You're implying that I've made an ass out of myself by talking aloud this whole time? Great!" Nayeli said put-upon, then realised that she had said even this aloud.

Deciding to put the tree to the test, she made a conscious effort to not say anything and thought of a simple question to ask. She settled on 'What's the name of your owl friend?'

Partly to her surprise and partly to her gratification, Willow only reacted to her earlier outburst, though. "You didn't know any better. And I wasn't a very good teacher, since I neglected to mention this lesson before."

Nayeli ignored that comment and harrumphed. "Didn't you hear what I asked afterwards?" she questioned out loud.

"No, sorry," Willow said. "What was it?"

"I asked what your owl friend's name is – telepathically. And you didn't hear me! But now that I'm speaking out loud again, you can. This means I'm right and you're wrong. I'm not able to communicate via my mind."

"Then how do you explain that I, a tree, can hear and answer you?"

Nayeli shrugged. "You're the expert here."

"And I do have an explanation for what you just experienced," Willow said. "After all, talking telepathically to someone doesn't lead to the recipient hearing all your thoughts."

"They don't? You can't?" Nayeli asked, confused.

The tree answered to the negative. "Telepathy isn't identical to mind-reading, but rather a communication tool, which you use to send messages to another person in the form of energy. The recipient only receives the messages clearly when you intend for them to be heard."

"But I did concentrate on what I wanted to say."

"Then do something real quick for me," Willow responded. "First, think about a fact you know. Merely the fact, nothing else. Then think of a second fact and direct it my way – maybe by imagining it reaching me like a stream of light would. You'll find that the second attempt will feel different since it's directed outward, unlike the first one, which is directed inward."

Sitting silently, Nayeli did as ordered.

Willow's response came shortly after. "I received the message that the skirt you are wearing today is blue."

"That was my second thought," Nayeli said, surprised. "The one I directed at you. You were right all along. I don't need to speak out loud to talk to you … Oh my God, I can talk telepathically!" Jumping up because she couldn't contain her excitement, Nayeli smiled from ear to ear and pumped her fist into the air. Only then did she realise that she must look even stranger than when she had seemingly soliloquised while speaking to a tree.

Sitting back down on the grass, Nayeli adjusted her skirt. "This is amazing!" she gushed. "I was friends with twins as a kid, and they said they could talk telepathically to each other. I was always envious of them and wanted to do it myself. And now I can!"

Willow laughed at her antics. "And you're doing a damn fine job of it. Especially considering you're still new to rediscovering your talent. Telepathy might be your true soul-language and is accessible to every human being at any point in their lives, but it often takes some time to remember how to use it again in a conscious manner."

Nayeli was about to ask why, when the tree forestalled her.

"The easy part is to send out messages. Everyone can do that. In fact, everyone *is* doing it all day, every day. What you humans have trouble with, however, is receiving energetic messages and information from others or the spirit world. Because your senses are too overloaded and cluttered. This makes using your clair-senses – via which telepathic messages arrive – difficult. You need to practise to quiet your mind's chattering first."

"By learning how to meditate and be present," Nayeli filled in.

"Correct," the tree replied. "You don't need to relearn telepathy, because the ability has never left you. You just need to remember how to switch your mind into receiving mode, so to speak, and learn how to listen again."

Nayeli grinned in enthusiasm. "So, are there any limits to speaking telepathically? Why haven't I rediscovered this talent before now? What if I want to talk to someone whose language I don't understand? And ..."

The tree laughed and halted her flow of words. "That many questions at once?"

"Sorry," Nayeli responded, not sounding sorry at all. "But I can't help it. This is all too interesting and new to me, and I want to know everything."

"And you will. To answer your last question first – you can use telepathy with anyone, even if they don't speak your language, and vice versa."

"But I'm still thinking in English, talking out loud or not," Nayeli argued.

"That's true. You're thinking in one language. But what you send out is nothing else but the energy of the message and the intention behind it. It's not the words themselves. Meaning, anyone can receive the information, and it will be translated into a language they can understand."

"Wow, that's amazing," Nayeli breathed. "Telepathy should be taught in schools over the planet, in that case. It would help bring a lot of people together and get rid of some barriers between us. I can't believe how easy it would be for people to understand each other better."

"Not so fast, my dear, not so fast," Willow said. "Understanding someone is much more complex than simply perceiving the words they say. And you humans have a hard time with that lesson, no matter if you speak the same language or not."

"How so?" Nayeli asked, bewildered.

"I'll gladly explain this to you in detail. But first, let me get back to another question of yours that I've yet to answer."

"Which one?" Nayeli asked, having all but forgotten what she had wanted to know, with all the news being revealed today.

"You asked," the tree said, "why you haven't used telepathy before. But you *have* used it before you met me."

Just when Nayeli was about to disagree with Willow, the tree briskly continued. "Not consciously, of course. But humans *do* use telepathy to some extent in their everyday life. For example, when you think of someone and then they call you, that was you picking up telepathically on their intention. Likewise, when you say the same thing as someone else at the exact same time. Or when, on the way home from work, you stop to get some ice cream, and your partner tells you that they've fancied ice cream all day."

The tree hummed. "I've noticed that a lot of humans expect a grand revelation when they start to actively use their intuition or telepathy. As if it needs to show up with fireworks and fanfares. But these natural talents come along more like a quiet whisper. You might even feel a bit let down by how unspectacular they are. And by how many times you've used these skills in the past without knowing it."

"That's amazing!" Nayeli said, dumbfounded, remembering a host of similar situations from her own life. She was so lost in thought that she jumped when Willow mumbled behind her.

"Anyway, was there anything else you wanted to learn about telepathy or should I move on to the next topic, as promised?"

"Can you lie when using telepathy?" Nayeli blurted out.

There was a short pause, followed by a snort from the tree. "Why? Do you want to? But to answer your question … it's difficult. Since you are aware that your message is a lie, you'd send an energetic vibration alongside it that's divergent to the content within. Thus, someone who's well-versed in this natural soul-language will immediately know that you're not telling the truth."

Nayeli cocked her head. "That all sounds hella complicated."

"Not when you've had some practise," the tree answered. "Everything becomes easier with training."

"That's true," Nayeli admitted. "But how can I practise telepathy once I need to go back home? If I don't have you around to talk to? Because I bet my mum and friends wouldn't believe it was possible, let alone try it out."

"Then why don't you practise with someone else who hasn't forgotten how to use telepathy and uses it all day, every day? I can promise that, aside from me, there are many others who would love to speak to you, too."

Curiosity and doubt filled Nayeli in equal measure. "Who?"

"That, my dear, is a question I'll gladly answer … after telling you another story that you might be interested in."

8. Cocoa, the Wild Ass

The darkness around Strix lifted somewhat and he became aware of a gently swaying motion – back and forth, back and forth, back and forth – in a rhythm that was very calming. He tried to open his eyes but didn't have the strength to manage it. Instead, he let himself drift deeper into the weird half-world surrounding him, not fully awake but not completely unconscious either.

Pictures emerged in front of his closed eyelids. At first, they showed random scenes that didn't make much sense, but then they pieced together into a clearer image. Or was it a memory? Strix thought he remembered the landscape. It was one he had travelled through shortly after he had left Plum, the warthog, behind.

***

Strix had travelled south-east, and the countryside had become rockier, the grass sparser and the air dryer. There had been nothing below him to catch his eye, no dab of colour that could disrupt the vast brown plains.

After flying like this for an hour or more, Strix was getting bored by the sombre wasteland, wishing himself anywhere but here. Or alternately wishing that he had, at least, a companion to talk to.

Luckily the universe was in his favour today because, when he turned his head to look behind him, he saw some movement on the horizon. Hope rose within him. Altering his course slightly, Strix aligned his path with the cloud of dust coming his way.

Once the group of animals drew near, his first thought was that they must be donkeys with their long ears. But he'd never seen some with black-and-white-striped legs before.

"Hey!" Strix called out in a friendly manner as he flew above the herd. "Would you mind if I accompanied you? I feel like I've been traveling alone forever."

"If you have nothing better to do," a shaggy female answered, "you're more than welcome to join us – if you can keep up, that is."

Singling her out as the chattiest of the bunch, Strix dropped back until he was level with her.

"I sure can," Strix said confidently. "I'm as swift as the wind when I want to be. My name's Strix and I'm a short-eared owl. And you are ...?"

"Cocoa, one of the last wild asses," she answered, giving him the once-over. "What brings a strange bird like you here, out of all places? I don't think I've ever seen one of your kind in my life."

"That's because I'm not from here. And most owls stick closer to home. But the longer I travel around, the more I question their decision. The world is an exciting place with lots of adventures to discover, and I wouldn't want to miss a single one of them!"

"Adventures?" Cocoa huffed. "If someone is saying the words 'adventures', what they really mean is trouble. Trust me. I'm talking from experience. And my experiences also say that it's best to stay as far away from any excitement as possible if you value your life. Familiar surroundings and routines are the way to go. Not to mention staying with your herd."

Strix quickly rejected that advice. "No, thank you. I've had enough boredom and routine to last me a lifetime. And before I go to the other side, I want to use the time I have here to its fullest."

Throwing him curious looks, the other members of Cocoa's herd snorted derisively but didn't otherwise respond. Unlike Cocoa who wasn't inclined to keep her opinion to herself.

"Then you're flying straight into a disaster, my plumaged friend," she retorted bitterly. Her eyes held a far-off look, as though she remembered something that had happened a long time ago.

"Why don't you tell me about your experiences?" Strix asked.

Cocoa shook her head to get rid of a few persistent flies. "All right, I'll tell you. Maybe it will be a lesson for you to stay out of any adventures in the future and to heed your species' habit of not travelling too far ..."

"Yes, yes," Strix said hurriedly, eager to hear her tale. "Of course, if you don't get to it soon, the suspense will kill me faster than any danger I could call upon myself." The last was said with a twinkle in his eyes and Cocoa's nostrils flared as she snorted in amusement.

"Keep your feathers on, I'm already starting," she said and drew in a deep breath. "Back in the day, I was still young and naive and totally clueless. I had just weaned from my mum when my herd came close to a human settlement. It's hard to avoid them, as you surely know, because humans are practically everywhere. They're taking over the land bit by bit and boxing us in. Anyway, my herd was drinking at a waterhole near them, and I sneaked off to the humans' living boxes. To my surprise, I saw a female ass standing in front of one box. But something about her was strange. She didn't look quite like the rest of us, and her accent, when she talked to me, was unlike anything I had ever heard. Later, I learned that she wasn't a wild ass at all but a donkey – our cousins who live with humans. But at the time I approached her I didn't know that, and this was my downfall.

"I had dared to advance too close, and suddenly there were humans all around me, cutting off the way back to my herd. They had some long, lifeless brown snakes in their hands, which they threw over me.

"I was in a panic and screaming for my mum. But before anyone could help me, one of the rough snakes was tossed over my neck and I was wrenched to the ground. The humans pressed me down and laid even more of these snakes around me until I couldn't move at all."

***

The grey fog dispersed, and Strix realised that there seemed to be a big fleshy snake wound around his middle, keeping his wings pressed to his sides. Trying to fight the tightness off, he soon had to admit defeat because the grip was too powerful and he was too weak to escape from it.

And so, when a soft voice told him to relax, and that everything was going to be fine, he was ready to follow the demand, sinking back into the murky waters of his memory and Cocoa's tale.

***

"Lying on the ground, I saw my family galloping off. My mother was in the midst of the herd, and the other members were pushing her along. To this day, I can hear the pain in her voice as she screamed for me when she was forced to leave me behind."

Cocoa swallowed noticeably. "I can't remember much of the following hours. I was in shock. I felt despair set in, as everything around me lumped together into a dark, foreboding cloud that hung above my head, threatening to crush me. The humans had taken me to a confined space. It was so small that I could barely turn around without touching the walls of my prison. There was no sky to be seen, no moon, no stars and no wind to caress my skin.

"Even worse than being held prisoner against my will was the hollow ache of loneliness I felt within me, though, after having been torn from everyone I loved. When I couldn't take being isolated any longer, I began to talk to the donkeys in the prison cells beside me. But this only drove the fact home further that there was no one who got the pain I was going through. These donkeys held such different beliefs and ideologies, and it made me feel like an intruder, an outsider, someone who didn't belong with them. Someone who didn't belong with anyone anymore.

"I don't remember clearly when I noticed the human foal standing outside my prison for the first time, but one day he was there. He wasn't nearly as tall as my other jailors but smelled similar to the men who had torn me away from my mum and my herd. So, I ignored him the same as the other two-legged whenever they brought me food. And I also continued to ignore him when he started to climb into my prison to sit with me.

"The female donkey in the cell next to me, the one I had seen outside on the day I had been captured, told me how stupid I was not to make friends with him. But I didn't care about her opinion, as she had been born among humans and was being brainwashed from an early age. She couldn't grasp the fact that they're evil. Quite the opposite. She actually enjoyed their care and attention. She was so attached to them that she even let them ride her or place loads on her back when they were travelling. She said that it made her feel useful. When I told her what it was like to run free beneath the endless sky and being able to go wherever you want, she responded it was safer and more comfortable here among the humans, and that she wouldn't swap her life for anything in the world.

"To this day, I seek to understand her point of view but can't fully comprehend it. And back then, I definitely couldn't. Just like the donkeys didn't understand me and why I was suffering ..."

"And how did you escape that prison?" Strix butted in, captivated by the story that was unfolding in front of his eyes. "It couldn't have been easy."

The herd of wild asses had stopped on the open plains to graze some sparse blades of grass, which sprouted from between boulders. Cocoa followed suit and threw Strix a dirty glance for so rudely interrupting her. Pointedly ignoring him and his question for the time being, she plucked some of the meagre grass and chewed it particularly slowly. Only when she had kept him in suspense for some time did she deign to respond.

"It was actually impossible," Cocoa answered gravely.

"But you must have managed it somehow, or otherwise you wouldn't be here, telling me about your time there," Strix pressed, baffled.

"No, I didn't escape," Cocoa answered earnestly. "But I'll come to that in a bit. First, let me get back to the little human foal. Cause he had a big surprise in store for me ...

"One day, the human foal was sitting with me again, as still and silent as always. But on this day, my patience had run out, and I forgot all my intentions to continue to ignore him. And, in my anger, I also forgot that humans can't understand us animals. Thus, I raised my head to look him straight in the eye and told him in no uncertain terms to leave me the heck alone.

"What I hadn't counted on, however, was his reaction. The human foal crossed his arms defiantly, telling me he would stay. I had already begun to turn my head away to stare at the wall again when I realised what had happened. I froze. 'Don't be surprised,' the human foal told me as I turned to him once more, a small smile twisting his features. 'Of course I can hear you. And I can see that you are in a lot of pain.' The message was so clear in my mind that I briefly doubted my sanity. I had never heard of a human who could speak our language, but there he was, sitting right in front of me. And as if a spell had been broken, he talked to me – not in his strange human language but in ours. He told me that he could empathise with my loneliness because he had lost his mother, too. And that he missed her every day.

"The whole situation was beyond weird, and I couldn't help but listen to him. The longer I did, the more my heart opened when I heard about all the suffering he had endured at his age.

For the first time since my imprisonment, I felt connected to someone again, and it made me break down. I felt all the fear and hopelessness rush up and consume me while the young human foal wrapped his little arms around my neck and cried out his own grief, his tears dripping onto me one by one until my mane was soaked."

***

When Strix's memory faded into the background, he noticed that his plumage was soaked through, and he was wet to the skin. Belatedly he became aware that the swaying motion had stopped, and he was lying on his back on the hard ground. He tried to open his eyes, but the sun was too blinding and so he closed them again. Then he felt, more than heard, heavy steps coming closer, which made the ground vibrate beneath him. When they stopped right in front of him, cool, fresh water trickled into his half-open beak.

Strix swallowed out of reflex as he felt the wetness hit the roof of his mouth. Feeling the water run down his parched throat, he sighed in contentment. Strix couldn't remember anything else that had ever felt this heavenly. Opening his beak even further to let more of it pour in, he gasped as the stream was cut off.

"Slow down," a warm voice said mildly. "Or you'll get sick."

Wanting to plead with whoever was standing above him to give him more water, Strix felt the murky blackness creeping up again, encasing him and pulling him under, right back into his memory of Cocoa's story.

***

"The little human foal continued to visit me every day. He was the one to name me Cocoa – something my mother hadn't been able to do because it is custom in our family to give our foals names when they turn into adults, and I was taken from her too early.

"And the young human was also the one who kept me company in my darkest hours. He sat beside me in silence or made the time pass more quickly by talking to me about everything under the sun. Over time, I began to enjoy our conversations as I always learned something new. But neither his presence nor his understanding nature prevented me from getting sick. My imprisonment and captivity, the lack of light and freedom and the separation from my family had, at long last, taken their toll on my body. I became sicker with every hour and was convinced that I would go to the other side soon.

"I wasn't afraid. On the contrary. I welcomed the thought with all my heart, because it meant I would be free again. But the human foal looked sadder and sadder the sicker I became. And his sadness and pain were the only reason I was still hanging on to life. I tried to tell him that everything would be all right if he let me go and that I would be happy again, but he cried harder every time I told him about my wish to leave. Then one day, I felt so weak that I couldn't stand up anymore. I was lying on the ground, breathing heavily, when the young human foal came to see me. I had expected him to be upset and scared, but a strange transformation was going on with him. Squaring his shoulders, he came straight over to me and used all his strength to force me up onto my legs. My knees wanted to buckle underneath my weight, but the small human wouldn't let me. Instead, he pulled me forwards and outside my prison.

"I thought that he wanted to show me the stars one last time before I left this body behind. Sure enough, when we walked out into the cool evening air, they were blinking brightly above me. Feeling awe at their beauty, I stared up at them, transfixed, while my nostrils caught the faint scent of myrrh on the breeze and my ears perceived the almost inaudible sound of a bat flying over our heads.

"My senses were overloaded by all these impressions, and I failed to notice that the human foal removed the last dead snake from around my head. When it was gone and he gave me a pat on my back, I startled.

"Turning around, I looked at him, confused, and he smiled sadly at me. But at the same time, he exuded a strength that I hadn't seen in him prior to this day. 'Go – you're free,' he said. He told me that he couldn't bear to see my suffering, and he didn't want to watch me die – which would happen sooner rather than later if I didn't get my freedom back.

"I didn't know what to say, but to my relief, no further words were needed. We understood everything that had been left unsaid at a glance. I bowed my head to him in thanks and staggered forward on shaky legs, leaving my prison behind. Along with my little human friend, who I knew I would miss for the rest of this life.

A life which, at the time, I didn't think would last more than a few hours. My chances of survival – being alone in the wilderness in my poor condition – didn't look great. But at least, I said to myself, I would die free.

"To my surprise, when I was trotting north, the movement revived me a bit, though, and when I came upon a pond and drank the clear water, I felt much better. It took me some time to recover, but every day I felt stronger and, eventually, I knew that I would stay here for a while longer."

"And you did," Strix said matter-of-factly, impressed by the wild ass's story.

Snorting loudly, Cocoa smiled. "I did. And I even found my herd again. Or rather, they found me. I can't tell you how happy I was to be reconnected with them."

"And the human boy?" Strix asked curiously. "Do you know what happened to him?"

"No, I haven't seen him ever since he released me. But we'll see each other again on the other side at the latest, and then we'll have lots of new stories to share."

"And here I thought that all humans were evil," Strix mused. "That's what my mother taught me when I was young. That, and to stay clear of them."

"Well, I wouldn't trust them all," Cocoa said. "Just because one of them understood me doesn't take away from the fact that others captured me without any qualms. So, it's best to heed your mum's advice."

"You're right," Strix said gravely. "And I'm sorry that this happened to you. It must have been terrible to be imprisoned."

"It was," Cocoa agreed. "But I'm at peace with it now. And hey, at least I've got a great story to tell my future foals."

***

Once again, Strix was pulled from the memory. He felt the surrounding blackness thin out, turning greyer at the edges until he was finally able to open his eyes. Groaning as terrible waves of pain hammered inside his head, he tried to sit up, but a claw pressed him back down onto the earth.

"Take it slowly," a male voice told him roughly. "That was a close call. If the elephants hadn't saved you, you'd already be on the other side."

Focusing his eyes on the bird in front of him, Strix took in his brown plumage, the featherless white head and his lively eyes.

"Elephants?" he croaked. "Where are they? And who are you? What happened? Where am I?"

The bird standing above him laughed. "If you are this curious when you're half dead, I don't even want to know how many questions you'll bombard me with when you're fully awake. But to answer your question, I'm a vulture. And the elephants had to continue on their journey. They left you here with me after they got some water into you and your body temperature went down. They do have young ones to take care of, after all. But don't worry – I'm a passable healer myself, you'll be well taken care of. And this near to the coast, the temperatures are also more bearable. But now, as your designated nurse, I'm telling you that you need more rest. So sleep!"

It was as if the last word held inner magic. Strix instantly felt compelled to follow the command, slipping back into the endless darkness. Only that now, it wasn't an old memory awaiting him there, but a deep healing sleep.

Animal Communication and Understanding

"Willow, are you implying that I can talk to animals? Is that what you meant when you said I could practise telepathy with many others who'd be glad to speak with me? But how is that possible?"

"Nayeli," Willow replied, mirth in the tree's voice – or, at least, in the imagined voice inside Nayeli's mind. "You *are* aware that you've just asked a tree this question, aren't you? A tree you're already talking telepathically to?"

Nayeli peered hard at the tree. "Yes, I haven't forgotten that little detail. But there must be a difference between talking to a plant and an animal – when my friend's dog is around, he never tries to talk to me. Or maybe you're an exception to the rule? Cause now that I think of it, my houseplants don't talk to me either ..."

"There's no difference at all. When using telepathy to communicate with an animal, you do the same as when you speak with me. Focus on a thought, send it out to the recipient and open yourself up to receive the answer. And as for your friend's dog – why would he talk to you? From when they are small puppies, dogs realise – just like any other pet – that you don't use your telepathic abilities or consciously understand the soul-language anymore. A situation to which they have adapted in their own way – by mastering the ability to observe you. They learn your body language, gestures, facial expressions and what the tone of your voice and certain words means. They use this information to communicate with you in a way you can understand: for example, by running to the door when they want to go outside or by whining at you or nudging you to get your attention. Because otherwise, a lot of their needs would stay unmet.

"For them, being raised in a human household is akin to an

Italian person moving to France without knowing a single word of French. And just like those people, dogs have two options. They can either learn the new language and will then be able to connect to you, or they refuse to adjust to their environment."

Nayeli groaned in embarrassment. "Our pets must think we're so stupid! They go to all the trouble of learning an additional language because we can't talk in the soul-language that connects all living beings and species."

"I think most of them are actually very understanding of the fact that you have trouble using telepathy, even if they aren't aware of the reasons."

"But now that I know how to use it, I can talk to any animal and they'll answer?"

"As long as you respect the animals' free will, yes," Willow replied. "Like humans, they aren't always in the mood to chat. They may want to be left alone. No animal should be at your beck and call, and they don't have to answer all your questions if they don't want to. But in my experience, as long as you respect them, most animals will be happy to talk to you. I think they'd be grateful that, finally, a human is willing to understand them better."

"Understanding is a big topic, isn't it?" Nayeli took up the cue. "It definitely was in Cocoa's story."

"It is. Forget about telepathy for a moment. You humans haven't only forgotten to speak the universal language. You've become blind and deaf to people who speak the same language as you. Have you heard the saying 'humans don't listen; they wait for their turn to speak'? That quote is, sadly, true in many cases. Humans have forgotten how to step into someone else's shoes and look at life through another person's eyes, to understand and feel and see and hear them ... And by hearing someone I don't only mean with your ears but also with your heart. You need to allow yourself to be truly present with another person when they speak, without being lost in your own internal world. Or aren't I right? Tell me, how often have you felt misunderstood by someone?"

"How often?" Nayeli laughed. "Blimey, I can't possibly answer that. A few million times probably?"

Nayeli fixed her gaze on a beetle landing on a flower. "And I have to admit that it's true the other way around as well. Sometimes I'm slow on the uptake when it comes to understanding others. But what are we doing wrong?"

The tree rustled loudly with its leaves. "You are concentrating too much on separateness, rather than on your soul's true nature of connectedness."

"But how? Why?" Nayeli inquired.

"Remember what your ego does day in, day out? It compares. It compares you to other humans, to things and situations."

"Is that a bad thing now?" Nayeli questioned, remembering that Willow hadn't made it sound like something negative to watch out for when the tree had first mentioned the ego.

"No, comparing things is a neutral fact. But put into practise, it can go two ways. You can use comparisons to create more disconnections in your life. Or you can switch your focus and use this natural inclination of your mind to find similarities with others as opposed to differences. You could, for example, think, 'I'm similar to my friend because both our parents divorced when we were teenagers.' Or 'I'm the same as my pet because we both love to be outdoors.' Every time you identify with someone else, you enable more understanding and, as a result, more connection and love. On the other hand, each time you focus on the differences, you create more disconnection."

"But we're all so different," Nayeli cut in. "You were right when you said that we're all individuals with unique soul-plans. So, maybe the gaps between some of us are too wide to bridge, and maybe we humans are too egoistical to be able to see things from another's perspective? I mean, looking at the world, fights and conflicts can be seen everywhere. Humans from different cultures and religions fight each other. People with different sexualities, genders or skin colours don't see eye to eye. Rich persons don't get the poor, older generations don't understand younger ones and vice versa. On top of that, in every group, individuals fight anyone who's different or who makes them feel threatened in any way. Colleagues have conflicts over promotions, siblings compete for their parent's approval and neighbours feel disturbed by the other's noise. Instead of searching for connections, it all has become about exclusion. I'm tired of it, now that I'm aware of this pattern. I'm tired that, in place of lifting us up and celebrating people for who they are, we're constantly pulling each other down and blaming us for what we're not."

Willow grunted. "It's true that humans have become masters at exaggerating the differences between each other. But remember that, once you look deeper, you'll find that you have a lot in common with others. Much more than you initially think."

"Are you saying that people who hate each other because of their differences are alike in some way?" Nayeli asked.

"Sure they are," Willow said business-like, the tree's statement ending in a chuckle. "They hate each other, as you so eloquently put it. And isn't that already a similarity that can't be denied?"

Rolling her eyes heavenwards, Nayeli couldn't help but laugh along. "Be serious here," she complained. "I'm trying to learn something."

"All right, all right," Willow gave in. "Let's use a simple example then, shall we? Knowing nothing about your father and your relationship with him, I'm confident that I can easily list fifty things you two share ..."

Taken aback at her father being mentioned, Nayeli needed to take a few breaths to compose herself. She didn't want to talk about that part of her life. But then she quickly reconsidered and let Willow carry on, as she knew the tree's example would fail spectacularly anyway.

Waving her hand for Willow to continue, Nayeli snorted derisively. "If you find *five* things I've in common with him that's more than I'd expect. We are *nothing* alike."

"Okay." Willow took up the challenge. "One, you both incarnated as humans. As such, you both breathe air and have one heart, unlike an octopus who has three. Second, you were both children who grew up into adults. Third, both of you have an ego, which makes you perceive yourselves as separate to everyone else in the world. Fourth, you have decided from a soul perspective to share part of your lives with each other. Five, both of you have felt negative and positive emotions that have shaped you. And, on top of all that, you share genes. Certainly, these are all generalities, as I don't know your father or anything about your past with him. Maybe there are a whole lot more examples than that. Maybe you have the same hair or eye colour. Maybe you tie your shoelaces in the same way since he might have taught you that. Maybe you both have a tendency to be untidy. Maybe you're both right-handed. Or maybe you share the same taste in music."

Willow lapsed into silence, letting Nayeli digest the list, before proposing another thought. "And maybe you don't see the similarities between you and him because you're too focused on the differences, hmm?"

Feeling mulish, Nayeli looked off into the distance.

The tree wasn't deterred by her stony silence, though. "If I could teach you only one thing today, this would be it: that every single similarity you find between yourself and someone or something else has the potential to bridge differences and to create more understanding and connection in your life!"

"Wait – *something*?" Nayeli asked, her mind stumbling over the one word that didn't fit with the mental picture she'd created.

"Of course. Why stop looking for commonalities when it comes to anything that isn't human or an animal? You can also find commonalities with plants, stones and anything else you can think of. Even an object like a stool can have a lot of parallels with you."

"A stool?" Nayeli asked disbelievingly, breaking out into laughter. "Now you're having me on, Willow, aren't you?"

"Not at all," the tree answered earnestly. "Just think about it. What traits do you share with one?"

Staring up at the willow tree, as if it had grown a second crown, Nayeli waited for a sign that the request had been a joke. But nothing of the sort came, and Willow remained silent. Finally deciding to humour her friend and play along, Nayeli thought hard about the question. But try as she might, she couldn't come up with a single idea. Giving up, she eventually shook her head. "I'm sorry, but there's nothing."

"Then let me help you along," the tree said, its voice cheeky. "How about the fact that a stool stands on legs – like you? And how about the fact that a stool often is made of wood, which is a living, breathing organism? How about the function of the stool? It is supportive: it holds up your weight while letting you relax. You do the same when you help someone else by being supportive towards them ... And these are only a few examples. Do you now see what I was getting at?"

Nayeli looked up, baffled. "I do. Wow. We've *really* forgotten how to stay connected to everything around us, haven't we? But how will finding similarities with others help me find the connection I crave? I mean, me understanding someone else doesn't automatically translate to them understanding me as well – or does it?"

"You have no control over someone else's free will and whether they'll respond in kind, that's right. But you can improve your chances as people are used to mirror your behaviour towards them. Approach someone with the attitude of judgment, and it's likely that they'll judge you back. Approach someone with the attitude of curiosity, and it's highly probable that they'll do the same.

"But let's play a game of pretend, shall we? Let's say you meet someone and you don't know how to connect to them on a deeper level. The other person does, though. They take the time to get to understand you, they take interest in your dreams, desires and wishes as well as your fears and worries. They treat you as if you were part of them and take all your needs into account. Just imagine how you would feel if someone did this for you. If they accepted you as you are and supported you on all levels. How would you react?"

"If someone were to make me feel thoroughly safe around them?" Nayeli asked in contemplation. "They'd have my endless loyalty and love in return. The kind of 'I'd bury bodies for you without asking questions' love and loyalty."

"Exactly," the tree agreed. "True understanding is a skill that rarely any human has mastered in this day and age, but which all crave for themselves. And this means people will flock to you when you become an expert in this field. Naturally, there's no guarantee that everyone will give back. Some people will only want to receive. But if one person cannot reciprocate the understanding you give them, look around. There are plenty of others who can and will. You simply need to be brave enough to take that first step to find the meaningful, safe relationships you desire. The alternative would be to stay lonely your whole life – to never build a deep connection to anyone. Is that what you want?"

Nayeli directed her gaze to the brook, which was glittering in the sunlight. "No, of course not! I just don't think I can do it. Or maybe I don't understand everything fully yet. How can I truly see and get someone else if I've never walked in their shoes? How can I know why they think the way they think when I haven't lived their life?"

The tree whistled a short tune before answering. "I could teach you one technique that enables you to join someone else's reality or for someone else to join yours. I call it the tree process."

"The tree process?" Nayeli giggled. "Of course! What else but a tree would a tree use as an example? Oh please, do tell me about that one."

Willow joined in her laughter. "Your wish is my command, you cheeky child. To do this exercise, you need to become present first. Then imagine that you are a leaf on a giant tree. Now, to enter someone else's perspective you need to move out of your leaf and let yourself become one with the source energy, which is making up the tree itself and all its branches and twigs. Move down your branch and towards another leaf that holds the perspective of someone you want to understand better. Move right into that leaf and the other person's reality. See everything from their eyes and delve into their awareness, which is based on all their previous experiences. Watch how everything changes from this vantage point. Once you've done this and gained a new understanding of their reality, take it with you while you move back to your own leaf."

"And if I can't do that? What if my meditation or imagination skills don't allow me to use this method?"

"Then you have another option. Ask the other person questions. Lots of questions. And listen to what they have to say. Essentially, become a private investigator. If you look at it from this angle, understanding is a skill that's actually fun to practise."

"How so?" Nayeli asked, intrigued.

"Think about it. What could be greater than discovering something new and delving deep into a universe no one has ever stepped foot in before?"

"I'm sorry, Willow," Nayeli began, "but we were on the topic of understanding people. Why are you talking about universes now?"

"Because that's what a person's internal world looks like. It looks like a unique universe that wants to be discovered by anyone willing to become an astronaut and venture into it. You'll find beautiful planets and landscapes yet unexplored within a person and strange creatures or ethereal beings who represent all of their internal parts. A person is made up of a multitude of different layers – so many that you'll never be able to fully explore all of their being, even if you spend your whole life doing nothing else. You humans are so complex that you cannot even completely know yourself – not in aeons and certainly not in one lifetime. And aside from this, you have to consider the fact that you constantly need to rediscover everything. These internal landscapes that constitute your being evolve and change as you grow.

"Any being is like a stream of water – always flowing, always changing. And just as you can never see the same river twice – because the water you saw yesterday is long gone – you are also never the same person. With every second that passes, you have a new experience, a new focus, a new perception. And thus, you have to get to know yourself and others all over again."

"That makes sense," Nayeli said thoughtfully. "But if we are that multilayered, why do some people become bored in relationships? Why do some couples who've been together for years stop talking to each other?"

"That," Willow responded, "is due to them keeping their relationship on a superficial level without delving deeper. Something you can avoid when you make another person a priority in your life and taking real interest in them."

Sighing, Nayeli looked up at the white clouds passing by. "You make it sound easy. But I don't believe it is. I only have to think about my mum and sister and how they have disconnected from each other this last year ... I don't know if they can repair what has been broken."

"I understand why you say that," the tree answered empathetically. "Moving out of your ego perspective and seeing things from someone else's view can be challenging. But finding a connection is possible when both parties are willing to create one. And it's definitely worth it. Because it's only by understanding each other that you humans will be able to heal the worst pandemic that has ever hit this planet: loneliness!"

Nayeli inclined her head. "I'm sure you're right. Even though I think it's unfair that we're at such a disadvantage when it comes to finding love and understanding, simply because our perceptions differ so much that we are constantly faced with misunderstandings."

"And because there are countless truths present inside this reality, some of which contradict each other."

"Countless truths?" Nayeli asked, confused. "But surely there can only be one!?"

"Far from it. Everyone experiences things differently, and the way you perceive a situation shapes your truth. But before I delve further into this topic, I'd best let Strix and Aqua have their say first ..."

9. Aqua, the Octopus

Strix had been flying around for days, but there was no sight of the elephants who had saved him.

While recovering from his heatstroke, he had questioned the vulture who was looking after him, keen to find out all that had happened when he had been unconscious. He'd discovered that an elder elephant cow had found him and made a detour with her herd. That she had carried him with her trunk for miles and given him water. And that she had travelled on with her family after making sure that he would survive.

Strix had wanted to follow her immediately, to thank her for all she had done for him, but he had been too weak to stand, let alone fly, for some time. And when he felt fit enough to take to the air again, the elephants were long gone.

Strix wasn't deterred, though; he was intent on seeing them for himself. This was what he had wanted from the get-go. Ever since his uncle had told him about his own journey to Africa, Strix had desired nothing more than to see these grey giants with his own eyes. And now that he owed them his life, his earlier interest had turned into an obsession.

He had no more clues than the general direction they had gone in. But the African savannah was crowded by wildlife, big and small, and Strix reckoned that someone must have crossed their path and could point him in the right direction. Only that the herd of elephants seemed to have vanished into thin air. No one he had asked since yesterday evening had seen them.

Strix sat down on the ground. It was time for a break and, beyond that, it was also high time to be brutally honest with himself:

He had lost the elephants' trail. Cursing loudly, Strix realised that they must have turned course and followed another hidden path at some point. But he had no idea when and where ... Feeling dejected at his failure to find them, Strix wondered what he had done wrong. Usually, he was better at tracking, and these giants should be an easy exercise, even if they had a significant head start on him. But despite that, he had been unable to catch up.

As his thoughts turned into a negative downward spiral, Strix became aware of a faint sound – a sound that had been present for a while now as a distant background noise, familiar and at the same time alien to hear in these plains. The sound of waves crashing onto a shore.

Understanding that he must be closer to the coast than he had realised, Strix quickly banished his dark thoughts to the back of his mind and took off. He was excited to lay eyes on the sea again and headed straight towards the noise of the rolling waves. Shortly after, Strix was close enough to smell the salty air, which he breathed in deeply, feeling both energised and comforted by it. Then Strix spotted the shore and, behind it, the endless ocean that melted into the azure sky. Being utterly mesmerised by the beautiful sight in front of him, Strix laughed happily as he soared above the sandy beach, carried by a fresh breeze.

"Help me! Please!"

The male voice was weak and faint, but the words were unmistakable. Someone close by was in trouble. Looking around, Strix tried to locate the source of the call, scanning the section of the beach beneath him with an urgency that surprised even him. He reckoned that it might be due to having been saved himself days ago. And if he wasn't able to locate the elephants and thank them, at least this way he got the chance to honour their deed by giving something back – if not to his own saviour, then to some poor animal who was in need.

But when his sharp eyes located movement beneath him and made it out to be a nest of wagging snakes, he wasn't sure whether his good intentions could hold up in light of the reality he was facing. No way did he want to get any closer than was absolutely necessary to a bunch of reptiles, which were most likely venomous if the black-and-white bands running across their elongated bodies were any indication.

The voice, which was sounding even more frantic, chose that moment to call out to him once again, erasing all doubts that it was coming from this nest. "Help me! Please, help me, bird. I'm going to die if you don't."

Circling above the nest, Strix wondered why only one of the snakes spoke, and the others remained silent. Then the sight in front of him shifted.

Instead of the black-and-white reptiles that had been lying on the sand, only one animal remained: a brown creature with eight long limbs sticking out from his middle. The stranger was beckoning him closer with two arms now, wheezing. "I need to get back into the water quickly. We octopuses can't survive for long on land before we dry out. And I've already been here too long. But the sand is so soft that I can't reach the water's edge. Please, pick me up and throw me in."

Normally, Strix would have thought twice about flying near such a weird stranger – one that could obviously change form by magic. But Strix also saw that the animal was speaking the truth. The octopus was weak and appeared to have trouble with breathing as his long arms coiled uselessly back and forth.

Without further ado, Strix ignored his worries and swooped down towards the creature. He grasped the squishy animal in his claws as carefully as he could, so as not to puncture the skin, and flew towards the open sea. The octopus was heavier than he had looked, and Strix had trouble gaining his balance for a breath or two. But then he righted himself and crossed over the lines of rolling waves, making sure he was a good bit away from the shore so that the animal would land in deep water.

The male octopus hung lifelessly from his feet, as if he had already perished. But as soon as Strix opened his claws to release him into the blue depths of the ocean, he came back to life.

Realising too late what was going on, Strix felt three of the arms wrap around his body as the animal dropped towards the water, pulling him down with his weight. Not being able to free himself from the octopus' death grip around his back and legs, Strix tumbled straight into the sea. The water closed above his head.

Strix was convinced that he would drown as the creature held on tightly and pulled him further into the gloomy darkness below. Gasping in fright, he swallowed a mouthful of the salty sea and began to struggle in earnest against the creature and the pressure of the water all around him, which was so unlike the air he was used to soaring in. To his relief it worked. Because the male octopus released his tight grip as suddenly as he had grabbed on to him.

Taking this chance, Strix beat his wings and legs to swim towards the surface, seeing the sunlight as a blurred ball above it, beckoning him up like a moth to a flame. It seemed to take an endless amount of time to reach it. And all the while, Strix felt the overwhelming urge to open his beak to inhale some air. But he kept it closed, desperately suppressing the cough that was rising within him. Finally, when the need became so overwhelming that Strix couldn't survive a second longer without inhaling some fresh oxygen into his lungs, his head broke the surface and he opened his beak. This made the tickle in the back of his throat even worse. Coughing out more salty water than he thought he had swallowed, Strix fought to hold his head above the small waves rolling past him and tried to shake off the panic that was keeping his body in a tight grip.

Eventually, after what felt like eternity but was probably only around a minute, his breathing settled into a more natural rhythm, and Strix noticed that the water kept him afloat when he paddled with his feet.

Despite that, he didn't intend to stay any longer inside the sea than necessary. Spreading his wings, Strix tried to fly high into the safety of the sky, but to his horror, his plumage was soaked through and too heavy for him to lift his weight. Feeling himself rise a few inches, Strix immediately sank back into the cold water. And when he tried to lift himself a second time, his wings just sprayed a fountain of water to each side as they slapped against the surface.

"No!" he called out disbelievingly as he tried to lift off a third time. But it was no use and he had to concede defeat. Strix continued to paddle with his feet to stay afloat, using his spread wings for added balance.

This was when he remembered the danger lurking unseen beneath him. The hostile octopus who had almost drowned him must still be in his vicinity. Feeling another panic attack lurking, Strix racked his brain to find a solution, wondering how he could get back to land and out of the waters before the creature got a second chance to attack him. But there was no plan coming to his mind, not even a vague idea, and a moment later all thoughts fled him as a body appeared beside him in the sea.

His eyes widening in fright, Strix looked at the spot where the animal was swimming, close to the water's surface. It didn't take him long to recognise his attacker. But to Strix's surprise, the sight of the animal washed away all his terror and replaced the feeling with burning anger. Anger strong enough that Strix was tempted to take a chunk out of the octopus's squishy flesh.

Until a moment later, when he noticed the suckers all over the octopus' limbs and realised why this small creature could have held on to him with such a death grip. Knowing that if he dared to swim into the range of these arms, the animal could easily pull him down into the deepest depths of the sea, Strix common sense told him to keep his distance – thus saving the octopus from being eaten.

"Thank you," the creature said heartfelt, as if having heard his thoughts.

Strix felt confused, as this strange greeting didn't seem to fit such a vicious beast. And he was even more confused by the octopus's next words.

"That was a close call. If it hadn't been for you, I wouldn't have survived," the animal declared. "I owe you one. My name's Aqua, by the way."

Staring at this weird creature, floating so innocently in the water beside him, Strix knew that the octopus must be intending to play with his mind to make him easy prey. Luckily, his attacker didn't know that Strix was too smart to fall into this trap, though, and that he could outsmart the octopus with ease.

"Are you serious?" Strix asked acidly. "You nearly drowned me, you stupid jelly-bag! Is that your way of thanking me for saving you? If it is, you can keep your goddamn gratefulness to yourself."

"Hey, stop making a fuss. It's not like I intended to pull you down with me. It was just a reflex to hold on when I felt myself falling."

"A reflex?" Strix asked incredulously. "A REFLEX? Is that all you've got to say in your defence? You ball of slime! Look at me. I'm in quite a predicament because of you. I can't take off from the water and the shore is far away. Who knows if I'll make it there!? And all because I had to play the saviour to some stinking animal who didn't deserve my help!"

"Come now, don't be so melodramatic!" Aqua laughed, not at all perturbed by Strix's rage. "This is an ocean, not the hell you make it out to be. And if you gave my home a chance, you might even grow to like it."

"Ha!" Strix cried. "I've already made closer acquaintance with *your home* than I cared to." Scowling at the octopus, Strix tried to shake off some of the water clinging to him.

The attempt was as useless as trying to dodge raindrops when it was pouring. But some of his anger dissolved, leaving him feeling depleted. "Since I do have a heart, I'll call it quits, though, if you can find me a ride back to the beach."

"A ride?" Aqua asked, amused. "Where the heck would I get a ride for you? You'll have to swim there."

Strix fixated the waves that were rushing towards the sandy shore. A shore that seemed to get further and further away from him the longer he looked. Strix swallowed hard. The weariness he had felt after his heatstroke was back with a vengeance and he wondered whether he could make it to safety before the ocean swallowed him whole.

"Don't you worry," Aqua added off-handedly. "It's not that hard to swim. And if you want, I can accompany you for most of the journey. Until we are close to the beach. Cause I don't want to risk being washed up on it again ... How's that?"

"Splendid!" Strix said angrily. His irony was lost on Aqua, though, because the octopus splayed out his arms in satisfaction.

"Great – then let's go. This is gonna be fun. You gotta know that I'm great company. And what's more, I can warn you of any approaching dangers."

Strix almost drowned a second time when his head went underneath the water. Sputtering, he came back up and paddled even harder to stay afloat. "Dangers? As in plural?" Strix croaked, doubtful that he wanted to actually know the answer to his question. He peered warily into the dark depths of the sea. "What kind of danger?"

"The usual." Aqua laughed. "Whales and dolphins and sharks and sea snakes and stingrays and jellyfish and all that. Oh, and don't forget about that cliff to the right of the beach – there can be strong currents there, which could smash you against the rocks faster than you can scream out 'help'. But other than that, you should be perfectly fine."

"You sure?" Strix asked, once again laying as much sarcasm into these words as he could muster.

But Aqua was as deaf to it as before and bobbed his head up and down earnestly. "Yeah, I'm sure of it."

Wanting to roll his eyes, and cursing the fact that owls couldn't do this, Strix took two deep breaths to calm himself down. "And what, pray tell, should I do when some of those sea snakes or stingrays approach? Fly off? Cause that's not going to happen."

"That's a no-brainer," Aqua said matter-of-factly. "Transform yourself into an animal they fear so that they won't approach. Preferably a venomous one."

"Transform?" Strix asked, bewildered, as another wave lifted him up and rolled on towards the beach.

"Yes, like this." And with those words, Aqua's brown skin took on some white stripes while he let his arms trail behind him, resembling spines. "Now I look like a lionfish," he explained. "A highly venomous creature you'd best avoid if you want to live."

"Wow," Strix said, his anger momentarily forgotten. He was amazed at how fast the octopus could morph into another species – a talent, not even the chameleon could compete with. But neither could he, Strix realised. Which meant his end, if a predator decided to show its face.

"I can't transform myself," Strix voiced the obvious.

"Why?" Aqua asked curiously as he changed back to the light brown tone he had been earlier and assumed his usual form. "With these sharp claws, you look like an apex predator of the sky, just like we octopuses are the apex predators of the sea. And this must mean that you can do more than the usual bird, no? Or don't you have any foes up there?"

"Naturally. But we use other techniques to evade them," Strix answered.

Floating in the water, Aqua smacked one of his arms on its surface. "Ha, I knew you birds were strange, but you're even more curious than I imagined. Why would you use anything less than shapeshifting to hunt your food or stay alive?"

"Strange? Us?" Strix asked, feeling amusement rise within him at hearing something this ridiculous. "And what would you call a weirdo like yourself?"

"We're normal," Aqua answered soberly. "And I can prove that to you by stating only one fact. We don't choose to live in sight of that fiery ball that dries you out faster than you can crawl back into the water."

"Do you have something against the sun?" Strix pried – partly because he was interested in the answer, and partly to distract himself from the feeling of dread uncurling in his stomach whenever he thought of the predicament he found himself in. "I concede that I'm not its greatest fan right now, since it almost killed me a couple of days ago. But normally, it's lovely to have its rays warm me on cold days."

"Lovely?" Aqua asked aghast. "The sun is more dangerous than anything else I listed. It's even more dangerous than the damn venomous sea snakes that creep up behind you. As is the sand, for that matter, and the dry land behind it. And the air, of course, which is toxic and kills anyone who is exposed to it for too long."

"The air?" Strix laughed, amused for real this time. "Don't be silly. The air is just another word for freedom and happiness and life. I would love to show you what I mean by flying some loops and soaring on the currents. But unfortunately, some idiot prevented me from doing so!"

He shot Aqua a glare, but the octopus simply bobbed up and down on the waves unimpressed. "Sorry, my feathered friend," he said confidently. "But you've got it totally wrong. The one thing that gives and enables life is water. That's where we all come from and where we belong. Buddy, give it a try. Breathe the water in like I'm doing. That's when you'll see the truth ..."

Wondering not for the first time if the octopus was sane, Strix swam a foot or so away from him to be on the safe side. Then he looked longingly at the beach in the distance. He couldn't wait to reach it – not only to get out of this sea as quickly as possible but also to escape Aqua, who was clearly not mentally stable.

"This is all stupid," he groaned. "I'm stupid for having helped you. And I hate water, I damn well hate it!"

Aqua grinned, waving two of his arms around. "That's because you're acting like a stubborn child. If you stopped arguing against reality and came down there with me, you'd be able to see paradise for yourself. You'd see the coral reefs, the forests created out of seaweed and the schools of fish swimming around. It's a manifold, multi-coloured and immensely beautiful world. A beauty none of you birds have ever laid eyes upon. Without a doubt, it has some negatives too – like the sharks hunting you or the toxic litter left by humans that is poisoning us and our environment. But there's always some hell where there's heaven, don't you think so? You can't tell me there aren't hunters and poison in the air ...?"

"There are and there is," Strix replied. "But it's still a hundred times more beautiful than being under the sea. Not to mention safer. So, quit your talk. I'm not falling into this trap. If you want another chance to drown me, you'll have to think up something better than to whitewash the truth."

"Are all birds this enamoured with conspiracy theories? Why don't you give me an hour of your time, and I will show you my home? I promise you'll never want to leave again."

"Yeah," Strix laughed humourlessly. "My body sure wouldn't leave the sea after a whole hour inside it. I'd be on the other side by then, you utter moron. Thank you for this kind offer, but I'm gonna pass."

Strix and Aqua stared at each other as though they had seen an alien life form. But then, as if a ban had been broken, they simultaneously broke out into giggles.

Aqua changed his skin colour to a sandy beige tone. "I guess, in the end, there's only one truth that we can agree upon, isn't there?"

Strix smiled, amused. "And it's that we disagree on everything!"

"Which is already false, since we just agreed on this," Aqua added lightly.

Strix shrugged. "That's true, too."

And with that, they doubled over, their laughter ringing out over the expense of the blue sea.

"I can see what you want to tell me with this story, Willow," Nayeli said. "That Strix and Aqua have two totally different perspectives and that they're both right in their own way. But this story is about two completely different species. An owl and an octopus – an animal that lives in the sky and on land and another animal that lives in the sea. It's obvious why they can never be of the same mind. What is important for one is dangerous for the other and vice versa. And the fact that one of them has lungs and the other gills makes it impossible for them to delve into the other's life and see things from the opposite point of view. But how can this apply to humans? Shouldn't we all have a similar outlook, since we all live in the same reality?"

"But do you?" Willow asked sweetly.

"Yes, we do," Nayeli said. "We all breathe the same air, we all walk on the same earth, we all eat the same foods, we all go to school as kids and get jobs later on in life ..." Stopping mid-sentence, Nayeli palmed her forehead. "Oh, dang. Forget what I just said."

Willow laughed knowingly. "Why?"

"Because I'm talking nonsense," Nayeli admitted as she realised the truth. "There are people who can't afford to send their children to school, while some other kids are home-schooled. And not everyone gets a job afterwards. We all eat different foods, depending on the country we live in, what religion we practise, how much money we have and so on. Not everyone can walk, as some people use a wheelchair. And even the air we breathe is different: big, smog-filled cities compared to salty sea air. You're right, Willow. We all do have different lives – and perspectives."

The willow tree let its lighter branches whip up and down so that they tapped on the grass in a rhythm that accentuated the song of a few birds bathing in the brook.

"You do. It will be impossible to find a second soul who agrees with you about everything you think, feel and believe. But let's look at an example to see how much one perception can differ from another one, shall we?"

Nayeli agreed all too readily, as she always understood the lessons best when Willow used some real-life examples to turn the theory into something more tangible.

"Good, so tell me, my dear, when you heard me talking about exit points, how did that make you feel? What did you think when you heard that our souls need to decide for us to cross back over, or that they need to at least agree when and how we are going to do this?"

Thinking back, Nayeli stared off into the distance. "In the end, relieved, I think. Because our souls have a wider perspective and should know what's best for us, even if it's painful from our human point of view."

"That's a valid reaction. But now imagine a mother whose child was murdered. She will be in a huge amount of pain, both because her child is gone and because it had such a violent, scary and inhuman death. If you were to tell her that the soul of her child agreed to die in this way and at this young age, she would not only not be able to understand this, it would also increase her suffering."

Nayeli felt deeply affected by the example that Willow had given her. "Because that would imply that her child actively chose to leave her in this much pain ...?"

"Precisely," Willow said. "The truth of the mother is that neither she nor her child knew about this exit point in advance. The child did not wake up that day, consciously aware that it would die. From a human point of view, this *experience* was unplanned and definitely unwanted. Of course, the child healed instantly when it crossed over, as it reconnected with its soul. But the mother didn't. She's trapped in feelings of grief and rage that her child was taken from her like this and can't possibly accept a reality that completely disregards her emotions. And because these are of such a low frequency, she's even more removed from the soul level truth than ever before.

"Luckily, most disagreements that stem from different perceptions of reality aren't as serious as this. But they can all cause suffering, disconnection and loneliness as we don't feel understood by others."

"Because we all add different meanings to everything we perceive?" Nayeli asked.

"That, and because you perceive things differently in the first place. One of the best examples to explain this phenomenon is colours."

"Colours?"

"Yes. Two people who look at the same red wall don't necessarily see the exact same shade. Maybe one person sees a shade slightly lighter or darker than the other person. Or one of them sees the colour more intensely. Maybe one human sees only one shade, whereas the other's eyes can make out different sub-shades. This is due to the fact that colours are not a property of an object itself. If you take two identical objects and place one in front of a blue background and the other in front of a yellow background, the first object will appear lighter and a bit more yellow and the second will look slightly bluer and darker. This is the case because colours are built inside your own mind, depending on your brain function that interprets the wavelengths that reach your eyes. And thus, colours are subjective – just like truth is!"

Contemplating this, Nayeli drummed her fingers against the earth, belatedly realising that she was using the identical rhythm that Willow had tapped out.

"Are you implying that objective truths don't exist? But there must be some that are absolute and rule out all others, no? Cause if I add 1 + 1, I always get 2."

"Not if you're a computer programmer. They have nothing else but the numbers 0 and 1 to work with, if I remember correctly," Willow joked before turning serious. "But to answer your question – yes, objective truths do exist. The lessons I'm teaching you here ... The fact that you are an infinite soul having a human experience, the fact that everyone has free will in addition to a soul-plan and the fact that telepathy is everyone's soul-language are all ultimate truths that apply to everyone. You don't have to remember them or believe in them for them to be right.

"Then again, by teaching them to you, I'm turning these objective truths into subjective ones, whether or not I want to. Every spiritual teacher you meet will differ in their teachings – in small or big ways – even when they're talking about the same thing. It doesn't mean that one is right and the other is wrong. It means that, based on their unique pasts and the meanings they apply, they see, hear and understand objective truths differently. And they prioritise different aspects of them."

Nayeli nodded. "You are saying that by thinking and speaking about a topic, our individual awareness lays a subjective filter onto it?"

"Exactly. Everything we think and say is filtered through our expectations and beliefs and the knowledge we have gained previously. Thus, objective truths exist, but outside of our awareness. They are simply the sum of all subjective truths, including all contradictory ones."

"Contradictory truths?" Nayeli questioned.

"Sure. If there are at least as many truths out there as there are souls present, then some of those have to contradict each other. But let's look at another example, shall we? One subjective truth is that dogs are dangerous. This belief can be formed when you are bitten by one as a kid. Or when your parents are afraid of dogs and you began to copy their behaviour. An opposing or contradictory subjective truth is that dogs are the most loving animals on earth. This belief can be formed when you have had positive experiences with dogs or even had one as a pet yourself, which was your best friend and constant companion. None of these subjective truths are objective truths that apply to everyone, however."

Nayeli puffed out a breath. "What would an objective truth be in that case?"

"The objective truth is that dogs are animals that react to their surroundings. They can be a man's best friend, they can be loyal and loving. Or they could become aggressive and bite when they feel threatened."

The tree smacked two of its branches together. Startled by the sound, some birds in the small stream took flight. Nayeli looked after them until they disappeared out of sight.

"You know, my dear," Willow said, sounding amused, "the most objective truth about truth itself is that truth is subjective. This reality in and of itself is already a contradiction. Your ego makes you think of yourself as separate from everyone else, while our souls know no disconnection. Likewise, any spiritual truth you encounter inside this reality comprises one or more contradictory truth at its opposing end, which are equally true. For example, the spiritual teaching of self-love contradicts the spiritual teachings that we are living inside an interdependent reality and need other humans to fulfil our needs, which includes the need to be loved. But both of them are right – for different people or at different times in human's lives. Let's say someone has low levels of self-worth. They would benefit greatly to learn how to love themselves. On the other hand, if someone shoulders too many responsibilities, they'd best take advantage of this interconnected reality to receive more support from others."

Nayeli leaned forward in interest. "Is that how it is decided what is true for us and what isn't? We are simply a match to one truth over the other because of what we need most?"

"That plays into it. In effect, this universe consists of a multitude of layers, each one holding different truths. And we're matched with the truth of the frequency we currently hold. Or, to put it another way, we come across the truths that make us feel better, while we don't recognise or exclude any others that make us feel worse. This happens when we're not yet ready to see a truth but also when we've grown and evolved from one that rang true for us before but doesn't anymore. To visualise this, imagine that your life path is a road on which you are walking. Anything you can perceive around you is true, while anything out of sight in front of you or behind you is not."

The tree swayed its branches from left to right and back. "In the end, contradictions are unavoidable inside this 3D reality. But that doesn't mean that they are always black and white. Sometimes things that seem to be contradictory can actually add to each other by approaching a scenario from two different perspectives. A prime example of that is your battle between religion and science. When you look closely at it, both are beholding the same ultimate truth: namely, that the source created this reality and everything in it, and that life came about by the process of evolution. Religion and science see the exact same thing from two opposite standpoints, with religion basing everything on a creator called God or Allah or whatever other name they choose to give, while science sticks to things that are provable, such as the Big Bang, which was the starting point of life here on Earth."

"You think that religion and science are compatible?" Nayeli asked, surprised.

"I do if you see the big picture. Look at it like a jigsaw puzzle. Both religion and science, respectively, are one piece of the whole truth. And when you put these together, you'll see that they fit quite nicely. The inherent problem is that humans don't do this as they are usually only a match to seeing one half, while opposing the other."

Nayeli nodded. "I haven't thought about it before but this also explains the situation between my mum and sister. They both see nothing but else but their own half of the whole truth, not the other's point of view."

Staring up at the patches of blue sky between Willow's leaves, Nayeli balled her hands into fists. "Y'know what, Willow? My mother could use the tree process, which you taught me earlier, to see my sister's reality and why she cut off contact without a word. When she sees my sister's truth – and when my sister takes the time to look at things from my mother's perspective – they could solve their problems. I need to tell my mum about this!"

The weeping willow shook out its crown. "Well, you can give it a go, but don't be disappointed if she isn't interested in hearing about this, my sweet child. Many humans are not yet ready to step out of their reality to see someone else's."

But Nayeli didn't heed Willow's warning. She hadn't even heard the last part, as she had jumped up and was halfway across the meadow before the tree had finished. Heading for her grandma's house, she was filled with a newfound sense of purpose: finally, she knew how to end the family fight that had troubled her mum for so long.

Finding her mother in the attic, where she was going through some old papers, Nayeli took a minute to watch her from the doorway. The last weeks had written more worry lines into her face than the last years put together. But despite the pain edged into her features, she was still radiating a source of inner strength.

Nayeli only hoped that she'd inherited that kind of fortitude.

Walking over to her mother, she knelt down on the other side of the open carton and sifted through the folders herself, glad to have something to do with her hands as she felt her way forward. "Mum?" she asked, not knowing how to broach the subject now that she was facing her.

"Yes, darling? What is it?" Laying a file aside, her mother looked up at Nayeli enquiringly.

Clearing her throat as she set out across what she regarded dangerous ground, Nayeli chose her words carefully. "I wanted to speak with you about my sister."

But she obviously hadn't been cautious enough.

Her mother's expression darkened. "What about her?" she asked, her tone defensive. "She's made her decision to stay as far away from me as she can, hasn't she? And I have no idea why. I mean, I've made mistakes – who hasn't? But for her to ignore me and not answer my calls ... I've done nothing to deserve this. I'm her mother, for God's sake, and I love her. I've done everything I could for her. And I don't get why she's this ungrateful now."

"I know," Nayeli interjected. "But what if I told you that there is a way for you to understand her reasons? What if you could see her part of the truth?"

Her mother interrupted her, not seeming to have heard a single word Nayeli had said. "I've told her countless times that I'm ready to talk to her. She's the one who doesn't want to sit down and address our problems. I've called her, I've written to her, I've gone by her place. But no more! If she wants to resolve this, it's up to her now. I just hope that one day, she'll need me and think about what she's done ..."

Nayeli sighed as she saw her mission crumble in front of her eyes. She knew that all further attempts to talk about her sister would be pointless if her mother was in this kind of mood. The underlying hurt and anger exuding from her mum were practically tangible in the air between them. So, doing the only reasonable thing she could think of, Nayeli admitted temporary defeat and quickly steered the conversation in another, safer direction.

Spending the next hour helping her mother organise stacks of documents into piles on the floor, they spoke about lots of things. How a cousin of Nayeli had caused drama when he had been arrested by the police, that her mother's neighbours were once again rebuilding their patio and what the latest altercations between

Nayeli's work colleagues had been about. Only one person was omitted from being mentioned again: Nayeli's sister.

***

The next day, when Nayeli ducked down under Willow's branches and sat in the grass below the tree's crown, she sighed theatrically.

"It sounds as if your plan wasn't successful?"

"No," Nayeli said, telling the tree about her mother's reaction as well as her sister's who she'd phoned later that evening. "As soon as I mentioned Mum to her, she closed herself off. She said she didn't want to talk about it. And then she hung up on me."

Gazing into the distance, Nayeli sighed again. "Willow, I don't understand my sister either. Sure, Mum's not perfect. But she's always done her best. And yes, there were a few arguments, but nothing that would explain cutting off all contact. Dammit, why does my family has to be this complicated? At least the three of us could stick together. You know, female power and all that. But no, we have to create problems where none exist ..."

Willow's branches swished in the warm wind. "I take it you mean the illusion of female power? Since genders and sexes don't exist on the soul level?"

"What?" Nayeli looked stunned. "But genders and sexes *do* exist. Maybe you trees don't have or understand them, but humans certainly do."

"I do understand that you chose a superficial outer expression for this incarnation. But I also know that your soul is genderless."

"It is?" Nayeli asked, intrigued.

"Mmm-mmm. I'll tell you about that in a minute. But first I want to let Strix have his say once more ..."

"Gladly. And who's the animal teacher this time?"

"A clownfish," Willow said seriously.

Nayeli exploded with laughter. "A clownfish? Are you telling me that Strix, after his last mishap, ventured underwater again? Cause I know for a fact that clownfish never go on land."

"I'm aware of that fact, too," Willow said, a smile visible in the tree's voice. "I might be a gnarled old tree, but my knowledge is still as fresh and young as Strix's wings that carry him high into the sky."

"Sorry," Nayeli said, sheepishly. "I didn't want to imply that you don't know what you're talking about."

"Don't worry, my dear. And you're right – Strix did his best to stay clear of deep water after his encounter with Aqua."

"But then, how did he meet a clownfish?"

"Did I say he met one?" Willow answered enigmatically.

10. Dusty/Ash, the Clownfish

"Come on, you can't be serious, Aqua," Strix exclaimed.

The octopus laughed heartily. "But I am. Seahorses *do* look like that. And the males *do* carry the eggs."

"Well, then I'll have to come back as a seahorse in my next incarnation to check that."

Strix had eventually accepted that there was no shortcut and that he had no choice but to paddle back to the beach the hard way if he wanted to reach dry land. He was now glad that the octopus was with him. It made the task seem less daunting, and Strix had capitalised on the time spent together by asking Aqua about all the creatures living in the ocean that he would never get to see himself. At least not in this lifetime.

The octopus had turned out to be a great companion, even if some of his stories were so far-fetched that Strix doubted every other word that left Aqua's beak. Like when he had told him about the horses without legs ...

Still, the tales distracted him from the monotonous sight and sound of the sea, which was tiring him out more than swimming. And the swimming was hard, too. It had been a cumbersome procedure to learn how to use his feet to manoeuvre and how to use his wings as oars, pushing through the water as he paddled forward inch by inch.

At first, it had seemed to Strix that he wasn't moving from his spot, no matter how much energy he put into paddling. And it was made all the harder by the wind picking up, making the waves even higher, with white caps dancing on top of them. Every time Strix had managed to make up some ground, another wave would rush in from behind, lift him up and throw him back, destroying all the progress he had made. By now, though, the beach in the distance seemed to get closer – admittedly not as fast as Strix would have liked, but at least he knew he was finally making progress.

"When you do come back as a sea creature," Aqua interrupted his thoughts, "you should come back as a clownfish, if you ask me."

"Why?" Strix asked, glad to turn his attention away from the cold wetness that seemed to seep into his very bones. "Because I'm funny?"

"No!" Aqua giggled. "Because then you'd have the pleasure of living as both sexes in one lifetime. If you're strong enough, that is."

Exploding with laughter at this baloney, Strix lost his concentration. His head went under as another wave rushed him, and when he came back for air, he coughed up half a bucket of salty seawater. Cursing the ocean to the deepest level of hell, Strix struggled to stay afloat. "Why is swimming so damn difficult?" he called out.

"It wouldn't be if you didn't fight the water. Let it help you instead." As if to emphasise his words, Aqua swam in circles around him and rode the incoming waves. Huffing in annoyance that the octopus could make something difficult look this easy, Strix glared at him.

"You owe me a damn good story for this hell you've brought upon me."

"I've already told you two," the octopus protested, watching Strix struggling.

"Then make it three," Strix panted sulkily.

"All right. Then let me tell you about how I met my friend Dusty, the clownfish. Or should I say Ash, the clownfish? In any case, it's a great story from my teenage years, when I thought I knew everything there was to know."

"Which is it then?" Strix interrupted his friend. "A story about Dusty or Ash? Or do I get two tales?"

"Nope," the octopus said, grinning. "It's only one, but it has a surprise ending. And if you hold your beak for a couple of minutes, I can start …"

***

It was a bright day, close to the Australian coast. The water was cool and clear, and the sun was painting patterns onto the watery ceiling above. Meanwhile, the sandy ground was inhabited by clams, shells, crabs and starfish, and the whole scenery was framed by coral reefs that stretched out in all directions.

Sliding out of a cave between two rocks where he had taken refuge from some hunting dolphins, Aqua found himself directly in front of a huge field of stinging anemones, ranging in colour from an electric blue over purple to bright pink. Having learned early on to stay clear of their venomous tentacles, Aqua turned his back to them and sank low to the sea bed while changing his skin colour to resemble the sand.

He was hungry and on the lookout for prey. But before he had spotted some suitable food swimming by, Aqua was taken by surprise when something pink sped straight past his head. It had come and gone so swiftly that it took him a moment to get his bearings. When he did, the only thing that remained was a small water vortex that told of a presence of something alive. And fast.

While Aqua was wondering if it would be worth it to get to the bottom of this mystery, he felt another small water current against his back. Spinning around, he saw the pink speck, which could be nothing else but a fish, turn around abruptly and dive back between the sea anemones.

Aqua's curiosity was piqued. He knew no one who would voluntarily take on these deadly tentacles. But then he vaguely remembered hearing about a species of fish – called clownfish – which had a symbiotic relationship with the anemones. Until this day, he hadn't met one, but surely that fact had changed today?

As if having been summoned by his thoughts, the fish in question once again shot out from its cover and headed straight for him. Aqua saw that it was pink with a bright white stripe behind its head and a grey dot on the backside. What was standing out the most, however, was the cocky glint in the male fish's eyes.

Swimming a circle above him, the clownfish laughed and darted back into the safety of the anemones.

"Hey!" Aqua called out at this audacious little creature. "Watch it. Some folks would like some peace and quiet to hunt. And if you chase away all the other fish with your crazy antics, I'll have no choice but to eat *you*."

The anemone fish laughed in response. "As if you could. You're so slow, I can swim figures-of-eight around you without you ever catching me. And besides, I'm much smarter and way braver than you."

Aqua was speechless. The impudent brat! Briefly considering whether he should catch and eat the creature like he had threatened, he abandoned the idea as quickly as it had come. The small fish would be a meagre meal. And, additionally to that, he was clearly crazy. Who knew what eating him would do to his mental health ...

Instead, Aqua decided to move on somewhere quieter where he could hunt in peace. Turning his back on the fish, he was about to pick up speed but was interrupted by the young clownfish calling out to him.

"Don't be a spoilsport," he said. "I was just joking – don't leave in a huff."

The anemone fish was swimming out into the open sea again, following him. This time, he was more careful to stay out of reach of Aqua's long limbs, though. Which meant that he wasn't quite as stupid – or suicidal – as Aqua had initially believed.

The fish then shouted questions at him, so nervously and fast that he almost stumbled over his own words.

"How old are you?" the young clownfish asked in a rush. "You look like you could be two hundred years old. I don't actually know if you can even grow that old, but you look like it. Oh, I forgot to introduce myself. I'm Dusty, a clownfish, or an anemone fish if you prefer that term. And you are? Of course, you must be an octopus. I've seen some like you before. Or, to be more precise, not exactly like you, because you look totally different. But they looked similar to you, if you know what I'm getting at? Anyhow, what species are you? And what's your name?"

Aqua groaned at this barrage of questions and wished with all three of his hearts for the fish to shut up.

A second later – and much sooner than he could have hoped for – his wish for peace and quiet was fulfilled. Because at that moment, a big shadow fell over them from above. The clownfish – Dusty, he reminded himself – jerked away and sped back into his favourite hiding spot between the anemones.

Aqua laughed out loud, turning back and grinning at the small fish, who was peeking out anxiously.

"Yes, you are a brave and smart one, aren't you?" he asked sarcastically. "That shadow was a sea turtle, nothing more."

"I'm seeking fun and friends, not danger!" Dusty defended himself and grinned widely at having attracted Aqua's attention. "Can I ask you something?"

"You just did," Aqua responded tiredly, already regretting having addressed the anemone fish in the first place. But it was too late to turn back time. And if Aqua was completely honest with himself, he was also curious to discover the reason why Dusty wasn't perturbed by his gruffness when, normally, all fish fled from him, even when he was in a good mood. Aqua sighed and yielded to his fate. "Go on, what is it you wanted to know. But make it quick, I have places to be."

"You're an octopus, right? I have heard many cool things about you. That you can use tools and that you can spray out ink to fog up everything around you and —"

Aqua knew he had to use this priceless opportunity that had been handed to him on a silver platter. "Do you want me to demonstrate this talent to you? I'd be more than glad to give you a performance and to engulf you into a cloud of ink."

"Hm, nah," Dusty answered impassively, not at all fazed by the threat. "I think I'll pass on that one, thanks. But do you use any other tricks you could show me? Like changing your skin pattern, as you did earlier?"

Offended by this question, Aqua curled and uncurled his arms reflexively, imagining strangling the life out of the impertinent anemone fish.

"That's not a TRICK, you little chit," he said haughtily. "It is art!

An art form, I should add, that I have honed until I reached perfection."

"Cool," Dusty said excitedly. "Life inside these anemones can get boring over time. Always the same faces to see, never any visitors, and I can't venture out far to search for other friends. Which means any diversion is welcome. Would you present one of these transformations? Pretty please? Can you turn into me, for example?"

Aqua did not know how to respond, because he didn't have a clue himself. He had never tried to replicate a clownfish. But what could it hurt to try? The answer would give him added knowledge that could be useful at some point in the future. Deciding to use this chance to find out the truth, Aqua folded his arms back alongside his body, sticking them out at the right spots to resemble fins while simultaneously changing into a light peachy pink with a white stripe behind his head and a grey dot on his back to make the transformation perfect. Examining Dusty closely, Aqua tried to replicate every colour, storing them in his memory.

"Wow!" Dusty gasped in wonder. "You look amazing. We could be twins. You've even got the grey mark on the back that none of my relatives have and which I was named for. That's so cool!!"

Hearing that the grey dot wasn't common among this species, Aqua quickly removed it. But dot or not, he wasn't entirely satisfied with the transformation, as it wasn't up to his usual standards of shapeshifting. "The pink colour is a bit off. And I'm way too big to be a convincing clownfish."

"Ach," the small fish said dismissively. "I think you look good. And besides, at your size, you'd make a super-great female."

"A great female?" Aqua asked, confused. But as he began to untangle his limbs again, he waved the question off. "Never mind. I'm not really interested in the answer."

Dusty dared to advance from his cover anew and swam a few excited circles around Aqua. "Then teach me how to change my colours," Dusty demanded.

"Teach you?" Aqua asked, laughing out loud as he realised that Dusty was serious. "I can't! You are a fish, not an octopus. And as a fish, you're at the bottom rung of the food chain, which means you don't get the ability to camouflage yourself or mimic other animals or use any of my other countless talents."

"Humpf," the clownfish answered. "I bet I could do it if I wanted to – I've learned that I can do anything at all if I put my mind to it."

"Little Dusty." Aqua sighed. "Don't get carried away by dreams that are impossible to accomplish. You know, when I was younger, I was like you. I believed that anything was achievable. But I'm wiser now. Dreams and play are great – but if you want to stay alive you need to be more realistic."

"Pah, realistic?" Dusty said disapprovingly as he somersaulted and freewheeled through the water. "But that's boring! Where did realism get you in life, heh?"

Feeling that he'd been put on the spot with that question, and not in a good way, Aqua glowered at the anemone fish. "I don't have any dreams anymore. Which is for the best because they only spell trouble. And you should follow my example if you are smart."

Stopping dead in his tracks, Dusty looked at the octopus, stunned, before wagging his tail fin. "I don't believe that. We all have some dreams, even if we aren't aware of them any longer. Think about it. And then tell me what the last wish is that you remember."

Aqua didn't care to share his innermost desires with a cheeky fish – so he was even more surprised than the clownfish when he found himself answering the question. "I always wanted to travel west and see the open sea. But that's a dangerous journey to undertake, into unknown territory with many predators lurking in the water ..."

Dusty smiled widely at the octopus. "I don't get why you doubt your abilities. You're a true master at defending yourself and don't even need anemones to discourage predators. So, if anyone can do it, it's definitely you!"

"Maybe, maybe not," Aqua said evasively, pondering how he could distract Dusty from delving further into his past and the long-forgotten feelings it brought forth. The answer promptly came to him. "And what is *your* biggest dream?"

Clearly excited that the octopus was showing an interest in him, Dusty picked up speed and whooped in joy. Only then did he calm down enough to concentrate on the answer. "I want to become a female!" he said enthusiastically, a spark gleaming in his eyes. "And my dad says, if I keep growing this fast, I might be strong enough to fulfil my dream one day."

Looking at the small clownfish in disbelief, Aqua couldn't help guffawing. But then he remembered that it wasn't nice to laugh at someone else's dream, even if it was as ridiculous as Dusty's. He thus swallowed the derogatory comment that had been lying on his tongue and searched for a milder reply instead.

"Dusty, you can't change your sex. It's been given to you by nature and you will be male from your birth until your death. This doesn't mean, of course, that you can't live out your female energy as a male. But other than that, I have to disappoint you. Which, I'm sure, you'll thank me for in a few years. Cause it's always better to know the truth early on rather than chasing after an impossible dream."

"But Dad says I can!" Dusty stared down at the octopus.

"Dusty, your dad is probably just humouring you. He doesn't want to dash your hopes. And he thinks that when you grow older, you'll forget about your dreams and not be as heartbroken when you realise the truth."

"I don't believe you," Dusty said, his voice firm. "I feel that I can do it and that it's in my future. And nothing you say, can make me doubt it."

Spreading his arms in a placating manner, Aqua stopped Dusty in his rant. "Fine by me," he answered, not really caring either way what the fish wanted to believe. "Go on and think whatever. But the day you turn into a female is the day that I will become a blue whale."

"Is that another dream of yours? Do you want to be a blue whale?" Dusty asked curiously, his upset at the octopus's earlier words seemingly forgotten.

"No!" Aqua called, irritated. "I do NOT want to be a blue whale. Why the heck would I want to be anything other than an octopus?"

"That's too bad." Dusty grinned. "Because you will be a blue whale soon. I'm not gonna wait forever to become a female, y'know?"

Aqua nodded tiredly, not interested in wasting any more time here. "Yes, yes, I can't wait. But now I gotta go. I'm hungry and your endless chatter is going to scare away any food."

Swimming away from the clownfish and the anemones that were his home, Aqua was sure he'd seen and heard the last of him when the pesky fish called after him. "Hey, you still haven't told me your name ..."

"It's Aqua," Aqua called back before swimming behind a large boulder and out of sight, all his attention being focused on finding the best hunting spot where prey would be numerous and predators scarce. And, most importantly, where no annoying clownfish would be present.

***

Over the next months, Aqua forgot all about his encounter with Dusty, until one fateful day it all came back in a rush.

Aqua was sitting on the sandy ocean bed, eying a strange transparent object. Perhaps it had fallen out of one of the human boats that sometimes crossed the water above. Studying the weird gadget intently, he felt movement behind him, followed by a small water vortex. Hearing laughter, he watched as a big pink clownfish vanished between the tentacles of a sea anemone not far from him.

"What the heck?" he called out, having a déjà-vu. "Can't I have some peace here?"

"Since when are blue whales interested in human inventions?" the anemone fish asked cheekily in a female voice.

"What are you talking about?" Aqua asked, dumbfounded. He began to wonder if all clownfish were crazy because of the venom of the anemones they were subjected to daily. "Have you never seen an octopus in your life? How can you mistake me for a blue whale?"

"Aw, now I'm hurt, Aqua," the female fish answered. "Don't you remember me?"

Aqua tried to place her but couldn't. He didn't have a lot of dealings with the fish community, as most of them didn't dare to come too close to an octopus. And try as he might, he couldn't remember ever meeting a female anemone fish in his life, only a male one. A male one with a distinct grey marking on his backside, similar to the one this female had. Remembering Dusty again, a realisation came to him.

"Wait, how do you know my name?"

Looking more closely at the female clownfish, Aqua watched her rush out from the anemone, swim some circles above him before diving back into the safety of her host, just as Dusty had done some months ago.

Her behaviour, calling him a blue whale, the marking – it all fit together perfectly. Apart from the little fact that it was impossible. Yet there was no denying the truth that swam in front of him. This female clownfish was Dusty!

Aqua's beak fell open in shock. He wasn't capable of forming a single coherent thought, let alone words that would make sense. "B-b-but ... that's not possible," he spluttered. "You can't be Dusty. Is this a trick? Are you a friend of his and he's hiding somewhere to laugh at me?"

"My name's Ash now and nope, no tricks," the female clownfish said cheerfully. "Remember? You told me that a fish isn't capable of using those ..."

"I ... I didn't mean ... I mean ..." Aqua stuttered, unable to take his eyes off the sight in front of him.

"It's okay," Dusty – no, Ash – said, "Mr Blue Whale!"

All his disbelief dissolved at these words and Aqua burst into laughter, followed by the little fish who wasn't quite as little anymore.

"This is amazing. I have no idea how you did that, but I'm happy for you."

"My dream wasn't all that unattainable," Ash admitted slyly. "You see, every clownfish is born male, and we all have the ability to change the outer expression of our sex. Whenever the female clownfish in a group dies, the biggest, strongest and most dominant male will take her place. I didn't know that back then, but I could feel the truth in my heart." Laughing brightly, Ash sped out from the anemone and swam another round above Aqua's head. "Mr Blue Whale!"

"You're never going to let me forget that I was in the wrong, are you?" Aqua asked good-naturally.

"Nope!" Ash said happily as she disappeared inside a gap between the anemones' tentacles, leaving another vortex and her high, clear laughter behind.

***

"And this," Aqua concluded, "is how I gathered my courage to come here. I thought that if Ash had been able to fulfil her dream, even though it had sounded utterly ridiculous at first, then maybe I could fulfil mine, too."

"And you did," Strix said, seeing Aqua with new eyes.

The octopus, who had appeared so strange and different at first, was rapidly becoming a confidant. And the more Strix recognised the things they had in common – such as their shared love of adventure and travelling, or their scepticism about believing things they couldn't see with their own eyes – the more he liked him.

"Guess what, Aqua?" Strix asked thoughtfully as he paddled with his legs and wings to cross another wave, the shore steadily coming closer. "My first instinct was to dismiss the story to be nothing else but another one of the fairy tales you made up to entertain me. But now I *do* believe that it's the truth after all."

Aqua acted surprised. "Why the change of heart?"

"Because," Strix said, "if there are animal species that don't even need air to survive, how much of a stretch is it that a species exists that can change its sex?"

"Are you ruminating about that topic again? We already established that we have different breathing organs, did we not?" Aqua responded.

"Yeah, but I wasn't talking about breathing this time, but flying," Strix explained. "It's an endless mystery to me how anyone can live happily without feeling the breeze ruffling their feathers when they soar up into the sky or without feeling absolutely weightless as they're carried by a gentle updraught."

Aqua's skin tone turned a greenish hue, as if he was feeling ill. "That's definitely something that I'll pass up on," he said. "Flying with you once was scary enough to give me nightmares for the rest of my life. It was way too high for comfort."

"High?" Strix laughed. "That was nothing. If you knew how much higher I can fly when I'm not carrying a heavy octopus ..."

"Heavy?" Aqua called out in mock outrage. "How dare you?!"

Smirking, Strix let his wings slap down onto the water so that a small wave splashed over Aqua, who gave back as good as he got, spattering Strix with four of his arms.

They only stopped their impromptu water fight as Aqua pointed to the beach that stretched out before them. "I can't come any farther than this or I'll risk being stranded again. And since you can't fly right now to bring me back, this is where I'll say goodbye. But if we ever cross paths again, I need to tell you about Caramel the camel. Now that's a story you shouldn't miss – it's about something super cool: a ship of the desert!"

"I doubt I will want to get back into the sea, but thanks for the offer." Strix grinned. "I'll keep it in mind." Floating on the waves, he watched Aqua wave two of his arms in a silent farewell before he disappeared into the blue depths of the sea.

Strix wouldn't have thought it possible when he had met the octopus, but he was a bit sad to see Aqua go as they'd begun to form a connection: something on which they could have built if only they didn't live in such different worlds.

Just then, a huge wave whooshed in from behind him, carrying Strix a few feet forward. His feet connected with the sandy beach and Strix hooted in joy that he'd reached the shore unscathed. Spreading his wings for added balance, he stood up and ran forward, letting himself fall into the dry sand.

"Finally!" he panted, lying with outspread wings, as the sun slowly dried his plumage. "Finally!"

Gender Energies and Equality

"Fine, clownfish can change their sex. I have known that since elementary school," Nayeli said. "But how does this translate to humans? Because we certainly can't. Unless we undergo a lot of operations, that is. Or do you mean that the gender we identify as isn't necessarily the sex we're born as?"

"No, although that can be true, too. As a human, you have both a sex that comes in the form of your body as well as a gender your ego identifies as – which can be the same or different. But on the soul level, neither of those exist. Or you could say that all souls are completely androgynous as they have an equal amount of divine female and male energy."

Nayeli was unable to keep up with Willow's explanation. "But if we have an equal amount of both on the soul level, why does our ego think of itself as either male or female?"

"Because parts of you are stored inside your subconsciousness, which you have no access to. If many female parts are stored there, you'll be more aware of your male energy. Or vice versa."

The tree continued its explanation calmly. "Anyway, every time you incarnate into a body, most of you choose one sex and identify as one gender only. But you can change that each time you come here."

"Wait, are you saying that I might have been a man in a past life?" Nayeli asked.

"Sure," Willow replied. "The likelihood is high that you've been both male and female several times throughout your incarnations. After all, you want to learn different lessons when coming here, and you choose the physical appearance and gender that best serve your purpose. If you want to experience giving birth, you'd do well to choose the female sex. On the other hand, if you decided to experience being a knight in medieval England, you'd have been wise to choose to be a man, since women weren't allowed to take on that role ..."

"That makes sense. But why were sexes and genders invented for this reality in the first place when we are really genderless as souls?"

"Part of the reason behind it is the dual reality we live in here and its need for opposites. And the second reason is that there needs to be a means for new souls to come into this world. And procreation via sexual intercourse followed by birth seals that deal."

"It does," Nayeli agreed. "But still, I don't find it fair that one of the two genders gets the short end of the deal – even though I don't yet know which gender is the bad one. Cause a few women in my life would say that men are awful, while some men would disagree with that and be convinced that women are the weak gender and inferior to them."

"What are you talking about, my dear?" Willow asked, bewildered. "Why do you think that one gender needs to be better than the other?"

"Me? You!" Nayeli said vehemently. "You just said that one of the reasons for genders existing is the two opposing ends inside a dual reality. And what I learned from you is that, for everything good, something bad has to exist. When the opposite of peace is war, and when the opposite of richness is poverty, one of the genders must be good and the other bad, no?"

Willow grumbled loudly at that. "Oh no! Female and male energies might be opposites, but they are equally important and valuable. But to stave off any more misunderstandings, I propose to tell you about the basics first ...?"

Agreeing wordlessly, Nayeli settled back against Willow's trunk. She didn't have to wait long for the tree's explanation.

"Female energy," Willow began, "is a reactive energy. Reactive, not passive, I might add – cause there's quite a difference. When you live in accordance with it, you're letting life flow while your intuition and emotions are your guiding systems. Female energy is a soft, gentle energy that helps you to take care of and nourish yourself and others. In contrast, male energy is an active energy. It drives you to success, lets you take things into your own hands and see them through. Male energy is, therefore, a go-getter type of energy that helps you to provide for and to protect yourself and others."

"But that's not necessarily what describes a woman or a man," Nayeli interjected. "A woman in this day and age can totally be assertive. And I know at least one man personally who's the born caretaker and has the most nurturing energy ..."

"Yes, undoubtedly. And this is the next issue I wanted to address. I've noticed that plenty of humans confound sexes and genders with the divine female and male energy. You might choose one sex over the other and identify with one gender when coming here, but you are not choosing one energy over the other. Instead, you always have both energies present within you, and you use both of them continuously.

"Think of male, or active, energy as the one that provides intent and direction. It is the thought and action you take to reach your goals. Meanwhile, the female, or reactive, energy provides the space and nourishment so that whatever you wish to create can grow and develop. If you don't have a canvas to paint on, it would be pointless to own watercolours and brushes. And if you don't have some earth to put seeds in, no plants can grow."

"These are all great metaphors, Willow, but how do they relate to our day-to-day lives? And how should we use these energies if they are both present within us?"

Willow rumbled. "There is no right or wrong answer, my dear. Because the options are as endless as there are souls present. For example, one person could live out their female energy in a healthy way in their job as a nurse or teacher, and take on male energy when playing football in their free time. Another person lives out their female energy when volunteering or when taking care of their kids or pets, and lives out their male energy when they run for a political office ..."

"When you say 'in a healthy way', I take it there are unhealthy ways to live out male and female energy as well?" Nayeli asked.

"Certainly. There can be healthy and unhealthy expressions of all things, including active and reactive energy. For example, one expression of healthy female energy is nourishment, while an unhealthy expression of it is letting people walk all over you. Meanwhile, a healthy expression of male energy is shown through protectiveness, while an unhealthy expression of it can be found in aggression. Be aware, though, that all these examples are nothing else but overviews. As I've mentioned before, female and male energies are constantly lived out in all areas of our lives, as they require each other.

"Based on everything I just told you, you might think that female energy is expressed when you hug someone, when you comfort a child, when you pet a dog, when you take care of your plants, when you let yourself be taken out on a surprise date or when you improvise when cooking. And you might think that male energy is present when you give a presentation, when you take charge in an emergency situation, when you provide financial help for others, when you plan a holiday or when you teach the family dog a new trick. You are not wrong when you think this. And yet, when you look closely at these examples, this strict separation between the two energies is false. When you water your plants, which is predominantly female because it has a nurturing element, the act of pouring water into the watering can is actually male energy. And while planning out a holiday is predominantly male energy, the daydreams and excitement that go along with it are naturally female. Every situation in life is built out of these two opposing energies, without exception. And you will be the healthiest and happiest when you accept and make room to live out both. Because, sadly, even in this day and age, the gender energies are unbalanced – inside individual humans but also on a wider social scale."

"How so?" Nayeli asked, intrigued.

"For centuries, the male energy has been dominant. Which wasn't all bad, mind you. Relying on your mind, on logic, analytics and science, you humans have managed in a short time to invent things like refrigerators, cars and computers, which allow you to live a more comfortable life today. But in the process, female energy – and, with it, emotions and intuition – got a bit of a raw deal. Regarding this, it's important to now support this energy once more and to bring these traits forward – without making the mistake of suppressing the male energy along the way."

Nayeli tapped her chin in thought. "Half an hour ago, I would have said that the feminist movement is already doing that. That we are fighting for true equality between the genders by empowering women."

"But?" the tree asked knowingly.

"But now I'm aware that the divine female energy isn't subjected to one gender only," Nayeli replied. "Reaching a state of equality is important, but it's not identical to balancing the two energies in our lives, correct?"

"Very true," Willow said. "Aside from the fact that equality in the sense of sameness doesn't exist in a reality that is based on individuality and free will. At least not when you look at the objective truth from the source perspective."

"Excuse me?" Nayeli flared up, meaning to vent her anger at hearing something this stupid. But she was stopped when the tree talked on, calming her with its next words.

"I want to make one thing clear from the beginning. I'm not saying that social injustices do not exist. Because they did, and they do. For a long time, black people were held as slaves by white men. This created an energetic rift between them, which has lasted even to this day. And today, women are still often paid less than men for doing the same job. This is based on a long history of women being treated as the property of men and not having the same social standing as them. Beyond that, children in poorer countries find it harder to access education than children in richer countries. LGBT+ people are still bullied and even prosecuted in some areas of the world. And abuse reigns freely all over the planet, through all social classes, religions, nationalities and cultures. All these facts and more cannot be denied. And I'm all for making these things a part of history. Although fairness isn't always as easy to implement as we might believe."

"Why not?" Nayeli crossed her arms in front of her chest defiantly. But before the willow tree got the chance to answer, she unfolded them again and brought her right hand up to rub her forehead. "Or wait, I think I know where you are going with this. Cause I've had my own hands-on experience. Earlier this year, we had to reduce our office working hours for a couple of months. Our boss said that everyone had to accept an equal cut in salary. She made this decision because she didn't want anyone to feel at a disadvantage or for envy to make the rounds. But my colleagues and I were split into two departments in the company. The department I belonged to had loads to do, and I could have easily worked eight hours a day. Meanwhile, the other department had practically no work. We were all paid for the same number of hours, but while some of us were stressed out to manage everything in the short time we had, the others only twiddled their thumbs. This made the whole matter unequal again."

"See, my dear? That's what I wanted to bring across. Depending on your perspective, the very same thing can be perceived as fair and unfair."

"Ha!" Nayeli called out, pointing a finger at the tree. "You just indirectly admitted that the concept of equality *does* exist after all and thus proved your own words from earlier untrue."

The tree corrected her. "I admitted that social injustices and unfairness exist. But even if you right all these wrongs, it does not change the fact that, by nature, we are all unequal inside a dual reality. And that you'll never be equal to others in every aspect for as long as you're incarnated here."

"Which you still haven't explained to me," Nayeli complained.

"Then let me do that now. The inequality that's at the base of this reality affects every level, starting with your bodies. Having the female sex enables you to give birth to a child, which makes you superior to anyone born with the male sex in this regard. A small child cannot carry the same weight as an adult, and is thus inferior in this aspect. A colour-blind human cannot describe the colours of a rainbow nearly as well as a person who has perfect eyesight. A trained musician would win every singing contest against someone who's never sung a note in their life and who has no musical ear. And no human can run faster than a cheetah, so you are all inferior to the cheetah when it comes to speed. That's why, in most sports, women and men compete separately. And why children are treated differently to adults."

As the tree swung its branches back and forth, some leaves brushed the earth. "If you were to judge a duck, a deer and a shark by how far they can fly, it will always be the duck who wins. But if you were to judge them for their ability to stay underwater for hours on end, neither the duck nor the deer would have any chance against the shark. And the same applies to you humans. A surgeon is superior when it comes to saving someone's life, but a mechanic is superior when it comes to repairing a car ... You all have areas of excellence. You are all superior and inferior in an infinite number of ways. And this changes not only in terms of who you compare yourself to; it also changes over your life path as you learn new things and lose interest in others. But this natural *inequality* is a blessing in disguise since your differences guide you down the path you have chosen for this life and to your unique purpose, in which you are unmatched. In the end, it's important not to focus on the things in which you are inferior but to tap into the talents and abilities that make you superior. So what if you aren't a great tech genius? Focus on being a great writer instead."

Nayeli gnawed on her bottom lip while thinking about this. "I understand that we're all unequal when it comes to talents, abilities and chances, considering that we also have unequal beginnings in life, as some people are born into rich families, while others start in poverty to name just one out of many examples. But no matter the differences, every human should still be valued the same, shouldn't they? And be supported equally?"

"They should," Willow agreed all too readily. "But to value humans the same inside a 3D reality, you need to support everyone's inequality. Or, to say it otherwise, the truest form of equality in this dimension is to help every single person to be safe and free to live a fully authentic life. If you manage to do that, everyone would be empowered to go for what makes them happy. In such a world, someone wanting to climb the corporate ladder and someone wanting to be a homemaker would be supported equally. Neither would stand above the other, and no one would look down on either of them."

"Are you implying that we don't embrace our differences enough?" Nayeli asked.

"You sure don't," Willow replied matter-of-factly. "I only need to survey your education system, which is based on the principle of not supporting individuals. Consider a child who is bad at maths but great at languages. What will most parents and teachers do? They'll give them extra help in maths, essentially forcing them to spend more time on a subject the child doesn't have any innate talent for, instead of letting them become an expert in another subject, which they are naturally good at. This is because your school system demands that every pupil passes every subject, even the ones that aren't important for the child's soul-plan."

"But isn't it beneficial that we learn a lot of different stuff in school?" Nayeli asked.

"Yes and no – there are obviously things that are important for each human to know. How to read and write and basic arithmetic, for example. Foreign languages are also helpful later in life if you are thus inclined. But why force every human to fit a template after you've learned the basics? Why does an actor need to know how to calculate a parabola? They'll never need that knowledge in their profession, and they'll soon forget it after leaving school anyway. And why would a doctor need to know who wrote *Hamlet* or what it's about if they aren't interested in English literature?

"Just imagine, my dear, what this world could and would look like if every human was enabled to focus on their area of excellence. When everyone could follow their dreams and passions and remain on track with their life path. When every job is matched to the right person, who'd be perfectly suited for it. Imagine how fulfilled everyone would feel. The world would be a much better and lighter place, one of happiness as opposed to one of pain and failure."

"You're right about that," Nayeli agreed, after thinking about the matter. "But how are we supposed to create a world in which we're allowed to be who we are?"

"There are two main pillars. One is to focus on the solutions instead of resisting the problem. Because, as you've learned, what you resist persists. Protesting against something has its place – protests raise awareness of a problem. But it can't end there. If protests aren't followed by action to create the shift you want, they're useless."

"And the second pillar?"

"The second pillar is based on another spiritual law that we'll discuss in-depth later. It's called the Law of Reflection and tells of the fact that the outer reality you perceive is nothing else but a mirror of your inner world. Thus, to create change, the best place to start is within yourself. In practice that means, in order to help the world balance the male and female energies, you need to allow both your reactive and active energies to express themselves in healthy ways and support them in equal measures."

The tree seemed to gather its thoughts and moved its branches apart before pulling them back together. Patches of sunlight danced on Nayeli's legs prior to being blocked out again.

"You know, my dear, I want to end this lesson with a beautiful quote based on a Cherokee proverb. It goes like this: 'A man's highest calling is to keep the woman safe so that she can follow her highest calling – to lead the man back to his soul.' For this quote to apply here, it only needs to be changed slightly: the person with the higher male energy should provide safety for the person with the higher female energy, who in turn leads the person with the male energy closer to his or her own female energy. And this can translate to two people or you alone. Let the male part of you provide safety for the female part so that it can take on her role."

"That does sound great, on one hand ..."

"But?" the weeping willow questioned, as Nayeli fell silent and stared into the distance.

"But," Nayeli continued slowly, her voice tinged with sadness, "on the other hand it sounds awful. When you say it like that, you make it sound as if we never need anyone else. As if we're whole and don't need other people to complete us. As if love is unnecessary and soulmates are outdated. And I did like the idea that I'd be able to someday find a perfect match, someone who brings out the best in me. A person I belong to. But, whatever. I'll just have to accept that soulmates are not real."

"Don't be too hasty in writing them off, my dear child," Willow said gently and dived straight into the next story without giving Nayeli any time to process these words or ask about their meaning.

11. Rose, the Swan

Strix had stayed near the beach for two days and nights to recuperate fully from his dip in the ocean. After which he had become restless again.

Flying northwards, Strix watched the savannah drift by underneath him, which presented itself in its wild beauty. The landscape was dominated by elephant grass swaying in the warm air, only interrupted by groups of Baobabs. Under one of these trees, a lone buffalo stood. And when Strix passed by him, he saw a river meandering into the west, populated with hippopotamuses that would occasionally open their huge mouths to show off their impressive incisors. It was a landscape that Strix could still admire, despite his earlier mishap of suffering a heatstroke.

Having learned from his mistake, this time around Strix took better care of his needs and made sure he wasn't out in the sun for too long, preferring to fly at night when millions of stars appeared overhead and littered his path. It was in these moments that he felt most in his element.

Strix acknowledged that he had never felt this alive prior to his near-death experience, nor as free. He revelled in the fact that he could go where he wanted whenever he felt like it, without anyone holding him back or controlling his actions – a freedom that was made all the better when he was carried by the night breeze, which let his thoughts disperse in the wind and let him enter a meditative state where neither worries nor troubles existed.

It was only when another morning dawned on the horizon that Strix came back to reality. Looking out for a suitable resting place for the day, Strix saw an oasis appear in his line of sight almost immediately. It was a small waterhole encircled by trees and inhabited by flamingos, pelicans and other birds of all sizes and colours that were either locals or stopping for a rest on their migration journey.

Strix was instantly smitten with the place.

In parts, this might have also been due to a beautiful female swan choosing this very moment to land on the water. The bird was sliding over the surface with a gracefulness that was unmatched by anyone else before bending her long neck in a perfect curve to drink.

Feeling as if he had been struck by lightning at the sight, Strix lost his ability to fly and almost crashed head-first into a tree. Missing the trunk by millimetres, he swerved around it and felt a twig graze his stomach. Wincing, Strix was relieved that it hadn't been one of the spiky branches and that, when he landed behind the tree, nothing else but his ego was bruised. But beyond this, his luck had run out. Because when he looked towards the waterhole to gauge whether the beautiful swan had seen his almost-crash, he noticed that the female bird was watching him with an amused twinkle in her eyes.

A moment later – and before Strix could compose an escape plan – she landed beside him.

"Hi," the larger bird said brightly. "I'm Rose. What's your name?"

Strix scrambled around for a name to give, but all information had fled his brain. It was only after a few endless seconds of searching the blackness that had once been his memory that Strix found the right answer. "Strix," he said, relieved, hoping she wouldn't think him rude or – even worse – simple for taking this long to respond. "My name is Strix."

Remembering his manners, he bowed. "It's very nice to meet

you, Rose. And what a beautiful name that is. Very fitting for a graceful swan like you."

Strix didn't know where those mushy words had come from, but he didn't have long to be mortified about them, because Rose was speaking again and her sweet voice captured his full attention.

"I saw your collision with the tree and wanted to ask if you're all right," she said.

Strix hoped for an earthquake to rip apart the ground at his feet and to be swallowed whole. Anything to release him from this hell. But nothing happened to save him from his embarrassment.

Nervously pawing at the ground, Strix decided on the second-best course of action: to downplay the incident. Aiming for a confident voice and displeased to find it squeaky and nervous instead, Strix raised his head. "Er, yeah, that was totally planned," he choked out. "It's always good to practise these aerial manoeuvres - you know, in case one day you need to swerve around a tree that's appearing out of nowhere. Not that they jump into your path. I mean, ... maybe some do. I've seen many weird things on my travels. It wouldn't surprise me to see a moving tree. And now I'll certainly be ready whenever I meet one!"

Only after the words had left his beak did Strix notice how absurd they sounded. If he could, he would have taken them back in an instant. But his embarrassment was forgotten when the female swan giggled lightly in answer.

Rose's laughter was high and clear and the most beautiful sound Strix had heard since he had hatched.

"I like you! You are funny!" Rose said.

Looking dreamily at the swan, Strix felt as if he had been enchanted. Meanwhile, his stomach tingled with excitement, as if a bee colony was dancing inside his belly. Not wanting to think too long about what this implied, as Strix felt totally out of his element whenever feelings were involved, he tried to concentrate on something else he *was* naturally good at – striking up conversations with strangers and becoming friends with them. Only that, right now, he couldn't think of anything to say to keep the ball rolling.

Rose didn't seem to mind his silence, though. She moved around to sit next to him and let her gaze drift out over the water where the other swans of her bevy swam. "It's beautiful here, isn't it?" She sighed blissfully. "Normally, we swans don't travel this far south to the African continent. But last year was an especially harsh winter, and when we reached this place we liked it so much that we decided to pay a short visit again this year before travelling back north to our wintering area."

Strix followed Rose's gaze and had to agree with her assessment. The small oasis was truly a paradise in this savannah, and the animals living here seemed to be of the same opinion. Birds were coming and going and there were some of the most colourful butter flies Strix had ever seen in his life. Not to mention the gazelles and zebras on the far side of the waterhole who'd arrived shortly ago to drink. Overall, the atmosphere was one of joyfulness, with everyone talking in a lively manner.

"Yes, it is," Strix breathed, thinking by himself that Rose's presence had a large share in transforming this place from merely charming to magnificently beautiful. He felt a connection to her so strong, as if the swan was a part of him that he had missed all his life, without ever knowing something had been lost. Their connection felt comforting but also new and exciting. And it felt as if they had years to catch up on. But, to Strix's dismay, time didn't seem to be in their favour. Because, just then, a big male swan chose to land in front of Rose, interrupting their intimate togetherness.

The male spread his wings to appear even bigger than he was, and when he spoke to Rose, his voice was deep and masculine. "Hello, my angel. You look lonely; as if you need some company. C'mon, don't be shy. If the others are making too much of a ruckus for you, we could steal away from them and have a nice one-on-one conversation. If you know what I'm saying?"

"I know exactly what you're saying, you big lump," Rose said, sounding fed-up. "And I've told you a thousand times that I'm not interested. When will that information sink in to your bird brain? Get lost and stop bothering me!"

The huge swan glared at Strix before swivelling his eyes back to Rose and puffing his chest out proudly. "Of course, if you'd rather spend your time with a scrawny owl instead of me, I won't stand in your way. You'll come to your senses sooner or later. But by then, it might be *too* late, because *I* won't be interested in *you* any longer. Think about what you stand to lose here. And don't wait forever!" Spreading his wings, he flew back and set down in the middle of the waterhole.

"Men," Rose said angrily. "They think they own the world and can have anything they want. But I'm not a prize! And if they can't understand the word 'no', my bill is certainly strong enough to drive that message home."

Feeling both attracted and a little frightened by Rose's fortitude, Strix coughed. "But surely not all males are like that?" he asked carefully.

Rose's huff turned into a sad laugh. "The ones I know are all stuck up and arrogant and stupid. You being the exception, of course," she added quickly.

Strix was relieved at hearing those last words, but the happiness setting in evaporated as soon as the swan continued to speak.

"But you don't count, since I only mean my admirers and possible love interests." The last words she muttered so sarcastically that Strix could feel derision drip out of them. "Whatever," she concluded. "Love is overrated, anyway …"

Normally, Strix would have agreed with that statement wholeheartedly. He had always thought that the importance of romantic relationships was exaggerated by everyone. But curiously, at this moment, his heart felt as if it was breaking apart. Not wanting to let his hurt show, though, Strix swallowed his feelings and forced a smile.

"That sounds like you're finished with love before you've even tried it. Did … did something bad happen for you to feel this way?"

Peeking sideways at Rose and seeing a closed-off look on her face, Strix hastily added: "I'm sorry if that's too intrusive. You know what? Just forget my question."

"No, no, it's fine. I don't mind telling you. I learned that love isn't for me when I was a cygnet. Because it hurts everyone involved, and I don't want to have any part in that."

"Why's that?" Strix asked, trying to make sense of Rose's words. "What happened to make you think relationships are hurtful?"

"My dad died when I was young, and my mum was in a lot of pain afterwards. It took her forever to get over his loss and find another partner. And on top of that, love has destroyed all my friendships. Once my childhood friends had got their mates, they stopped having time for me. They're way too busy staring into their soulmate's eyes and preparing nests for their future cygnets. Not that I begrudge them their bliss, but ..."

"... it feels as if you're being abandoned and left behind by everyone." Strix felt compassion for the swan because he'd been in the same boat as her.

"I suppose." Rose sighed. "You know, you're the first who's understood me. I have many admirers who are all doing their best to woo me. But none of them ever take the time to ask me what my dreams and hopes are. So why should I even consider them?"

"Maybe you just haven't met the right partner yet?" Strix asked, unable to keep a tone of hopefulness out of his voice.

"Yes, maybe." Rose shrugged. "But I definitely won't settle for anyone who's as superficial as that stupid cob over there. Being alone is the better alternative."

Rose looked sideways at him. "And what about you, Strix? Is there a nice female owl waiting for you back home?"

Immediately, an image appeared in Strix's mind, but he quickly dislodged it. "No, no one," he said neutrally. "Hey, we should form an alliance. The two birds who have sworn off love. That is, unless you still hope you'll find Mr Perfect ...?"

"Yeah, right." Rose laughed. "I'll most likely find him the day that trees grow legs and walk."

Being reminded of his earlier blunder, Strix felt the embarrassment come back in a rush. He scraped at the ground, avoiding the swan's gaze. But when Rose nudged him good-naturally and laughed brightly, Strix couldn't help but join in, infected by her merriment. He also couldn't help but notice how her bright tone mingled perfectly with his deeper timbre.

***

Over the next few days, Strix and Rose cemented their bond as they alternated between flying north with the swan's flock to their wintering ground and resting near ponds or at the beach, sharing their memories and experiences from childhood and their travels.

After yet another long day's journey – one that made Strix realise he didn't envy migratory birds who had to keep up with the group and couldn't choose their own pace like he did when flying alone – they arrived at a small wadi that was currently carrying water.

As soon as Rose had laid eyes on it, she had offered to help him fish a morning meal, but Strix had only taken one quick look at the water and declined, opting to hunt for his food on land instead.

When he arrived back at the wadi after having filled his stomach with an excellent meal, Strix chose a vantage point on a rock from where he could watch Rose. Seeing her glide over the surface as elegantly as always, Strix thanked the universe for having led him to her, as he treasured every minute he spent with the swan. He knew that life couldn't have turned out any better for him.

It didn't take long for Rose to notice that he'd returned and she headed straight towards him. Beaming as she landed on the ground beside him, the female swan shifted restlessly from one foot to the other, oozing excitement. "Don't you want to ask me what happened this morning when you were off hunting? Come on, ask me!"

Ready to play along with any wish Rose uttered, Strix matched her smile. "Yes, all right. What happened this morning?"

"Strix," she said happily, pausing for added effect. "I think I've fallen in love!"

Hearing these words, Strix felt his heart jump into his throat. It was beating so strongly that he believed any animal for miles around must hear it. Meanwhile, his thoughts were doing cartwheels inside his brain, making Strix wonder if Rose's feelings finally matched his own. Until the swan dashed all his hopes.

"He arrived an hour ago, and he's the most beautiful swan I've ever met. And I don't only mean his appearance with that, but his character. He's attentive and caring and thoughtful and witty and smart and funny. He's perfect, and I don't know what to do."

A deep sense of sadness and disappointment – which replaced the hope he had tasted so briefly – came faster than Strix could have anticipated. And seeing Rose's vibrant eyes that shone with adoration made him feel even worse. Averting his gaze, Strix stared at the ground instead.

"Why?" he croaked out. "He sounds like the one. And if he's that great, you shouldn't waste any more time but grab onto him. It could be a once-in-a-lifetime chance. Go on, what are you still waiting for? Tell him how you feel. I'm sure he'll be delighted. And if he isn't, he's an idiot and doesn't deserve you."

The last shred of hope that this foreign bird wasn't interested in Rose or was already spoken for crept inside Strix's mind, but it was shattered before it could fully blossom.

"Oh, he feels the same," Rose responded excitedly. "He says he's never met anyone like me in his life." Not noticing Strix's pain at her words, Rose closed her eyes in bliss. "You would need to experience this yourself to understand it. 'Magical' is the sole word I can use to describe this feeling. When I look into his eyes, I feel as if I'm coming home; as if something inside us draws us together."

Strix was tempted to tell Rose he knew exactly what that felt like. That he had fallen madly in love with her on first sight and felt an intimate connection with her so strongly that he thought he was going crazy at times. But at the last possible moment, he swallowed the words. It would be unfair to her, since she clearly didn't feel the same way about him. And maybe that was even for the best. For whoever had heard of a healthy, functional relationship between a swan and an owl? They were simply not meant for each other, and the most loving thing he could do was to let Rose find happiness and love on her own. Even if it wasn't with him, and even when she would never know the sacrifice he had made.

Strix pulled himself together, ignoring the sadness and hurt that was filling him up. And when he spoke, he tried for a deliberately joyful tone of voice.

"That sounds great," Strix said. "What are you still doing here? Go and get your cob, Rose."

"You're right!" she agreed happily, straightening up. "This is my chance at love. One I thought I wouldn't get in this life only last night. I should go with him."

"Wait, go with him?" Strix asked, feeling as if he had got punched in the gut at this news.

"Uh-huh, his flock's wintering grounds are a bit west of here and he asked me to come along and join up with them. From what he's told me, the place is utterly beautiful. Mountains and valleys and lots of meadows with babbling brooks. I can't wait for him to show me everything!"

"I'm glad for you," Strix said and was surprised to find that it was the truth. While part of him was shrouded in pain, another part was happy to see Rose like this: blissful and practically glowing. It suited her.

"Thank you, Strix," she said gratefully. "You know, you could come with us. I'm sure there are lots of mice for you to hunt where we're going, and maybe you'll also meet some other owls there. Come to think of it, maybe you'll meet *the* owl."

For a split second, Strix toyed with the idea of accepting her offer, but then he thought about having to see Rose every day, building a life with someone else. He promptly shoved the image away from him, replacing it with others from his past adventures.

"No, thank you. My wings are itching to get going again and to continue my own journey. There're still many things left to do and an endless sum of countries to travel to. I want to make the most of my freedom and independence."

For the first time in his life, these words were a blatant lie, but he wisely kept this knowledge to himself. Or, at least, Strix hoped he hadn't let his true feelings show. Because when he looked up at Rose, he saw concern for him reflected in her eyes.

"Promise me something, Strix, will you?"

"Hmm?" He didn't trust his voice anymore, fearing it would break over the first word he spoke.

"When true love enters your life," Rose said pensively, "don't let it pass you by. We both know that I've thought along the same lines as you. That romantic love is useless and a waste of time. But all that changes when you meet the right soulmate you are meant to be with."

Looking off into the distance, Rose smiled. "And your perfect match might be closer than you think. Just keep your eyes and heart open, all right?"

"Right. I won't rule it out completely, but I do believe that love isn't for me," Strix said, repeating Rose's statement from the day they'd met.

"We'll see." Rose smiled and opened her wings. "But now I gotta go. He's waiting for me."

This time, Strix could not conceal his sadness. "Have a safe journey, then. And a good life."

"Hey!" Rose called, upset. "This doesn't mean that we'll never meet up again. You can visit us and we can visit you as soon as I know where you'll be settling down. And if you don't … next year at about the same time we'll fly to the oasis again where we met. And I would love it if I could talk to my best friend then." Rose gently touched her bill to Strix's forehead in a sign of affection.

Strix choked back a few tears at this, keeping his answer vague. "Yes, maybe we can do that." He knew in that instant, though, that there wouldn't be any reunion between him and Rose in this lifetime. And it would be better this way for both of them.

"Well, then. Until next year," Rose said as she leaned over and gave him a second peck on the cheek. "I'll miss you."

"I'll miss you, too." Strix sighed forlornly, but by the time he had uttered the words Rose was already gone, settling elegantly down on the water near a tall male swan.

Deciding not to make this goodbye any harder than it had to be, Strix quickly flew up and turned east, away from the swan who held his heart. He only allowed himself one last glance back towards the wadi. Tears were blurring his vision, but his sight was still sharp enough to see an image, which he feared would be stuck in his mind forever. It was of Rose and her soulmate happily bending their necks towards each other, forming the shape of a heart.

Soulmates and Soul Contacts

"That's a sad ending!" Nayeli complained while looking up into the canopy and the blue sky beyond. "Did Strix see Rose ever again?"

"No, not until this day. But the story isn't so sad once you know its real ending …"

"You mean there is more to it?"

"There's much more to it," Willow promised.

"Well, tell me about it," Nayeli demanded.

"All in due course. For now, you simply need to be aware of the fact that Rose wasn't Strix's true love, as he believed at that time."

"Then why did Strix have such a crush on her, if she wasn't the right partner for him? Why meet her at all and go through this heartbreak if they were both meant to be with someone else? If they aren't each other's soulmate?"

"Oh, but they are soulmates," Willow answered.

Nayeli thought she could hear a grin in the tree's voice and rolled her eyes.

"Can you please make up your mind? First you say they're not soulmates and then you say they are. Are you trying to confuse me, or do you simply not know what you're talking about?"

"I never said they weren't soulmates. I only said they weren't meant to be romantic partners in this life – quite different, my dear. Nobody is meant to end up with every one of their soulmates or be romantically involved with all of them, for that matter. That would truly result in chaos."

"Wait, Willow," Nayeli said. "You make it sound as if everyone has several soulmates, instead of just one."

"You have more than one for sure. In fact, every single soul is your soulmate if you break it down that far."

"Humpf. That wasn't exactly what I had in mind when I said I wanted one. The colleague I can't stand at work and my noisy neighbours are definitely not people I feel I belong to, if you know what I mean."

"I do know what you mean!" Willow said earnestly. "But don't judge this matter before you've heard all the details. Let's see, how can I best explain this to you?" The weeping willow let its lighter branches rub together above Nayeli's head. "Hmm, yes, imagine source consciousness as a giant tree with thousands of branches and millions of leaves."

Nayeli couldn't help poking fun at her friend. "Another tree example? You aren't very imaginative today, are you?"

Laughing with her, the tree shook out its branches. A few leaves rained down upon Nayeli. "Hush, you naughty girl. Or you won't hear my explanation. Where was I? Oh yes, the tree. Picture an immense tree of life with many, many branches that fork out into twigs, which all have countless leaves growing on them. On this tree, every leaf is a soul. And every soul is connected to the others because they're all part of the same tree – or rather, part of the same source consciousness. But naturally, some leaves grow closer to you, some even on the same twig, while others grow further away, some on the other side of the tree. And just like that, you'll notice that you're closer to some soul-family members, while you are not quite as close to others."

Nayeli flipped her hair over her left shoulder. "Are you saying that the people I get along with great are my closer soulmates, and everyone else is a distant relative, so to speak?"

"Not quite," Willow replied. "You can't recognise a soulmate by how you feel about them. You can only recognise them by the intensity of the emotion they evoke in you or, to say it otherwise, by the importance they have in your life."

"Come again?"

"Your close soulmates take on varying roles in your life. They can be parents or siblings or children or friends or romantic or sexual partners. Or they can be your enemies and adversaries. An abusive partner, for example. Or a boss at work who takes advantage of you."

Gasping in shock at this revelation, Nayeli clamped a hand over her mouth. "But why? Why would our soulmates decide to be our enemies? Why would we come here and do that?"

"A soulmate's main priority in life is to help their soul-family grow. And inside a dual reality, one of the fastest ways to achieve this is through hardship," Willow explained. "Now, if you decide to experience being bullied, you need to meet a bully. And what would be better than getting help from someone you trust on a soul level? This might be a terrible concept from your human perspective. But from the source's point of view, it is really an act of love. After all, your soul-family wants you to achieve the dreams you've set for this life. And those will be put into motion by overcoming the corresponding trauma."

Nayeli blew out the breath she had been holding. "That's just great," she muttered, her voice laced with sarcasm. "Cause my worst enemy is *definitely* not the kind of soulmate I wanted, either. Isn't there *some* good news you can tell me about my soul-family?"

The tree chuckled in answer. "How about this: as you move along your path and heal past traumas, you'll meet fewer soulmates who will create negative situations for you. Once you integrate a part of yourself that was lost inside your subconsciousness, you no longer need to be taught that lesson. And when that happens, you will attract more relationships that belong into the blessing category and which are harmonious and loving."

Nayeli stretched out her legs. "That does sound better. And having lots of soulmates means that I have at least several shots at finding a partner who will be a perfect, or an almost perfect, match for me, or isn't that right?"

"Indeed. Not to mention that you *need* more than one option in this 3D reality. Imagine having written in your soul-plan that you'll meet your future spouse in your twenties and that you'll then spend the rest of your life with them. This meeting is agreed by both your souls before birth and written down in a soul contract. But when you incarnate, only you decide to follow your soul-plan, while the other person decides to stray from their chosen path. Maybe, due to these changes, you'll never meet in this incarnation. Or maybe, the other person will already be married to someone else when you do meet up. Or they might simply be in such a low vibrational place in life that they're not ready for a relationship. You'd end up alone because of the free will of someone else – and this is a total contradiction to the universal law, which says that everyone can create their life as they wish ..."

"What's a soul contract?" Nayeli interjected. "You haven't explained those before ..."

"It's easy to understand. Since you are not an island, you must coordinate parts of your soul-plan with other members of your soul-family. You'll have soul contracts with the souls of your incarnated parents, with your siblings, with teachers and work colleagues, with your children, platonic friends and with your romantic partners to name just a few. In those contracts, you will decide when and how you'll meet and which role you will play for each other."

Nayeli lifted her eyebrows in surprise. "And you are saying that, if the soulmate I planned to marry and spend the rest of my life with decides to become a monk, both our soul contracts are rewritten while we are here?"

"Correct. Since your soulmate's free will to change their path cannot affect your free will to continue to follow yours, you will meet another soulmate who'll take the place of the first one. To do this, your higher self will find another member of your soul-family who is incarnated, and together both souls will agree on how you two will meet instead. This way all souls get the experience they create for themselves, whether this is to experience life as a monk or to experience having a deep, loving bond with a partner. This re-writing of existing soul contracts happens all the time since the free will of humans creates changes. But it's always done in a way that benefits everyone involved. And in the end, it all harmonises and flows perfectly together."

Frowning, Nayeli summed up Willow's teachings. "So, we all have a soul-plan as well as soul contracts, which are written prior to our birth. But we also have free will that messes up these plans constantly and forces our soul to rewrite them countless times. And this means that everything is confusing as hell and no one can ever understand why something happened the way it happened?"

Willow's branches whipped up and down as the tree laughed. "Sounds about right."

Chuckling herself, Nayeli thought about everything she'd just learned. As she once again pictured the giant tree of life with thousands of leaves, an idea came to her that she hadn't previously considered.

"Willow, what about the leaf that's growing closest to me on the tree of life? Couldn't that be my one true love match? Better than any of my other close soulmates?"

"Yes, and no. Spiritual people call this person your twin flame or mirror soul. It is essentially your closest soulmate."

"My twin flame?" Looking up in interest, Nayeli rubbed her hands together. "Now, that sounds like what I was looking for all along ..."

"Not so fast, my dear," Willow answered. "Your twin soul *does* come closest to the general idea of a soulmate that most of you humans hold. The relationship you have with them can be harmonious and loving on top of being liberating and exciting. If you are ready for that part of your journey, the bond you two share can be the most accepting, supporting and loving you can possibly imagine ... But that doesn't mean they are the perfect romantic partner for you in every incarnation."

"But why?" Nayeli asked, feeling let down at this news.

"It's obvious why, when you think about it. Apart from you, they are the soul who's most invested in healing you. In other words, this person will do their utmost to make you aware of all your unhealed wounds by creating situations that will trigger your traumas."

"Which will be painful," Nayeli concluded.

"Very painful," Willow agreed. "When you meet your twin flame before you're ready – before you've healed most of your past wounds – it can be a real rollercoaster ride. IF you can even meet them, that is."

"Why shouldn't I be able to?" Nayeli asked, puzzled.

"Not all twin flames incarnate at the same time. It's actually been the standard procedure for thousands of years that most mirror souls take turns."

"Because?"

"Because a twin flame relationship is intense and the two people involved will accelerate their healing. And, in turn, the healing of the collective consciousness, which would lead to a huge shift in the world. The dormant-lying abilities they'd awaken in each other would lift the world into a much higher vibrational state. And since most humans have not been ready for that in the past, twin souls took turns to incarnate to ensure they wouldn't meet too soon. Something that's starting to change now. But there's no guarantee that *your* mirror soul is currently incarnated."

"But they could be? So I could try to search for them?" Nayeli needled the tree, not yet being able to let go of the idea of meeting her closest soulmate.

"You could, but I'd advise you against it. For the reasons I already mentioned. And because placing too much importance on the term *twin soul* can quickly become a pitfall. Imagine you feel a deep connection to someone, but after a year or two, they become abusive towards you. You might then excuse this behaviour by saying 'it has to be this way, it has to be painful, they are doing this to heal me'. But this is nonsense. You, my dear child, are not meant to stay in destructive patterns after you've become aware of them. What you are here to do is to create happy and fulfilled relationships. Which you can do with any closer soulmate, not just your mirror soul."

"But won't my twin soul get jealous if I get together with anyone but them?"

One of Willow's longer branches tickled Nayeli's leg. "First off, on the soul level, it isn't possible to feel jealous because jealousy is a lower vibrational emotion. And second, no – the opposite is true. Your twin soul wants you to be as happy and fulfilled as you can possibly be. They are rooting for you to sail through this life and to find all the love you can. Just like you do for them."

Nayeli blew out the breath she had been holding. "Right, okay, so I shouldn't embark on a quest to meet my twin flame, come hell or higher water. Only, what does this tell me? That true love is something that we have no real control over? And that it might not exist for all of us in each of our lives?"

"No. Everyone can create harmonious and loving relationships in their lives – without exception. Some of your soul-family members join you on your path specifically for that purpose – to show you what close soulmate connections and the unconditional love that's present within them feel like. And to show you why your desire for love couldn't be quenched until now ..."

"You make these relationships sound like the most beautiful thing on Earth. But what do they feel like?" Nayeli questioned.

"They make you feel completely safe and free at the same time. You feel as if you've found a person with whom you belong, someone who accepts and understands you on all levels. It feels like you're coming home!"

Part 2 - The spiritual journey continues

Prologue – Relationships and Belonging

The sun was rising, casting a warm orange glow over Willow's meadow.

As Nayeli walked over the dew-wet grass, many thoughts were swirling through her mind. Thoughts about her past and how she had come to be here, of all places. Thoughts about how crazy her present life was, as she visited a tree every day, which told her about souls and the universe and life itself. And thoughts about her future and what blessings or catastrophes it might still hold.

She was so lost in contemplation that she jumped when the tree addressed her.

"Hello, Nayeli, do you have somewhere else you need to be today?"

Looking up and becoming aware that she had already passed the small hill the weeping willow stood on, Nayeli quickly turned around and swept some of the branches aside to walk through them into the shadowy cavern beneath the tree's crown. "Sorry," she said. "I wasn't paying attention to where I was."

Willow murmured. "I noticed as much. What were you thinking about?"

Shrugging, Nayeli searched out a spot on the grassy floor and made herself comfortable. "My family again. My mother hasn't heard a peep from my sister since the funeral. And that this separation happened in the middle of my parent's divorce is an additional burden for my mum."

"Your parents are separating? I'm sorry to hear that."

"No need," Nayeli replied offhandedly. "It's long overdue. They've not been on good terms for ages. And with ages I mean for as long as I can remember." Sighing, Nayeli pinched the bridge of her nose. "I simply don't get why relationships have to go downhill for no reason. They're messy in the best case and painful in the worst ..."

Willow let its branches wave about in a steady rhythm. "But maybe it's not quite as hopeless as you make it sound, hmm? Sure, no relationship is perfect. People hurt us. They make mistakes, the same as we do. And even though they may have the best intentions, their words or actions can trigger us, just as we do them, making us feel angry or jealous or impatient or all kinds of other negative feelings. But relationships are not all bad, are they? They can also be loving and supportive."

"I guess," Nayeli said mulishly. "When you're lucky. Which my family apparently isn't."

"There's no luck involved here, only the free will of everyone involved," the tree replied. "That's the bad news. Everyone in a relationship automatically has the power to hurt the other person."

"What do relationships have to do with power? That seems a strange thing to say."

"It might seem strange, but the two are closely related. And this is one of the hardest truths to swallow about relationships. You need two people's free will to build a connection, but one person is enough to end it. Imagine it like a rope strung between you and someone else. If you cut the rope on your side, the bond will be cut, no matter how much the other person holds on to their end."

Willow let the words sink in before continuing. "This makes it difficult for humans to create new relationships or to deepen existing ones. They fear being powerless, as this is one of the lowest frequencies you can possibly hold. Many people aim to avoid feeling it at all costs. And so they try to be the one in control – either by not starting a relationship in the first place or by ending it as soon as the first problems appear. Before the other one has a chance to abandon them."

"And it's feeling powerless that makes me hurt when relationships turn bad?"

"It's part of the pain," the tree explained. "But there's also the disconnection itself to consider. Since humans need connection above all else, experiencing the opposite, like loss, loneliness, rejection or abandonment, is very hard to bear. And if a relationship does not end well and someone leaves you, you have two of the most painful experiences at once. You face the pain of the loss itself and, on top of that, you have to face your inability to control the situation – and the other person involved."

"Which only leaves one conclusion," Nayeli declared. "It's best to avoid relationships altogether. Besides, once you get used to being alone, it becomes comfortable. And safe! I for one have learned to enjoy my solitude."

"But remember, you aren't an island, my dear child, and will always need other people. Or do you want to tell me that you think you're independent?" The tree chortled.

Nayeli nodded earnestly, wondering why Willow – the tree that seemed to be omniscient and had an answer to anything – needed to ask something this simple.

"Of course I am. I live in my own flat, which I clean by myself. I have a full-time job to pay my rent and bills. I'm neither financially dependent on anyone nor do I have a romantic partner on whom I can rely on emotionally. I'm alone in life – at least, as alone as an adult can be whose parents are still alive. So what if my mum takes me along on a shopping trip, or if my friends help me paint my room? I could do all that stuff on my own, if I had to. Meaning that, yeah, I *am* saying I'm independent ..."

"And I know why you think that. I've noticed that you humans have a skewed perspective regarding independence. But I'm sorry to tell you, you're wrong. Any human who thinks they're independent is wrong, because that couldn't be further from the truth."

"You are having me on, right?" Nayeli asked, uncertain whether or not the tree was serious.

Willow shook its crown, illustrating its point patiently. "Let me start to explain this matter by talking about a toddler. Did you know that humans are born prematurely? Nature has designed it this way so that babies can fit through the birth canal. The downside to this is that you're more helpless and dependent than any other species on Earth. The young of zebras or giraffes can run hours after birth. The young of mice, rabbits or foxes, who all live in dens, leave their nests and tunnels after a few weeks at the latest. Dolphins or sharks can swim almost immediately after being born. And birds don't need more than a couple of weeks to be able to fly and hunt.

"What can human babies do after days or weeks, though? You can't even crawl by then, let alone walk or find food. If your parents or other primary caregivers didn't provide for you for years on end, you would die – simple as that. And this shows how dependent you humans are ..."

"I agree that human children depend on their parents. But when we become adults, surely that changes?!"

"It doesn't change all that much," Willow argued. "Even if humans teach you the opposite at times. I know that you learn that when you have to deal with adult stuff like rent and taxes and insurances, you're more or less self-reliant. But that's a far cry from being truly independent. You humans require services from others all the time, not only to survive but to fulfil all your wants and needs, which you can't meet by yourself."

"Like what?" Nayeli asked, perplexed.

"There are endless examples ... You might need service from an insurance company or a car repair shop or a plumber. And let's not forget your need to eat. Do you want to become both a farmer who grows crops and a baker who makes bread? Would you be able to rent a home, send your kids to school or have the internet if you were completely independent and didn't rely on anyone else?"

"But I pay for all these services," Nayeli objected. "They're deals I negotiate myself."

"Exactly, you make deals. And you cooperate with other humans that provide what you need. Hence, my answer is still the same. You are never independent for as long as you are here."

"All right, if you want to be that nit-picky about it," Nayeli concluded, acknowledging Willow's way of seeing things.

She looked towards the trees on the horizon, which were presenting themselves in all shades of green as the sunlight sparkled through their foliage. "But there are exceptions to this rule, aren't there? If I said goodbye to civilization and went off to live in the woods, collecting and hunting my own food, building my own shelter ..?"

"No," Willow disagreed. "Because everything in your life is a relationship. And by that, I don't just mean the connections you have with your partner, parents, friends, co-workers and countless other humans like your family doctor or your postman. I also mean that you have relationships with pets and wild animals, with nature itself, with the trees and oceans, the wind and the ground you walk on. Beyond that, you have a relationship with your house, your neighbourhood, the shopping mall you go to, the town or city you live in and your local community. You have a relationship with your workplace and your profession, with your finances and with objects you own. And you have relationships with your higher self, with your soul-family and with the source. Which is me only naming a few examples out of many.

"Being incarnated as a human being entails having an ego. And having an ego leads to you perceiving yourself as separate from everything and everyone around you. Now, anything that is separate is linked to all other things in some way. Accordingly, anything outside you is in a relationship with you and vice versa. If it's not a human farmer providing you with food, it can be the apple tree itself. But either way, you depend on others for your survival and to meet your needs."

"Thus, I'm stuck having to find compromises when I wish for something because my free will is constantly at odds with the free will of others?" Nayeli asked, realising that she felt no joy at the prospect of having to keep feeling the emotional pain that came along with human connections.

"I wouldn't call it compromises, but cooperation or co-creation," Willow said firmly. "Compromises have a negative connotation. They imply something is taken away from one or both persons involved, and that no one is pleased about the end result. Meanwhile, co-creation means you get together to accomplish an out-come that's for the best of everyone. Let's say, for example, that neither you nor your partner likes to cook. But since you want to eat freshly cooked meals, you take it in turns to stand at the stove. That's a compromise where no one is truly happy. On one hand, it's better than having to cook every day but, on the other hand, you still have to do something you hate."

"But what other solution could there be?" Nayeli asked.

"Countless ones, depending on the individual situation. You could decide to eat at a restaurant every day if you think it's worth the expense. Or, if your families lived close by, you could take turns eating with them and spend more time with your parents and in-laws. In return, you could help them with gardening, which is something you love but they don't care for ..."

"I understand," Nayeli said slowly. "A compromise gets two people on the same page by making concessions. It results in a win-lose or a lose-lose outcome. And it would be healthier if we can find solutions that make everyone feel they have won."

Turning her head up to look into Willow crown, Nayeli frowned. "That all sounds easy when you explain it. But I also think that finding practical win-win solutions in life is difficult to do."

"Most things are easier said than done," the tree agreed. "But it's definitely possible. As long as you take care of all three parts of the relationship you want to sustain or improve."

"Wait," Nayeli said, puzzled. "Three parts? Didn't you just say that a relationship is between two parties?"

Willow's bark groaned and creaked as the tree stretched. "No, I do really mean three. Any relationship includes you, the other person or entity involved and the relationship itself – which is the combined energy of the two of you."

"Ah, okay. And we can improve that how?" Nayeli came back to Willow's earlier statement.

"Imagine, once more, a relationship between you and someone

else like a rope stretched between you. The closer you stand and the looser it is, the better your relationship is. On the other hand, the more tension the rope is under and the further apart you stand, the more easily it can snap. By meeting your partner's needs, you are essentially asking them to step closer to you, just as you are being pulled closer to them each time they look after your wants. Something that, even if it sounds simple, can get confusing for humans. I've often seen you lost because you mix up what you give to yourself, what you give to others and what you give away without anyone benefiting from it ...."

Nayeli gave the tree a blank look. "Well, I'm definitely lost right now. Can you give me an example?"

"Sure. Let's say you met your partner because you both ran the identical route each morning. You both liked to jog and your relationship, which turned into a romantic one, was fed through this shared hobby. But as it happens, people and situations change over time, and now the sole reason you continue to jog with your partner each morning is to make them happy. You wouldn't jog for yourself anymore, but you don't want to take away from this quality time. Now, as chance would have it, your partner has changed, too. When you'd ask them, they wouldn't want to get up early and jog any more than you and are only doing it for your sake. In this example, continuing to jog together each morning does not feed the relationship: both of you give energy to it, but no one feels like they are receiving what they want or need."

"So, what is given is essentially lost?" Nayeli asked for clarification. "Because we aren't communicating enough with each other?"

"Yes. And because you need to learn about how the other person ticks and how they receive – and feel – love. For this, you have to be aware, though, that relationships are fluid and that the needs of the people inside them vary, depending on the situation they find themselves in. Someone who usually loves hugs might not want one when they're in the middle of watching an interesting movie. And when someone is ill, they might prefer you cooked them soup than gave them a present, even when normally they love getting little gifts."

Nayeli pulled her knees to her chest and wrapped her arms around them. "What I gather from this is that we have to accept that our interpretation of love can differ from how someone else receives it. And that I should consider that maybe they don't get what I'm saying or doing is for them. In other words, we need to be clear on our needs and wants and adjust the way we show love to others if need be?!"

"I couldn't have said it any better," the tree responded, pleased.

"Man," Nayeli said, puffing out a breath. "I knew that relationships were complicated. But I didn't know they were *this* much work ... Isn't there some good news about them?"

"You make it sound like what I've told you thus far is bad news. Which it isn't. But all right, I can up the ante. Relationships are paving the path to the greatest feeling you can experience here on Earth – belonging!"

"Now that sounds more akin to something I'd like to hear about." Nayeli grinned.

"Then let me satisfy your curiosity! Belonging and connection is the number-one need of any soul, and especially of humans. You humans are one of the most social species alive, and your need for connection is even more important than your most basic physical needs, like food or shelter. Take a grieving person, for example. Are they interested in eating regular meals? Or isn't it rather the case that they forget to eat or not care about food anymore?

"Every human needs to feel that they belong somewhere. You need people who understand, support and accept you. This is – without exception – the greatest source of happiness for all. Give a human all the money and success they want, but take away their family, friends and pets. They'd be in a hell built out of loneliness and disconnection. They'd suffer immensely."

"That's true," Nayeli said, remembering how desolate she had felt when she had heard of her grandmother's passing about a week ago. Which had only been the latest farewell in a long series of goodbyes. "I've had to experience many losses in my life and I've felt lonely often. Which is not a nice feeling to have. And when I look at the world, I can see that it's not merely me. I think everyone alive has suffered a loss in one form or another and knows how painful loneliness is. People who are living alone and who have no one in their lives anymore – no family, no partner, no friends. People who are connecting over the internet but who have no one living close by when they want some personal interaction. People who have social anxiety and trouble building new connections. People who are betrayed or abandoned by a loved one. Not to mention all the old people in retirement homes who don't get any visitors ..."

Willow's voice was firm when the tree expanded on that list. "And don't forget all the people who, on the outside, have family and friends, but who feel lonely despite that because neither their partner nor anyone else is capable of truly seeing into them.

"When all is said and done, loneliness might only be an illusion from the source's perspective since your soul always stays connected to it, but here, in this reality, it's a real and painful pandemic –

the worst that has ever hit humankind."

"But Willow, how do I find out where I belong? Or with whom?"

"A good question, my dear, a very good question. Essentially, if you can be yourself around someone and they accept you as you are, you know you've found the right kind of person. Saying that, belonging isn't just a positive thing, however. You can belong to groups that you perceive as negative, too. As a human, you have a habit of placing yourself and everyone else in boxes. These can be labelled 'I'm a woman', 'I'm an adult', 'I'm bisexual', 'I'm Hispanic', 'I'm a father', 'I'm a college graduate', 'I'm poor', 'I'm an INTJ', 'I'm a teacher', 'I'm a cancer survivor' and so on and so on. Some boxes are temporary – for example when you were a basketball player at school but stopped playing afterwards. Meanwhile, some other boxes last for your whole incarnation here – for example, when you are an empath."

"And what do these boxes have to do with belonging?"

"Simple. When you call something 'my' or 'mine', it has already become a part of you. When you say 'my dog' or 'my boyfriend' or 'my phone' or 'my job' or 'my back pains', you're identifying with that person, animal or thing, whether you like it or dislike it."

Nayeli voiced the first thought that came to her mind. "Is that the shadow side of belonging? That we identify with things that we perceive as negative?"

"No, the shadow side isn't that you identify with things you don't like. The shadow side is the opposite of belonging, namely separation. You need to know that there are two types of energetic movements in this universe: pushing something away or pulling something closer. Acceptance, understanding and love enable more connection, while feelings like fear or hate create further separation.

The latter is something you humans practise a lot, I might add. You build up walls around yourself to stop others from hurting you, you wall out anyone who doesn't belong to your group of people, you put up walls against anyone who you think is unlikely to understand you and you wall out all those who you don't understand."

At first, Nayeli sat quietly, digesting all that Willow said. But then she shifted around in unrest.

"What is it, my dear?" Willow asked, as always sensing when something was amiss. "What are you thinking about?"

"What you just said – it reminded me of one of my cousins who's gay. He lives in a region that still has a pretty high percentage of homophobic people and the places he feels safest to be himself – apart from at home – are LGBT+ establishments. But isn't that the kind of separation you are talking about? A form of exclusion? Is that supposed to be a bad thing now?"

"No, not necessarily. If you look for a group of like-minded people who have had similar experiences and can relate to you, that's a positive thing first and foremost. It's the easiest way to find connection in this world. It's only when your underlying intention is to exclude others who don't *fit* or *belong* in that circle, that it can become detrimental because then you're in a state of resistance. And as you know, resistance brings forth the energy of the very things you are resisting."

"It's my intention that's crucial?"

"Indeed. Your intention and your focus. They can make a great difference in any relationship. Shall I tell you how?"

Nayeli made herself comfortable. "Yes, please."

"Let's take young love as an example. When you fall in love with someone, you see the other person through rose-tinted glasses. You are deeply invested in that new bond and want to know everything about them. You take an interest in who they are and what they dream about. You ask them lots of questions, spend quality time with them and enjoy discovering all the commonalities you share. When you learn that they share a love for soccer, going to games together will make you feel more connected. And if you find out that you are both only children and missed having a sibling that is a reason to feel closer, too. The similarities you can find with other people are endless and they allow you to connect to each other on different levels – emotionally, intellectually, physically and so on. To sum it up, your whole focus in these early months is on creating connection by pulling the other person closer energetically.

"Only, have you noticed that this feeling does not last forever? That sooner or later, relationships tend to go downhill? Either temporarily, because of fights and misunderstandings, or permanently when you split up?"

"Yes," Nayeli said.

"That's because your focus has shifted. From connection to disconnection. From love to separation. From the positive things you share to the negative things that are opposites. Your focus is all that decides how connected or disconnected you are in your relationships. And you humans have learned to let your awareness shift towards the negative end of the scale. To explain this better, let's fast-forward the romantic relationship from our example a few years when everyday life has taken over and the little faults come to the fore. You might start to dislike that your partner spends hours in the gym each week instead of with the family. You might feel fed up that they are constantly leaving unwashed dishes sitting on the countertop. Or you might fight over where to go on the next holiday because you want different things. This shift of focus is a recipe for disaster in any relationship. It's the point in time where some couples go their separate ways, while others stay together but detach emotionally. Instead of continuing to be connected, they live alongside each other, not with each other."

"But what can we do differently, Willow?" Nayeli interrupted the tree.

"The first thing to do is focus on the similarities you share with the other person again."

"And what if that isn't possible? Because I've drifted too far apart from someone else?"

"Then you have to consider that you might be incompatible."

"Incompatible? What does that mean?"

"It means that the gap between what you both need is too great to bridge and that no solution can be found that's in the best interests of everyone involved – whether the incompatibility has been there from the beginning and you simply didn't see it before or whether it arose during the relationship because you grew apart. Now, most differences are small enough that they don't pose a problem. If your partner prefers coffee to tea, while you always drink the latter, you simply get a coffee maker *and* a water kettle; simply as that."

"And what if the differences are bigger? Are you saying that we need to end our relationships in that case?"

"No, if that's what you're worried about, I can set your mind at ease," the tree answered softly. "There's no need to end most relationships. You only need to do that when they're abusive in any way."

"Are you sure about this?" Nayeli asked doubtfully. "Cause I know many people who have separated because of differences that arose. And not all of these relationships were abusive."

"I'm aware that this happens a lot. But it's due to you humans living in a throwaway society, which you extend to your relationships. When you're led by your ego, you might choose to give up on someone instead of mending your connection. Which is always a possibility, when both people are willing. You can start to feel into them again, to see and hear them and to understand their needs. Or, if you're too immersed in your own take on the problem to see a solution that serves both, you can ask a third party, who will be more objective, to help you. It's only when this does not work that you need to look for a different solution."

"To end the relationship?" Nayeli asked once more.

"Not necessarily. You can also change it."

"Change it?" Nayeli asked. "How?"

"Why, by altering the status between the two people involved, of course. Let's say that you're in a romantic relationship. Your partner wants to have children, but you don't. That might be an issue you can't find a solution for. Might and not must, mind you, because every situation is unique. But in general, it can be said that if one partner has to give up their innermost desires for another person, it's likely to breed bitterness in the long run and the relationship will be doomed. But even if you don't work as romantic partners anymore, you can still be close platonic friends. Your partner can then find another person who does want to start a family with them, and you can find someone who doesn't want to have kids. You'd keep each other in your lives, you'd stay connected and love each other, but you'd also follow your own soul-plan, honouring your desires and feelings. And *that's* the best win-win you could hope for in a case like that ..."

"I get all that. But doesn't that imply that we need to change a whole lot of relationships in our lives? And isn't it unlikely that we'll find a partner who'll stay with us until the end?"

"Well ..." The tree laughed. "I'm not a statistician. I don't know how likely it is, as both scenarios are possible. You may find a match who grows alongside you. But then again, there's no guarantee that this will happen What I do know is this, though: you can absolutely build and uphold loving relationships, no matter if they change over time. And please, my dear child, keep in mind that a great relationship is not based on how long it lasts. It's about how much you take the other person's interests to heart, just as they do the same for you. When doing this leads to the relationship changing, there's no *failure* involved. Quite the contrary. It's a lot better than continuing to hurt each other."

Nayeli rubbed her forehead. "So we shouldn't throw away relationships needlessly, but we should alter them if we're not happy?"

"That's right," Willow replied. "And if you do need to end some, you can be sure that there are plenty of other people with whom you can build connections. Because, in the end, there's not only a few people who will accept you but many. Don't forget that no human can escape their need to be connected. Which means millions of people share the identical desire as you – to belong! What's left for you to do is to select people you're on a wavelength with. Your compatibility with other people is actually the secret of upholding long-lasting relationships. No one will always be fully on your side and share all your opinions and beliefs. But if you match with someone who has similar desires, someone with whom most of your needs won't clash, the understanding that results from this will lay the groundwork to connect to this person on a deeper level. And because of this, a great compatibility comes closest to feeling unconditionally loved – the infinite state of the source itself."

"Are you indicating that unconditional love doesn't exist on Earth?" Nayeli asked sadly. "There's nothing else but a fake copy of it in the form of compatibility?"

"The answer to that is both yes and no," Willow said. "But before I delve more deeply into this topic, I first want to share Buttercup's wisdom on it ..."

12. Buttercup, the Crocodile

Strix was flying east, with no intent or purpose. He remembered how he had revelled in the feeling of utter freedom just before meeting Rose. But now, he couldn't dredge the emotion up anymore, no matter how hard he tried to get rid of the depression that clung to his feathers.

Not having the energy to talk to anyone or take much interest in his surroundings, the days blurred into one, and Strix let his thoughts drift. Memories arose within him. Of Rose and the time they'd spent together. Of how the swan had looked in the evening light when the sinking sun had bathed her white plumage a soft orange tone. And of her infectious laughter and how she had giggled at his jokes with such delight. But most of all, he remembered his dreams of a future with her.

Strix would have loved to be there when her eggs hatched, to see her face light up when she first laid eyes on her cygnets. He felt certain that she would be a great mother one day and the knowledge that he wouldn't be at her side to witness it made his emotions resemble a burned wasteland filled with sadness.

Gazing up, Strix registered the blanket of dark clouds above him. It had begun to rain, a steady drizzle that reflected his mood – as if the sky was displaying its empathy by crying along with him.

The droplets hit the water in a riverbed beneath him and created small ripples on the surface. Strix followed the flowing water on a whim and soon spotted some green-scaled bodies in it. The sight of the crocodiles reminded him of another one he had met, after leaving Olive in Costa Rica. A crocodile who had been as caring and loving towards her children as he imagined Rose would be. And one he had misjudged greatly at first glance ...

***

It was hot and sultry in the swamp.

The humidity made Strix feel more tired than he should have been, considering the short distance he'd travelled since leaving the sloth behind. But his fatigue proved to be convenient, as he was hesitant to brave the wide expanse of the Atlantic Ocean lying ahead of him. And so he was glad to find any excuse to prolong his stay on this island for a little while longer.

Strix searched out a suitable resting place and circled above a few trees. Landing first on a branch that overhung the water's edge, he changed his mind at the last second and fluttered down to settle on a bare patch of earth instead, a fair bit away from the murky-looking water.

Immediately after vacating his spot on the tree, another colourful bird took his place and hunkered down to sleep.

It was the moment all hell broke loose.

A large, green-scaled body catapulted out of the water and lifted itself up, reaching the branch with an ease that belied its massive appearance. Then the beast fell back down, its mouth clamped tightly around the lower half of the unfortunate bird, which screeched loudly. A cry that was abruptly cut off when both animals disappeared underneath the surface. And just like that, the scene reverted back to the peacefulness it had presented before.

Strix breathed heavily, being painfully aware that *he* could have been eaten by the crocodile if he had stayed on that branch. A cold shiver of fear ran down his spine at his narrow escape and rooted him to the spot. Meanwhile, his eyes were glued to the area where the reptile had disappeared with its prey. But no sight of it remained.

Wondering if this place was as safe as he had initially thought, Strix craned his head in every direction to watch out for more danger approaching. But the only soul he saw was a female plover sitting on a sandy patch of earth nearby. She was calmly cleaning her plumage, as though nothing out of the ordinary had happened.

"Hey!" Strix called over to the bird. "Did you see that?"

"What?" she answered emotionlessly.

"The monster that ate one of our cousins, of course."

"Monster?" the plover asked, perplexed, before shaking off the sand in which she had bathed. "Ah, you mean Buttercup!"

"Buttercup?" Strix couldn't help but chortle, despite the terror still clinging to him. Surely, there couldn't be a more absurd name for such a dangerous animal. "You call this ... thing ... Buttercup? Have you taken a good look at it? Cause the name sounds great for a colourful butterfly or a sweet bunny or even a cow, but definitely not something like *her*!"

Puffing herself up angrily, the female bird glowered at him. "That *thing* is my friend and a great and gentle soul, and I won't have you badmouth her."

"I'm sorry," Strix said, taken aback by her response. "But the fact remains that she killed one of our kind. You can't possibly condone that?!"

The plover hopped a few paces closer to him and tilted her neck sideways. "She was only doing what her nature dictates – nothing more, nothing less. We all need to eat, don't we? And I'm convinced that the mice you hunt stare at you with the same horror as you look upon her. But are you a monster because of that?"

"No," Strix muttered, not knowing what else to say to her convincing argument. "You really do like her, don't you?"

"I do," the smaller bird replied in a matter-of-fact tone. "When I met her, she saved my fledglings from another predator."

Strix squinted his eyes in doubt. "And she did that out of the goodness of her heart?"

"No," the plover admitted, "she was hungry and ate the beast. But it was still the beginning of our friendship, and I don't regret meeting her for a single second."

Strix wanted to ask the bird even more questions about the crocodile. But he was prevented from following through with his idea when the reptile in question appeared yet again. And this time Buttercup was swimming straight towards them.

Hooting in fright, Strix dived behind a large boulder. From there, he peered at the dangerous predator to see whether she would attack him.

But Buttercup did no such thing. After climbing out of the water, she lay on the sand and opened her giant mouth, her teeth gleaming white and deadly in the sunlight, the blood from the bird having been long washed off.

"Would you mind?" she asked the plover.

Strix was surprised when the small bird he had been talking to hopped towards the crocodile without hesitation. And then, to Strix's utter amazement, the plover jumped straight into the reptile's mouth and picked between her teeth, not seeming to be aware that she would be caught in a deadly trap if Buttercup closed her jaws.

Holding his breath, Strix watched tensely, waiting for his feathery acquaintance to be swallowed whole by the beast.

But Buttercup lay peacefully while the plover flittered here and there, first cleaning the reptile's throat before taking care of the scales along her back. It took her about half an hour; then the plover fluttered off and sat down beside the huge predator.

Peering out from behind his hiding place, Strix stared at the female bird. But instead of seeing a distant feathered relative, she seemed to be more alien than animal to him.

"You … what … how … why weren't you eaten?" Strix asked, once Buttercup had disappeared back into the water.

"Why would I be?" the plover asked. "I told you that Buttercup and I are friends. All right, it started as a trade-off. She would protect me, and I would help her out with cleaning – a win-win situation. But it turned into so much more when we decided to forgo all our differences and approached each other's needs, as if they were our own. When we started to hold space for each other without passing judgment. And now she's my closest friend and confidant."

Strix's eyes had grown rounder in wonder with every word the bird said. He couldn't comprehend being this close to an apex predator. But if his eyesight hadn't failed him – which it never did – everything the plover said must be the truth.

"You'd be smart to stay out of her path, though," the smaller bird continued. "There might be a lot of love between us, but Buttercup does need to eat. Meaning, she won't extend the exception she makes for me to all my acquaintances."

"Doesn't that bother you?" Strix asked again.

Shrugging, the female bird looked after a turtle that was swimming near the water's edge.

"I just tell the ones I love to stay away from her. And I teach them how a crocodile can kill them. When you know the danger facing you, you're much better equipped to avoid it, or isn't that right?"

Strix gulped. "Ehm, how can she kill us?"

The bird chirped happily. "She can catapult herself straight out of the water as you saw earlier. Aside from this, she's a fast walker on land – at least compared to other crocodile species. And she can use her long tail to hit a tree trunk so hard that birds and other animals sitting on the branches fall off."

"Splendid," Strix responded, his voice oozing with sarcasm. "And that's all?"

"Aside from not going anywhere near or inside the water because she could easily seize you – yes."

Proving the bird's words true in this moment, Buttercup shot forward from the hidden spot she'd been lying in and grabbed the turtle by the shell, disappearing with it underneath the water in seconds.

"That was quick," Strix said tonelessly and wondered if he was in a state of shock, as he felt strangely indifferent to the killings going on in front of his eyes.

The female plover waved her wings about. "I know that Buttercup appears to be scary, if not evil. But if you have a couple of days to spare, I can show you how I see her. As a great mum who loves her offspring unconditionally. She's a great role model from whom we can all learn a lot."

Strix took his time to think about the proposal. Part of him itched to get going and discover the old world – but his reservations about his flying ability held him back, making him wonder if he could make it across the wide ocean.

Weighing the pros and cons, Strix's fatigue finally won out. "I'll stay for now."

"Great!" the female bird called and yawned heartily. "Would you mind, in that case, looking out for danger approaching while I take a nap?"

"No problem," Strix said, more than happy to provide this little favour in the hope of it being returned when he needed to close his eyes for an hour or two.

The plover didn't take long to nod off and Strix used the time to inspect the swamp and its residents more closely. There were a few other turtles in the water he hadn't noticed before, alongside a multitude of different birds flying to and fro. Not to mention the countless midges and other insects swarming around. And then there was, of course, Buttercup, the crocodile.

The only part of her that was visible right now was her eyes, peering over the water's surface. The rest of the reptile's body was hidden underwater, lying still and calm.

Strix was reasonably sure that Buttercup did so to bide her time as inconspicuously as possible until there was another chance to attack an innocent animal.

Keeping one eye on the crocodile, the humid head made Strix drowsy as the minutes ticked by, and he had to flap his wings several times to stay awake. After almost slipping off into sleep yet again, he jerked upright and scanned the swamp in front of him. He could see no sign of Buttercup.

Alarmed, Strix gazed from left to right, searching for a ripple in the water or a pair of gleaming eyes. When he did spot the crocodile, he saw that she was moving as a shadowy outline underneath the surface. At once, Strix was undecided whether should feel glad about knowing where she was or frightened, as Buttercup was swimming quickly in his direction.

Hiding behind the big stone once again, Strix hissed at the female plover. "Hey, wake up, something's happening."

By the time the smaller bird had opened her eyes, Buttercup had reached the water's edge. As the reptile emerged, she did so bit by bit. First, her long, pointy snout became visible, the teeth innumerable and sharp. Then her massive body appeared, her scales looking like armour and enhancing her muscles. And at last, her tail was displayed, swishing dangerously to the right in one long arc.

Lazily, Buttercup walked past them, more nimbly than Strix would have imagined for a beast of her size and weight.

At first, Strix didn't know where the crocodile was heading or why, but then he heard the sound. A faint melody of many voices calling out. Listening closely, Strix realised they were coming from underneath a mound that had been built not far from where he sat.

Seeing no entrances or holes inside it, Strix wondered how anyone could live there. But before he could question the plover about it, Buttercup had already halted in front of the area and begun to dig so fast that soil and organic matter flew to both sides. Soon, she'd uncovered a clutch of eggs, some of which were moving a little, as if the animals inside were impatient to get out.

"Oh no, she's not going to eat a whole nest of baby animals who haven't even been born yet, is she? I know the bird and turtle must only have been a snack for her, considering her size. But still ..."

"Who said she's hungry?" the plover beside him asked cheerily.

"What else is she gonna do with all these eggs but eat them? Look, she's taking one."

True enough, Buttercup scooped one of the eggs up and held it between her sharp teeth, applying pressure to the shell.

Strix knew it would not hold up long under the strain, and when it broke in half, he wanted to avert his gaze to not watch the bloodbath that would ensue. But something kept him from turning his head. And a second later, Strix gasped in surprise as a baby crocodile appeared between the broken eggshells. Lying on Buttercup's tongue, the little hatchling peered out of its mother's mouth at the new world it had arrived in, its eyes filled with innocence and curiosity.

The huge reptile repeated the process with the other eggs, helping all of her young ones to hatch, before carrying them towards the water inside her open mouth, from where she let them swim out.

Some hatchlings climbed quickly onto her back and head while the boldest of her young was nearing one of the turtles in curiosity, splashing around in the water as it tried to coordinate its limbs.

"They are kinda cute when they're this little." Strix grinned, turning around to look at the plover. But he must have spoken louder than he'd intended because, instead of the female bird, it was Buttercup who answered him.

"But, unfortunately, being *little* means they also have a lot of natural predators. Like birds. In short, you'd better stay away from them. Or, trust me, I'll make you wish you'd never been born!"

Spooked at her words and the way she fixated him with her gleaming eyes, Strix took an involuntary step backwards, almost toppling over a tree root sticking up from the ground. It didn't take long for his fright to cease, though, because Buttercup was way too concerned with her hatchlings to be any danger to him right now.

Strix's fear was then replaced by embarrassment at having been caught talking about someone behind their back. Wanting to make up for his blunder, he thought of something nice to say.

"Surely they don't have to worry about that? With such a powerful mother to love and protect them?"

"I do all I can," Buttercup answered. "But I don't harbour illusions that all of my young will reach adulthood. They make their choices and some of those will turn out badly. That's life."

"But you must have some influence on them? You raise them, after all, and can guide them in the right direction. You can teach them everything they need to know to stay safe."

Buttercup glowered at Strix. "The words of someone who isn't a father yet ... Let me give you a word of advice, little bird. Once you have kids, don't believe that they're an extension of you. They don't come into this world to fulfil your needs or dreams. They come here to take their own journey. They have their own soul-plan and a free will that can take them far from where you would like them to be. Yes, they are your hatchlings, but they are not your clay to mould. You can take care of them to the best of your ability and show them everything they need to know to survive. But that's where your power over their life ends. Because they need to decide for themselves what lessons they want to accept and in what way. And to enable them to live their authentic truth is the most unconditional loving thing you can do for them."

The female plover cut in at that point. "It's true. You can never shape your young after your wishes. But if you accept them and love them as they are, you can learn from them as much, if not more, than they can learn from you."

"Eh, thanks for the advice," Strix said, taken aback by the passion in both of their voices. "But it's unnecessary in my case. Cause I'll never be a dad."

"You say that now, bird," Buttercup responded patiently, "but wait until your chosen one lays eggs and the first ones hatch. You'll remember my words then."

"My chosen one?" Strix chortled. "No way! Not only will I never be a father, but I'll also never fall in love with anyone!"

***

Tears stung Strix's eyes, and his blurry sight made him see the crocodiles beneath him only as shadowy outlines, letting him imagine it was Buttercup swimming in the river, despite her being miles away to the west, beyond the great ocean.

Her words still reverberated so vividly inside his mind, as if they had been spoken yesterday. And that he had been so wrong about one half of Buttercup's prediction made Strix wonder, if maybe, the second part would come to pass as well, and that he would someday be a father. But then Strix brushed that silly notion aside. Of course, he wouldn't be. Rose had been his one true chance at true love in this life, and he'd never have another. The thought saddened him even further, if that was possible.

Strix wasn't sure if the wetness on his face was due to his tears or the constant drizzle of rain. Not that he really cared. Feeling a new wave of depression surge up inside him, Strix decided to fly away from the river, from the foreign crocodiles lying there and from the memories they brought forth.

He wanted to head for a place where he could forget both Buttercup and her talks of parenthood as well as Rose and his feeling for her. Someplace that would help him erase the entire last few weeks of his miserable life.

Unconditional Love and Oneness

"Willow, why did you imply that unconditional love doesn't exist in this dual reality?" Nayeli immediately took up her line of questioning from earlier again. "Buttercup sure seemed to love her young with all her heart."

"She does. But that doesn't mean she can always be unconditionally loving inside this reality. But let me tell you the fundamentals first, my dear child. Unconditional love is nothing else but a vibration – the vibration of the source itself. It is the emotional reflection of oneness and an infinite state of pure positive focus: a focus that is reflected to you by the feeling you call love.

"Unconditional love isn't easy to describe in the human language, but I'll do my best ... Feeling unconditional love for someone or something feels, in a physical way, as if your heart is expanding to take in all they are. You take them on as part of you until there's no separation left. They are you and you are them. You love them completely: all their strengths and weaknesses, all their talents and flaws, all their character traits, all their opinions, beliefs and actions – if you loved their entire being holding nothing back, then you would love them unconditionally. If, however, there are small things you aren't fond of or things they do that you don't agree with – when there are moments where you are not positively focused towards them – then you are not in the frequency of unconditional love."

"But then no human would be unconditionally loving," Nayeli declared. "Not even a mother loves her child every hour of every day. Everyone gets fed up sometimes and dislikes certain character traits or actions, although you love the other person overall."

"That's correct," Willow agreed, as a soft wind whispered through the tree's leaves, underlining its next words. "No human can be fully unconditionally loving in this day and age. You can experience it for fleeting moments or even longer periods of time. But always, without exception? No, I have to disappoint you on that. Ultimately, that's because unconditional love is nothing else but the source energy itself, and any time you experience it towards someone or something in your life, you are simply holding the identical frequency as the universe.

"The inherent problem is that you humans will have moments when you're in a lower frequency due to your ego. Moments, in which you feel anger, hate or fear. Moments, where your unhealed wounds will be triggered. Moments, where your own needs oppose those of another person. Moments, in which their decisions cause you pain or when yours hurt someone else. All these moments that are part of the dual reality and belong to the human experience.

"You can, however, move your energy upwards more often and for longer when you practise unconditional love. Every second of every day, you have the choice of tuning in to this frequency and bringing it to your relationships. Your focus and awareness will unlock this experience – for you and anyone else who feels ready for this part of their journey."

"So, unconditional love is not an objective, but more akin to a process?"

"Yes. It's the road, rather than a destination. And learning how to have these moments is the most beautiful journey you could ever undertake."

"Then how do I start?" Nayeli asked, poking Willow's trunk as if the tree would reveal the answer faster that way. "How do I learn to love unconditionally?"

"First, you must tune in to the other person, listen to them, understand them, find the things you have in common and look for the ways you are connected, as love is a natural by-product of positive focus. Then, you'll notice that the other person's needs and wants automatically *become* your own. If unconditional love is present, their wants can actually become indistinguishable from yours. Even if you wanted to, you could not not take them into account because doing this would hurt you. If unconditional love is present in a relationship, you don't just feel happy when they're happy. It means that whatever is done to them is done to you and vice versa."

Nayeli looked up, surprised, feeling as though a lightbulb had been switched on inside her mind. "Is that also the reason why people get defensive over all kinds of things? Because we identify with a person, animal or thing in some way and feel their hurt, as if it were our own when they get attacked?"

"Precisely, my dear. When you love something or someone, you take it or them on as an integral part of yourself. A shark-lover who has studied all the species and their behaviour feels hurt when someone misunderstands and discredits sharks. And a person who loves a band gets defensive when someone else criticises them. Or, to name a different example ... Let's say you have a dog you love with all your heart. Imagine that another person is aggressive towards it, threatening to kick it. You'd instantly feel threatened yourself. No way could you stand back and do and feel nothing when your pet is hurt."

As Nayeli tightened her lips, ready to cut in, the willow tree quickly continued speaking. "By the way, this example also shows how disconnected some humans have become from recognising unconditional love. Because a lot of people would think, 'it's only a dog'. And even the person hurting your dog could think they aren't hurting *you*. They might say they love you as they don't see that your love for your dog makes it an inseparable part of you ..."

"If someone hurt a pet of mine," Nayeli said hotly, "I'd want nothing more to do with that person. I'd toss them out of my life faster than they could say the word 'love' – because it would be clear that they didn't care about me."

Feeling anger creep up, merely thinking about such a scenario playing out, Nayeli clenched and unclenched her hands. "But isn't this sad? That we leave a state of unconditional love behind and come here to experience this fake copy that we call human love?"

"But that's the whole point. You didn't come here to learn how to love unconditionally, my dear child. You already know how to do this because your souls – as part of the source – are always in alignment with this vibration. You – as incarnated humans – came here because you wanted to experience what conditional love feels like and what the process is like to move back towards unconditional love from it."

"Then tell me about this conditional love," Nayeli urged. "How is it different and how is it alike?"

"Conditional love is another term for attachment. When you love conditionally, you put your own needs the highest and you give love to someone else when they make you feel good in any way. Let's say that you've been in a romantic relationship for some time and your partner gets an offer for their dream job. If they take it, they will have to move away – something you can't do unless you give up your own profession, which you love. When you hear this news, if you love them conditionally, you'd feel scared or threatened, because you can see that your wishes conflict with theirs and that your sense of security and happiness might be in danger if they accept the job offer."

"But how would that change if we loved each other unconditionally?" Nayeli asked. "We'd still be at a stalemate, wouldn't we? Even if I let them go because I recognised how important the job was for them? Or they chose to stay for me?" Shifting, Nayeli absentmindedly raked her hand through her hair while waiting for the tree's verdict. It didn't take long.

"But that's the thing – with unconditional love present, the situation could not play out like this. 'Unconditionally' really translates to not needing someone else and not being hurt by their decisions. The moment you feel pain because of another person's actions, you're not holding the frequency of unconditional love anymore."

"But then unconditional love is even more painful than the other kind," Nayeli complained. "And it's not something I would want in my life."

"Why not?" the tree asked, bewildered.

Nayeli sat up and opened her arms wide to encompass the clearing. She shrugged, as if the answer should be obvious. "Because your explanation of unconditional love sounds lonely to me. I mean, if I'd be equally happy when someone is with me or when they're gone, then how can you call it love at all?"

"Ah, but that's because you've been traumatised in terms of abandonment and rejection, my dear child," Willow answered. "Once you heal those wounds, you will be able to recognise that unconditional love is one of the most beautiful experiences in the world. Imagine knowing that the sole reason your partner or friend stays in your life is that they love you – not because they're afraid to be without you, not because they're forced to stay with you by circumstance or any unhealed traumas within them. It's pure, unadulterated love for you that makes them stay."

Nayeli inclined her head. "Okay, when you put it like that, it does sound appealing," she conceded. "But still, you said that most humans are incapable of unconditional love. And I'd rather not wait for something that will never happen. And therefore, I'm gonna be stuck with the attachment style of love."

"The attachment style or the transactional kind of love," Willow corrected.

"There's even more?" Nayeli asked, letting her eyes dart around, as if the answer to her question could be found in the meadow. "What's the difference?"

"Children usually hold an attachment-style love towards their parents. When you are a baby or child, you need your primary caregivers in order to survive. You depend on them to fulfil your needs and your attachment to them is your priority. Many parents also have an attachment-style love for their children – when they use them to fulfil their own needs. Because people have children for all kinds of reasons, and not all reasons are to help another soul come into this life and to support them on their unique journey. Often, the reasons are more selfish. People have kids to have someone around to nurture and take care of. Or they want their genes to live on. Or they do what is expected of them because starting a family at a certain age is the norm. And these are only a few examples ... Now, you can see that parents are attached to their children when those grow up or move out to build their own life. When the parents feel the pain of separation, some try to counter it by clinging on to their children more tightly, unable to let them go. They continue to treat them like children, no matter how old they are. And they won't accept their child's decisions if they stray too far from their own wishes and expectations.

"Furthermore, a co-dependent relationship between adults is another form of this attachment style. When this transpires, you are simply shifting your need to be taken care of and be provided for into your adult relationships, and then you grow dependent on your partner as opposed to your parents. In this case, your spouse or even your friends become your security blanket."

Willow paused for a moment and the twittering of some birds filled the ensuing silence. Then the tree continued to speak and the sound reverted into the background once more.

"A lot of other adult relationships are mainly transactional, though, as they're built on invisible contracts."

"How can contracts be invisible?"

"Similar to your business deals such as employment contracts, you have tons of *silent deals* and *agreements* in your relationships. They're often not recognised as such because you don't put them down in writing, but they do exist. The terms in these contracts differ from relationship to relationship, with some of the most common ones being 'I'll help you with the housework so that you'll give me affection in return', 'I'll have sex with you because I want you to love me', 'I'll buy little gifts for you and expect you to appreciate me' or, and this is often born from loneliness, 'I'll stay with you if you agree to stay with me; that way neither of us will be alone'. And so on and so on. People in relationships do things for each other because they know they'll receive connection when they do so."

Nayeli wrinkled her forehead in thought. "That's a tough judgement to make, Willow. It sounds as if attachment or transactional love is somehow less than unconditional love. Less important. Less meaningful. Less *real.*"

Willow rumbled. "It's not my intention to make it seem less. I just want to show you that there's even more love and a deeper connection to be found than you've encountered till now. In the end, conditional love and unconditional love are not an energetic match; you can't feel one if you feel the other. But the kind of love you have for someone can change at any second. One day you will love someone unconditionally, the next you'll love them conditionally and an hour later you'll switch back into the frequency of the source again."

"Right, that makes sense," Nayeli said. "But how can we recognise when we truly love someone, as opposed to being attached to them?"

"The answer is easy. Imagine you had everything you needed. You have the house you've dreamed about, lots of money, the chance to travel anywhere you want, great hobbies and a profession you love, a purpose in life, close friends and deep connections, all the romance and sex you want, and you're healthy, secure, free, happy and fulfilled on top of that. Now, if you have all that, would you still want to have this person around? For them, not for what they can give you? If the answer is yes, then you love them. And if the answer is no, you need to ask yourself *what* you love about them. What do they give you that you need and which you receive only from them?"

Nayeli was silent as she turned that idea over in her mind to look at it from all sides.

"You seem sad." Willow interrupted the silence after some time. "Why is that?"

Nayeli watched the water in the brook ripple over the pebbles. "You just disillusioned me a bit, I guess. I've never viewed love in this light. I hadn't realised that most of our relationships, which are loving at first glance, are this superficial. And that we are missing out on being truly connected ..."

Nayeli wanted to say more but her words were lost in a yawn.

"You are sleepy," Willow said. "Why don't you go home? We'll talk more tomorrow, hm? When you feel more refreshed. I know that it's a lot to take in."

Nayeli was about to contradict the willow tree that she was fine and that it was barely noon, but as soon as she tried to speak, she had to stifle another yawn. Registering the tiredness spreading inside her body – a tiredness that was filling her extremities with lead and which was clouding her mind – she yawned a third time.

"Fine, you win," Nayeli relented as she stood up. "But tomorrow you'll have to answer more of my questions."

Feeling bone-weary all of a sudden, Nayeli simply focused on placing one foot in front of the other until she was standing before her grandma's house. Entering the living room, the only goal in her mind was to soak in a warm bubble bath. But the voices of her mother and uncle directed her steps to the kitchen instead.

Watching her mother unload the dishwasher, Nayeli felt like she could really see her for the first time in a long while. She saw the love and care her mother had given freely to her children and how she'd tried to do everything right by them. But she also saw the many mistakes her mother had made. Nayeli saw the dreams her mother had to give up to raise them. And she recognised all the good experiences she'd gained from that decision. A feeling of deep love overcame Nayeli at that moment, rushing into her body and filling up her heart.

Then Nayeli's uncle swept out of the room and she came face to face with her mother, whose haggard face immediately turned softer when she spotted Nayeli. As her mother tried for a bright smile that didn't quite reach her eyes, Nayeli stepped forward and hugged her.

Clearly surprised by this display of affection, her mother hugged her back. This time, her smile did reach her tired eyes. "Hey, how was your day, sweetie?"

"Good," Nayeli answered. "I had a talk with someone who put some things into perspective for me."

"Oh?" her mother asked, sounding interested. "Was that, by any chance, the secret love interest of yours that you still haven't introduced to me?"

"Mum!" Nayeli cried, exasperated, rolling her eyes heavenwards.

Her mother wasn't deterred, though. "Why don't you bring him over? I could bake a cake – how does that sound?"

Stopping herself from laughing aloud at the idea of digging up Willow and using a wheelbarrow to move the tree to her grandma's garden, Nayeli bit her lip before answering in what she hoped was a neutral tone.

"Um, the cake does sound great. But my friend isn't that agile."

"A wheelchair wouldn't be a problem. There are only three steps in front of the door and I can help you carry him in."

"It's a bit more complicated than that," Nayeli answered vaguely, pondering how to distract her mother from this topic. She might have accepted by now that she was able to talk to trees, but she wasn't ready to tell anyone else about it.

Seeing some papers that appeared to be land registries and

other official documents piled on top of the kitchen table, she snatched a few of them up and leafed through them. "Why don't I help you with those? I'm pretty adept at that kind of paperwork, considering I handle similar stuff all day at work ..."

Looking at her, as if seeing right through Nayeli's distraction tactic, her mother nodded after a minute or two. "Ah, I see. It's not a problem, really. I get that you'd like to keep him to yourself for a little while longer. I'm just glad that after all these endless years of you being single and hiding at home, you are getting into the dating game." Winking at her over the top of her glasses, her mother smiled. "You can always introduce him to me later, when it's getting serious."

"Mum," Nayeli groaned, her feeling of love quickly being replaced by irritation. But since it would be better to let her mother believe in her new boyfriend in favour of the truth, Nayeli forced a smile onto her face and turned back to the kitchen table. "So, what about it? Do you need any help?"

The next two hours, they worked together through the pile of forms and lists, after which they were both ready for a pause. Starting on the batter for the promised cake, Nayeli used the time to quiz her mum on the newest recipes she had tried out. It was a topic that distracted her mother sufficiently enough that, to Nayeli's satisfaction, her *secret boyfriend* wasn't mentioned again for the rest of the day.

***

Once Nayeli reached the crest of Willow's hill, the sun was already shining brightly from the crystal blue sky.

She felt a lot more relaxed than the day before, which wasn't only due to the best night's sleep she'd had in some time, but also because she had been able to spend a few peaceful hours with her mother – for a change without any arguments.

Realising that she had been more upset by their fights than she'd wanted to admit, even to herself, Nayeli had treated herself to a lavish breakfast with her mother and uncle this morning before bounding out of the house, full of energy and ready for the day and the lessons it would bring.

Letting herself fall onto the grass beside one of the tree's roots, Nayeli couldn't contain her excitement. "I'm back, Willow! So, what's the next thing you wanted to teach me?"

"Slowly, slowly." The tree stretched its branches, as if waking from a dream. "First you're gonna have to tell me why you're in such a great mood today."

"I had an epiphany," Nayeli explained. "My mum loves me and I love her. And you know what? That's the most important thing in life, no matter what kind of love it is. So what if I'm attached to my mum? If that ensures I get to keep her in my life, I'll take it. And I like the transactional relationships I have with my friends, as well – it shows we're helping and supporting each other in all kinds of ways. Which, when it comes down to it, does sound like love to me. And besides, this is all I'm ever gonna have in this life, so I'll do good to appreciate what I can get."

"What makes you say that 'this is all you're gonna have in life', my dear child?" the tree asked, surprised.

"I mean that I agree with Strix's stance on romantic love. That ship has sailed for me long ago."

"Why, though? I hear bitterness in your words. And hopelessness in your voice. But you are young. Why have you given up on finding love already?"

"Because I'm thirty-three years old and I've never had a partner. Not one boyfriend. Or girlfriend, for that matter. No one, do you hear me? As a tree, you might think I'm still young. But in the human world, everyone at my age has had a few partners, at least."

"Then why haven't you?" Willow asked. "Because I have the impresssion that you're interested in finding one? Or am I wrong? Are you aromantic or asexual?"

"No, yes, I don't know." Nayeli closed her eyes. "I can't be aromantic because I do have romantic feelings. And I do find myself attracted to people now and then. I also long to have that one special person at my side who I mean the world to. But despite all that, I've never really looked for a boyfriend." Nayeli huffed. "It's complicated. And how can anyone hope to figure it out if I don't even get it myself?"

"I could help you uncover the underlying cause, if you want?"

Shrugging, Nayeli shook her head in dismissal. "Don't bother, Willow. I'll have to accept that I'll die a spinster and that romantic love – whether it's of the conditional or unconditional kind – will have to wait for my next incarnation."

Nayeli moved around until she had found a more comfortable position. "But now enough about me. I'd rather use this day for more of your teachings."

Not sure if the tree would demand to dig deeper into her lack of love life, Nayeli breathed out a sigh of relief when Willow followed her lead.

"Then let me extend on why you humans are yearning for love and connection in general. When love is the frequency of the source, then loneliness, disconnection and isolation signify that you're as far removed from your soul as is humanly possible. So, that's what love is in the end. It's your soul's way of calling you to reconnect with it."

"That sounds interesting. Can you tell me more about this?"

"Certainly, just let me think about where to kick off." The tree remained silent for a while. The only sound in the meadow was the distant calls of birds and the buzzing of insects flying around Willow's branches. But then one of the tree's longer branches tapped the earth excitedly. "Ah, I know. Do you remember me telling you that you have soulmates and that you create soul contracts with them?"

"Yes. What about it?"

"On one dimensional level, this is true. But on another, contradictory, level all of that is false ..."

"What?" Nayeli asked, perplexed.

"On the most fundamental level, the universal truth is that of oneness." Willow began to talk. "When you break it down, everything is energy. You are energy, the grass littering this meadow is energy, a thought you think or a feeling you feel is energy. And so is any physical object, like the kitchen table in your home or the car you own. And since there is only one source of energy – which, as I mentioned before, can be called the source or the universe or God or anything else you want to identify it as – nothing can exist outside of it. Which begs the question, how can we be anything else but individual expressions of source itself? The answer is – it's impossible."

After days of talking to the willow tree, Nayeli shouldn't feel bewildered when Willow came out with yet another surprising statement, but she still raised her eyebrows at this revelation. "Are you trying to tell me that I'm God? And that you are as well, and that this yellow butterfly that just flew by me is God, too?"

Sniggering, the tree tickled Nayeli's legs with one of its lighter twigs. "I know that it must sound a bit weird to you at first but, essentially, the answer is yes. And what's more, you are not solely an expression of source. You are everything there is. If you say goodbye to your individual perspective, which makes you perceive yourself as separate, you'll see that there is one simple equation: If you're nothing but source energy and the source is also me, then ..."

"Then I'm you," Nayeli concluded, confused, because this opposed her sense of logic.

"At which point, we're back to the truth of oneness," Willow said, not letting Nayeli think too long about this latest insight. "You are every human, every animal and every single atom from the past, present and future. Everything is one. Everything is you ... and you are everything. Which means that the soulmates I mentioned are not separate souls from you – they are essentially you, but with different soul-paths as the source divided itself to experience different realities."

"Ah," Nayeli said in realisation as the dots connected. "And when it comes to our soul-plans, I didn't choose a more difficult path than someone else who chose easier lessons. Because I chose every experience – that of being a butcher and that of being the butchered lamb, that of being the bully and that being the victim ... I just experience them at different points in time."

"That's right. See humanity as if it were an anthill. An anthill is not, as most people believe, only home to the ants that live there. It is a living organism in and of itself – it breathes and grows. And any ant who lives inside that colony is one small cell of this super-organism; a single, but integral, part of the big picture. Now, similar to ants, souls can be seen as singular cells of one giant consciousness."

"And that's why we're desperate to belong to others, to be loved? Because we subconsciously remember being part of this oneness, where nothing exists outside us?"

"Yes – whether you have already *awakened* and are aware of where your desire comes from or whether you're still *sleeping*, you'll subconsciously remember the truth of the oneness and the feeling of being complete. Ultimately, you do miss it, and this gives rise to the desire to feel whole again. And the closest you can come to that feeling while you're incarnated here is to find connections to other souls. For this reason, love and belonging are not only your most important needs but your most natural desires – a desire that no one can ever escape. Sure, you can push it down and reject it until, consciously, you're barely aware of its existence anymore. But it never ceases to exist, no matter how faint its voice has become."

Nayeli was pensive, looking out over the green meadow that stretched to the line of trees on the horizon. "What you said ... it does ring true. But it poses another question – one I don't know if I should ask."

"You can ask me anything you want, my dear," Willow said in a relaxed manner. "I hope you know that by now?"

"I do ..." Nayeli said hesitantly, her voice ending in a waver. Noticing as much, she sat up straighter and plucked up her courage. "If this longing to be loved and find connection is the longing to be back in this oneness ... doesn't that imply we're longing for *death*?"

"No, don't worry," Willow said tenderly. "Wishing for love

doesn't indicate you're secretly suicidal."

Nayeli heard the tree's trunk creak behind her as the tree bent forward.

"To better grasp what I mean, imagine life as if it were a holiday. When you're at home, you can't wait to go. As you pack your bags and plan your journey, you get excited about relaxing by the ocean or discovering a new culture and great food or doing lots of fun activities. And when you arrive at your destination, the first days or weeks are great – the beautiful weather, the landscapes and sightseeing you do ... But then something will happen that doesn't feel good. Maybe there's a storm and you can't leave your hotel for a few days, or the other tourists annoy you. By then, you'll be thinking of home and miss it – along with the family and friends you left behind. But will you cut your holiday short because of that? Will you leave the jungle and its old temples or the sunsets in the mountains? Something you've looked forward to and are enjoying immensely despite the negative moments that are part of any experience? No – you'll still enjoy your holiday, you'll savour it to its fullest even while being homesick at times, and you'll be grateful for all the beautiful memories you'll take back home once the trip is over."

Nayeli leaned her head back against Willow's trunk. "We always want what we can't have, don't we?" She laughed. "When we're home, we want to travel and experience other things. And when we're on the road, we get homesick."

"True." Willow joined in with her laughter. "But the great news is, you don't have to be completely separate from the source while you're away from the other side, so it's not like you have to make an 'either or' decision. Connection and love do bring a piece of the source to us while we're here – like the partner you go on holiday with. Or the new friend you make as soon as you arrive. And the more you are awakened and the more conscious you become of these facts, the better you'll learn to build these deep connections, to other humans and animals, who are your travel companions, and to the universe itself."

Nayeli chuckled. "It's kind of hilarious when I think about it, that we're all suffering from amnesia every time we go on a new *holiday*. We think that the beach town we're staying in is our home. And it's only when we wake up that we see the whole truth: namely, that this incarnation is nothing else but a short stop on our journey and that we have another home that we come from and will go back to."

Stretching to work some kinks out of her shoulders, Nayeli exhaled loudly. "You know, Willow, everything you've told me makes sense on one level. But on another level, it's also completely blowing my mind. I mean, I don't even get why my sister thinks and acts the way she does most of the time – how then can she be a different expression of me and I of her? And how can we both be the source and a flower?"

Breaking into raucous laughter, Willow took a few seconds to calm down before responding. "I know that it's a difficult truth for your human mind to grasp. And you'll likely never understand the full magnitude of it while you possess your ego. But you don't need to understand every detail of how you came to be here to enjoy your holiday and make the best use of it, do you?"

Nayeli snorted. "It does introduce a couple of other questions, though," she said. "For example, how can there be oneness when there's also time and we can't be everywhere at once? And are there any other ways – apart from unconditional love – to connect back to our soul while we're on this holiday called life?"

"I'll gladly answer you both questions," the tree promised. "For now, let me tackle the last one you mentioned and go on from there, all right?" Not waiting for Nayeli to respond, the weeping willow continued without delay "To answer it, I need to tell you a bit more about how your interaction with your soul works and how you can use the emotional scale to find out how far removed you are from it. Or, to say it otherwise, how close you are to the 'happy' end of the scale, and why happiness is your north star."

Nayeli heard the grin in Willow's voice and knew that her friend must be proud to have answered her question this cryptically. Whereas she felt even more lost. "The emotional scale? The happy end of it? The north star?" Nayeli asked, unsure what to think about all this.

Willow shuffled its crown. "Yep, this all belongs to a topic that, I think, Sunshine can shine some light upon ..."

13. Sunshine, the Dolphin

Depression had settled inside Strix and it seemed determined to stay as he soared aimlessly east. Strix vaguely registered how the landscape changed from rugged, mountainous rims to a desert beneath him, but he couldn't dredge up enough energy to care.

It was only when the land gave way to the open sea that he felt the first stirrings of an emotion within him that wasn't born out of his sadness.

Groaning pitifully at seeing such a wide expanse of water stretching out in front of him, Strix had half a mind to turn around. But, knowing his bad luck, he might cross paths with Rose again if he did that. And he didn't want to be around when she showed off her perfect little family, which was probably already in the works. The mental image alone made him feel lonelier than ever, and Strix promptly decided to brave the ocean instead.

The sound of the waves and the smell of the salty sea air did nothing to help him relax, however. Quite the contrary. Images rose in his mind's eye of an octopus pulling him into the dark depths of the ocean and of him almost drowning as a result. When his nerves began to act up and Strix began to tremble with anxiety, he remembered the sloth he had met at the start of his journey and how she had told him that breathing deeply would help him calm down.

Following the advice, Strix let the air travel deep into his belly while he beat his wings in a steady rhythm. In an instant, he felt some relief.

But it was short-lived as a cackling pod of dolphins emerged in the waves beneath him, their slender bodies ploughing through the water effortlessly. Occasionally, one of them would jump into the air and land with a splash, which was met with loud squeaking that accentuated their endless chatter.

There was no way Strix could concentrate on his breaths with that ruckus going on. And all of a sudden seething anger filled him – anger at fate bringing him here, anger at these unwelcome passers-by and anger at the awfulness of life in general.

Giving up on his venture to calm down, Strix used the dolphins as an outlet. He cursed colourfully at them for disturbing his quiet and being so obnoxious, hoping it would be enough to drive them away.

But, instead of being deterred by his rage, one of the younger dolphins even had the nerve to call up to him. "Hey, why are you in such a grumpy mood? Life is loads of fun. You just gotta join in."

"Leave me alone and swim somewhere else!" Strix called angrily and sped up to lose the annoying individuals.

Only that they were as fast as him and easily kept up.

"I'm Sunshine," the adolescent exclaimed. "And you are?"

Strix doggedly ignored the dolphin's presence and kept his eyes on the horizon, hoping to find some land where he could lose the juvenile and his family.

Sunshine was silent for some time, perhaps waiting for an answer. But when the young dolphin realised he wouldn't get one, he happily chatted on. "You aren't talking to anyone, are you?" he asked, amused. "I see how it is. When I was a calf, my mum always told me not to talk to strangers, too. But I'm nice, I promise. And so's my family."

Strix groaned in annoyance and flew lower to give the adolescent a piece of his mind or, if need be, to show off his impressive claws. But before he could follow through with that plan, Sunshine had catapulted himself into the air. And when the dolphin dived back in, he triggered a fountain of water, which was rushing directly at Strix.

Trying to swerve out of the way, Strix knew that he wouldn't be fast enough, a split second before the shockingly cold water drenched him.

"Bloody hell!" he shouted, following that up with a few more choice words he was surprised to have in his vocabulary.

For a moment, he feared that his plumage would be too wet and heavy to fly on and that he would need to swim once more – this time being even further away from any shore. But luckily, when he shook himself, he felt himself gain height as a warm air current lifted him. He soared away from the dolphins, who were laughing.

"Can't you watch out, you stupid fish?"

"I have to disappoint you," another dolphin chimed in. "We are not fish, we are mammals. Something a wise owl like you should know."

"I do know it," Strix bit out. "I'm not stupid. But I can call you whatever the heck I want. And if you don't like being called fish, then you're free to swim somewhere else and get lost. The ocean is big enough, after all. Fish!"

"Okey-dokey." Sunshine laughed lightly. "You've made your point. You're angry and want to take out your bad mood on someone else."

"I don't want to take out my bad mood on anyone," Strix corrected rudely. "I want to be left the hell alone. Is that so difficult to understand?"

To Strix's dismay, it obviously was – or maybe the dolphins were just too stubborn to follow orders as they proceeded to swim beneath him.

"It's not healthy to wallow in these negative feelings, y'know?" Sunshine said after a while, even though nobody had asked him what he thought.

When Strix didn't react to the dolphin's opinion, the young mammal observed him closely. "Looks like you don't want to talk about what's upset you," Sunshine concluded. "Yeah, I figured ... Fine, if you don't want to unload your troubles, it's gonna have to be Plan B. You need some cheering up. And guess what? It's your lucky day. Because I bet I can make you laugh. I'm the best joke-teller the world has ever seen. Soooo, do you wanna hear one?"

Strix refused to answer, but the young dolphin didn't seem to mind his stony silence and continued to chatter happily. "Okay, listen," he squeaked, "I'm sure you haven't heard this one yet. What do you call an owl in a bad mood?"

Flapping his wings faster in order to escape this godforsaken sea and all its inhabitants, Strix hoped to find an island or a coastline where the pests below him couldn't follow. But there was nothing to be seen. No rocky cliffs, no trees, no beaches, nothing that promised a safe haven.

When Sunshine caught on to the fact that he wouldn't get a response, he gave the answer himself. "A scowl! Do you get it? Owl? Scowl?" The adolescent chortled and the whole pod of dolphins joined in and cackled loudly. The sound of their laughter was even more irritating than their endless chatter, and Strix clenched his beak in irritation.

"And that was supposed to make me laugh?" Strix groused.

"Didn't you like it?" Sunshine asked a little hurt. "No worries then. Cause I have lots more jokes where that one came from. And I bet we'll find the right one for you. How about this one? What does a wolf with a speech impediment do?"

Sunshine only waited a split second before blurting out the answer. "He owls! Think about it ... howls, owls ..." He broke into a fit of laughter, and the group of dolphins squeaked in chorus.

Sighing in misery, Strix realised that he needed to alter his tactic in order to get rid of the mammals and addressed Sunshine directly. "Ha-ha, how funny," he muttered dryly. "I've never heard a better joke in my whole life. I feel much happier. Your job is done. Why don't you search out someone else who's in a bad mood and help them, too? Cause you can perform miracles with those jokes."

"Why don't I believe you one bit?" Sunshine said in a sing-song voice. "Hmm, maybe because you look as grumpy as before?"

Strix tried to put on a fake smile, hoping it would convince the pesky individual. But luck had deserted him long-term.

"Right, the third joke then," Sunshine exclaimed brightly.

"No ..." Strix groaned painfully. "Please don't!"

But the young dolphin wasn't to be deterred. "This one I adapted from some jokes a human told when I swam near his boat." Turning around to one of his friends, he spoke quietly to him, after which his eyes darted back to Strix. "Ready? Well, ready or not, here it comes ... Knock knock."

"Who's there?" the dolphin Sunshine had talked to answered.

"Who!" Sunshine responded simply.

"Who who?" his friend asked.

"Who who who!"

Breaking out into laughter, the two dolphins leapt so high that spray reached Strix's claws once they dived back into the sea.

"Isn't that genius?" Sunshine asked excitedly once they'd calmed down. "It sounds like the noise an owl makes. And you can keep it up infinitely."

Strix shook his head in despair but couldn't help a tiny smile from crossing his face. "Do you only know owl jokes, or what?"

"No, I know lots of others, too," Sunshine said proudly. "Do you want to hear some?"

"Don't you dare!" Strix warded him off. "Your jokes are getting worse by the second." But his tone was already lighter because Sunshine's continued cheerfulness was proving to be stronger than the anger Strix tried to hold on to. And the longer he was around these high-spirited beings, the better he began to feel. He was, in fact, feeling happier than he had ever since he had left Rose behind.

Being reminded of the swan brought back the emotion of sadness, but this time Strix let it wash over him. And when he breathed in deeply, he could practically feel the depression seep out again, dissipating like a cloud of black smoke.

"See?" Sunshine smiled knowingly. "That feels good, doesn't it?"

"Hmm," Strix mumbled noncommittally and tried to keep from smiling to not give the dolphin any satisfaction – or, even worse, make Sunshine believe that his jokes were actually helpful.

But the juvenile didn't need his validation. He grinned up at Strix. "You're welcome," he beamed while flinging himself out of the water and doing a pirouette.

Just then, Strix saw the contours of an island appear on the horizon ahead of him. It looked tiny, but good enough to rest his tired wings and get some peace and quiet.

Looking down, Strix eyed the young dolphin. "It was nice of you and your family to keep me company. And to brighten up my day. But this is the moment I have to say goodbye. I'm knackered and if I don't take a break soon, I'll probably fall into the sea and drown."

An excited twinkle stole into Sunshine's eyes at these words, which didn't bode well at all in Strix's opinion. "Y'know, you mentioning death reminded me of another great joke ..." Sunshine paused briefly to build up the tension. "Why aren't owl jokes dead yet? Eh? What do you think? C'mon, don't be a spoilsport. Give me an answer. Why aren't owl jokes dead?"

Turning his head away so that Sunshine wouldn't see him smile at his exuberance, Strix gave the dolphin one last concession, now that his rescue was near. "I don't know – maybe because you don't let anyone forget them?"

"Wrong!" Sunshine laughed before giving the correct answer. "Because they're a hoot!"

The pod of dolphins laughed out loud. And this time, Strix couldn't help but join in.

"I told you," Sunshine said happily as they reached the shallower water. "Sharing laughter with friends is the easiest way to reach happiness. And you can find us whenever you need someone to lift your mood."

"Thanks! I'll keep that in mind," Strix said and was surprised that he meant it.

Heading straight for a grassy spot behind the dunes, he settled down and looked out at the group of dolphins.

They were swiftly disappearing into the vast expense of the sea, their laughter growing fainter the further away they swam.

Soon, the little island was draped in silence that almost made Strix miss the constant chatter of his fish-reeking companions. Pausing at that crazy idea, he fluffed up his feathers and hunkered down. No way had he taken a liking to the dolphins. But before he could convince himself of that fact, tiredness overwhelmed him, and Strix postponed all further thought until later in favour of a deep, dreamless sleep.

***

When Strix woke up, he felt better – in body and spirit. Stretching, he noticed that his overstrained muscles were restored and that the sadness had finally lifted.

Rising into the air to watch the glistening sun sparkle on the water, Strix thought about where to fly next. He wanted to leave the ocean behind for good but didn't have the slightest clue where he was and how far it stretched into each direction. And there was no animal in sight to ask, either.

Belatedly, he realised that he had wasted the opportunity to ask the dolphins – they would have certainly known where the next coastline was. But it was too late. The pod was presumably long gone by now.

Having no option but to pick one direction at random and to trust his instinct that it would be the right one, Strix decided on a north-east course, praying that this route wouldn't lead him further into the open sea, and took off from the island.

Not much had changed in the last couple of hours. The ocean was still as blue and endless as ever, and Strix didn't particularly enjoy crossing it. But he didn't feel quite as threatened anymore. If he could look at the sea from the land, he might even grow to like the serenity it radiated.

Watching his own shadow, which painted a darker shape on the water, Strix flew in arcs and did some crazy aerial manoeuvres, to see it dance on the crests and blend in with the troughs of the sea.

Immersed in the sight, Strix didn't notice the many slim bodies until they were directly underneath him. There were several of them, and Strix wondered if they were the same dolphins he'd met yesterday before quickly casting the idea aside. That would be too much of a coincidence.

But then one body broke the surface to breathe fresh air and Strix's doubts proved to be false. He had found Sunshine and his family again.

"Hey Sunshine!" he called out happily as he flew lower to greet the young dolphin. "Short time no see, eh? You know what? It's fortunate that we've met again. I thought up some dolphin jokes this morning to match yours. And I came up with this one: Why are dolphin jokes so great?" Strix burst out with his answer so fast that Sunshine didn't even have the chance to respond. "Because there's nothing fishy about them! Good one, right?" Flapping his wings excitedly, Strix waited for Sunshine's approval.

But the dolphin only smiled up at him half-heartedly. "It was a great one. Thanks."

"What's wrong?" Strix asked, concerned, only now becoming aware of the sadness lying in the eyes of Sunshine and his whole family. Something bad must have happened to turn this joyful pod into such a glum group in less than a day's time.

Sunshine's next words confirmed his suspicion. "We had a loss last night. My aunt died and we are all mourning her."

"I'm sorry," Strix said heartfelt, thinking back to the time his father had crossed over. Not even the knowledge that he would see him again had eased the pain of the loss. "I'm really sorry," he repeated. "I know how painful goodbyes are. I hope you remember that she's waiting for you when your time comes, though?"

"Sure," Sunshine answered. "I haven't forgotten the other side. But I'll still miss her in this life and the joy she spread. Y'see, she was usually the first one to laugh when I told a bad joke ..."

"Do you do that?" Strix asked, attempting to lighten the gloomy mood because he was at a complete loss what else to do. "And here I thought you only knew the funny ones ..." To Strix's surprise, his strategy seemed to work as Sunshine's smile grew a little brighter. But then the dolphin sighed. "This actually reminds me that I have to apologise to you."

Opening his beak in surprise, Strix looked down at the young mammal, baffled. "Why?"

"Because I pestered you. I didn't listen when you said you wanted to be left alone. I didn't even know why you felt bad – whether you were mourning or whether there was some other reason. But in the end, it doesn't matter. I should have accepted you weren't happy. It's fine not to. I see that, now that I'm feeling down myself. It's made me realise that we need to value the whole range of our emotions, including the ones of a lower frequency."

"It's no problem," Strix muttered. "Your light-heartedness did me a lot of good, even if I didn't want to admit it at the time. And you were right to be persistent. I should have let go of my bad feelings cause I kept wallowing in them when their usefulness had long passed, and that's not healthy either."

"That's true." Sunshine grinned, a faint spark returning to his eyes.

Seeing the twinkle, Strix should have known what was coming, but he was still taken by surprise at the young dolphin's next words.

"When *owl* is said and done, *owl* we need to do is to allow *owl* our feelings to express themselves, but to release *owl* of them when it's time to move on. Or isn't that true?"

"Seriously?" Strix laughed at Sunshine. "That's the best you've got?"

"Sorry," Sunshine grinned, not looking sorry at all. "I'm not at the top of my game today. But I promise that when we meet next, I'll make up for it by re-telling the funniest owl jokes you've ever encountered. Deal?"

"Deal!" Strix extended his right claw. He then realised that the dolphin had no leg to shake it and pulled it back self-consciously, grinning down at the mammal. "But until then ... can you tell me where I need to go to reach the next coast? Cause I'm totally lost."

"Turn a bit north and you should reach land in about half an hour."

"Thanks." Strix flew higher and turned in the direction indicated, wishing there was more he could do for Sunshine and his family, but knowing that the best thing he could give them was the space to work through their grief in their own time.

Letting himself be carried by the sea breeze, Strix wondered at how quickly emotions and life itself could change. Only yesterday he had been hanging on to his feelings of loss and now he was looking forward again, excited about all the new adventures that awaited him. He knew that not all would be perfect and that feelings of grief and sadness would be visitors in the future because there would be many more goodbyes in his life. But somehow, he thought, that was all right. As there would be just as many new beginnings – since there couldn't be one without the other.

The Emotional Scale and Happiness

"Hey, I thought you wanted to tell me a story about happiness, but you turned it into a sad one about loss and grief!" Nayeli complained.

The tree shrugged. "As Strix said, a beginning can't happen without an end. And you can't feel happiness if you haven't been on the opposite end of the emotional scale. It's all connected."

"What is this emotional scale you keep talking about, Willow?"

"It is your compass in life. And happiness is the compass needle that points north, towards the desires of your soul-plan."

Willow let its lighter twigs brush against each other. "You already know that we live in a world of dual reality and that everything has an opposite. This holds true for emotions as well. Imagine it as a scale: one end holds the emotion with the highest energetic frequency, while at the other end there is the emotion with the lowest vibration. In other words, on one side, you have the emotions of happiness, empowerment and freedom. And on the other side, you'll find hopelessness, grief, fear and panic, which are some of the most disempowered emotions you can possibly hold."

"Oh, I could tell you about *that.*" Nayeli laughed humourlessly. "Panic attacks are the most horrendous things to endure ..."

"That sounds as if you have made acquaintances with them?" Willow prodded gently.

"I've had them for ten years – not only a few here and there. But fifteen or twenty in a day and bad ones at that ... You know, Willow, the physical side-effects of panic attacks aren't a walk in the park either: they can range from extreme back pains or stomach cramps to nausea, tremors and hot flushes. But compared to the feeling of panic itself, they're nothing. These attacks always made me think I was dying because the emotion is so awful that I felt I couldn't endure it another second. It turned me into a crying, shaking mass of nothingness and made me cling to the floor or wall or anything else nearby because I felt like I was gonna cease to exist at any moment. And the sole thought in my mind was 'please, make it stop somehow'." Shuddering, Nayeli crossed her arms in a weak attempt to imitate a hug that would bring her some comfort. "After living through that for such a long time, I'm convinced it's the worst feeling any human can go through. And I wouldn't wish it on my worst enemy, not even for one minute!"

"I'm sorry you had to experience this, my dear," Willow whispered. "That can't have been easy."

Nayeli nodded, then shrugged. "Well, it's over and dealt with, there's no use crying over spilled milk. And I'd rather we get back to what you were telling me regarding this scale."

"What else do you want to know about it?"

"Uhm, what's the feeling above fear?"

"Anger," Willow said. "Above fear is anger."

Frowning, Nayeli rubbed her forehead. "Are you sure?"

"Positive," the tree replied. "Why?"

"Because any feeling that's higher on the scale should feel better than the one below it, no? But anger doesn't feel better. It's not as debilitating as panic, I'll give you that. But it's still an awful emotion, both when you're on the receiving end of it and when you're experiencing it yourself. I for one despise it!"

Willow let its branches swoosh through the air. "Although anger doesn't feel good, it's higher on the scale because someone who is angry feels some form of power through it. Their anger fuels them into action, which enables them to create change. That's also why people who have no healthy boundaries often show anger when one of their lines is crossed. In comparison, anxiety and fear are powerless states, which is why they rank below. And as for your opinion that anger is an awful emotion you don't want to deal with – how you feel about any emotion has to do with your upbringing and past wounds. Some people learn as children that anger is not okay. These people have forgotten how to express it healthily or how to respond to it when they see it in other people, and they thus feel unsafe when they are met with anger. But not everyone feels that way. Some people learn the complete opposite in their child-hoods. They might have learned that showing anger was acceptable, while showing any form of *weakness* was to be avoided. And others might have had the advantage to be enabled to express all their emotions as children.

"When all is said and done, emotions are never bad, not even those on the bottom rung of the scale. They're natural and, what is more, they're valid because every feeling has a good reason to be present. It's only when you act on any emotion in an unhealthy way that it can become detrimental – to you or others."

Nayeli contemplated the matter. "I see. Just because I accept that anger is a part of me, I don't have to let it make me do anything hurtful. And although I have little choice about the emotions I feel, I have every choice about how to express them in a healthy way."

"You got it, my dear," the tree said proudly. "Don't let the negatively perceived emotion control you, but let it do its job and guide you closer to your higher self."

"Eh, Willow? You've lost me there. What does all of this have to do with moving closer to my soul?"

"Sorry. I'm explaining this poorly. I should have been clearer from the get-go since you're new to this topic. Let me begin afresh ... I've already told you that when you're incarnated you are two points of perspective, right? You continue to be a soul and you have the second perspective of a human being here on Earth. Now, when you come here, you'll eventually experience something negative, most likely sooner than later. When this happens, your human ego perspective becomes a match to the lower vibrational end of the scale and you experience anger or fear or powerlessness. After you've experienced these lower frequencies, you'll then automatically long for the positive emotion that's on the opposite end of the scale. For example, if you're born into a poor family that barely scrapes by each month, this might make you desire to feel powerful. And if you had parents who cluttered your calendar with piano, ballet and soccer lessons on top of school, you might long to feel freedom.

"The problem is that the manifestation of a desire into your reality takes some time. As a human, you won't instantly have your wish fulfilled. Your higher self, on the other hand, isn't held back by anything. That means when you feel the desire to be loved, your eternal self immediately moves into that higher energy of experiencing love in its purest form. And when you give rise to the desire to feel free, your higher self is immediately in the frequency of freedom. This creates a distance between your human self and your higher self because one is stuck in the energy of the unfulfilled need, while the other has already reached fulfilment. Your task as a human is to then close that gap so that both of your perspectives are in the same space once more."

"In short, I'm playing a catch-up game with my higher self?"

Nayeli asked.

"Spot on, my dear. A catch-up game that's going to keep you occupied your entire life. For every human has several desires simultaneously and every time you fulfil one it gives rise to even more."

Nayeli rubbed her chin absentmindedly. "But what if someone is the exception to that rule and doesn't have any wishes?"

"That's not possible. There is no human alive who doesn't have several desires present within them. It doesn't matter if they want something big like a baby or a house, or something smaller like trying out a recipe or watching a new movie that came out. You always have an array of unfulfilled wishes. And your higher self is always fulfilled, pulling you in that direction like a magnet. The only thing that can happen is that desires become stuck inside your subconsciousness and you're not aware of them any longer. But that doesn't mean you don't have any."

"Right, then say I don't have access to mine. What do I do then?" Nayeli questioned.

"Let me first tell you what to do when you know what your soul's desires are. Imagine your desire as the needle in a compass pointing north. When you know where north is in relation to where you stand, you can go there directly and take appropriate steps to get what you want. For example, when you know that travelling is your ultimate desire, you can pack your bags and buy an airline ticket. Which is where we come back to your question ... if you're not sure what you want and where north lies for you, then find out where south is. It is often easier for you humans to figure out what you *don't* want. When you realise that you hate being employed, look for what you dislike about it – what your personal south is – and then go for the opposite to arrive at north."

“Sounds logical,” Nayeli said thoughtfully.

“You have to become aware, though,” Willow continued seamlessly, “that sometimes desires you have can be misleading.”

“How so?”

“Sometimes your ego can get in the way and create desires that seem to come from your soul but actually don’t. Desires you think are important, but which aren’t. These can lead to some detours on your road where you move east or west instead of north.”

“Great,” Nayeli said sarcastically. “You’re saying ‘follow your desires but be aware that they’re not always leading you in the right direction’. That’s a lot of help, Willow. Not!”

Laughing, the tree pulled its branches together in front of Nayeli to block out the meadow beyond. “Since you like it this much, I have a second piece of wisdom for you ... ‘Follow your happiness as it’s the best way of moving closer to your higher self, but remain aware that making joy your sole focus can lead you in the opposite direction at times’.”

“Come again?” Nayeli said.

“I mean,” Willow chuckled, “that happiness can potentially keep you stuck where you are or let you slide down even further from where you want to be. An addict might feel happy when they use the substance they’re addicted to, although they’re endangering their health long-term. And someone who doesn’t want to face their dysfunctional relationship might lie to themselves about their partner cheating on them – a deception that makes them feel more positive in the short term but which will hurt them in the long run. In these and more cases, it would be better if you first faced your problems head-on, by actively going backwards on the scale and dealing with the lower frequency emotions.”

"But then, how can I discern between the two?" Nayeli asked, confused. "How am I supposed to know when it would be better to move backwards and when to move forwards?"

"Generally speaking, it's always a good idea to move backwards first, to heal the underlying traumas. For example, when you are stuck in anger, it often makes no sense to try to go further upward without dealing with the fear and powerlessness that are at the root. But there can also be times when it's useful to move upward, despite not having healed the core wounds yet. If you're often stuck in the frequency of anxiety, fear and powerlessness, it could actually be an improvement to move towards anger, because that would feel more empowering and would enable you to take action and create changes in your life. In the end, you need to listen to your intuition, regarding what would improve your situation long-term."

Nayeli inclined her head in agreement, as this was something she could get behind. But the next second, she was pulled up short by a new thought. "Wait, Willow, are you saying that every single time someone feels anger, there's fear or pain beneath it? Cause there's no way that can be true. Have you never experienced how hateful some people are? I'm not saying you're completely wrong, but fear and pain are not at the root of all aggression. The people I'm thinking of don't feel any weakness ... the bullies, the narcissists, the xenophobes or homophobes, people who enjoy bringing others down."

"Then let's see if I can convince you otherwise," the tree said cheerfully. "Let's imagine an alcoholic man who beats his wife and children. The victims in this situation are the wife and children, wouldn't you agree?"

Answering to the affirmative, Nayeli wondered what Willow was trying to get at.

"But now let's switch perspective and look into the childhood of the man. Maybe he has been beaten himself. Maybe he was the family scapegoat. Or maybe he was starved of affection."

"But none of that excuses his later behaviour," Nayeli said steadfastly. "We can't all go around and hurt others because we've been hurt in the past. That would result in a landslide effect of endless pain."

"Which is exactly what's happening in the world," Willow replied matter-of-factly. "My dear, I'm not excusing anyone's behaviour here. Every single person is responsible for how they act. But I'm asking you to understand what's happening and why. For without an awareness of the core reasons behind a problem and without the willingness to see the underlying truth, there can be no change towards a better reality. And to gain that awareness, I want to ask you to move in the perspective of this boy again. Forget what he becomes in later years. Think only of the child who is hurt and in pain. Isn't he the victim when he's young, because he's dependent on his parents or caregivers?"

"Yes," Nayeli admitted. "But still ..."

Shaking its crown, the weeping willow continued, as if it hadn't been interrupted. "The abuse and violence that's happening worldwide are due to people becoming victims of victims. Because we've all been hurt by others. Even the most hateful person has unhealed traumas within themselves, and whenever these wounds are triggered, it reminds them subconsciously – if not consciously – of their past pain. This leads them to feel threatened. And since they cannot endure feeling *weak*, they need to project the issue outwards and make someone else responsible.

"Therefore, my answer is yes. All emotions can be traced back on the emotional scale. The ones that are of a lower frequency cause the ones above. And since powerlessness, fear and sadness are all below anger, all anger results from them. Many people aren't aware of this pattern. But just because the underlying feelings aren't felt and heard any longer doesn't make them disappear. On the contrary. They'll fight their way back to the top. Which results in the anger and hate getting stronger to drown them out anew." Willow whistled softly. "You can look at aggression as an overcompensation for feeling out of control. It lets people pretend they're fearless, even to themselves."

Nayeli began to see what the tree meant. "Hmm, I guess you're right, after all." She rolled her eyes heavenward and added with a deep, put-upon sigh: "Again!"

"Was there any doubt about it?" Willow asked cheekily.

"Smartass," Nayeli replied, smirking.

The tree chortled. "I would prefer 'wise' and 'all-knowing'. But whatever works for you, my dear child, whatever works for you."

Nayeli snorted. "If you're all-knowing, then you can surely tell me the solution to this problem. How can we stop humanity from using aggression and abuse?"

"I can suggest the perfect solution that would work in theory," the tree replied promptly. "The perfect solution is to make every single person feel safe and happy at all times. Imagine no one felt threatened anymore. Imagine that every human had everything they needed and could get anything they wanted whenever they liked. There would be no need for envy and greed. There would be no need for hate or fear. When everyone would be in the top range of the emotional scale, to put others down would lead to them walking backwards on their own scale, reducing their happiness. And who'd want that?"

"But wouldn't that result in a lasting feeling of happiness? And wouldn't that defeat the purpose of the emotional scale and the whole game of tag I play with my higher self?" Nayeli asked.

Willow swung its branches affirmatively, losing a leaf in the process, which landed on Nayeli's head.

Plucking it off, Nayeli turned it over and over as the tree continued to speak.

"That's why I said it would work *in theory*. In this dual reality, the best solution we can work towards practically is to develop understanding. You need to understand yourself and your core wounds and triggers, first and foremost. Then you need to develop an understanding of others and why they think and feel and act the way they do. If everyone did this, the world would already heal so much it would be headspinning. And we'd take a huge leap towards ending all prejudice and hate."

"This call to action sounds great in theory," Nayeli concluded. "But not everyone will be ready to see it this way, will they?"

"No," the tree answered. "You're all on different paths on your journey, and not everyone is ready to hear this truth yet. But every person who does find more understanding, on top of following their happiness and heading north on their scale, is already making a difference."

Nayeli massaged a tense muscle in her neck. "And if I'm stuck in a place where I feel I can never be happy again? What am I supposed to do then?"

"Then, my dear, you train your happiness as you'd train a muscle in your body. But why don't we look at your life in particular to make this clearer? Tell me, when was the last time you felt happy?"

The answer came instantly to Nayeli. "Last year, when I was on holiday. I found a secluded bay where I spend my time. And one day when I was in the water, I was visited by a group of dolphins who swam near me. It was a magnificent experience, and one I'll never forget."

"And since then you haven't felt happy once?" Willow asked.

"Well, I was happy last month when I got around to reading a new book I'd wanted to delve into for the longest time," Nayeli admitted.

"And in the weeks since then?"

Nayeli shrugged helplessly as she fumbled for the answer the tree was fishing for. But try as she might, she didn't know what her friend wanted to hear. "It's not like I've had many reasons to be happy recently. But now that I think about it, my mum did bake an apple pie yesterday and I had a piece this morning. Does that count?"

"Was it tasty?" Willow asked.

"Fantastic," Nayeli replied. "No one else can bake better than her ..."

"Then it does count," the tree answered. "And if you needed to make a list of what else has made you happy today?"

"Just today?" Nayeli asked. Considering the matter, she couldn't think of a single thing at first. But then a memory emerged, and she smiled. "That I can spend my day with you and talk about such interesting topics."

There was a long silence before the weeping willow responded. "And that's all? You're only happy about two things – the pie included – this whole day?"

"I ..." Nayeli said, unsure. "I guess so ... at least, I can't think of anything else."

"Then I'll tell you a few things that make me happy," Willow declared. "I'm happy that I can talk to you and spend my time with you. I'm happy that I can teach you new things. I'm happy that you're already more in tune with your soul-path than when we met. I'm happy to call you my friend, Nayeli. I'm happy for the sun shining on my branches, which revives me. I'm happy to have the brook running beside me. I'm happy for the cool wind that makes my leaves rustle, and I'm happy that this sound – together with the birds' voices – creates such a beautiful song. I'm happy that Mother Earth provides for me and that I'm always connected with her via my roots. And those are merely a few of the things that came to me ..."

Finally, the meaning behind the tree's questions revealed itself to Nayeli. She grinned ruefully. "You're saying that humans tend to oversee the little moments that could bring us happiness, right?"

The tree's bark croaked behind Nayeli's head as Willow raised its branches skywards. "Yes, when you tell humans to practise happiness, the mistake that's most often made is that they only look for the big, memorable situations that bring them joy. Meanwhile, they become blind to all the small blessings that litter their path day after day. When you practise happiness, it's not the time to differentiate between good and better or small and big. And it's not the time to compare yourself or your situation to anyone else's or to your past or future self, either. Happiness is about appreciating what you have or what is good at any given moment. And when you do this, you become aware that there's much more joy to encounter in this world than many humans realise."

Willow nudged her with a twig. "So, try again. What else makes *you* happy?"

"The flowers on this meadow," Nayeli began hesitantly. "They appear in all colours of the rainbow and I'm feeling more joyful just looking at them. Then there's the fact that I'm wearing my favourite dress today, which I thought to bring along. I'm happy to have got some fresh orange juice with the pie this morning that my uncle made. My uncle who, by the way, is helping my mum so much these days. And, last but not least, I'm happy that you've been able to open my eyes to all these little moments of happiness."

Silence hung between Nayeli and Willow in the meadow. It was amicable and peaceful and didn't need any words to fill it.

But then it was broken by the sharp cry of a bird and the tree rustled its crown, as if waking from a trance. "So, tell me, my dear, is that a problem you generally have? Do you have trouble recognising things that could make you even happier?"

Nayeli grimaced. "I don't know. Maybe. I can obviously laugh and put aside work to play. But for some reason, I do it way too seldom. And it feels like I should be happy more often."

"You're one of these *serious people* then, are you?" Willow teased.

"Yeah, I'm guilty of that. Sometimes I actually take happiness seriously. As in 'I have to be happy now', as if it's a task I need to set for myself."

Willow laughed at that and Nayeli followed suit. "I suppose I'm not that great at finding the balance between being serious and having fun. Just like it's tough to accept all of my emotions and to hear them out, but at the same time to distinguish between what still serves me and what holds me back from my desires."

"But you don't need to go looking for balance," the tree said, sounding surprised at her revelation.

"Don't I?"

"No, you definitely don't ..." Willow replied cryptically.

14. Forest, the Squirrel

"It's the owl's turn to sing us a song now."

The request came from a green bee-eater, and it was mirrored by the other birds sitting in the circle.

Having all eyes on him, Strix felt put on the spot. He glanced uncomfortably at the centre stone where a sunbird had just finished its ballad and was vacating its place for the next performance.

Strix had met this ragbag group of birds when flying through the forest and when asked to join them for the evening, he hadn't hesitated. Travelling around alone for longer periods of time always left him with the desire to connect to others. But when he had accepted the invitation, he'd had no idea that everyone would be asked to perform. Knowing that his singing voice was nothing to write home about, Strix scratched at the ground nervously. "Uh, I'd rather not."

"Come on," one of the smaller birds called out. "You've listened to all of us. You can't bow out."

The other birds agreed unanimously.

Feeling the pressure built, Strix walked slowly to the rock while trying to think of a solution to escape his predicament. It was only when his claws touched the cold surface that an idea took shape. He raised his head to stare at the assembled birds.

"You don't want to hear me sing, trust me. But how about I narrate a tale instead? I've travelled far and am a much better storyteller than a bard."

Looking at each other, the birds didn't know how to respond at first, but then a kingfisher spoke up. "Show us what you've got then."

Relief surged through Strix and he searched his memory for the right tale. At long last, he settled on an experience from his time in England, which had happened shortly after he'd left Brownie, the badger, behind.

***

As Strix flew over the forest that stretched out in all directions below him, he could almost imagine being back home, so closely did the trees resemble the woods behind Willow's meadow. He missed his old friend terribly and wondered what the tree was doing right now and who was keeping it company. But then Strix pulled himself out of his nostalgic thoughts; he knew that, no matter how much he missed his home and everyone he had left behind, he would never see them again in this lifetime. He'd burned all bridges when he had flown off without a word. And there was nothing for him to return to.

Thus, instead of letting himself get trapped in any regrets he might harbour, Strix came back to the present and tried to look for all the small differences that set this area apart from the place he had lived in for most of his short life. He noticed a couple of plants that he didn't know from home, in addition to some birds that looked different. Moreover, half of the squirrels he saw here were red, unlike the bigger grey ones that populated his birthplace.

Sitting down on a branch of a birch tree, Strix watched as two red squirrels chased each other in what appeared to be a strange courtship ritual, skipping around the trees, running up and down the trunks and jumping from one branch to the next with skill and elegance.

He knew how difficult it could be to keep his footing on the thinner twigs when they swung in the wind, but these two rodents were keeping their balance with an ease that was unparalleled by any other creature he knew. And when they flew from one tree to the next – their bushy tails stretched out behind them – they landed safely, not even needing a breath or two to collect themselves before running head-first down another trunk. What was more, they managed to jump such great distances between the trees that they appeared to be flying.

Captivated by the two nimble animals, Strix noticed a third one almost too late and ducked just in time to avoid a collision.

The rodent in question jumped over him and scurried further down the branch.

Turning his neck to glare after the rude animal who hadn't even called out a warning, Strix shook his head in outrage. It was only when the male red squirrel disappeared out of sight behind the tree's trunk that Strix looked back towards the two rodents he'd watched before. But a moment later, the third squirrel come barrelling back, once again barely missing Strix's head, as he jumped onto the branch above him.

"Hey!" Strix called out as he ducked a second time. "Can't you pay attention? Or are you blind? Didn't you see me?"

"What's your name?" the squirrel asked tersely, coming to an abrupt halt.

"Strix," Strix answered, taken aback by the unexpected question and the rudeness of the tone.

"Good, Strix, you listen to me now. It must be real nice for you that you have this much free time on your claws. But I'm busy. I need to find food for the winter to survive. So, look for another place if you want peace."

Strix gazed up at the few deciduous trees surrounding him in the mostly coniferous forest, which had just started to wear green.

"Um, finding food for the winter?" Strix asked, dumbfounded. "Aren't you a bit early? I reckon it's going to get warmer in the next weeks and there must be ages until the first snow comes. Which means that there are probably no nuts or seeds or anything like that to be found at this time of the year, either."

"It's never too early to prepare for the worst case," the squirrel rudely threw back while his teeth chattered in irritation. And then, without another word, he was gone, jumping into a conifer and disappearing behind its trunk.

"Don't mind Forest," the female red squirrel he'd watched earlier called out, her suitor seemingly having disappeared while Strix had been distracted. "He's a little ... how should I say this ... different to the rest of us."

"What are you talking about?" Strix asked curiously and fluttered over to sit beside her.

"Forest was born three years ago, and his first winter was a harsh one – the harshest in the last decade. Not to mention that he lived up north, where it was worse than here. Many squirrels and other animals didn't survive, including his mum. He was left all by himself and would have died if it hadn't been for a grey squirrel who had lost her whole litter that year. She took him in. Normally, the only things the greys give us are their stupid viruses and death. But fate was with Forest that day when she found him, as he wouldn't have made it otherwise."

"And that's why he's strange?" Strix probed. "Because he was raised by a grey squirrel?"

The female rodent looked off into the distance. "We'll never know for sure, but I can't help wondering sometimes if his foster-mum did him any favours in taking him on. Or if it would have been better for him to cross back over like his mother did. You see, she taught him all these weird customs the grey squirrels have, and he's adopted them without question. But he isn't faring too well – although he believes he's a grey squirrel, he isn't one, and he'll never become like her."

"And what customs are you talking about? I thought all you squirrels acted alike?"

"Not by a long stretch." The female said. "To name an example, the greys bury nuts in various stashes, while we tend to make one large pile. Which makes it less stressful to find them again come winter. You just have to watch Forest to know what I mean. He's trying to copy his foster-mum, and it's not working. He's jittery and absent-minded and anxious a lot of the time, not to mention forgetful – about anything in his life. I'm actually amazed that he remembers his own name."

The female squirrel laughed mirthlessly. "As great as he is balancing on the thinnest twigs, his mind is not balanced in the slightest. It's a mess – if I'm allowed to speak that bluntly."

"But why does he stress himself out this much?" Strix asked, still not getting why Forest would go to such lengths to find food supplies that hadn't even grown yet. He has weeks, if not months, until the first cold days. Why not save his energy for autumn and put in a bit more work then?"

The female squirrel shrugged. "Yeah, that would be the smart thing to do. But Forest is too scared to be smart. He fears experiencing another winter like the one in which he lost his mother. That, and the hunger afterwards, are so deeply ingrained in his brain that he tries to stock up whenever he can, no matter the season."

"Hm, it must have been difficult," Strix said, feeling compassion for Forest. Looking after the red squirrel in question, who was nothing else but a distant blur by now, Strix made a snap decision. He flew up into the air and into the direction the rodent had disappeared in.

"Hey, Forest," he called when he had caught up with the squirrel. "Wait, I'm gonna help you."

But the squirrel ignored him.

Left with no other option, Strix landed directly in front of him on a thin branch.

Making angry noises, Forest was about to turn back the way he had come. But before he had a chance to do so, Strix spread out his wings in a sign of peace. "Wait up, will ya? If you told me what you're searching for, I could help you."

"Who are you, Sir?" Forest asked while looking him up and down. "And why are you keeping me from my important work? I need to stock up on my food supplies for the winter, and I need to do it quickly."

Strix was confused at the red squirrel's weird behaviour. Not only was Forest repeating the same words from earlier, but he was also staring at Strix, as if he was a stranger he had never seen in his life.

But then Strix remembered the female squirrel's words about Forest's memory and how bad it supposedly was.

"I'm Strix," Strix said, trying to gauge whether Forest was showing any signs of recognition. "We met a few minutes ago."

"Don't talk such rubbish," Forest replied impatiently. "I don't know you. Do you think I'd forget a rude bird like you, who keeps me from my work? What was your name again? Never mind; I need to get going. The faster, the better. Because once the autumn comes, every squirrel will give me a run for the nuts. I need to get a head start and bury anything I can find before then."

"Right," Strix drawled, watching the red squirrel with big eyes. He only now understood what it must be like for Forest to live like this, day in, day out, and felt sorry for the squirrel and the hard lot he had been dealt for this incarnation.

Forest, meanwhile, had turned around and was running up the next tree trunk. Then, sprinting down a lighter twig, he soared through the sky and landed on a neighbouring tree. There, his body froze and he squeaked in joy.

Curious about what had delighted Forest this much, Strix followed the squirrel and saw a few pine cones lying on the forest floor. The squirrel was heading straight for them.

Diving into the task of digging holes in the ground, Forest filled some of them with the cones, while leaving others empty, after which he covered them all up with earth.

Believing he'd made a mistake, Strix cleared his throat and voiced his concerns to the squirrel.

"That's not a mistake, mister," Forest responded curtly. "I do that for a good reason. Who knows how many squirrels or other animals will come across my stashes in the next weeks and months? And when they smell that something is buried here, they'll dig out holes. But if I keep some empty, they might not find all my nuts because they'll be fed up to dig out the empty ones."

"Ah, clever," Strix responded, amused at the squirrel's logic. "Can I help you?"

"No," Forest said assertively. "I don't need anyone else to know where I hide my food. Especially some stranger I've never met before and who could be a thief, intending to steal from me. So, turn your back or be gone."

"I'm not a thief and I'm certainly not interested in these cones," Strix replied, feeling his amusement turn into indignity. "If I were, I could have taken any of yours prior to you burying them."

"Maybe," Forest replied absentmindedly, already seeming to have forgotten what they had talked about. He snatched up the second to last cone lying behind him and dug a hole for it a bit further away.

Shifting his weight from one foot to the other, Strix watched Forest bustle about. "So, do you remember in which holes you've stored the food and which holes you left empty, come winter?"

"I don't," Forest admitted with a crooked grin, acting more amicably now that he had successfully completed his task. "But that's all the more reason to make this many stashes. That way, I have a chance to find at least a few of them to get me through the cold season."

Strix inclined his head. "Why don't you store food in one stash, though? Like the other reds do."

"No way – I'd be screwed if anyone found it before me. And besides, that would go against our ancient treaty with the forest."

"Your ancient treaty?" Strix asked, his interest piqued. "What's that about?"

Forest looked off into the distance dreamily. "When I was growing up, my foster-mum told me that our squirrel ancestors negotiated this treaty with the trees and nature itself."

"And what is it about?" Strix asked for a second time, figuring the squirrel must have forgotten his question when he didn't continue to speak.

"My mother told me that the treaty is an old tale that is passed on from generation to generation. And it's still fresh in my mind ..."

Hiding a grin at that comment, Strix wondered if Forest was really able to remember something he'd been told such a long time ago when he couldn't even recall a name he had heard minutes earlier. But he swallowed the question, for fear of tearing the red squirrel out of his memory.

"It says," Forest went on, "that the first squirrels that existed had a great memory. The best memory in the whole animal kingdom, to be exact. But, because of their great memory, they were in serious trouble. Every year the squirrels stocked food for the colder winter months. And, unlike today, they found every single cone and nut they had buried. None were left in the earth come spring and because of this, no new trees were able to grow. As a result, over the years, there weren't enough young trees to replace the old ones that were dying. And thus, the woods thinned out, which scared the squirrels and other animals that depended on them.

"To prevent this cycle of death, the squirrels searched out some of their wisest leaders who were assigned the task to find a solution. Many suggestions were made and a lot of experiments were set into motion, from starving every other winter to not gnawing the tree's bark anymore. But even though every squirrel promised to take part in these trials, most of them were doomed almost as soon as they began. For they wanted to save their environment. But when their stomachs rumbled in hunger or their teeth grew too long, all their resolutions were forgotten.

"This made the wisest of the squirrels think of the treaty with

Mother Earth. To protect the woods in the future, all squirrels agreed to give up part of their memory. Instead of finding all the nuts and seeds they had buried in the autumn, they would merely remember some of their stashes. And ever since that day, my foster-mum told me, our forgetfulness has been a blessing in disguise that we should honour."

Huffing sadly, Forest stared down at his front paws. "I don't know if she just came up with the story because she wanted me to feel better about my bad memory, or if it's true. But either way, I'm glad she did. And I'm glad that all the seeds I don't find will, come spring, grow roots and become new trees. It's my way to give back for the food I receive from Mother Earth and to restore the balance."

"That's an interesting tale," Strix said.

"It's why my mum named me Forest," the squirrel added seamlessly. "She said she named me that as a reminder that we squirrels are the rangers of the woods. And since I'm the best ranger, or so she said, I deserve to have that name."

Taking the last cone and holding it between his paws, Forest stripped away its outer layer to get to the seeds within, which he ate with relish.

"That was thoughtful of your mum," Strix replied, touched.

"What was?"

"The name she gave you," Strix elaborated.

"What name? Mine? That doesn't have to interest you. Specially since I dunno yours," Forest mumbled, his cheeks bulging.

"It's Strix," Strix reminded him. "Seriously, how can you forget it so fast, but recount a story to me that your mum told you years ago?"

"I don't know about any story I told you, Mister," Forest interrupted him. "I've just met you, after all. And besides, I don't have time for any tales. It's all fine and dandy if you have the leisure to chat, but I'm in a hurry and have to save food for the coming winter."

Strix coughed to hide a chuckle, being all too aware that it was useless to talk to the squirrel when he was like this. "You know what, Forest? If I were you, I wouldn't bother. You won't remember your stashes anyway and will have to trust your nose to find food. Which begs the question: Why don't you let the other squirrels do all the work and steal their supplies?"

"Why are you so disparaging, bird?" Forest chattered angrily. "I've got a great memory! Shall I prove it to you by telling you how I got my name? That's an ancient tale and I still remember all the details."

"Never mind," Strix said, chuckling for real this time. "I'll be on my way again if there's nothing I can do to help you. Good luck for winter, Forest. And may you always find enough food!"

"Thanks," Forest chattered absentmindedly, already looking around for more nuts that he could bury. It was only when Strix had risen into the blue sky that the squirrel stopped dead in his tracks. "Hey, how do you know my name, Sir?"

Strix hid a grin as he shouted back. "I just know that you are the ranger of the forest and that you're doing a great job!"

Obviously satisfied by that explanation, the red squirrel turned around and sprang onto a pine tree beside him, running upwards onto the lighter branches from where he jumped into a neighbouring tree.

As Strix flew higher, he looked down at the running squirrel one last time. Wondering how many of his stashes Forest would find come winter and how many would turn into new trees, Strix became aware how everything in nature fitted together to create a bigger picture that was perfectly balanced.

"That is, if I remember the story correctly," Willow added seamlessly.

"Willow!" Nayeli called, appalled. "It's not nice to make fun of someone who's got a bad memory."

"Sorry," the tree mumbled, feigning innocence.

Nayeli sniggered. "What am I supposed to do with you, hmm?"

"Maybe forget that I ever said anything?" the tree deadpanned.

Nayeli rolled her eyes. "Y'know what? I give up. You've won. Let's just get back to the topic at hand, shall we?"

"I'm ready when you are. What do you want to know?"

"Is it true what Strix said at the end of the story? That nature is perfectly balanced? Because there are a lot of catastrophes and chaos everywhere ... And how can that be when what you say is true?"

Willow didn't answer immediately, and the meadow sat silently under the relentless summer sun, which made the air hot and heavy. But when the tree did speak, there was a firmness in its voice that Nayeli had seldom heard.

"The natural state of Mother Earth is to be balanced in every aspect, and that's what life gravitates towards at all times. But it can become unbalanced through outside sources, and it often is. Over the past couple of hundred years, this has mainly been down to human actions. Just think about all the animals and plants that are dying out. And how the younger human generations might not even realise how quickly this happens."

"What do you mean by that?" Nayeli questioned.

"I mean the fact that you automatically behold everything that happens inside your short lifetime as *normal.* But that you only see five butterflies and hear three species of birds while walking an hour through nature is *not* normal, but the result of a mass extinction taking place. If the older generations were attentive, they'll remember that only a short time ago it was normal to see 15 butterflies and to hear 10 species of birds in the same amount of time.

"Saying this, nature always tries to compensate for any deviations from the centre, though. And even the chaos and catastrophes that you mentioned can be a way to reach a natural state of balance again, for example, by reducing a species, which overpopulates an area."

"And with that, you're talking about us humans, aren't you?" Nayeli questioned. "Cause we are definitely overpopulating this planet."

"That fact cannot be denied," the tree agreed. "But I'm speaking on a more general note here. To make this clearer, let me recount a story that was told to me by a woman – a woman who was sitting in the same spot as you are today. Her name was Ferenwe. Or maybe it still is – who knows? Anyway, she told me that near where she lived at the time, the whole countryside was changed over a few years. She said that soil erosion lessened dramatically and that the stream's water-table was raised. All because a couple of wolves were reintroduced to the area."

"No way!" Nayeli said in disbelief. "No wolf can influence a stream. How are they supposed to do that? Building a dam like a beaver or performing a rain dance?"

"But it *is* possible. Wolves had been extinct in the area for more than fifty years, which created a ripple effect. Ever since the last wolves had been killed, the elk population had risen to overcapacity. Because there were so many, their territories grew smaller and smaller and they didn't move around as much. This turned out to be detrimental to my brothers and sisters, the willows and other trees that surrounded the stream. Their bark was being eaten and damaged by the elk constantly rubbing their antlers against it. A lot of the trees died, which in turn was fatal for the beavers who needed them to survive – to build dams, as food and to shorten their ever-growing teeth. Thus, they began to decrease as well. And as the dams began to disappear, the erosion of the landscape got worse. But when the wolves returned as the natural enemy of the elk, their herds were diminished and they wandered around once again. This enabled the trees to recover and the number of beavers to grow. And thus, order was restored and nature balanced itself..

"Now, this is a simplistic approach to explain what happened as there are plenty more factors that play into it, for example, the coyote populations. But it shows how nature needs balance to function like humans need air to breathe. If you take one species away, it can have dire consequences for everyone and everything else – not only for the animals that prey and for those that are preyed on by it, but for all. The ecosystem is incredibly complex, and everything ties together so perfectly that the tiniest change can create a whole landslide of repercussions that aren't foreseeable."

"Like the butterfly effect, right?" Nayeli asked, remembering having heard of this phenomenon at school. "It says that the wingbeat of a single butterfly could potentially result in a tornado on the other side of the world if a lot of variables came together."

"Yes, it signifies that something small can create a huge backlash."

"And we humans pollute the air, wipe out lots of species and are responsible for global warming to name just a few problems ... You know, Willow, I'm sorry that humans are this stupid and that we have detached so much from nature that we don't even understand that we're hurting ourselves when we hurt Mother Earth. I'm sorry that we're ruining the natural balance for us and for everyone else."

"It's not a good position we find ourselves in, that's true," Willow agreed. "But there's no use in beating yourself up over it. Especially since it wasn't your choice alone, but the choice of the collective consciousness. Maybe the current situation was necessary so that more people could wake up to the fact that something has to shift if you want to continue to incarnate here on Earth."

Nayeli felt subdued. "Is there even a way back now? Or are you saying that we have to wipe ourselves out to restore the balance? As in, 'first we mess up, and now it's time we paid for it so that Mother Earth can become healthy again'?"

"Nothing this drastic, no," Willow said mildly. "It's not too late to turn it all around and live in harmony with nature once more."

"Then it's more a question of it being the time to give something back now? After only taking for decades? To actively restore balance in this way?" Nayeli asked, still not knowing what the tree wanted to convey.

"Well, it's definitely a good idea to give back to Mother Earth and all her inhabitants whenever you can. But don't do it with the intention to restore balance, as it isn't something you can create artificially. Balance is a natural process, which you'd best leave to Mother Earth."

"Willow, can you decide what you want? First, you tell me how important balance is, and now you say that I shouldn't go and create it?" Nayeli looked hard at the tree.

The willow tree wasn't at all deterred, though, and laughed brightly. "It is important. But what you humans need to do in your lives is to practise inclusion, not balance."

"I'm sorry. You're going to have to explain this one to me," Nayeli replied.

"Looking for balance means searching out the middle ground, while leaving out all extremes. That's like putting the brakes on when driving. And it will take you a long time to get anywhere you want to go. What you can do instead is to extend your consciousness to encompass extremes. By doing this, you're helping the natural balance to create itself. Just think of the emotional scale we talked about. The negative experience that gave rise to your desire has already happened, hasn't it? Thus, balance is restored by going for the most happiness you can find."

"My gosh, you're right. Balance would be counterproductive regarding the emotional scale. We don't want the middle-scale emotions; we want the good ones at the end. This is why happiness should be our advisor ..."

Nayeli fanned herself in a weak attempt to get some cooler air. "But what about our relationships, Willow?"

"What about them?" the tree asked back.

"Some people run themselves into the ground by continuously giving to others, while others only ever take. And that's unfair."

The tree used one of its longer branches to point at her. "That's a superficial view of the balance between give and take. Or give and receive, which is the term I prefer to use, simply because taking has a negative ring to it, bordering on force. In comparison, when you receive, you open yourself up to invite all that flows naturally to you."

"Does it matter what words we use?" Nayeli asked.

"My dear, words can make a huge difference, which is something I'm gonna explain to you soon in more detail. But now I want to come to your earlier statement ... In reality, everyone is constantly giving additional to receiving. That's a universal law that cannot be bypassed. What can happen, however, is that a perceived imbalance is born based on what kind of energy you receive and what kind of energy you hand out. When someone gives something positive, while getting back nothing else but negatively charged energy, they'll feel as if they don't get back anything at all. But they do, even if it isn't what they want. Let's look at someone who has traumas around not being seen and heard. They might only want to talk about themselves but never ask how others are doing. Thus, they might give back the energy of insensitiveness. Or, to name a different example ... a stingy person who has had past traumas surrounding money might accept invitations from friends but will never return the favour. They might then give back angry words when confronted about this."

"And that's unfair," Nayeli repeated her earlier statement. "And it's not a balanced relationship. If I give out good and get back something bad, how is that equitably?"

"From the human perspective, it isn't. But the source does not divide energy into 'good' and 'bad' or 'positive' and 'negative'. Energy-wise, anything that is given out must result in something being given back. How that looks for you in detail, though, is based on your free will and your manifestation work."

"Manifestation work?"

"I'll come to that in a minute. But before I do, let me get back to the topic at hand because there's another important detail to consider here. The belief that giving is more virtuous than receiving."

"Which isn't true, I suppose, after all that I heard just now?" Nayeli guessed.

"Correct. There are two reasons why this belief is false. For one, a healthy relationship – and you've already learned that anything at all in your life is a relationship – needs both. Think of it in terms of friendships. When you are always there for a friend, when you are listening to their problems, helping them out and supporting them but they never do the same for you – do you think that's a healthy bond? Do you feel respected by them? The answer is no. They don't care about you in the same way you care about them. And why would you waste your time letting yourself be exploited instead of finding someone else who values you?"

The tree swayed its branches from side to side. "But don't get me wrong, my dear. I'm not saying that you should keep count. In any relationship, there are times where one or the other person will need more attention and help. It's only when it never happens the other way around that a relationship becomes one-sided or even abusive."

"And what's the second reason?" Nayeli asked curiously.

"That you *need* to receive in order to give and vice versa. If you were to just give and never allow yourself to receive, you would eventually run dry and become ill until you aren't physically, mentally or emotionally able to give any more. You can give nothing else but the energy, time, money or whatever else you want to pass on that you have first allowed yourself to receive. On the other hand, you first need to give to provide the necessary space in yourself to receive again.

"This process of giving versus receiving is taking place on all levels, down to the physical one. Or how do you think your breathing functions? Your body takes in fresh oxygen and breathes out the old, stale air. It is, in fact, not possible for your body to inhale until you've made room for the new air to flow into your lungs. Or, if you want a mental image to better visualise this – think of a full wardrobe. It's filled with clothes you have received from others as gifts or which you have bought yourself with the money you allowed yourself to receive previously. Now, if you don't clear out your wardrobe from time to time, you'll soon have no space to receive any more clothes."

"I could buy another closet," Nayeli suggested flippantly.

"For which you would need to give up money as well as space inside your flat," Willow replied. "It would simply delay your original problem."

"All right, all right, I get it. That we need to give to receive and receive to give is an endless cycle taking place, one that we cannot escape from while being incarnated here."

"Yes. But the truth goes even deeper than that. Because you don't only receive *something,* but *what* you send out energetically. That's what the Law of Attraction is all about – the law that our reality here is based on."

"The Law of Attraction?" Nayeli asked, her interest piqued. "I think I've heard of that before, but I can't remember much about it ... It does have something to do with the manifesting work you mentioned earlier, right?"

"Right. And if you want, I'm happy to refresh your memory."

15. Crim and Son, the Red Pandas

As Strix flew farther east, the wilderness of the continent alternated between woods, plains and mountains, interspersed by some human settlements, so that the sight never became boring to his eyes.

One evening, after a long, restful sleep, Strix saw yet another mountain range appear on the distant horizon, its crests layered in snow. And before those, densely wooded slopes stretched out, creating a green carpet that looked as if it had been rolled out just for him.

Unable to get enough of the view, Strix absorbed all of it: the reddish-orange moss that shone through between the green foliage, the song of the many birds drowning each other out and the long bamboo poles that created entire forests by themselves.

Flying over a big tree that towered over all others, his eyes were suddenly drawn to a movement inside it that piqued his curiosity. Strix circled above it, noticing that the animal he had spotted was a male, about the size of a raccoon and owner of a bushy red-and-white-striped tail that fitted his reddish coat and the mask-like markings on his face perfectly. Swooping lower to take a closer look, Strix was careful to stay out of sight of the animal, remembering one of the first lessons his mother had taught him, namely to be wary of strangers if they might pose a danger to you – a precautionary measure that was specially called for when the animal in question had such sharp claws as the one below him.

Luckily, Strix's ability to fly silently made him capable of remaining unseen if he wanted to stay hidden, even during the day and especially in the gloom of twilight that was descending now. But to his surprise, his stealth didn't seem up to his usual standards today, as the red and white animal saw up, startled, and scanned the sky.

Knowing he had been found when their eyes met, Strix wasn't sure what reaction to expect. He reckoned that the animal might be scared and call out a warning to others. He deemed it possible that the furry mammal might threaten Strix to not come any closer or attack outright. And he also considered that the creature might extend an invitation to join him on the branch and swap stories. The only thing Strix hadn't expected was for the raccoon-like creature to stiffen, let go of the green stick he was holding in his front paws – and then tumble right after it.

Shocked, Strix drew in a sharp breath.

For a long moment, all he could do was watch as the fluffy animal fell through the canopy of leaves, hitting a branch here and there on the long way to the ground. Then Strix folded his wings and dived himself, landing on the forest floor a few seconds after the young male had hit it.

The creature had rolled himself into a tight ball and lay lifeless on some dry leaves.

"Are you okay?" Strix called, in too much of a frenzy to tell whether the animal was still breathing. "Please say you're alive. And that you didn't hurt yourself."

Hearing a whimper come from the furry bundle, Strix sighed in relief. But his relief quickly morphed into concern as the sound turned into pitiful moans.

Too scared to touch the male for fear of hurting him any further, Strix hopped around the stranger, unsure what to do. But when the whimpers didn't cease, he plucked up his courage and nudged him with his beak.

The animal promptly recoiled. Looking unscathed, he jumped to his feet, faster than Strix would have thought him capable of and dived straight into a bush standing nearby.

"Go away!" the young male pleaded while sheer terror shone out of his eyes, which were visible through a small gap between the leaves. "Please go away and leave me alone."

"What?" Strix asked and craned his head around to see if anyone else was standing behind him. When he saw nothing even remotely scary, he turned his head back and faced the fearful eyes.

"Me? Do you mean me?" Strix asked, irritated by the animal's odd behaviour. "You don't have to fear me, you know? I'm Strix, and I'm friendly. Besides, you're way too big for me to eat you."

"It's not that," the male said tearfully. "You owls bring bad luck wherever you go. You're omens of death and pain to come. Look how far I fell from that tree. I could have broken all my bones, not to mention my neck. I want you gone. Now! Go!"

Perceiving the young animal's terror-stricken face, Strix knew instantly that it would be pointless to reason with him. Instead, he nodded and opened his wings in what he hoped was a calming manner. "All right, all right. Don't throw a fit. I'm already gone. Forget that I was ever here."

He felt the animal's eyes bore into his back until he was way up above the crowns of the trees and out of sight.

Flying a bit further, Strix then landed on another tree, trying to make sense of what he'd just experienced.

Being so immersed in his own thoughts, Strix only became aware of a presence behind him when he felt a hot breath touch his neck. Hooting in alarm, Strix fluttered up and turned around to see who had sneaked up on him.

The animal he came face to face with looked almost exactly like the one he had left behind, covering in the scrubby bush. It might be slightly larger than the other one and certainly less fearful of him, but otherwise, the two of them could have been twins.

"Boo!" the red-and-white animal said jokingly and broke into a fit of laughter, her voice being higher than that of the young male. "Sorry if I startled you, but how could I resist? You don't often get a chance to creep up on an owl in this region. It was too good an opportunity to pass up." Grinning at him, the animal bowed her head. "I'm Crim."

"Strix. Nice to meet you," Strix answered, not entirely convinced that he was speaking the truth, as this entire species seemed to have lost its marbles one way or the other. Exercising caution, he landed two branches above the weird animal until such a time as he'd be able to figure out whether the female was simply a jokester or a loose cannon. "By the way, you have an unfair advantage over me since you know what species I am, but I have no idea what you are. Care to tell me?"

"Why, a red panda, of course. Haven't you ever met one of us?"

"Actually, I have." Strix coughed. "About three minutes ago, a bit west of here. But even though he looked like you, he acted totally different. He babbled something about owls bringing bad luck – after falling out of a tall tree and hiding inside a bush from me, I might add. Consequently, he didn't want to answer any of my questions."

"That's my son," Crim said. Her voice was carefree by all appearances, but Strix thought that he could detect a faint echo of worry in her words. Which was confirmed by her next question. "Is he all right? Did he hurt himself?"

"Physically he seemed fine," Strix said slowly. "I don't think he broke any bones, and he sure as hell was fast in getting away from me. But emotionally, he seemed to be rather unstable. He was shaking in terror, unlike any animal I've ever encountered before. Maybe you should check upon him ...?"

"That's nothing out of the ordinary," Crim said, sounding relieved. "He's always fearful and jumpy. Especially when he sees owls. Or vultures. Or snakes. Or frogs. But otherwise, he's doing okay – more or less."

"But that's not normal, to be scared of such a long list of animals – or is it?" Strix tossed in. "I mean, I've watched some human pets from a distance that were psychologically unstable, but I always put that down to the fact that they're living around the two-legged and adopting their unhealthy behaviours. Wild animals don't usually hang on to traumas. We shake them off and move on."

"Pff," Crim shrugged. "What IS normal in this world, anyway? My son was badly traumatised as a cub when humans came into this forest and stole his sibling right from underneath our noses. Considering this, who can blame him for not being wholly healthy? I think he has every right to feel how he does, and I'm not only saying that because he's my flesh and blood."

"What happened?" Strix asked in consternation.

"We were living here, in the top of these trees. Him, his little sister and me. The two cubs were a few weeks old. When I heard the strangers coming, I tried to hide us between the orange mosses. But as I was pulling my son deeper into the leaves, one of the two-legged spotted my daughter. He climbed up the tree and put her in a cage. I was rooted to the spot and could do nothing else but look on in horror as they carried her away. She was screaming for me the whole time, and I felt as if I couldn't breathe. My son and I awoke from our paralysed state only once she was out of earshot. He was as badly shaken as me and felt guilty for what had happened. He thought that if I had tried to hide my daughter first, not him, she would not have been taken. He could never fully rid himself of his guilt and self-hatred, no matter how often I told him he's not to blame. Despite my best efforts, his panic attacks started shortly after that ordeal – and he still has them to this day."

Strix felt deep compassion for the young male with the terror-stricken eyes he had left sitting in the bush. "That must have been terrible to live through for such a young one. But what does this story, as awful as it is, have to do with him fearing owls?"

"The first time my son saw – and heard – an owl was a few minutes before the humans came to steal his sister. Ever since then, the two things have been connected in his mind, and he thinks that owls are the bearer of bad news. This pattern has continued even to this day. Only last week, a snowy owl came through here. The moment my son saw it, he choked on a bamboo stick and almost suffocated."

"Oh gosh, that's terrible," Strix said, knowing how daunting life must be for Crim's son if he always expected the worst in every situation and was stuck in a downward spiral of fear and dread, based on his self-fulfilling prophecies.

Crim looked sad as she went on. "I've tried to help him. I let him stay here and share my territory with him so he's not on his own, and I support him in any way I can. But until he starts to create positive change for himself, there's nothing else I can do ..."

"I'm sure you are helping him a lot, just by being there for him," Strix said confidently, seeing how much Crim cared about her son.

"I hope you are right." Crim sighed, wrapping her long, bushy tail around herself. “And I also hope that one day he'll heal. You know, it's the bamboo, which makes me optimistic that he'll eventually rid himself of all his traumas and fears – even if he seems to be as stuck inside them as ever.”

“The bamboo?” Strix asked, bewildered. “Why would a plant give you hope?”

Crim seemed to struggle over how to answer that question, but then she sat up straighter, giving off an air of determination. “I assume you haven't heard the bamboo tale yet?”

”No, I can't say I have. What is it about?”

“It's about the truth behind manifesting whatever you want into your life,” Crim whispered, as if she was scared that someone would overhear her. “Every great panda and red panda alive has heard this tale. We absorb it with our mother's milk. It's a secret we all guard with our lives. One that makes us successful.”

“Will you recount it?” Strix pleaded. He'd always been interested in the lore of other species. And especially in stories that were sold this compellingly.

”Well, I think I can make an exception for you this once. But you've got to promise not to tell it any animal which preys on us. We don't want to give them an edge, after all.”

“I promise,” Strix said solemnly and raised his right wing to confirm his oath.

Crim seemed satisfied by that and looked around to make sure there wasn't anyone eavesdropping. “Strangely, it's a story from a human perspective. But it still fits life quite nicely. The story starts with a man who wanted to grow his own bamboo plants – a very smart specimen if you ask me ...”

“Why?” Strix asked, puzzled by this statement.

"Haven't you listened to me? He's growing bamboo," the red panda explained.

But when Strix only looked at her questioningly, Crim rolled her eyes heavenward. "Bamboo is the tastiest food on Earth, and there's way too little of it for everyone. So, whoever wants to grow more of it must be hella smart!"

"Right." Strix grinned. "I've never been keen on all that veggie stuff myself. But whatever floats your boat, right?"

"Hmpf, philistine," Crim said. But then a mischievous twinkle stole into her eyes. "Which is all the better for us. The more philistines who live in the world, the more bamboo is left for those of us who value its worth. As much as I like the taste of some fruit or a bite of fresh meat from time to time, there's nothing tastier than it. Although, right now, I'm more in the mood to eat a nice juicy egg ..."

"Which you can get, right after you've told me the story," Strix said impatiently.

Crim cocked her head at his eagerness. "If you are this impatient, you'll never find the hidden message in the story, no matter how many times you hear it."

Strix was about to say that he wasn't impatient at all and that Crim should leave it to him to interpret the lore correctly. But before he could do so, the red panda had taken up the thread of the story again.

"Anyway, this human buys seedlings and takes good care of them. He plants them in the most nutrient-rich earth he can find, in such a way that they will get the perfect mix of sunlight and shadows, he waters them whenever the earth is too dry and he protects them whenever the rain falls too heavy. Despite all that, after a year the seedlings have grown into nothing more than meagre green stalks, which have barely risen above the ground. The man isn't deterred, though. He renews his efforts the next year, taking even better care of his plants. He watches over them and sees that they have all they need to grow. But after the second year, the small bamboo plants haven't grown more than a few inches. It goes on like this, year after year, the man never giving up. And then, suddenly, it happens."

"What?" Strix asked eagerly as Crim stopped talking. "What happens?"

Crim smiled knowingly. "The bamboo shoots spring upward. And after a few short weeks, they are as tall as the biggest bamboo plants the man's ever seen in his life!"

"But how is that possible?" Strix asked, flummoxed. "Why haven't they grown before that?"

"Oh, they did," Crim said, bemused. "And that's the crux of the story. They've grown the same height every single year in all that time."

Noticing his confused look, the red panda continued her explanation. "In the first years when the man didn't see any growth, the bamboo was growing downwards. The roots grew bigger and longer every year beneath the earth, until the bamboo plants were so stable that they could grow *above* the earth. If they hadn't built such strong roots in advance, the first gust of wind could have snapped them in half or uprooted them. But since they were firmly embedded in the earth, they could grow into these huge plants, like the ones you see all around here."

"You're saying that we might not always perceive results immediately, but that this doesn't mean there aren't any? That they are just invisible to us, like the roots?"

"Yes, my friend. And we need to be patient and not give up if we want to achieve the results we hope for."

Strix had the impression that the red panda wanted to say even more, but Crim was distracted by something falling past Strix and landing on the branch that the red panda was sitting on. Or, better yet, splattered. Because the egg that had fallen from the sky had broken open upon impact and the yellow yolk was running out of the cracked shell.

Gaping upward, Strix tried to see if there was a nest above them, but he could discern nothing of the sort. What he saw instead was the silhouette of a big bird circling above them, barely visible in the quickly darkening sky if it hadn't been for his great eyesight. Then the truth became apparent to him: the bird must have dropped the egg, likely after stealing it from a nest himself. But it was Crim who was reaping the benefits and licking up the spilled yolk.

Remembering with sudden clarity how she had wished for an egg only minutes earlier, Strix opened his beak in wonder.

"You ...?" he asked unbelievingly, letting his gaze wander from the egg to Crim to the sky and back. "How did you do that?"

"What?" Crim said innocently, holding a large piece of the shell between her paws and slurping up the liquid protein. "I asked for an egg, you heard that."

"Yes, no, but ..." Strix got out, unable to organise his thoughts into words that made any sense.

"Why are you asking, anyway?" Crim asked, interrupting his stuttering. "Do you want one yourself? Then order your own from the universe, because my egg is not large enough to share it."

"No, thanks," Strix said, dumbfounded by the fact that someone had mastered the Law of Attraction in a way that they could ask for something and have it handed to them a short time later.

But then Strix realised that it wasn't only Crim who was creating her own reality. He had done the same in the past. Sure, he hadn't been as conscious as the red panda. But looking back, Strix had managed to attract a whole lot of things – good and bad experiences and everything in between.

The first thing coming to his mind was a memory from his childhood when he had gone flying with his friend Nuktia, another owl. He had been so cocky that day and had wanted to impress her. Which had worked out at first, but then his underlying nervousness that something would go wrong had foiled his plans because he had flown head-first into a tree and then landed in a puddle on the ground, fuelling his embarrassment to even greater heights.

With hindsight, Strix had managed to laugh at his little mishap, but at the time he'd wanted to curl up and die, and neither Nuktia's attempts to cheer him up nor Willow's words of wisdom had helped him feel better.

Feeling another flash of homesickness bombard him at the thought of both of his friends, Strix only allowed the feeling of longing to consume him for a short while before forcing himself back to the present and to Crim, who was watching him with inquisitive eyes. "Is everything all right? You seemed lost there. As if you were miles away."

"Miles and aeons," Strix corrected and quickly changed the subject. "Listen, Crim, didn't you say that another owl came through here a few days ago? Do you know where it went by any chance?"

Assuming that talking to another owl might be all he needed to alleviate his increasing homesickness, Strix decided that tracking the snowy owl would be on the top of his to-do list for now.

"I remember it was a female by the name of Pearl," Crim replied pensively. "And I remember that she wanted to fly south to a place where it's freezing, as she said. But that's all I know. Sorry. That's not very detailed, but I'm not particularly knowledgeable at geography, since I've spent my whole life in this place."

Looking up from her feast, Crim gave Strix the once-over. "Hey, if you want to find that snow owl, why don't you ask the universe to guide you to her? Like I asked for that egg to come to me?"

Strix wasn't entirely sure if he could succeed in such an endeavour, as he wasn't nearly as skilled as the red panda to create his reality consciously. But on the other hand, what could it hurt to try? He could give it his best attempt, at least.

"I will think about it," he therefore said. "Thanks so much. For the story and everything else."

"It was my pleasure," Crim answered and winked up at Strix after which she returned her full attention to the egg lying in front of her. Picking up another large piece of the shell, she held it between her front paws and licked off the gooey yolk running over her arms, a gleam of relish in her eyes.

"You want to say that there's no luck and that I create everything that happens to me?" Nayeli began to put her thoughts into words. "But then, what about people who are followed around by bad luck – someone who attracts anything and everything that can possibly go wrong – like Crim's son in your story? Are you saying that's what they *want* to manifest?"

"No, I'm not saying that. They simply don't know how to use the Law of Attraction to their advantage and are therefore stuck with the shadow side of it. Which can be a disaster."

"Wait, Willow, what shadow side? I thought we use the Law of Attraction to attract positive things and to manifest a better life for us ... Does it also create things that are unwanted?"

"Both can happen," Willow declared. "The Law of Attraction is a universal law that reacts to the energy you send out, which in turn is based on your focus. It doesn't discriminate or judge what energy you hold. You are in the driver's seat, so to speak, and the universe is nothing more than your co-driver, who reads the map to you. You can follow its advice or you can ignore it and find the way yourself. But whether or not you listen to your higher self, you are always the one who's driving. And the source responds in kind to your decisions, respecting your creative power and free will."

"Now that's just great," Nayeli complained, incensed. "We come into this life, forget all about how the Law of Attraction works, use it in a way that's detrimental to us and then the universe doesn't even step in when we create awful situations for ourselves?"

"That's the world that the collective consciousness created, yep," Willow agreed. "But remember that, from the perspective of your higher self, negative experiences aren't necessarily a bad thing, because of the desires they give rise to. Moreover, sooner or later, every incarnated soul will come to a point where they recollect that the Law of Attraction exists. And it's here that you can turn your life around. If you learn how to work with this law, it becomes your best ally – instead of your enemy."

"Fine then, share your great wisdom with me, Willow. How do I benefit from this Law of Attraction?"

"To explain this universal law, let me give you an example that's used often ... Imagine that you throw a red apple into the air. It will always be a red apple that falls back down, not a green one nor a pear."

"Unless you sit underneath a pear tree and the apple you throw up hits one of the branches and gets stuck, and a pear falls down instead," Nayeli tossed in jokingly, only to be met with an appalled gasp from the tree.

"Hey!" Willow called, outraged. "You're ruining my little example!"

"Nope." Nayeli laughed. "I'm just pointing out the flaws in your analogy."

As Willow's trunk rumbled with laughter and the tree's branches swept through the air, Nayeli quickly leaned back to not be hit by one of them.

"All right," the tree said, after calming down, "you win this round, Mrs Stickybeak. The example might be faulty, but what I wanted to show you through it is that the Law of Attraction does not act by itself. It's a reactive law; it can't change the frequency of the energy that's sent out."

"I already understood that, but how do I work with it?" Nayeli asked a second time. "Is it difficult to master?"

Rustling its leaves, Willow seemed to think about the matter. "Yes, and no. In theory, this law is one of the easiest tools you can use. It gives you what you focus upon – that's it! It's akin to manually adjusting a radio channel. You switch yourself to the frequency you want, and then you hear the music playing there. In the best case, you're focused on something positive that you want to draw into your life, and in the worst case, you're focused on something you don't want."

"Thus far, this law sounds pretty straightforward. Now, where's the catch?"

"What makes this universal law more complicated is you humans – you're too complex to keep anything simple that's simple by nature."

"What do you mean?" Nayeli asked curiously.

"That you humans are not like an ordinary radio channel." the tree debunked its own illustration. "You are more like a mixing console in a recording studio. A mixer unit where every button or switch represents one aspect of yourself. Your emotions are the voices you record, your thoughts are the instruments you can hear, your intentions are the lyrics that are sung, your actions are the synthesisers you use and so on. Furthermore, every control that adds an effect – that makes a tone louder or softer, or that makes a voice sound deeper or higher – influences the energy you send out. And to send out the desired energy, you'd need to adjust all the buttons correctly."

"Then I become the best sound engineer there is – what's so difficult about that?"

Willow guffawed knowingly. "That half of the buttons and

switches are invisible, and you can't feel them or hear their effects until you make them visible."

"Come again?" Nayeli said.

"They represent your subconscious and everything that is hidden inside it," the tree explained. "That's what makes using the Law of Attraction tricky. Because whether or not you are aware of a fragment within yourself, all parts of you send out energy. And it's the sum of all that you'll attract back."

As silence reigned between them, Nayeli thought about what the tree had told her thus far, all the while being uncomfortably aware of how her dress stuck to her body in the humid summer air and how she was itching, thanks to the sweat coating her skin. With every day, the air felt hotter, and even breathing became a task. The one thing that kept her from melting was the fact that she sat underneath Willow's leaves, which created a shadowy cavern.

Nayeli wished that it would rain soon to wash away the oppressive heat. Closing her eyes, she momentarily lost herself in the daydream of cool air on her skin and the fresh smell of water as it hit the earth.

But then Willow resumed speaking, and Nayeli opened her eyes again.

"To show you how the Law of Attraction can go wrong despite your best intentions, imagine you have a job interview coming up. The many different aspects at play inside you will send out their own specific energy. One part might be excited at having this chance because it's your dream job. But there might be other aspects that work against this one. There might, for example, be one part of you, which is nervous about the interview because it has social anxiety. There might be an aspect that doubts you'll get the position and which belittles you. And there might be yet another part that's constantly replaying a past interview inside your mind and is embarrassed because you misunderstood a question back then. And so on and so on. In the end, if the majority of your aspects are focused on not getting what you want – for some reason or another – that's what will happen."

Letting its branches dance to a tune only known by the tree, Willow created patterns of shadow on the green grass.

"In other words, all those different parts are pulling me in different directions and I'll get nowhere because of them?"

"Precisely. It's like an endless game of tug of war within you, which no one ever wins. It's true that, when you focus on what you desire with the majority of your being, you will attract it into your reality. But since your subconsciousness makes up half of you and you don't know what these parts want, you need to do more than just focus positively. You need to look at your resistance, heal your past traumas and wounds and integrate the aspects within you for them to act together, not against each other."

Sighing, Nayeli peered through a gap in Willow's foliage. She noticed that the blue of the sky was slowly being concealed by a blanket of white clouds moving in their direction. But then the change in weather was pushed to the back of her mind by a more important thought.

"And are there any more problems relating to this *easy law* that I should be aware of?"

"There is indeed one more," Willow said. "There's a time lag. What you attract doesn't manifest instantly – it might take hours or days, if not more, to appear physically. And this leads to misunderstandings about cause and effect."

"Wait, Willow," Nayeli interrupted her friend. "Why do some manifestations only take hours, while others need longer to come to pass? Why the difference, and how do I know when I can expect my results?"

"There are two factors that come into play here. One, you cannot manifest something into your physical reality while you are still resisting it. If you are worried about an outcome, fear a change that needs to happen or hold tension regarding an unfulfilled desire, these things don't match the desire; they oppose it. And this focus on the negative end of things blocks it from coming to you. So, depending on what limiting thoughts and beliefs you hold about something, the time it will take to successfully manifest your desire can range from a few hours to decades. To release resistance to something you want to attract could happen next month or tomorrow. It depends on you ..."

Nayeli leaned forward, eager to hear more. "And what's the second reason?"

"The second thing that influences how long a manifestation takes is the frequency you send out. The higher the vibration, the closer you are to the source energy, and the faster you can manifest because you are less linked to the perceived 3D space-time reality. It's a bit like water. When it's in the form of ice, it has a low vibrational energy, which makes it move slowly. But when the water turns into steam, it moves more rapidly. Just like that, the time required to manifest something varies. But no matter how high your energy is – since you exist in this 3D reality and since you are yet unhealed – it does need *some* time. Because of this, occasions that seem to be totally unrelated at first glance are often linked to each other.

"Imagine, for example, that you live with an abusive partner who drinks excessively and gets violent when they do so. As a result, you feel victimised and powerless inside your relationship. Now, imagine that one day you are about to drive into a parking spot but someone else wants it as well and barrels in there before you. They stomp over to you, acting rude and aggressive, threatening you for intending to take their spot. And as a result, you might be scared and feel victimised and powerless. But wait ... doesn't this sound familiar?"

"Sure," Nayeli said. "I'd feel the same way I feel at home. But how do these two events relate? They feature different people and settings."

"These two situations might appear to be unrelated at first glance. But energetically they are not. When you send out the energy of fear, the universe responds in kind and sends you more situations that will make you scared – since, from the perspective of the source, you clearly want to experience more anxiety as you are this focused on it. This can manifest in any way. By letting you miss the bus and making you late for work. By letting you find a massive spider in your flat. Or by letting you worry about your cat, which goes missing for two days ..."

"You make it sound as if anything bad that happens is my fault," Nayeli said indignantly. "And that sounds a lot like victim-blaming to me."

"It's not my intention to do that," the tree replied softly. "You are not responsible for the actions of anyone else; that's on their head. But what you have control over is what you are a match to energetically. Your mind functions like a magnet. If you constantly think of worries, that's what you'll attract. Likewise, if you are focused on joy, you'll more often find yourself in situations that bring you happiness. It's an automatic process taking place. The situations you receive back, based on your energy, will make you feel the same way again, which in turn makes you focus on the same things and tunes you into the same frequency, which you then send out. This is detrimental when you are stuck inside a negative downward spiral or useful when you're in the middle of a positive upward spiral."

"You know what, Willow?" Nayeli said pensively. "This actually makes a lot of sense. Why people who seem to have bad luck all the time never catch a break. And why so-called lucky people are always successful. But what can we do if we're stuck in a downward spiral?"

"Break out of the cycle by following three steps," the tree explained. "First, you need to heal and integrate anything within you that needs to be healed and integrated. Second, you need to change any limiting thoughts and beliefs. And as a third step, you need to focus on what you desire."

"And if I do all that?"

"Then you can manifest anything that you wish into your outer reality. Riches, love, success, health – whatever you dream of having or being. There are no limits unless you create them."

Nayeli smirked. "And what if I want to ride a dragon?"

Willow broke into a fit of laughter, which Nayeli could feel as a faint vibration in the trunk behind her.

"You smart aleck, you," the tree scolded her. "Of course, you can't meet a real-life dragon in this reality, since they don't exist here. But if that were really a desire of yours and you dig deeper, you'll find a wish underneath it that *is* possible to achieve. Maybe it would be the desire to feel childlike happiness again or to experience the freedom of flying – and these desires can be met in lots of ways, not just by riding a dragon."

"Hmm," Nayeli said to fill the silence as she reflected on what else she wanted to ask the tree. But before she could come up with a question, she was pulled out of her mind by a cool wind that had picked up. Shivering as the breeze touched her sweaty skin, Nayeli looked up and noticed that the formerly white clouds had been replaced by a blanket of heavy grey ones that promised rain.

True to her thought, the first raindrops started to fall at that moment. At first, they were sparse but, after a minute or two, the rain became heavier. Buckets of water splattered loudly against Willow's crown and quickly transformed the small brook beside the hill into a churning stream.

Still mostly protected by Willow's leaves – since the tree had pulled its branches together to shield her – Nayeli watched in awe as steam rose from the grass and listened to the birdsong being drowned out by the insistent patter of the rain hitting the earth, which was soaking the water up until nothing more could be absorbed.

It rained so hard that Willow's branches could not shield Nayeli for long. Within a few minutes, she was drenched and began to shiver.

"You'd better run home," Willow advised.

"But you hadn't finished telling me about this spiritual law," Nayeli complained. "And I wanted to hear more."

"You will. Tomorrow."

Grumbling for a second at the unfairness of life, she ultimately acquiesced to Willow's wisdom and sprinted through the downpour.

Running through the rain reminded Nayeli of her earlier wish for it and she pondered whether she had somehow manifested this summer storm into reality, just like Crim had manifested the egg falling from the sky. She hadn't come to any conclusion by the time she'd reached her grandmother's house, aside from the fact that the matter was worth some research ...

***

The next day, when Nayeli returned to Willow, the rain from the day before had been soaked up by the earth and the grass on the hill wasn't as wet as she had feared. Nevertheless, she pulled out the red-and-blue checked blanket she'd brought as a precaution and laid it down. Sitting cross-legged on it, Nayeli then waited for the tree to acknowledge her presence.

"There you are again, my dear. How are you?"

"Good," Nayeli answered brusquely.

"What's wrong?" the tree asked. "You appear to be distraught ... Is anything wrong?"

"There is kind of something," Nayeli admitted and mustered her courage to say what was bothering her. "It's about the Law of Attraction. I couldn't stop thinking about it. And since my time with you has been cut short yesterday, I used the evening to surf online to see what other info I would find. Then I came across this site where someone explained why it can't exist. They used the physical law of magnetism to support their facts, saying that it's verifiably not true that like attracts like. It attracts the opposite, similar to the two opposing ends of a magnet. When it comes to science, it's a fact that identical charges always repel each other. And when I look at human relationships that tends to hold true, too. Sometimes people are attracted to people who are the total opposite of themselves. My friend, for example, who's an introvert and a bookworm is with an extroverted man who likes to go to parties and never reads. And they complement each other perfectly."

"My dear," Willow said in a voice that was as soothing as ever and not at all indignant, "the site you found is correct when it says that opposites attract each other."

"But how can you say that?" Nayeli asked, frustrated. "You spent hours yesterday telling me the complete opposite – that we get back the same energy that we send out. That like attracts likes. Willow, I don't understand anything anymore!"

Chuckling, the willow tree shook out its leaves so that a few rain droplets fell down on Nayeli, who squeaked, startled, as the cold water hit her warm skin.

"I never used the words 'like attracts like', though," Willow said seriously. "And opposites attracting each other does not contradict the Law of Attraction at all. These two laws exist fine alongside each other, no problem."

"How?" Nayeli asked, puzzled.

"Sometimes, because of the Law of Attraction, you become a match to someone who is your complete opposite because, to give you back the same energy that you send out, the universe has to send you contrary situations and people. Let's say that you were sending off the energetic vibration of feeling caged. How can the universe send you more situations in which you can feel that way without sending someone who restricts your freedom? And when you send off the vibration of being knowledgeable, what better way is there than to send you people to whom you can pass your knowledge on to? By having the opposite reflected in your outer reality, you attract the same energy back internally."

"Ah!" Nayeli said, in comprehension. "That makes sense."

"Don't sound so surprised," the tree quipped. "Most of what I've said thus far has – or isn't that right?"

Nayeli grinned at that. "You're always right. Better?"

"Much better," Willow said, satisfied. "But keep in mind that, sometimes, my version of 'right' might not always be yours."

"Well, that hasn't really happened until now," Nayeli responded. "Which is a relief because it means I can ask you even more questions and get answers that ring true for me. And guess what? Coincidentally, I have such a question."

"Then out with it. Let's hear what it is."

Nayeli wasn't sure how she could best phrase the thoughts running through her mind, but then she threw all caution to the wind and let the words tumble out as they came to her. "When I was in bed last night, I was thinking about how some people easily manifest everything they want without being the slightest bit spiritual. For example, when I was in college, one of my fellow students was ridiculously rich. And the last I heard, she's going on holidays several times a year and living the best life. But I doubt that she's ever heard of manifestations, let alone how those work. Not to mention that this shouldn't be possible ... Cause didn't you once say that everyone needs to experience the opposite first to create a desire? So, how can someone be rich if they weren't poor previously?"

"You are mixing up two entirely different things here. When someone is rich from birth, being rich is not a desire but a reality that's built on the person's past. They're automatically attracting more money because their beliefs and thoughts are lined up with the fact that they'll always have enough. This doesn't entail, however, that this person can easily manifest something else they *do* desire. Maybe they feel they're lacking in the relationship department because they had toxic relationships with their parents who've spent money on them but weren't emotionally available. Or maybe they have difficulty finding a purpose in their life that fulfils them ... In the end, you're all born with different preconditions. And what one person desires is another person's reality. But the Law of Attraction works alike for everyone.

"Saying this, it's certainly possible to use this law and manifest things you want without knowing about the underlying workings. You can't cancel out the spiritual laws any more than you can cancel out any of your physical laws, whether you've gone to school and learned about them or not. Or can you suspend the law of gravity when your sandwich falls off the table, so it doesn't hit the ground?"

Nayeli shook her head, grinning.

"See, it's no different from the spiritual laws. It's only a matter of being able to actively use the law to the best of your ability once you become aware how it works – just like engineers used their knowledge of the physical laws to build aeroplanes."

Nayeli shifted around to find a more comfortable position. "Are you saying that the reason I failed so spectacularly at successfully manifesting things in the past is that I wasn't aware of this law before?"

"Oh, but you didn't fail. Failure does not exist when it comes to the Law of Attraction, as everything inevitably manifests – either as a lesson or as a gift. The end result might not have been to your liking every single time – especially if you manifested something subconsciously – but you can learn from that and use your past knowledge to create a better future reality for yourself. When all is said and done, you can never *not* create as you're always sending out energy. You've already manifested your entire life and created your reality prior to being born and every single second since then. And at every moment, you create your future, based on all of your thoughts, beliefs and emotions, based on the actions you take and based on the focus you hold."

Nayeli scrunched her nose up. "It's my own fault then when my life goes wrong?"

The weeping willow nodded with its branches before shaking its crown. "I wouldn't put it quite like that, as there are many more factors at play that we haven't talked about yet. But you're not entirely wrong either ..."

"Marvellous," Nayeli said sarcastically, sounding discouraged. "That ensures I'll stay unfulfilled my entire life."

"Why do you say that, my dear child?"

Nayeli cast her eyes down to the ground. "Logically, everything you said made sense. But I still don't know how to implement the whole process into my life. And no matter what you say, I feel as if I'm failing over and over again. I've wished for love for years now, and haven't received it. I have longed for money so that I can give up my job – but nothing! I haven't even been able to manifest a dog into my life, for God's sake, despite it having been my number-one dream since I was a kid. And now I feel like it's my fault and I'm not worthy of having any of my wishes come true."

"I'll gladly help you with any questions you have about the steps you need to take," the tree interrupted her. "But please, don't doubt your own power. You have to internalise the knowledge that whatever you dream about is meant to be yours!"

"It is?" Nayeli asked, surprised.

"Yes, everything you desire is included in your soul-plan. It was either written into it before you came here or it was added when you altered your course while being incarnated. But whichever it is, your dreams aren't only achievable; you've got everything you need to reach these goals. Once you are fully healed, any desire you focus on is fulfilled automatically. It's never about forcing it to happen. It's about clearing away the blocks that are preventing your dreams from becoming reality, as they should. In other words, if you want love and money and a dog, then it's a telltale sign you're meant to have all three in your life in the future. And it's totally within your ability to create these things – if they are things you *actually* want, mind you, not substitutes for something else."

"Come again?"

"Manifestation works best when you take the direct approach," Willow explained patiently. "It doesn't work nearly as good to manifest something *so that* you can get something else – because you might still hold resistance to the underlying desire. For example, let's say that someone says they want to manifest lots of money ... They should then ask themselves *why* they want it. Is there an underlying motivation? Do they maybe want the feeling of safety that comes along with being able to buy anything they need? Or do they want the freedom to travel around the world? Or do they want to feel powerful? In all these cases, money is not the real desire; it's a means to an end. And in terms of the Law of Attraction, you can much more easily manifest a core desire like a journey around the world than the money you need to finance a trip around the globe."

"But isn't that the same thing?" Nayeli asked. "You do need the money to get started after all, so why does it matter what we manifest?"

"Ah, but you don't necessarily need the money for any of these underlying reasons," Willow disagreed. "You can also see the world by using travel and work agencies. Or you could visit friends around the globe who let you stay with them for free. You could take on a job that enables you to travel to exotic locations. Or you could win a round-the-world-trip. The universe has an abundant array of ways to bring you what you want."

"Ha!" Nayeli laughed humourlessly. "I don't believe *that* for one second."

"What?" Willow asked, confused. "What don't you believe?"

"That there's abundance, of course. Just take my desire to write books, Willow. In order to write, I need time. Time I don't have because I need to go to work forty hours a week. A full-time job that only lets me scrape by every single month, mind you. That's proving the opposite, if you ask me."

"Wanna bet?" The tree laughed. "Cause I can tell you a story, which I think will convince you that the universe and everything inside it *is* truly abundant."

"I want to see how you're gonna do that," Nayeli muttered.

Accepting the challenge all too readily, Willow began to talk, the tree's voice blending in with the insects buzzing on the meadow.

"It was a sunny day when Strix visited me. And, as usual, he was full of energy and curiosity, eager to explore all the wonders he had yet to experience for himself. Which is why I sensed trouble the moment he landed on one of my branches …"

16. Goldie, the Bumblebee

"Willow!" Strix beamed in greeting as he landed on one of the tree's branches. "How has it been going for you, my old friend?"

"Good," the willow tree answered before returning the question. "And you? Any trouble you've run in to?"

Sensing an undertone of resignation in the tree's voice, Strix acted offended. "Trouble? Me? I have no idea what makes you think that."

"No," Willow said sarcastically. "You are innocence personified. Not! So, spill the beans, Strix. What is it this time? Are you hiding from Nuktia again?"

"I have never hidden from her," Strix said indignantly. "Your memory must be off."

"Maybe yours is," Willow retorted. "Or do I have to remind you about the last time she flirted with you? You were scared out of your wits and hid behind my trunk for ages until she had left."

"I was resting there because it was cold and rainy that day and your branches were dry and comfy," Strix replied.

"That's weird. I distinctly remember it being so sunny at the time that I feared my leaves would dry out ..."

Strix only huffed at that and kept silent.

"You can defend yourself all you want," Willow continued, "but even a tree with no eyes can see that Nuktia is infatuated with you. And you are with her, for that matter. You're simply too scared to admit it."

"Ha! I'm not scared of anything," Strix said loudly, raising himself to his full height. "And you're fantasising. Nuktia is just a friend, nothing more."

"Says you," Willow retorted. "But don't forget that I'm older and wiser. And that I know things you can't even comprehend at your young age. You wait and see, Strix. And in a few years, when it's been proven that I was right all along, you will be free to admit my superiority."

"I suppose by that you mean your ability to detect a love story everywhere you turn, which is a habit that gets worse the older you get?"

"Hey!" Willow replied, feigning indignity. "I know what I know. And I'm not dottled yet."

Just then a gust of wind swooshed through Willow's leaves, and Strix was almost thrown off as the tree used the opportunity to shake its branches a good deal more than was necessary.

Barely managing to cling on to his branch, Strix stared angrily at Willow's trunk.

"Watch it, will ya?" he called out, but then he couldn't help joining in with the tree's giggles.

"In any case," Willow said, once their laughter had died down, "Strix, you better tell me right now what trouble you're in. I'll find out either way. And you don't want me to worm the answers out of your beak."

"There's no trouble, I promise," Strix said defensively. "I've been the most well-behaved bird in this hemisphere."

"For how many minutes?" Willow asked dryly.

"And besides," Strix continued, as if the tree hadn't interrupted him, "I never go looking for trouble. It just somehow tends to find me."

Willow barked out a laugh. "If you truly believe that, then you're more detached from reality than I thought. The truth, please, young bird. What are you thinking about?"

Strix stalled for another minute or two, but then he began to talk, hesitantly at first, before gaining momentum. "I had a nice chat with one of the black bears who live around here. We talked about the bees and the nectar they gather. He said that it's the tastiest food in the whole world, especially if you get some proteins in the form of pupae, larvae and eggs along with it. He says that no one has lived until they've tried it. And he painted the sweet taste and texture and the creamy consistency in such vibrant pictures that I gotta have a sample of the nectar. But I'm not sure how to get my claws on it."

"Why? What's so difficult about this? You fly over to the nearest hive and ask nicely if the bees would share some of it with you. The worst that can happen is that they'll say no."

Strix shifted his weight and gripped Willow's branch even tighter with his claws. "Nope!" he said adamantly. "Can't do that. You see, the bear warned me that the honey bees who have a prosperous amount of nectar are all living near the two-legged, and I'll most certainly not fly into their cities and towns. And as for the wild bumblebee colonies around this meadow ... he said they all keep a jealous watch over their nectar as they don't collect a whole lot. Every drop is so valuable to them that they guard it with their lives. And if I were to ask them for some, they might attack me without further ado. They have attacked the black bear in the past. To him that's not life-threatening as he's bigger than me and protected by thick fur. But think of a hundred bumblebees stinging me at once; I'll probably die of an allergic shock. No, it's impossible for me to get the sweet nectar this way. I'll be safer if I think of something else ... I could lure them out of their hive, for example. And when it's empty,

I snatch the nectar and will be gone, long before they know what happened."

"Strix, I don't know," Willow put in. "There has to be a better way. One that doesn't include trickery and stealing. Besides, how do you think they'll react once they find out what you did?"

"But they won't," Strix said. "If all goes to plan, no one will see me and they won't suspect an owl of having stolen from them. Maybe they'll think it was the bear again."

"And what if they take it out on him? Could you live knowing that you sicced a raging bumblebee colony on him?"

Shrugging uncomfortably, Strix looked away from Willow. "It's not that I have much of a choice, do I?"

"There's always a choice," Willow reprimand Strix. "And, pardon my bluntness, but this sounds like a terrible decision you're about to make."

Strix brushed aside his friend's concern with a dismissive wave of his right wing. "I'll admit that I'm not great at making plans, but this is the best one I could come up with. I *need* to taste the nectar. And I can improvise as I go along if I have to – that's my strong point, anyway."

Taking off from the branch, Strix flew a quick circle above Willow's crown. "Don't worry about it. I'll be fine with a bit of luck." And before the weeping willow could say anything else, Strix soared off, letting himself be carried by the soft summer breeze that ruffled his feathers.

He knew exactly where to find a bumblebee hive as he'd flown past it several times on his way to and from Willow's meadow. It was on the other side of the woods, where they ended in a field. There, beneath the trees, was an old abandoned mouse hole, which a queen bumblebee had occupied this spring to raise her brood.

Flying straight towards it, Strix chose a tree with thick foliage nearby that would not only hide his presence but also make for a great observation point. The first part of his plan consisted of spying on the bumblebees to find out all of their weaknesses, which he then could use against them.

In the first hour, there wasn't much to observe, though.

A few bumblebees flew into the hole in the ground while others flew out, disappearing between the tall grass and flowers. There was a constant coming and going but at no time did the bumblebees leave their hive unguarded.

Agonizing over what to do and how he could lure out the insects without them realising what he was doing, Strix suddenly noticed something curious.

One of the female bumblebees who had flown out earlier had come back, laden with pollen, and was now dancing in the sky above the hive. She was drawing the attention of other females in the colony, who watched her movements intently after which they left the hive and flew in the direction the bumblebee had come from, seeming to have been hypnotised by her.

Strix felt excitement built up inside him as more bumblebees had flown away this time than in the entire last hour put together. Of course, some had remained behind. But Strix figured that he might be able to copy the dance and thus hypnotise them, too. Not hesitating a moment longer, he flew out of his cover and neared the hive.

The bumblebees in front of it were instantly on alert and monitored his every move, ready to intervene if necessary.

Staying a safe distance away from their stingers, Strix flew a big figure-of-eight. It was more difficult than he had expected, and he needed to fly in such a large curve that the tips of his wings almost touched the leaves of the surrounding trees. But he didn't let himself be deterred by that and continued to dance in the sky until more and more bumblebees had come out of the hive to watch him. Glad that his trick with the hypnotic dance seemed to work, it took Strix some minutes to notice that the bumblebees weren't leaving as he had anticipated. Instead, they were busy laughing at him.

Not knowing what he had done wrong, Strix dropped to the ground and glanced inquisitively at the insects who were cracking up.

Eventually, the female bumblebee who'd demonstrated the dance first took pity on him. Choking back her laughter, she looked Strix up and down. "Why are you imitating my waggle dance? And why, pray tell, are you copying it wrong?"

Her words slammed into him like a sledgehammer. Strix's first instinct was to defend his actions, but then he closed his beak with a snap, as he couldn't very well announce his reason for having made an utter fool of himself. So, taking the next best course of action, he took to the sky and fled the scene without a word.

Flying straight back to Willow and diving underneath his friend's low-hanging branches. Strix's chest was heaving from having crossed the distance in record time.

"What's wrong?" Willow asked immediately, obviously sensing his distress.

"Nothing," Strix tried to gloss over the situation. "Everything's perfectly fine."

"Yeah, and I'm an owl. Hoo-hoo," Willow responded. "Come on, tell me. It can't be any worse than the time you fell out of a tree and onto a porcupine, can it?"

"Thanks for reminding me, I'd successfully forgotten about that," Strix said, upset. Then he sighed. He knew that he could never keep anything from his friend for long anyway and so informed the tree of what had happened.

"Strix," Willow said sympathetically once he had finished. "Don't you know that bumblebees don't do this dance to hypnotise the others? It's how they tell where they can find the best flowers and pollen."

Strix flapped his wings in irritation. "How would I know that? And how come you do? Why do you always know everything important, and I don't?"

"Because you're a couple of years my junior?" the tree answered in its most innocent tone of voice. "Strix, don't let your head hang. It's not the end of the world. They'll soon have forgotten about it. And if need be, you could tell them that you were drunk because you accidentally ate a fermented fruit."

Feeling an idea being sparked by his friend's words, Strix looked up, a gleam in his eyes. "Willow, you are amazing!"

"What did I say?" the tree asked guardedly.

"Whatever would I do without you?" Strix simply said, ignoring the weeping willow's question and flew off.

Finding fermented fruit at this time of the year wasn't easy. But after a thorough search, Strix came upon a berry bush beneath which lay some rotten fruit that would surely do. Bumblebees weren't big, after all, and even though there were a lot of them, a few berries should be enough to make them all drunk. And then he would have ample time to sample their nectar ...

Clasping the fruits in his claws, Strix flew back to the hive where everything had quietened down. Dropping the berries in front of the hole in the ground without slowing down, Strix flew past the surprised bumblebees and landed on a branch near them. Nodding at them, as if the embarrassing incident an hour ago had never occurred, Strix grinned. "I brought you a present. Dig in!"

Looking down at the berries and then back at Strix, the female bumblebee he had talked to earlier spoke up. "I'm sorry, but what are we supposed to do with these?"

"Eat them," Strix said matter-of-factly. "They're tasty, I promise. I've tried some myself."

"That's a nice gesture, Mr ..."

"Strix."

"Mr Strix," the female bumblebee, who introduced herself as Goldie, said. "As I said, the sentiment is appreciated. But we don't eat any fruit. We only eat pollen and nectar."

Strix felt dejected as his plan crumbled before his eyes "You won't even try them? They might be to your liking."

Goldie declined the offer a second time and Strix tried not to let his irritation show. His thoughts were chasing each other around and he was desperately searching for something else that he could do or say that would get him the sweet gold.

"Right, right," Strix said, improvising. "I knew that, of course. And the berries were simply an excuse to come here."

"Why would you need an excuse?" Goldie asked in bewilderment.

"To warn you," Strix said, having a flash of inspiration.

"Warn us? Of what? Or whom?"

"Of something terrible that's about to happen this evening. You see, I was flying around, enjoying the beautiful day and minding my own business, when I overheard a couple of skunks. They said they want to team up to attack your hive. They said they want to catch you unawares and kill you all."

Goldie apparently wasn't convinced by his story. She looked Strix up and down. "Ah, and why are you telling us that?"

"Out of the kindness of my heart," Strix replied. "You've been my neighbours for so long, and I couldn't live with myself if I let a massacre like this happen. Not if I could have done something to prevent it ..."

"In that case, thank you."

The female bumblebee began to clean her translucent wings and was the picture of calm, not seeming at all perturbed by the news..

Waiting for something – anything – to happen, Strix glanced from her to the other bumblebees who had heard his warning as well.

"Aren't you going to do anything to stop them?" he asked, growing increasingly restless.

"What would you advise us to do?" one of the other bumblebees asked.

"You could fly out there together and attack them. Attack is the best defence, right? And you have a big advantage because they're not expecting you. Which means the faster you act, the better. And I can tell you where to find them ..."

"No," Goldie answered firmly. "That's not possible. We can't leave our hive unprotected. Our queen and eggs would be exposed to any enemy that approached."

"So, you're just gonna wait until they come?" Strix asked, annoyed at her passivity. Then his mind caught up with Goldie's words. "Wait, does your queen never leave the hive?"

"No," Goldie answered. "She stays in there and lays eggs while we get the pollen she needs. Why?"

Ignoring her question, Strix ruffled up his feathers as he found it easier to think that way. If only one bumblebee remained in the hive, it wouldn't pose a huge problem for him. But since the others were adamant to not leave their queen alone, he had to draw them away somehow. Only that nothing he had tried thus far had worked.

Getting more and more frustrated, Strix almost wished it were true that some skunks were rallying up to attack the hive. Then he could wait for them to act and take what they left behind. Sighing loudly, he realised that there was merely one last straw he could grasp at.

"You know what? I could keep an eye on your hive and your queen while you all fly out. How does that sound?"

"I'm sorry," Goldie said, shaking her head. "But this is our job, and we take it seriously."

Dejectedly, Strix bowed his head. This was it, he thought. There was nothing else up his feathers, no further ideas, no stroke of genius. Angry at himself for not being smart enough to get past the bumblebees, Strix was about to say his goodbyes and hole up somewhere to lick his wounds when he was interrupted by Goldie.

"Why don't you ask us?"

"Ask what?" Strix said, too preoccupied with his failure to note what the female bumblebee meant with her words.

"Why don't you ask us for the nectar you want instead of coming up with one lie after another?" Goldie questioned, softening her harsh words with a kind tone.

"B-b-but ..." Strix was taken aback, struggling to find the right words. "But one of the black bears told me that you don't give it away freely. And he has quite a lot of stings to prove that."

"Naturally, we won't share our nectar with him. Cause that's not the only thing he's after. He also wants to eat us and our young ones."

Deciding it would be wise not to inform Goldie that he wouldn't say no to a nice protein meal himself – at least, if it didn't sting him – Strix ignored that comment.

"Not to mention," Goldie continued, "that the bears take it from us by force all the time and damage our hives with their big paws. Which makes us not inclined to let them have our gold."

"Then why do you want to share some of it with me?"

The little bumblebee shrugged. "I've kinda taken a liking to you."

"But I tried to betray you," Strix said sadly as his shame caught up with him.

"Everyone makes mistakes." Goldie said. "The important thing is to learn from them." Looking him up and down, the bumblebee buzzed loudly. "Anyway, how is it? Do you want some? Or not?"

Strix wondered whether he could accept such a gift, after what he'd been prepared to do to the bumblebees. But as usual, his curiosity won out and so he flew over to the furry insect.

Not long after, he was the proud owner of a bit of nectar that was encased by some wax. Strix picked it up carefully with his beak, At once, a sickening sweetness spread over his tongue.

"Uhh, tha' awfell," he mumbled, barely able to get the words out because of the gooey consistency of the nectar. "Sory."

"I figured you'd say that," Goldie laughed out loud, "since owls aren't exactly known for their culinary expertise."

"Thenn wy didnd yuu telll me tha' befoor?" Strix asked, offended.

"And would you have believed me?" Goldie returned pitilessly.

"Or wouldn't you have rather tried to come up with another 101 ideas to trick us? At least, now you know that it isn't worth to raid our hive in the future ..."

Strix had half a mind to tell Goldie exactly what he thought about her manipulative nature. But the knowledge that he hadn't acted any better than her made him pause. And then he was prevented from saying anything further because he was too busy trying to spit out the sticky mass that was filling his beak.

Abundance and Prosperity

"And that's how Strix arrived on my hill again," Willow concluded. "His beak and front feathers, where the nectar had dripped down, were sticky as heck, and he needed to take a good long bath in the stream to clean himself. Consequently, he was in such a bad mood that everyone avoided him for the rest of the day. Let's just say it was the first – and last – time he ever tried the bumblebee's gold. But it taught him a valuable lesson."

"And what lesson would that be? Cause it certainly wasn't one about abundance," Nayeli tossed in. "You said yourself in your story that the wild bumblebee colonies don't have enough nectar to share it with everyone ..."

"Then let me try to convince you otherwise. Because this universe can't exist in any state *but* abundance. Look around you, my dear. Look at the stars present in this solar system alone. Look at every single snowflake that falls in winter, each of which is unique to all others. Look at every leaf on me and on my brothers and sisters. Look at the infinite droplets of water in the oceans and the grains of sand in the deserts. Watch how the grass re-grows days after it has been cut. Look at how quickly a meadow is covered in wild flowers once spring comes. Nature and life itself are always prosperous and give without asking for anything in return. The sun doesn't want payment for the warmth and energy it bestows on us day after day. And neither does the stream for the water it carries. Nor the earth for providing us with all the nutrients we need."

"It might be true that nature is abundant," Nayeli cut in. "But it definitely isn't true for all living beings that inhabit her. And especially not for us humans as many don't even have enough money to get their most basic needs met …"

"All right, first off, being abundant relates to more than your finances. Abundance is more profound and can relate to anything in your life. It can mean having lots of great friendships, it can mean an abundance of free time or an abundance of interests or hobbies. It can mean having an abundance of creativity or beauty or having lots of trees in your garden that are bearing fresh fruit. On a deeper soul level, true abundance is closely related to safety, because being abundant on all levels translates to being secure in the knowledge – not the hope, but the knowledge – that every need you have will be met.

"And secondly, I have to disagree with you. As abundance is a universal law and since you humans are part of this universe, you are automatically subjected to it, too. Just like the universe, you can't live in any state *but* abundance."

Nayeli crossed her arms in front of her chest defiantly. "Then this is the first time you are wrong, Willow. Cause the fact still stands that merely some areas of our lives match this abundance. And how can that be? How can someone have lots of time but a lack of education? Or countless friends but a lack of purpose? Shouldn't everything in our lives exist abundantly, if what you say is true?"

"But that's the case, my dear, that's the case. Don't forget that you live inside a dual reality and that, therefore, this law works in both directions, which is where we come to your perceived lack in certain areas."

"What's your point?" Nayeli asked, tilting her head back.

"My point is that abundance doesn't indicate only good things exist unrestricted. That's not how it works. Alongside an abundance of money and wealth, there can also be an abundance of poverty or bills. At the other end of an abundance of health is the abundance of illness. And opposing to an abundance of love, there can be an abundance of loneliness or rejection. The types of abundance you can attract are as infinite as everything else. But abundant you are, in every aspect of your life."

"Oh!" Nayeli whispered as she comprehended what the tree was telling her. "I've never seen it from this perspective. But ... okay, that's true."

"And isn't that good news?" Willow sniggered. "That you are an abundant being and know no lack ...?"

Laughing at Willow's flippant reply, Nayeli clamped a hand over her mouth as a bird, which had been pulling a worm from the earth near her, fluttered up, startled.

"It would be great if I found a way to pick the abundance I want to have, though, thank you very much."

"And you can," Willow responded.

"By using the Law of Attraction, right?" Nayeli asked.

"Yes. But there's further knowledge to be gained here ..." The tree's voice held a promise, but before Willow could say more on the matter, they were interrupted.

"If I may interject," a voice cooed to Nayeli's left, almost too softly to hear.

Jerking upwards, Nayeli looked around but wasn't able to detect the source right away.

"Down here," the timid voice said. "On the flower."

Following the indicated direction with her eyes, Nayeli spotted a small bumblebee sitting in the middle of a yellow blossom. "Hello, how are you doing?" Nayeli said kindly.

It was only after she had spoken that Nayeli realised she hadn't blinked twice at the insect talking to her. Having spent days in Willow's presence and listening to a tree must have made her more accustomed to strange occurrences than she had wanted to acknowledge till now. But she had no time to contemplate the matter further because the little bumblebee was addressing her again.

"That's the thing I wanted to speak to you about. I couldn't help overhearing you and the willow tree talking, and I thought this would be my one chance to speak to a human who would understand me and my dire situation."

Curious, Nayeli inclined her head to the bumblebee. "What situation do you mean?"

"It's about your race. And mine. And the relationship between us. You see, our ancestors enjoyed an abundance of healthy flowers that crowded the meadows. But our current abundance isn't one of pollen and flowers. Every summer, we have fewer of those and more abundance of illness. There's a lot of pesticide pollution now, even if we fly a good bit away from your fields. Our flowers and the earth are being poisoned and our survival is in danger."

The little insect buzzed loudly before continuing seamlessly. "One time, I saw a pair of humans walk by and heard them talk about your honey bees and how they are suffering and need to be helped. But it's not just them who are dying. It's all of us, including the wild bumblebee species. And we are fertilising at least as many plants as your domesticated bees."

"I'm sorry," Nayeli whispered, her voice laced with sadness. "I know that we're endangering not only our abundance but the abundance of all living beings. I do wish there was something I could do to help ..."

"But there is," the little bumblebee said assertively. "I can't because I'm a tiny insect and no human will listen to me. I tried to speak to the pair I mentioned earlier, and others, but no one hears me. They simply wave their hands to fend me off or they ignore me altogether. But you are one of them. You can speak their language and can tell them what I told you. You can tell people that they're hurting themselves when they wipe us out. Because if we become extinct who will be left to pollinate the plants you and your cattle eat each day?"

"That's all true. But I'm one single woman – my voice won't carry far ..."

Willow rumbled indignantly at that moment, but Nayeli quickly quieted her friend. "I know that Willow has a different opinion but, even if you're both right, it would take forever for me to influence enough people to make much of a difference."

"You could try," the bumblebee pleaded.

Watching the small insect, so steadfast in its conviction, Nayeli was strangely touched by the trust this animal had placed in her. And suddenly, a thought was planted in her mind. A crazy idea, but one that might not be impossible after all.

"Okay, I will try," Nayeli pledged, making up her mind. "I can't promise that people will hear me, but I'm gonna do my best!"

"Thank you," the little insect answered, relieved. It then spread its translucent wings and buzzed around her head once, after which it weaved through the willow tree's branches.

"Huh," Nayeli said as she watched the bumblebee fly out of sight. "That was unexpected."

"What did you mean by the promise you gave that bumblebee?" Willow asked. This time it was the tree's voice, which was filled with curiosity.

"Well, it has to do with my newfound passion for writing. But I'm not too sure about the details yet and I'd like to think things through a while longer before telling you about it – if that's all right with you? Cause I do want to know what you think about it, as soon as I've figured everything out ..."

"Certainly – that sounds intriguing," Willow said tenderly. Then the tree chuckled. "You definitely have an abundance of secrets right now, my dear child. Which gets us back to the topic of how you are an abundant being."

Eager to hear what else the tree had to say on the topic, Nayeli inched back to rest more comfortably against its trunk. "And I can genuinely have any kind of abundance I want?"

"You can," Willow answered. "You can't change the fact that you are in a state of prosperity at all times, but you can swap one form of abundance for another if the one you hold is not in alignment with your path or your desires."

"And are some things easier to manifest than others?"

"Why would they? The collective consciousness created this whole world. It created the physical laws, black holes, evolution, mathematical formulas that no one but a few geniuses can grasp and even something as complicated as the human ego. Letting a million dollars or the love of your life come your way is child's play for the source energy. Just remember that everything in existence is energy. And it can either be attracted or repelled by you. That's the whole secret behind it and it always works alike, no matter what your desires are.

"Think about a puppy. Imagine it's scared of rubbish bins and doesn't want to walk past one. What are you going to do so that the puppy will come with you? Are you going to pull it along, with brute force? You could do that, of course, but it will not erase the puppy's fear. It will rather increase its panic, and the puppy will struggle all the more. It will resist and pull back, making things as difficult as possible for you. And the same happens when you use force to draw something to you energetically. The more force you use, the harder you'll make the process and the more you will repel what you want. The other option you have is to go down to the puppy's level and show it that the rubbish bin is safe. You can encourage the puppy and take advantage of its curiosity, making it want to examine the bin for itself. If you do this, instead of the leash being strung tight between you, it will hang loose and you will receive the result you desire more quickly and easily. Or don't you think that enticing the puppy will lead to more positive results than pressuring it?"

"Without a doubt," Nayeli said, not having to think about it. "It will, most likely, take a little longer in the beginning, but it's the much better option all around. And it will ensure that the puppy will not only come with me but that it will also want to stay with me afterwards. Because it trusts me."

The tree agreed. "The trick is to align your life in a way that the energy you wish to gain would feel welcome and happy to join you."

"You mean I should basically make myself attractive to whatever I want to attract?"

"Precisely. And you do that by improving your relationships with the things you want to draw into your life."

Confused, Nayeli held up her hand. "Hold up, Willow, why are you talking about relationships now? We've covered those already, haven't we?"

"We did," Willow answered. "And I think I clarified that you are in a relationship with everything outside yourself? Even your financial situation, if we stick with this example? Any relationship – whether it's to people or other things – is healthier the more you take the other party's needs into account and vice versa. Accordingly, your relationship with prosperity in the form of money will improve when you take better care of it."

Nayeli rubbed her eyes tiredly. "I'm sorry, but I still don't know what I'm supposed to do here ..."

"It's simple. Think of money as if it's a person. And now ask yourself the following questions. If you were that other person, would you like to be treated the way you treat your money? Would you want to be around you? Or would you rather leave and look for a person who's taking better care of you and who appreciates having you around? What relationship *do* you currently have with your finances? Are you saying that this *other person* is not good enough, that they are not doing enough for you? Are you resenting them for staying away, or are you angry that they seemingly like other people more than you? Do you sometimes wish they didn't exist in the first place? Are you clinging to them? Or are you giving off an air of being uninterested in them?

"And if you have these, or similar, thoughts about money, why do you think the energy of financial abundance would want to come to you? I'm telling you – it won't! If you want more of it or more of anything in your life, then make the thing you'd like to attract your friend. And turn the unhealthy relationship into a relationship that is beneficial for everyone involved. For you and for whatever it is you want to pull closer."

"That does make sense ..." Nayeli said, amazed at how easy some things were if they were explained in the right way.

The tree rubbed its leaves together, creating a crinkling background noise with them. "In the end, the only thing you have to do to make the reality you want your reality, is to make it a reality before it is your reality."

"Woah – what?" Nayeli laughed and shook her head, as if that would help to clear her mind.

"To say it with other words, you need to fake it till you make it! As long as you hold the energy of searching for something, you can't be a match for the energy of finding it."

"And I assume the universe doesn't make advance deliveries either?" Nayeli joked. "And that it's no use bargaining with it to give me the abundance I want prior to doing my part?"

Willow snorted. "Not likely. It does not help to sit on your sofa and ask the universe to please send you a million dollars while saying that, in return, you'll change your limiting beliefs and feelings concerning prosperity later. No, first you need to change your inner world to allow a shift to occur in your outer reality. And the better you are at convincing yourself that you are already in the space of what you desire, the faster it will arrive."

"But how can I do that?" Nayeli asked. "I can't ignore the fact that I'm scraping by, can I? Am I supposed to buy myself lots of things using credit cards and then hope the universe brings me the money in time for me to pay back my debts?"

"Not at all," Willow said. "Having debt is another way of ensuring that you stay on the energetic side of lack. No, what you should do is to use visualisation techniques."

"Visualisation techniques?" Nayeli asked. "Daydreaming is supposed to help me gain more prosperity? Are you serious?"

"Absolutely, my dear. It's true that, regarding your ego and thus your human perspective, there's a distinct difference between the outer reality you live in and the images you create inside your mind. But regarding the universe, there's no such distinction. It reacts to the frequency you send out, no matter the reason behind it – something we'll talk more about later, I promise. But for now, you just need to know that visualisation does work. And the more details you can think up and see and feel and perceive with all of your senses, the better. Let's take your wish to have a dog as an example ... To help this desire become your reality, imagine what your life would look like when you have one. How would you structure your day? When would you get up in the morning and where would you go for your first walk? Imagine how and when you would play with your dog, what food you would feed him and what you would experience together. How does the fur feel when you cuddle him? How wet would his nose be if he poked you to get your attention? Let a whole day play out in front of your eyes. Feel the love and happiness for your dog and imagine having him by your side with all your senses."

"But what if I can't visualise it? What if that isn't a talent I have?"

"You think you can't visualise?" Willow asked surprised.

Nayeli shrugged. "Maybe, maybe not. I've never done it."

The tree chortled. "Then you've never read a book and envisioned the scenes play out before your inner eye? You've never thought about what you need to get from the supermarket and have seen the aisles in your mind? And you've never revisited a memory and watched it like you would a movie on the screen? All these and more examples are nothing else but you visualising, my dear. Sure, some people are naturally better at it than others but almost everyone can do it, at least to some extent. And in case you're one of the humans who really can't visualise, there's another method you can use ...”

“What’s that?” Nayeli asked when Willow didn’t follow that statement up with an explanation.

“A topic that Nuktia can tell you quite a lot about,” the tree replied cryptically.

At first, Nayeli was annoyed that Willow was being this vague, but then the realisation hit her upside the head. “Nuktia? You mean *the* Nuktia? Strix’s Nuktia?” Nayeli asked, excited at the prospect of hearing more about this mysterious female owl.

“The very same,” Willow promised.

Interlude B: Nuktia

When Willow felt the unmistakable sensation of owl claws wrapping around a branch, the tree almost greeted its old friend Strix. But then Willow remembered, just in time, that he wasn't here anymore. That he had left for his trip around the world from which he might never return.

Strix had flown off a few weeks ago and Willow hadn't heard a peep from him since, as the young owl had somehow closed himself off from their energetic bond and all the tree's attempts to communicate with him.

Obviously, Willow would realise when he crossed over to the other side, as the tree's connection to source was as strong as it had ever been. But knowing that Strix must be alive didn't alleviate the worries about whether he was safe and happy. And neither did it help to answer the question of whether he had found a place to settle down or if he was still travelling from one country to another.

Sighing deeply at the thought of never hearing his hoots or his laughter again in this life, Willow felt overwhelmed with sadness. But then the tree pulled itself together and concentrated on Nuktia instead, whose claws were digging into the wood of a low-hanging branch.

The young female owl was unusually silent.

Willow didn't know her quite as well as Strix, but good enough to sense that something was amiss. "What's wrong, Nuktia?"

Shrugging, the short-eared owl craned her neck around. "Nothing much," she said, trying to sound indifferent, but failing spectacularly at it. "I just had a huge row with Whisky and needed to get away."

"Whisky? Is that the young albino owl who lives around here, the one you are friends with?"

"Yes," Nuktia answered. "But our fight was so bad that I think our friendship is over."

"What were the two of you fighting about? If I may ask, that is."

Willow could feel Nuktia restlessly shifting from one leg to the other.

"I wanted to play hunting to take my mind off things and to practise our skills some more. Y'know, that game where one of us plays at being a mouse and hides somewhere and the other needs to track them. But Whisky wasn't feeling up to it; she never is these days. The only thing she wants to do is sit around and talk. She tells me constantly that I need to get my sorrow and anger at Strix leaving off my chest ... It's annoying! She's annoying! I'm fed up talking about Strix. Besides, it would benefit Whisky to exercise more. She's getting a little plump around the middle, which slows her down when flying."

"If she manages to hunt enough food to get plump, she can't be all that slow, now can she?" Willow joked. But when Nuktia didn't join in the laughter, the tree quickly became serious again. "Maybe you should speak about all this with someone, though? It's not healthy to bottle your feelings up."

"Don't you start as well!" Nuktia called out angrily. "I don't need a second pseudo-shrink who knows what's best for me."

"Sorry," Willow said. "I didn't mean to boss you around. I simply suggested it because I thought it would help."

Nuktia puffed her feathers up. "No, I'm sorry. None of this is your fault and it isn't right for me to take my bad mood out on you. It's just ... when Strix left, I actually thought that talking about my feelings would help. But when all my attempts ended badly, I eventually gave up."

"Badly?" Willow asked. "Why?"

"Do you know another owl around my age that lives here? She's dark brown."

"Your friend Brandy? Yes, we have met. What about her?"

Nuktia rocked back and forth on Willow's branch. "We're not friends anymore, either. Our relationship ended in a huge argument when she wouldn't listen to me. Every time I tried to make her see what I'm going through, she suggested we should do something to get my mind off things. Like flying over to that old forest up north where the fog never fully clears or to the big river in the west to try ourselves at fishing. That's not being a good friend, is it? She wasn't there for me when I needed her ..."

"And yet, you're angry with Whisky for doing what you wanted from Brandy?" the tree asked gently. "Nuktia, I know that you've been going through a rough patch these last few weeks. But what I don't get is why you're searching for the things you need in all the wrong places. I've heard that Whisky is great with emotions and talking things through. And that Brandy is always up for an adventure and fun. Which begs the question – why aren't you taking advantage of what they're naturally gifted at and what they love to do? You're saying they're bad friends for not being there in the way you want them to be. But you can't see that they're being the best friend you could wish for in another way."

Nuktia let out a hoot and loosened her tight grip on Willow's branch. "I never saw it like that. But you're right. That's exactly what I did." Shifting her weight, she groaned in despair. "I feel so stupid. I've ended two friendships over nothing – I've accused them both of having ruined our relationship and told them not to bother me in the future. But all the while, *I* was the one who was being a bad friend to *them*!"

Willow let the branch Nuktia sat on sway in a soothing rhythm and shushed the owl. "Ssh, don't say that, Nuktia. You were in pain and not seeing things clearly. Besides, you can set things right now."

"You think so?" the young owl asked, sounding unsure.

"I know so," Willow answered confidently.

Nuktia remained sitting, obviously mulling this new revelation over in her mind. But then she soared up into the sky with new-found resolution. "I hope you're right. And now excuse me; I have some apologies to make."

"Godspeed!" Willow called after her, but Nuktia was already gone, flying towards the clearing where Whisky and Brandy could usually be found.

***

Less than two days later, Nuktia returned.

Willow felt her claws set down on a branch once again. But it didn't feel quite the same because this time, she stood on one foot only.

The reason for that became apparent when Nuktia raised the other leg to her beak and ripped off large chunks of a dead mouse she held clutched, devouring it in less than two minutes.

"Mmm," she mumbled happily. "Tasty! How are you doing, Willow?"

"I'm fine," the tree replied and added jokingly, "although I feel better when there aren't pieces of dead mice clinging to me."

"Sorry," Nuktia said, chastised, as she swallowed her last bite and cleaned the branch where a few pieces had fallen down.

The willow tree chose that moment to playfully whip its branches up and down, which made Nuktia cling to the one she sat on with both claws. "Hey," Nuktia called out, startled. "You think it's wise to upset my stomach after I've eaten a huge meal?"

Willow stopped abruptly and let out a sound of disgust. "Don't you dare throw up on me!"

"I won't if you don't play merry-go-round with me," Nuktia promised before laughing brightly.

"You seem in a much better mood today," Willow said. "I take it, your talks with Brandy and Whisky turned out all right?"

Nuktia bounced happily. "Better than all right. Which I have you to thank for. If you hadn't brought me to my senses, I would have lost them forever. And I'm really, really glad I didn't. I can count myself incredibly lucky to have three such fabulous friends in my life."

"Three?" Willow asked in confusion.

"Yeah. Whisky. Brandy. And you!"

If Willow had been physically able to blush, the tree would have done it. As it was, Willow was lost for words, which was an unusual occurrence.

"Thank you, that means a lot to me," the tree eventually said. "And just so you know, I regard you as my friend, too."

Hemming and hawing in answer to that, Nuktia turned her head sideways. "I guess, in that case, I won't bother you if I come around here more often in the future?"

"Bother me? Definitely not! Why would you think that?"

"Because I'm not Strix. And I can't replace him."

"No one is replaceable," Willow muttered. "But saying this, we can fill the holes that are created by our losses with entirely new friendships. And I am grateful to be included in your circle."

For a while, silence fell in the meadow between them as each one dwelled on their own thoughts. But then the female owl sighed. "Why did I have to fall in love with such an idiot?" Nuktia complained.

"Strix isn't *that* bad, is he?"

Laughing hollowly, the short-eared owl tightened her grip on Willow's branch. "He ran … er … flew away the second I told him I loved him. So yeah, he *is* that bad."

"Oh, Nuktia," Willow said sympathetically. "I know better than most how stupid Strix can act sometimes. But maybe he just needs a little while longer than the average owl to realise what a precious gift he's letting slip through his claws, hmm? Don't forget we're talking about a male here, after all ..."

Nuktia snorted. "Or maybe I was fooling myself this whole time when I believed something was growing between us. Maybe he never cared about me."

Willow was surprised at the direction Nuktia's thoughts were taking. "No, Nuktia, you're wrong! Even if he doesn't have romantic feelings for you – which I doubt – he cares about you a great deal. Trust me. I know Strix. And I know when he feels deeply for someone. You were always at the top of that list, from the moment he met you."

The young owl hooted out loud in response. "I remember that day so vividly. The fear I felt when I found myself all alone outside my nest, practically on a silver plate for any predator walking by. And the feeling of comfort when Strix arrived on the scene and got me back to safety. My mum was so grateful that he'd saved my life, she actually trusted him to take care of me whenever she had to go hunting in the next weeks. And once I grew my feathers, she let him teach me how to fly. Ah, everything was perfect in these first few weeks and the months afterwards. Damn, why did I have to tell him about my feelings? If only I'd kept my beak closed. Then we would still be the bestest of friends and he wouldn't have left ..."

"You were true to yourself and being authentic, Nuktia," Willow answered. "That's a good thing, and Strix will come to terms with his emotions in his own time. Wait and see."

"Hmm, maybe," Nuktia mumbled.

"You disagree?" the tree asked.

"I'm not sure, Willow. I know that you're wise and all that, and I'd like to believe that he'll come around. But there are so many unanswered questions inside my head – about why he left and what this means for me. Currently, I feel adrift and don't even know what I want anymore or what is right for me."

"Then maybe you should be grateful for this *you-time* that Strix has given you. It gives you the opportunity to find the answers to the questions that are plaguing you, without him being here to distract you."

"And that's something I should be grateful for? That he left and made me suffer? You must be kidding!"

"I'm not."

Nuktia flapped loudly with her wings. "Are *you* grateful that he's gone, then?

"No," Willow replied. "I do miss Strix and will continue to do so, for as long as he's not here. But I've learned to focus on the silver lining in every situation."

"Like what?" Nuktia asked curiously. "What could be the silver lining in the situation we find ourselves in?"

"There are many positive things we can focus upon," the tree replied. "I'm grateful, for example, that Strix and I spent the first year of his incarnation together, talking and joking about everything under the sun. I'm grateful that he gets to learn and grow a lot while being away. I'm grateful that there's still a chance he might come back someday. And, what's more, I'm grateful that now I got the chance to build a closer connection with you."

Nuktia closed her eyes for a moment and nodded. "Y'know what, Willow? Strix has the best friend in you. And whether or not he comes back to me – he would be really stupid not to come back to you."

And with those words, Nuktia opened her wings and flew off, leaving an overly emotional Willow in the meadow.

Gratitude

"And did he?" Nayeli asked when Willow stopped talking. "Did Strix come back to you and Nuktia eventually? Or did she move on from him?"

"That's something you'll find out in due time," Willow said. "But first, tell me, what has this story taught you? And why would I choose to recount this episode of Nuktia's life?"

Nayeli waggled her eyebrows. "I think, you either want to tell me how amazing mice taste, or you want to teach me how important gratitude is."

"The latter," Willow answered quickly. "Definitely the latter. I don't get how some animals can eat meat and enjoy the experience. I've never been gladder to be a tree who can live on water and the nutrients in the earth alone."

"I absolutely agree. I've been a vegetarian for five years, and I don't miss meat at all."

"See, my dear? That you don't miss it, is already the first thing you can be grateful for. And now that we're on the subject of gratitude, let me explain what it means. Gratitude is a state of complete non-resistance. As such, gratitude is the energy that is most closely matched with abundance and prosperity."

Nayeli stretched out her legs in front of her. "And since, in order to manifest what we desire, we need to stop our resistance first, we can use gratitude to get what we want, is that it?"

"Yes. Gratitude is a way of focusing on the frequency of abundance, by shifting your focus from the negative side to the positive end, which in turn creates more wealth in your life – wealth of happiness, wealth of love, wealth of health or wealth of any other kind you are searching for. The best news is, though, that it's one of the easiest tools to utilise."

Blinking into the bright sun that shone through a gap in Willow's crown, Nayeli shielded her eyes with a hand. "So, don't keep me guessing here ... what do I need to do to practise gratitude?"

"First and foremost, you need to realise that you can be grateful in almost any situation in life."

"For almost anything?" Nayeli asked doubtfully. "I don't know, Willow. Why should I be grateful for my car breaking down? Or for my house burning to ashes?"

"You misunderstood me, my dear child. I didn't say you can be grateful *for* anything in your life but *in* almost any situation. That's an important distinction. To understand this, you have to become aware of one basic truth. Which is that gratitude is not an emotion, but a state of being. It transcends emotions and exists outside the emotional scale you learned about. Thus, it can exist alongside positively perceived feelings as well as alongside negatively perceived ones."

Nayeli scratched her nose absentmindedly. "Are you sure that gratitude isn't an emotion?"

"Think about it for yourself – how good can you control your feelings? Can you stop being afraid just because you decide you don't want to be anxious anymore? Can you be happy because someone else asks you to? The answer is no. We can't directly control any of our emotions. They come automatically based on the situations we're in, based on the thoughts we think and based on the beliefs we hold. And we can only change them indirectly by changing our thoughts, beliefs and actions. On the other hand, gratitude is solely based upon our focus, which *is* controllable. You can be happy about your upcoming holiday *and* feel gratitude for the opportunity to travel to a foreign country, which has been at the top of your to-visit list. Or you can grieve the loss of a person close to you *and* be grateful that they were such an integral part of your life. It doesn't matter what emotions you hold at any time; you can always experience gratitude on top of them."

Willow's bark creaked and groaned as the tree moved. "So, to come back to your examples – you obviously won't be grateful for your car breaking down or for your house burning to the ground. But you can feel gratitude alongside the anxiety or sadness or grief or anger or whatever other emotion you're experiencing in these situations. When your car has engine trouble, you could be grateful that you noticed it in time before you crashed and hurt yourself or others. You could be grateful that you know a great auto mechanic who'll repair it in no time. Or you could feel gratitude because now you've got the great opportunity to finally buy the new car, which you've had your eye on for some time. Likewise, when your house burns down, you can feel gratitude that you and your loved ones got out safely. Or that you had a USB flash drive in your jeans pocket with files and photos that are not lost. You can feel grateful that you have insurance that will cover the costs. Or that you have nice neighbours who immediately offered to help you out."

Nayeli stared into space in thought. "But what if there's a situation where nothing at all is positive?"

"Something like that doesn't exist," Willow answered firmly. "No matter how dire a situation is at first glance, nothing is ever black and white. You'll never find something that's beneficial to everyone. Nor will you find something that's entirely bad. There are always grey areas in the middle, and you always have the choice to change your focus to look at the things that *are* positive about the situation you find yourself in.

"It can, of course, happen that you can't see a silver lining because you're too involved in the drama, but in that case you can simply ask someone else to help you shift your perspective. And when neither you nor an objective third party can think of a single thing to be grateful for, you can, at least, feel gratitude for the lesson you've learned. Cause you can be sure that everything that happens to you, without fail, is enabling you to grow and to become the person you are meant to be."

"You're trying to help me recognise that the glass is half-full instead of half-empty?" Nayeli questioned the tree.

"No," Willow said seriously. "I'm teaching you to see the glass as fully full. Even if it's only half-full of liquid, the other half is filled with air, isn't it? Which you should value. You humans can spend a few days without water, but no more than a few minutes without breathing in oxygen."

"Ha ha," Nayeli replied dryly. "Your analogies are getting worse, you know that?" But she said it with a smile.

Shifting around, she leaned back on her arms and let her gaze sweep over the gaps in the foliage above her and the blue sky beyond. "What I don't yet get is why you said that we can feel grateful in almost any situation. Why not in all? According to your explanation, I should be able to utilise gratitude at all times, no?"

"No. Gratitude is a great tool to help you, no question about that. And most humans don't use it nearly often enough. But gratitude is not the solution for everyone in every situation. To get my point, look at someone who's depressed, someone whose life is bleak and dark with no light at the end of the tunnel. To tell them to shift towards the positive blessings that could come out of their situation would be akin to giving someone a single grain of rice when they are starving. It would only increase their desolation and hopelessness. You can't spray water over the desert and hope a lake appears. You need to get out of the desert first to see that there are places that hold water."

"Ah, so the technique itself is useful but we need to assess when it's helpful for us and when not?"

"Indeed. In the end, that's true for every single lesson and technique I tell you about. They're all helpful for everyone *but* at different times. After all, we're all on different sections of our journey."

Nayeli blew out her cheeks. "Why is this whole spiritual business so hard, Willow? I feel that, no matter how long I study these subjects, I'll always do something wrong because there's too much to consider ..."

"I'm aware that it can all be confusing at first," Willow said in a soothing tone. "But you'll get there, don't worry. The more you practise, the easier everything will become. Just take one step after the other."

"Are you kidding?" Nayeli asked incredulously. "I can't do this slowly. If there's one thing I don't have in abundance, it's time. I feel like it's running out faster than ever, the older I get. And I already fear it's not gonna suffice for me to achieve all my goals and dreams."

"My dear, I know that your human ego can get caught up in the illusion of passing time, but the only time that exists is eternity. And that's more than enough to achieve every wish you could possibly dream of."

"What do you mean with an illusion of passing time?" Nayeli

asked, playing with the edge of the blanket she was lying on.

"I mean that time does not exist," Willow said. "But before I delve further into this topic, let me first tell you a story about a tortoise who knows at least as much about time as I do, if not more ..."

17. Cherry, the Tortoise

Strix was getting tired. After having flown off from Crim, he'd headed south, hoping to spot the snowy owl on whose trail he had set out on. But as the woods had alternated with farmland, there had been no sight of her.

A few other animals he had met in the last days had crossed the snow owl's path and could direct him onward, letting him know that he was still flying in the right direction. But no matter how hard he tried to get more mileage out of his wings, he was always a couple of days behind.

By now, it was time for Strix to acknowledge two things: one, the snow owl had too much of a head start for him to catch up easily, and two, his aching wings were in desperate need of a rest.

Strix's last section of the route had included crossing some open water, with no place to stop. This made him all the happier to see a coast appear up ahead. Flying inwards, Strix followed a stream. The clear water of the river soon gave way to a swamp, surrounded by trees that were casting the place into shadow. Mosquitoes were buzzing around everywhere and the air felt damp and moist on his plumage.

Wondering if there was any suitable resting place here, Strix was relieved when he saw a medium-sized rock on the ground and promptly headed for it. Settling down on the stone, he folded his tired wings and closed his eyes with a contented sigh. But his rest was short-lived as an earthquake jolted him awake only seconds later. Feeling the rock beneath him shake and move, Strix opened his eyes, alarmed.

As he tried to get his balance, Strix unfolded his wings, ready to fly off until the ground would calm down once again. But before he could take to the air something made him stop dead in his tracks. The swamp around him wasn't affected at all by the earthquake, as neither the trees nor the water was moving.

Just then, Strix noticed that the rock he had landed on had grown four feet and a wrinkled neck and head, which was turned backwards to fixate him.

"Ah, a blind passenger," the female tortoise he'd landed on said, looking delighted. "It's been forever since I had my last one ..."

Stuttering in embarrassment, Strix managed to get out an apology. "I'm so, so sorry that I landed on your back. Are you all right? Did I hurt you? Damn, I must have been more tired than I thought." Bowing his head, Strix was gathering his remaining energy to take off from the tortoise when the old reptile spoke up.

"Stop! Where do you think you're going? You can't wake up an old lady and then be so impolite as to leave without having introduced yourself."

Strix felt his embarrassment increase at her reprimand. "My name is Strix. And I'm going to fly off now. I'm so sorry to have landed on you in the first place."

"Ah, balderdash and hogwash! You're doing no such thing. You, my owl friend, are staying exactly where you are. Don't move a muscle. Is that understood? Look at you. You're so tired that you're practically swaying, and there isn't even a breeze. My, you young ones push yourself past all your limits, don't you? But where are my manners? Excuse me! It's nice to meet you, Strix. My name's Cherry. But all my close friends call me Chérie. They got that from my late partner Turquoise. He was returned to the wild by humans after he spent his first years in a French zoo. At least, that's what he called it.

Anyway, he had some strange customs and a funny accent, which is why he butchered my name. But I grew to like it and then it stuck. Oh, but I'm blabbering on about myself here, and you surely don't care to hear the life story of an old lady like me."

Strix waited out the tortoise's long monologue. Cherry tended to pause between each sentence and took her time to pronounce each of her words clearly, letting them ring out and listening after them, as if an echo would somehow complete her speech.

As tired as he was, Strix feared that he would be lulled to sleep by her voice. But when the tortoise stopped and watched him expectantly, Strix shook off his drowsiness to clear his mind. "So, Mrs Cherry—" he got out before learning that the tortoise could also talk incredibly fast if she wanted to, as she quickly interrupted him.

"Shh, none of that Mrs stuff!" Cherry interjected. "I'm not exactly fresh out of the shell, but being called Mrs makes me feel older than I am. And didn't I just tell you that my friends call me Chérie? That applies to you too, young Strix."

Despite her admonishing words, her tone was gentle and her eyes gleamed with humour.

Strix inclined his head. "Chérie, then. Do you really not mind me sitting on your shell? I'm quite heavy, after all."

"Heavy?" Cherry laughed. "Please, you're a featherweight. I can carry imps like you around for ages without a problem. It was only you landing on my back that jostled me a little. If my shell wouldn't be so sensitive, I wouldn't even have realised that someone had knocked on my door, so to speak. Don't worry, though, I'm happy to welcome any visitors I get. It happens seldom enough in my old age. But who can be faulted for that, heh? No one wants to hang around with a wrinkly old granny. The young ones have much better things to do. I mean, a dapper, fit bird like you can have any lady he wants, isn't that right?"

Feeling himself blush under her intense eyes, which raked up and down over his figure, Strix cleared his throat. "Eh, are you flirting with me?" he asked, surprised.

"I very well might be. I would be stupid not to when I'm face to face with such a cutie, no? What? Do you think we become blind with age?"

"No, of course not." Strix grinned playfully, bowing low in true gentleman mode. "But it is I who is overwhelmed at having the pleasure of making your acquaintance, madam. For your beauty and grace are out of this world, and you look as fresh as a flower in spring."

Laughing out loud, Cherry jerkily moved her head back and forwards. "Aw, you're an enchanter, darling. I think I'll never let you go if you carry on giving me compliments like that – even if plenty of them are lies. My wrinkles and crinkles are silent witnesses of all the years I've watched pass me by."

Strix cocked his head to one side as he answered. "That may be true. But I think that they suit you. They add a depth and wisdom, which is hard to find in this fast-paced world."

"Now it's decided," Cherry said, determined. "You'll have to stay here with me until the end of my days and whisper sweet nothings in my ears all the time."

For a split second, Strix worried that the tortoise meant what she was saying. But then he was soothed by the sparkle of laughter he saw in her eyes. Playing along with his host, he winked at her. "All right, then. I'm ready to spend my future with you. Where are all your friends? We've got to tell them the good news."

The tortoise grimaced. "No way are they gonna meet you – or you them. Why give them the chance to steal you from me? Nope. We old ladies are anything but slow when we find fresh meat. Because when all is said and done, we don't have a lot of time left, do we?"

Laughing loudly, Strix's next question slipped out before his brain caught up with his beak. "How old are you anyway?" Quickly biting his tongue as he remembered his mother scolding him that it was rude to ask a female their age, Strix would have done anything to take the words back. But it was too late.

Luckily for him, Cherry didn't make a big deal out of his question, though. She giggled merrily and lowered her voice. "I'll have my 89th birthday soon."

Still embarrassed to have asked about her age in the first place, Strix decided to make up for his blunder. "Since that's merely 87 years older than me, I do see a chance for us," he joked. "It's not that much of an age difference, after all ..."

When Cherry joined in his laughter, her whole body shook, including the shell Strix sat on. "You're not only a pretty owl, but a witty one, too! What a catch!"

Strix meant to give back the compliment but his answer was lost in a yawn, as he was unable to keep his tiredness at bay any longer.

"You are exhausted," Cherry stated the obvious. "Which isn't surprising, considering it's the middle of the day. Aren't you owls asleep at this hour?"

"Often, but not always," Strix replied, impressed at her knowledge of his species. "You are well-informed about us, aren't you? How come?"

"I know an awful lot about almost everything," Cherry said.

"That's the best thing about getting old. You can add all kinds of facts to your tomes of awareness and wisdom. Which reminds me, I haven't learned a lot of new things today – something you can change. Tell me, why are you flying around at this hour and where are you flying to?"

"I'm travelling to see the world," Strix said. "And because I'm in a bit of a hurry currently, I flew the last two days without barely any pause. Which proved to be too much for my wings. And my senses. Hence my little mistake earlier. If I'd been more awake, I'd have noticed that you are way too pretty to be a rock, my lovely Chérie."

"Smooth ending you did there." Cherry's eyes twinkled. "But tell me, why were you in such a hurry? There should be enough leisure during your travelling to enjoy your surroundings and to stop and meet others, don't you think? What fun is it otherwise to see all these places if you don't take the time out of your day to savour them? Have you never heard the saying that the journey is the destination?"

"I agree with that," Strix said and yawned a second time. "And I usually take things slower. But I'm following a snow owl, who I want to catch up with. You haven't met her by chance? She must have come through here at some point."

"No, I can't say that I've seen her. But tell me, who is she? Your lover?" The tortoise bobbed her head sadly. "And here I thought you would be different from all the other males. I thought you'd be faithful to me. We've known each other how long? A couple of minutes? But you're already looking forward to having an affair with another owl. Or do you intend to break up with me for good?"

Grinning, Strix shook his head. "Never! A mere snowy owl could never have my heart because, alas, I've already given it to you. I'm just following her because I would love to talk to one of my distant cousins after weeks of not seeing another owl."

The answering grin on Cherry's face upon hearing these words made her wrinkles emerge even more prominently. "I'm so relieved to hear that I'm the only one for you. And in that case, I could ask a few of my friends if they've met her?"

"That would be lovely," Strix said in the midst of another beak-splitting yawn.

"And you, my young Strix," Cherry continued sternly, "will take a nice long nap in the meantime. You know what? Why don't you sleep on my back? I can speak to my friends while giving you a ride. This way you don't have to fly the whole distance. How does that sound?"

"That sounds heavenly," Strix said, dumbfounded by Cherry's generous offer. "You'd do that for me?"

"Sure," the tortoise said as she stood up. "You simply need to tell me in what direction you were heading."

Doing as asked, Strix bowed his head in thanks once more, relieved not to have to search for another resting place. "Thank you, Chérie. That's very kind of you."

"Ach, nonsense. And now find a snug place to perch, my charming little Strix, because your transport will start in three … two … one … now."

Cherry moved forward, mindfully setting her feet onto the ground and turning southwards.

Standing precariously on the tortoise's shell, it took Strix a short moment to find his balance, but the steadiness of Cherry's steps made it easy for him to adjust to the rocking movement. Settling down in the middle of her back, Strix ruffled his feathers and looked at his surroundings with bleary eyes. The last thing he saw before he closed them was a small hill in front of them with a lone tree standing on top of it – not unlike his friend Willow, so many miles away.

His mind having made the connection when falling asleep, Strix was soon dreaming of his home. Of Willow standing tall and proud on the hilltop, of the brook meandering through the landscape and of the woods behind the meadow, where Nuktia lived. In his dream, Strix rode on a calm breeze over a flowery field. And Nuktia flew right beside him, so close that the tips of her right wing touched his left and their shadows intermingled on the ground below. They flew like this forever, enjoying the relaxed silence between them as the sun slowly gave way to the moon and stars, and as the heat of the day cleared the way for the cooler night's breeze.

Just when the full moon was painting its picture across a lake they were flying above, Strix woke up.

He needed a few seconds to remember that he was half a world's journey away from his home meadow and from both Willow and Nuktia. The sadness of not having them around hit him full force. To distract himself from that feeling, Strix gazed around and noted that he was still sitting on Cherry's shell, being carried over the muddy ground. What he hadn't expected, however, was how long he must have slept. For the day had turned into evening and the first stars had become visible in the gaps between the tree's crowns.

Yawning heartily and stretching, Strix looked more closely at his surroundings. At the swampy water to his right and at the small hill with the lone tree sitting on top of it behind them.

Freezing, Strix opened his beak in a silent gasp. The hill with the lone tree looked exactly like the one Cherry had set out to climb at midday when he had slipped into sleep. And they'd passed it by. But only by a few feet.

"Chérie?" Strix asked, feeling his way forward. "That hill there – is this the one that was right in front of us when I fell asleep? Or is the landscape here identical, everywhere you turn?"

"Ah, you are awake again, lazybones ..." Cherry said, craning her neck backwards to glance at him. "Good evening. You slept for so long that I was worried you might have crossed over to the other side. Not that I would deny you the pleasure of going there, but carrying a dead body around on my back was not how I imagined my last years would go. It's not becoming to smell of rotten flesh."

"And why is it," Strix added another question, "that you seem to have lost quite a bit of your charm in the last hours? You were a whole lot nicer before I went to sleep. But maybe that was me dreaming?"

"If next time you dreamed about me instead of a cute owl called Nuktia, I'll be more charming when you wake up," Cherry responded. But her eyes twinkled as cheekily as ever as she said so.

Remembering his dream, Strix coughed. "Um, did I talk in my sleep? What did I say?"

Cherry gave a perfect expression of feigned outrage. "Nothing much apart from her name – over and over again. But you made it pretty clear that you like polygamy and that I'm not the only female in your life. Or heart. Were you planning to ever tell me about her, you little Casanova?"

"There's nothing to tell, Chérie. I can promise you that the owl I dreamed about is not my mate." It was with a softer tone of voice that he added the next words: "She definitely isn't."

"Things can always change," the tortoise responded, suddenly serious. "Don't give up hope yet. Any owl would be lucky to have you as a partner."

"No, no, you got this wrong," Strix defended himself. "I'm not in love with her. Why would I be? Just because she's been my friend since forever and she's funny and smart and pretty doesn't mean, I have romantic feelings for her. It would destroy the great bond that we have – that we had …"

"Had?" Cherry asked, unable to hide her curiosity. "Did something happen between the two of you?"

"Apart from the fact that she told me she had fallen in love with me out of the blue? Nope, nothing else happened," Strix said uncomfortably.

Smiling knowingly, Cherry swayed her head from side to side. "Ah, I see! That's why you had to go on that world trip of yours, is it?"

"There's nothing to *see*," Strix said. "She's a friend. There was never anything more between us, there isn't now, and there will never be."

"Relax," Cherry said in an appeasing tone. "You don't need to bite off my head. I'm sure it is exactly as you say. You know best what your feelings are for this mysterious young owl, after all."

"Damn right," Strix replied fiercely. Then, hearing after his words, he cringed at his own tone. "Sorry, I didn't want to come across so severe."

"It's all right," Cherry said.

Strix wasn't sure if she was speaking the truth, though, because the tortoise quickly averted her gaze to look ahead. Feeling bad for having ruined the flirty atmosphere between them, he could have kicked himself.

Working out an apology inside his mind, Strix was just about to give voice to it, when Cherry brought the conversation back onto safer ground.

"By the way, regarding your question from earlier, yes, this is the hill we saw. Why are you asking? You didn't believe I would be that fast, right? Admit it. Ha, I'm used to surprising everyone with my speed. I'm the fastest tortoise around here – not even younger ones can keep up with me."

Not knowing if Cherry was joking or being serious this time around, Strix coughed loudly to cover his laughter. "Em, yeah. I'm surprised," he said, in the most neutral tone he could manage. And it was the truth. Because he'd had no idea that an animal as big as Cherry could walk this slowly.

But the tortoise either didn't notice or chose to ignore Strix's underlying irony. "I'm sure I could have reached that tree over there, too," she added, pointing with her head to a mangrove that stood close by, "but then I met a couple of friends and took a few breaks to gossip with them. You slept right through all of that, by the way. Sadly, they couldn't help with your mysterious snowy owl. But they did have some other interesting news to share ..."

Strix perked up, always enjoying a bit of the latest gossip. "Like what?"

"The moth I met, for example ... He's the great-great-great-great-great-great-great-great-great-great-great-great-great-great-great – where was I? – anyway, he's a descendant of the first moth friend I ever made when I was little. He told me he's found a new flame in his old age and he's head over heels in love with her. In his old age, he said ... can you believe that? He was only born earlier this year. I would have asked him more about her, but his kind is always so hectic, fluttering around here and there, never taking the time to sit down and talk for a few days. What kind of life is this where you are constantly in a rush, I ask you?

"Anyway, afterwards I met another friend of mine, a mouse-deer. She told me that her latest young one has just been weaned. That's her ninth fawn since I've known her ... they're really doing their best to breed like the rabbits. Not that I judge them, mind you. To each their own. I simply don't get why she's not enjoying motherhood for longer. If I could give birth like their species and breastfeed my young, I'd prolong that time for as long as possible. The world already moves so swiftly – we don't have to match it, do we? Life is not a race. You don't win if you arrive at death the fastest."

Shifting his weight to a more comfortable position, Strix cocked his head to the side. "Do you think I should slow down, then? Should I stop chasing after the snowy owl? Cause I've wondered about that myself. I've questioned whether it's a waste of time to follow a phantom. But – and I don't know why – it somehow feels as if it's part of my destiny to meet up with her. It feels important for some reason."

Cherry's eyes twinkled with something that could be merriment or hidden knowledge. "You might not be aware of the answers right now, but give it some time and they'll come to you. And if it's part of your destiny to meet up with that snowy owl for whatever reason, it will happen. At the right time. You can never be too late for that meeting, no matter how many weeks or months you need to find her, and no matter how many rests or detours you take."

Thinking about that, Strix inclined his head. "You're probably right," he said, heaving out a sigh. "I know I need to stop pushing my body beyond its limits, either way."

"And I," the female tortoise said abruptly, stopping midstride, "know that this is the perfect time to catch a few hours of sleep. Which I really deserve after my strenuous journey today."

Strix grinned as he thought about the short distance Cherry had covered, which he would have been able to travel in less than a minute. He marvelled – not for the first time – how time could be perceived so differently by two beings living on the same planet. But then he was startled out of his thoughts as the tortoise lay down where she stood, making Strix lose his footing on her back.

Opening his wings, he wobbled for a beat or two before finding his equilibrium again. His stomach chose this moment to growl in hunger.

"And I also know," Cherry continued, speaking in the slow ebb and flow of words that was in her nature, "that it would be a good time for you to find yourself a snack."

Not having noticed how famished he was until now, Strix felt a gnawing sensation in the pit of his belly at Cherry's words. And yet Strix hesitated.

"What's the problem?" the old tortoise asked, picking up on his reluctance.

Shrugging uncomfortably, Strix looked off into the distance. He couldn't help but feel a twinge of sadness as he realised his inevitable farewell from Cherry loomed over him. Although he'd got used to saying goodbye over the last couple of months, he hadn't felt this unwilling to move on in a while. He liked the tortoise and the way she made him feel.

"It's just that ... leaving you is one farewell I'm not looking forward to. Even in this short time I've known you, you've become an important part of my life."

"Time is irrelevant when it comes to the matter of the heart." Cherry smiled wisely. "But don't be sad, my little Strix. Us saying goodbye is what we need to do, to allow us to say hello again, isn't it? And what could be better than that?"

"Right," Strix said, not convinced that he could see the situation this positively. Nevertheless, he knew that prolonging something didn't reduce its pain. So, taking heart, he soared up into the air and circled above the tortoise. "In that case, I promise to come back in the future and share all my adventures with you. It will be my turn to tell you some gossip."

"That it will," Cherry laughed, and her wise old eyes crinkled up even more. "And now, let the wind carry you wherever you need to go next. Trust the flow. And take your time – one flap after another."

Heeding her advice, Strix turned south and looked back at the tortoise one last time, before his view would be blocked by the trees.

Cherry had already withdrawn her head into her shell and did her best to imitate a stone once again.

Smiling nostalgically, Strix averted his eyes. He was filled with sadness at having to leave, but underneath the sense of loss was also a newfound hope that Cherry's view of the future would come to pass and that he'd not only find the snowy owl when the time was right, but that his wings would one day lead him back to the tortoise.

"Hearing this story was definitely time well spent," Nayeli joked. "But it doesn't answer all my questions. For example, why time doesn't exist. Cause in your story, it definitely did."

"Oh, time does exist in this 3D reality and you are subjected to it for as long as you are incarnated. But when you look at it from the source perspective, it's nothing else but an illusion. On the other side, there's no such thing as the linear space-time continuum we have here on Earth."

Out of the blue, Willow voiced a request. "Do me a favour and think back to your math classes at school."

"I'd rather not." Nayeli groaned, grimacing as if in pain. "It's always been one of my worst subjects."

But when Willow ignored her complaint, Nayeli resigned to her fate and squared her shoulders. "All right, What about it?"

"Can you remember being taught that every spatial extension has to have an end when it has a point of beginning? The same can be said about time. If it had a beginning, there would also need to be an end. But neither exists. And thus, eternity, which is at the base of this universe, is a single point inside which everything happens simultaneously."

"Okay, wow." Nayeli laughed. "I think my brain just somersaulted, trying to follow you there. It's so difficult to conceive ..."

Willow bobbed its branches up and down. "I can imagine. The human ego isn't particularly skilled at seeing anything outside the illusion it's stuck in. But that's not a problem. You simply have to grasp one thing – that time exists solely in the present moment."

Nayeli raked her fingers through her hair. "Since everything else you've told me so far has been true, I'm just gonna believe you on this one, Willow. But there's something else you *can* try to explain to me further, which my brain might be able to grasp. You say that this linear timeframe we live in is an illusion in order for our egos to put everything into neat little boxes labelled past, present and future. But if it were just our minds telling us that time exists, how can we measure it? How can I tell you that I've been sitting here underneath your branches for about three hours today? How can I tell you that the first day we met was Friday? And how can I tell you that I've been incarnated for thirty-three years in this body? And beyond that, how can we prove scientifically that every second takes as long as the next one?"

"Don't forget that there are multiple truths, my dear. That the objective truth from the universal standpoint says one thing does not imply it has to be true here, for anyone being incarnated. Since you live inside the illusion, everything that's part of it will seem real for you – so much so that you can measure and prove it scientifically. In some instances, the universal truth of timelessness can penetrate this reality, though. For example, when you notice that time flies, if you want to hold on to a moment. Or when it crawls by, if you want something to be over. It's your perception of time that creates it in the first place. And because of this, an objective timeline cannot exist outside of someone's subjective awareness of it."

"Are you saying that time is different for all of us?"

"Naturally. Do you think that every species perceives time as you do? That it is the same for a tortoise or a mayfly? It's not. When you enter a different awareness, the perception of time changes alongside it. And just like it differs between species, the perception of time can also differ between individuals. Often, older human generations will perceive time to move faster than younger people, for example."

"Yes, I've actually heard about that ... Since children learn many new things and aren't stuck inside a repetitive routine yet, their memories don't blend together, and this in turn lets them perceive the passage of time more slowly."

Leaning her head back against the tree's trunk, Nayeli closed her eyes as she tried to wrap her mind around the topic. But when her brain failed to grasp the concept of timelessness, she soon concentrated on another question, which she thought would be easier to tackle. "Willow, if time is only real for everyone incarnated that implies that, on the other side, no time at all passes between my birth and my death, right? Or between my grandma's death and my own, for that matter, although they could be decades apart here on Earth?"

"That's true, my dear. Since every life happens simultaneously – not to mention all moments inside these incarnations – what you might be most relieved to realise is that every goodbye is also an illusion. Some people will leave this physical dimension before you and some will still be here when you cross back over. But on the other side, without the illusion of time, you don't have to wait for anyone who's incarnated here because our souls are all there, connected eternally."

"That *is* comforting to know," Nayeli said. "I just wish I could experience something alike while being here: feeling connected to everyone I love, no matter if they are currently at my side or not."

"I know this reality can be incredibly painful at times," the tree replied empathically, "but remember that we created it like this for a good reason. The illusion of time is a necessity, not a luxury."

"Why? If we don't need it on the other side, why here?"

"We need the concept of time here because it gives us the delays we need when manifesting something."

"That's a stupid reason," Nayeli complained. "Why did we decide that we need to wait for the things we desire? It would be nice to have a huge pile of money, the moment I think of it …"

"And would it also be nice to have a robber mugging you because you walk down a dark alley and become afraid of such a thing happening? If things manifest immediately and there's no time buffer, they have to manifest in exactly the way you imagine them. There's no time to translate your energy into another track or to soften the blow. What you think is what you get. That's the status quo on the higher dimensions. You think of something there and it exists at that very moment. But imagine what this would look like down here. Since you humans aren't healed yet and many of you have no grasp of the Law of Attraction, the world would go haywire. Therefore, time is a gift that's given to you. A gift that makes you adapt and learn and change your vibrations along the way, so that you can manifest a better reality."

"I see …" Nayeli said, finally understanding the tree's point.

"But?" Willow asked, apparently sensing her unvoiced reservations.

Nayeli looked up. "I just thought about something else you implied earlier."

"Then out with it."

"Our souls have eternity at hand to achieve everything they want to learn, that's fair enough. But it doesn't help me in this incarnation, now does it? Cause I only have a limited amount of years to fulfil my desires and walk this soul-path prior to crossing back over and choosing another incarnation. And each of my days doesn't have more than 24 hours out of which I need to sleep and eat and work. Which means the amount of free time I have at my disposal is limited."

"That's correct. The illusion of time is not subjected to the Law of Abundance, simply because it is an illusion, not reality. But something else does exist abundantly and that's your choices to use your time however you like."

The tree fell silent and let a few seconds tick by. "I want you to do something for me, my dear Nayeli. Go back to your grandma's house, or wherever else you'd like to be, and spend the rest of the day as you want. Only eat when you feel hungry. Only go to sleep when you feel tired. And fill all the hours in between by following your desires."

"But the day is still young," Nayeli objected. "And there's a whole lot left you need to teach me ..."

"Yes, but nothing can be rushed. And this is a lesson right here, which you'll understand better when you experience the results first-hand. So please, do as I ask and then come back tomorrow morning and tell me what you learned."

Hesitantly agreeing, Nayeli left her blanket underneath Willow's crown and walked across the meadow, back towards her grandma's house. The whole way, Nayeli thought about what she would like to do, now that she had this much free time on hand, but she wasn't any wiser when she reached the front door. Or when she walked into the living room that was in disarray, with dozens of moving boxes stacked in front of the sofa.

***

Close to two hours later, Nayeli arrived back at the meadow and sat down on the blanket beneath Willow's crown.

"You're back," the tree greeted her neutrally. "Tell me, what have you done?"

"First, I thought about helping with packing my grandma's belonging. But since you made it clear that today I'm only supposed to do what I like that was against the rules. Which is why I tried to read a book I brought along, but I couldn't concentrate on the story. And when I became restless, I took the bus into the city because I felt like seeing something else than this town for a while. But then, when I arrived, nothing seemed right. I didn't want to go shopping or sightseeing or anything else. And when I asked myself, what I wanted to do instead, the answer came as clear as day. To come back here and hear more of your stories."

The tree bent forward. "And you shall. But first, share with me what this time away taught you."

"I'm not sure," Nayeli muttered. "But based on the fact that I was bored and didn't know what to do with all these hours – maybe that we have more time on our hands than we realise in our busy day-to-day lives? I mean, on a normal working day, I'll constantly say how little time I have – and that's definitely true. I jump out of bed in the morning and rush to do everything I need to do prior to work. Then I'll spend eight plus hours in the office, slaving away for someone else. And when I get home, I have to cook and wash up and go grocery shopping and do all the other chores piling up. In short, I barely have any time to relax. Add to that the fact that I'm exhausted in the evenings and that all I can do is to collapse in front of the TV and zap through some shows that don't really interest me, and the day is gone. It's sad when I think about it. Neither do I have enough energy to meet my friends as often as I'd like nor do I have any zest to pursue my hobbies. And the next day is a repeat of the one before. Honestly, Willow, I'm living for the weekends and holidays. Or am I doing something wrong? Can you tell me how I can improve my life and get more out of my days?" The last part Nayeli said hopefully, not yet daring to believe that such a solution existed.

"Initially, that wasn't what I wanted to tell you with this exercise. But if you want, I can give you some pointers on that, too. To begin with, you need to take a close look at what you do each day and where you lose valuable minutes and hours. Throw these tasks out of your calendar or delegate them to someone else who actually enjoys doing them."

"But that's the thing," Nayeli said indignantly. "I can't stop doing any of those tasks. Nothing I listed is unnecessary. I need to go to work unless I win the lottery. And I do need to clean my home. And I do need to eat and sleep."

"That's might be true, but you don't need 24 hours to do all of it, do you? Let's say you need eight hours of sleep each night and you need ten hours for work, including breaks and commuting. Add another two for doing the housework and any other necessary things like eating. That still leaves four hours each day for leisure or for you to do something that interests you. Now, do you make the most of these four hours? No? That's because you have included time-wasters in your daily routine."

"Of what kind?" Nayeli wasn't able to come up with a single thing that took up that much time.

"Why don't you tell me again, in detail, what you do each morning before leaving for work? Maybe then we'll find one or two of them," Willow suggested.

"All right," Nayeli agreed and started to list everything in order. "I get up. I brush my teeth and take a shower. Then I eat breakfast while scrolling through my e-mails and the messages on my social media accounts. After that, I make my lunch, pack up everything I need and drive off to work."

"And how long do you scroll through your social media channels?" Willow asked, interested.

"Not that long," Nayeli defended herself. "Not more than about fifteen minutes. I'm not a phone addict, unlike some other people I know."

"It might not be more than fifteen minutes each day, my dear. But if you do that every day, you spend close to two hours in a week doing nothing else. In a month that's about seven and a half hours. And over the course of a year, that's more than ninety-one hours! Think about how many pages you could write in that time. Or how you could eat dinner with your friends every week instead. And this is only fifteen minutes each morning, not counting the other three hours and forty-five minutes that you lose by zapping through TV shows or doing other things that are not important to you."

"I see what you mean," Nayeli said. "When I fill my life with things that don't really interest me, I'll feel as if I'm wasting my time. But as I previously said, sometimes it's not even a lack of time preventing me from doing things, but a lack of energy."

"There's little difference, as a lack of energy often tells you that you have deviated from your soul-path and you're not making the most out of the time you have. Look at it like this: Loads of people want to improve their work-life balance, as they call it. This isn't an optimal solution, though. A better option would be to fuse your profession with whatever brings you joy. If you let your happiness be your guide and find a job you love doing and which fulfils you, then pleasure would already be part of your working life. And by doing what you love, day in, day out, you'd remain energised and could use your free time to do any of the other things you desire to do."

Willow paused. "This is where we come back to the reason for your little exercise. No matter how long each of your incarnations lasts, it's important to prioritise your time. And to fill your life with things that are part of your purpose and that make you feel good. There's actually a widely known illustration concerning this, involving a glass, some large rocks and sand. The glass is your life, the rocks are everything that you love doing and the grains of sand are the tasks that don't bring you any joy. Now, when you fill the glass up with sand, that's all you'll have at the end of your lifetime. But if you fill it up with rocks first, you can still fill the gaps in between with sand that represents all the tasks you dislike but which you can't delegate."

Nayeli inclined her head. "At least I can comprehend this, not like all the eternity stuff from earlier, which totally blew my mind."

Willow chuckled. And when the tree answered, its voice was as cheeky as a child's who had stolen a cookie from the cookie jar. "Then maybe you'd like an opportunity to challenge your mind some more?"

"With what?"

"With the fact that there's not only eternity to consider, but that we also live in a multiverse with an infinite number of alternative realities ..."

"What are you talking about, Willow? Are you saying that there are other planets and solar systems that we don't know about yet?"

The tree vibrated with energy. "No, I'm getting at the fact that there are layers of parallel realities that exist alongside each other, based on the countless potential life paths of all living beings."

"Er, can you give me an example?" Nayeli asked hesitantly, not understanding a single word the tree said.

"Sure, imagine that you decide to get a takeaway pizza before you go home to your mother and uncle this evening. This is one decision out of many you could make. Another decision you could make is to get some sushi. Or you could go straight to your grandma's home without getting any takeout. Or let's say that you fulfilled your wish to get a dog and picked out a Labrador at the shelter. You could have decided on a poodle from a breeder instead, or a cat or a hamster, or no pet at all. Humans make decisions and take actions all the time. And each time you do, you exclude all other eventualities from becoming your reality inside this dimension. But the universe isn't limited to one life path. It sees the potential of all decisions made by all souls and wants to experience them all. So it does. Every time you decide on something, countless other alternative versions of you exist in parallel realities, which choose differently."

Nayeli gasped at this new revelation but was prevented from asking a question when the tree resumed speaking. "There are billions of parallel realities that resemble the one you live in and are only differing slightly by little decisions you make each day. Then there are some that differ a great deal because you had different childhood traumas in them or met other soulmates you haven't met here. And last but not least, there are alternative realities that were created so early – long before your ancestors incarnated on Earth – that they are starkly different from this world. Realities where a linear timeline does not exist, realities where physical matter and bodies do not exist and realities where none of your known physical laws exist. And, of course, all varieties of realities in between."

"Wow," Nayeli said, taken aback.

"You know what the best thing is about these parallel realities, though?" Willow asked, providing the answer itself. "You can travel between them. In fact, you do that regularly without realising it."

"Excuse me?" Nayeli laughed. "We humans can do a lot. But if you're insinuating that we have time-travel machines or any such thing, I have to disappoint you. These only exist in science fiction novels, not in real life."

"No, I mean a subtler form than sitting inside a machine," Willow answered. "To understand this, you have to know that every single reality has a unique frequency, the same as any incarnated being living in it. And when you change your frequency, you automatically shift into a reality that's once again a match to you. Saying this, you obviously don't wake up in another reality where your history never happened or where a continent is wiped off the map. Instead, you will be in a reality that closely resembles your last one: a world in which you won't perceive any big changes with your physical senses or your mind, but in which you might notice small differences when you tune in energetically.

"You know the days where nothing goes right and you got out of bed on the wrong side? Where you get stuck in a traffic jam on the way to work, spill your coffee down your shirt and are generally in a bad mood all day? During those days your frequency is lower than usual, just like the reality you woke up in. On the other hand, on a day where you are full of energy and everything goes smoothly, you hold a higher frequency, the same as the reality you've moved to."

"These shifts only happen at night then?" Nayeli questioned.

"No, that was simply one example. You are also moving into different realities during your waking hours. Which is most noticeable when you are having a déjà-vu. You could see these as a glitch that exists between the different realities, which makes you experience a moment twice."

Willow shifted its branches together in front of Nayeli's face before moving them apart, creating a gap through which Nayeli could observe the meadow. "And isn't this great news? That you can travel between realities and through time? Without needing to invent any strange gadgets first?"

Nayeli squinted as a ray of bright sunlight shone into her eyes. "I don't know, Willow. It sounds pretty far-fetched, if you ask me. And, even if it were true, it's not like this would help in any way, would it? Since we can't really control where we travel to?" Raising her head, Nayeli pointed at the tree. "And why travelling through time? You haven't said anything about us being able to move back and forth to the past or future while jumping realities."

"Oh, you can definitely travel through time. You can, for example, travel to any future possibility and watch what the outcome would look like for you."

"Future possibility?" Nayeli asked, feeling as if her brain was fried by all the mind-boggling concepts the tree was throwing her way.

"Yes, the future is never set in stone. It's rather an endless sum of options. Which is why no one can predict it for sure. What some people *can* do is to look at the streams of possibilities and tell which life path is the most likely to be taken in this dimension, based on where you currently stand. But with every decision and action you take, you can change that course and another possibility can replace the one that was the likeliest to happen thus far."

A few birds were twittering as they flew over the meadow and Willow remained silent until they had passed.

"Yet another reason to travel through time is to revisit your traumas in order to heal them. You essentially travel back to the moment they happened and change the outcome of the situation that created the wound in the first place."

"Tell me about that," Nayeli demanded, keen to hear more on this subject.

"Soon," the tree promised. "But there are still some other topics I need to tell you first."

"For example?" Nayeli looked at the sky, noticing the passage of time by the sun's steady descent. "Because, speaking of the illusion of time, I have only enough left to hear one more story tonight."

The tree raised some of its branches, one after the other, as if counting with them. "I could tell you about thoughts and how they work. Or maybe you'd first like to hear about changes and how they influence your life?"

"I don't know what I want to hear," Nayeli replied. "The sole thing I know is that I want it to be an important lesson because I don't have nearly enough time left inside this incarnation and I need to get a move on if I want to awaken further."

The tree shook its branches. "My dear, even if you wanted to, you can't control how fast you move along this ascension path of yours. And, I believe, the best way to explain this further would be to tell you about kundalini energy."

"Kunda ... what?" Nayeli asked. "I've never heard of that. What is it?"

"I could tell you what it means. Or I could first tell you a story about someone who's the epitome of kundalini energy."

"The story first, please," Nayeli requested and closed her eyes, letting herself be transported into another place and time by the tree's gentle voice.

18. Rainbow, the Snake

Strix was hiding inside a thorny bush in the Australian grasslands, cursing the fact that he'd ever come here.

The moment he had reached the coast he had been accosted by some saltwater crocodiles and, as if that hadn't been bad enough, his current predicament was even worse. Peeping out between two twigs in front of him, Strix saw that the female snake was slithering towards him through the long blades of grass, which were moving in the warm breeze. Terrified of the reptile and her sharp fangs, which glittered in the light of the sun, Strix took an involuntary step backwards, only to feel a warm draught of air on his tail feathers, which now stuck out on the other side of the bush. Jumping forward to draw them back into his pitiful hideout, he noticed that the move brought his beak dangerously close to a gap in front of him, where the branches were growing sparsely.

Watching the reptile move closer, Strix wished himself anywhere but here. But there was no escape: the thorny bush he had chosen as a shadowy sleeping spot to wait out the hottest hours of the day had turned into his prison, as it prevented him from quickly opening his wings and flying off.

He had known, from his experience in Africa, that he couldn't stay out in the bright sun for too long if he didn't want to risk another heatstroke, and this shady place had seemed like the best option to rest until the night closed in. A choice he regretted now as his ragged breaths proved.

On closer inspection, the brown snake moving towards him looked hurt – maybe from a past fight – as a few pieces of skin hung loosely from her body. That didn't comfort Strix in the slightest, though, because he knew that a wounded animal could be even more dangerous than a healthy one.

Unable to avert his gaze from the reptile, Strix's beak clacked as he trembled in fear. Meanwhile, his mind was filled with all the stories about venomous snakes his mother had told him when he was little. Stories about how futile it was to escape these reptiles if they'd got as close as the one before him. Stories about how painful it was to be bitten. And stories about the slow death that followed.

What he could not recall, however, was how to find out if a snake was venomous or not. And having no idea whether the reptile in front of him belonged in that category only reinforced Strix's panic.

The brown snake chose this moment to halt a mere inch from him, raising her head sensually while the split tongue flickered out to taste the air.

Strix huddled down and closed his eyes, hoping against hope that the snake hadn't noticed him and that it was simply a coincidence that she'd stopped here.

But the female reptile promptly shattered his silent prayers "Get out of there, birdie," she sing-songed, "Or you'll become good friends with my teeth and the venom in them ..."

As Strix opened his eyes and looked out, the iridescent slits of the snake's eyes bore straight into his own with a scary intensity, shimmering in all colours of the rainbow and nailing him to the spot.

"I-I-I taste awful. And I'm skinny. I haven't eaten in days." Strix quickly choked the words out. And when that didn't help, he bypassed all the reasons he could think of and opted for plain begging. "Please don't kill me. Please!"

The brown snake didn't answer right away. Instead, she

rounded the bush, hissing all the while.

Strix trembled like a leaf. He reckoned that she would lunge forward and bite his back or one of his legs at any moment.

Eventually, the snake had completed her examination and come back around to face him, halting on the same spot as before. Then she lunged forward.

Hooting loudly in terror, Strix flinched, almost skewering himself on a thorn when recoiling backwards. But the female hadn't intended to bite him. Yet! Realising that the brown reptile was playing with him and his fear, Strix gulped two times after which he dared to look at the snake again. Something that wasn't easy with her unblinking gaze being fixed on him.

"Are you really venomous?" Strix asked as the snake drew her head back, his voice a squeaky whisper.

"I am." The reptile smirked. "And my hit rate is 100 per cent. If I want a piece of prey, I get it. But I'll make a deal with you. If you get lost in, let's say, five seconds, I'll spare you this once. If, however, you need a second longer, you'll feel my venom spread along your veins, paralysing you and crippling your nervous system. Your breaths will slow until no air at all passes into your lungs, leaving you gasping. And, aside from that, you will writhe in unbelievable pain that is still unknown to you. How does that sound?"

"Please," Strix begged, cowering even further into the bush.

"Five," the female started to count, unimpressed by his plea for mercy. "Four, three ..."

Spurred into action, Strix scrambled backwards and wormed out of the gap he had come through earlier that day. It was a tight fit, and he could feel thorns graze his sides, one of them catching a feather and ripping it out. But right now, Strix couldn't care less about that. He fell over his legs in his haste to get away from the brown snake, who watched his every movement out of cold, calculating eyes.

"Two and one."

Quickly flapping his wings, Strix lifted into the sky and out of harm's way.

The snake grinned smugly and slithered into the bush Strix had vacated.

"Hey!" Strix called out, irate, as he realised what had happened. "Are you serious? You drove me out of there because you wanted the place for yourself? You didn't even intend to bite me?"

"Don't get on my nerves, birdie," the female reptile snarled from inside the bush. "Go on, be off with you. Or I will reconsider and kill you, after all."

Strix huffed in annoyance at the nerve of the snake. But he told himself that it couldn't turn out well if he picked an argument with her. Especially since she held such a huge advantage over him with her venom.

Thus, grumbling underneath his breath, Strix turned southwards to continue his journey when he heard a voice calling out to him. Spotting a boulder not far away, he saw another brown snake on it, sunbathing. It looked very similar to the one that had evicted him from the bush, aside from the fact that this one was a male.

"I couldn't help overhearing what happened with Rainbow over there," the snake said, appearing to be friendlier than his kin. "Would you like to sit here with me instead? The stone is casting quite a shadow and you can sit behind it and wait there until the sun sets."

Flying above the place, Strix saw that the reptile was speaking the truth. There was indeed enough space for him to sit comfortably. And yet he hesitated. His gut instinct was screaming at Strix to stay as far away from any snake as possible. But then his mind switched on and called him a scaredy-cat. This reptile was obviously nice, and it wouldn't do to lump them all together just because he'd had one bad experience. Making his decision, Strix flew down and landed behind the stone on which the brown snake lay.

"Thank you," Strix said gratefully.

"No problem," the reptile answered dismissively.

"It sure was a problem for your cousin over there. I think you mentioned her name is Rainbow?"

"Yeah, but don't take offence. Normally, she isn't that aggressive or rude. The thing is, it's her time to be reborn and that process makes all of us extra-sensitive, which in turn makes us prone to anger to cover that up. We simply don't have the patience to deal with anyone else when we're going through a huge change. We need to conserve our strength for ourselves."

"Being reborn?" Strix asked curiously, his beak gaping in wonder. "Are you saying that she'll travel to the other side and choose a different body? Is this thorny bush where Rainbow has chosen to die in peace?"

At first, Strix couldn't place the weird hissing sound that emanated from the snake. But then it dawned on him that the reptile was sniggering. Strix felt outraged to be laughed at.

"Sorry," the snake said, but couldn't keep from hissing further. "But you birds are funnier than you think." Raising his head, he let his tongue flicker out. "To answer your question, no, we don't need to make that detour. We do something better. We release our old body and get ourselves a new one right here. One that's more robust and, at the same time, more flexible."

"You mean you change your skin, right?" Strix said as a flash of inspiration hit him. "I've come across old snake skins before that your kind has exchanged for new ones. But is it that difficult to do?"

"Yes, that's what I mean, and it's definitely not the most pleasant experience you could have. Not at the beginning, when the skin is stretched too tight but not quite ready to peel off yet. And not when it does peel off, but parts of it stay stuck to the new, sensitive skin underneath. It can be damn itchy and irritating. Which is why we stay hidden somewhere safe, quiet and preferably dark when we go through that process. And when we're bothered during that time, we can get quite volatile; I'm the first one to admit that."

"How long does that take?" Strix asked curiously.

"It depends. Usually only a couple of days. But it can take up to two weeks. By which time we're ravenous ..."

"Ravenous?"

"We don't eat during the time we moult," the snake declared.

Strix stared at the reptile, aghast. "You don't eat for two weeks? You must be joking. How the heck do you survive that long without food? That's impossible!"

"No, it's not," the male reptile answered lightly. "And I am living proof of that as I've undergone quite a few transformations in my life, already."

Strix was impressed by that revelation and wanted to probe further. But then he was distracted by the sidelong glance the snake was giving him. If he didn't know any better, he would have described the stare as hungry and something about it triggered a thought in his mind. But before Strix could grasp it, it was gone, which is why he concentrated on the next one instead.

"That certainly explains Rainbow's bad mood," Strix said compassionately, imagining what it must be like to spend entire days not only uncomfortable but starving. "But tell me, if this whole transformation business is so difficult, why do you do it in the first place? Why not keep the old skin? It has served you for a long time, after all?"

Laughing out loud in hissing waves, the snake looked him up and down. "You want the short answer or the long one?"

"Both?" Strix demanded smartly.

"Do you want to stay where you are your entire life, never learning, never growing, never evolving?" the snake shot back.

When Strix negated the question, the reptile grinned knowingly. "Ha, that's what I thought. The process might not always go smoothly, but something good comes from it when we dare to transform ourselves into a better version. Just like when we let the snake within us uncoil – the snake we all carry, no matter what species we decide to incarnate as."

Strix craned his neck around. "Was that the long or short answer?"

"The long one," the snake smirked. "The short answer would be that our skin gets too tight because it doesn't grow with us."

"Ah, of course," Strix said and yawned. Despite having rested the whole day, his fear had drained his energy, making him bone-tired.

"You can close your eyes if you want," the brown snake offered. "I'll keep an eye out for any dangers as long as you nap."

For a fleeting moment, Strix was convinced that the reptile was gazing longingly at his body. But then the snake's friendly smile and easy demeanour were back.

Strix blinked, surprised. If his eyes were starting to deceive him, he must be even more fatigued than he had thought. Or maybe, he considered, it was the sun at fault again and these were the first symptoms of heatstroke? Yet another reason to accept the snake's gracious offer to rest here and wait out nighttime.

"Thanks," Strix, therefore, said, grateful he had found such a nice specimen. He had already blinked his eyes closed when the thought that had evaded him earlier came back full force. Opening his eyes, he looked sideways at the male reptile, who was sunning himself on the hot stone, and cleared his throat. "Since you're being this nice to me, I presume you aren't anywhere near the time of your own change, right? In other words, you *are* currently interested in food?"

"I suppose." the snake responded dryly. "Why?"

"And when ..." Strix swallowed hard, "when did you last eat?"

"A while ago," the snake answered, uncoiling and keeping his eyes glued to him.

It was only his quick reflexes that saved Strix. He took off, not a moment too soon, as the snake catapulted himself forward, his jaws snapping shut a feather's width beneath Strix's feet.

Hooting, alarmed, Strix gained some height until he was out of range, in case the snake attacked again.

"What the hell?" he called out in a rage that was fed by his fear and shock. His anger was so immense that his vision was dotted with red spots as he glared at the reptile. "Is this your idea of hunting? Making conversation with your prey and lulling it into a false sense of security to then treacherously attack? How NICE of you!" His words dripped with sarcasm.

"Hey, don't judge me," the snake defended himself. "We all use the skills available to us to feed ourselves. And my repertoire happens to include intelligence."

“Intelligence, pah!” Strix spat. “I think ‘cunning’ and ‘guile’ are the words you were searching for. You snakes are all alike. I should have listened to my mum and given you all a wide berth. You slimy long worms!” It did Strix’s heart good to scream out his rage and fear, and so he continued to throw insults at the reptile, knowing he was safe from his fangs up in the air.

But then he realised he was facing an entirely different problem now. Although the sun was slowly descending and would soon give way to the cooler hours of the night, he still had a few miles to fly through snake-infested land. And, if what he’d heard about the size of this continent was true, he presumably wouldn’t be able to cross the whole distance in one night. Then, tomorrow, the hot sun would come out again, just as much of an enemy as the venomous reptiles if he didn’t find shade or water.

The knowledge that it would be best to make haste, combined with his subsiding anger, let Strix stop mid-rant. “Why do I even bother? You aren’t worth any more of my time.” Rising higher into the air, he turned towards the thorny bush once more, calling out loudly: “None of you are!”

Kundalini Energy and Chakras

"Wait, what?" Nayeli asked, much more interested in the snake's teachings than Strix had been. "A snake that's inside all living beings? What does that mean?"

"Kundalini energy," Willow said matter-of-factly, "is also called the serpent energy. And the mental image most spiritual people use to explain it is of a snake lying coiled at the base of the spine. A snake that's waking up and rising within you as soon as the kundalini energy is activated. Only that this image is wrong for one important reason. Since kundalini energy is simply prana – or life energy – it is present within everyone at all times. It is in each of your cells, in each of your chakras, in each layer of your aura, and it doesn't need to be activated in order to exist. It's, of course, true that you can't access all your powers and spiritual gifts like your clair-senses at all times. But that's because you have put up blocks within you. Blocks that prevent you from seeing or using these natural abilities."

"And what happens when we get rid of these blocks?" Nayeli asked curiously. "What if this kundalini energy can move freely?"

"Then it transforms you on every level – physically, emotionally, mentally and spiritually – by raising your frequency from the 3D to the higher 4D dimension. And this can either be a beautiful, amazing experience or a painful, scary one. Or both. Depending on how you look at it."

"It sounds amazing," Nayeli said, fascinated. "How can something like this be painful or scary?"

"It can be when some blocks remain and the kundalini energy hits traumas, wounds or any areas where a lower vibrational energy resides. Working through these can result in lots of different symptoms, ranging from emotional and mental ailments to physical pains. Depending on where the area is located, you might have problems remembering things or your emotions might overflow, which will make you feel depressed or anxious. You might have a bloated belly or headaches or skin problems or flu-like symptoms. Or you might have trouble sleeping or notice a lack of energy. The symptoms are as varied as each person ..."

"Then why the heck would I even want to *activate* this energy," Nayeli asked, "if there are this many side effects? Listening to you, I think I'd rather put it back to sleep. Or to influence it in another way that slows down or stops the entire process."

The tree let its leaves swing in the air. "First off, my dear, you can merely influence this process indirectly. The more you practise your spiritual abilities, the faster you'll reach the point where your kundalini energy becomes available to you in full. But that's as far as you can control it. And as for stopping it ... no, that isn't possible. Once awakened, there's no going back. It wouldn't happen if you could not deal with the experience, though. Even if you still have dense energy to work through and don't feel ready, it can only happen at the right time in regards to your own unique journey.

"Saying this, more and more humans are ready at this time than ever before. Since the world is now ascending into the 4D reality as a whole, so will a lot of incarnated beings. It's a landslide effect: the more people awaken, the higher the frequency of the combined consciousness will be, and the stronger the pull for others to follow suit. Which accelerates the whole process."

Nayeli narrowed her eyes. "And we just have to accept any side-effects?"

"There's no saying if you'll have any negative symptoms at all," Willow responded. "If you have healed many of your past traumas before your kundalini energy awakens in full, there will be few blockages left. And if there are any, you can weaken the symptoms by working with the energy instead of against it."

Nayeli looked up expectantly. "How?"

"By accepting the process and reducing your resistance towards it. In practice, that translates to eating healthy foods and to exercising regularly, to reduce stress and to get enough sleep. If you don't fight the process, you can even enjoy some of the amazing symptoms that can accompany the awakening of kundalini energy."

"Which are ...?" Nayeli asked, her interest piqued anew at this revelation.

"Everyone has different ones but some of the most pleasant symptoms I've heard about from humans are currents of energy running up and down your body, the sensation of your heart chakra expanding or the heightened ability to use your telepathic skills."

"Well, I already know how to do *that*," Nayeli said as she remembered the lesson on telepathy and how she had realised that she'd been using this skill prior to actually learning about it.

"That you do," the tree answered happily.

"Sooo, say I want to support this process – what techniques should I use to help this energy move within me?"

"Using any spiritual tool from meditation to training your clairsenses is helpful. But there's one integral part we haven't covered yet and that's working with your chakras."

"What are those, Willow? You've mentioned them a couple of times now ..."

"Remember what I told you about auras and that each of your

bodies has an auric field? Your chakras are the corresponding energy funnels to these. But let me start at the beginning ... Throughout your whole body are nadis – points which pass on the prana, or life energy, that flows through you. And these nadis are concentrated in some areas, which are then called chakras. They are the main energy centres in your body, which receive and circulate energy within you. You could visualise them as spinning funnels or as swirling vortexes. You have hundreds of those chakras and thousands, if not more, nadis – in your feet and hands and ears and everywhere else. But the seven main chakras are along your spine. It is through these that most of your energy travels.

"The first of these is your root chakra. It sits at the lowest point of your spine and corresponds with your physical body. It helps to keep you grounded and enables you to feel secure when it's healthy. At the level of your lower belly is your sacral chakra, which corresponds with your emotional body. It governs your emotions, creativity and sexuality. And at the level of your upper belly, where your diaphragm is located, sits your solar plexus chakra, which corresponds with your mental body. It is related to thoughts and logic and can help you achieve a healthy self-esteem and self-worth. These three are the lower or physical chakras.

"The fourth chakra is the heart chakra, inside your chest, which is concerned with the relationships in your life. It helps you to give – and receive – love and compassion. It is also the balancing chakra between the three lower chakras and the three higher ones, which correspond with your higher bodies.

"The first of these is your throat chakra, at the level of your throat. Above that is your third eye chakra, between your eyebrows, and your crown chakra, at the top of your head. Your throat chakra enables you to speak your truth, to be authentic and to communicate. Your third eye chakra helps you to visualise and to receive intuition, and your crown chakra connects you to your soul and the collective consciousness.

"Every chakra has its own tasks to fulfil. And it's important that they are all healthy and open so that energy can move freely through them."

"And how do I know that they are working right?" Nayeli asked. "Or how do I manage to open them if they are closed, or close them if they are too open?"

"There is no such thing as a chakra that's *too open*, my dear. You can't take in more energy than you can process. If a chakra is completely open, it simply means it's healthy and functioning. Now, when a chakra is almost shut and little amounts of energy moves in and through it, you'll notice this by being unhealthy yourself. In the case of your sacral chakra being blocked, you might have physical ailments relating to your womb, kidneys or bladder. Additionally, you might have emotional problems since this is the chakra that corresponds with your emotions. You might feel a lack of passion or sexual energy or you might have difficulty being creative."

Willow moved about. "It's normal in this time and age that the chakras of most humans are not as open as they should be. Some might even be almost fully closed and work only well enough to keep you alive, but not anywhere near healthy. Due to the many traumas you humans have accumulated, there are lots of blockages and leaks of energy within you – especially since few humans are aware of these energetic levels and they don't actively take care of them, like you take care of your physical bodies. But the good news is that anyone can learn to cleanse, heal and replenish their chakras, similar to how you can learn to cleanse, heal and replenish your auric fields."

"I can do that myself?" Nayeli questioned curiously.

"Yes. It's not difficult. The only thing you need to know is the corresponding colour of your chakra and its position in your body. The root chakra, for example, is associated with the colour red, while your heart chakra is green. To heal and recharge your root chakra, you envision a red flower at the base of your spine, which blossoms open and spins clockwise. And if you want to cleanse and charge your heart chakra, you envision a green flower at the level of your heart spinning clockwise and opening. The first time you do this might take a bit longer – because you aren't used to the technique yet and because, over the years, you've collected quite a few blocks. But the more often you work with your chakras, the easier it will become and the healthier they'll be."

Nayeli tilted her head sideways. "I'm sure you're right and that a lot of humans can do it. But I doubt that I can."

"And what are you basing that belief upon?" Willow queried.

Nayeli raised her chin. "I don't know. There isn't any real reason I can name. I just don't think I'm good enough to do it. And that I'd better find someone who's more experienced and talented at these things."

"You can choose to do that, of course," Willow said. "Energetic healers can help you cleanse your energetic field. But don't diminish your own power, my dear. You are so much more capable than you think you are. It's simply your negative focus, thoughts and beliefs that make you doubt yourself. Which is truly one of the main problems when it comes to humans: you can have the life you dream of, if only you learned how to interrupt the cycle of debilitating beliefs you are currently stuck in. But before I tell you more about this, I believe it's time for you to go home?"

Looking up at the darkening sky, Nayeli saw that the crescent moon was already visible between Willow's branches, framed by the first stars blinking into existence. She sighed regretfully, wishing she didn't have to wait until tomorrow to hear more. But she also knew that it wouldn't help to delay the inevitable.

***

The next morning, Nayeli let herself collapse underneath Willow's crown.

"Hey," she said tiredly in greeting. "I'm back."

The weeping willow tree let its leaves swoosh through the air, which felt stifling yet again. "I noticed. But you seem exhausted. Aren't you well?"

"I'm fine, it's just that I didn't sleep all that many hours," Nayeli mumbled. "My mind was racing with everything you told me yesterday, and I wasn't able to switch off my brain."

"Ah yes, thoughts ..." Willow chuckled knowingly. "They can be quite noisy sometimes; isn't that right?"

Nayeli nodded. "And I can imagine what solution you're gonna recommend in a minute – meditate and let them drift by."

"That's wise advice," Willow said cheekily. "Wherever did you get that from?"

Nayeli only grinned and poked the tree playfully.

"But no, that actually wasn't what I was going to say. Meditation has its benefits, but it's not the universal solution for everything. If you were to use this technique to ignore your thoughts – and what they're telling you – it would be a recipe for disaster in the long run. You know, you do need to listen to that little voice inside your head from time to time. But before I explain this in greater detail, let me first introduce you to Lemon and his beliefs on this topic."

19. Lemon, the Platypus

The stars began to fade – a sure sign that the night would be over soon.

After his narrow escape from the snake, Strix's mind had been occupied by one thought only: to put as much distance as he could between him and the crazy reptiles that lived here. But by now, he had flown for hours on end, and his strength was waning while his wings began to ache.

Resting was out of the question, though, unless he could find a safe place to close his eyes. Or another animal who was friendly enough to let him stay around, warning him of any approaching snakes in time.

Deciding to search out one such specimen, Strix let his gaze sweep over the eucalypt woodland spreading out beneath him. A small river wound itself through the landscape, and on both sides of it, grasses and shrubs grew between the trees.

While being on the lookout, he followed Crim's example and put into words what he needed. Although he wasn't quite as capable of using the Law of Attraction as the red panda, he figured that it couldn't hurt to ask the source nicely to help him. Composing the sentences inside his head, Strix finally spoke them out loud. "Please let the next animal I encounter be nice. Maybe more of a bird than a reptile ... Yes, yes, laying eggs alone is obviously not sufficient, since snakes do that, too. But if the animal lays eggs *and* has a bill that would be great. Or even a nice furry mammal, for that matter. But one on the smaller side, and maybe one who lives near the water. That way I can kill two mice with one claw since I'll have a place to appease my thirst. And for all that's holy, please don't let it be venomous!"

Repeating this wish continuously in his mind, he flew further south, following the river until he saw movement inside it. Strix focused on the area to see if the animal in question posed any danger to him. But to his immense relief, his prayers appeared to have been answered. Because the species he saw was a funny-looking bird with a broad, duck-like bill, which was diving underneath the surface and emerging shortly after.

Swooping down to observe the animal from up close, Strix landed on the bank. Some oddities immediately caught his eye. Instead of wings, this strange bird had four legs. And, as opposed to the feathers Strix had expected to see, it was covered in fur and had a tail that reminded him of a beaver, which didn't seem to fit the sleek otter-like body.

For a moment, Strix wondered if he had been scraped by the snake's teeth after all and if a tiny amount of the venom was coursing through his blood, making him hallucinate.

But then the otter-beaver-duck climbed out of the water and sat down beside him, where it shook itself.

Water droplets rained all around and Strix was hit by more than a few. The shock of the cold water made it unmistakably clear that he was awake and that the weird specimen in front of him was as real as the eucalyptus trees standing all around.

Up close, the animal looked even funnier. But Strix did notice that it had webbed feet, which seemed to prove his assumption that this was nothing else but a deformed duck. And besides, it was meeting all the requirements he had listed: or, at least, all that he could see. And that the animal was nice on top of that was proven true a second later when the stranger introduced himself.

"Hi, I'm Lemon. A platypus."

"A what?" Strix asked, perplexed.

Grinning, the weird creature sat down and emptied his cheek pouches onto the ground between them, pushing out shellfish as well as some gravel from the riverbed.

"A platypus. We're mammals. But we also have a lot in common with birds or reptiles – like the fact that we lay eggs, for example."

"You do?" Strix asked, amazed at his own manifestation power, feeling all limiting beliefs from earlier being spirited away on the breeze.

"We do," Lemon confirmed, using his broad duck-like bill to scoop up one of the shellfishes, along with a few small rocks. He munched on those, as if it was the most delicious feast. "Do you want something?" the platypus asked, pointing at the rest of the offerings lying between them.

Strix declined politely.

The male platypus shrugged and continued to eat while mumbling. "Sometimes I think that, throughout evolution, our ancestors simply took the best out of all worlds and now we're a combination of everything."

"You're unique, that's a fact," Strix agreed, amazed that the creature was obviously eating the pebbles additionally to the seafood. "I have travelled through a lot of countries now, but I've never seen an animal as curious as you." Strix looked off into the distance, feeling wistful all of a sudden. "Y'know, I sometimes wish I could be more special. Instead, I'm just a bird like any other ..."

"I'm sure that's not true," Lemon replied empathetically. "Everyone has special talents and abilities. And everyone can do things that no other can. The only question is, do you believe in yourself?

Your self-image influences your whole life, positively or negatively. If you tell yourself that you aren't special over and over again, that's exactly what your life will reflect to you. But if you truly believe that you deserve anything you ask for, that's what you'll see manifest."

"Maybe, maybe not," Strix said, uncertain. "Or maybe I'm just as average as I seem to be. I mean, I can fly fast and soundlessly but my aunt is faster, and my dad was the quietest owl I've ever known. He could creep up on any of us if he wanted. And even though I'm a great hunter and can detect the tiniest mouse under a deep pile of snow, my best friend from childhood usually hears them a second before I do." Strix let his forlorn gaze rake over the surrounding area, whispering the next words more to himself than to Lemon. "Nuktia deserves someone better than average, better than me ..."

"Is that the name of your partner? Nuktia?" Lemon asked, sounding interested, He scooped up another shellfish and some more stones.

Strix cocked his head. "What makes you think I have one?"

"I just figured, since you're the second owl who's come past in so many days, that you two belonged together. We normally never see your species otherwise."

Alert, Strix sat up. "You saw another owl? A white one?"

"Yes, yes, it was a snowy owl. But shouldn't you know that if you're travelling together?"

"We're not," Strix explained. "But I am trying to find her. Can you tell me where she went?"

"As far as I remember, she said she wanted to fly south to another continent she'd heard stories about. One that is as cold as the one she comes from up north, where snow and ice reign. Not a pleasant destination, if you ask me. But to each their own."

"Right, right," Strix said absentmindedly, already planning how to catch up with the female owl. "I've been on her scent for weeks, but every time I seem to get near her, she's moved on. I don't know what I'm doing wrong."

"Ah, but if you keep telling yourself that she's a few steps ahead, you'll never catch up with her," the platypus replied offhandedly before fixing him with a gaze. "Do you even realise how powerful your thoughts are and how much you could achieve if you changed the way you think?"

"Should I?" Strix asked.

"Why yes, it's important. Cause your thoughts shape your beliefs and your beliefs influence your whole life. Shall I tell you a story about an adventure I had, not long after I was born? I think that would shed some light on the topic ..."

"I'd love to hear it," Strix said, excited to learn something new. Fluffing up his feathers, he hunkered down comfortably and watched the platypus.

Lemon's eyes turned glassy, as if he was seeing the scene play out in front of his inner eye. "As I mentioned, I was young when it happened. My sister and I had just begun to venture out past our burrow and explore the surrounding area a day or two ago. Normally, our mum wouldn't have left us for long in our nest but an unfamiliar platypus had crossed into our territory and she needed to chase him away. Thus, we were unprotected and unguarded, apart from the shelter the burrow provided. Which was not preventing a hungry snake from coming inside, looking for prey."

"A snake?" Strix interrupted Lemon, hissing out the word. "These slimy long worms create havoc everywhere they slither!"

The platypus shrugged. "They live according to their nature, as we all do. Anyway, this snake entered our burrow and approached our nest. It must have sensed our movements and the warmth our bodies gave off. It could have devoured us with one bite and our lives would have been over in an instant – *if* it hadn't been for my blind trust born out of naivety. Of course, I noticed that the body in the burrow wasn't our mum. It smelled and looked different. But I had never heard of snakes or the danger they presented. And so, my curiosity won. I scrambled over my sister, who was huddling close to the wall, and ventured closer to the reptile. Maybe it was the clumsy way in which I moved. Maybe it awoke some motherly feelings in the reptile, or maybe it reminded the snake of itself when it'd been little. Whatever it was, it didn't attack me. Instead, it waited patiently to see what I would do.

"I remember that I stumbled up to the snake and cuddled against it. Its skin was different to my mum's – smooth and a bit cooler because it had no fur. But I still enjoyed the safety of having an adult there to protect us. Back then, I was sure the snake had nothing else in mind but to watch us while my mum was gone. I felt so secure that I even licked the snake's skin, forgetting for a moment that it wasn't our mother."

"Hold up!" Strix interrupted Lemon, his voice filled with disbelief. "You lick your mother? Why the heck would you do that?"

Lemon glanced at Strix quizzically. "Because we are thirsty, obviously, and want some milk. Why else would we do it?"

Strix smiled condescendingly. "Look," he said, "I have a lot of mammal friends, and if you are intending to pass off as a half-mammal yourself you should get your facts straight. Females have nipples that produce the milk. That will make your tales more believable in future ... And in case you want to keep this part of your story, then you could maybe pass that off as a strange family custom or something ..."

Lemon shook his head "The only weird family custom is that my mum gave us all names that make no sense. She says that an odd name is fitting for a species that's the epitome of oddness itself ... Be that as it may; I'm talking about actual facts here. Your other mammal friends might not lick each other's skin, but we do as the female platypuses have special glands that make milk pool in their wrinkles, which the young ones then lap up. And if you don't believe me, you can fly upstream and search out a burrow on the other bank. A female platypus lives there, and she can verify what I said."

Feeling uncomfortable under Lemon's penetrating gaze, Strix shifted from one leg to the other. "No, there's no need for that," he relented after a breath or two. "I'll take your word for it. I'm sorry that I came across this distrustful. Cause if there's one thing I've learned on my travels, it's that nothing is impossible when it comes to Mother Nature and her creations. It's just that I had a bad run-in with a snake lately and ever since, I've been wary of pretty much everything I'm being told ..."

"That's fine," Lemon said generously. "But speaking of snakes, where was I with my story? Ah yes, the reptile looked stunned at my strange behaviour and stared at me with eyes as big as the sun. Maybe it thought I was crazy. Or maybe it was shocked because it believed I wanted to eat it. I'll never know for sure because right then our mum came back, spitting with rage at seeing a snake this close to us.

"In hindsight, the reptile could have taken her down with ease, but instead of attacking my incensed mother, it slithered away, searching for prey elsewhere. I watched my mum as the snake disappeared and the expression of terror on her face is one I'll never forget. Afterwards, she told me about the danger we'd been in, which is when I started to build the belief that all snakes are dangerous – the big ones that can break our spines with no effort, and the small, venomous ones. In a split second, my thoughts had shifted from childish innocence to believing that danger lurked everywhere. It transformed my whole worldview. I was terrified at having been this close to death's door, and if a snake would have approached me during that time, I think I would have been rooted to the spot, making a perfect meal for it."

"But you're still here," Strix interjected. "If you speak the truth and your thoughts shape your reality, shouldn't you have fallen prey to a snake by now?"

"No, because I changed my thoughts and beliefs yet another time," Lemon replied. "When my mum noticed how fearful I had become and how powerless I felt because of that, she took me aside and revealed a secret to me. Namely, that I have a great defence technique myself, which I stole from the snake who had visited our nest. She told me that when I licked its skin, a bit of its venom had entered my bloodstream and accumulated inside my sting."

"Yeah, right." Strix laughed, amused. "The stories our mums tell us when we're kids ... But if it helped you transform your beliefs about being powerless and enabled you to survive, the white lie was worth it, right?"

Lemon looked at him, as if gauging how he should respond. "Obviously, I know by now that what she told me was rubbish. All male platypuses have stings, whether or not they lick snakes. But at the time, my mum's version made a lot of sense to me."

Remembering the order he'd placed with the universe and how

perfectly his requirements had been delivered thus far, Strix laughed out loud. "You platypuses are for sure strange mammals with your bills and webbed feet, but you're definitely not venomous. No way!"

Lemon turned around and presented his hind legs to Strix.

The rising sunlight caught the sharp stingers that protruded from them, and Strix's laugh caught in his throat. Squeaking in fear, he reared back and flung himself into the sky faster than he would have believed possible, feeling gratitude for the fact that this weird species at least didn't have wings to follow him there.

He then stared down at the platypus who was clearly not as harmless as he had pretended to be.

It was all too much to take in.

"What the ..." Strix said disbelievingly to himself as he beat his wings, catching a rising thermal and flying away from the dangerous individual that had seemed friendly till now. "But I specifically asked to meet a non-venomous animal, dammit. How did this happen? What did go wrong?"

Strix was so occupied with his thoughts that he didn't register Lemon's last words, which the platypus shouted after Strix.

"Hey, what's the matter with you? I'm not carrying any venom right now, since the mating season hasn't started yet. And even if I were – I don't use it to kill birds ..."

The words drifted by Strix, being carried away on a gust of wind, while his own belief solidified that this country was full of dangerous and venomous animals that were after his blood.

Thoughts and Affirmations

Having lain down, Nayeli had watched Willow's top branches stir in the warm summer wind while listening intently to the story. But by now, she was sitting up again, frowning.

"Why did Strix attract Lemon into his life after ordering what he did? He's right that this doesn't make any sense. Cause he specifically asked to meet an animal that wasn't venomous. And a platypus is venomous – at least for some time of the year."

"But it does make sense, my dear child, because the universe doesn't recognise negations."

"Sorry?" Nayeli asked.

Willow laughed at her bewilderment. "If I ask you to *not* think of a green bunny, what is the first image that comes to your mind?"

"A green bunny?" Nayeli answered.

"Indeed. And the reason for that," Willow explained, "is that the word 'not' doesn't exist on the energetic planes. If you say that you don't want to be sick, the universal language translates that into you wanting to be sick. And when you repeatedly think that you don't want to date another macho, guess what kind of guy you'll meet ...? In order to manifest something you want, you need to word it positively."

Nayeli grinned as she understood Strix's little misunderstanding with the universe. "A mammal that lays eggs and isn't venomous ... That's brilliant. Of course, source would send a platypus to cross Strix's path after he'd made that order. But then, affirmations are not as easy as I thought – or are they?"

"They are easy. Alongside visualisations – where you picture the outcome you want instead of using words to ask for it – affirmations are actually one of the easiest tools to improve your manifestation work. You merely need to know three rules about them."

Nayeli latched on to that. "So many? See, I told you, it's complicated."

"Wait until you hear them." The tree laughed good-naturedly. "These three are simple, all things considered. The first rule we already talked about: Do not use negations. The second one is to state everything as if it's happening this instant because if you affirm something for the future, along the lines of 'I will be healthy', the universe will take that to mean that you don't want to be healthy right now. And since the linear passage of time does not exist on the other side and everything happens in the same moment, that *healthy future* might never arrive. And the third rule is to only affirm what you believe you can manifest."

"Er ... what?" Nayeli asked, surprised.

"This is where we come to your thoughts and beliefs," Willow explained. "And where I first have to tell you how those two fit together."

"I do know what thoughts are," Nayeli objected. "They are all the words in my head that keep me awake at night or that bother me when I need to concentrate on something."

"And do you also know that it's true what Lemon told Strix? That thoughts turn into beliefs? Because this is exactly what happens. Beliefs are thoughts that you have decided are true and which you've thought so many times that they've become second nature to you. You don't question them anymore. Nor do you remain aware of them all, since a lot of those thoughts have moved from your conscious to your subconscious mind."

"I understand that, but what does this have to do with only affirming things that align with my beliefs? Doesn't that restrict me unnecessarily? I mean, if I know I'm poor, but I want to be rich, I need to affirm something that's outside my belief system, don't I?"

"Many people try to do that," the tree answered. "And they all fail. Because your beliefs override any affirmation."

"Can you give me an example of that?"

"Sure. Let's say that since childhood, the following beliefs have been installed in you: 'money is hard to come by', 'I'm poor and can barely make ends meet', 'if you're born poor, you'll always remain poor' and 'money is a limited resource'. If you now tried to affirm winning a million dollars in the lottery, you can say this to yourself over and over again, but you won't believe it. Something inside you will balk. You'll feel uneasy, and you'll have negative thoughts that are triggered by these affirmations. Thoughts like, 'that's not true', 'such nonsense', 'this will never work' and so on. These thoughts will come quickly, and you won't be able to shut them out. And by the end, as opposed to having affirmed money, you'll have affirmed a greater lack of it. You might even end up in a lower vibrational state than you were before. Because when your manifestations are unsuccessful, you'll doubt the Law of Attraction, which in turn will strengthen your limiting beliefs."

"Right, and what would I need to affirm instead if I wanted to win a million dollars? Cause telling me what doesn't work is so not helpful ..."

"That's the problem, my dear. There is not one affirmation that would work for everyone. An affirmation that brings *you* more money could have the opposite effect for someone else if they hold resistance to that thought. The bottom line is this: To affirm something successfully, you have to listen to your intuition and choose sentences that make you feel good. You could tell yourself, for example – if we stick with the topic of money – that you deserve to be rich. But only if your ego doesn't have any arguments against it."

Nayeli furrowed her brows. "Correct me if I'm wrong, but what I take from this is that I need to think thoughts that are a step towards what I want, but which conform with what I believe, to ensure that my ego doesn't intervene and negates my affirmations. And then I can build up from there, affirming bigger and bigger things?"

"That's accurate," the tree answered. "Because the more you create your reality, the more you'll believe in your ability to manifest whatever you want. Which means that, in time, you can aim higher – without your mind cutting in with all these negative thoughts."

"That sounds like it's gonna take a long time, though," Nayeli said grumpily, being all too aware of how impatient she was. "Isn't there a faster way to do it? Or what if I can't manage it at all? What if I still have negative thoughts when affirming something, no matter how minuscule my steps are?"

"To answer your first question – you can work directly on your limiting beliefs and change those. But that's a whole other topic I'll defer until later. And as for your second question – if you have any negative reaction to an affirmation you make, it's better to not use it. You can then see it as a wake-up call instead, which is alerting you to something that needs to be healed within yourself."

Nayeli scooted over so that she was sitting snug between two of Willow's roots. "You keep saying that I need to think or say what I want and believe that it will come true, and then it will happen ... But what about my feelings or my intentions or my actions? Don't I need to transform those as well to manifest my desires?"

"Yes and no, my dear," Willow said kindly. "Let me unravel this for you. At first, you have a desire. The moment you decide to make it your reality, you create an intention that this is what you want to manifest. These steps are important, but you complete them prior to your actual manifestation work. They're the foundation for it, so to speak. Meanwhile, the manifestation itself can be equated with your focus. And when this transpires, there's a cycle that happens over and over again in your life. This cycle has three steps: thoughts, emotions and actions.

"When something happens in your outer reality, it generates a thought. And since thoughts always attract more thoughts, you'll soon have a whole array of them running through your mind, each of them triggering the next. Let's say that you're visiting a zoo and a tiger breaks out of its cage, roaming among all the panicking people. Your thoughts in that situation could be 'the tiger's gonna kill me', 'I need to find a place to hide' or 'please someone help me'. But it doesn't stop there, as thoughts not only trigger other thoughts but are also translated into emotions. If a tiger is roaming about, those emotions might be fear or sheer panic. And the third pillar besides thoughts and emotions is actions. Once you feel the emotions that are a direct answer to your thoughts, you are going to be compelled into a reaction. In a dangerous situation, your survival instinct will kick in – resulting in a fight, flight or freeze response – while in other situations it may be a more calculated action. In this example, with the tiger, your reaction could be to climb onto a roof.

"Now, to complete the circle, the action results in a new reality, which in turn creates new thoughts. When you're sitting on the roof, looking down at the tiger, your next thought might be 'this is not going to help me, since tigers are great climbers'. To sum it up ... your thoughts make you feel certain emotions, the emotions make you react and your actions create new thoughts."

Nayeli played with a strand of her hair while reflecting on what she had heard. "Got it. But why do you put this much emphasis on thoughts in that case, if they merely make up a third of this cycle?"

"Because thoughts are powerful. Your thoughts determine where your focus is. And what you focus on is what you'll attract. Yes, your feelings and actions are important, too. Your feelings act as an indicator of whether your thoughts will attract something positive or negative to you. And the action you take will either support the process or work against it. In the end, if you don't feel abundant or if you sabotage yourself by not taking guided actions towards what you desire, then you can think affirmative thoughts all day long and nothing will happen. They'll just be empty phrases as the rest of your frequency does not match them. But saying this, thoughts are the simplest way to tackle the problem of being stuck inside a negative downward spiral and to break this cycle."

"Why?" Nayeli asked the tree in interest. "I mean, I agree with you that changing the emotions would literally be impossible. When I'm thinking scary thoughts, I feel anxious, whether or not I want to. But the action step ... breaking the cycle at this point seems workable. At least, when I'm acting consciously and not reacting instinctively to a perceived threat."

Willow rustled loudly with its leaves. "I didn't say it's impossible to initiate change at the action step, but it's harder for most people ... Imagine you're terrified of flying and every time you board a plane, your mind constantly tells you that you're gonna die while your emotions make your turn into a shivering bundle on the floor. I can tell you that most people would do their utmost to avoid flying and to pick holiday destinations closer by. Or, if they can't avoid it, they'd do their best to drown out their fear with other thoughts that comfort or encourage them.

"Of course, to name a different example, some people are fine hitching rides with strangers, despite having all these mental images of being murdered by them. But for most people, it is difficult to change the action step before changing their thoughts because the action you take can potentially pose a threat to your survival."

"Ah, I understand," Nayeli interjected. "It's easier to start with my thoughts because I can then adjust my action steps gradually, which makes me feel safer than taking a wild plunge into the unknown."

"Quite right, my dear. When you first build up the belief to be capable of migrating to another country, you're more likely to put that plan into motion than if you're anxious about being on your own in a foreign land. The bottom line is this: Your thoughts can make or break any action you take, and because of this you'd do well to turn them into your allies."

"I agree with all you've explained thus far," Nayeli said firmly. "Except, Willow, you don't seriously think that thoughts are this powerful, do you? They're just thoughts, after all, nothing more."

"Nothing more?" the tree asked, sounding shocked. "Don't you know that everything in existence – every invention and creative outlet – was first a thought that was then born into our reality? Thoughts are the foundation of all you can see, hear, touch, smell, taste and feel because everything's that ever been created – including this world we live in – existed as an idea prior to becoming *real*. Which means that, yes, thoughts are powerful. And so are words, by the way, as they direct your thoughts and the energy present in them outward to others."

Willow extended its branches before drawing them back, tickling Nayeli's legs with the longest ones. "This reminds me of an experiment that humans carried out using two house plants. Have you heard of it?"

"I can't say that I have," Nayeli responded. "What was it about?"

"Two plants of the same species, of a similar height and width, were kept in the same external conditions. They were given the same amount of sunlight and clean water, in addition to the same earth and nutrients. The only difference was that everyone who walked past Plant A had to say something nice to it – for example, that it was beautiful or that it had grown a lot in the last few days. Meanwhile, each time someone walked past Plant B they had to say something derogatory to it – that it was ugly or weak or something along those lines. Now, what do you think happened?"

Nayeli looked up into Willow's crown. "The way you say it, I surmise that Plant B came off badly compared to Plant A?"

"That's an understatement," Willow answered. "Plant B wilted and withered, its leaves turning brown and falling off, while Plant A flourished. And it's not merely plants that react to words. Other experiments have shown that words can also influence crystals and water. There was one experiment where the crystalline structure of water was photographed after being exposed to positive respectively negative words. The water exposed to the positive speech was more symmetrical after having been frozen than the water exposed to negative comments.

"Words carry energy, my dear child, and any energy influences everything around it. Which is one of the reasons, by the way, why a lot of people bless their food before they eat it. And when words can have that much influence on plants and crystals and food, which don't even have ears to hear the physical component of the negative energy being used against them, think how negative thoughts and words affect humans – both the people who think and speak them and the people who are on the receiving end."

"But what about our free will, Willow? I thought that can't be overridden by anyone else. So, it shouldn't matter what someone says to me?"

"The words of someone else can't force you along a path you don't want to walk on, but what they can do is to influence you. Imagine that your teachers constantly complained that you were lazy at school and could have done better. You'll eventually adopt these beliefs about yourself, either consciously or subconsciously. And in the worst-case scenario, this leads to low self-worth, which hinders you from using the Law of Attraction to your advantage."

"Ah," Nayeli said as her puzzlement turned to comprehension. "Your point is that negative speech can influence someone else to form debilitating beliefs about themselves, turning them in a direction that's detrimental to them? Just like my own disparaging thoughts can influence me negatively?"

"Yes. Sadly, when humans grow up, the truth that thoughts and words are powerful is replaced with the belief that 'it's only thoughts' or that 'those are just words'. But that doesn't detract from their importance. On the contrary. The more unaware you are of the thoughts you have and the beliefs they have installed within you, the more damage they can do. Therefore, always choose your thoughts and words wisely. And change any that are not to the best of all involved."

Nayeli felt pensive at the tree's warnings. "I promise that from now on, I'll reflect more about what I think and that I'll be a lot more conscious of the words I speak, so they don't result in any catastrophes – for me or others."

"A wise choice, my dear child," the tree replied. "A very wise choice. One that can result in many positive outcomes when you put it into action. Which is where we come to the last step of the cycle that we haven't talked about in detail yet ..."

20. Sandy, the Kangaroo

"I think I'm going to be sick!" Strix groaned pitifully.

"Oh no, you don't," Sandy said in indignation, coming to a halt. "Not in my pouch!"

"I told you not to let a foreign species use it," one of Sandy's friends called out as she hopped past the kangaroo.

"And I told you that it was my decision and you should keep out of it," Sandy returned.

Strix tried to follow the disagreement between the two kangaroos, if only to distract himself from his nausea. In the first hour of riding in Sandy's pouch, Strix had felt nothing more than a slight uneasiness, but as the rocking motion of the kangaroo's jumps continued, he'd had more trouble to keep his stomach in check. Repeatedly having to swallow the bile rising in his throat, he concentrated on breathing deeply. Which helped temporarily – until the next wave of nausea hit.

Sandy looked down at him with a questioning gaze. "Better? Can I move on? I can't lose the rest of the mob, y'know? Already, they're a good bit ahead. And they won't wait for me just because you feel sick. They don't get why I took you with us, anyhow."

Strix nodded bravely. But when he answered, his voice was subdued. "I'm sorry for being such a bad guest and complaining about everything. You saved my life, after all, by allowing me to travel in your pouch. And I am grateful for that because I know this is the safest and fastest way to get to the coast. I'm simply not used to all these leaps, and they're upsetting my stomach."

"But do you have it under control again?" Sandy asked dubiously. "Otherwise you could always use your wings and fly the rest of the way. It isn't far now."

"Come out of here?" Strix squeaked fearfully. "No way! You can't make me." Strix burrowed himself so deep that his eyes were only just peaking outside, registering the dry, parched barrenness all around them. "I will not leave the safety of your pouch until I see the damn coastline with my own eyes. I've had enough of being almost eaten and poisoned and whatever else the weird animals that live in this 'Land of Nope' want to do to me."

"Are you shaking?" Sandy asked incredulously.

"Me?" Strix said. "No. Never. I'm not shaking. I'm not scared at all." But his body proved him a liar, as he felt his legs tremble uncontrollably.

Sandy grinned knowingly, apparently feeling the vibrations inside her pouch. But to Strix's relief, she didn't comment any further. Instead, she leaned forward and placed her front paws on the ground, taking a huge leap. She did so as gently as she could but her pouch was still moving a great deal, and Strix had to suppress the urge to gag.

He desperately tried to distract himself from the swaying motion by thinking about everything that had brought him here ...

***

After leaving the eucalyptus forest behind, Strix had reached a conclusion. If at all possible, the Australian continent was even hotter than the African one – or maybe it was the timely distance that deluded him into thinking this. To Strix, the weather always seemed the most extreme whenever he was directly faced with it, while everything else paled to a faint picture in his memory.

But whether his impression was born out of reality or his imagination, the fact remained that the merciless sun was his worst enemy right now. And Strix knew that, if he wanted to survive, he had no other choice but to find a shady place soon to wait out the day,

Luckily, he saw the outskirts of a small town emerge on the horizon. Normally taking big detours around human settlements because they were too loud and smelly, not to mention filled with the two-legged, Strix decided to make an exception today. Because, as scary as humans were, they had no natural defence mechanisms like beaks and claws, and based on this they would surely make a wide berth around any places where crocodiles and snakes and platypuses and other dangerous creatures resided.

Nearing the town, Strix hid in the foliage of a tree in a park-like area and made himself comfortable on his perch. From there, he peered at the strange two-legged beings who were bustling about. Strix was amazed at the humans' weird habits and physical attributes. Some of them had grown round things beneath their feet and, instead of walking, they raced by his tree. Meanwhile, others touched their cheeks with rectangular, hard devices and talked to themselves. But the strangest of them all was a pair right underneath his tree who appeared to be arguing. Despite laughing the whole time, they were pushing and shoving each other, walking back- and forwards and rounding each other in circles, as if to gain the upper hand. They did this for a couple of minutes until the larger human, a male, had won and bent the smaller female back-wards.

Strix had observed something like this twice before, the rare times he'd dared to go near humans. Once he'd watched a band of long-haired musicians play a number of songs on the street, and behind the crowd that had assembled two of the two-legged had moved in circles while having their arms wrapped around each other. And another time, he'd seen a female in a white dress, who seemed to have only one real leg, the other foot looking like it was made of some kind of metal. Despite that, she had given as good as she got from the slightly taller male, dressed in black, who was twirling her about.

He remembered now what the humans had called it – dancing. Strix tried to figure out what it was done for. But as his memories blended in with the sight of the couple below him and the heat lulled him into a dream-like state, Strix felt his concentration slip.

His rest was short-lived, however, when a loud voice called out a warning to him.

"Hey, owl, get out of that tree! Quick! There's a big snake behind you!"

Strix catapulted himself forward so fast that he almost landed face-down on the ground. Spreading his wings to catch his weight, he soared up into the sky and looked back at the tree. True to the warning, a large green snake was coiling over the branch he had been sitting on and glared angrily, first at him and then at the bird who had warned him in time of being choked to death. The snake then hissed before pulling itself back into the green leaves, where it became invisible once more.

Gulping, Strix flew towards his saviour, a bird slightly smaller than himself. "You saved my life! How can I ever thank you?"

"Ah, there's no need, my friend. We birds need to stick together, don't we? And I've had a score to settle with that snake anyway. It killed my fledglings last summer ..."

"I'm sorry to hear that," Strix answered earnestly.

Shrugging, the female bird fixated the tree where the snake was hiding. "It's the course of life. Birth and death in a never-ending circle. It's what we all signed up for when we chose to come here."

Letting her gaze rake over him, she tilted her head sideways. "Anyway, I dare say, you're not from around here. Am I right? You're too careless to survive long in sunny Australia, my boy. If you want a piece of advice from me – you'd better stay away from all snakes. Not all of them eat owls, but many of them are either venomous or can crush your spine with ease."

Strix was about to say he already knew that because he'd made his own bad experiences with these reptiles up north, but by the time he'd opened his beak, the other bird had gone without saying a word of goodbye.

Perplexed, Strix looked about. Then she shrugged and moved on himself. Deciding that he would stay clear of any trees and bushes since the snakes could blend in too well with those and lie in ambush, Strix also ruled out any man-made settlements as the presence of humans obviously didn't guarantee a safe spot to sleep, either.

Flying underneath the burning sun, Strix felt even more exhausted than before having nodded off, and this made him all the happier to come upon a small stream, which was carrying fresh water. After carefully scanning the vicinity for any dangerous reptiles, he circled down to quench his thirst. Being able to see for miles in each direction, Strix was reasonably sure that this time nothing could go wrong. But he had underestimated the hazard known as Australia. Because as soon as he had taken his first gulp, a high-pitched voice called out to him.

"Watch out, owl, a venomous spider is crawling out of a hole behind you!"

Gasping in fright, Strix rose up fast and high and nearly collided with another bird flying past. Peering at the ground, he saw that there was indeed a huge spider walking over the spot he'd been sitting on a moment ago. Turning around to look for his saviour, he spotted a gecko sitting on the other bank.

"What the bloody hell is this place?" Strix asked, hooting indignantly.

Laughing, the gecko curled up. "I suppose you're not from here, heh? Everyone knows that the deadliest creatures on Earth live in these regions. But don't you worry, you'll get used to them. That is, if you survive that long ..."

Strix didn't deign to answer the small lizard, but turned around and flew on, away from this place and the dangers it held.

On his way, he spotted a careless mouse running over the ground. Trusting his experience that at least these rodents were never poisonous, he swooped down on the unsuspecting animal and gulped it down. But even this meal and the bit of water he had drunk didn't help in alleviating his exhaustion. And the sun shining from the cloudless sky continued to worry Strix. He felt way too hot and he knew he was in danger of another heatstroke if flew on in broad daylight.

It took a lot of energy for Strix to stay airborne. The adrenaline that had coursed through his body was diminishing, and the resulting exhaustion made it hard for Strix to keep his eyes open, which began to droop repeatedly. Soon, he was wavering in fatigue and the next thing he knew was that he had flown smack into another, bigger animal.

Screaming in fear, Strix pushed against the warm body and tried to put some distance between himself and the potential danger. But he was too panic-stricken and almost crashed to the ground instead.

"Hey hey, easy," a caring female voice said.

Strix looked up to see a grey animal with a huge tail and immense back feet. "I'm sorry," he said, stumbling over his words in his haste to get them out. "I didn't mean to fly into you. Please don't kill me!"

"It's okay, no one's going to kill you," the female animal said soothingly. "Why would you think that? If you don't mind me saying, you seem a bit stressed out. What's wrong?"

Strix didn't know where to begin, without revealing too much to a stranger, which could yet turn out to be a predator. At that moment, a warm gust of wind hit him, and fatigue made Strix plummet clumsily to the earth. He quickly righted himself and tried to lift off to get away from any snakes or spiders that were lurking around, but was too tired to coordinate his wings.

"I take back what I just said. You don't look a bit stressed out. You look like death warmed up. You poor thing! It's a wonder you are still conscious. Why don't you sit down and rest?"

"I can't. Too dangerous." Strix said, his voice laced with fear. "As soon as I sit down anywhere, I'm gonna be dead. I need to keep flying until I reach the coast."

Gazing all around, the larger animal shrugged. "I see nothing dangerous here. I think you will be safe."

"I didn't see anything the last times either, but then I was almost eaten."

Closing her kind eyes, the animal smiled winningly as she opened them again. "Or maybe you'd be interested in another option?"

"Anything!" Strix cried. "If you know any safe place where I can rest, I'll owe you, big-time!"

"In that case ..." The female animal reached down with her front paws and opened a fold in her stomach. "Surprise! You can rest in here. We're going your way – my mob is moving towards the southern coast and I could take you with me."

"What ... what is that?" Strix asked, perplexed. "And are there any venomous stings inside it?"

"It's my pouch," the female explained. "All kangaroos have one and even some other species. And no, it's not dangerous. It's where we keep and nourish our young ones until they're old enough to stand on their own feet. It's the safest place for them. But mine is still empty because my first joey hasn't been born yet."

"No kidding?" Strix asked as he wavered on his feet. "I can really rest a bit in there? You'd allow me to do that?"

"Sure," the kangaroo said. "Go ahead, hop in."

"Stop right there, Sandy," another female kangaroo chimed in. "You can't let a stranger inside it. Who knows what parasites he carries ... And have you seen his claws? If they cut you open, you could die. Together with your unborn child."

"Will you stop being so damn negative? It will be fine. Look at the poor bird. He's exhausted."

"And you're being irresponsible," Sandy's friend replied. "And driven by pregnancy hormones. In a while, you'll have your first newborn. There's no need for you to mother strange birds."

"Nonsense," Sandy said, once again opening her pouch and indicating for Strix to hop in. She gave her friend a stern gaze. "It's entirely my own decision. And I have set my mind, no matter what you say. Now, let's stop this pointless debate. The others are moving on."

True to her word, kangaroos of similar size and colour to Sandy and her friend were hopping away, following a bigger male who was obviously the leader of the group.

Strix spared them only a short glance before diving head-first into the safety of Sandy's pouch, not wanting to give the kangaroo the time to reconsider her offer. "Thank you, Sandy," he said, his head reappearing at the top. "I promise that I don't have any parasites and that I'll be careful with my claws. And if there's ever something I can do for you in return, simply say the word, yes? My name's Strix, by the way."

"It's nice to meet you, Strix," Sandy responded while her friend snorted and turned away from them, a disapproving look in her eyes.

When Sandy leapt forward, Strix tried to find a good position in the pouch to not fall out – without hurting his nice host with his claws. He was relieved to have found the kangaroo and this foolproof way to travel to the coast.

***

When the relief of feeling safe had given way to nausea, Strix had begun to wonder if it had been such a clever idea to accept Sandy's offer. But then again, he thought, it wasn't like he'd had many alternatives to act on. And so he let these deliberations go, concentrating instead on calming down his upset stomach, which was acting up more with every jump the kangaroo took.

And Sandy was achieving a great number of those as she followed the other members of her mob in giant leaps.

Strix was just about to ask how much longer they had to go

when it happened. Opening his beak, Strix retched and brought up a pellet of all the indigestible parts of the mouse, which he'd eaten prior to meeting the kangaroos. He threw it up so quick that he didn't even have time to poke his head out over the fold in Sandy's stomach.

"Ew," Sandy uttered, and stopped abruptly, eying the pellet Strix had heaved up.

"I'm so, so, so, so sorry," he said, ducking his head in shame.

The other kangaroos had stopped as well, some of them watching Strix curiously, while the rest of the group began to graze off the sparse grass growing all around.

"Is everything all right?" the big male called over.

"Sure," Sandy responded, having already reverted back to her happy-go-lucky self. "You know what?" she said, facing Strix once more. "It's not a problem. At least this way, I've some practise in cleaning my pouch in advance of my joey moving in. Who knows what mess they'll make in there over time, eh?"

"You're awfully calm about this," Strix said uncomfortably, beyond embarrassed by what had happened.

Shrugging, Sandy laughed. "There's nothing we can do about it now, is there? What's done is done. The main thing I'm interested in right now is getting my pouch clean again. And for that, you need to move out for a bit."

"Onto the ground?" Strix whimpered.

The kangaroo took her time to check the sandy patch of earth she had stopped on and then looked in all directions for good measure. "Strix, I don't see a single living animal here aside from us, least of all a venomous one."

"O-kay," Strix said, still unsure, but knowing it was the least he could do. Hopping up, he unfolded his wings and floated down to sit in the long shadow Sandy cast on the ground. He watched her bend over as she emptied her pouch with her front paws and was suddenly reminded of the humans he had seen and how they had moved underneath the tree he had been sitting on.

"Hey, Sandy," he said, "have you ever heard of dancing?"

"Dancing?" Sandy asked in surprise. "I'm sorry, but I've no idea what that means."

"It's a human custom to cement a friendship," Strix answered confidently, ignoring the fact that he didn't know the real reason that two-legged did it. "Shall we try it out?"

"Why not?" the female kangaroo agreed willingly. "It can never hurt to actively improve a new relationship, now can it?"

"Great," Strix said, excited to attempt this strange rite for himself. He hopped up and down before the kangaroo as he tried to think of the movements they needed to copy. "We need to stand in front of each other and sway our bodies from side to side. Yes, like that. And now I hop backwards and you need to take a step towards me."

Strix craned his neck around, watching out for anything that could creep up on him from behind. He was so intent on looking out for venomous animals that he nearly missed Sandy leaning forward on her front paws and taking a huge step towards him.

It was only in the last possible moment that Strix sprung to the side, preventing her from crushing him underneath her weight.

"I'm so sorry," Sandy said apologetically. "I didn't mean to hit you. But you did say you were gonna take a step backwards ..."

"I did," Strix defended himself. "But I said a step, not a mile. Never mind. I forgot how big you are and that your steps are longer than mine. Why don't we do it the other way around? This way I won't risk being stood on."

"You want me to move backwards now?"

"Yeah," Strix answered. "And I'll hop forward."

"Right," Sandy agreed, tensing the muscles in her hind legs.

But she didn't move. Instead, the kangaroo's eyes grew round and big as she stared down at Strix.

Hooting in fear, Strix soared up into the sky and gazed all around for any dangerous animal preparing to attack him. When he saw nothing, he looked at Sandy questioningly. "What is it? What did you see? Was there a snake? A scorpion? A huge spider? Why didn't you say anything? Don't just stand there like a statue."

"I ... no," Sandy stuttered. "It's ... I-I-I can't."

"What do you mean, you can't?" Strix asked. "You can't what?"

"Step backwards," Sandy explained. "I don't think the way my hind legs are formed allows me to move that way. Or maybe it's my tail that gets in the way. Whatever it is, I can't do it.."

Strix heaved a sigh of relief that he wasn't in any immediate danger. But then his happiness turned into worry for his new friend when Sandy's shoulders drooped in sadness.

"Hey," Strix said empathetically, searching his mind for something to say to cheer up the kangaroo. "Who needs to dance anyway, right? It's only a stupid ritual that humans do. I rode inside your pouch for a few miles. And what could be better to cement a friendship than that, I ask you?"

"That's true," Sandy had to agree, a small smile evicting the sadness from her eyes. "Pouch friendships are so much closer than dancing friendships."

"And besides," Strix continued encouragingly, "you're capable of so many things that I couldn't even dream of. Like making those giant leaps? It's impressive, especially since you pull it off this effortlessly."

"For real?" Sandy asked, flattered.

"For real," Strix answered. "I wish I could do that. Figuratively, at least, if not literally. To never look backwards, to keep my eyes focused on the goal in front of me and move towards it, without being side-tracked by any doubts ..."

Speaking about doubts immediately triggered thoughts of his home. And Nuktia whom he had abandoned. Wondering if flying off without a word would be the last memory of him that Nuktia would carry around for the rest of her life, Strix felt sick to his stomach again, but this time for an entirely different reason.

"Hey, what's wrong?" Sandy asked, concerned. "You don't look so well. Is your stomach still troubling you?"

"No. Yes. I don't know." Strix groaned. "Sandy, I think I made a big mistake in my past. One that I can never set straight."

"Nonsense," Sandy answered. "It's true that you can't change past decisions. But you can act differently today when you see that your choices don't align with your goals anymore. To do that, you don't have to take giant leaps either. Just take it step by step, at whatever pace suits you."

"And what if I don't know what the right action is?"

"Then you can always ask for some guidance and help," Sandy replied. "Isn't there anyone in your life who would understand what you are going through and could add some wisdom?"

The question sparked a picture in his mind's eye of the snow owl he was following. After all, she wasn't only a distant cousin. Beyond that, she'd also decided to take on the same adventure as him by travelling the world. Figuring that if anyone could understand his situation it would surely be her, Strix felt as if his reason for flying after the owl had finally been revealed to him.

"You're right, Sandy," he said, all of a sudden feeling a burning desire to move on, now that he knew what he was looking for. "Thank you for everything. But I do need to get going now. I have to be on time for a meeting with someone who doesn't know about it yet. Someone I hope can give me the answers I seek."

Sandy smiled down at him. "Good luck in that case. And safe travels. I hope you find them. And if you ever come back here, visit me, agreed? I might even take you on another ride in my pouch if it isn't occupied by one of my joeys at the time."

"No frigging way!" Strix cried, causing both of them to burst into laughter.

Some of the other kangaroos who were grazing nearby glanced up curiously to see what was so funny. But Sandy and Strix were too busy catching their breath to pay them much attention.

Once Strix had calmed down, he soared up into the sky and flew a few circles above Sandy's head. "I honestly don't know if I'll ever dare to come back to Australia, since you have been the one bright spot on this godforsaken continent. But if I do, I'll sure visit you again." And with those words, he flew higher into the air and turned south, with the intention to only look forward from now on, not back. At least not before he hadn't found the snowy owl.

Taking Action and Letting Go

"Wait, Willow," Nayeli said as soon as the tree had ended its tale. "Before you explain the message behind this story, let me venture a guess. Because I think I've figured this one out." Drumming her fingers on the earth in a staccato rhythm, she looked up into the tree's crown while struggling to keep a straight face. "You're telling me that kangaroo rides are worse than any roller coaster, aren't you?"

The tree chortled loudly. "That's certainly some useful information to take from this – in case you ever get invited to travel in a kangaroo's pouch."

"Hey, do you think that's impossible?" Nayeli asked, mock-offended. "Then wait until I manifest such an invitation into reality. Cause some tree I met recently told me that anything is achievable – when I want it to be."

"Did it?" Willow said light-heartedly. "Hmm, that tree might have lost its marbles ..."

"Oh no," Nayeli said at once. "I think it's very wise. But seriously, I do believe I know what you were trying to tell me here. Meditating and visualising and affirming what I want is all well and good. But beyond that, I need to take guided action if I want to get anywhere., right?"

"You are getting quite good at figuring out the messages in the stories," Willow replied. "Or maybe I'm getting more obvious, who knows?" Laughing, the tree wiggled its branches. "Anyway, you're right. That's what I wanted to talk to you about. Because you do need to take matters into your own hands and take appropriate steps to get where you want to be, alongside doing all the internal, energetic work. While the universe and your higher self will always help you and work in alignment with your wishes and dreams, they can't do everything by themselves. You need to fulfil your part of the deal."

"And what part is that exactly?" Nayeli asked, unsure what the details entailed, even though she had understood the overall message.

"Essentially, everything physical that the universe and your higher self cannot directly influence, since they have neither hands nor vocal cords," the tree replied. "To give an example ... Let's say you want to move into a bigger house. The universe can line you up with one. It can guide you to buy the paper where you'll find an ad for that house. It can guide you to walk down the specific street where you see an estate agent sign. Or it can guide you to speak to a friend who's heard of a house being sold. But what it can't do is to replace your home for your dream home when you are asleep. And it can't pick up the mobile or sign any contracts, either. Or, to use a different example, if you manifest a soulmate relationship, the universe will set up the opportunity for you to meet one of yours. It will guide you both to be at the same place at the same time. But if you don't take action and talk to them, your paths are going to move in different directions before your relationship can begin. Because how can it come to pass otherwise? This, by the way, ensures that your free will takes effect. No matter where source guides you, you can always turn away and take a different route instead, which you might find to be equally beneficial."

"Ha!" Nayeli called out. "I doubt that."

"What?" Willow asked, confused. "What do you doubt?"

"Why, that I could decide on a different course and it would turn out in my favour. Whatever decisions I make, they end up being the wrong ones ... Just look at my life, Willow. I have a job that I hate because I decided to quit university when money got too tight and because I accepted the first position I was offered. And work isn't the only thing that sucks. There's my decision to move away from my home town, which cost me some dear friendships. Not to mention my decision to give up on my writing till now. So, how many decisions could I have made that have been to my advantage?"

"Millions." the tree answered matter-of-factly before delving into an explanation. "You make hundreds of decision each and every day. When you eat a snack, you don't merely decide to eat it; you decide which snack to get, to eat it at that specific time and that the food is worth its price. You decide what to wear every day, when to leave for work, whether or not to switch on the radio in the morning, what film to watch in the evening and so on and so on. And even if you do nothing at all apart from staring at a blank wall, you have decided to do nothing else but to stare at the wall.

"But what is more, every time you make a decision, you decide *against* hundreds of different options. When you decide to wear a green shirt, you automatically decide to not wear a yellow or red or black one. And when you decide to go jogging, you decide against watching TV or painting or dancing or sleeping. As an incarnated human, you can never escape making choices. And you generally make a lot of good decisions among a couple of bad ones."

"Then I must be the expectation of that rule," Nayeli replied mulishly. "Cause my decisions are poor at best. At least, when it comes to the more important ones."

Willow grunted. "It's true that not all decisions weigh identical. There are simple ones as well as big decisions that have consequences, which will impact your future. And if you make a bad decision on a life-changing event, then it will have a bigger effect than a hundred small decisions that turn out to be less fortunate."

"See?" Nayeli interrupted the tree petulantly. "Consequences do exist. And I always receive the worst ones."

Willow's voice remained as gentle as ever when the tree answered. "I never said that consequences aren't part of this reality. They do exist. And sometimes they are plain awful. But don't make the mistake of thinking that these are dished out by the universe. Consequences are a side-effect of your free will and thus based on your own actions."

"But that's not true, Willow. That consequences are always my fault, I mean," Nayeli pointed out. "If I'm held at gunpoint by a robber, they have taken away my freedom and force me to comply with their wishes, haven't they?"

"No, my dear. Even in such a dire situation where force is used on you, your free will is still in effect. You can comply and hand over all your money or you can refuse to do what they say. The only thing that someone else can do is to put so much pressure on you that you comply because you want to avoid the resulting consequences if you were to refuse their demand. But in the end, it *is* your decision ... And the same holds true for less extreme situations than being held at gunpoint. Imagine, for example, that parents tell their children for years that they will never amount to anything. To survive, a child needs a close relationship with their caregivers more than a positive self-image. So, in order to form a closer connection, these children will eventually agree with the parent's opinion. In this case, the child will – subconsciously if not consciously – choose with its free will the consequence of low self-esteem and self-hate over the consequence of being disconnected and lonely."

The tree hummed underneath its breath. "You have to realise that making a decision doesn't necessarily amount to having a good and a bad option. At times, all decisions you make will lead to good outcomes. While, at other times, you only have the choice between two scenarios that are both painful. Let's say that you are a teenager living at home and that your parents are divorcing and moving into separate houses halfway around the world. And now they ask you who you want to live with. If you love both of them, there is no decision you can make that wouldn't be painful in some way."

"So, sometimes there's no way to win at life?"

"Not always, no," Willow answered. "But on the bright side, seemingly bad or painful decisions teach you some of life's greatest lessons. You'll never learn more about yourself and what's important to you than when you have to choose between the devil and the deep blue sea."

"Hmpf," Nayeli said, not at all happy about this revelation.

Just then, a ladybird landed on her knee, and Nayeli was distracted by the insect scurrying down her leg before returning to the sky. Watching it fly towards a flower where it sat down, Nayeli redirected her thoughts back to everything she had learned today.

"This might all be true, Willow, but I still don't see me making any big decisions easily. I mean, there are days when I can't even choose what book to read next. And if I'm that indecisive, how can I be trusted with any high-stakes decisions on my own?"

"Since you're never completely on your own, you don't need to do that," Willow responded softly. "If you're unsure of a big decision, ask for guidance from your higher self or the universe and it will be given to you. Then let the matter go and leave it up to the source to help you in whatever ways it sees fit."

"Let it go? But I thought we were talking about taking action here and that I need to do my part of the deal?"

A gust of stifling air rushed through Willow's branches and made Nayeli feel the full heat of the summer day.

"Letting go is part of the deal we're talking about. Sometimes letting go is the actual action you need to take. While you're the one person in control of your desires, intentions, thoughts, beliefs and actions when manifesting your reality, the universe is much better equipped to deal with all the details that follow. And messing with that would restrict the flow from the source. Because of this, the best thing you can do, my dear, is to leave the 'how' up to the universe and not stress about it. You don't need to have a clear plan in what way something will arrive in your life. It's a lot better to stay flexible, like a tree bending in a strong wind so as not to break."

"But Willow, this doesn't make sense," Nayeli said, confused. "Why would it block my manifestation when I say specifically what I want?"

"Let me explain this based on the topic of soulmates we talked about previously. You already know that there are several of your soulmates incarnated at this time who'd be a compatible romantic match, right? But then again, there are only so many million people on this planet, which indicates the selection isn't limitless. Now, you might have one soulmate with black hair who'd be a perfect match and another with blond hair who's an almost perfect match. But because you prefer a certain type, you ask for a soulmate with blond hair. Since the universe has to factor in your free will and bring you what you ask for, adding any unnecessary detail will not be beneficial for you when you look at things from a wider perspective. And the manifestation might not arrive as quickly as it otherwise could, either. For example, when you want money and you ask to win five million dollars in the lottery that restricts the universe. In contrast, if you simply asked for money and left the 'how' up to the source, the universe could send it to you by whatever means is the fastest at any given time. And that makes its job easier."

"Ah, you're saying that we need to be specific on the important parts we desire, but not on the surface-level stuff or even on the way it's gonna come?"

"Yes. Having a higher awareness, the universe sees how everything fits together. And it can respond more effectively when you give it some room to navigate. Then the sole thing left to do is to not block the intuitive guidance you receive.

"But let me tell you about the natural pulse of life that's at the base of all things – including this universe and everyone living inside it – as this explains everything you need to know ... This endless cycle consists of four steps: Expansion, a short stasis, contraction and another short stasis. When you're expanding, you are in the creation phase by taking action and sending out energy, which is based upon the focus you hold. After that, there's a short pause, which you should use to let go so that the universe can 'process your order'. Then, there's an inward contraction where you receive the results of your manifestation work. This is also the point where you come back to yourself and bring into your core everything you learned, gaining a new awareness and perspective. This step is followed by another short pause, in which a new desire is born. And this will once again lead to an outward expansion in which you manifest your new reality thanks to the new focus you hold."

The tree waited for a beat or two before continuing. "This

process happens simultaneously for anything you create in your life. There are always some parts of you that are expanding, while others are contracting. And to not resist that natural rhythm is the best action you can possibly take."

Nayeli narrowed her eyes. "Which is great. But this leaves me with a problem. Cause no matter if it would be beneficial to me or not, I can't let go and move with the flow. Giving up control feels like a threat to my very survival. Maybe because I've learned not to trust anyone else. For good reasons, I might add, since my trust has been broken repeatedly in the past."

"I'm sorry to hear that," Willow replied earnestly. "Do you want to tell me about it?"

Shrugging, Nayeli leaned backward. "I could give you countless examples. One that comes to me immediately is that one of my so-called friends stole some song lyrics I once wrote. She knew some people in the music industry – which is why I showed them to her in the first place. But then she sold them as her own ..."

"Are you writing songs additionally to stories now, my dear?" the tree asked surprised. "What's next? Movie scripts?"

"I don't know," Nayeli laughed, instantly taking a liking to that idea. "Back in the day, I was trying out different styles of writing, but when my lyrics were stolen it was the beginning of the end. I felt so discouraged, and my creativity ground to a halt for years. Until now, that is."

"I'm sorry to hear you experienced that," Willow said a second time. "And I understand your reluctance to give up control in that case. But surely you know, based on the fact that you've already encountered panic attacks in your life, that sometimes you have to give up control in order to gain control?"

"What?" Nayeli asked, bewildered. "What kind of nonsense is that?"

"It's not nonsense," the tree replied patiently. "Don't you remember what helped you most when you had your panic attacks?"

"Not resisting them," Nayeli answered without having to think about it. "But what does that have to do with anything?"

"The more time you spend fighting your fear, the more it increases, resulting in the panic attacks getting stronger. But when you stop trying to control these attacks, when you accept them instead, their tight grip on you will loosen. And by doing so, you are suddenly the one who has power over them. Yet another example to explain this would be a company that employs several people. What do you believe would happen if a manager was set on controlling all their subordinates' work?"

"I don't have to venture a guess about that, since that's exactly what my boss does. She doesn't trust any of us to do our work properly and supervises every step when she's around. Even thinking about it makes me feel caged. I hate to be controlled and to be constantly told not only what I need to do, but how I need to do it. If she gave me some leeway, I would be better at my job, and I would also be much more inclined to commit myself to the company. But as things stand, I'm not interested in doing anything more than strictly necessary."

"See? By trying to control everything, your manager hinders your dedication and thus loses control of the success of her business," Willow added. "And that's what I mean. Sometimes you need to trust and give up your tight grip to remain in the driver's seat."

Nayeli sighed. "It's hard, though, to change something when you've done it differently your whole life."

"Change isn't easy, that's true," Willow agreed. "But at times, it is needed. And since we're already on this topic – Strix has had a huge change creep up on him. And I'm not merely talking about the change from the burning heat of Australia to the freezing cold of the Antarctic ..."

21. Arctic, the Penguin

It was beyond cold. The Antarctic wind was biting as it blew through Strix's plumage and the freezing air was hard to breathe into his lungs.

Strix had initially thought that his feathers would give him enough protection from the frost, but it was decidedly colder here than what he was used to back home in a normal winter. On top of that, the icy air seemed all the more extreme after the heat of Australia.

At first, Strix had been more than glad to escape the relentless, burning sun, but the further south he had flown and the more biting the wind had become, the more he had questioned his judgement to travel here. Especially since the sky had been obscured by thick clouds that promised a blizzard when he had reached land – if one could actually call it that because it was nothing but a layer of thick ice, covered in snow.

In a vain attempt to keep warm, Strix kept flapping his wings as fast as he could, all the while looking out for the snowy owl who had supposedly travelled here. But even if the white owl was anywhere near, it would be impossible to find her, for everything in this land was white: the ground with its snowbanks and the sky with the gusts of snowflakes that coated his feathers in cold.

To make matters worse, the blizzard was picking up and, soon, every wingbeat required a great deal of effort as particularly strong blasts pushed Strix backwards. Finally admitting to himself that it was madness to continue to fly around in this icy no-man's-land – a land which was just as much a hell as any fiery pit of doom – Strix came to the hard decision to go back the way he had come and turned around.

He was sad that his plan to find the snowy owl had failed, but giving up was the only reasonable choice to make, as he had no way of knowing how far this continent stretched and whether he would survive crossing it. All the more so as the snowstorm was growing ever stronger, reducing his senses to a bare minimum: Strix's field of vision was narrowed down to less than a meter while any potential noises were drowned out by the howling wind in his ears.

From one minute to the next, it wasn't about what Strix wanted anymore. Instead, it had become a fight for survival.

He kept flying for what felt like hours without seeing any proof that the coast was coming nearer. Then Strix could continue no longer. Landing exhausted, he tumbled down a snowbank.

As his feet touched the freezing ground, Strix flinched. But since he was too tired to fly on, he simply fluffed up his feathers to create some air pockets between them and hunkered down to provide at least the illusion of warmth. Choosing to wait out the storm in this way, he hid his face in his plumage as well as he could.

Jerking awake some time later, Strix realised to his surprise that he must have fallen asleep, despite the coldness seeping into his bones. He felt chilled to the core, as if ice – instead of blood – was running through his veins. Shaking himself to get rid of the last traces of sleep, and throwing off the snow and ice crystals clinging to his plumage in the process, Strix looked about. The storm had abated a bit and the view was better, but there was still nothing to see apart from the blinding white plains that extended in all directions.

He spread his wings and beat them a few times to warm up his muscles, determined to tackle the last miles lying between him and the coast before his growing hunger would sap his strength completely. But as Strix tried to take off from the ground, he was yanked back by a sharp pain in both of his legs.

Looking down, confused, he tried to lift first his left leg then his right, but, to his absolute horror, neither of them moved an inch. His feet were frozen solid to the ice, which was hidden underneath the thin layer of snow he was sitting on.

Feeling a sense of desperation creep up on him, Strix tried to take off a second time. Flapping his wings, he pulled up from the ground with all his strength, intending to rip his feet from the ice. But the only result was another pain travelling up his body, sharp enough to steal his breath. Strix was almost glad of it, though, because it told him that there was still life inside his legs – other than in his cold feet, which he couldn't feel at all anymore.

Realising with sudden clarity what a hopeless situation he found himself in, Strix tried with all his might to remain calm and to find a solution for his predicament – only that none existed. There was simply no whitewashing the truth that he was unable to fly off, let alone protect himself from the elements. And if the weather wouldn't cause him to cross over to the other side, his growing hunger would likely seal that deal.

It wasn't in his nature to succumb to hopelessness, but here he was, with no other option but to wait for his end. Huddling down, a single tear slipped out of Strix's right eye and instantly froze to the feathers on his cheek.

To keep the despair at bay that threatened to consume him, Strix started to hum an old lullaby. It was the one his mum had sung to put him to sleep when he had been a little fledgling. His voice was croaky and uncertain, but the action did calm his racing heartbeat and helped him cope to face what was unavoidable.

Strix sang until his attention was caught by a loud gabbling sound.

Wondering what or who was making it, Strix closed his beak and listened intently. Immediately, a sliver of hope began to rise within him that he wasn't alone in this icy desert, after all; a hope that someone out there might be able to help him cheat death.

He noticed that the noise sounded like many voices, with individual calls standing out here and there. A slightly mismatched, yet at the same time well-rounded, choir.

Lifting his head as high as he could and craning his neck to look behind him, Strix's gaze fell on a large group of black-and-white birds that were waddling up a snowdrift behind which they had been invisible till now. Strix's eyes widened in wonder. He couldn't remember ever having come across such an immense gathering of birds at any location. And certainly not a group that wasn't flying in a formation, but toddling clumsily over the ground. His wonder was quickly replaced with horror, though, when Strix realised that the colony would pass him by if they continued on their course.

Strix called out to them but it was to no avail. No matter how loud he hooted, the group of birds took no notice of him as their own voices drowned out all other sounds. Collecting his breath for a second round of cries for help, Strix waved his wings for added effect.

"Help!" he called. "I'm stuck here – help me!"

At first, it appeared as if the colony would proceed without taking notice of him, but then one of the birds turned its head in his direction and stopped abruptly, making another bird walk straight into its backside. Calling out to the others in the group, the bird then waddled straight towards Strix, the others following close on its tail.

"Are you all right?" the male called out when he was in earshot. "What happened?"

"My feet are frozen to the ground!" Strix answered. "I can't move or fly away. Can you help me?"

"In my whole life I've never seen a penguin's feet stuck to the ground," the bird chattered as he reached Strix. "Not even the youngest or most reckless ones could manage that …"

"A what?" Strix asked, perplexed, never having heard that word before. "A pengwing?"

"Penguin, not pengwing," the bird, who introduced himself as Arctic, corrected him. "That's what we are."

Looking questioningly at the black and white colony members behind him, Arctic waved his short wings about. "Does anyone have any idea what to do?"

But he was met with equally clueless faces and a lot of head-shakes.

After some time, an older female member of the group squeezed through the bodies in front of her and spoke up. "We could form a tight ring around him and warm him up that way. And then one of us will slide our own feet under his, bit by bit."

"That's a brilliant idea," Arctic said happily and gestured the members of his colony over. Everyone shuffled around Strix, getting into position.

Strix gave off a sigh of relief. It felt good to be surrounded by hundreds of warm bodies, not only because they kept the icy wind at bay but also because he didn't feel as alone anymore.

"You know," Arctic, who was pressed against Strix's left side by the many bodies behind him, said, "if this fails we can bring you some fish from the sea. That way you won't starve until we can think of something else."

"Thank you," Strix answered, grateful for the offer and for how warmly the whole group had welcomed him into their midst. "But I hope that won't be necessary because I want this plan to work. I don't want to be stuck to this ice forever."

"Don't worry, it's gonna get warmer in the next months. The summers aren't as frosty as they were when our grandparents were alive. They're getting warmer every year. We actually fear that, someday, all the ice will thaw and leave us without a home. Hopefully, that will be stopped before it happens, though ..."

"A few months?" Strix asked aghast. "I can't stay stuck here for that long."

"Let's not lose any sleep over that before we haven't used up all other options," Arctic said. "We'll find a way to change your situation for the better. Somehow ..." And with those words, he pushed ever closer towards Strix and warmed him up with his body heat. Unfortunately, it didn't help to unstick Strix's feet, however, which continued to resemble icy clumps that were glued fast to the ground. None of the penguins had managed to detach them even a little.

"This isn't working," one of the males behind Strix finally stated the obvious. "Our feet are too cold to thaw the ground enough for him to move away. That's probably why we don't stick to the ice ourselves."

"You tried your best," Strix said dejectedly, attempting to sound brave, although he felt anything but. "No one could ask for more."

"Hey," Arctic cut in, "if you think we're going to give up that easily, you're mistaken. We stick together – always. No one is left behind. And you're an honorary penguin now."

Moved to tears by Arctic's declaration and at all the other penguins around him murmuring in assent, Strix was momentarily lost for words.

"I have a new suggestion," another female cut in at that point, raising her voice to be heard over the never-ending cackle of the black and white birds. "You remember the human boat we saw, heading for our coast? We aren't far from there. If we manage to get to them before they wander off, maybe we can lead them here."

"To what end?" a smaller penguin piped up. "What will they be able to do that we can't?"

"I don't know," the first penguin shrugged. "But they've loads of weird ideas. Remember those things that made the clicking sounds? They didn't serve any purpose, but despite that the humans were constantly looking at them. They might be able to think of something that we haven't considered. It's certainly worth a try."

"No!" Strix called out loudly. "No humans! Please. They are the only creatures that scare me more than crocodiles. I've learned that they can't be trusted further than they can fly."

"Why do you say that?" Arctic asked. "During all our encounters with them, we've never been in danger. Yes, they are weird. They are, for example, trying to squawk at us in our language all the time – which they fail at spectacularly, mind you. But it's a nice attempt. In any case, what I wanted to say is that humans are okay to be around."

"I don't know," Strix said, unconvinced. "I've heard such terrible things about them. And I can't even fly away this time when they come near."

"But you don't have a lot of choices left," Arctic retorted. "As far as I can see, you can take your chances with the humans or stay stuck to the ice for a couple more months while we bring you fish."

Strix felt his stomach plummet at these two options, which both sounded less than ideal.

Arctic, meanwhile, seemed to take his silence as approval. "Then it's a done deal, right? We'll go and bring the two-legged here?"

"Sure!" hundreds of voices echoed back.

Strix was still mulling over the fact that it might be preferable to cross over peacefully to the other side instead of attracting any human's attention. But when he raised his head to say as much, it was too late.

The colony of penguins was already leaving, marching away in unison and disappearing behind a high snowdrift.

When Strix couldn't spot them anymore, he let his head hang. This was going to end terribly; he knew it would.

The next minutes felt like an eternity to Strix, who fluctuated between hope and despair. And just when the thought wormed into his mind that the penguins must have abandoned him and wouldn't come back, he heard the first distant call. Staring bleakly at the spot from where it had originated, he soon spotted a huge moving mass that divided itself into many individual birds the closer they came, toddling fast in his direction while looking back every few steps.

It wasn't until the penguins were near enough for Strix to make out who was who that he saw three humans following them at some distance. Trembling in fear that had nothing to do with the cold penetrating his bones, Strix's eyes widened at the sight of the two-legged. His instinct told him to take to the air and the safety it provided but, of course, that was impossible. The only thing he achieved by flapping his wings was to attract the men's attention.

Seeing that one was pointing straight at him, Strix renewed his efforts to get away as panic engulfed his entire being.

Shortly after, the humans were upon him.

Strix covered away in fear and opened his sharp beak to hack at one of the men's hands. But not even his attack impressed them sufficiently to stay away.

Instead, one of the men threw some sort of fabric over him and pressed his wings against his sides, robbing him not only of his sight but also of any form of movement.

Suddenly, Strix felt a wet warmth over and around his feet, which melted away the top layer of the ice. His fear momentarily forgotten, he hooted in joy as feeling – and pain – crept back into them.

Once Strix's feet became unstuck completely, he would have liked nothing better than to fly away. But one of the humans was still holding on to him. Wondering when they would release him, now that he was freed from the ground, Strix was surprised when he was being moved around – it felt like the two-legged who was holding him was standing up and walking away.

The realisation of what was happening came slowly, but when it did, Strix screamed.

"No!" Strix called out loudly, squirming and wriggling to get out of the human's grip. "Arctic! Please help me! Please don't let them take me away and imprison me – or do even worse than that. I knew this was a bad idea! Please, anyone, please help me!"

The second he uttered the words, Strix knew that his pleading with the penguins was pointless, though. For what could they do against the two-legged? Although there were hundreds of them, their bills and claws were no match against these giants. And their small feet on which they wobbled around didn't measure up with the long strides of the men, especially since the black-and-white birds had yet to prove that they could fly.

Strix heard the penguins call out to him.

Artic shouted words of encouragement that everything would turn out fine, and the other birds of the colony seconded that, creating a ruckus of noise.

But the further away Strix was carried the more the penguins' voices blended into a cacophony, which grew softer and softer until Strix was surrounded by a dark, foreboding silence that was only interrupted by the heavy breathing of the three humans.

Changes and Coping Mechanisms

Nayeli was shifting around impatiently by the time Willow had finished its story. "What did the humans do to Strix? Is he all right?"

"All in good time, my dear child, all in good time. If you are patient enough, you'll learn that these circumstances Strix is caught up in are a blessing in disguise because they will lead to something he's wanted for weeks now ..." The tree emphasised the last words, as if they should reveal a deeper meaning.

When Nayeli failed to see what that was, she furrowed her forehead in confusion.

"To meet the snow owl he's been following, of course," Willow said when the silence had stretched on for too long.

Nayeli couldn't contain her excitement about that prospect. "He met her? That's great! Has she been captured by the humans, too?"

"Not exactly." The willow tree chuckled. "But before I tell you that story, let's talk about what you could learn from this one first."

"Well, the fact that jumps out immediately is that life can be scary. Maybe not for our souls who are safe on the other side. But for us, stuck in this dual reality? Heck, yeah! Just look at Strix – ending up as a captive. His situation might be even worse than it was before ... and this story is supposed to make me want to embrace change? Are you serious?"

Nayeli blew a strand of hair away from her face. "Cause I've come to some conclusions in my life. One – change is scary. And two – it isn't needed as we can survive without it."

"These are some interesting conclusions," Willow responded mildly. "Why indeed is change needed when we are all creatures of habit? Why should seals hunt hares on land when there's enough fish in the water to eat? Or why should a mole move to live above the ground when it has adapted perfectly to a life beneath it? Why would any animal change their behaviour, habits or environment out of fun if the ecological niche they occupy makes them thrive? The obvious answer is that they change exclusively when they're forced to adapt by external circumstances. That's what evolution is, by the way – the adaptation to change over generations."

"See?" Nayeli said. "Change isn't natural and we should avoid it at all costs!"

"Not so fast, my dear," the tree murmured. "Change *is* natural. It happens constantly, and on every level – even down to the cellular one. Your liver, your skin, every cell regenerates itself and after a few years, your entire body is renewed. Additionally, life is continually undergoing shifts, and you transform into new versions of yourself as you grow older. No, no. In the end, change is not only natural but also inevitable for all living beings. And especially for humans!"

Nayeli crossed her arms in front of her chest. "Why are you implying that it's different for us humans?"

"I'll come to that in a moment. But first, let me explain why changes are needed in general ... Change is necessary for any kind of growth to take place – for your own growth as well as for the growth of the collective consciousness. If there were no changes in your life, it would stagnate and you'd stay where you are. But that's not what you came here for. You are not a tree with your roots rooted deep inside the earth. You have legs to move forward. So use them!"

Nayeli frowned. "But animals have legs, too. Which brings me back to my question: why are we different?"

"You are different because you have a fully grown adult human ego. This enables you to undergo changes much faster and much more often than any animal. You do not need several generations to create big changes in your life, and neither do you need to wait till you have no other choice left. You can transform your life how you want whenever you want. Which, by the way, is one of the main reasons you chose to come here as a human and not as a giraffe or a squirrel – to grow at this rate.

"Sadly, though, many humans don't use this birthright as few people willingly initiate changes until it becomes necessary – or at least not until the positive aspects far outweigh the negative ones. Generally speaking, a situation has to become unbearable for you to brave venturing out of your comfort zone."

"Yeah, because my comfort zone makes me feel safe," Nayeli declared.

"But it also makes you a prisoner," Willow countered, extending its branches as far as they reached. "For it prevents you from reaching any of your goals, which are outside of what you know and are accustomed to. When you always do and think the same things, you'll always stay in the same reality. You need to risk making changes to get different results."

Nayeli sighed. "All right, all right, you can stop trying to convince me. I *am* starting to see the benefits of creating shifts in my life, but there's still a huge difference between understanding this in theory and applying it in practice ..."

"Of course, there is. And you aren't the only human who's faced with this problem. Many people know that living a healthy lifestyle would be beneficial to them, and yet they don't start to exercise and eat a healthy diet until they get ill. And all your talk about averting a climate crisis? That wasn't done decades ago when the problems began, but now when you humans are standing with your back to the wall and have no other choice left."

The tree let the words sink in. "But this is precisely why it's beneficial to change before circumstances force you to. Just think about the two alternatives ... When you wait till the last possible moment, you have little time to build your reality. If, however, you introduce changes yourself early on, you can decide how you want the shift to look. It's the difference between being passive and between actively creating your future. Now, what sounds like the better option to you, my dear?"

"The latter," Nayeli replied. "Definitely the latter. But Willow, I get the impression that you believe changes are merely scary. Which isn't true – they can be dangerous, too. And I can prove that based on something one of my friends went through. At one point in her life, she quit her job in favour of being self-employed. But the business she started didn't do well and it caused a landslide effect, making her lose not only her money but also her home and her partner. If her parents hadn't let her move back in with them, she would have been out on the streets and might have never got back on her feet. Thus, when we open ourselves up to changes, we open ourselves up to the possibility of failing and losing everything, don't we?"

The tree whipped its branches up and down in silent confirmation. "Any drastic change can have big consequences, that fact can't be denied. But you can always take the safer route, start with smaller changes and built upon them step by step, which is what I'd recommend for most people anyway. At least, until you've developed an unshakeable belief in your ability to create anything you desire. No matter, if you prefer big or small changes for your own life, though, you should allow for *some* shifts. Instead of settling for a life that doesn't bring you happiness."

"What are you getting at?" Nayeli questioned. "You make it sound as if we actively choose to stay in situations that are not for the best of us – which is not the case. We do want a better reality; we simply don't know how to create it or are too scared to take the first step."

"I beg to differ," Willow replied, the tree's words sounding firm while its voice remained loving. "Based on the fact that you even go so far to create coping mechanisms as a means to endure something long-term that's detrimental to you."

Nayeli observed some birds that were crossing the meadow while addressing the tree. "What kind of coping mechanisms?"

"Anything that will reduce your stress levels. Coping mechanisms are habits that act to soothe you. By using them, you are avoiding or reducing the stress you are exposed to. When you read books in order to escape a painful reality, that can be a coping mechanism for you. When you go into freeze mode as soon as someone raises their voice, this too might be a coping mechanism. And when you are reducing your stress by smoking cigarettes, it can also be a coping mechanism."

"So, addictions are coping mechanisms?" Nayeli asked, surprised.

"Oh yes, addictions are prime examples of those," the tree said. And this includes every addictive behaviour – from playing sports or watching TV shows to practising meditation or overeating. Saying this, having an addiction isn't necessarily bad as we can have countless harmless ones during our lives. Up to a certain point, they are even useful as they provide something we currently need. Maybe the comfort of eating sweets is more important to someone right now than the long-time consequences of gaining weight."

"But addictions can become detrimental?" Nayeli cut in.

"Undoubtedly – any coping mechanism can."

"And how do we recognise when this happens?"

"When an addiction or other coping mechanism overtakes our lives, we can best see it by a lack in another area. When someone spends most of their time working, that isn't necessarily a destructive behaviour yet. But when their social or family life takes a back seat in a way that's hurting them, they have established a destructive pattern of working too much. A smoking addiction might manifest in a lack of health. And an addiction of always staying at home might lead to a lack of connection and relationships.

"But the worst thing about coping mechanisms is, like I mentioned, that they prevent you from changing anything in your life for the better. They make your present reality bearable enough for you to stay in it, even though you could have a much happier and more fulfilling life."

Nayeli looked off into the distance where the birds had disappeared between the trees, believing to know how this correlated. "This is part of the reason why we are so reluctant to initiate change, isn't it? Because the coping mechanisms we installed are perfectly suited to help us with the original problem that generated them, but they might not prove as useful for any new issues that arise?"

"That's correct, my dear."

"Hmm, now that you say it like that, I think I've fallen prey to this myself in the past ... Cause when I was a kid I was bullied in one of the schools I went to before we moved away to another state. I didn't tell my parents or teachers about it – instead I just avoided the group of students by staying inside during the breaks or by leaving the school grounds. I mean, speaking up about it might have made things better, but then again, I couldn't be sure that it would lead to an improvement. Maybe I would have got out of the frying pan and right into the fire ..."

"Yes," the tree agreed. "No one can say beforehand if a change won't make some things worse, too. And because of this, familiar, awful circumstances often feel a little safer than the unknown because you've already survived those for some time – letting you know it's possible to continue to do so. But as I said previously, if you don't dare to take a leap of faith eventually, you'll never get where you want to be."

Reflecting on this, Nayeli closed her eyes for a moment. "Okay, let's say I'm gonna follow your advice and start to create changes in my life. What exactly would I need to do then?"

"The first thing that's essential is to see your reality for what it is and to be honest with yourself. You need to be brave enough to recognise the truth even if it's painful. When you ignore the fact that you and your partner are incompatible in a romantic setting, you cannot find solutions for that problem. And when you refuse to recognise that drinking several bottles of alcohol each day is bad for your health, you won't ever think about stopping or reducing the amount.

"To this end, you also need to become aware of your coping mechanisms and what those stand for. If you're addicted to eating cheese that could, for example, indicate that you lacked motherly love and are subconsciously craving to be nurtured. Find out what the root cause of the addiction is and begin your healing journey there. Because it's no use at all to force yourself to stop your addictive behaviour when you don't change the situation that generated the coping mechanism in the first place. If you do, you'll risk a relapse into your old coping mechanism or you will create different ones, which aren't any healthier. If you binge-eat every time you feel lonely and manage to stop doing it but don't find a solution for your lack of relationships, the pain of the disconnection might drive you to do excessive sports instead. And if you take heroin because you are in an abusive relationship and come out clean after rehab, but go right back to the person who abuses you, it won't take long until you are using again."

Nayeli chewed on her bottom lip. "In short, to successfully stop a coping mechanism and move on from a destructive pattern, we need to find out what we are compensating for, meet our unmet need and thus heal the underlying cause?"

"Indeed, very good, my dear," Willow said happily, satisfaction oozing out of the tree's voice.

Nayeli could have felt pleased at the praise, but instead she hunched her shoulders.

"What's wrong?" Willow asked, immediately sensing her distress.

Nayeli threw up her arms. "I just don't know how I'm supposed to do this all. There's so much to learn and do. All this information is overwhelming. Maybe it's too much for one person alone. Maybe it's too much for me!"

"But who says you have to do it alone?" the tree asked gently.

"I am! Because whenever I ask for help, it turns out badly," Nayeli muttered darkly. "I'm not sure why, because it seems easy enough for some people. But somehow, I always mess it up. Either the person I ask refuses. Or they don't deliver the help they promised. Or I give up on the idea to ask for help before I get the opportunity to speak to the person – because I know they'll let me down anyhow."

"I know that it can be tricky sometimes to ask other humans for support or to receive the right kind of help from them, simply because they have their own agendas, lives, perspectives and problems. Which leaves the question – why not ask someone else instead? Someone who stands above any 3D problems and has a wider perspective?" the tree asked.

"Like who? Do you mean my higher self? Or the source itself?"

"No, I mean your spirit guides. They are available to offer their help to you at any point in time. Not as a replacement for human relationships, mind you, but by being a valuable asset to them."

Nayeli looked up. "In that case, why don't you introduce me to some of them?"

Willow laughed. "Coming right up."

22. Pearl, the Snowy Owl

Strix figured he could have done worse in this incarnation. At least, he'd had a loving family and friends, including his parents, the weeping willow tree and Snowflake, his fox friend, who was probably roaming their home meadow right about now. Then there were the great friends he'd met on his world journey: like Hazel, the wolf, or Cherry, the tortoise. And of course, there was Nuktia. Nuktia, whose plumage shimmered so beautifully under the pale moonlight. Nuktia who had the loveliest voice of all owls. Nuktia, who always knew what she wanted and how to get it. Nuktia, who he'd have liked to see one more time ...

But it was not to be.

Having been brought onto the human's ship and locked up in a cage, which was so small that it prevented him from unfolding his wings properly, Strix was acutely aware of how trapped and powerless he was. All of his attempts to hack or claw open the strong metal bars had failed, and his desperate hoots for help had fallen on deaf ears. Which only left him with one option – to accept his destiny. Strix was certain that the journey back into the spirit realm was imminent, and his last remaining hope was that the two-legged would make his passing as painless as possible and that they wouldn't draw it out.

Pressing his head against the bars of his prison, Strix was glad that his emotions couldn't be contained by them like his body was because he wanted to feel them all one last time. Letting his mind wander back to the past, he let himself fully experience the grief, happiness, longing, love and sadness that were rising up, letting each emotion run its course before saying goodbye to it and welcoming the next.

The one that occupied his mind the longest was regret. Regret that he had left everyone behind whom he loved and that he had so carelessly thrown away the great friendship he'd had with Nuktia. But no matter how much he second-guessed his decision to leave, there was nothing he could do to revoke his mistake now. His fate was sealed.

Strix closed his eyes. He needed to prepare himself for this last leg of his journey by making his peace with all that had happened in this lifetime. But just when he felt the negative emotions ebb out of him, his cage was shaken. Silently cursing the humans for not letting him have this last moment to himself, Strix opened his eyes, expecting to see one of their faces looking in at him. But what he saw instead was a black beak that was almost entirely covered in white feathers.

Rearing back in surprise as far as the bars allowed him to, Strix opened his own beak to say something. But all his words were stuck in his throat as he watched the female snowy owl balance on top of his cage.

"Cat got your tongue, kiddo?" She grinned down at him. "Or have you never seen an owl before?"

"Are you Pearl?" he asked the first question that popped into his head, simultaneously realising how unlikely it was that two snow owls had strayed this far south.

"I am," the female owl responded. "Can I ask how you know my name? And what's yours?"

"Crim told me about you and that you wanted to travel here. I actually tried to find you but had no luck. And then I was captured by the two-legged, as you can see. Oh, and my name's Strix."

"My, how long has it been since I saw Crim and her son?" Pearl pondered out loud. She then shook herself and diverted her attention back to Strix. "They are real nice, aren't they? Well, they are if you overlook Crim son's phobia of owls." Laughing, Pearl contemplated him more intently. "Pray tell, how did you get yourself into this predicament, though? Why didn't you fly away when you noticed that humans were coming? Are your wings broken?"

"No." Strix sighed. "I was stuck to the ice and they freed me from it. But instead of letting me go afterwards, they imprisoned me. Do you know how to open this cage? All my attempts have been useless."

"I don't," Pearl said slowly, her eyes lightening up a moment later. "But I know someone who does for sure. Let me get in touch with them, and we'll see if we can't get you out – before the humans do whatever they've planned. Agreed?"

"Yes." Strix hooted softly, not daring to be too loud with the two-legged being this near. A sliver of hope was rising within him that he could be freed from this prison after all. And he would not thoughtlessly squander it by attracting the humans' attention to the fact that another owl was sitting on his cage. They might want to catch her, too, and thus destroy his only chance of survival.

"Please fly as fast as you can to your friend and ask them, then come back in a flash. I don't know where they're taking this boat. So, the faster you are, the easier it will be for you to find me again."

Worried that the humans would change course, or that he wouldn't be alive once Pearl returned, Strix tried to stress the importance of her leaving immediately. But to his utter disbelief, the snow owl simply nodded in agreement and then closed her eyes, hunkering down on top of the cage.

"What are you doing?" Strix called out to her. "Every second counts. You must leave right now and ask your friend. If you sleep first, it could be too late for me."

Opening one of her eyes a fraction, Pearl looked down at him through the bars. "What are you talking about? I'm already on my way. Lighten up and let me do my job."

The snowy owl closed her eye again, giving no indication that she would fly off anytime soon.

"Pearl," Strix said softly, being all too aware that he didn't have much time left. "Why aren't you taking to the air?"

"For heaven's sake, Strix, show a little owl understanding, would you?" Pearl called out, this time opening both her eyes. "Can't you manage to stay quiet? I need peace to concentrate here."

"Shh," Strix said quickly, turning his head in both directions to see if any of the two-legged had heard the snow owl's loud hoots. Luckily, none of them were showing their faces and Strix breathed a sigh of relief. It was only then that Pearl's words registered in his brain. Puzzled, he wanted to ask her what she had meant with them. But the snowy owl had already huddled down and closed her eyes once more, and Strix didn't dare to address her a third time, fearing that she might backtrack on her offer to help him if he annoyed her too much.

Sighing forlornly, Strix shifted his weight to get more comfortable and decided to wait her out. And wait he did.

For almost half an hour nothing happened.

Strix was growing increasingly restless with every second that passed by and shifted from one foot to the other. At long last, he had got so nervous that he was almost ready to poke Pearl with his beak to wake her up. But before he could put his plan into action, the snowy owl finally stirred and gazed down at him through bleary eyes.

A second later they sharpened and she turned her head sideways to inspect the cage in greater detail. "There!" she called out happily. "Do you see that thing that sticks out in the middle? That's called a latch, and I need to pull it to the right for the door to open."

"Wh …?" Strix began, perplexed. "But I thought you had no idea how to get me out of here and wanted to ask your friend?"

"That's what I did." Pearl fluttered down and landed on the boat deck in front of him. Eyeing the cage from this perspective, she stretched one of her legs out to grasp the bars and used her beak to bite the latch. It slipped off a couple of times, but then she had a solid grasp and pulled it back and sideways.

As if by magic a door opened where only seconds ago firm, unforgiving bars had been.

In his haste to get out before the opening could close again, Strix almost knocked down Pearl, who quickly leapt aside.

Strix took to the sky and didn't stop until he'd reached a height from which the boat looked like a miniature. Soaring on the cold winds, he was able to breathe deeply for the first time since his capture. Although the icy air had blown through the cage bars and ruffled his feathers the whole time, he'd felt close to suffocating inside his prison. Which was a total contrast to having nothing else but the endless sky above him. Strix revelled in this freedom – a freedom which he'd thought lost forever only seconds ago – and grinned widely.

Pearl, who was flying beside him, had an amused expression on her face. "Better?"

"Yes, thank you," Strix breathed. "I don't think I've ever felt this good in my entire life." And to prove his point, he hooted with joy.

Noticing that two of the tiny humans below were nearing the now empty cage, Strix hooted another time, as loudly as he could.

The men turned to stare up at him. One of the two-legged glanced between them and the empty cage, dumbfounded, while the other simply smiled and waved.

Irritated by this odd behaviour, Strix turned to Pearl. "Come on, let's get away from here and search for some land. I need a long sleep and a nice meal after all this stress – and I don't mind in which order."

Agreeing with his suggestion, Pearl told him about a small island that wasn't far from their current position.

They flew towards it in a comfortable silence for some time, and Strix looked down at the deep blue ocean. The sea didn't feel threatening to him any longer, now that he'd survived being captured by the two-legged, which was the worst-case-scenario that he could possibly imagine. Instead, it was a tranquil experience to watch the gently rolling waves beneath him.

Eventually though, the peacefulness was brushed aside by the pending questions inside his mind, and Strix's endless curiosity gained the upper claw once more.

He turned his head sideways to look at Pearl. "What the heck was all that about?"

"What do you mean?" the snow owl asked innocently. "I was only doing what I promised. And successfully, don't you think so?"

"But you didn't talk to anyone," Strix objected. "You did nothing else but sit there and sleep."

The snowy owl laughed loudly and joyously. "Oh, Strix, do you really have no idea what I did? Have you never flown to you're ancestors or other spirits to ask them for guidance?"

"Flown to my ancestors?" Strix asked, thinking about declaring Pearl insane. "No, my wings are strong and can carry me far, but they won't let me cross over into the higher energetic planes."

"I'm not talking about your wings, Strix," the snow owl corrected him. "I'm talking about your mind. Even if your body can't travel there, your spirit can."

"And that's what you did? You ... you travelled to the spirit world to get the answer?" Strix asked, dumbfounded. "How? And who did you talk to?"

"Archangel Uriel," Pearl answered his last question. "Once, curiosity made me fly through an open window of a country house. But when I was inside, I panicked and couldn't find my way out. Then I heard my mum's voice in my head, reminding me that if I ever needed a practical solution to a problem, I should call on this archangel. So I did, and Uriel helped me to find my way out before the humans returned. Ever since that day, I've had chats with several angels whenever I needed some help."

"Wow," Strix said, impressed. "That sounds intriguing. I've never even thought about talking to anyone on the spirit planes till now. And I wouldn't know where to start, either."

As Strix flew at Pearl's side over the vast expense of the ocean, he eyed the older owl and marvelled at all the things she knew. Wondering what else he could learn from her, Strix began to quiz her on her life, and soon they were both engrossed in conversation about their different adventures.

Becoming aware that Peal was practically overflowing with enthusiasm whenever she recounted tales about her travels, Strix smiled knowingly. "You've found your calling in journeying, haven't you?"

"Definitely," Pearl said with conviction. "I love it more than anything else in this world. But why do you ask? Don't you enjoy it?"

"I do," Strix said, noticing that his own enthusiasm was laced with hesitation.

"But?" Pearl prompted.

"But I kinda think ... maybe I should return home. Maybe it has been a mistake all along to come here. Maybe I only chose this path as an escape from something I was too afraid to face. No, scratch that. I *did* run away from something that scared me."

"It must have been a dangerous opponent if you fled that far... Was it a bear? I saw one last year, and it was huge and scary."

Strix couldn't help grinning. "No, it wasn't a bear. It's someone much scarier than that."

"A crocodile, then? They can attack rapidly."

Turning his head, Strix let his gaze drift to Pearl. And in his mind's eyes, her image transformed into that of a smaller, brown owl. Nuktia.

"No, it was my best childhood friend. She told me she loved me. And I freaked out and left her sitting on the branch while I fled halfway around the world. What an idiot I am. If that isn't an extreme reaction, I don't know what is." Strix huffed sadly. "I might even be the most cowardly of all owls ..."

"Don't be this hard on yourself, Strix. Have you never considered that it was right for you to fly away *at the time*, but that this is now the right time for you to return?"

Strix grinned lopsidedly. "You're saying that the insights I've won – they wouldn't be there without all the experiences I've had over the last few months?"

"Yes, you can see this journey as you running away. Or you could see it as a vital task you needed to undertake to reach the awareness you have now."

"Hmpf," Strix muttered. "Did one of your spirit friends tell you that?"

"Hey," Pearl said, mock-offended. "I don't need a friend for that. Being wise comes is in my job description as an owl, kiddo. Something you should know yourself!"

Looking at each other, Strix and Pearl burst into laughter.

"I don't know," Strix eventually said, still giggling. "I certainly don't feel very wise when I look at all the mistakes I've made in my life."

Pearl flew a loop and winked at him. "But merely the wisest of us realise that we aren't wise all the time. And you are thus wiser than me because you know how unwise you are."

"Ow, now you're poking fun at me," Strix complained, but he did so good-naturedly.

Then he fell silent. Mulling over what Pearl had said, Strix took a good look at his past decisions before plucking up his courage to ask himself the question he hadn't dared to face until now. What if he flew back, only for Nuktia to be angry with him? What if she'd already moved on? And what if she didn't want to see him anymore or let him explain? But, on the other hand, what if he continued to run in fear? Wouldn't it be amazing to have his inner peace back and not to have all those 'what ifs' chasing each other around inside his brain?

Just then, a new thought slammed into Strix's awareness. A thought, which was so shocking that he almost lost his balance and crashed into the waves below.

"Oh my gosh," Strix muttered under his breath. "I love her."

"And you didn't understand that till now?" Pearl asked jokingly.

Looking at the snowy owl in confusion, Strix opened his beak to ask what she meant, but Pearl beat him to it. "Strix, your eyes lit up the second you mentioned her. It was as clear as day."

"Well, it wasn't to me." Strix defended himself, before grinning brightly. "I need to go home and see if there's anything left between us."

Strix wished that all the miles between Nuktia and him would shrivel up into nothingness and that he could be back by her side this instant. He groaned in dismay when he realised that another few months and countless countries lay between his current resolve to return and actually laying eyes on Nuktia again. Months in which she could build a new life in which there'd be no place for him. And months full of new dangers that could prevent him from reaching his destination.

But then Strix quickly cast these gloomy thoughts aside and berated himself for letting his mind go there. He should be content. He finally had a real direction to turn in, and that was enough to take on anything that stood in the way of his happiness.

Just as he thought this, the island Pearl had mentioned appeared on the horizon, with its promise of food and sleep. It would be the first step to prepare himself for the long journey that lay ahead. A journey he was more than ready to embark on ...

"Willow, are you implying that there are beings in the energetic realms apart from the souls who incarnate here? That there are angels and the likes? Cause I don't know if I can believe such a thing. I've never been religious, and the thought is alien to me, to put it lightly."

"I can understand your reservations. But don't dismiss this aspect of spirituality before hearing about it, hmm?"

Shrugging, Nayeli yielded to the wisdom of her friend. "Bring it on, then. Convince me – or not, as the case may be."

"Fine, fine." the tree droned, satisfied at having got its way. "Let's see, where should I start? Ah, yes ... There are many different spirit forms and everyone can find one or more they can relate to, based on their background, religion and culture. There are angels like your guardian angels and the archangels, for example, the Archangels Michael, Raphael and Gabriel. There are the ascended masters, which range from Buddha to Jesus. There are gods and goddesses – for example from the Egyptian or Celtic cultures. And there are, of course, all the spirit animals.

"While all the incarnated souls have decided to live through their experiences from a first-hand perspective to grow their consciousness, the spirits are expanding by guiding us in our physical lives from the other side, and they are thus happy to lend us their knowledge – whenever we ask for it."

"All right, I see why they'd like to help me in that case, as they apparently get something out of it. But what's in it for me? If these angels don't have any ideas about the obstacles here on Earth because they aren't incarnated themselves, how can they give me the solutions I need?"

"Remember what we talked about when we were on the topic of your higher self, my dear child? The same holds true for the spirits. They are not confined to a physical body nor to the illusion of a space-time reality. Thus, they can see a bigger picture than you – one that includes the past, the present and any alternative future roads, on top of all the different interrelations between you and other souls. These all make them great mentors in guiding you along the best path you could take. What's more, they can look at your problems from an outsider's perspective. Just think how easy it is for you to give someone else advice when you're not in the middle of the drama ..."

Silence settled in the meadow and, after a minute or two, the tree continued in its kindest voice. "Don't get me wrong, though. Spirit guides aren't all-knowing. It's correct that they do not have a full-blown ego like you incarnated humans, but they *do* have a form of consciousness and, with it, a perception of a separate self. Which makes their knowledge subjective, too."

Nayeli jutted her chin. "Then what good does it do for me to communicate with them if anyone I ask gives me another solution instead of the objective truth? And how do I even decide who to ask?"

The tree's trunk thrummed with energy. "If you remember us talking about truth, you'll also remember that everything is true on some level and that you move through different layers of it during your life. What is true for you one day can be wrong the next. Spirit guides recognise where you stand and what you need to hear to move onward. The answers you receive from them are in harmony with your present level of reality.

"And if they say something you don't agree with, you simply use your free will to say 'no thanks'. You shouldn't take anyone's advice – whether this is from another human or someone on the energetic planes – without checking for yourself whether it's right for you."

Nayeli shifted to a kneeling position and sat down on her heels. "Fine, so let's say I decided to work with the spirit guides, how do I do that? Do I ask them while meditating, or what?"

"That's one option. You can connect to the spirit world via various forms of meditation. You can travel to the higher planes via astral travelling or by going on a shamanic journey, which are both lessons in their own right. Or you can use tools like oracle cards or auto-writing to channel messages. Answers can come through any of your clair-channels, or as signs or messages you see in your 3D reality, from a newspaper article to a song you hear on the radio. You just need to remain open to detect the answers when they arrive, in whatever form they appear."

Nayeli let her gaze sweep over the row of trees on the horizon. "And what group of spirits should I work with first?" she repeated her earlier question.

"The answer to that is a matter of preference and will be different for everyone. You should ask your intuition instead of me, because whoever you feel drawn to work with will be right for you. This can even change as you progress along your path. But if you want my opinion ... I've noticed that you have a great connection with animals. Hence, spirit animals could be a safe bet."

"What do you mean by that?" Nayeli inquired.

"Many humans, like you, are atheists and raised to only believe in science. They might not have had any past dealings with angels or goddesses and think of them as legends, not real. But a whole lot of humans have an affinity with animals. You share this planet with all these different species after all. And this makes it easy to work with their counterparts in the spirit world, the spirit animals, as establishing a connection to them comes naturally to you."

Nayeli agreed with that assessment. "Now that I think of it, I've heard about spirit animals before. I think it was in relation to Native American tribes. The spirit animals are sacred messengers for them, and especially for the shamans, aren't they?"

"Not solely for them," Willow corrected. "There are, for example, totem animals in several African tribes as well. Animal guides are at the core of many native cultures. But you are right that the term 'spirit animal' is best known in regards to the American shamans, who have known about and worked with these messengers for a long time. In the end, everyone has spirit animals, though, independent of what culture you were born into. They are happy to work with anyone who is ready to connect with and learn from them. And they can teach us all so much, if only we learned to truly listen to them ..."

Thinking about this, a revelation crossed Nayeli's mind. "Wait, where all the stories about the animals Strix met on his travels messages from the spirit animal world?"

"The stories carried messages, that's correct, and if any of them resonated with you, the inherent lesson is of importance for your path. But saying this, the animals we met in these tales weren't archetypes of their species. They were all individuals with a name and character and a unique life path. Therefore, the answer is no, those weren't spirit animal messages."

Nayeli arched her eyebrows. "What do archetypes have to do with them?"

"Like humans, all incarnated animals are individuals. They all have different characters and quirks. Just look at my dear friend Strix and his cousins. Most short-eared owls migrate in irregular patterns that are based on finding food sources. The likelihood that one short-eared owl would talk to a sloth, a kangaroo and a giraffe is slim to none. Unless you are named Strix, that is, and have chosen an abnormal amount of adventurousness in your soul-plan for this incarnation. This begs the question, if they're all so different, what does it tell you if you have the short-eared owl as one of your spirit animals? With one preferring to stay close to its nest, while another one is being more adventurous, how can you relate that to your own life? Which of the two animals tells the truth? The answer is that a spirit animal is always the archetype of the animal it represents, meaning it portrays the usual behaviours and traits that belong to the species."

Nayeli cleared her throat. "Are you saying that if I have an owl as a spirit animal, it will embody what we associate the most with owls? Like having wisdom?"

"That could be one of the messages. But maybe I should give you a more in-depth example?"

"Please."

"Since you're familiar with Strix, let's stick with his species ... The short-eared owl is a widely distributed bird whose main habitat is grasslands where it nests on the ground. Like all owls, it can rotate its neck two hundred and seventy degrees and it can fly almost silently."

"So?" Nayeli asked when Willow stopped. "That told me nothing important. Why do I need to know where they live and nest? Or that they can rotate their necks? It's not as if I can dislocate my spine ...

And I don't want to move from my nice, warm home to live on some grassland, exposed to the elements. I thought these archetypes of spirit animals were supposed to give us messages that we humans can relate to?"

"And they do," Willow said fondly. "There were, in fact, lots of messages hidden in this small summary. That the short-eared owl is a bird, and at home in the air, tells you about your connection with that element. The air is the realm of thoughts, ideas and dreams and having the owl as your spirit animal could mean that you're highly innovative or creative or that your daydreams hold important messages for you. But then there's the fact that this owl likes to sleep and nest on the ground, which translates to the grounding aspect and that staying connected to the earth will be important to you, as well. Another fact is that the owl flies almost silently: this could relate to you keeping your ventures secret until you're ready to let them be seen by others. And the owl's ability to turn its head could mean that you have the ability to see things that others can't. Or that your throat chakra, which stands for truth, communication and self-expression, is of great importance to you at this time. You might need to heal it or work with it specifically.

"Do you see what I'm doing here? So far, I've only spoken about the fact that the short-eared owl is a bird who nests on the ground, is stealthy as heck and can see what's going on behind it. I haven't even touched on their eating and mating habits or their physical features yet. It would take an entire book to write down all possible characteristics of the short-eared owl alone and of all the meanings that could be applied.

"Because, naturally, everyone will relate to different attributes and will uniquely interpret those. Maybe someone's favourite story as a child was about an owl and they are fond of them. What they think of owls will be different to what someone who is scared of birds thinks of owls. And if you were raised in Asia, where the owl is seen as a messenger of death and bad omen, you'll see owls differently than if you were raised in a culture where the owl is seen as wise."

"And what's more important? The archetype of the animal? Or the meanings I apply to it?"

"Both. All your subjective experiences matter just as much as the archetype of the animal because your meanings individualise the messages you are receiving. But in order to apply those meanings, you first need some knowledge of the animal in question ... Or can you tell me your subjective opinion of a desert mole rat?"

Nayeli shook her head. "I have absolutely no clue what it would mean to me since I don't know a thing about them. I couldn't even say what colour their fur is or what they eat ... Ah, I get your point. If we know nothing about an animal, we can't interpret the signs. But when we have all the facts, we can apply them to our own lives and filter out what we need."

"Yes. To work with messages from spirit animals, first look at what you associate with them and what your intuition tells you. Then you can read up on the animal itself, how and where it lives and what traits it has. Look at all the facts that stand out to you and think of what it could mean for you personally. Then, as a third step, you can also check the literature about spirit animals and see if there's anything else that resonates with you, which you've overlooked. And as the last step, you can look for any deviations from the norm that appear in your reality."

"Deviations from the norm?" Nayeli asked, not being able to

keep up with the tree's mental leaps. "But I thought working with archetypes leads to excluding all abnormalities?"

"It does at first," Willow clarified. "But once you know an animal's *normal* behaviour, you can recognise any exceptions. When a species shows different traits and behaviours around you, then those can hold a strong message for you. If, for example, you know that an owl species normally flies at night and you see a lot of them during the day, this is an important sign. In fact, the more important a message is, the more visible and stronger the sign will be. And one way to grab your attention is to do something different from the norm."

Nayeli settled back against the tree's trunk and smoothed out her skirt while thinking about what she had learned. "That makes sense. But there's one question I still don't have an answer for. How do I decide what spirit animal I need to work with specifically? Is it the wolf because I've loved wolves all my life? Or the finch, because I see and hear them all the time, wherever I go?"

"Both can be your spirit animals," the tree replied. "But first let me make something else clear from the beginning. You are not the one who chooses your spirit animals. It's the other way around. They chose you. You have several of them throughout your life. Some of them stay for your whole incarnation, while others only travel with you for a bit to teach you the lessons you need at that specific time. There's no limit to how many spirit animals one person can have. And the more you listen to them, the more might cross your path. Now, as for how you recognise them ... many of your spirit animals evoke strong feelings within you, either because you love them – or because you hate or fear them."

"Fear? Then a spider could be one of my spirit animals, too?"

Nayeli asked aghast.

"If you have a phobia of them, then yes," the tree answered earnestly. "A spider or snake you fear can be just as much a spirit animal of yours as a lion or panda you love. They are your so-called shadow animals and represent your subconscious parts."

The weeping willow waited for a beat or two, a grin being visible in its next words. "And knowing this, you must have an idea what Strix's shadow animal is?"

Nayeli opened her eyes wide. "Even Strix has one?"

When the tree answered in the affirmative, she recalled all the stories she'd heard about Willow's feathered friend. Immediately, one animal stuck out. "A crocodile? He seems to see those wherever he goes and has had quite a few negative experiences with them."

"It's indeed the crocodile, very good," Willow said proudly. "Which is where we come to the other ways in which spirit animals can show themselves to you. Apart from evoking strong feelings, they can appear repeatedly in your dreams or in your life. When you've noticed that you see one bird or insect species more than any other when you are walking outside, or when you constantly stumble across a specific animal species in magazines or in TV spots, that's a sure sign it's a spirit animal of yours, too."

"And what about our pets? Do they also count as spirit animals?"

"Not in the same way as wild animals," Willow answered. "Usually, a pet represents its wild form. That means if you own a dog, your spirit animal could be a wolf, coyote or fox. And a cat can represent a tiger, lion or leopard. What pets have in common with spirit animals, though, is that they teach you valuable lessons – lessons like how to love unconditionally or how to be truly happy in the present moment. They just use a different technique: they incarnate and live alongside you instead of offering you help from the spirit world."

Accepting this gracefully, Nayeli leaned her head back and closed her eyes, letting all the new information settle on top of the lessons she'd learned over the past few days. She was lost so deep in thought that she only came back to the present when she heard the sharp cry of a distant bird of prey. The call triggered a question in Nayeli's mind that had already been lurking around the edges of her consciousness for some time.

Sitting bolt upright, Nayeli furrowed her forehead.

"Willow, if Strix got out of that cage, why isn't he here? He must have told you all these stories after coming back. And I've been sitting underneath your crown for a week now and haven't seen him once … Not in the mornings, not during the day and not in the evenings when I leave. Or did he not arrive? Did something happen to him on his journey home and he has crossed over to the other side? Has he told you all these stories from there? And, come to think of it, I haven't seen Nuktia around, either."

Willow chuckled cheerfully. "You don't expect me to reveal the answers this early, do you? I mean, I left it when Strix was still on the other side of the world. There are so many meetings with other animals lying between him and his possible reconnection with Nuktia. Don't you want to hear about all his adventures first? Before I tell you about where he is now?"

"Absolutely. I want to hear everything," Nayeli answered. "I just thought … I thought that maybe Strix's story is over?"

Willow's next words were full of promise. "Not by a long shot, my dear Nayeli. Strix's journey isn't over yet – and neither is yours."

Nayeli grinned in delight at these words, but a moment later her grin was replaced by a frown as another, darker thought blocked out her joy.

"What's wrong?" the tree asked, as usual sensing the change in her emotions.

Nayeli slumped her shoulders. "It's just, in a week I have to go home, which is halfway across the country. I've only got two weeks off from work and half of that time is already gone. Which made me wonder – will the time we have left be enough? I don't want to say goodbye to you. And it would be even worse if I had to go when you have still more lessons to teach me. Yes, I know what you want to say – that I should stay present and not worry about the future because time doesn't exist either way. But I can't help it. There are moments when these fears are just too overwhelming ..."

"I know," Willow said empathetically. "And it's okay. You shouldn't ignore or deny how you feel – your emotions are always valid. Especially when they are acting as your internal alarm bell when one of your past traumas has been triggered."

"You've mentioned something along those lines before," Nayeli said. "That traumas from our past get triggered, and we need to heal these and integrate all the parts of ourselves. But what does that all entail, and how do I do it?"

"I'll gladly tell you all about it," Willow promised. "But it will have to wait for tomorrow because it's getting late. The warmth of the day is fading with the sun and it will soon be completely dark. Thus, it's better to end here and continue once you're rested. If you'd like to come back?"

"Of course, I want to!" Nayeli said steadfastly.

Standing up, she waited for the tree to part its branches to walk through the gap. Raising her hand in a silent farewell, Nayeli then walked down the small hill and followed the babbling brook towards the village, noticing the faint outline of the moon hanging in the darkening sky above her.

Tonight, while walking towards her grandma's house, Nayeli was filled with the knowledge that there would be more to come: more stories, more laughter, more tears and more lessons. And, above all, more time to spend with her new friend, the weeping willow tree.

Appendix 1 – Practical Steps

Nayeli's introduction

When I met Willow, who quickly became a close friend and confidant, I was going through one of the hardest times in my life. It was truly a blessing that I walked across the tree's meadow that day and sat down beneath its branches because Willow helped me in a lot of ways. The tree helped me to heal and to let go of my fears. It helped me to have trust and faith again – not just in the universe but also in myself. And it helped me to see the bigger picture and to reconnect to my soul.

What is more, Willow also reawakened my passion as a storyteller. Hearing all the tree's tales about Strix, the short-eared owl, and his adventures made me remember my past dream to be a writer. A dream I had given up on because I had no idea how to go about it or what to write about. And because I believed I'd never be successful. But then my passion was roused and, when I met a little bumblebee, an idea was sparked inside me: the idea of collecting all of Willow's stories so that other people could receive the same help the tree gave me in my time of need.

I'm very happy with the book that Willow, Strix and I have created together, but I still felt that a piece was missing when I finished writing it ... Then it came to me what it was. When we only read a cookbook but never try out any of the recipes, we'll never taste the dishes. And when we read Willow's stories but practice none of the tree's teachings, there'll be no growth.

Now, being a human myself and having the first-hand experience on what it means to have an ego, I know how difficult it can be for us to translate spiritual lessons into our day-to-day lives. This is why I wrote this appendix 'Practical Steps', which can be seen as an addition to the stories and includes tips and tricks. You can read it from front to back or jump straight to the matters that interest you most.

I have tried out all these techniques myself and they've helped me in one way or another. But since we're all different, with unique experiences and beliefs, not every part might ring true for you. So, see them as suggestions for you to alter, add to or ignore. Because, in the end, spirituality is not a destination but a journey. And this appendix isn't intended to take you anywhere. Instead, it's meant as a guide to accompany you.

Seven basic meditation tips

1. There are hundreds of different forms of meditations. The first thing to do is to try out different techniques and see what works best for you. Play around and be open to the experience.

2. External circumstances can greatly influence meditations. Some people can relax better when sitting cross-legged or on a stool because they fall asleep when lying down. Others need the comfort of a bed or sofa. And a third group will feel too restless to sit or lay down for any length of time and need to walk while meditating. Likewise, some people will get better results by practising outside in nature, while others receive better results in their homes, where they are undisturbed. And even the time of day can affect how successful your meditation practice will be. Find what works best for you and stick with that.

3. No matter what form, time, place and position you choose, it's a good idea to introduce a ritual beforehand to program your subconscious mind. When you *teach* your body that every time you do this specific ritual, you will follow it up with a meditation, you'll eventually become accustomed to relaxing as soon as you start your preparations. This, in turn, will help you reach a heightened awareness state more easily.

A ritual can look different for everyone, and the following examples are just some ideas: play a certain song, light a candle, dance or sing, drink a glass of water with lemon slices, hold a crystal and let it warm up in your palm or do stretching exercises.

4. Another good tip to master meditations is to take some time beforehand to write down your thoughts in order to get them out of your head and onto paper. This will help your mind to let go more easily, without having to worry about forgetting anything important. You can also combine this with the step before and make this practice your ritual.

5. If your mind is still full of thoughts when meditating and won't calm down, don't blame yourself or your ability to stay present. It is quite natural for thoughts to arise, and meditation time can be a great opportunity to watch those. And if you're doing that, you are already in a state of awareness and thus meditating successfully.

6. You have various options on how to react to the thoughts that arise during your meditation time.

- The first option is to take a back seat as a spectator and watch the thoughts, as if they are a movie playing out in front of your inner eye.
- The second option is to let your thoughts drift by without taking a closer look at them. To do this, imagine your thoughts as clouds in a blue sky. If a thought stays around for too long, imagine the wind picking up and pushing it along. Or, if you'd rather work with words than with images, express your thanks to the thought that arrived but at the same time say that it isn't needed right now and that you'll come back to it later.
- The third option is to run with any thoughts that arise. Maybe you sat down, intending to meditate, but what you really needed at that moment was to relax enough so you could figure out an answer to a problem or get a new idea.

7. Practise makes perfect. No baby can walk or talk immediately. They need to spend hours and hours learning the basics first. The same holds true for anything new that you try out, including meditation. So, don't be discouraged and know that meditating for just a few minutes each day can already make a big difference.

Seven different forms of meditation to try out

1. The breathing meditation

The most basic meditation form is to concentrate on your breath. Draw in air and feel it travel down into your belly. Pause for a moment, and then slowly exhale. Pause again and take another deep breath in. You can facilitate this process by counting your breaths or by thinking 'inhale' and 'exhale', to stay focused on the pattern of your breath.

Congratulations! You have just meditated. Meditation has become such a big, scary word that people shy away from it because they think it's difficult to do. But being aware of your breath is all it needs. You can also do this anywhere and at any time because you always have your breath with you.

2. Some advanced breathing meditations

- There are hundreds of different breathing mediations. A great technique is the 4-7-8 breathing pattern. Breathe in while counting to four, hold your breath while counting to seven and breathe out while counting to eight. This technique, by the way, can also help when you're having trouble relaxing or falling asleep.
- Then there's the alternate nostril breathing meditation. Find a comfortable position in which your spine is straight. Relax and bring your right hand (if you are left-handed, you can reverse the hand) to your face. Place the index and middle fingers of your right hand on your third eye between your eyebrows. Then put your thumb against your right nostril and close it off. Inhale through your left nostril slowly and steadily. Then hold

your breath. While doing so, take your thumb away from your right nostril and seal your left nostril with your ring finger. Exhale through your right nostril. Pause briefly, then inhale through your right nostril. Hold your breath and seal your right nostril with your thumb while taking away your ring finger to exhale through the left nostril. Repeat this pattern a few times.

- A third breathing meditation is the ujjayi breathing meditation. To try this one, find a comfortable position, close your eyes and relax. Take a few deep breaths in through your nose and exhale through your mouth with a *haaaaaaa* sound. Once you've done this a few times, close your mouth and breathe in and out through your nose. Now listen to the sound of your breath as it flows through your nasal passages – it might sound a bit like Darth Vader or waves crashing on the shore. Deepen your breath with every inhale and slow down on the exhale, trying to make each one last longer than the one before. But be mindful not to strain yourself, and to keep your body relaxed while doing so.

3. The body scan meditation

Sit or lie down in a comfortable position and notice your breath for a moment. Are you breathing shallowly or deeply? Are you breathing through your nose or mouth or both? Now deepen your breaths and concentrate on any sensations you feel: how the air is cooler when you breathe it in and warmer when you breathe it out. How it flows through your body from your nose to your belly and back up. Lay your hands on your belly and feel how it rises and collapses with each breath. Then withdraw your mind from your breath and let it travel to other parts of your body. Are your feet warm or cold?

Are your legs relaxed or tense? Is there any tightness in your body? Any pain? If so, where? Scan your whole body and relax each part in turn, starting with your toes and moving up to your head.

4. The sensing meditation

This is a beautiful meditation technique to do outside in nature, but you can also use it anywhere else. Stand, sit or lie down, then close your eyes and breathe deeply into your belly a few times. After that, start to take in everything around you with any sense you want to focus on – or with all senses, one by one. When you focus on your hearing, what sounds can you make out? Are there birds singing? Do you hear insects buzzing? Or the wind whispering? Is there the sound of cars driving by or an aeroplane high up in the sky? Can you hear a TV or a dog barking? The murmur of a river or the faint sound of the refrigerator? And what about your breathing? Can you hear the sound of your inhales and exhales?

Likewise, what can you see, smell, taste and touch? How many different flowers are there? What colours are dominant? Can you smell cookies baking in the oven or the pine trees when standing in a forest? Can you taste the salty sea air? What texture has the sand or rug underneath your feet? How do your clothes feel against your skin?

5. The object meditation

Chose any object – or anything else you can perceive like a sunset or the alternating shapes of clouds as they drift by – take a few deep breaths and relax. Now block out your surroundings by focusing all your awareness on this object. Let's say it's a crystal. What colour has it? Does the hue of colour change as the light falls on it? In what way? Pick it up in your hand and feel it – is it smooth or rough? Warm or cold? Turn it over and look at it from all angles. Use any sense you can to examine the object.

6. Guided meditations

There are countless guided meditations to be found online or on CDs where you can listen to a voice that will carry you to lush, green meadows or peaceful bays facing the ocean, as well as into unknown fantasy lands or space. The only job you have to do is close your eyes, relax and follow the directions.

7. Some active meditations

- If the above meditation techniques sound too boring, try an active meditation instead. The most natural active mediation is the dancing meditation because the energy we are made of is always in movement. It flows and ebbs in an endless rhythm. We only seem to be static because the energy moves very slowly when condensed in physical form. To start this meditation, put on some music you like and stand still in the middle of the room. Do not consciously move your body, but let the music flow through you for some time. After a while, you'll feel a natural movement set in. It can be something simple, like swaying from side to side or nodding your head. Allow the movement to take over your body and flow with it. Also, pay attention to how your movements change when the music does.
- You can also try out yoga, which is basically nothing else but meditation in motion. The point of yoga is not to master the different positions but to move in harmony with your inhales and exhales.

- Or you can try out any other sport where you need to focus your awareness, such as tai chi or Qigong, or archery or a simple walking meditation. If you want to try the latter, become aware of your steps as you walk. Concentrate on their rhythm, time your breathing with them or count the steps inside your mind.

Seven thoughts about thoughts

1. Aside from using meditations you can use regular breaks from your busy life and your constant media intake to declutter your mind. Use this time to read a book, meet a friend, try out a new recipe, paint a picture or do anything else you find relaxing or fun. Make these breaks a regular thing in your life – for a holiday, a weekend or simply for a few hours.

2. Thoughts can present a problem when they are limiting or restricting. They can prevent you from going after your dreams by setting up walls that block your path. The good news is that you can change any negative thoughts, no matter how deeply ingrained they are. You just have to become aware of them and exchange them for more empowering ones.

3. One way to stop your thoughts from going into a negative downward spiral is to put up a mental 'stop' sign. Just say 'stop' in your mind whenever you catch yourself being needlessly anxious or worried. In the beginning, you'll have to do this every other second because thoughts are persistent by nature. But with time and perseverance, they will take longer to come back and can eventually be replaced by thoughts that serve you better.

4. Once you put a stop to a negative thought, think of other thoughts that are more objective. Often, negative thoughts are born out of worries and fears and paint the 'worst-case scenarios' in bright colours, which will probably never come to pass. To get out of this pattern, look at the situation and yourself from an outsider

perspective, like you are watching a movie. You can also talk to yourself, as if you were giving advice to a dear friend. Don't deny the truth of the situation, but don't fall prey to seeing bigger problems than those that are currently present.

Let's say you can't stop thinking you will be fired because you made a mistake at work. After putting up the stop sign, think about how many other mistakes you have made in the past, which had no consequences. Think of all the similar mistakes your colleagues made, who are still at the company. Think about the fact that, even if you do get fired, it's not the end of the world: You're competent and a hard worker and you'll find another job fast. Think about the fact that your health and your relationships with your family are much more important than keeping this job. Think of anything that makes you feel better – without denying the fact that you made a mistake that could potentially have consequences.

5. Bear in mind that you look at everything from your limited perspective only. Your thoughts are based on your past experiences and installed beliefs. Thus, any thought may be false if your beliefs are also untrue.

If you ruined the first cake you baked and were told that it tasted awful, you might believe that you are a bad baker and can't follow even the simplest recipe. But the truth might be that you are actually a good baker; you've just never permitted yourself to hone your skills.

6. Use affirmations to reprogram your thought patterns over the long term. To do this, choose a thought to replace a negative thought and repeat it to yourself a few times daily. You could also

use this affirmation as an online password so that you're forced to type it repeatedly.

Pick words that are both positive and believable. For example, if your goal is to eat more healthily, but you tend to snack on sweets, it won't do you any good to say 'I'm eating only healthy foods from now on', because every time you cheat on your diet, you'll feel worse. Another bad affirmation would be 'I'll not eat sweets from now on', because the universal language doesn't recognise negations and you'll thus affirm that you *will* eat sweets from now on! It also won't help to choose 'I'm trying to eat healthily' because 'trying' is not the same as doing something. You could however say 'I'm much more aware of my food intake', as this is a positive thing that is always true, even if you have a cheat day.

7. Become aware of where the thoughts you are thinking come from. What you perceive as your thoughts can come from two different sources. One is your ego, which keeps chattering away at you. The other is your higher self, which can use clairaudience among all the clair-senses to send you messages. To tell these two voices apart, you just need to look at the thoughts, what they entail and how they are brought forth.

Your ego's primary job is to keep you safe to ensure its survival. Because of this, it tends to look at everything that could go wrong and comes from a place of fear and worry. It's the voice that comes up with all the worst-case scenarios and negative talk. Meanwhile, your higher self comes from a place of love, so it will say things that are positive, uplifting, understanding and supportive.

Seven starting points to recognise and train your dominant clair-senses

1. These are the eight clair-senses you can access:

Clair-sense	Meaning	How it appears most often
Clairvoyance	clear-seeing	Seeing mental images in the mind's eye
Clairaudience	clear-hearing	Hearing a voice or sounds inside the head
Clairsentience	clear-feeling	Feeling sensations inside the physical body, having a 'gut feeling'
Claircognizance	clear-knowing	Knowing the answers, without knowing how you know them
Clairgustance	clear-tasting	Tasting something without there being any physical source
Clairsalience	clear-smelling	Smelling something that is not currently present in your surroundings
Clairtangency	clear-touching	Knowing facts about a person or object when you touch them/it
Clairempathy	clear-emotion	Sensing the emotions of others

2. To find your main clair-sense or senses, think about what physical sense is dominant within you. Do you have exceptional eyesight? Do you hear the softest tones, to which others are deaf? Do you smell something long before others are aware of it? Do you have strong gut feelings?

Also, think of any problems you have with regard to your senses, as those are also relevant. For example, do you suffer from misophonia or find many noises too loud? Do you need to wear sunglasses because the light is too bright? Do you get headaches when you smell perfumes or cleaning products? Do you have any allergies?

3. Another way to recognise your dominant clair-sense is to think of your favourite film. What comes to your mind first? The beautiful scenery and how the characters look? Or the voices and songs? Or the emotions the film generated in you? Or the plot of the film and what you learned from it?

4. You can also look back at your childhood. How do your memories appear? Do you see pictures in your mind's eye? Or is the thing you remember most clearly the voice of your mum as she read you a bedtime story? Is it the taste of freshly baked cookies? Or the scent of roses?

5. And if you are still unsure what your dominant clair-sense is, use the intuitive answer method. To do this, take a magazine, a book or anything else you like and ask your higher self to tell you what the first word on page 222 is or the first image you'll see when you open the magazine on a random page. Tune in to the way you get the answer. Do you see an image in front of your inner eye? Does a thought appear in your mind that you 'hear'? Do you have a feeling in your gut? Do you maybe just *know* what it is without knowing where that knowledge comes from?

6. Once you have worked out what your main clair-sense or senses are, you can train those by training your corresponding physical sense. When your dominant clair-sense is clairaudience, you can tune in to different sounds regularly. Listen to the buzzing of the refrigerator or the birds singing outside. And when you put on a song, try to listen to each of the instruments separately. To train your clairvoyance, switch between near and far focus repeatedly or 'sunbathe' your eyes by turning your face up to the sun with your eyes closed. And to train your clairgustance you can, for example, try to detect various ingredients in a dish.

7. You can also train your clair-senses by focusing on them directly. Here are some tips for the four most prevalent ones:

- To train your clairaudience, imagine hearing different sounds. To do this, find a quiet place, close your eyes and relax. Now try to remember what rain sounds like when it hits the window. Imagine hearing the purring of a cat, a thunderstorm, laughter or music you like.
- To train your claircognizance, learn automatic writing. Ask yourself a question, then write down on a piece of paper the thoughts coming to your mind. Don't judge what you put down; just observe the words flowing out of you. It can, by the way, be useful to use your less dominant hand for this, as it is less linked to your ego.
- To train your clairvoyance, work on opening your third eye and on seeing different levels of the auric field.
- To train your clairsentience, feel into your body regularly, for example by using the body scan meditation explained above. Or learn how to feel your aura.

Seven facts about auras and how to see, feel, heal, cleanse, protect and recharge them

1. If you want to see auras, the first step is to open your third eye. There are, of course, several ways to go about this. But the following is one of the most common methods: First, close your physical eyes and relax. Then imagine a third eye sitting between your eyebrows. The eye is closed at this point. Now imagine it opening while your physical eyes stay shut. Since the third eye and third eye chakra are associated with the colour indigo, it can also help if you imagine the iris of your third eye having an indigo colour. After you have done this, open your physical eyes and continue with any of the following steps.

- One of the easiest things to see with your third eye is the energy that constitutes everything in this universe, including us. You can see this so-called Orgon-energy most easily when you look up into a cloudless blue sky and soften your gaze. Chances are, you'll soon start to see silvery-white dots flitting around (depending on the light conditions, they can also appear black at times).
- Another easy way to train your third eye is to look at lamps (especially streetlamps when it's dark outside) and let your eyes go soft. Several phenomena can now occur. Often the glowing light grows larger and brighter. You might also start to see other colours, such as reds, greens and blues at the edges. Or you might see structures and patterns inside the light.
- A simple way to see an aura is by using plants as props. Place a plant in front of a monochrome background and allow your gaze to get soft while you look at it. You might soon start to see

a swirling fog or a pulsing light around the plant as a whole or around a single leaf (depending on what you are focusing on). In the beginning, this fog will appear to be slightly translucent or white, but with practice, you can see different colours. You can also hold your own hand in front of a monochrome background. Or you can look at animals, other humans or even objects while letting your gaze get soft.

2. If, after trying all these techniques several times, you cannot see any aura layers, it is likely that clairvoyance is not your primary sense. If this is this case, you can use another clair-sense to perceive auras – for example, clairsentience. To do this, rub the palms of your hands against each other until they get warm. Move your arms apart but hold your palms parallel to each other. Then slowly move your palms closer together, but without letting them touch. At some point, you'll start to feel a resistance between your hands. This is an aura layer you're feeling. Other sensations you might feel include either a warm or cold feeling in your hands, a tingling or a prickling sensation or – when you are very sensitive – you might also feel something akin to a mild electric shock, which travels up your hands and forearms.

Once you can feel an aura layer, move one of your thumbs above your other palm, painting symbols or letters in the air. You may be able to feel these as if you are touching your physical skin instead of your energetic body.

3. To heal and cleanse your auric field, you can use a white light meditation. Breathe deeply into your belly a few times, relax and imagine that you're standing underneath a waterfall. But instead of

water, a pure white light is raining down on you, flowing into your physical body and your subtle bodies and filling these up. Let it wash away all the dense, dark, negative and stagnant energies that have accumulated.

4. You can protect your aura against lower energies. To do this, imagine that you are inside a sphere of pure white light. It surrounds you and only lets through higher energy of positive intent while reflecting everything else. Use this image daily – for example, when waking up or leaving the house as this protective shield only lasts for a few hours.

5. Recharge your aura by filling it with an energising colour, which you choose intuitively. Imagine inhaling this colour and seeing it fill up your body and aura in your mind's eye, or place yourself under the waterfall again. Let this colour flow into all of your bodies, but especially into any areas in your aura that lack energy.

6. Another great and easy way to cleanse your aura is to take a shower or to walk outside in the rain. Meanwhile, being in sunlight recharges your aura as nothing else can.

7. If you don't yet feel capable enough to heal your auric field by yourself, you can visit an energetic healer who specialises in aura healing.

Seven chakras and how they correspond with the seven auric layers

1. Root chakra/Etheric body
   - It relates to your physical body and your physical senses (seeing, hearing, smelling, tasting and touching).
   - When it is healthy and open, you are grounded and will feel secure in your life. You are connected to your body.
   - What you can do for it: Alongside using grounding techniques, you can do anything that directly relates to your body and senses. This includes doing sports, enjoying a nice meal, listening to music, sleeping, taking a bath, surrounding yourself with pleasant-smelling candles and so on.

2. Sacral chakra/Emotional body
   - It relates to any emotions (positive and negative) that you have towards yourself. It is also the place of your clairsentience.
   - When it is healthy and open, your emotions flow freely. You can easily express yourself creatively and have good access to your passions. And you have a healthy sexuality.
   - What you can do for it: Feel your emotions and express them. Use creative outlets and self-loving techniques.

3. Solar plexus chakra/Mental body
   - It relates to your thoughts and mind. It is the place of your self-worth.
   - When it is healthy and open, you have good self-esteem and are confident. You thrive when it comes to learning new things. It's easy for you to bring order and structure into your life.

- What you can do for it: Read, learn new things and train your memory or logical thinking skills. Also, make plans and lists, use affirmations and change your thoughts and beliefs so that they are more positive.

4. Heart chakra/Astral body
- It relates to any emotions (positive and negative) you have towards others as well as your relationships with them. It is also the balancing chakra/body between your three lower and your three higher chakras/bodies.
- When it is healthy and open, you have healthy relationships and can be intimate with others. It also helps you to create a healthy balance between giving and receiving.
- What you can do for it: Create and maintain healthy connections with others. Be compassionate and kind. Allow yourself to receive from and give to others. Also, practise understanding.

5. Throat chakra/Etheric template body
- It relates to your ability to manifest. It's the place of your free will and your soul-plan, as well as your authenticity and truth. It is also the place of three of your clair-senses: clairaudience, clairsalience and clairgustance.
- When it is healthy and open, you will find it easy to manifest. You can communicate clearly. And you stand fully in your authenticity, being able to express your truth.
- What you can do for it: Discover your soul-plan and learn how to become more authentic. Communicate your truth, develop your corresponding clair-senses and use manifestation techniques.

6. Third eye chakra/Celestial body

- It relates to awareness. It's the place of visualisations, dreams and meditations. It is also the place of your clairvoyance.
- When it is healthy and open, you can easily meditate and visualise. You also have the ability to lucid dream.
- What you can do for it: Train your clairvoyance. Use meditations and visualisation techniques.

7. Crown chakra/Causal body

- It relates to oneness and to being connected with your own soul. It also relates to wisdom and teaches you to access the Akashic records, which is the collective knowledge of all souls – past, present and future. It is also the place of your claircognizance.
- When it is healthy and open, you have direct knowledge, insight and epiphanies.
- What you can do for it: Learn techniques like astral travelling to have out-of-body experiences to access the Akashic records and to connect to source.

Some extra info:
Often, something can relate to more than one chakra and auric body. Inspiration, for example, can be part of the seventh chakra/body when it comes in the form of claircognizance, or it can be part of the sixth chakra/body when it comes via dreams or through your clairvoyance sense. And doing puzzles can train both the third chakra/body (by using logical thinking skills) and your sixth chakra/body (when it's a meditative practice).

No	Chakra	Chakra colour	Position in the body and how to recharge the chakra	Aura	Aura layer meaning	Chakra/ Aura function	Some related body parts
1	Root chakra	Red	Imagine a red flower at the base of the spine opening and spinning clockwise	Etheric body	Body	Being grounded, secure, present	Feet, legs, lower back, bones, immune system, sexual organs (men)
2	Sacral chakra	Orange	Imagine an orange flower below the belly button opening and spinning clockwise	Emotional body	Emotions	Emotions, Passion, Healthy sexuality	Kidneys, bladder, appendix, sexual organs (women)
3	Solar-plexus chakra	Yellow	Imagine a yellow flower between the navel and the breastbone opening and spinning clockwise	Mental body	Mind	Thoughts, Logic, Healthy self-esteem	Stomach, liver, gall bladder, pancreas
4	Heart chakra	Green	Imagine a green flower at the centre of the chest opening and spinning clockwise	Astral body	Relation-ships	Intimate relationships, Understanding	Heart, lungs, circulatory system, upper back, shoulders, arms, hands
5	Throat chakra	Blue	Imagine a blue flower in the throat opening and spinning clockwise	Etheric template body	Authenticity	Authenticity, Truth, Manifestation	Throat, thyroid gland, mouth, teeth, ears
6	Third-eye chakra	Indigo	Imagine an indigo flower between the eyebrows opening and spinning clockwise	Celestial body	Awareness	Awareness, Visualisations, Dreams, Meditation	Eyes, face, brain, nervous system
7	Crown chakra	Violet	Imagine a violet flower at the top of the head opening and spinning clockwise	Causal body	Oneness	Wisdom, Oneness	It transcends the physical body

Seven game-changers regarding time

If you think all these tips regarding meditations, developing your clair-senses or working with your auras and chakras are all well and good, but you don't have any time for them in your busy life, you might profit from some of the following tips:

1. Incorporate spiritual practices into your life instead of setting time aside to do them. For example, many meditation practices can be done while cleaning. Do a sensing meditation when washing the dishes: notice the temperature of the water, feel how the washing-up liquid changes the consistency of the water and watch the bubbles reflect the light. Or when you're vacuuming, do a breathing meditation, timing the back and forward movements of the vacuum with your inhales and exhales. Likewise, you can train your clair-audience by listening to music while folding the laundry or recharge your aura when gardening.

2. Find your wasted moments. Keep a record for a couple of days in a row and write down everything you do and how long it takes. Then read through your lists and see where and how you can save time, either by delegating tasks to others, by reducing the time you spend doing them or by tossing unnecessary tasks out of your life completely.

3. Do things you're feeling stressed about immediately. When you think about doing something, use this as your wake-up call to do it. If you spend three hours thinking about folding the laundry and ten minutes folding the laundry, you'll have wasted three hours think-

ing about an unwanted task – time you could have used to do something more fun or relaxing.

4. Use your unique energy levels. Some work best in the mornings, others in the evening. Organise your day according to your needs. If you are prone to slipping into a post-lunch slump, incorporate a nap or other relaxing activity during that time. And if your imagination is at its peak in the evening, use that time on creative ventures.

But also, do any tasks you dislike as early in the day as possible. That way you'll feel a sense of accomplishment, which you can enjoy all day long, knowing you've already done your part.

5. Write to-do lists. This has two benefits. First off, you get the tasks out of your head and onto paper, making room in your mind for more important things. And secondly, it creates a sense of accomplishment when you can cross out the items on the list and see how much you got done. Make these lists as detailed as possible and also include fun, relaxing activities on them. Don't be fooled to think that these are only a bonus. They're just as necessary as the 'real' tasks if you want to stay healthy.

6. When you feel that time slips by too fast, one reason for that is that we're constantly stuck in either the past or future and spend rarely any time in the present moment. If that's the case for you, be present more often. A great practice for that is to become more aware when eating. So often, we scarf something down without really tasting the food. Which is neither healthy for our mind nor our body. So, take the time to enjoy each bite. Notice the textures,

the flavours and how they harmonise with each other, as well as the smell and the colours. Celebrate this experience.

7. Being present isn't something we should only do when we're alone. It is, in fact, a great practice to use when around other people because it's essential to create more understanding and the key to healthy, happy relationships. So, spend quality time with your loved ones, during which you put your phone away, tell your persistent thoughts to wait until later and truly listen when they talk. Hear, see and feel into them.

Seven guidelines to gain more understanding

1. There's a maxim you can keep in mind to better grasp the topic of understanding. As soon as you need to raise your voice, you know that you have moved further away from someone and are trying to bridge that gap with a louder tone. But this does not equal understanding. Understanding happens quietly, and the softer you can be with someone, the more connection there is between you.

2. One tool to gain more understanding is the tree process. Imagine that every soul is one leaf on a giant tree. Now, to see things from someone else's perspective, imagine retracting your consciousness out of 'your' leaf. Leave all your habits, beliefs, fears and wishes behind while you travel into the tree trunk, which is the equivalent of oneness. From there, move towards another leaf that represents a person whose perspective you want to share. Imagine entering that leaf. Accept all that you see, hear and feel – without judgement. Once you are finished, retract your consciousness once again and travel back into the tree trunk before moving back to your own leaf, taking the knowledge you gained with you.

3. Understanding is most easily obtained when you find similarities between yourself and others. So, make it a regular habit to find things you have in common with other humans, animals, plants, objects, ideas or anything else you can think of. One day, think about what you have in common with a giraffe. The next day, choose a loaf of bread. And the day after that, your bus driver or an invention. The more you focus on these connection points, the easier it will be for you to delve into someone else's perspective.

One example to jumpstart this process: a clock is an instrument to measure time. You measure your surroundings with your senses, too. Your eyes measure the distance between you and an oncoming car. Your skin measures the temperature of the bathwater and tells you whether it's too hot or too cold. Besides that, a clock needs energy or it won't run. So do you, both in the form of food and sleep. Otherwise, you will get sick and be unable to function properly. And these are just some points — can you think of more?

4. When you argue with someone, try to switch perspectives with them. Pretend to be advocating for their opinion and find arguments that support their truths and vice versa. You can do this verbally or by writing down all the points and then read them to each other. For example, when you disagree about where to go on holiday with your partner – they want to do a city tour of Rome, while you want to go on a cruise around Norway – list all the pros for going to Italy. Or, if you have different political views, pretend to be a supporter of the opposing party and come up with any and all reasons why you could vote for them.

5. If you can't consider someone else's perspective by yourself, let them help you – no one knows their reality better than the person living inside it 24/7. To this end, ask them questions. Lots of questions. Be curious about them. The more you ask and listen to the other person, the better you will understand where they are coming from. Take the time to discover their dreams, hopes and fears. See where these differ from your own and where they are similar.

6. Another important step in understanding others is to hold space for them. Don't jump into problem-solving mode immediately when someone opens up about a problem or worry. Be aware that they are vulnerable in this moment and that just being with them without passing judgement makes them feel safe and understood.

7. Understanding others is important, but don't make the mistake of forgetting yourself. Take the time to delve deep into your subconscious mind and discover new talents and interests. Look at your dreams and worries, watch your thoughts and learn to recognise your feelings when they rise to the surface.

Seven ways to better understand your emotions

1. Make a list of all emotions you can think of. Which emotions do you know? Which are similar to each other? How do they differ?

2. Think about what the emotions on the list mean to you personally. What past situations and experiences do you connect with them? What thoughts and memories arise when you feel a certain emotion? What physical sensations do you feel when you feel that emotion? Where in your body do you feel them? Which emotions do you feel most often? How intense are they? When do they appear? Which do you like, and which do you dislike?

3. When an emotion arises, take the time to feel it. We spend most of our lives inside our mind, even when it comes to emotions. And the above steps are a prime example of that. We think about emotions, categorise, interpret and analyse them. But in this step, you have to be fully present with the feeling by merging with it. When you're happy, allow yourself to really *be* happy. And when you're sad, delve even deeper into the sadness without distracting yourself from it.

4. After feeling the emotion, name it. If necessary, take the list you made and find the feeling that best matches how you feel now.

5. Talk to your emotion. Once you know what you are feeling, use this chance to get to know the feeling even better. Or, if it is a negatively perceived emotion, ask it directly why it has come and what it needs from you.

If you are good at visualisations, you can use an imaginative café or any other place for this step. Imagine sitting at a table, waiting for your emotion to enter. When it does, notice everything about it. What does it look like? Does it, for example, look like your mother or a teacher you know? Or like a stranger? Does it look like an animal, or is it simply a colourful dot? Is it big or small? Is it soft or hard-looking? Does it walk with an air of arrogance, or does it look threatening? Every image holds further messages about what this emotion is trying to tell you.

6. Meet your emotion's needs. Once you have talked to your emotion and know what it wants, find a solution to the underlying problem. What changes can you make in your life?

7. Make it an automatism to become more aware of your emotions in everyday life. Choose a specific time or activity – for example, every morning when you wake up or every time you turn your computer on – and spend a minute checking in with yourself. Become aware of whatever emotion you hold at that time. If this becomes a daily habit, you'll soon be able to tune in to your emotional body fast and naturally.

Seven things to consider when you don't feel beautiful

1. Sometimes, it doesn't take much for a negative emotion to arise. Seeing an unflattering photo or catching a glimpse of yourself in a mirror and thinking 'I'm ugly' may be enough. But, as we've already learned, our thoughts are not always right. And this one definitely falls into this category because the most important fact about beauty is already in the name: to *be you*. Expressing beauty means being authentic and thus everyone is beautiful when they show their true self.

2. Despite that inherent truth, any thought you think has a valid reason for existing. So, don't let yourself be persuaded to think of yourself as beautiful, come hell or high water, even when you feel anything but. This is neither healthy nor helpful because you'd be denying and rejecting the part of you, which believes that you – or one of your features – is ugly. And that belief will only be amplified if you resist it.

3. See any parts of yourself that you perceive as ugly or which you are self-conscious about as a blessing, not a curse. Anything inside our dual reality has a positive and a negative side to it. Maybe the 'flaws' that you see in your mirror save you from shallow people. Maybe they'll prevent you from wasting precious time with some-one who's not compatible with you – or maybe they are there to teach you to love yourself more or to erect stronger boundaries.

4. Enhance any parts of yourself that you find beautiful and build on them. Accepting your flaws doesn't mean you have to show them

off to the world. If you feel prettier when you dress a certain way, wear make-up or have your hair coloured, do that. But only if that's what *you* desire. Don't be talked into it by outside sources as that would block your authenticity further.

5. Real beauty is always internal. You will realise this once you've fallen in love with a person you weren't initially attracted to. When you meet someone who doesn't fit your type and begin to love their character and personality, you'll notice that the more you love them, the more attractive they'll become. This also means that you shouldn't judge other people on their appearance – their beauty might only reveal itself to you once you get to know them.

6. If you cannot find any beauty within yourself, create beauty in the outside world: for example, by painting, writing, singing or dancing. Sometimes, parts of ourselves are stored inside our subconscious, to which we have no access. But based on the Law of Reflection, anything that is within you is also outside of you and vice versa. So, you can use outside ventures to reach these forgotten parts and draw them out.

7. When you continuously think of yourself as ugly, you are not in the space of loving yourself. Change this by starting to treat yourself to good things and experiences. And make your wants, needs and wishes a top priority in your life.

Seven messages on how to apply changes in your life

1. Change is scary. There's no getting away from that fact. But it is also necessary – for our growth as well as for the growth of the collective consciousness – and therefore unavoidable in life. If you find that you're resistant to change as a whole, or a specific change, deal with that resistance first. Ask the anxious part within you what exactly it's scared of and what it needs to feel safer. Then find ways to provide for those needs.

2. Start to see change as the opportunity it is. You can't control much outside of yourself. You can't control relationships or other people because of their free will. But you can have complete control over your own life – once you stop reacting to situations and start to actively seek the changes you want to apply. By choosing to create change early on, you can manifest your goals and desires much more easily because you are placing yourself in the driver's seat.

3. If necessary, take baby steps. You don't have to create big changes out of nothing. Take it slow, feel your way forward.

4. Changes imply leaving your comfort zone, which makes you feel secure. One great way to get used to that is to do everyday things differently. Take another road to work, eat something you've never tried before, pick up a book from a genre you haven't read yet or try out a new sport or hobby. In short, extend your horizon beyond what you already know and change your routine.

5. Use the five-second rule to jumpstart change. This rule is simple. When you think about doing something that's outside of your comfort zone, do the very first step within five seconds. When you're scared of jumping into a pool, your anxiety will increase the longer you stand on the diving platform. Likewise, if you're worried about starting a big project, use the five seconds after you've decided to do it to pick up the phone and make that first call, to open your web browser and research what is needed or to make a list of the first things you need to do.

6. Failure does not exist. Maybe you'll find out that the changes you applied in the past weren't so positive, after all. But they were still needed to bring you to this point of awareness. Honour the learning experience and change any previous changes if you see that they aren't to your liking. Remember the old saying, 'a master has fallen more times than a novice has even tried to walk'.

7. A vital part of applying change – and of any manifestation process, for that matter – is to let go of anything that doesn't serve you any longer. This is an active step to create the necessary space in your life to receive new and better things.

Seven parts of the manifestation process

1. Be clear about what you want. If you don't know what you desire, look at all the things you *don't* want, as these are often easier to recognise. Then turn around and go for your dreams, which lie in the opposite direction.

2. Heal yourself and change any existing resistance or limiting beliefs regarding the things you want to manifest. The more your inner parts work in harmony towards a goal, the easier it will be for you to manifest your dreams. Also, be mindful that what you send out is the total sum of your conscious and subconscious parts. So, work with your subconscious: delve as deeply into it as you can and get to know yourself and all your buried desires, dreams, needs and fears.

3. Ask for what you desire. Talk to your higher self or the universe, pray to God or ask the spirit guides for help. Be specific but not too specific as you don't want to place any unnecessary limitations on the source and its ability to bring you what you want.

4. Visualise what you want in as much detail as possible and with as many senses as you can. What does the desired result look, feel, smell and sound like? Imagine a full day in your life, as if you have already achieved what you want. What would you do? Set aside a few minutes each day to do this. The more you do this, the faster it can manifest. Essentially, make what you want your reality before it is your reality.

5. Take any guided action that is necessary to manifest what you desire. If you want a new home, look for ads or estate agent boards. If you want a better job, start to read job ads and send out applications. The universe can do a lot, but if you don't take appropriate action steps, your wish won't be fulfilled.

6. Step back once you have done all you could, and let the universe handle your order however it deems best. Concentrate on another part of your life while the universe brings you what you asked for.

7. Look at how successful you were in manifesting your desires. If something doesn't become your reality, no matter what you do, examine your wish. Is it really what you want? Then you still have traumas, blocks and limiting beliefs stopping you from achieving it. Or is it an overlay of another wish? For example, a desire to travel could be the desire to have more excitement in your life or more relaxation. Manifest the underlying desires directly by repeating the steps mentioned above.

Seven tricks to manifest more abundance

1. One of the main reasons rich people stay rich (even if they aren't consciously aware of this pattern) is that they spend a lot of money. Energy-wise, the universe receives the message that they think of themselves as prosperous and aren't worried that they could run out of it. And so they receive even more.

This is what you want to do as well. Of course, you can't spend as much as a multi-millionaire. But what you can do is to *imagine* spending lots of money. Imagine that every time you look into your wallet, hundreds of new banknotes appear, faster than you could possibly spend them. Imagine walking into a shop and buying anything you like, whether that's ice cream, new shoes or a yacht. Imagine with every sense how you would indulge in the experience. Imagine the taste of the pizza you got, imagining looking into the mirror and marvelling at your new hairstyle, imagine living on your dream ranch. Dive as deep and as often into imagining this as you can.

2. Use higher frequencies to your advantage. The higher the frequency you are in, the faster you can manifest. When you are awake and your brain is engaged, it is normally in the frequency of beta waves or, sometimes, in the frequency of gamma waves, which means you are hyper-alert, stressed out or even panicked. In contrast, alpha brainwaves are active when you are relaxing while still being aware of your surroundings: for example, when you are daydreaming or in a light meditation. Theta brainwaves occur when you are in a REM sleeping phase or a deep meditation. And delta brainwaves appear when you are in a deep, dreamless sleep.

Use the higher brainwaves by affirming or visualising directly before you go to sleep or right after waking up. You can also use sound frequencies to reach these higher states more easily during the day.

3. Another great tool to manifest is to use water, as it is easily influenced by energies. And since our bodies are about 60% water, our own energy is easily influenced by any water we take in. To use this to your benefit, simply charge your drinking water with crystals that have the properties you need – and which are safe to add, as some crystals can corrode, rust, dissolve or contain minerals that shouldn't be ingested. Do your research into which crystal is right for you, clean it under running water, then place it in a container with your drinking water overnight, so that the crystal infuses it.

Or use the two-cup method. For this, you need a piece of paper and two glasses, one full of water, the other empty. Write on the paper any positive affirmations that you wish to manifest and place it under the empty glass. Now pour the water from the full glass into the empty one and drink it while focusing on your affirmations.

4. Start to believe in the manifestation process by recognising how often you've already successfully manifested something in the past. Did you get that job you applied for? Did you find a flat when you moved away from your parents? Did you receive the present you wanted as a kid on Christmas Day? Every second of your life was manifested by you, either consciously or subconsciously. And by placing your focus on the times you were successful to draw into your life what you wanted, you can create a positive landslide effect of attracting even more of your wishes.

5. When you're spending money, you can do so with two attitudes: with an attitude of resentment or an attitude of gratitude. When you pay for something with an attitude of 'I'd rather use the money for something else', 'I don't have enough' or 'It's too expensive', you're in a lower frequency that's a match to the lack of prosperity, which will create more of the same: more expenses, more resentment and generally more lack in your life. Instead, practise being grateful for the fact that you can spend the money, no matter what it's on. For example, when you have to pay your rent, take a minute to think of all the good things you get in return for the money, like a roof over your head for a full month to keep you and your possessions warm, dry and protected.

6. Abundance has its own feeling signature, which means you can use the areas in which you are already abundant to gain abundance in others. For example, when you have an abundance of ideas or an abundance of energy, focus on this feeling and let it fill you up completely. Then imagine this energy flowing into any areas of your life where you don't feel abundant yet.

You can also use memories that come closest to what you imagine the fulfilment of your desire would feel like. For example, if you have a lack of feeling safe and secure, think back to any moment in your life in which you have felt the safest and securest. Was it a purring cat curling up on your lap? Was it huddling under the blanket in your bed as a child? Was it the sound of white noise putting you to sleep? Remember the situation in all details and then zero in on this feeling you felt at the time. Let it fill you up to replace the feeling of lack.

7. For some people, using manifestation tools drives home the fact that they lack what they desire even more. And by focusing on this lack, they attract more of it into their lives. If this is the case for you, forgo all manifestation tools aside from concentrating on the action steps you can take to fulfil your dreams, such as taking classes in a certain field, or going out more often so you can meet the guy or girl of your dreams. Trust the universe and your higher self to handle the rest and simply be grateful for their help.

Seven life hacks regarding gratitude

1. Start to notice and appreciate the small blessings in your life. Gratitude and happiness go hand in hand: when you focus on one, you amplify the other. Sadly, we are used to only recognising big, memorable things to be happy about and have become blind to the smaller details, which we take for granted. But it's the smaller things that create a life full of gratitude.

There's your oven, which bakes the bread rolls just right. There's the smell of coffee that fills your kitchen. There's the multitude of colours in the sky outside the window when the sun rises. There's the fact that one of your favourite songs is playing on the radio. And these are all things you can be grateful for before you've even finished breakfast ...

2. Gratitude is a great energy to manifest your desires as it is not only based on positive focus but also a state of complete non-resistance. To use this to your advantage, try scripting. This is a type of journaling where you write down your goals and wishes in the present tense, including sentences that show your gratitude.

For example, if you want to buy a house you could write the following: 'I'm so grateful that I own this house. It's so comfy and everything I imagined it to be. The turquoise colour I picked out to paint my bedroom makes me feel as If I'm underwater. It's so soothing and relaxing. Every day when I come home from work, I feel joy when I step through the front door. And on the weekends, I love to do the gardening or read a book on my terrace, which is my favourite place ...'

3. Use a gratitude jar. Each evening, write down on pieces of paper three things you've been grateful for that day and put them in the jar. Soon, your jar will be full of reasons to feel gratitude, some of which you've probably already forgotten by now. Read through what you've written and feel the gratefulness rise up in you again.

4. Gratitude is an energy that increases if you share it with others. So show gratitude to the people in your life. One of the easiest ways to do this is through words, either said aloud or written in a note or letter. Another way is through actions, from buying a gift or spending quality time with others to helping someone with a task or giving them a hug. Think about what the person would prefer and act accordingly.

5. You can extend your gratitude to the spirit world by thanking the angels, ascended masters and spirit animals for being by your side and helping, healing, guiding and protecting you. Since words – either spoken or thought – carry energy, any spirit guide can easily receive those meant for them. You can also show your gratitude by sending out love or healing to other people, animals, relationships, situations or the world at large. Or you can take practical actions – for example, planting trees as a gift for Mother Earth.

6. Don't forget to show gratitude to yourself! We can often get caught up in thanking others for what they do for us, but, in the end, we are the ones spending 24/7 with us from birth until we cross back over to the other side. So, treat yourself to nice things and experiences.

7. Write a gratitude letter to your past self. Pick any age and think back to what happened at this time in your life. What problems were you dealing with? What made you succeed and get to where you are now? Think about all the things you handled well and how you came out stronger. Your past self paved the way for your present self, and you wouldn't be here now to follow your happiness if it weren't for them.

Seven factors to consider when you need more happiness in your life

1. Follow your inspiration, desires and passions, as these automatically lead to happiness. Take time out of your day to do what you love. And if you cannot do it as a profession, at least make it a hobby.

2. Surround yourself with happy, positive people. Think about how contagious laughter is. The same can be said for a positive mindset because your aura intermingles and exchanges energies with the auras of people around you. When the people that are in the same room with you have a higher frequency, you'll automatically adopt some of those positive feelings.

3. Use the Law of Attraction to your advantage. You don't have to create happiness all by yourself. Watch a funny film or your favourite comedian or anything else that makes you laugh. When you do so, you are sending out the energy of happiness to the universe, which will respond in kind, bringing more things into your life that you can find joy in.

4. If you can't find anything to be happy about, look for what makes you unhappy. Since survival is key for humans, we tend to place a lot of our daily focus on the negative situations in our lives and any potential threats. That means it's usually a lot easier for us to be sure about what we *don't* want than what we do want. And the more you can rule out, the better. When you realise that neither cooking, reading, knitting nor painting brings you joy, look for what

these activities have in common. For example, staying at home might not be to your liking. In that case, try a sport or any other activity that gets you outside.

5. We live in a dual reality, so remember there must be something positive in everything – even if you can't immediately see it. Start to look for these hidden blessings while being careful not to deny anything bad that happens. If your house burns down, you can stay stuck in the negative perspective of loss and fear regarding what will come. But you can also see the positive aspects – namely that you and your family and pets got out unhurt or that you had insurance, which will cover the cost of rebuilding.

6. Realise that every emotion has a good and valid reason for being in your life. When you are not happy, listen to what other emotion is predominant in your life right now. Why is it there? Accept it and don't try to change it by force, as that will lead to denial. And repressing the feelings you don't want to experience will only increase those.

Also, if you suffer from depression or another ailment that's blocking you permanently from accessing happiness, heal this first instead of putting on a superficial outer layer of happiness. It's okay to not be happy at all times.

7. If you want to master happiness, watch animals and small children. They can teach you a lot more about being happy than any monk or spiritual teacher ever could. This is because they don't have an adult human ego and live fully in the present moment. Learn from them and become more grounded in the moment, too.

Seven grounding practices to help you become more present

1. Imagine being a tree. Imagine that roots are growing out of the soles of your feet and entering the ground below, moving through all layers of the Earth deep into its core. Imagine that core as a crystal of pure golden light. Imagine breathing out all the negative energy that you have accumulated, as if it's black smoke flowing down through your roots and into this crystal, where it is renewed into pure, clean energy. Then imagine the golden energy flowing up your roots and filling your entire being.

2. Heal and strengthen your root chakra as this is your grounding chakra, connecting you to your body and the physical planes. Remove any blockages inside it. When meditating on it, visualise a red flower opening and spinning clockwise at the base of your spine.

3. Connect to nature by spending more time in it. Hike through woods or visit places where there's water, be it lakes, rivers or the ocean. Watch the wildlife, smell the flowers, listen to the birds singing and look at the clouds or stars. The simple act of stepping out of your home and into a natural setting already brings you closer to Mother Gaia. And if you cannot easily go into nature because you live in a concrete jungle, bring nature to you by buying plants for your balcony or living room. This doesn't just have the effect of improving the quality of the air; the act of taking care of the plants is grounding in and of itself. Alternatively, you could look into getting an allotment.

4. Walk barefoot on natural surfaces like earth, grass or sand whenever possible. Just as our houses are a barrier to the natural elements, our shoes are barriers that prevent our feet from directly connecting to Mother Earth.

5. Hug a tree. The reason this works so well is that our aura intermingles with the auras of other beings, which include trees. As soon as this happens, an energy exchange takes place. Since the tree's roots reach deep into the earth, they are perfect for keeping you grounded. And when your senses are already fine-tuned to the energetic layers, you can even feel the energy flowing into you.

6. Eat grounding foods. This means any plants that grow in the earth, such as potatoes or carrots. Chose natural, organic foods, as any chemicals like food colouring or flavour enhancers reduce your energy in an unhealthy way.

7. Take a salt bath with natural salts like sea salt or Himalayan salt. Water and salt both cleanse your aura and wash away any negative energies that have accumulated inside it. You can also add grounding essential oils to the bathwater or carry around grounding crystals – for example agate, jasper, shungite, hematite or smoky quartz.

Seven suggestions for how to find your way back to your soul-path

Once you are grounded, you'll have a much easier time finding your way back to your soul-path – and staying on it. That's because spiritual awareness grows by fusing spirituality with your physical day-to-day life.

1. The first technique you can use is to think back to your childhood and remember any dreams and wishes you had (or you can ask your parents/caregivers if you can't remember anything yourself if they're available). Why did you want to have the job you desired as a child? What would it have given you? What did you like about it? How did it make you feel? What need of yours would it have met?

2. Another option is to remember what story – from a book or film or TV show – you were obsessed with as a child, and why. Which character was your favourite? What did they dream about? The answers you get will hold true for you as well and tell you about your innermost desires, as you wouldn't have otherwise identified with the character and storyline.

3. If your memories of your childhood are blocked and there's no one available to ask about your early years, *become* a child again and follow their example. Be curious about life and all it has to offer. Try out as many new things as possible. Learn to change a car tyre, go skiing, write poems – find out where your talents lie.

4. Follow your happiness. Happiness is the number-one indicator that you're going in the right direction. Your soul path always plays into both your expertise and your interests.

5. Think outside of the box – don't limit yourself unnecessarily. When we grow up, we adopt lots of limiting beliefs. We learn to be 'reasonable' when it comes to our dreams and not to aim too high. But what if you are meant to do something completely new and ingenious? If no existing professions are to your liking, the reason for this could be that you're simply not meant to work in any of them. Someone always needs to be the first to invent something new, break away from the herd. And who would have thought, two decades ago, that people could make money by running social media accounts? Or that a device would need to be invented to rid the oceans of plastic waste?

Be bold. Finding your life path doesn't start with logical thinking and strategic planning – those follow afterwards. Instead, it starts with ideas and big dreams.

6. Don't be discouraged by obstacles and detours that appear in your path. At times, things you perceive as impediments are actually blessings in disguise that make you reach your dreams all the quicker. They might hone skills you'll need later on, connect you to people who'll jumpstart a change or open up possibilities that you haven't even thought about yet.

7. Ask yourself what you can give to others. We are not islands, and whatever you set out to do will help souls who need that product or service. So, thinking about your skills can lead to the answer

what you desires are in a roundabout way. And if you aren't sure what you are good at, ask your friends, family or partner. What do they think you are talented at? What do they wish they could do that you can? What do they appreciate most about you? And what have you given them in the past that they value?

Seven answers regarding the core values of male and female energy

Incarnated humans are individuals and thus, their desires and needs differ greatly. But there is one value at the core of each woman and each man respectively, which I'll disclose right now.

(I'll explain this by using the example of a relationship between a man and a woman. But it can also be applied to a relationship between two women or two men, one of whom has more access to their male energy and one who has better access to their female energy. Or it can play out within one human only as we all have both male and female energy present within us.)

1. The one value that's important for all women is safety. If you ask a group of 100 men (who don't belong to a minority) how many feel afraid every day, almost no one will raise their hand. But if you ask a group of 100 women how many feel afraid every day, close to or even all of them will raise their hand. Women have been made to feel afraid, anxious and unsafe in their lives for generations, and this has become deeply ingrained in them. So, the number-one thing you can do for any woman is to make her feel safe with you.

2. Be aware that there are many kinds of safety. There is physical safety, but there is also mental, emotional, financial or sexual safety. When a woman is anxious about talking on the phone, you could offer to call the doctor for her – and follow up on that promise. You could let her sit in the corner of a restaurant and take the outer seat yourself to be between her and any possible danger. Or you could provide for her financially.

3. Any type of safety you can provide will be greatly appreciated. But there's one level that's neglected often, despite it being one of the most important forms of safety for any women: emotional safety! Attune to a woman and understand her. Make her feel that she can tell you anything and that she is appreciated and supported instead of judged and rejected.

4. The one value that's important for all men is their need to be appreciated for what they can provide as men gain confidence and self-worth by what they do,

For generations, men were in charge. They built the house their family lived in. They brought home money or food and thus provided for their wife and children. And they rode into battle to protect their loved ones. This has changed because women in this day and age do everything that men do: they work, they provide for themselves and their families, they drive cars, vote and do so many other things that seemed unthinkable before. At times, this doesn't leave a clear role for a man in a woman's life, which in turn makes them feel useless. And because of this, the number-one thing you can gift a man is an active place in your life for which you value them.

5. This role can be anything at all. If a man loves working with his hands, ask him to build a shelf you bought or to do DIY at home. If he likes to drive, let him drive you around. Let him cook for you, let him mow the grass, let him organise barbecues or board game night with friends. The possibilities are endless ...

6. Make sure that the role you give the man in your life is one that he can fulfil, though. It wouldn't do any good to give a man the task of repairing the TV if he's terrible at it, while you are more tech-savvy. That would only end in a broken TV and lots of anger and fights.

7. Of course, knowing all this, there's one optimal scenario between a man and a woman that serves both equally: for the man to fill the role of the woman's protector. This way, the woman receives the safety she needs and longs for and the man gets the recognition and appreciation, which he needs to gain a greater sense of self-worth.

Seven words of advice on how to improve your relationships

1. If you know how to create harmonious relationships, you are winning in life. Relationships are something we can never escape from while incarnated, as we are in relationships with everything around us, from other humans and animals, your house plants, your home, your bed, your car, your income, your health, your liver, your logical thinking skills, your eating habits, your back pain, your limiting beliefs and your hobbies to Mother Nature, the sun, the rain and the source itself. And that's just a few examples.

To understand how important relationships are, choose one of yours to examine each day. Analyse your role in the relationship and how you respond to the other party or thing involved. For example, your car. Do you like it? Is it comfortable? Does it have all the amenities you wanted? Or are you dissatisfied with it because the motor acts up at times? Is the fuel consumption too high? Would you rather exchange it for another? Are you planning to get rid of it in the near future? Could your relationship be better?

2. Everything in this world is made out of energy, including your relationships. So, if one of your relationships is not to your liking, simply change the energy between yourself and the opposing party. To do this, copy what you do in healthy relationships. If you have a great relationship with your mum but a poor one with your health or home, look at what you are doing differently. What changes could you apply to improve the unhealthy relationships in your life?

3. Any outer relationship you have is nothing else but a mirror to the relationships you have with parts of yourself. If you are in an abusive relationship in your outside reality, it means one aspect within yourself is acting abusively towards another aspect within you. And if someone in your life is constantly criticising you, that's because one part of you is highly critical of another part of you. The outer reality exists to make you aware of these unhealthy internal relationships. And to improve your relationships in the outside world, you first need to heal any discord within yourself.

4. When you are too involved in a relationship that is going badly, ask a third party to help you resolve any conflict. The more objective this person is, the better they'll be at finding a solution that works for all involved.

5. Change relationships. Humans fear change – especially when it comes to potentially losing connections to loved ones. We stay too long in situations that are not serving us any longer. But change doesn't equal loss. Just because you and your romantic partner have drifted apart and have different goals for the future, doesn't mean you won't make great friends. Be honest when you look at your relationships, and adapt when one needs to be re-arranged.

6. End relationships. Some people are not meant to stay in our lives forever. When a lesson has been learned, it may be time to not only change the relationship but to end it. This is especially true if the relationship has become unhealthy and abusive. In that case, don't prolong the misery but move on and make room for something better.

7. After ending a romantic relationship, wait before starting a new one. When we are in a relationship with someone, our energies begin to merge to some extent, and it takes time for our subtle bodies to clear away the energy that doesn't belong to us. If you jump into another romantic relationship right after leaving your previous partner, they'll subconsciously be attracted to this mixed energy, not to the unique energy of your authentic self. And because of these wrong expectations, you will have trouble finding soulmates who are a match for you.

Seven notes on soulmate relationships

1. Be careful what you wish for, as not every soulmate is a suitable romantic partner. Often, soulmates come in the form of mentors, friends or even enemies who shake up our world, act as a catalyst for a big change, then leave as soon as we've learned the lesson. If you want a romantic relationship with a life partner, then ask for that specifically.

2. If you're in search of a romantic soulmate, one of the best tips is to stop dating. When we're dating, we try to present a perfect picture of ourselves to attract the person we're interested in. We dress up, go to restaurants we wouldn't otherwise visit or buy flowers as presents to woo them. If you were to continue these habits after you'd entered a relationship with the other person, that would be fine. But the problems start when you stop buying flowers once you are married and only wear sweatpants in your day-to-day life. In that case, the person your partner fell for turned out to be a 'false persona' – you were hiding your authentic self underneath a mask. This is one of the main reasons relationships fail. People cannot see if they are a match when no one shows who they are from the get-go.

3. Develop good communication skills. While we're in this reality, we all have an ego to deal with. And so we all have trouble sometimes to understand another person's perspective. Close soulmates are usually much better at this than other couples, but even they can go wrong and misunderstand each other if they don't communicate their truth.

4. Take risks. No relationship is 100% safe, because every person can choose to end one at any point. But not taking the risk of losing someone means being lonely from the beginning.

5. Don't try to force love. Love is a natural state that we move into as soon as we perceive another person to be a part of ourselves. When we love someone or something, it's because we understand them on a deeper level. So, in the end, *understanding* is the road to true intimacy and should be your top priority in all your relationships. Feel, see and hear the other party involved and hold space for them by being present with their feelings, needs, wants and wishes as if they were your own. This is the most loving thing you can do for them, and it will create more love in your life than anything else.

6. Cherish the moments of unconditional love in your life. Since you have an ego, you cannot always be in the energy of the source. But you can extend and increase the times you love unconditionally by extending and increasing the moments you are positively focused towards someone else.

7. If you're wondering how you'll know that you've met a close soulmate, the answer is: there will be no questions as the connection you will share is deeper than anything else you have experienced before. You'll feel comfortable, safe and at home in their presence. Being authentic and honest around them will be easy and, if you're lucky, you'll even be able to experience a telepathic bond with them.

Seven practical tools to develop your telepathy skills (including animal communication)

1. Since sending information is easier than receiving messages, the optimal situation for beginners would be to find a partner who's already able to receive telepathic messages clearly so you can first practise sending. If you don't know anyone who can speak telepathically, take turns sending and receiving.

2. To send a message, imagine your energetic connection like a rope strung between you. Now, concentrate on one simple fact: for example, a colour or a number you see in your mind's eye or a name you repeat over and over again inside your head. Once you have focused on something, imagine this image or word travelling across the imaginary rope to your partner and for them to receive it.

3. If you are playing the role of the receiver, use a meditation technique to become present and clear your mind as much as possible. Let any thoughts drift by or imagine a box in which you can place them for the duration of this practice, to bring back out later. Then wait for any image, thought or feeling to appear without actively searching for one. Say out loud anything that comes to you, no matter how nebulous or unclear it is. Let your partner give you feedback on how close you were regarding what they sent you.

4. Don't be discouraged when you get something wrong. Often, there are more overlaps between the message sent and the message received than might seem apparent at first glance. If you thought of the colour red and your partner says they received the colour blue,

you might both have imagined a very bright or very dark colour. Or maybe the colour red holds the same meaning to you as blue does for your partner ... And even if you don't get anything right to begin with, remember that practise makes perfect.

5. You can also practise with an animal, either with a pet or a wild animal. A lot of the time, this is even easier than practising with a human because animals, unlike most humans, use telepathy daily as their natural language.

The only thing you have to do is to respect their free will. If they don't want to talk to you because they're busy or they don't like talking to humans, don't try to force a conversation with them or pester them with questions.

6. Even if you cannot receive messages yet, use telepathy to send messages to your pets or other animals and watch their reaction. For example, tell a bird that's sitting on the sidewalk that it can stay where it is; you will detour around it. Be mindful, though, that telepathy doesn't recognise negatives. When you tell your dogs *not* to worry as you'll be back in ten minutes, you are telling them the exact opposite: namely, that they do need to worry.

7. Keep your questions and messages short when talking to animals and expect equally short answers from them. Since animals live so much in the present moment, a dog will not elaborate on the fact that they 'love it when you throw the ball because they enjoy chasing after it as their hunting instinct gets triggered, which is exciting' when you ask them what their favourite game is. The answer will be more along the lines of 'blue ball flying'.

Seven steps to find and work with your spirit animals

1. In addition to improving your relationships with your incarnated animal companions, you can also create better relationships with your spirit animals. To find out who these are ask yourself what animals you have strong feelings about. It could be an animal you fear (e.g. a spider) or an animal you love (e.g. an elephant or wolf). Also, when an animal appears repeatedly in your life and/or dreams, it is one of your spirit animals as well: from the dragonflies that constantly cross your path to the beaver that visits you in your dreams and the shark you see everywhere on adverts and in magazines. They appear in your life because they have a message for you.

2. If you are still unsure what your spirit animals are or which you should work with at this time, you can also go on a shamanic journey into the lower world or try astral travelling (see "*Willow and Strix – A healing journey*") to meet up with one or more. Beforehand, simply state your intention to meet the spirit animal who has the message you need to hear most right now.

When you meet your spirit animal via journeying, use this opportunity to ask the animal directly what messages, answers or advice it can give you. Ask what it can teach you. Or you can simply sit with the animal and get to know it better, creating an even deeper bond between you.

3. Once you know what your spirit animal is, ask yourself what this animal means to you specifically. How does it make you feel? Do you like it? Do you have any past experiences with it? Did you read any stories about it as a child that have stuck with you? How is

it seen in your culture and your myths? Your feelings about it tell you as much as the facts that you can find about the species. Because the meanings you apply individualise its messages.

4. The next step is to pick up a biology book or go online and read up on the animal. Learn about its characteristics, attributes, habits, traits and behaviours. When does it sleep? Does it live in a pack? Is it carnivorous? How many young does it have? The more you know about the animal, the easier it will be for you to see what message it's trying to convey to you.

5. Once you know the habits and characteristics of the species, ask yourself how those can apply to your situation. To do this, become present and listen to your intuition. Then ask yourself the following question: Which facts jump out at you the most? What traits of the animal could you replicate and how would that help you? What should you stop doing?

6. Only when you've exhausted all other steps should you read up on what others say the messages from this spirit animal could mean. There are diverse online sources or books on spirit animals for that. You could also visit my spirit animal blog at https://awakansspiritanimals.wordpress.com/ or turn the pages to the second appendix 'Spirit Animals'. Read up on the spiritual meanings and look for anything that you missed that resonates with you.

7. Give back. A healthy relationship includes both giving and receiving. If you want to deepen your relationship with your spirit

animal, who gives you valuable information and insight, give back to it. How? Sometimes it can be something as simple as sending light or loving energy to the species. Sometimes it could be giving a little money or time to help a non-profit organisation related to your spirit animal. Or you could choose to do something practical that will help them. For example, if your spirit animal is a dolphin, shark or jellyfish, you could stop using single-use plastics because this would help to protect the oceans.

Enclosed, you'll find seven 'Gaia life hacks' to give you some pointers on what kind of changes you can implement in your own life:

- One basic principle is that anything bad for your health is also bad for the environment. This holds true for plastic or chemicals to name just two examples. So, avoid plastics if possible, whether this is bags, takeaway coffee cups, children's toys, food packaging or household items. And avoid using chemicals, whether it is in food, in hygiene products or in cleaning supplies.
- Adjust your buying behaviour. You might say that you're only one human and can't create big changes. But customers hold power. What the consumers demand is what the companies need to provide if they want to stay in business. So, for example, buy more local, seasonal and organic foods. These are not only beneficial for your health but also the environment, as it cuts back on the fuel for transportation and thus the pollution of the air or water.
- To stop deforestation, only buy sustainable-made wood products that are certified to this end. You can also plant more trees if you own some land or donate to a charity or environmental

group to plant some. Additionally, inform yourself, which cultivations are mainly responsible for the global deforestation and avoid the products that include these ingredients.

- Dispose of any rubbish in an environment-friendly way. Recycle paper, don't put hazardous waste in the normal waste bin, and don't flush old medications or chemicals down the toilet as residues end up not only in the groundwater but also, as a result, in our drinking water.
- Be aware that holiday experiences, which allow a direct contact with wild animals, are usually – if not always – detrimental to the species involved. For example, there are places where groups of tourists can cuddle tigers or other big cats. These animals are heavily medicated and/or abused; otherwise, you wouldn't be able to walk out of these enclosures alive and with all your limbs intact. Then there's the whole 'riding on elephants' business. You might think that this doesn't pose a problem because they are big animals that can surely carry a tiny human or two ... But that's false. Unlike a horse's spine, which curves downwards, an elephant's spine curves upwards. And this means that any extra weight on an elephant's back can cause severe spinal damage. Not to mention that the elephants in question are also often abused from an early age.

  On the other hand, most adventures where you only watch the animals from afar are indirectly beneficial to them: for example safaris. The money these countries earn from tourism helps their people to survive. And the better they are doing, the fewer poachers and hunters there will be.

- If you want to experience closer contacts with animals on holidays, there is another great option. Look up any animal welfare organisations in the country you are travelling to and offer to help them. That way you'll even learn a bit about the species in question while doing something worthwhile.
- So often, we are intrigued by animals that live far away and ignore the fauna that's in our back gardens because we dismiss these animals are 'boring' and 'normal'. But you don't have to look far afield to do some good. Find out about the native animals that live near you and do something for them. For example, you could install a bird nesting box on your balcony or a bird feeder in your garden. You could plant indigenous, bee-friendly plants. Or you could stop using any chemical fertilisers and insecticides.

Appendix 2 – Spirit Animals

Strix's introduction

When my friend Willow told me about this book and asked me if I thought that tales about animals would be a good way to convey messages to humans, I agreed immediately, because I learned that many of the two-legged can relate to us.

To this end, it also helped that Willow and Nayeli chose to give the animals I met some human attributes to make the lessons more relatable. I mean, in reality, no warthog cares about their appearance and no giraffe feels superior about their farsightedness – animals lack the adult human ego to think along those lines. Which doesn't mean that my experiences were altered in any big way, mind you. Willow has done an incredible job of reciting my journey around the world and Nayeli did a terrific job of writing it all down. We made sure to keep the animals' habits and characteristics as accurate as possible and only took liberties here and there when necessary.

But taking these liberties also made me think of the idea to include this appendix on spirit animals. We animals are more than happy to guide you humans by adjusting to your life and your ways of communication. But we have even more to offer you, if only you took the time to look at things from our perspective every so often and invest energy in trying to understand how we live.

So, take a step out of your awareness and enter our world. Choose any animal you like, or read up on all of us. Let our lives be your teacher and let me help to translate these messages for you, so you can apply them to your life. The kingdom of animals awaits you!

Spirit animal Brown-Throated Sloth

(*Bradypus Variegatus*)

Animal Facts	Some spiritual meanings
The sloth is reputed to sleep all day long. But this is, in fact, not true. Wild sloths only sleep for about nine to ten hours a day, which isn't all that much longer than humans. Sloths only seem lazy because, even awake, they don't move a lot. And when they do, they're slow about it. The brown-throated sloth is built for life in the treetops. It spends most of its time hanging upside down from branches, which it clings to with its long claws. This technique doesn't require much energy and it's been known that, even after death, sloths can continue to hang suspended from their branch for some time. Sloths do almost everything hanging upside down from trees, from the moment they are weaned from their mother to whom they cling for the first months of their lives. They sleep, eat, mate and even give birth while hanging upside down. The reason sloths can remain in this	When the sloth has come into your life, note that it lives the majority of its life up a tree. Therefore, the elements air and earth are important for you. Stay grounded while you reach for the sky. Sloths hang from tree branches by their long claws. Do you hang on to things for too long? Do you need to let go of something? Or are you giving up too easily when situations can still be resolved? The fact that sloths mostly see the world upside down provides

position for such a long period is that their internal organs are fixed to their rib cage so that they don't weigh down their lungs. That the brown-throated sloths don't need to move much is a good thing because they need to preserve their energy, as their diet is low in	you with a unique view of life. Are you able to see things from a different perspective? Do you need to?
nutrients. Unlike two-toed sloths, which also snack on fruits and insects, the three-toed sloths – to which the brown-throated sloth belongs – only eat certain types of leaves, which are low in calories. They digest these leaves so slowly – they need around thirty days to digest one – that they only need to climb down once a week to use the forest floor as their bathroom.	When eating, the sloth only needs to pluck off the leaves growing all around it. Do you have easy access to what you need? Or do you not feel prosperous? What blocks do you have concerning abundance?
Toilet breaks are one of two occasions when sloths voluntarily leave their trees. The only other time they do so is to find a partner. Mating begins with the female sloth emitting a long, high-pitched call that attracts males from a radius of 700 metres around her. Mating itself is also the only time that sloths make an exception to the rule of doing everything at a snail's pace: once they've found a partner, the whole	Sloths spend the majority of their lives in solitude. Do you need more time for yourself and your ventures? Or are you feeling too lonely? Do you need more connections?
mating ritual is over in about five	When slots move, they

seconds, after which they go back to their natural state of solitary unhurriedness. Visiting the forest floor is dangerous for sloths. For one, because they are slow and clumsy on the ground. As the sloth's hind legs are weak, it has to dig into the earth with its long front claws to pull itself forward, dragging its belly across the ground. This makes them even slower than usual and unable to evade any predators, which consist mainly of eagles, jaguars, snakes and, of course, humans.	are slow about it. Do you need to slow down? Are you rushing into things without thinking? Or do you move too slowly? Are you maybe standing still, not moving forward at all? Use your energy wisely and don't over-exert yourself.
The second reason why sloths are much more vulnerable on the ground is that their main defence does not work – up inside a tree, sloths are protected by camouflage as green algae grow on their fur, making them blend in with the surrounding trees. Add to that the fact that a sloth has no body odour and does not sweat, and they are almost invisible. Which is why most sloths die during their toilet breaks, during which they lose up to a third of their body weight.	Sloths use camouflage to melt into their surroundings. Do you feel that you are seen and heard? Do others maybe treat you as if you're invisible? Or do you feel too exposed? In that case, create healthier boundaries to feel safe.
Melting into the trees isn't the algae's only advantage, though. It also contains important nutrients that three-toed	Sloths live in symbiotic relationships. Look at your own

sloths need to supplement their diet. And the algae plays host to sloth moths. These enable faster algae growth and therefore more nutrients for the sloth. In return, the moth larvae survive on the sloths' excrements – a perfectly symbiotic relationship between the two animal species. A little-known fact about sloths is that they are surprisingly competent swimmers: they can swim three times faster than they can move on land. They can also hold their breath for up to forty minutes. Finally, three-toed sloths can turn their head up to 270 degrees – as far as an owl. This is due to the fact that they have additional vertebrae in their neck. Together with the manatees, they are thus an exception among the mammals who usually only have seven.	relationships. Are they healthy? Do you give as well as receive enough? What could you do to improve them? Since the sloth can turn its neck up to 270 degrees, sloth people often have a great connection to their throat chakra and the clair senses associated with it. Is your throat chakra open? Can you speak your truth? Are you authentic? Or do you need to heal it?

Spirit animal European Badger

(*Meles Meles*)

Animal Facts	Some spiritual meanings
European badgers are nocturnal and usually seen alone when about. But they're social as well, living together in clans – called cetes – of up to fifteen individuals inside their large underground setts that consist of a maze of tunnels, chambers and entrances. Some of these setts are centuries old, being reused by badgers over generations.	European badgers are both social and self-reliant. Do you enjoy your own company? Do you take enough 'me-time'? Or are you too lonely? Do you need to socialise more?
Sometimes, European badgers even share their setts with other species, such as foxes or rabbits, which then inhabit their own part or level of the sett. This can, of course, lead to disagreements, especially in the winter when the European badger goes into a torpor state and blocks all entrances to the sett to prepare for this. This torpor state is not a full hibernation. Badgers go into a deep sleep and slow their metabolism. But they regularly wake up to eat before going back into the next torpor phase.	The badger is an expert digger. Do you need to unearth the root of a problem? And are you grounded enough in your life? Since a badger spends a large part of its life under the earth, it's seen both as the keeper of healing herbs and as a gatekeeper to the subconscious.

Another preparation they make to survive the cold winters is to gain fat in advance. That way they can withstand the months when they find fewer food sources that consist of earthworms, grubs and other insects, small mammals, birds, reptiles, carrion and eggs as well as roots and fruits. As European badgers spend much of their life below ground, they are perfectly adapted to that environment. They have a third eyelid that protects their eyes from flying dirt and thick hairs in their nostrils and ears to keep those clear of debris. Last, but not least, they have strong front legs that end in shovel-like paws with sharp claws, which they use for digging their chambers and tunnels. Badgers are remarkably fast diggers, and when faced with a predator, they can dig a hole and disappear into the earth in a matter of seconds. European badgers prefer to avoid confrontations, but when they or their young are threatened, they are fierce opponents who will take on much bigger animals, such as wolves or bears. To that end, they have strong jaws that	If a badger has come into your life, you might be called to a healing profession. Also, are you suppressing your feelings and thoughts? Dig deep to uncover and integrate your subconscious parts. Badgers are physically tough and fierce when it calls for it, but they prefer to retreat into the earth when attacked. Are your lines being crossed repeatedly? Do you need to create healthier boundaries? It might be beneficial for you to withdraw from emotionally charged situations and to first heal yourself. The strong jaws of the badger are an

are muscled in a way that prevents dislocation and which lets them hang on easily to anything they bite. Another added protection the badger possesses is its fur, which is not only thick but also hanging loose so that it's difficult for a predator to grip.	expression of language and thus tales. What is your life story? Is there a story you've heard recently that holds the answers you are seeking?
European badgers are very clean animals. They toss out their used bedding – consisting of grass, straw, hay, bracken, leaves and moss – regularly throughout the year. Or they'll take it out on a dry, sunny day to 'air' and to kill off pests before retrieving it later on. They also use communal latrines outside the setts, so as not to dirty their home. And, finally, when a badger dies inside its home, other cete members either seal the chamber shut or carry the body outside and bury it there.	Also, as your words hold power, be mindful which ones you use, both towards yourself and others. Badgers are very tidy animals. Is your life in order? Or do you need to 'tidy up' any unresolved issues?
Badgers can mate several times over the course of one year, and yet the females only have one litter with two to five cubs in winter or spring, due to delayed implantation. The European's badger's fur is mostly grey, apart from their white face with the two large black stripes that give them a mask-like appearance.	The mask-like markings of the badger might hint at the fact that you hide behind a mask as well. Do you need to be more authentic? Or are others around you not showing their true selves?

Spirit animal Grey Wolf

(*Canis Lupus*)

Animal Facts	Some spiritual meanings
The grey wolf is a social animal that lives in a pack, which is led by an alpha pair and can have between 3 and up to forty members, including the offspring from previous years. The pack members live in a hierarchy and each wolf fulfils a specific role inside the group for which they are perfectly suited. The social structure inside the pack can change when a wolf that's lower down in the hierarchy challenges the alpha wolf or another wolf standing above them and wins. But aside from these fights for dominance, wolves settle any existing conflicts between the pack members in a gentle way. A subtle signal like a glance, a different posture or a light growl is usually all that's needed to assert dominance and restore harmony. Being such social animals, wolves communicate in a number of ways – by leaving scent marks, by making a variety of sounds such as growling, whimpering,	Wolves are very social animals and create close emotional connections with their pack-mates. When the wolf is your spirit animal, ask yourself the following questions: Have you found a community in which you belong? Are your relationships harmonious? Do you wish to create a closer connection with someone? Or is loyalty missing in your life? Do you need to be more social? Are you feeling lonely? As wolves use complex communication skills, which consist mainly of

barking or sighing, and by using complex body language, such as posturing or positioning their tails and ears in specific ways. They also communicate by touch, using their snouts, teeth or paws. Combining all these communication tools, wolves can understand hundreds of different messages. One of the wolf's most distinguishing characteristics is, of course, its howl. Wolves howl to contact separated members of their group, to stake out their territory and to connect and bond with each other. But even better than their hearing is the wolves' sense of smell as they have 280 million olfactory receptors with which they can perceive odours that are hundreds to millions of times fainter than what humans can detect. This ability also helps them to find suitable prey.	subtle hints, you can allow yourself to be gentle with others. Are you communicating clearly? Do you recognise what's been left unsaid? Are you not voicing things that need to be expressed? Are you maybe too aggressive in your reactions? Or do others react aggressively towards you? Also, do you need to assert your dominance in a certain situation or with a certain person? Create healthy boundaries with others.
Wolves hunt co-operatively inside the pack. This enables them to kill much larger animals – like deer or moose – than they'd be able to bring down on their own. But hunting such large prey can be dangerous, as the wolves could be speared by sharp antlers or kicked by	The wolves' sense of smell is exceptional. Can you sniff out anything wrong in your environment? Trust your intuition when something feels

hooves. Because of this, they have to assess the herds carefully to choose which individual to go after. They look for any signs of weaknesses and factor in conditions like the terrain or the weather, which could affect the hunt. Sometimes wolves also strike up symbiotic relationships with ravens. Ravens scavenge on the wolf's carcasses and feed on the leftovers after the wolves gorged themselves. Meanwhile, wolves follow ravens that lead them to nearby prey or carcasses that are so frozen that the ravens' beaks cannot penetrate them.	off. Wolves are great hunters who assess the situation and their abilities correctly. Be observant and embrace opportunities when they arise. But also learn to let go when something proves to be unprofitable.
Wolves have great endurance and stamina, which they need to patrol their territory, to defend it against rivals and to hunt for food. But wolves also take rest seriously. And raising their young. Only the alpha couple is allowed to reproduce inside a pack, but all members are involved in the upbringing of the pups: they play with them and teach them how to hunt; they regurgitate pre-digested meat for them and they babysit them while the other wolves of the pack go hunting.	The wolf has great stamina. Are you persistent when you go after your goals? And do you feel energised enough to see things through to the end? Or do you give up too soon? Take enough breaks and include time for rest in your day-to-day life.
Wolf pups are born deaf and blind. They	Wolves are well

stay in the den with their mother for the first weeks, then they start to explore the world outside. But they only make longer journeys with their pack-mates once they are about six to seven months old. When they are between one and two years old, the young wolves have to make an important decision: to either stay with the pack and accept their social role in it or fight for a higher position. Or to leave the pack and find, or form, another one with the chance to reproduce. It's also possible that they might end up as a 'lone wolf' without having a pack to rely on. Leaving an existing pack holds many dangers, and a lot of wolves die during this time. They might cross territories of other wolf packs and be injured or killed by those, or they might be killed by humans.	organised: they teach us about the distribution of roles and how you can trust both yourself and others. Have you found a role that suits your abilities? What is your field of expertise? Which tasks fill you with joy? What tasks could you delegate to others? Also, how can you benefit from each other's talents and work as a team towards a shared goal? Learn to ask for help when needed while trusting in your own strengths.

Spirit animal Golden Eagle
(*Aquila Chrysaetos*)

Animal Facts	Some spiritual meanings
Golden eagles are birds of prey that are found all over the northern hemisphere. They were named for the golden-brown feathers on their heads and necks, which stand out from their otherwise brown plumage. Golden eagles live in diverse habitats, from grasslands over woodlands to mountain ranges, preferring to nest on cliffs or trees as building their nests high up helps to keep their eaglets safe. But sometimes, they also nest on the ground or in human-made structures such as windmills and towers. The golden eagle pair collaborates: the male collects the nest material and the female builds the nest before lining it with greenery and aromatic leaves. These have a disinfectant property to help keep the nest clean, and they are also believed to keep insects away. Golden eagles mate with the same partner for several years, if not for life. To raise their young, they reuse their	The eagle is a messenger of the element air, which represents the mind, intelligence, thoughts and ideas. The golden eagle is also a messenger of the sun, which gives life and is a symbol of fire and passion. So, use your passion and wit to create the life you want. You have the power to do so. Golden eagles raise their young together. Do you have people in your life you can depend on? And can others depend on you? Do you receive help when you ask for it? Do

nests of which they often have several, rotating between them and mending them regularly. The female lays one to four eggs, and the pair takes it in turns to incubate them. Later, when the eaglets are born, the male golden eagle will hunt for food while the female guards the young. The mother is unable to ward off one danger, though, because it comes from within the nest. If two or more eggs have hatched, the strongest eaglet will often attack and kill the weaker ones to ensure its own survival. Once the surviving eaglet or eaglets have fledged and have learned all the skills they will need to survive on their own, the golden eagle pair will expel the young from their territory. Like all eagles, the golden eagle has excellent hearing and eyesight. The latter especially during the day when they can utilise their great colour vision. Just like an owl, their eyes cannot move in their sockets, but they can turn their heads up to 270 degrees. Golden eagles are so effective at hunting that they spend little time doing so. What they hunt depends on their habitat and	you even ask for it? Eagles have strong beaks that can cut and tear easily. You could potentially hurt someone by cutting and tearing them with words. Or are you too easily hurt by what other people say? Eagles have excellent vision and hearing, even though their ears aren't visible. This translates to you being capable of hearing your inner voice. Are you listening to it? Also, can you see what's ahead of you? Do you have a clear vision of your future? Eagles create a natural balance by capturing

can include small to medium-sized mammals, other birds, reptiles and fish. They have also been known to eat carrion at times, to supplement their diet, or when they can't find enough prey. Golden eagles are opportunistic hunters. When they spot possible prey, they swoop down at high speed and strike it with their talons before they tear into it with their sharp beak. Sometimes they also work in pairs, with one eagle driving the prey towards the waiting partner who then kills it. And golden eagles have even been seen snatching birds in mid-air. The other time golden eagles exhibit aerial stunts is during courtship rituals. To impress their chosen one, the golden eagle will emit shrill, high-pitched calls and 'sky-dive', meaning it will repeatedly switch between steep dives and upwards swoops. Golden eagles also engage in aerial play with objects like sticks, stones or dead prey. They carry these up into the sky, drop them, and then fly down to retrieve the object before it hits the ground. Overall, the golden eagle is a majestic	weak prey or eating carrion. If you have the eagle as your spirit animal, you might be a natural healer. Do you need to heal yourself? Or can you provide healing for others? Eagles might spend a lot of time in the air, but they are still connected to the earth and its resources via the food they hunt. Are you staying grounded enough in your life? Or do you need to take wing? The golden eagle relies mostly on surprise attacks. Do you make the most of the chances you are given? And can you

bird in flight and possesses astonishing agility and manoeuvrability for its size. On top of that, the eagle can fly long distances without needing to stop, as soaring and gliding on thermals rising from the land takes up little energy.	easily adapt? Or do you need to be more flexible? Use your intuition to sense the right time to make a move.

Spirit animal Mediterranean Chameleon (*Chamaeleo Chamaeleon*)

Animal Facts	Some spiritual meanings
Chameleons are known best for their ability to change their skin colour. The Mediterranean chameleon can show colours from bright green to dark brown and grey or tan, with various patterns. In addition, it generally has two lighter stripes along each side of its body, which can be continuous or broken into a series of spots. Even though most of the colours the Mediterranean chameleon can show off help them blend in with their surroundings, camouflage is not the reason for their skin tone changes. They change colour to regulate their temperature, to adapt to humidity and to communicate with other chameleons: for example when mating or when defending their territory. The Mediterranean chameleon is usually solitary. Males only leave their territory to find a female – preferably a large one, as those tend to produce more eggs – which is also when they get into fights	Most of the chameleon's colours help it blend in with its surroundings. Having this spirit animal means you don't need to stand out in order to thrive. Just like the chameleon is sensitive to its environment, you are connected to your sensitivity. Can you sense anything amiss? Tune into your intuition regularly and trust what it tells you. The colour changes of the chameleon are partly due to their emotions. Are you allowing your

with rival males. In these fights chameleons can move surprisingly quickly. But otherwise, they move slowly through life, using a swaying back and forward motion. This has two benefits: For one, it helps their eyes focus and zoom in on an object. And secondly, it helps them to camouflage better by imitating the leaves around them, which move in the wind. The Mediterranean chameleon is an arboreal species, meaning they live most of their lives in trees. They're expert climbers, which is made possible by the chameleon's unusual feet with toes that are grouped together on both sides. These work similar to our thumbs and allow them to firmly grip the branches they walk on. On top of that, the chameleon can wrap its prehensile (Latin: able to grasp) tail around tree branches when climbing. Sometimes chameleons drop from the tree they are sitting on, as if dead. They have not lost their grip, however. The truth is that they use this technique to avoid being killed by a predator, which includes birds of prey, snakes and cats. Yet another survival technique is for	feelings to come to the surface? And do you let others see how their words and actions affect you? Like the chameleon, live life at your own pace. Slow down if necessary, take a step back and study your situation carefully before moving forward again. Are you patient enough? Or are you overcautious in your ventures? As a chameleon person, you don't need to rush to reach your goals. Chameleons are masters of versatility. Likewise, you are adaptable. Embrace this talent and allow yourself to be calm and relaxed one moment, then extroverted the

them to puff themselves up to look as big and intimidating as possible and hiss threateningly. But no matter how fast a chameleon moves when trying to defend itself or fight for its rights to reproduce, it can never be faster than its own tongue, which is one of the fastest in the animal kingdom. This long elastic muscle – which is twice the length of the chameleon – shoots out when the chameleon sees suitable prey like grasshoppers, flies, wasps, ants, other insects, spiders and sometimes even fruit or smaller chameleons. Its tongue is coated in mucus that sticks to the prey when the chameleon retracts it – all in the blink of an eye. In order to aim their tongue so precisely, the chameleon utilises yet another unique feature. Their eyes can rotate and focus separately from each other, which gives the chameleon a 360-degree view and the ability to zoom in on two objects at the same time. With those eyes, the chameleon can access the ultraviolet light range, additional to the colour spectrum that's visible to humans.	next. Are you enabling all of your parts to come to the surface? Chameleons can extend their tongues incredibly fast to catch prey. Are you quick to pull in what you need when the opportunity arrives? The chameleon can use both eyes separately and focus on a potential threat and food source at the same time. Are you focused on what you need to see? Can you zoom in on a problem and notice the little details? Additional to having a literal third eye, the chameleon can also see in the ultraviolet light range.

A little-known fact is that the chameleon, like most lizards, also has a third eye. This sits on the top of its head and is called a parietal eye. It can only detect light and dark but works well enough that the chameleon can, for example, see the shadow of a bird of prey flying overhead.	This tells of your great psychic abilities. Clairvoyance and seeing auras might come easily to you. Is your third eye open? Do you need to work with it?

Spirit animal Common Warthog

(*Phacochoerus Africanus*)

Animal Facts	Some spiritual meanings
The warthog is named after the wart-like bumps on its head, which are a combination of bone and cartilage and which help to pad and protect its face and eyes in fights. Especially in the mating season, males, called boars, fight over their right to reproduce, which is why they have bigger and more bumps than females, called sows.	The bumps on the warthog's face act as a protective layer. Have you added unnecessary protective measures in your life? Or do you need to create stronger boundaries?
Older boars often live alone, while younger males live in bachelor herds. Meanwhile, females live in so-called 'sounders', which include several generations of their female offspring and can contain up to forty members. Litters contain two to eight piglets, and warthog mothers are protective of them when it comes to their long list of natural enemies, such as lions, African wild dogs,	The sows are known to be caring mothers. Do you have any ideas or projects that need your attention and care? Look at what you need to nurture in your life right now.
hyenas, crocodiles, leopards and cheetahs. When faced with these predators – which the warthog mostly detects with	Warthogs prefer to back into their burrows when threatened. Do you have a place to

their great sense of smell and hearing as they have poor eyesight – they prefer to flee and hide in their dens. They back into their burrow, backside first, and defend themselves and their piglets with their long, razor-sharp tusks, which are simply canine teeth. These can cause serious wounds and rip open a lion's belly with ease.	which you can escape when feeling overwhelmed by life? Or do you feel cornered? Also, do you need to take on what's lying in front of you?
As well as using their tusks for fighting and as a defensive tool, they use them for digging up roots to supplement their diet of grass, plants, berries, fruit and bark. During times of scarcity, they also eat insects and meat from carcasses they find. When grazing, warthogs do so with their forelegs bent because of their short	The warthog will fiercely protect itself and its piglets when attacked, even taking on much larger enemies. This means you can successfully take on large projects.
necks and – in comparison – long legs. To protect their knees when kneeling, they have calloused pads on them. Even though they could also use their tusks to dig their own burrows, warthogs are opportunistic animals and prefer to use holes that have been made and abandoned by other animals, mainly aardvarks. Apart from protecting them from their enemies, these burrows shelter	Using burrows made by other animals tells of the warthogs' opportunistic nature. Can you accept gifts? Are you ready to seize chances? Or are you too inflexible to act quickly? Do you maybe feel that you don't deserve what

warthogs from the elements. The only real fur of a warthog is a mane-like stripe on their back, similar to a horse's mane, and a tuft of hair at the end of their tail, which they stick straight up into the air like an antenna when they run. This lack of fur means that they are sensitive, both to the cold at night and to the burning sun. A method the warthogs use to protect themselves from the latter is to take regular mud baths. Like other pigs, they have no sweat glands, and they use mud to help them regulate their body temperature and keep cool. This is why they prefer to live near waterholes, as the mud also has the benefit of preventing sunburns and protecting them from insects. On top of that, warthogs form symbiotic relationships with bird species, which eat the parasites that crawl on their skin.	you've been given? The erect tail of the warthog when running looks like an antenna. This speaks of your own link to the higher planes. Are you listening to the intuitive messages you receive? As well as being an expert digger, the warthog is connected to nature by taking mud baths. Are you grounded in your life? Also, is there anything hidden that you need to dig up?

Spirit animal Masai Giraffe

(*Giraffa Tippelskirchi*)

Animal Facts	Some spiritual meanings
The most prominent feature of the giraffe is, of course, its long neck, which – despite its length – has the usual seven vertebrae that are typical for mammals. Their long neck not only enables the giraffe to reach leaves at the top of trees, but it also helps them to spot predators such as lions, leopards, hyenas and crocodiles well in advance. Even though a fully grown giraffe is safe from these natural enemies, due to its size, younger giraffes are still worthwhile prey. When attacked, a grown giraffe can kill a lion or other predator with a well-placed kick, but they're flight animals first and foremost and seek refuge from danger by running away, being very fast over short distances. Giraffes are one of the few animals to change their gait when running, exchanging the swinging, camel-like pace where they move both legs on one side at the same time for the diagonal step	As the tallest animal in the world, the giraffe has the gift of far-sightedness and foresight. This tells of your ability to not only see the present but also your future. Can you see clearly what lies ahead of you? Or are you too concerned about the future? Have you lost sight of the goals on your horizon? You can aim higher than you thought possible and easily achieve things that seem out of reach when you take action and follow through on the ventures you foresee.

sequence used by most mammals, swinging their front and rear legs in unison. Newborn giraffes can run with their herd a mere hour or two after their birth, which happens with the mother standing up. So, the first thing a calf experiences in this life is a drop of about two metres to the ground. Additional to helping the giraffe reach higher food sources and making them farsighted, their long necks are also used by the bulls to fight with each other and assert their dominance: to this end, they slam their necks against the opponent's head and neck, which is called necking. Sometimes they also use the two hair-covered horns on the head as extra weapons. These are called ossicones just like the third one in the centre of the giraffe's forehead, where the third eye is located, which isn't as pronounced as the other two and only visible as a lump. Usually, giraffe fights end peacefully, with one of the bulls admitting defeat and walking away. But, at times, the necking can become so fierce that the loser can be knocked out or die. In short, the giraffe's long neck has many	The giraffe is able to change its gait. Just like them, you can adjust your pace to your needs. Are you going forward too hastily? Or are you too cautious? Are you not moving forward at all? Are you maybe running away from something? A giraffe's ossicones resemble antennae that tap into the spirit realm. Additionally, the third ossicone is directly located above the third eye. Are you using your natural psychic gifts? Do you need to open your third eye? Clairvoyance might be one of your dominant clair-senses.

advantages, but it has one disadvantage, too. Since water is on the ground, giraffes need to lower their heads to drink. There's a common misconception that they'll pass out if they raise or lower their heads quickly. This is wrong because giraffes have an installed safety measure in form of a jugular vein containing a series of one-way valves that prevent excess blood flow to the brain. But despite this, bending down to drink still makes them vulnerable. Because, as long as their necks might be, they are still shorter than their legs. Therefore, they need to splay their front legs or bend their knees, meaning they need a few second to get back up in case of a threat. The good news for them is that they rarely need to drink because they can get most of their water intake from the plants they eat. In fact, they can go for weeks without drinking water – needing it even less frequently than camels. Being ruminants that eat for up to fifteen hours each day, giraffes have to be mindful about which trees they munch on, though. Mopane or acacia trees, for	The giraffe is most vulnerable when bending down. Do you have trouble being vulnerable around others? Are you most insecure when you lose sight of your goals? This spirit animal tells you to stand tall and proud in your beliefs. Learn to keep your head up. Giraffes can survive long periods without drinking. Are you using your own resources wisely? Also, make sure you drink enough water and keep yourself hydrated. Giraffe people need to look at their throat chakra, as the neck holds much importance. Is your throat chakra

example, generate bitter compounds as soon as they are fed upon and send messages to other trees with the wind saying that they are under attack. The leaves of these trees will then be unpalatable for some time. This process is called 'Jasmonation'. So, to feed, the giraffes need to walk upwind. Apart from bending down to drink, the other most vulnerable position for giraffes is lying down. This is why adults prefer to sleep standing up. On top of that, giraffes only sleep between thirty minutes and four hours each day and usually for only five minutes at a stretch – a very short time compared to other mammals. Of course, it also benefits giraffes that most live inside a herd so that some members can look out for danger while others are resting. Not all giraffes live inside groups, though, as older bulls are generally loners, only joining the herds of females – known as 'towers' – during the mating season. Meanwhile, most of the younger bulls will join bachelor herds when they leave their mothers. But giraffe groups are not as close-knit	healthy? Are you speaking your truth? And are you using creative ventures to express yourself? The neck is also the connection between the head and the torso, and thus a symbol of balancing your higher self with your ego self. Do you stay grounded enough? Or do you have your head in the clouds? Most of a giraffe's sounds are in the infrasound (low-frequency) range. This means that giraffe people tend to be on the quiet side. Do you speak up when you need to? Also, can you perceive the little nuances and hear what's been left

as those of most other herd animals and can change every day, with members leaving or joining them. To communicate with each other, calves will emit snorts and mewing sounds – in the range that humans can hear – while adult giraffes hum in the infrasound range. Alongside using this vocal communication, giraffes also use their good eyesight to recognise other members – as no two giraffes have the same coat pattern. The spots on their hide are as unique as human fingerprints. Additionally, a giraffe's coat pattern also helps them with thermoregulation. Around each spot is a large blood vessel that branches off into smaller vessels, and a giraffe can send blood through these into the middle of the patch to release heat.	unsaid by others? Sometimes power can lie in silence. Distinguish when it's better to not voice an opinion. No two giraffes are alike, as their skin pattern is unique. Distinctiveness is important to you. Are you true to yourself? And do you allow yourself to be seen? Or do you try to hide in a crowd? Know that this world needs your unique talents that no one else can replicate.

Spirit animal African Wild Ass

(*Equus Africanus*)

Animal Facts	Some spiritual meanings
The African wild asses are the ancestors of all modern domesticated donkeys. They live in a flexible social system. Some wild asses are solitary, while others live, temporarily or permanently, in herds of up to fifty members that can be made up of females only, males only or both sexes. Generally, though, younger males join bachelor groups, while females and their foals form separate herds. This is also why male wild asses can often be seen near water sources, as this is one way they can ensure to meet the females who pass through their territory. If necessary, wild asses can live a few days without water, as they can absorb some through their food, which consists of grass, herbs, bark and leaves – thus being perfectly adapted to the rocky, dry deserts or semi-deserts they live in. A wild ass can sustain water loss of up to 30% of its body weight, which can be	The wild asses' legendary stubbornness is, in reality, a sign of brains coupled with vigilance. Wild ass people are intelligent and know how to use their wit to their advantage. If you're ever in doubt about how to proceed, simply stop and re-evaluate the situation before moving forward. The wild ass can survive in barren landscapes. You are effective and able to thrive even if you have few resources at your disposal. The asses' ears are

replenished within a few minutes once they find a source of water. Because temperatures usually rise very high during the day, wild asses are most active between dusk and dawn and rest in the shade by day. To cool down, the wild ass radiates excess heat through its large ears like their domestic cousins, the donkeys. And the same as donkeys, they also share the tendency not to bolt when threatened. The asses' first reaction is to freeze and to find the source of the threat. This habit led to wild asses' reputation for being stubborn. But in reality, this tendency is simply their way of finding out what's wrong and why, and it has the benefit of saving energy. If the threat turns out to be a predator, the asses' next step is to either flee or to defend themselves by kicking out with their hind and front legs. Their kicks are so powerful that they can easily break bones. Males also use their powerful kicks when fighting with each other. Wild asses are territorial and defend areas of up to fifteen square miles, which they mark with their dung. But because	funnel-like, which means they can hear sounds over great distances. Wild ass people are usually good listeners. Can you hear what others can't? Do you hear all that's been left unsaid? Also, are you tuned in to your inner voice? Or do you let other people make choices for you? Do you listen to them more than to yourself? Clairaudience might be your dominant clair sense. Its careful evaluation of its surroundings can make the wild ass slow to react. But when it does, it shows great courage. Are you too set in your ways and routines? Do

that's a lot of terrain, they usually tolerate the presence of subordinate males, as long as those accept their status and don't approach females to mate with them. Wild asses do not have a fixed breeding season, but they prefer the rainy season. Gestation lasts for about a year, after which the female gives birth to a single foal that can stand up and nurse a mere thirty minutes after being born. To communicate, wild asses use vocalisations, visual signals, smells and physical contact. But they are probably best known for braying, which can be heard up to three kilometres away, with the males being loudest during the mating season. The main thread to wild asses is not lions, leopards or hyenas. The main threat is humans, who are not only responsible for habitat loss but who also endanger wild asses by interbreeding them with domestic donkeys. Today there are only a few hundred wild asses left, which makes them critically endangered.	you tend to weigh something up for too long before deciding what to do? Or do you embrace the changes coming your way? Wild asses do not shy away easily. Humans who share this trait are often burdened by too many responsibilities. Does this sound like you? Do people take advantage of your helpful nature? Say no to others when you have to and stand your ground. The braying of the wild ass is loud. Invoke the help of this spirit animal when you need to be heard.

Spirit animal Mimic Octopus

(*Thaumoctopus Mimicus*)

Animal Facts	Some spiritual meanings
Like other octopuses, the mimic octopus has three hearts that pump blood through its body. This blood is not the usual iron-based red tone of many species but blue, thanks to a copper-rich protein that helps the octopus' body transport oxygen more efficiently. On the downside, this causes the octopus to be very sensitive to any changes in water acidity: If the water's pH dips too low, not enough oxygen can circulate. This in turn means that climate change might have dire effects on the octopus population. Two of the mimic octopus' hearts pump blood only through the gills, while the third pumps blood through all other organs. This third heart actually stops beating when the octopus swims. They thus prefer crawling, as it's less exhausting.	As the mimic octopus lives in the water, this element holds immense meaning to you. It's the element of emotions. Meanwhile, being underwater is a symbol of the subconscious. Are you aware of your emotions? Do you listen to them? And are you able to express them? Also, do you need to bring forward what's hidden in your subconsciousness? Dive deep within yourself to uncover what you have forgotten.
That two hearts exist solely to pump blood through the gills, with which the octopus breathes underwater, shows	The octopus is very sensitive to its environment.

how important those are for its survival. The mimic octopus, like all octopuses, cannot survive out of water for long.	Do you allow your sensitivity to shine?
Under ideal conditions, when their body and gills remain moist, they can survive for half an hour on land. But in most cases, they can only survive for a few minutes. This is because they depend on water for the exchange of oxygen and carbon dioxide and because on land their gills eventually collapse. Still, on rare occasions, octopuses do choose to leave the water to find prey such as mussels or crabs. But the preferred habitat of the mimic octopus is warm, shallow water near river mouths, where they hunt and forage for small fish, crabs, other crustaceans and worms. There, the water is sandy and murky, which makes it easier for the octopus to hide from its many predators, such as whales, dolphins, eels, birds, sharks, barracudas and other large fish. Since they have so many natural enemies, the mimic octopus needs an arsenal of abilities and techniques to defend itself. These include camouflage, mimicry, jet propulsion, spraying ink and using tools as well as their strong arms	The mimic octopus lives in an environment that's always moving and changing. And just like the water, the octopus itself is a master of transformation. Are you flexible and open? Are you able to go with the flow? Or are you too rigid to navigate life easily? Be daring enough to change any situations in your life that are not satisfactory. You have all the capabilities you need to see these changes through to the end. When hunting, the octopus uses camouflage. Be stealthy in your

and beak. One of the octopus' best-known strategies is, of course, their ability to camouflage themselves. Unlike the chameleon, which changes its colours and patterns due to emotions and weather conditions, the octopus can deliberately change colour to blend in with its surroundings. But the mimic octopus takes this talent to an entirely new level, as it can also realign its arms to copy different animals. This ability, which is called mimicry, is similar to the camouflage technique but has a different goal. Instead of blending in with their surroundings to become invisible, the mimic octopus changes its colour and shape to mimic another animal, to trick predators or prey into thinking they are facing a different species. For example, they can scare a predator away by mimicking a poisonous animal or lull their prey into a false sense of security by mimicking one of their kind. The mimic octopus has mastered this so well that it is named after this talent. This technique also shows their high intelligence: the mimic octopus does not	ventures and you will receive a positive outcome. Don't announce your presence prematurely; stay hidden until you've reached your goal. Also, do you really see what you think you are seeing? Or are you being deceived by others? The mimic octopus has mastered the art of mimicry. Can you see and feel things from someone else's perspective? As an octopus person, you have the talent to understand others and are likely highly empathetic. Octopus people have a superb intellect, are quick-thinking, imaginative and

choose its disguise randomly. Instead, it actively chooses the animal that is the most appropriate for the attacker or prey it faces. Another option the octopus has to evade predators is to use jet propulsion, which funnels water from its gills through its siphon. Using this technique, the octopus can reach a high speed over a short distance to propel itself away from danger. The so-called ink the octopus produces contains a compound called tyrosinase, which momentarily blinds the enemy when sprayed into their eyes while also dulling their sense of smell so that the octopus can escape. And if all of that doesn't help to get them out of harm's way, octopuses can squeeze into the tightest spaces as they have no skeleton, making them one of the most flexible animals on Earth. The only hard part of their bodies is their beak – so if this fits through a hole or gap, the rest of the octopus can get through as well, effectively escaping a bigger predator. In general, octopuses prefer to avoid fights. They would rather hide or flee.	creative and are known to be great problem-solvers. Are you using these abilities and talents as well as the tools that are available to you? Your wit can easily overcome any problem you face, and your creativity can bring you unique solutions. Don't limit yourself. Think outside the box when the situation calls for it. Just like the octopus, you can squeeze through the smallest gap and get past obstacles you didn't think possible before. You can also show your strength by being soft and pliant whenever a situation calls for it. The octopus can use its arms separately.

But they can also use tools they find on the seabed or fall back on their strong limbs. The octopus's eight arms are flexible, with two rows of suction cups - called suckers - on each. These are made out of tiny complex muscles with which the octopus can apply a great deal of pressure - enough to tear flesh, break a prey's spine or suffocate a predator. But the mimic octopus can use its arms for more than that. The octopus has a whopping nine brains, one central brain that controls their nervous system and a small brain in each of their eight arms. As a result, the arms can act separately and carry out different tasks at the same time, and they can still act and react after being severed from the body. At great need, the octopus can detach one of its arms to distract predators. Then, once it has escaped, it will regrow a new limb. Despite their amazing abilities, mimic octopuses are not invulnerable. Generally, their life ends after mating, which is the only time these solitary animals come together. The male's hectocotylus - a specialised arm with	This means you have the power of focus and are effective at time management. Beyond that, the eight arms of the octopus represent the number eight, which stands for eternity and abundance. Are you feeling abundant? Or do you need to heal any limiting beliefs around prosperity? When you tap into the octopus medicine, you can gain an endless supply of energy and financial success. The octopus's arms can regrow if they are detached. This translates to you being naturally good at the healing arts. Do you need healing? Or can you provide

which it deposits the sperm into the female – falls off, which leads to his death. Meanwhile, the female octopus will carry around the eggs – up to 500,000 – in strings, guarding them against predators and blowing currents of water over them so that they get enough oxygen. She does this until the larvae hatch, when her body undertakes a cellular suicide, resulting in her death.	healing to others? Also, do you need to 'cut off' anything that doesn't serve you any longer? Have you learned how to let go? Or do you 'cut things off' unnecessarily instead of resolving the underlying issue?

Spirit animal Pink Skunk Clownfish

(*Amphiprion Perideraion*)

Animal Facts	Some spiritual meanings
The pink skunk clownfish is also known as the pink anemonefish, salmon clownfish, white-maned anemonefish and white-banded anemonefish. And, as its name suggests, it is a pink or peach colour with a white stripe along its dorsal ridge. The name 'anemonefish' originates from their symbiotic relationship with the sea anemone, which is a plant-like animal and acts as their host. This relationship is, as with every symbiosis, mutually beneficial for both species. Anemonefish clean the sea anemone by eating its parasites and dead tentacles. They help to circulate the water around it and thus provide it with much-needed oxygen. They lure other fish towards their host as prey for the sea anemone. They drive away predators of the sea anemone. And they also provide nutrients in the form of their waste. In return, the sea anemone provides food –	Having a fish as a spirit animal tells you that the element water is important in your life, and the emotions it represents. Are you in touch with your emotions? Can you express them? And what's hidden inside your subconscious that you need to bring to light? The pink skunk clownfish is best known for its symbiotic living arrangement with its host anemone. This means that you can gain much by creating symbiotic relationships in your life. What can you give to

in the form of parasites and dead tentacles – and a safe home as its venom protects anemonefish from attacks by predators.	other people? What do you need from them? How can you support each other?
Pink skunk clownfish are dependent on their host anemone and seldom leave the protection of it, venturing only a short way away to feed so that they can quickly swim back to safety if a predator comes near.	Recognise your own areas of excellence but also the expertise of others and what they can bring to the table.
The clownfish is immune to the lethal sting of the sea anemone due to repeated exposure to it. From early on, they continually touch the anemones, which results in a thick layer of protective mucus forming on the clownfish's bodies.	The sea anemone is the home of the clownfish, who hides inside it whenever danger comes near. Do you feel too exposed?
The pink skunk clownfish rarely migrate to other anemones but stay with their host anemone for their entire life. But they are one of the most mellow clownfish species, with the dominant adult pair allowing other non-breeding adults and juveniles to share the edges of their host anemone. These groups are called shoals and the most notable feature of such a shoal is that every anemonefish – apart from the dominant female – is male.	Or are you not daring to venture out enough? Dare to leave your comfort zone to fulfil your dreams. But also create a safe haven for yourself to which you can retreat when necessary. Clownfish are social animals that live in a

In fact, every clownfish is born male, including the dominant female. It's only when the current female clownfish of a shoal dies that the largest clownfish of the group changes sex and becomes the dominant female himself. The next biggest clownfish of the shoal then becomes her mate. On rare occasions, it's also been noted that clownfish can change sex when two males become mates. In that case, the larger, more dominant fish will change sex and become female. The male of the dominant pair does most of the work when it comes to taking care of the offspring by preparing and cleaning the nest, by guarding and fanning the eggs and by eating any eggs that are infertile or damaged. After the eggs hatch, the larvae drift away before turning into juveniles, which then search out a host anemone. And once they have found one, they touch it repeatedly to become immune to its venom.	clear hierarchy. Do you socialise enough? Or are you feeling lonely? Also, do you allow yourself to lead yourself and others? As a clownfish person, you have a healthy connection to both your male and female parts. Take care of and nurture both of them. While the venom of the anemone is deadly to most animals, the anemonefish is immune to it. This translates to you being able to easily change any toxic situations in your life.

Spirit animal Mute Swan

(*Cygnus Olor*)

Animal Facts	Some spiritual meanings
A lot of birds stay together to raise their young for a season, then move on to a new partner. Some species even mate with more than one bird during a breeding season. But most swan species, such as the mute swan, mate for life once their courtship ritual ends. There are only a few exceptions – for example, if one partner dies. Yet another reason for them to part would be a few bad breeding seasons in a row. While polygamy in the animal kingdom has advantages – such as distributing genes more widely – the mute swan has found the benefits of staying faithful to its partner. For one, if a bonded pair raises one clutch after another, they'll become better at nurturing their cygnets by learning from their successes and failures. To this end, it has been proven that when a swan needs to find a new mate, they raise fewer cygnets in the first	The swan is a large water bird and as such both at home on the water and in the sky. These two elements combined speak of great creative and inventive energy. When you link the ideas and thoughts of the air with the emotions and intuition of the water, you can accomplish great things. Spread your wings and fly. Both water and wind are in a cycle of endless flowing energy. Do you go with the flow? Or do you fight against the natural rhythms of life?

years because they make more mistakes. What is more, the risk of not finding another mate or contracting a sexually transmitted disease is pretty high if they decide to leave or 'cheat' on their partner. The mute swan pairs share responsibilities. The male swan, called a cob, helps the female, called a pen, to incubate the eggs and care for the young, giving her a chance to rebuild the fat reserves that she used up when she laid the eggs. During the moulting phase, which takes a few weeks, the mute swan cannot fly. Because of this, a breeding pair moults one after the other, so that one of them can always protect the cygnets and find food. When the mute swans' cygnets are threatened by a predator, like foxes or minks, the pairs can become quite aggressive. Their defensive tactic begins with a loud warning hiss. And if this doesn't drive off the opponent, they follow it up with a physical attack, smashing their wings at their enemy and snapping at them with their bills. Even though mute swans are one of the	The swan mates for life. When you have the swan as your spirit animal, partnership is important to you. Are you ready to settle down with someone? Do you commit fully to relationships? Are you truly intimate with the people around you? Do you need to take your relationships to a deeper level? Or do you feel that loyalty is missing in your life? Having the swan as a messenger might also mean that a new relationship is awaiting you. To allow it to take off and fly, the swan's bones are hollow. This shows that every situation in life has

biggest birds alive, they are not strong enough to break a bigger predator's bones, though. The reason for this is the swan's own bones. Like with other birds, those need to be hollow so they can fly. And since swans are one of the largest birds that take to the air, their bones need to be extra-light. Especially since most mute swans living in Asia and Europe migrate. When migrating, the mute swans congregate with other swans and form a bevy, flying inside a V formation to save energy. Some mute swans are also social outside of these migration journeys, living in colonies with more than a hundred pairs of other swans if there is enough food for them all. Meanwhile, other pairs have their own territory. But during the breeding season, all mute swans become territorial. Despite their name, mute swans are anything but mute; they can hiss, grunt, honk, peep and gurgle to communicate with each other. They were given their name simply because they are less noisy than most other swan species.	advantages and disadvantages. Are you aware of your strengths? Do you need to shift your focus accordingly? The migration pattern of the swan speaks of great endurance, while the V formation they fly in tells of collaboration. Are you persistent in your ventures? Or do you give up too soon? Also, do you receive enough help from others? And do you help those close to you? The long neck of the swan speaks of a balance between the higher and lower realms. Is your life balanced?

Spirit animal Cuban Crocodile (*Crocodylus Rhombifer*)

Animal Facts	Some spiritual meanings
As reptiles, Cuban crocodiles are ectothermic, which means cold-blooded. As such, they cannot regulate their body temperature themselves. Instead, they are dependent on external sources like direct sunlight or the heat radiating from the ground. This is why they can often be found basking in the sun, especially in the morning, when they are still cold and groggy from the night, or after a meal, to help speed up their metabolism. But when crocodiles lie with their mouth wide open in a cooler, shadowy place, it means that they are too warm. As crocodiles do not have sweat glands, they cool off via the mouth, like dogs. Cuban crocodiles have little webbing on their hind feet and long legs, which lets them do the 'high walk' they are known for. This enables them to be more agile on land than most other crocodile species. But their strong legs also help them in the water. The Cuban crocodiles use	The crocodile is an ancient creature – it was alive when dinosaurs still roamed the Earth. It is therefore seen as the guardian of ancient knowledge. You might have easy access to the Akashic records or could benefit from ancestral healing. Living both in the water and on land, the crocodile is a master of both the emotions and the rational. Do you allow your emotions to come to the surface? Or are your emotions so overpowering that they control your life?

them, along with their powerful tail, to jump out of the water and leap straight upwards – for example, to snatch prey from overhanging branches. Additionally, the Cuban crocodile uses its tail to hit tree trunks so that birds and other small animals, as well as eggs, fall out. The diet of the Cuban crocodile varies depending on its age and size. Juveniles eat mainly small fish, insects and arthropods while adults hunt fish, small mammals, crustaceans and birds. The main source of food for the Cuban crocodile is turtles, though. To this end, they have broad back teeth that are adapted to easily crush the hard shells. When hunting land animals that go near the water to drink, the Cuban crocodile swims underwater or with only its eyes and nostrils above the surface. It sneaks up on its prey before lunging forward and quickly pulling it under. There they do what is known as the 'death roll': they tense up and use their hind legs to rotate their body quickly in the water, tearing chunks of flesh off their prey in the process.	Also, do you overthink matters? Listen to what your thoughts have to tell you but don't let them control your life. The crocodile is strong and powerful. Are you using your innate power? Can you be assertive without being snappy? Crocodiles lie submerged in the water and wait patiently for prey to come along. Be patient and not rush into things. Stay hidden until the time is right. Also, be careful of anything unexpected. Do not get dragged under when you find yourself in murky waters. When feeding, the

Crocodiles cannot chew, as their jaws are not able to move sideways. So they need to swallow chunks of flesh or the whole animal if it's small enough.	crocodile can't chew but has to rip off chunks of flesh from its prey or swallow it whole.
Like other crocodiles, the Cuban crocodile also swallows stones. These help with digestion: the stones scrape against each other and the bones and shells in the crocodile's stomach. Additionally, the stones enable the crocodile to be better balanced in the water when it lies in wait for new prey.	Do you have trouble letting go once you've sunk your teeth into a project? Are you too stubborn? Be careful not to bite off more than you can chew.
Of course, when eating stones, some teeth may break off. But this is no problem for a crocodile, as their teeth are continuously replaced throughout their lives.	A crocodile's teeth regrow repeatedly. So, even if all seems lost at first glance, you have the ability to recover and start anew.
The territory of the Cuban crocodile includes areas with freshwater sources, such as rivers, sawgrass swamps, marshes, lagoons and mangroves. They prefer those to saltwater, even though they could survive in the oceans – other than their distant cousins, the alligators that don't have glands in the tongue to excrete salt from their bodies as crocodiles do.	Being underwater a good part of the day, the crocodile represents your subconscious. Is there anything floating to the surface right now? Do you need to dive deeper inside yourself?
It has been observed that Cuban crocodiles can occasionally work in a	

team or group, for example, when pack-hunting a large animal. This ability to coordinate speaks of their high intelligence. But for the most part, Cuban crocodiles live a solitary life and are territorial, defending themselves aggressively when feeling threatened. And this is especially true for females during the nesting phase, as the Cuban crocodile is known for its cannibalistic traits, meaning that they eat the young or eggs of their own species.	When crocodiles lie waiting for prey, only their eyes are visible. You can see and observe a lot without having to endanger yourself. Clairvoyance might be dominant in people with the crocodile spirit.
Female Cuban crocodiles use organic matter to camouflage their nests, which are built in trenches, holes or specially built mounds. The female lays a large number of eggs to compensate for the high mortality rate, as the hatchlings are easy prey – not just for adult crocodiles but also for other reptiles and birds.	The crocodile is unusual among reptiles because it has excellent mothering skills. Are you attentive to your projects and ideas? Do you nurture them enough? Also, you might be ready to have children if that's what you want.
When they're ready to hatch, the young crocodiles emit sounds to alert their mother, who helps them to free themselves. To do that, she carefully cracks the shells between her teeth and then carries her young to the water. Whether the hatchlings are male or female depends on the temperature of	Young crocodiles call out when they are about to hatch to receive help from their

the nest they hatched in, which can be influenced by the mother crocodile. Research has shown that if the nest temperature is 30–32°C, mainly male crocodiles will be born, and if the temperature is below 30°C or over 32°C, mainly females will be born. The Cuban crocodile is a critically endangered species because of two major threats – illegal hunting and the hybridisation with the American crocodile.	mother. Are you able to ask for help? Do you let others know how they can support you? And do you support those who ask you for help? Just like the crocodile, develop a tough skin but remain gentle and caring with your loved ones.

Spirit animal Common Bottlenose Dolphin (*Tursiops Truncatus*)

Animal Facts	**Some spiritual meanings**
Even though they spend their whole lives in water, the bottlenose dolphin is, like all dolphins, not a fish but a mammal. As such, dolphins have lungs instead of gills, and they need to surface regularly to breathe. Naturally, as mammals, they're also endothermic, which means warm-blooded, as well as viviparous, which means they give birth to live young whom they feed with milk. But dolphins have also perfectly adapted to the element water. Unlike land mammals, which can breathe through their mouths as well as their noses, dolphins can only breathe through their blowholes, which are an evolved nose on the top of the dolphin's head to make it easier to take in air when at the surface. This prevents the dolphin from inhaling water into its lungs, reducing the risk of drowning. Sometimes, dolphins can also be seen holding up weak, sick or old members of	The dolphin is a mammal but its habitat is the water, which is not only the place of emotions and the subconscious but which is also moving continuously. Are you in touch with your emotions? Do you express them? Is there anything you need to bring to the surface? And do you go with the rhythm of life instead of working against it? Dolphins are social animals and most live inside cooperative pods, where healthy members take care of the old, weak and ill. Do you have people in

their group between them who don't have the strength to swim by themselves any more, so that they can breathe. And they do the same for newborn dolphins. After a calf is born, the mother breaks the umbilical cord by swimming swiftly away from it. Then she swims underneath the newborn and lifts it to the surface so it can breathe in air for the first time.	your life you can rely on? And can others rely on you? Or do you need to be more social? Are you feeling isolated? Having this spirit animal means that you might be called to help others. But you also need to learn how to receive help.
The need to go to the surface to breathe about every ten minutes has an immense effect on the dolphin's life. They can never fully go to sleep, as they would drown. Instead, they rest by switching off half of their brain and keeping the other half active, alternating between the two sides. This also enables them to watch out for any potential dangers while 'resting'. Threats include predators such as sharks or whales but also human hunters and boat propellers, with which they can collide when surfacing.	Dolphins need to regularly come to the surface to breathe. Do the same by taking regular breaks. Also, do you breathe too shallowly? Learn meditation techniques to breathe more deeply.
Of course, they also face the danger of not being able to find enough food because of overfishing, suffocating on plastic waste or falling prey to chemicals or oils that leak into the oceans.	When dolphins sleep, half their brain is still alert. This tells us how vigilant dolphin people

And ships pose yet another threat to dolphins because they make the ocean a very noisy place. This is a problem because dolphins depend a lot on sound – for hunting, for communicating and for navigation. They use a process called echolocation, which works like a sonar system. Dolphins produce many high-frequency clicks that travel through the water. When the clicks meet an object, they bounce off of it and return as an echo. Using this technique, dolphins can determine the location, shape and size of an object or animal, even in complete darkness. And the time it takes for the sound waves to come back helps them to determine how far away it is. Knowing this, fishing nets can also pose a problem for the dolphins because they're often too thin and amorphous for sound waves to bounce off. This makes dolphins not perceive them as an obstacle. And when they swim into a net and get tangled in it, they'll drown. Because one thing the dolphin cannot do is swim backwards, due to them moving their flukes up and down, not sideways like fish do.	are. But at times, your brain can also be too alert, making you overthink and worry. Is that a problem you have? Or do you tend to ignore your thoughts completely? Listen to what your thoughts have to tell you, but don't get bogged down in fears that will never come to pass. Like the dolphin itself, dolphin people are usually good communicators who can express their truth clearly. Additionally, the echolocation speaks of a high auditory connection. Use sounds – inspiring music, spoken affirmations, humming

The good news about the anatomy of these flukes is that dolphins can pick up speed quickly when escaping a predator or when hunting. Meanwhile, the flippers of the dolphin are only used for steering and balancing. This is important because dolphins have delicate skin, which can easily be injured by scraping against a hard surface. On the upside, their skin is also quick to heal, and their cells are replaced as often as every two hours. This makes their skin smooth and sleek, enabling them to easily glide through the water, despite not having scales like fish. Fish are on the bottlenose dolphin's main menu. But they also eat squid, crabs, octopus, shrimps and other small creatures living in the oceans. These they swallow whole, as their rows of sharp teeth are good for catching and holding on to prey but not for grinding it. Bottlenose dolphins, like all other saltwater dolphins, do not just need food for the nutrients, though. They also get the water intake they need directly from their food sources, as drinking salt water would lead to death from dehydration. When hunting in groups, dolphins show	chanting or binaural beats – for your benefit. That dolphins 'see' via echolocation tells you to trust your intuition and inner guidance. Ignoring it might take you off the right path and into a dead end. Also, do you like what you get back? Change your focus to receive different results. The dolphin is very sensitive when it comes to its surroundings. Do you allow yourself to be sensitive? Or are you too sensitive and need to create healthier boundaries? Also, that the dolphin's skin heals so quickly might mean that you are talented at the healing arts.

their high social intelligence. They swim around a school of fish, driving them into a smaller and smaller space, then the dolphins take turns to swim in and catch a mouthful. Additionally, dolphins are one of the rare animal species that have learned to use tools: they cover their snouts with sea sponges, for example, to protect those when foraging.	Dolphins are inventive and intelligent. Do you use your wit and resourcefulness to get what you want? Use anything at your disposal to ride the tides of success.
Bottlenose dolphins live in fluid social groups, called pods, which can also congregate to form larger herds if food is plenty. There are nursery pods with mothers and their calves, but which may also include elderly dolphins. And there are juvenile pods of mixed gender. Meanwhile, an adult male will often form a pair-bond with another adult male and come and go to mate with the females. After a calf is born, it will learn to distinguish its mother's whistle and those of the other pod members before developing its own. These unique signature whistles are like our human names and allow dolphins to recognise each other by sound alone. A lesser-known fact is that dolphins are one of the few animal species to practice	Dolphins are well known for their playful nature. Do you allow yourself to have fun? Are there any areas in your life that prevent you from being happy? Have you become so laden down with responsibilities that you've forgotten how to let loose? Or are you too childish? Should you take things more seriously? Dolphin people might need to heal their inner child and connect to it once more.

foreplay: they use the act of copulation not only to reproduce but also to have fun. And fun is important to dolphins, even outside mating. Dolphins like to incorporate playfulness into their routine. They will leap out of the water, play football with an octopus or pufferfish, do seaweed tag games or blow bubble rings. Their playfulness is only matched by the dolphin's curiosity, which makes them approach other species, including humans.	The dolphin is a very curious species, which doesn't only show compassion with its pod members but also with other species. Approach others with curiosity, and they'll most likely respond in kind. Also, explore new hobbies and activities and try yourself out.

Spirit animal Red Squirrel

(*Sciurus Vulgaris*)

Animal Facts	Some spiritual meanings
As an arboreal species, the red squirrels spend most of their lives up in trees, which is also where they build their nests, called dreys. These are constructed out of twigs, leaves, bark and grass and have at least two entrances – in case they ever need to escape out the 'back door'. Red squirrels build several of these dreys in case one of them is damaged or needs to be abandoned, for example, when it has become too full of fleas. Their nests are important for the squirrels, as they spend long hours inside them when it's cold outside. But they do not hibernate during the winter. This is why they need to plan ahead and store food to survive the cold season when food sources become scarce. Despite common belief, the red squirrels rarely bury the nuts and seeds they find. This behaviour is mostly seen by the bigger grey squirrels, which are scatter-hoarders and native to the American	Red squirrels nest in dreys, which have two entrances through which they can escape if need be. Do you have a second option up your sleeve? Do you maybe need a backup plan? Also, do you feel unsafe in your life? What can you do to change that? Squirrels gather nuts and seeds for the winter months. Do you prepare for what lies ahead? Are you saving up enough resources? Or are you worried that you'll never have enough? Do you have traumas around

continent, but which have, by now, been introduced to the Old World as well.
This, by the way, causes problems as many greys carry a virus called squirrel pox to which they are immune, but which kills the red squirrels.
Unlike greys, the red squirrels store most of their supplies like nuts, seeds and cones in piles above the ground or in hollow trees. In winter, they return to these spots to feed from their stashes.
Squirrels are infamous for being forgetful, but they actually have an average to a good memory. And, what is more, they have an exceptional sense of smell, which doesn't only help them find their own food stashes but also those of other squirrels.
Of course, piling up nuts for the winter has its risks because squirrels could go hungry if their stash is found by other animals. Or their food could be hidden under a pile of snow or go bad for some reason. That's why the red squirrel has developed some backup plans. They gather fungus, which they hang out in trees to dry. And they also harvest maple syrup in winter. To do this, they cut the maple's bark with their teeth, letting the

abundance?
Just like the squirrel, you are resourceful and adaptable. Don't hold on to the past. Declutter your life of all things that don't serve you any longer and trust in your ability to manifest anything you need.

People with the squirrel as a spirit animal are usually great investors. They are determined and do not give up easily. They are also excellent planners and organisers.
If you put in the work now, you will reap the rewards later.
Are you sowing the right seeds in your life?

Squirrels learn by observing and copying others.
Are you observant of

sap leak out, and return to it once it's dried up. Despite their vegetarian stores of food, red squirrels are opportunistic omnivores and will also eat insects, eggs, young birds and other small animals. The red squirrel produces one or two litters each year, with two to three young in each, which are called kittens. The female raises these alone, as adult red squirrels live solitary. They do socialise with other squirrels in neighbouring territories to some extent, though, and copy their behaviour or newfound techniques – for example, to crack open nuts. The red squirrels exhibit a variety of sounds to communicate with each other, which range from territorial barks to chattering, screaming or purring. Aside from this, squirrels communicate through body language – for example, by stamping their feet, which warns others of a threat. When fleeing from their predators – such as hawks, martens, feral cats or eagle owls – the red squirrel runs in a zigzag pattern, searching for shelter in the trees. This doesn't help them to get out	your surroundings? Or are you missing anything going on around you that could be helpful? Having the squirrel as your spirit animal means that you might get the best results when you live according to the motto 'learning by doing'. Try out different things and see what works best. The squirrel is known for its boundless energy, running to and fro while racing up trees or flying from one to the next. Do you feel that you have enough energy? Do you take regular breaks to recharge your batteries? Or are you often exhausted because you're trying to do too

of the way of an oncoming car, however, and since houses and streets are being built closer and closer to woodlands, this causes a lot of squirrel deaths. In comparison, they are perfectly adapted to their home environment, the woods. Red squirrels have padded feet that cushion their landings when flying from tree to tree, and they can use their fluffy tails as parachutes to soften falls.	much? Squirrel people are known to be productive. But make sure you don't scatter your energy in too many directions at once.
The tail, which is the red squirrel's most prominent feature, can be used in other ways, too. It's used to balance themselves when running on twigs, by swinging it from one side to the other. During winter, a squirrel will wrap its fluffy tail around itself to keep warm. And in summer, it will use its tail as a sunshade, by holding it over its head. The squirrel will also pump more blood into its tail to lower its body temperature.	With its long, bushy tail, the squirrel is a master of balance when bounding over the thinnest twigs. Are there any areas in your life that feel unbalanced? Do you need to work less and play more? Or are your relationships not harmonious?
Apart from the bushy tail, red squirrels have a second prominent feature: ear tufts. They shed those annually and regrow them in time for their thicker winter coats. What red squirrels do not lose, however, is their four front teeth, which never stop	The squirrel's ear tufts translate to their connection to the higher planes. Are you connected to your higher self? Do you understand its

growing throughout their lives. This means they have to continuously wear these down by gnawing the bark of trees or by cracking hard nutshells.	messages clearly? You might also have a natural talent for clairaudience.

Spirit animal Chinese Red Panda

(*Ailurus Styani*)

Animal Facts	Some spiritual meanings
The red panda, which is also called the lesser panda, cat-bear, bear-cat, Himalayan raccoon or firefox, is, despite its name, not closely related to the giant panda. The giant panda is classified as a bear, while the two species 'Chinese red panda' and 'Himalayan red panda' belong to their own taxonomically unique family, the *Ailuridae*. The closest living relatives of the red pandas are the *Mustelidae*, which include weasels and otters.	The red panda's mask-like colouring reminds you to watch out for masks. Are you wearing one yourself, not showing your true colours? Or are others around you not being authentic? Do you see what has been hidden from your eyes?
In many ways, red pandas have more in common with the giant panda, though, and these similarities go beyond the mask-like markings on their faces. Since the two species share similar environments and enjoy the same food source, they are subjected to a phenomenon, which is called convergent evolution. This means two unrelated animals evolve similar traits and features. In the case of the giant and red	The red panda is a solitary living animal. People with this spirit animal are usually introverted and self-reliant. Do you feel capable of meeting your needs? Or are you trying to be too independent? Do you know how to use

panda, they both have a ‘false thumb’, which is an extended wrist bone that’s used to grasp bamboo – their favourite meal. The red panda does not eat bamboo exclusively, though. It is a herbivorous carnivore, meaning it eats a mainly plant-based diet despite being a carnivore. Young bamboo shoots and bamboo leaf tips form 85–95% of a red panda’s diet, being supplemented by roots, leaves, flowers, acorns, fruits, insects, eggs and small mammals or birds. The bamboo is such a nutritionally poor food source that the red panda needs to spend a lot of their waking time eating and can still lose weight quickly in winter. In very cold temperatures, which aren’t unusual in the mountainous temperate forests in which they can be found, the red pandas actually become dormant. They lower their metabolic rate and only raise it every few hours to wake and look for food. The red pandas’ thick, reddish-white coats are perfectly adapted to their habitat. Not only do they help the pandas	this interconnected reality to receive more support from others? Also, do you spend enough time alone to rejuvenate after socialising? Or are you alone too much and need more connections? Despite being classified as carnivores, they eat a mainly vegetarian diet. Are you doing things ‘your way’? Or do you follow the crowd without questioning what is right for you? Also, look at what nutrients you need and adapt your diet accordingly. The red panda spends most of its life up a tree, where it sleeps, eats, plays and mates.

to blend in with the branches of their preferred fir trees, which are covered in reddish-brown moss, but they also perfectly insulate their bodies, including their feet, which are covered in fur as well. Another option they have to keep themselves warm is to wrap their bushy red-and-white-striped tails around their bodies. These tails also help the red panda to balance when walking along branches. Meanwhile, their ability to rotate their ankles and their sharp claws, which are semi-retractable, aid them when climbing. The red panda, which is nocturnal, lives most of its life high up in the tops of trees without ever needing to touch the ground. They use them as a place to eat and sleep, to sunbathe, to play and to groom themselves – which is done similarly to how cats do it – by licking their front paws and then using them to wipe down their fur. They also mate and give birth in the trees. Females, called sows, usually bear two to four cubs at a time and raise them alone, as adult red pandas are solitary animals. When they do meet each other, red	Thus they are connected to the element air while staying rooted to the earth. Are you rooted in your life? Or do you need to be more grounded? Is your head in the clouds? Also, do you need to dream bigger and use the element air to bring your ideas alive? Just like the red panda you might be a 'night person'. Use these hours for work and creative ventures to attain success. The red panda teaches us about the power of touch, as it spends a lot of time grooming itself. Are you starved of touch?

pandas communicate using body language as well as several sounds. They hiss, grunt and twitter, they make whistling sounds to warn of danger and they use a loud vocal expression called a 'huff-quack', which sounds like a bear's roar. This they use when they are defending themselves. When attacked, the red pandas also use their sharp claws by standing on their hind legs and striking out. And if that doesn't keep the threat at bay, the red panda can release a strong odour – the same that they use to mark their territory – from scent glands at the base of their tails to scare off its opponent, as a skunk does. Fully grown red pandas are preyed upon by leopards, while smaller red pandas also fall prey to hawks, owls and other birds of prey. The main threat is humans, however, who hunt red pandas for their fur and also deforest large parts of their habitat.	Booking a massage or learning self-massage might be beneficial. Red panda people are usually good communicators and can express clearly what they need to say. Do others hear you? And do you listen to what others have to say? The red panda has sharp claws as well as a scent gland to defend itself. It thus teaches you about self-respect. Do you respect your boundaries as well as those of others? And do others respect yours?

Spirit animal Golden Northern Bumblebee (*Bombus Fervidus*)

Animal Facts	Some spiritual meanings
The bumblebee is part of the bee family, which has one of the most important jobs in the animal kingdom: they are responsible for pollinating the majority of plants on the planet. And while among the thousands of species only the honey bee is used by humans as natural livestock for honey production, bumblebees also pollinate various plants such as apple and cherry trees, tomatoes, cotton and mustard – among many others. And bumblebees are particularly effective pollinators because they use more than one technique. Like other bees, they fill the pollen baskets on their hind legs with pollen, some of which will stick to their hairy bodies. Then, when visiting other flowers, grains will fall off, effectively pollinating the flowers they fly to. But they use yet another method, which is called 'buzz pollination'. Because of their large bodies and their strong flight	The bumblebee belongs to one of the most important animal species alive, as they pollinate a large number of plants. They are thus messengers of service. Your services or products might be extremely useful for a large group of people. Do what you are passionate about because by fulfilling your own needs, you will help many. At times, bumblebee people can become workaholics. Is this a problem you have? Or are you not

muscles, bumblebees can make the flower they are sitting on vibrate and are thus effectively dislodging more pollen from it.	productive enough? Are you disorganised? Decide what's essential and what's not.
Other than honey bees who produce large amounts of honey, bumblebees only store small amounts of nectar – just enough to feed their own colony. Since this nectar is usually consumed rapidly, it does not have the time to go through the transformation process that would turn it into honey. But it is still searched out by other animals, such as bears or skunks, which raid bumblebee hives for the sweet treat as well as for protein in the form of larvae, eggs and adult bumblebees.	Also, make time to savour the honey of your endeavours and extract the sweetness from life. Even though the bumblebee is able to sting people, this insect is generally peaceful. It only shows its warrior energy when protecting itself and its colony.
Bumblebees are generally peaceful insects but they can get aggressive when they feel threatened or their nest is attacked. The males, called drones, don't have a stinger. But the females have a smooth stinger with which they can sting more than once.	Are you too aggressive around others? Or do others tend to react aggressively towards you? Can you communicate your boundaries clearly without needing to attack?
To communicate, bumblebees have several choices. As well as doing 'waggle dances' to tell other bumblebees where good sources of nectar can be found, they also leave pheromones on the	The antennae on the bumblebee's head tell of

flowers they visit. Other bumblebees	your direct link to the
then use their antennae to smell these	higher planes.
scent marks.	Do you use your
It has been said that bumblebees defy	intuition to receive the
aerodynamics and that they shouldn't be	messages being sent to
able to fly because they are too heavy for	you? Are you connected
their four delicate wings. But this	to your higher self?
mystery has been solved: bumblebees	
not only flap their wings rapidly – at	Just like the bumblebee
more than 130 beats per second – but	seems to do the
they also flap their wings back and forth	impossible by flying
rather than up and down. This way, they	with tiny wings
create a mini-hurricane underneath each	compared to their body
wing, and the lower air pressure helps	size, you can
them to stay aloft.	accomplish seemingly
The bumblebee also uses its wingbeats	impossible goals.
to cool down its nest when it gets too	Dream big.
hot. They hover over the top of the nest	
to circulate the air, just as a ceiling fan	Bumblebees are one of
does. And they use their wings to do the	the few insects that can
opposite, too. Despite insects being	control their body
classified as ectotherms, meaning that	temperature to some
they can't regulate their body	extent and thus teach
temperature themselves and are	you to become the
dependent on outside sources for heat,	master of your own
bumblebees can generate some heat	body.
through shivering in order to fly – if the	Are you taking good
temperature of their environment is not	care of it? Are you
too cold.	sleeping enough and

This makes them one of the first insects to fly out, come spring, when other bee species still have to wait in their hives. Golden bumblebee nests are built close to, or in, the ground, under piles of wood or dead leaves or in abandoned mouse holes. Their colonies are much smaller than honey bee hives, with a maximum of 400 workers. A colony is started in early spring by a bumblebee queen who has hibernated the winter months. She flies out to drink nectar, then searches for a suitable place to build her colony. Once she finds it, she collects pollen from flowers, lays eggs and shivers to keep them warm. When the eggs hatch, the queen feeds the larvae pollen. Then, when they are two weeks old, the larvae spin cocoons around themselves in order to develop into adult bumblebees. The bumblebees born in spring and early summer are always female workers. From the moment these first worker bumblebees hatch, the queen bumblebee never leaves the nest again. Her only job now is to lay more eggs. Meanwhile, the worker bumblebees	eating healthily? Do you exercise regularly? Having a spirit animal that lives inside a colony means you would thrive living in a community where the emphasis is laid on cooperation and sharing resources. Do you need more connections to others? Are you too lonely in your life? The bumblebee is a master of responsibilities and fulfils important tasks for the colony. Do you feel you have too many responsibilities at once? Are you burdened down? Also, do you not feel valued enough by others?

leave the nest and collect nectar and pollen. They also take over the chores of guarding, cleaning or fanning the nest as well as feeding the larvae and the queen bumblebee. Towards the end of summer, the queen lays eggs from which drones and new queen bumblebees hatch. They all fly out from the nest and mate with drones or future queen bumblebees from other nests, respectively. While future queen bumblebees prepare to hibernate to build a new colony in spring, the male bumblebees die after mating.	Or do you not value what others provide? Bumblebees teach us about prosperity, as they visit many flowers and take as much pollen as they need. Are you seeing the prosperity in your life? Is there a lack in any area? Do you need to work on your belief system regarding abundance?

Spirit animal Asian Forest Tortoise

(*Manouria Emys*)

Animal Facts	Some spiritual meanings
The Asian forest tortoise is the largest tortoise in Asia, with males weighing up to 37 kilograms. They can live more than a hundred years, thanks to their slow metabolism and they are believed to be one of the most primitive of all living tortoises, not having changed much over the past 55 million years. One reason for that is that the Asian forest tortoise lays its eggs in the nest above the ground, instead of burying them. Females construct nests out of leaf litter. They will add new nest material frequently, which helps to mask the smell of the eggs, especially when it rains, making the leaf pile smell damp. Unlike most tortoises, the female then stays near the nest to protect her eggs. When a predator approaches, the tortoise has several options. She can pull back into her shell while lying on top of her eggs, presenting this to the attacker.	The Asian forest tortoise isn't only a primitive species but is also known for its longevity, which translates to them being the keeper of ancient knowledge and wisdom. Are you continually learning new things? Do you access your inner well of wisdom? You might need to get in touch with your own past and heal childhood traumas. The tortoise can draw back into its shell whenever it needs to. Find security within, instead of outside yourself.

This method is not foolproof, however. The tortoise's shell, which is made up of bones and covered by plates of keratin, might seem hard. But it is, in fact, sensitive, as it has countless nerve endings inside it, which are directly connected to the tortoise's spine. This means that a tortoise feels any small poke, rub or scratch on their shell, let alone someone biting into it or lifting the tortoise by pulling on it. Another option the tortoise has when attacked is to run away. Even though tortoises are famous for being slow, the Asian forest tortoise can actually reach a human's walking speed. But they rarely do so and a female will most often prefer yet another method to protect herself and her eggs. She will first hiss a warning and, if that isn't heeded, she follows it up by biting intruders away. The tortoise has strong jaw muscles, with horned ridges that are sharp and can cause serious damage. These ridges are also effective for crushing their food since tortoises have no teeth. They mainly eat grasses, leaves, seedlings, herbs, fruit and fungi, but their	The tortoise's shell is strong and provides protection, but it is also very sensitive. Are you connected to your sensitivity? Or are you too hard on yourself? Do you let others put too much pressure on you? Create healthy boundaries and communicate those clearly. The tortoise is known for moving slowly through life. Is your life too hectic? Are you impatient? Do you rush into things? Do you need to slow down? Or do you think too long instead of taking action? Are you indecisive? Pace yourself. When you become too

diet can be supplemented by protein sources such as carrion, invertebrates and small amphibians The latter they find easily, as the Asian forest tortoises live near water sources like ponds, lakes, rivers or swamps. They generally prefer a habitat with high humidity and will often spend the warmest parts of the day either half-burrowed in soil or water. The Asian forest tortoises live solitary and males seek out females only during courtship rituals. To court one, the male bobs its head and adds vocalisations ranging from rhythmic grunts to loud bellows. A rarely known fact is that, when a tortoise goes into its shell, it empties its lungs first. One can hear them exhale when they are startled and pull inside to hide. This is because their solid shells cannot expand or contract and their ribs are firmly locked to it. To breathe while inside their shell, they have to rely on muscles around their lungs, which contract and expand those. But they can also hold their breath for a long time if needed.	stressed, slow down and focus on the essentials. Remember, slow and steady wins the race. Since a tortoise always carries its home around with itself, tortoise people are often travellers. Do you feel as if your life is lacking adventure? Or are you scared to venture out of your comfort zone? Do you feel insecure and have problems giving up control? The tortoise medicine speaks of breath being important. Learning different meditation techniques might be beneficial to you.

Spirit animal Northern Brown Snake
(*Pseudonaja Nuchalis*)

Animal Facts	Some spiritual meanings
The northern brown snake, also known as gwardar, is one of the western brown snakes living on the Australian continent and shouldn't be mistaken with the nonvenomous North American brown snake because the Australian species is one of the most venomous reptiles in the world. Even juveniles can give deadly bites. The northern brown snake's fangs, which are folded back into the roof of their mouth when not in use, are quite short, however, and so it prefers to take cover rather than facing any natural predators, which include the king brown snake and birds of prey. But when it doesn't have the option to retreat, it will rear up into an S-stance and show off its fangs. If provoked, it will then strike fast and turn around to escape. The northern brown snake's prey consists of small mammals, amphibians, birds and eggs as well as reptiles, including other snakes.	The northern brown snake is venomous. When it attacks, it's fast and accurate. Do you tend to strike out at people when you feel cornered? Or do you feel attacked by others? Do you need healthier boundaries? Also, are there any toxic situations or people in your life that you need to heal or cut out? As the snake continuously tastes the air with its tongue, smell is an important factor for you. Do things smell right in your environment? You might have a talent for clairsalience. Or try

To find prey, the snake relies on its smell, sight and on the vibrations it senses. In order to smell, it flicks out its tongue to taste particles in the air, which are then processed by the 'Jacobson organ' in the roof of its mouth. A snake's tongue is forked, and the two tips 'taste' different amounts of chemicals, allowing it to tell which direction a smell is coming from. It also picks up vibrations with the bones in its jaw, enabling the snake to detect sound waves despite not having external ears. On top of that, snakes can see infrared light as well as the heat signature emitted by other creatures. To protect their eyes, instead of eyelids, they have a single transparent scale called a brille. When the northern brown snake is hunting, they strike quickly, biting the prey with their fangs and injecting deadly venom. Then they secure the animal until the venom takes effect. Since snakes cannot chew, they eat their prey whole. To this end, they hunt mostly smaller animals, but they can eat prey three times their size.	out aromatherapy. The snake has an unblinking stare since it has no eyelids. Its gaze seems intense. Are you perhaps too intense? Do you need to relax more? As a snake person, you might be good at holding people's attention and have a natural confidence that others find attractive. You might also find it easy to do shamanic journeys for which you go into a trance-like state. Snakes can stretch their jaws far apart. Having a snake as your spirit animal means that you can easily digest any knowledge you take in.

Contrary to popular myth, snakes cannot dislocate their yaws. But since their upper and lower jaws are not attached by bone but by stretchy ligaments, they can open their mouths wider than their own bodies. Digesting their prey can take up to a few days, depending on its size, after which they need to hunt again. The only things that the snake's digestive system cannot dissolve are hairs, feathers and claws, which are regurgitated. Snakes also regurgitate their food if they are threatened shortly after a meal, so they can escape more quickly. Since snakes never stop growing – even though their rate of growth slows as they get older – and their skin doesn't grow with them, they need to periodically exchange it for a new one, which is called moulting. Another benefit of getting rid of their old skin is getting rid of all the parasites, such as mites and ticks. Before moulting, a snake stops eating and moves to a safe and preferably dark place to hide. Yet another obvious indication that his process is about to start is that the old skin becomes dull and the snake's eyes look cloudy. When	Snakes moult regularly because their skin does not grow with them. This is a symbol of rebirth, transformation and life changes. Are you allowing yourself to grow and transform? You might also be in a transition phase right now. Are you putting off making the changes you need to make? Or are you forcing change too quickly? Along with moulting, the snake gets rid of parasites. This is a sign of great healing abilities. Are you in need of healing? Or can you provide healing to others? Take a look at the different types and

moulting, the inner surface of the old skin liquefies, which causes it to separate from the new skin beneath it. This process is uncomfortable, and during it, the snake will feel itchy and tender. When their old eye caps separate, this also reduces the snake's ability to see, which makes it more vulnerable. The moulting period usually takes a few days, after which the eyes clear and the snake crawls out of its old skin. A lesser-known fact is that, as well as their skin, snakes have another feature that needs to be replaced pretty often: their fangs. When the snake breaks off one, it grows another fang to replace it. When the northern brown snake is not hiding during the moulting phase, it needs – like any cold-blooded animal – the warmth of the sun to regulate its body temperature. This is why they are often seen lying on stones, as these absorb the sun's heat. Therefore, the northern brown snakes are usually diurnal hunters, too. The exception is during very hot days when they'll hunt at dusk or dawn or even during the night. The northern brown snakes are able to	choose the one you are most drawn to. Before moulting, a snake's eyes cloud over, but afterwards they clear and the snake sees the world anew. Can you see all that you need to see? Or Is something creeping up on you unnoticed? Try to understand others by seeing things from their perspective. You have the power to shift your awareness. Slithering over the ground, the snake always stays connected to Mother Earth. Do you feel that you are grounded enough in your life? You can feel more secure by using grounding techniques

climb trees but prefer to spend most of their lives on the ground. They are typically uniformly brown, as their name suggests, but they can be patterned with flecks or bands or display several other colours. It has also been observed that they change colour, both depending on where they live and on the season. For example, they are most often darker during the winter months, to help them absorb more heat, and a lighter brown in the hotter months, to reduce the risk of overheating.	regularly. When you have a snake as your spirit animal, your kundalini energy might be awakening right now. Support this process instead of resisting it. It might also be useful to retreat for some time to focus on taking care of yourself.

Spirit animal Platypus
(*Ornithorhynchus Anatinus*)

Animal Facts	Some spiritual meanings
Animals are subdivided into classes depending on their attributes. Among the vertebrates, these classes consist of mammals, birds, reptiles, amphibians and fish. Mammals, for example, are endothermic animals with three bones in the middle ear and a four-chambered heart that give birth to live young. Meanwhile, birds are endothermic, egg-laying animals that have feathers and toothless beaks or bills. But the platypus doesn't care about these rules; it has been proven that they possess genes and properties of mammals, birds *and* reptiles. Even though it is classified as a mammal and has fur on its body, the platypus also has a bill. And it lays eggs, like birds and most reptiles. On top of this, males are also venomous at certain times – an attribute that is commonly found in reptiles, amphibians, fish and non-vertebrate species but which is seldom	The platypus is one of the most unique animals alive since it has attributes of diverse species. It teaches you to embrace your uniqueness. Do you live your authenticity? Do you express your emotions, thoughts, beliefs, wishes and needs to others? Are these recognised? Or do you hide who you are? Do you feel that you need to be someone you are not? Since the platypus doesn't fit wholly into any animal category, belonging and being

found among mammals. A platypus's legs are splayed, just like a crocodile's, but they do rotate their legs in their sockets, just like other mammals do. In short, the platypus is truly unique. The main reason why they are classified as mammals is due to one trait that only animals in this class possess: they produce milk to feed their young. But even this is done in the platypus's unique way. Instead of nipples or udders, the female platypus has milk glands. When milk flows out of those pores – similar to other mammals producing sweat – the young lap it up from the skin. The two most surprising facts about platypuses might be the following, though: For one, it belongs to the small group of monotremes, which can be translated as 'single hole'. This hole, known as the cloaca, serves as both the anus and urogenital opening. And, secondly, platypuses do not have a stomach. Instead, their oesophagus is directly connected to their intestine. This means that the platypus has a very fast digestive system and needs a constant supply of food – at least 20–30% of its weight each day. Because of this, the	accepted by others is a very important topic for you. Have you found a group of people where you belong? Or do you feel like an outcast that no one understands? And are you able to understand others? Do you maybe try to change them? Learn how to love and support yourself by accepting all your parts – even the ones that are negatively perceived – and integrate those. By doing this, you'll attract people into your reality that'll follow suit. Since the platypus doesn't have a stomach, it needs a constant supply of food to give it energy. Do you feel low in

platypus spends a lot of its waking hours hunting prey, which consists of crustaceans, earthworms, shrimp, molluscs, fish, eggs, tadpoles and insect larvae. They hunt for their food in freshwater sources such as rivers, streams, ponds or lakes.	energy often? Do you take the time you need to replenish your reverses? Do you eat healthily? Do you sleep enough?
A platypus catches prey in its bill or dives to the bottom of a stream to dig for food in the riverbed. When inside the water, the platypus closes its eyes, ears and nose. Since it's deaf and blind when diving, the platypus uses its sensitive bill to find its prey. This bill is equipped with thousands of electroreceptors and mechanoreceptors that allow the platypus to sense the electrical currents that are created by their prey's small muscle movements.	The platypus's bill is so sensitive that it can hunt with its eyes, ears and nose closed, relying entirely on its electroreception. Do you allow yourself to be sensitive? Do you regularly tune in to yourself to see whether you feel 'off', and why?
Once they've caught something, they store it in their cheek pouches and swim back to the surface, where they eat. Since platypuses lose their teeth before becoming adults, they have to come up with another solution to chew their food. So, as well as having rough grinding pads inside their mouths, they scoop up gravel from the bottom of streams to mash their food into digestible pieces.	Losing their teeth early, adult platypuses had to come up with another method to eat. Just like the platypus, you are inventive. Combine your ideas to create something new. Are you thinking outside the box? Are

Platypuses are good swimmers. Their webbed front feet act as paddles and help them swim. And their back feet and tail are used for steering, like a rudder. But that's not the tail's main use; the platypus stores about half its body fat in its tail, in case of a food shortage. Platypuses have thick waterproof fur, which they groom like otters do to create air bubbles inside. This further insulates them from the cold. But despite being this perfectly adapted to the wet element, platypuses spend a great deal of time on land, too. Unfortunately, their webbed feet make walking on land pretty difficult and they're thus using up 30% more energy than when they're swimming. They have at least one feature that helps them when outside the water, though. The webbing between their front paws is retractable, which enables them to use their sharp claws to dig in the earth. They use these claws to dig burrows near the water, which usually have two entrances as well as chambers for sleeping and nesting. When pregnant, females seal themselves inside one of the burrow's chambers and	you brave enough to venture out of your comfort zone? Focus on your strengths to be successful. The platypus divides its time between the water, which is the element of emotions and the subconscious, as well as the earth, which symbolises all things physical and material while lending support. Do you listen to your emotions? And do you stay grounded while doing so? Or is there anything you're suppressing that's been trying to come to the surface? Also, do you feel supported in life? And are you supportive of others?

typically produce one to three soft, leathery eggs. Males play no part in rearing the young, as platypuses live solitary. The platypus is also territorial, so they generally only meet during the mating season when males are often seen fighting each other and inflicting wounds using their venomous spurs.	As a platypus person, you work well on your own and enjoy solitude. Are you self-reliant? Do you trust in your own abilities? Or do you need more connections?
Both sexes are born with hollow spur buds on the back of their hind legs. But the female's spurs will drop off in the first year, while the male's spurs remain. These are attached to a venom-secreting gland, which is seasonally activated: it only produces venom during the mating season, which indicates that it is intended for fending off competing males. But platypuses can also use it to defend themselves when faced with a predator and the venom is potent enough to kill a medium-sized dog.	The platypus is a living paradox. Having this spirit animal means that you can easily hold several truths and perceptions at once, even if these contradict each other. Can you see all the layers of truth that make up your reality? Use awareness techniques to capitalise on this talent.

Spirit animal Eastern Grey Kangaroo

(*Macropus Giganteus*)

Animal Facts	Some spiritual meanings
The Eastern grey kangaroo is endemic to Australia and belongs to the group of marsupials. Kangaroos are the largest mammals that hop when moving around. This is an energy-saving form of travelling, well-suited for covering great distances in little time. Hopping actually requires less energy the faster a kangaroo moves, enabling it to pick up speeds of up to 64 km/h. And their bodies are perfectly adapted for hopping. Aside from using their long, muscular tail to keep their balance and steer when jumping, they use it as a fifth leg to propel themselves forward. Additionally, they have tendons in their hind legs, which act like rubber bands being stretched, releasing energy as soon as they contract. When moving more slowly, for example, when grazing, the kangaroo uses its shorter forearms as well as its tail to support its weight while moving its hind	Hopping allows the kangaroo to cross great distances while using up little energy. Kangaroo people are known to have good stamina. You don't need to overexert yourself to reach your goals. Trust in your abilities; you'll gain momentum the farther you go. Kangaroos can only move forward, not backwards. Now is the time for you to jump ahead and take a leap of faith – the bigger the better. Are you afraid to move on? Are you maybe hanging on to

legs forward. This is called crawl-walking. What kangaroos cannot do, however, due to the shape of their legs and tail, is to walk or hop backwards. Kangaroos eat grass, flowers, leaves, ferns and moss. Like cows, they have chambered stomachs so they need to regurgitate their food and chew it again before it is digested. Eastern grey kangaroos are social and live in groups that are called mobs, courts or troops, which comprise up to twenty animals of both sexes. A mob has a dominant hierarchy. The dominant male – known as a buck, boomer, jack or old man – is the only one allowed to mate with the females in the group. Whenever two male kangaroos fight over dominance and breeding rights, they kick and box at each other with their hind- and forelegs. Meanwhile, when they're faced with a predator, aside from kicking it or fleeing at high speed, kangaroos also have a lesser-known strategy to defend themselves. If there's a body of water nearby, they jump into it and use their	something from your past? Or you anxious about the changes you need to make? Don't look back at what has been. The present is what paves your road to the future. Males are boxing each other when they are competing for the right to mate. Do you know what you want and take action? Or are you too competitive? Focus on your own strengths instead of on other people. The kangaroo has great mothering skills. Nurture and protect what you hold dear to your heart. Do you need to birth new projects? Or do you need to

front paws to hold their opponent underneath the surface until they drown. Knowing this, it makes sense that kangaroos can swim. While they can't move their hind legs separately from each other when they are on land, they can kick each leg independently when in water.	nurture existing ones? You might also be ready to take on the responsibility of parenthood when the kangaroo hops into your life.
Usually, when it's too hot during the day, kangaroos will rest in the shade. They also lick their forearms, which have blood vessels just underneath the skin. And when the moisture evaporates, it cools their body down.	The kangaroo gives birth to immature young. Ask yourself if you are giving 'birth' to things too early.
A widely known fact about kangaroos is that the females – which are called does, jills or flyers – have pouches. They can have two young, called joeys, at the same time, at different developmental stages. An older joey who lives outside the pouch but who is still drinking its mother's milk and a younger joey, which lives in its mother's pouch. Additionally, they can carry an embryo, which is yet waiting to be born. Female kangaroos are almost always pregnant, as they can delay birth for as long as necessary until the pouch is empty. Additionally, they can also delay gestation – for example,	Do you need to take more time before you show your ideas to the world? Or is this the best method for you – getting your ideas out while they are still a work in progress? The nipple swells to fix the younger joey's mouth in place. This tells us of the fact that more growth is yet

when there's a drought or famine – which is called diapause. The mother provides her young with two types of milk: a high-protein milk for the younger joey, which needs to grow fast, and a high-fat milk for the older joey since it's already active and needs more calories. A joey is born when it's basically still an embryo and only as big as a grain of rice. From the birth canal, it blindly crawls upwards into the pouch. There it feeds and grows, attached to a nipple, while being protected from outside threats. A female kangaroo has strong muscles around her pouch, which she can tighten when taking big leaps so that her young won't fall out. When the joey is older, it'll start to spend more time outside of the pouch, exploring the world. But they stay close to their mother in the beginning and dive head-first back into the pouch when they're frightened.	to come. Take the time you need to heal your inner child and nurse it. The kangaroo's nipples provide different milk, depending on the needs of the joey. Are you receiving what you need? Also, adjust your diet according to your activities. The joey jumps in and out of the pouch for some time before being weaned completely. You might not want to commit to one path yet. Stay flexible, as even better opportunities might come along.

Spirit animal Adélie Penguin

(*Pygoscelis Adeliae*)

Animal Facts	Some spiritual meanings
Only a minority of penguin species live in the Antarctic and the surrounding coastal islands. The small Adélie penguin is one of them. The most striking feature of the Adélie penguins is the white ring around their eyes, which develops when they become an adult. Aside from this, they share the familiar black-and-white tuxedo-like colouring for which penguins are famous. This colouring – black on the back and white on the belly – was created by nature for a good reason: camouflage. When penguins are in the water and a predator approaches from above, the penguin's black feathers are hard to see in the black depths of the ocean. And if a predator approaches from beneath, the penguin's white belly feathers merge into the pale sky, making it equally hard to see them. This is why they are in most danger when they jump into or out of the water.	With its black-and-white plumage, the penguin is well camouflaged. Do you feel too exposed or unsafe in your life? Do you fear being attacked? Or are you too daring and forget to take necessary precautions? Create a secure environment and install healthy boundaries. You can then allow yourself to be more open and to express yourself. The water is the element of dreams, additional to emotions and the subconscious, and the penguin jumps into and out of it

Leopard seals, the Adélie penguins' biggest threat, hang around the coast to hunt them. That's the reason why they stay close together in big groups when going in or out of the water, as this makes it harder for the seals to single out an individual. But penguins also have a second problem concerning getting out of the water: the tide and global warming. If they jump into the water and the ice ledge they used breaks off or the water level drops, the penguins will be unable to get out of the sea at the same spot. It can take penguins a lot of time and energy to find a suitable place where they can jump onto land again. But they can't avoid going into the water because that's where they hunt. Adélie penguins feed on aquatic creatures like krill, fish and squids. Water is undoubtedly their favoured element. Penguins are one of the few bird species that cannot fly in the air, but they make up for that by 'flying' in the water. They have dense, not hollow, bones, which makes it easier for them to dive deep down, and they are excellent	repeatedly. Having the penguin as your spirit animal means that you might be able to move effortlessly between the physical and spiritual planes. Do you take the time to dive deep within yourself? Do you allow your emotions to arise? Are your dreams holding important messages? Or do you ignore what's trying to come to the surface? Also, you might be gifted at lucid dreaming and astral travelling. The penguin is one of the rare birds that can't fly in the air. But its ability to 'fly' in the water is unmatched. You don't have to do things the same way as

swimmers, with their torpedo-shaped bodies that can reach a top speed of 75 km per hour. Meanwhile, on land, Adélie penguins use their feet and flipper-like wings for tobogganing. To this end, they lie on their belly and either slide downhill or push themselves forward. This is an efficient, rapid way of moving that requires much less energy than walking. And Adélie penguins need to have a proficient method of crossing wide stretches of ice because they are migratory birds, moving from hunting grounds to breeding grounds and back again. When they come in from the sea, they build nests in large colonies, which can consist of up to 250,000 individuals. These nests are mounds of stones so they won't be flooded if the ice melts. The stones are collected painstakingly, and penguins sometimes even steal some from other penguins' nests. The Adélie penguins usually mate for life and the female lays two eggs in the nest, which both partners care for. They take turns incubating the eggs while the other one goes out to hunt and eat.	others. Find your own style while adapting to your surroundings. By doing this, you can ride the waves of success. The Adélie penguins travel over great distances. This means you have great endurance and are resilient, being able to survive the worst conditions. Are you aware of your strengths? Do you believe in your abilities? Or do you need to work on some limiting beliefs that prevent you from doing so? Trust yourself and know that you are capable of navigating through life easily. The penguin spends several weeks hatching

After the chicks hatch, one parent stays with them while the other hunts for food, feeding the chicks by regurgitating fish for them. Then, after about three weeks, the male and female both leave for the sea to hunt for food. During this time, the chicks gather in large groups for safety. These groups are called crèches. Young Adélie penguins only start to swim and hunt for themselves once their downy feathers have been replaced by the waterproof adult plumage. This plumage is periodically replaced in a moulting process that is called a catastrophic moult. Unlike most birds, the penguin doesn't just lose a few feathers at a time; it loses them all at once. They then have to wait until their new feathers grow before they can go into the water again. Apart from being waterproof, their plumage also effectively protects them from the cold by storing insulating air chambers between the feathers. Additionally, Adélie penguins have a thick layer of fat, called blubber, under their skin, which helps them to keep warm. This all works so well that a	its eggs by sitting on them. Do you take enough time to nurture your ideas and projects so that they hatch? Or do you act too rashly and try to put them out before they are ready? Your ideas might come to fruition sooner if you sit on them for a while and think things through. Many birds only lose a few feathers at a time when they moult. Not so the penguin, which moults all at once. Are you going through big changes right now? Do you feel ready for those? Or are you wary of creating the necessary change in your life? Call on the penguin when you feel that you

careless penguin can even overheat on a sunny day.	can't keep up.
What's always only a few degrees above freezing is their feet, though, which is the reason that those don't stick to the ice. This is possible because the blood flowing into the feet is cooled down, while the blood travelling upwards towards their organs is warmed up. They also have another feature that is perfectly adapted to their icy environment. Since the Adélie penguin has little access to freshwater sources, it drinks both from freshwater pools when ashore and from the salty sea. To this end, they have special glands underneath their eyes that filter salt from their body before it can travel into their organs. The salt is then expelled through their nasal passages and drips from their bills.	The Adélie penguins are social animals, taking advantage of their great numbers. They thus teach us about community. Are you involved in your local community? Do you have a social circle where you feel you belong? Or are you too isolated and need more connection with other people? You might also benefit from living in a community setting.

Spirit animal Snowy Owl

(*Bubo Scandiacus*)

Animal Facts	Some spiritual meanings
The reason for the snowy owl's name – it is also called the snow owl, great white owl, polar owl or Arctic owl – is obvious: their plumage, unlike that of other owl species, is white. Male snowy owls get even whiter as they get older, while females always retain some brownish or grey markings. Their appearance helps them to blend perfectly into their main habitat, the Arctic tundra. Snow owls are perfectly adapted to this environment. They have a thick layer of down underneath their outer feathers as well as feathers on their legs and talons, which keeps those warm. What the owls don't have is eyeballs. Instead, they have eye tubes, which don't allow them to move their eyes. To make up for this, the owl has increased mobility in its neck and can turn it 135 degrees in either direction, giving an amazing total of 270 degrees of movement. This is possible because owls have fourteen vertebrae in their necks –	The snow owl is mostly white, which is the colour of purity, innocence and peace. And, as a bird, the owl is also a messenger between the Earth and the higher planes. Is peace missing in your life right now? Connect to your eternal soul to enable more of it in your life. Also, astral travelling might be easy for you. Being able to turn its head 270 degrees, the owl can see what's going on behind it. Can you see things from all sides? Change your perception to recognise different

double the number humans have. Of course, moving their neck this far could potentially cut off blood circulation to their head. To prevent this, the owl has a system of small blood vessels that allow an uninterrupted blood flow to the brain when one artery is blocked. Despite not being able to move its eyes, the snowy owl has extraordinary night vision and far-sightedness as well as depth perception. The latter is due to its binocular vision – meaning it can see an object with both eyes at the same time since its eyes face forward. Additionally, they have bristles on their beak, which function like mouse whiskers and help them feel nearby objects. Owls have three eyelids. They have an upper and lower eyelid, the upper closing when the owl blinks and the lower closing when the owl sleeps. The third eyelid is called a nictitating membrane. It closes diagonally across the eye, from the inside to the outside, to clean and protect the surface of the eye. Despite their amazing eyes, the real work when hunting is done by an owl's ears, though. Their ears are placed	layers of truth and ask the snowy owl for guidance when you need clarity. The owl is able to see in the dark. This speaks of your ability to delve deep into your subconscious. What have you forgotten that you need to bring forward? Are there any parts you need to integrate? The owl's ears are not visible. This represents your need to listen to your inner voice rather than listening to the advice of others. Do you trust your ability to discern what's important? Can you access your inner well of wisdom? Also, can you hear what

asymmetrically on their head, which gives the owl an exceptional ability to pinpoint the location of a sound. Additionally, the snowy owl's flat face funnels sound to its ears so that the owl can detect even the slightest rustle underneath the snow. Owls are also known for being silent fliers. This is because they have broad wings that allow them to glide and minimise flapping. They also have special flight feathers with fringes on the front edge, as well as soft, downy feathers that minimise air turbulence and thus sound when they beat their wings. Even though snow owls are excellent fliers and agile in the air – they are so good that they can catch birds mid-flight – they mostly hunt opportunistically. The snowy owl prefers open landscapes where it perches and waits patiently for prey while giving off the impression of being half-asleep. The snowy owl's prey consists mostly of lemmings: a snow owl can eat up to 1,000 lemmings each year. Apart from these, they also hunt birds, fish and other small mammals such as	is left unspoken? What tone are people using? Do their actions contradict their words? You are not easily deceived as you notice subtleties. Also, your clairaudience might be dominant. The owl's wings allow it to fly silently. Do you announce your presence too soon? Be silent if you want to be successful. Don't let everyone know about your plans in advance. The snowy owl is an opportunistic hunter. Do you grasp the opportunities that present themselves to you? Or are you too rigid? Do you need to become more flexible? As an owl person, you

voles and rabbits while supplementing their diet with eggs. If the prey is small enough, owls swallow it whole. Otherwise, they tear off pieces of it with their sharp beaks. Afterwards, the owls regurgitate pellets that contain all the indigestible parts of the animal, such as feathers and bones. Even though the snowy owl prefers to stay in its Arctic environment, for which it is perfectly adapted, a lack of food can sometimes drive it south. The owls living on the American continent can migrate as far south as Florida or California. Snow owls usually pair for life. To nest, the female will choose a mound or boulder on the ground, where she scrapes out a hollow in which she lays the eggs. After incubating those, the female will stay with the hatchlings to keep them warm and safe. Meanwhile, the male will provide food for the female and owlets. Both males and females are territorial and will aggressively defend their young when necessary, for example by dive-bombing any predators, such as Arctic foxes or wolves that are coming too close to the nest.	can trust yourself to make the right move at the right time. The snow owl sits quietly and observes its surroundings. Are you conscious of your environment? Do you see what is going on around you? Or do things take you by surprise? Are you maybe unprepared for the changes that happen in your life? Take the time to sit still and examine your situation. Having the owl as your spirit animal means that the neck is of great importance to you. Is your throat chakra healthy? Or are there any blockages you need to heal or remove?

Spirit tree Weeping Willow

(*Salix Babylonica*)

Tree Facts	**Some spiritual meanings**
There are more than 400 species of willows, with the weeping willow tree being one of the best-known. This tree got its name because raindrops that fall to the ground from its drooping branches look like tears. The great diversity of willows is partly due to the fact that they cross-pollinate with one another so that there are constantly new varieties forming, both naturally and via cultivation. Most of these species are found in the northern hemisphere and can be either trees or shrubs. The bark of the weeping willow is generally grey or brown as well as rough and furrowed while the foliage is plentiful. The weeping willow is a deciduous tree, which means it sheds its long, thin leaves each year. These are usually green on top and whitish on the underside but change to shades of yellow before falling off. Weeping willow trees are also dioecious:	Just as you can have spirit animals, you can have spirit trees, spirit flowers and spirit crystals. If you have a spirit tree, this tells of the importance of grounding. Are you connected to Mother Gaia? Or do you need to spend more time in nature? The weeping willow is pliable and its branches bend a long way without breaking. Are you flexible enough? Or are you too rigid? The stronger your roots are, the more flexible

In spring the weeping willow produces catkins that contain flowers, which are either male or female, depending on the tree. These provide an important early source of pollen and nectar for insects like bumblebees, as weeping willows are one of the first plants to bloom in spring. The fruit of the willow tree is a small capsule containing numerous tiny seeds that are easily dispersed by the wind. Additionally, willow trees can also reproduce by creating genetic copies of themselves, via branches or twigs that fall off and take root. Weeping willows are usually found near water sources, such as ponds, streams or lakes. But, even though they prefer moist, cool conditions, they can withstand droughts and are tolerant of most soil types. The willow is a fast-growing tree – it can grow up to eight feet a year – and it is widely used in medicine, by both humans and animals. Deer, for example, will often rub their new antlers against the willow tree's bark to relieve the itching. They do this because the bark produces a pain-relieving substance	you can allow yourself to be. This tree also speaks of immortality since it can grow anew from a fallen branch. Are you aware of your immortal soul? Do you need to connect to it once again? Apart from the element earth, water holds great importance for you, as willow trees prefer to grow near sources of it. Do you fully feel all of your emotions? Do you need to reach a greater understanding of them? The willow tree is adaptable – it can survive in many different environments. Are you adaptable? Do you allow changes in your life?

called salicin, which is an ingredient in the drug aspirin. Humans from native cultures also chewed the bark of the willow tree to treat fever, headaches, inflammation, toothache and pain. Besides this, willow wood is used to make various products, including furniture, toys, musical instruments such as flutes and whistles, baskets, fishing nets, paintbrushes, arrow shafts and dream-catchers. Additionally, sketching charcoal is often made from processed willow bark.	Or do you try to control everything? Willow trees are valued for what they can provide. Have you found the skills and talents that you can pass on to others? Do you feel valued enough? And do you value others for their areas of excellence?

Thank you to

- My mum – For always standing by my side, especially during the most challenging times. Without you, I wouldn't be here today.
- My dog – For teaching me the most valuable life lessons. Without you, I would have a hard time knowing how to stay present, find happiness and love unconditionally.
- All my past pets – For sharing your lives with me. I will see you again on the other side.
- My friends – For never abandoning me and for accepting me as I am.
- My other soulmates – For all the lessons you taught me and for showing me what I needed to heal.
- Any reader of this book – For travelling a part of your journey with me. The road is always easier when you've got great company.
- Jane Hammett, my editor – For polishing my draft to make it shine. You did an amazing job and any mistakes the readers find are my fault alone.
- And last but not least, to the one I called brother – For turning my whole life upside-down when you helped me to awaken.

About the author

A. Wakan first got in touch with spirituality in 2010, when she went to a shamanic healer. But it wasn't until 2015, when she met a close soulmate of hers, that she delved deeper into these subjects and made it her mission to learn everything she could. "Willow and Strix – A spiritual journey" is A. Wakan's debut novel and the first volume of the two-book series called "Willow and Strix".

You can follow the author on her 'Spirit Animal blog'
https://awakansspiritanimals.wordpress.com/
and on her social media profiles
https://twitter.com/Nayeli_A_Wakan
https://www.instagram.com/nayeli_a_wakan/

Coming soon

Willow and Strix – A healing journey

In this second and last part of the two-book series, Willow teaches Nayeli about energetic healing, the subconscious and the inner child. The tree will reveal what the meaning of life is and why authenticity is important. And it explains shamanic journeys and astral travelling.

Meanwhile, Strix will take you along on his journey back home, on which he meets a butterfly, a black jaguar, a frog, a buffalo and elephants – among many other friends and foes.

Printed in Poland
by Amazon Fulfillment
Poland Sp. z o.o., Wrocław

75941104R00430